HAYDEN HERRERA is an art historian and biographer. She has lectured widely, curated several exhibitions of art, taught Latin American art at New York University, and has been awarded a Guggenheim Fellowship. She is the author of numerous articles and reviews for such publications as *Art in America*, *Art Forum*, *Connoisseur*, and the *New York Times*, among others. Her books include *Mary Frank*; *Matisse: A Portrait; Frida: A Biography of Frida Kahlo*; *Frida Kahlo: The Paintings*; *Arshile Gorky: His Life and Work*, which was nominated for the Pulitzer Prize; and *Listening to Stone: The Art and Life of Isamu Noguchi*, which won the *Los Angeles Times* Book Prize for Biography. She lives in New York City.

D1427700

ALSO BY HAYDEN HERRERA

FRIDA

HAYDEN HERRERA

BLOOMSBURY PUBLISHING
LONDON · OXFORD · NEW YORK · NEW DELHI · SYDNEY

BLOOMSBURY PUBLISHING
Bloomsbury Publishing Plc
50 Bedford Square, London, WC1B 3DP, UK

BLOOMSBURY, BLOOMSBURY PUBLISHING and
the Diana logo are trademarks of Bloomsbury Publishing Plc

First published in Great Britain 1989
This edition published 2018

A catalogue record for this book is available from the British Library

ISBN: PB: 978-1-5266-0531-3

2 4 6 8 10 9 7 5 3 1

Printed and bound in Great Britain by CPI Group (UK) Ltd, Croydon CR0 4YY

To find out more about our authors and books visit
www.bloomsbury.com and sign up for our newsletters

For Philip

CONTENTS

Preface

IN APRIL 1953, less than a year before her death at the age of forty-seven, Frida Kahlo had her first major exhibition of paintings in her native Mexico. By that time her health had so deteriorated that no one expected her to attend. But at 8:00 P.M., just after the doors of Mexico City's Gallery of Contemporary Art opened to the public, an ambulance drew up. The artist, dressed in her favorite Mexican costume, was carried on a hospital stretcher to her four-poster bed, which had been installed in the gallery that afternoon. The bed was bedecked as she liked it, with photographs of her husband, the great muralist Diego Rivera, and of her political heroes, Malenkov and Stalin. Papier-mâché skeletons dangled from the canopy, and a mirror affixed to the underside of the canopy reflected her joyful though ravaged face. One by one, two hundred friends and admirers greeted Frida Kahlo, then formed a circle around the bed and sang Mexican ballads with her until well past midnight.

The occasion encapsulates as much as it culminates this extraordinary woman's career. It testifies, in fact, to many of the qualities that marked Kahlo as a person and as a painter: her gallantry and indomitable *alegría* in the face of physical suffering; her insistence on surprise and specificity; her peculiar love of spectacle as a mask to preserve privacy and personal dignity. Above all, the opening of her exhibition dramatized Frida Kahlo's central subject—herself. Most of the some two hundred paintings she produced in her abbreviated career were self-portraits.

She started with dramatic material: nearly beautiful, she had slight flaws that increased her magnetism. Her eyebrows formed an unbroken line across her forehead and her sensuous mouth was surmounted by the shadow of a mustache. Her eyes were dark and almond-shaped, with an upward slant at the outer edges. People who knew her well say Frida's intelligence and humor shone in those eyes; they also say her eyes revealed her mood: devouring, bewitching, or skeptical and withering. There was something about the piercing directness of her gaze that made visitors feel unmasked, as if they were being watched by an ocelot.

When she laughed it was with *carcajadas,* a deep, contagious laughter that burst forth either as delight or as a fatalistic acknowledgment of the absurdity of pain. Her voice was *bronca,* a little hoarse. Words tumbled out intensely, swiftly, emphatically, punctuated by quick, graceful gestures, that full-bellied laughter, and the occasional screech of emotion. In English, which she spoke and wrote fluently, Frida tended to slang. Reading her letters today, one is struck by what one friend called the "toughisms" of her vernacular; it is as if she had learned English from Damon Runyon. In Spanish, she loved to use foul language—words like *pendejo* (which, politely translated, means idiotic person) and *hijo de su chingada madre* (son of a bitch). In either language she enjoyed the effect on her audience, an effect enhanced by the fact that the gutter vocabulary issued from such a feminine-looking creature, one who held her head high on her long neck as nobly as a queen.

She dressed in flamboyant clothes, greatly preferring floor-length native Mexican costumes to haute couture. Wherever she went she caused a sensation. One New Yorker remembers that children used to follow her in the streets. "Where's the circus?" they would ask; Frida Kahlo did not mind a bit.

In 1929 she became the third wife of Diego Rivera. What a pair they made! Kahlo, small and fierce, someone out of a Gabriel García Márquez novel, if you will; Rivera, huge and extravagant, straight out of Rabelais. They knew everybody, it seemed. Trotsky was a friend, at least for a while, and so were Henry Ford and Nelson Rockefeller, Dolores del Rio and Paulette Goddard. The Rivera home in Mexico City was a mecca for the international intelligentsia, from Pablo Neruda to André Breton and Sergei Eisenstein. Marcel Duchamp was Frida's host in Paris, Isamu Noguchi was her lover, and Miró, Kandinsky, and Tanguy were admirers. In New York she met Stieglitz and Georgia O'Keeffe, and in San Francisco she was photographed by Edward Weston and Imogen Cunningham.

Thanks to Rivera's mania for publicity, the Rivera marriage became part of the public domain; the couple's every adventure, their loves, battles, and separations, were described in colorful detail by an avid press. They were called by their first names only. Everybody knew who Frida and Diego were: he was the greatest artist in the world; she was the sometimes rebellious priestess in his temple. Vivid, intelligent, sexy, she attracted men (and took many as lovers). As for women, there is evidence that she had lesbian liaisons too. Rivera did not seem to mind the latter, but objected strenuously to the former. "I don't want to share my toothbrush with anybody," he said, and threatened to shoot one interloper with his pistol.

In talking to those who knew her, one is continuously struck by the love people felt for Frida Kahlo. They acknowledge that she was caustic, yes, and impulsive. But tears often form in their eyes while they recall her. Their vibrant memories make her life sound like a short story by F. Scott Fitzgerald—full of fun and glamour until its end in tragedy. The truth is bleaker. On September 17, 1925, when she was eighteen, the bus that took her home from school was rammed by a streetcar in Mexico City. She was literally impaled on a metal bar in the wreckage; her spine was fractured, her pelvis crushed, and one foot broken. From that day until her death, twenty-nine years later, she lived with pain and the constant threat of illness. "I hold the record for operations," she said. She lived as well with a yearning for a child she could never have—her smashed pelvis led only to miscarriages and at least three therapeutic abortions—and with the anguish of being often deceived and occasionally abandoned by the man she loved. Frida flaunted her *alegría* the way a peacock spreads its tail, but it camouflaged a deep sadness and inwardness, even self-obsession.

"I paint my own reality," she said. "The only thing I know is that

I paint because I need to, and I paint always whatever passes through my head, without any other consideration." What passed through Frida Kahlo's head and into her art was some of the most original and dramatic imagery of the twentieth century. Painting herself bleeding, weeping, cracked open, she transmuted her pain into art with remarkable frankness tempered by humor and fantasy. Always specific and personal, deep-probing rather than comprehensive in scope, Frida's autobiography in paint has a peculiar intensity and strength—a strength that can hold the viewer in an uncomfortably tight grip.

The majority of her paintings are small—twelve by fifteen inches is not unusual; their scale suits the intimacy of her subject matter. With very small sable brushes, which she kept immaculately clean, she would carefully lay down delicate strokes of color, bringing the image into precise focus, making fantasy persuasive through the rhetoric of realism.

The results pleased the Surrealists, who welcomed her into their number in the late 1930s. The paintings also appealed to a few discerning collectors—Edward G. Robinson, Edgar Kaufmann, Jr., A. Conger Goodyear, Jacques Gelman—but for the most part they languished in undeserved obscurity, until recently.

In the fall of 1977, the Mexican government turned over the largest and most prestigious galleries in the Palace of Fine Arts to a retrospective exhibition of Frida Kahlo's works. It was a strange sort of homage, for it seemed to celebrate the exotic personality and story of the artist rather more than it honored her art. The grand, high-ceilinged rooms were dominated by huge blown-up photographs of incidents in Frida's life, which made the jewel-like paintings look almost like punctuation points.

The art—the legend Frida herself had created—won out in the end, however. Because her paintings were so tiny in relation to the photographs and to the exhibition space, the spectator had to stand within a few feet of each one to focus on it at all. And at that proximity their strange magnetism exerted its pull. Taken from separate, poignant moments in her life, each was like a smothered cry, a nugget of emotion so dense that one felt it might explode. The paintings made the photographic panels mounted on an architectural structure in the middle of the room seem as precarious and piecemeal as a house of cards.

On November 2, 1978, to celebrate the Day of the Dead, one of

Mexico's most festive holidays, the Galería de la Raza in San Francisco's Mission district opened its own "Homage to Frida Kahlo." It was an exhibition of works in various media by some fifty artists (mostly Chicano), who were invited to send contributions made "in the spirit of Frida Kahlo's symbolism." Against the back wall of the gallery was the traditional *ofrenda*, an altar to the deceased, covered with candles, candy skulls, straw crosses, "bread of the dead" shaped like human bones, a coffin containing birds made of sugar, and a toy bed on which lay a miniature Frida. Filling the remaining walls and the room itself were the works of the artists, many of whom juxtaposed their own portraits with Frida's, as if to identify with her. Frida was portrayed as political heroine and revolutionary fighter, as suffering female, mistreated wife, childless woman, and "Mexican Ophelia." Many saw her as a person plagued by but defiant of death. One of the artists explained her reverence: "Frida embodied the whole notion of culture for Chicano women. She inspired us. Her works didn't have self-pity, they had strength."

Since then, Frida Kahlo's audience has been growing: a retrospective of her work traveled to six U.S. museums in 1978–1979, and in 1982 London's Whitechapel Art Gallery organized an exhibition entitled "Frida Kahlo and Tina Modotti," which traveled to Germany and to New York. For women, especially, the extremely personal and female nature of Kahlo's imagery, and her artistic independence, have become significant. In her art, she neither competed with nor deferred to Rivera, and there are not a few astute critics who feel she was the better painter. Indeed, Diego himself was often heard to say as much, flourishing the letter in which Picasso said of her, "Neither Derain, nor I, nor you are capable of painting a head like those of Frida Kahlo."

Frida would have been gratified by the multifarious memories she left behind. She was, in fact, one of the creators of her own legendary stature, and because she was so complex and so intricately self-aware, her myth is full of tangents, ambiguities, and contradictions. For that reason, one hesitates to disclose aspects of her reality that might undercut the image she created of herself. Yet the truth does not dispel the myth. After scrutiny, Frida Kahlo's story remains every bit as extraordinary as her fable.

PART I

PART 1

Chapter 1

The Blue House on Londres Street

THE STORY OF FRIDA KAHLO begins and ends in the same place. From the outside, the house on the corner of Londres and Allende streets looks very like other houses in Coyoacán, an old residential section on the southwestern periphery of Mexico City. A one-story stucco structure with bright blue walls enlivened by tall, many-paned windows with green shutters and by the restless shadows of trees, it bears the name Museo Frida Kahlo over the portal. Inside is one of the most extraordinary places in Mexico—a woman's home with all her paintings and belongings, turned into a museum.

The entrance is guarded by two giant papier-mâché Judas figures nearly twenty feet tall, gesticulating at each other as if they were engaged in conversation.* Passing them, one enters a garden with tropical plants, fountains, and a small pyramid decked with pre-Columbian idols.

---

* Designed to be exploded on Sábado de Gloria—the Saturday before Easter—such figures stand for more than the betrayal of Christ by Judas. They have also come to signify the betrayal of the people by powerful oppressors, and they take many forms: some represent policemen, soldiers, politicians, and landowners—"anyone who had earned the hatred of the people" (Bertram D. Wolfe and Diego Rivera, *Portrait of Mexico*, p. 51).

3

The interior of the house is remarkable for the feeling that its former occupants' presence animates all the objects and paintings on display. Here are Frida Kahlo's palette and brushes, left on her worktable as if she had just put them down. There, near his bed, are Diego Rivera's Stetson hat, his overalls, and his huge miner's shoes. In the large corner bedroom with windows looking out onto Londres and Allende streets is a glass-doored cabinet enclosing Frida's colorful costume from the region of Tehuantepec. Above the cabinet, these words are painted on the wall: *"Aquí nació Frida Kahlo el día 7 de julio de 1910"* (Here Frida Kahlo was born on July 7, 1910). They were inscribed four years after the artist's death, when her home became a public museum. Another inscription adorns the bright blue and red patio wall. *"Frida y Diego vivieron en esta casa 1929–1954"* (Frida and Diego lived in this house 1929–1954). Ah! the visitor thinks. How nicely circumscribed! Here are three of the main facts of Frida Kahlo's life—her birth, her marriage, and her death.

The only trouble is that neither inscription is precisely true. In fact, as her birth certificate shows, Frida was born on July 6, in 1907. Claiming perhaps a greater truth than strict fact would allow, she chose as her birth date not the true year, but 1910, the year of the outbreak of the Mexican Revolution. Since she was a child of the revolutionary decade, when the streets of Mexico City were full of chaos and bloodshed, she decided that she and modern Mexico had been born together.

The other inscription in the Frida Kahlo Museum promotes an ideal, sentimental view of the Rivera-Kahlo marriage and home. Once again, reality is different. Before 1934, when they returned to Mexico after four years of residence in the United States, Frida and Diego lived only briefly in the Coyoacán house. From 1934 to 1939 they lived in a pair of houses built for them in the nearby residential district of San Angel. After that there were long periods when Diego, preferring the independence of his San Angel studio, did not live with Frida, not to mention the one year when the Riveras separated, divorced, and remarried.

The inscriptions, then, are embroideries on the truth. Like the museum itself, they are part of Frida's legend.

The house in Coyoacán was only three years old when Frida was born; her father had built it in 1904 on a small piece of land he acquired when the hacienda "El Carmen" was broken up and sold. But the heavy walls it presents to the street, its one-story structure, flat roof, and U-shaped plan, with each room giving onto the next and onto the central patio instead of being linked by hallways, make it seem to date from colonial times. It stands only a few blocks from the town's central plaza and the parish Church of Saint John the Baptist, where Frida's mother had a particular bench that she and her daughters occupied on Sundays. From her house Frida could walk by way of narrow, often cobblestoned or unpaved streets to the Viveros de Coyoacán, a forest park graced by a slender river winding among trees.

When Guillermo Kahlo built the Coyoacán house, he was a successful photographer who had just been commissioned by the Mexican government to record the nation's architectural heritage. It was a remarkable achievement for a man who had arrived in Mexico without great prospects, just thirteen years before. His parents, Jakob Heinrich Kahlo and Henriette Kaufmann Kahlo, were Hungarian Jews from Arad, now part of Rumania, who had migrated to Germany and settled in Baden-Baden, where Wilhelm was born in 1872. Jakob Kahlo was a jeweler who also dealt in photographic supplies; when the time came he was wealthy enough to be able to send his son to study at the university in Nuremberg.

Sometime around the year 1890 the promising career of Wilhelm Kahlo, scholar, ended before it had begun: the youth sustained brain injuries in a fall, and began to suffer from epileptic seizures. At about the same time, his mother died, and his father married again, a woman Wilhelm did not like. In 1891 the father gave his nineteen-year-old son enough money to pay for his passage to Mexico; Wilhelm changed his name to Guillermo and never returned to the country of his birth.

He arrived in Mexico City with almost no money and few possessions. Through his connections with other German immigrants, he found a job as a cashier in the Cristalería Loeb, a glassware store. Later, he became a salesman in a bookstore. Finally, he worked in a jewelry store called La Perla, which was owned by fellow countrymen with whom he had traveled from Germany to Mexico.

In 1894 he married a Mexican woman, who died four years later as she gave birth to their second daughter. He then fell in love with Matilde Calderón, a fellow employee at La Perla. As Frida told the story, "The night his wife died, my father called my grandmother

Isabel, who came with my mother. My mother and my father had been working in the same store. He was very much in love with her and later they got married."

It is not hard to imagine why Guillermo Kahlo loved Matilde Calderón. Photographs of her at the time of her marriage show that she was a strikingly beautiful woman with enormous dark eyes, full lips, and a determined chin. She was "like a little bell from Oaxaca," Frida said once. "When she went to market, she gracefully cinched her waist and carried her basket coquettishly." Born in Oaxaca in 1876, Matilde Calderón y González was the oldest of the twelve children of convent-bred Isabel González y González, the daughter of a Spanish general, and Antonio Calderón, a photographer of Indian descent who came from Morelia. According to Frida, her mother was intelligent, though unlettered; what she lacked in education she made up for in piety.

It is somewhat more difficult to imagine what attracted the devout Matilde Calderón to Guillermo Kahlo. The twenty-six-year-old immigrant was by birth Jewish, by persuasion an atheist, and he suffered from seizures. On the other hand, his light skin and his cultured European background must have had a certain appeal in those days, when anything European was considered superior to anything Mexican. Moreover, he was intelligent, hard-working, and rather handsome, in spite of his protruding ears. He had thick brown hair, a beautiful, sensitive mouth, a fine mustache with pointed ends that twisted upward in just the way they should, and a slender, agile body—he "was very interesting and he moved in an elegant way when he walked," Frida said. If the look in his huge brown eyes was a little too intense—and it became more disturbingly agitated over the years—his gaze was also romantic.

Matilde, at twenty-four several years beyond the usual marriage age, may have been particularly susceptible because of a previous affair that ended tragically. Frida recalled that when she was eleven years old, her mother showed her a book covered in Russian leather "where she kept the letters from her first boyfriend. On the last page it said that the writer of the letters, a young German, had committed suicide in her presence. This man continued to live in her memory." It is natural that the young woman would have been attracted to another German, and if she did not love him—Frida said she did not—she at least thought she was making a good match.

It was Matilde Calderón de Kahlo who persuaded her husband to take up photography, her own father's profession. Frida said that her grandfather lent her father a camera, "and the first thing that they did was to go off on a trip around the Republic. They produced a collection of photographs of indigenous and Colonial architecture and they returned to install their first workshop on Avenida 16 de Septiembre."

The photographs were commissioned by José Ives Limantour, the secretary of the treasury under the dictator Porfirio Díaz, and they were to illustrate a series of large-format luxury publications for the 1910 celebration of the centennial of Mexican Independence. The job took four years to complete. From 1904 to 1908, using fine German-made cameras and more than nine hundred glass plates that he prepared himself, Guillermo Kahlo recorded the architectural heritage of Mexico, earning the accolade "first official photographer of Mexico's cultural patrimony."

Indeed, Limantour had chosen well: Guillermo Kahlo was a fastidious technician with a stubbornly objective approach to what he saw; in his photographs, as in his daughter's paintings, there are no tricky effects, no romantic obfuscation. He tried to give as much information about the architectural structure he recorded as he possibly could, carefully selecting his vantage point and using light and shade to delineate form. An advertisement for his work printed in English and Spanish said: "Guillermo Kahlo specialist in landscapes, buildings, interiors, factories, etc., and who takes photos on order, be it in the City, be it in any other point of the Republic." Although on occasion he took fine portraits of members of the Díaz government and of his own family, he said that he did not want to photograph people because he did not wish to improve what God had made ugly.

Whether Guillermo Kahlo knew the humor of such a statement is hard to say, but when Frida's contemporaries speak of him they almost always also recall his utterances, and usually the quote is at once direct, sardonic, and in a wonderfully deadpan way, funny.

This does not mean that Frida's father was a lighthearted man. To the contrary, he was a man of few words, whose silences had a powerful resonance, and there was about him an aura of bitterness. He never really felt at ease in Mexico, and although he was anxious to be accepted as Mexican, he never lost his strong German accent. As time went on, he withdrew more and more. Frida recalled that "he had only two friends. One was an old *largote* [tall man] who always left his hat on top of the armoire. My father and the old man spent hours playing chess and drinking coffee."

In 1936 Frida portrayed her birthplace and her family tree in the delightfully whimsical painting *My Grandparents, My Parents and I* (figure 2). She presents herself as a small girl (she said she was about two) standing naked and self-possessed in the patio of her blue house; her child-size chair is at her feet, and she holds the crimson ribbon, her bloodline, that supports her family tree as easily as if it were the string of a prized balloon. The portraits of her parents are based on their wedding photograph, in which the couple floats like angels in the sky, framed by an aureole of clouds. This old-fashioned photographic convention must have amused Frida: in the painting she has placed the portraits of her grandparents in similar soft cumulous nests. Frida's maternal grandparents, the Indian Antonio Calderón and the *gachupina* (of Spanish extraction) Isabel González y González, are situated above Frida's mother. On her father's side is a European couple, Jakob Heinrich Kahlo and Henriette Kaufmann Kahlo. About the origin of Frida Kahlo's most striking physical characteristic there can be no doubt: she inherited her heavy, joined eyebrows from her father's mother. Frida said she looked like both her parents: "I have my father's eyes and my mother's body." In the painting Guillermo Kahlo has an uneasy, penetrating gaze, a look that, in its unsettling intensity, was to appear again in his daughter's eyes.

Frida has faithfully copied every ruffle, seam, and bow on her mother's wedding dress from the original photograph, creating a humorous foil for the pink fetus, well along in development, that she has placed on the virginal white skirt. The fetus is Frida; that it may also refer to the possibility that her mother was pregnant when she got married is typical of Frida's delight in multiple meanings. Below the fetus is a mock wedding portrait: a big sperm, trailed by a school of smaller competitors, penetrates an egg: Frida at the moment of conception. Close by is another scene of fecundation: a crimson, U-shaped cactus flower opening to receive pollen carried by wind.

Frida has set her house not in the suburbs but in the cactus-dotted plain of Mexico's high central tableland. In the distance are the ravine-gashed mountains that were often the landscape setting of her self-portraits; just below the images of her paternal grandparents is the ocean. Her Mexican grandparents were symbolized by the earth, Frida explained, and her German ones by the sea. A humble Mexican home adjoins the Kahlos' house, and in a field beyond there is a still more primitive dwelling, an Indian's adobe hut. In a childlike vision, the artist has subsumed the entire town of Coyoacán into her own home, which she has then placed apart from the rest of reality, in a wilderness. Frida stands in the middle of her house, in the middle of Mexico, in the middle—one feels—of the world.

Chapter 2

Childhood in Coyoacán

MAGDALENA CARMEN FRIDA KAHLO Y CALDERÓN, the third daughter of Guillermo and Matilde Kahlo, was born on July 6, 1907, at eight-thirty in the morning, in the midst of the summer rainy season, when the high plateau of Mexico City is cold and dank. The first two names were given to Frida so that she could be baptized with a Christian name. Her third name, the one her family used, means "peace" in German. (Although her birth certificate says "Frida," Frida spelled her name the German way, with an *e*, until the late 1930s, when she dropped the *e* because of the rise of Nazism in Germany.)

Shortly after Frida's birth, her mother became ill, and the infant was suckled for a time by an Indian wet nurse. "I was nursed by a nana whose breasts they washed every time I was going to suckle," she told a friend proudly. Years later, when the fact that she had been nourished by an indigenous woman's milk became crucial to her, she painted the wet nurse as the mythic embodiment of her Mexican heritage and herself as an infant at her breast.

Perhaps because of Matilde Kahlo's health—as she neared middle age, she began to suffer from "seizures" or "attacks" resembling her husband's—or perhaps because of her temperament, Frida and her younger sister, Cristina, were cared for largely by their older sisters, Matilde and Adriana, and, whenever they were at home, by their half-sisters, María Luisa and Margarita, who had been placed in a convent when their father remarried.

Three years after Frida's birth, the Mexican Revolution broke out. It began with uprisings in various parts of the country and with the gathering of guerrilla armies in Chihuahua (under Pascual Orozco and Pancho Villa) and in Morelos (under Emiliano Zapata); they were to continue for ten years. In May 1911 came the fall and exile of the old dictator, Porfirio Díaz. The revolutionary leader Francisco Madero was elected president in October 1912, but in February 1913, after the "tragic ten days," when opposing troops in the National Palace and the Ciudadela bombarded each other, causing much destruction and death, Madero was double-crossed by General Victoriano Huerta and murdered. In the north, Venustiano Carranza rose to avenge the death of Madero. He took the title of first chief of the Constitutionalist Army and, with a small body of troops at his disposal, set out to overthrow Huerta. The vicious jockeying for power and its inevitable bloodlettings did not finally cease until the inauguration of President Alvaro Obregón, one of Carranza's generals, in November 1920.

In her diary, written in the last decade of her life and now on display in her museum, Frida proudly—and, one suspects, with considerable poetic license—recalled being witness to the battles of the opposing revolutionary armies that bore down upon Mexico City.

I remember that I was four years old [actually, she was five] when the "tragic ten days" took place. I witnessed with my own eyes Zapata's peasants' battle against the Carrancistas. My situation was very clear. My mother opened the windows on Allende Street. She gave access to the Zapatistas, seeing to it that the wounded and hungry jumped from the windows of my house into the "living room." She cured them and gave them thick tortillas, the only food that could be obtained in Coyoacán in those days. . . . We were four sisters: Matita, Adri, me (Frida) and Cristi, the chubby one. . . .

In 1914 bullets just hissed. I still hear their extraordinary sound. In the *tianguis* [market] of Coyoacán propaganda in favor of Zapata was made with *corridos* [revolutionary ballads] edited by [the printmaker José Guadalupe] Posada. On Friday these ballad sheets cost one centavo and, enclosed in a great wardrobe that smelled of walnut wood, Cristi and I sang them, while my mother and father watched out for us so that we could not fall into the hands of the guerrillas. I remember a wounded Carrancista running toward his stronghold [near] the river of Coyoacán. From the window I also spied [a] Zapatista with a bullet wound in his knee, squatting and putting on his sandals. [Here, Frida drew sketches of the Carrancista and the Zapatista.]

To Frida's parents, the revolution was not an escapade but a misfortune. Guillermo Kahlo's commissions from the Díaz government had given him enough money to build a comfortable house on a plot of land in a fashionable section of Coyoacán; the fall of that government, followed by a decade of civil war, brought him penury. Photographic commissions of any kind were hard to come by; as Frida said, "it was with great difficulty that a livelihood was earned in my house."

Matilde Calderón had married a man with prospects; now she found herself having to scrimp and save. Her husband had no head for money and was often unable even to buy photographic supplies. They mortgaged the house, sold the French living room furniture, and at one point had to take in paying guests. As Guillermo Kahlo became increasingly taciturn and misanthropic, it was his matronly wife who kept the household on its feet, grumbling at servants, bargaining with shopkeepers, and complaining to the farmer who delivered the milk. "She did not know how to read or write," Frida remembered. "She only knew how to count money."

Matilde Kahlo knew more than that. She taught her daughters the domestic skills and graces that go with a traditional Mexican upbringing, and she tried to pass along to them the religious faith that meant so much to her, shepherding them to church every day and to retreats at Eastertime. Frida did learn to sew, embroider, cook, and clean at an early age—and all through her life she took great pride in the beauty and order of her home—but both she and Cristina rebelled against the traditional piety of their mother, their older sisters (Margarita became a nun), and their aunts. "My mother was hysterical about religion," Frida said. "We had to pray before meals. While the others concentrated on their inner selves, Cristi and I would look at each other, forcing ourselves not to laugh." She and Cristina attended a catechism class in preparation for their First Communion, "but we escaped and went to eat haws, quinces, and *capulines* [cherry-like fruit of the capulin tree] in a nearby orchard."

When the time came to go to school, Frida and Cristina went together. "When I was three or four years of age they sent Cristi and me to a kindergarten," Frida remembered. "The teacher was old-fashioned, with false hair and the strangest dresses. My first memory is of this teacher. She was standing in front of the dark classroom holding in one hand a candle and in the other an orange and explaining how the universe worked, the sun, the earth, and the moon. It made such an impression on me that I urinated. They took off my wet pants and put on the pants of a girl who lived across the street from my house. Because of this, I took such a dislike to the girl that one day I brought her near my house and I began to strangle her. Her tongue was already out of her mouth when a baker passed by and freed her from my hands."

No doubt, Frida exaggerates her devilishness, but she was definitely a prankster. Once her half-sister María Luisa was sitting on the chamber pot. "In play I pushed her and she fell backward with the pot and all." This time, the victim retaliated. "Furious, she said to me, 'You are not the daughter of my mother or my father. They picked you up out of a trash can.' This statement impressed me so much that I changed into a completely introverted creature. From then on I had adventures with an imaginary friend."

Such rebuffs did not deter Frida for long. She even dared to tease her father, poking fun at his punctilious German ways by calling him "Herr Kahlo." And it was she who played a leading role in the episode that perhaps more than any other demonstrates the unhappiness in the Kahlo household during the years when the sisters were growing up. Frida told the story:

When I was seven I helped my sister, Matilde, who was then fifteen years old, to escape with her boyfriend to Veracruz. I opened the balcony window and later closed it again so that it looked as if nothing had happened. Matita was my mother's favorite, and her flight made my mother hysterical. . . . When Maty left, my father did not say a word. . . .

For some years we did not see Matita. One day while we were on a streetcar, my father said to me, "We'll never find her!" I consoled him and in truth my hopes were sincere [for a friend had told me], "There is a married woman who looks very much like you living in the Doctores section of town. Her name is Matilde Kahlo." In the back of a patio, in the fourth room off a long corridor, I found her. The room was full of light and birds. Matita was bathing herself with a hose. She lived there with Paco Hernández, whom she later married. They enjoyed a good economic situation and they did not have children. The first thing I did was to tell my father that I had found her. I visited her several times and I tried to convince my mother to see them, but she didn't want to.

It was a long time before Frida's mother forgave her eldest daughter. Matilde used to come home bearing gifts of fruit and delicacies, but since her mother refused to let her in, she left her offerings at the door. Later, when Matilde was gone, Señora Kahlo would take the presents into the house. Not until 1927, twelve years after Matilde ran away, could Frida write to a friend that "Maty now comes to this mansion. Peace has been made."

Frida's ambivalence toward her mother—her love as well as scorn— showed itself when, in an interview, she described her mother as both "cruel" (for drowning a litter of rats) and "very nice, active, intelligent." And although the inevitable battles with the woman she called *"mi Jefe"* (my Chief) became more intense as both grew older, when her mother died Frida "could not stop crying."

As a small child, Frida was a chubby imp, with a dimple in her chin and a mischievous glint in her eye. A family photograph taken when she was about seven shows a marked change: She is thin and gangling; her face is somber, her expression withdrawn. She stands alone behind a bush as if she wished to hide.

The reason for the change was illness: when Frida was six years old, she was stricken with polio. She was to spend nine months confined to her room. "It all began with a horrible pain in my right leg from the muscle downward," she remembered. "They washed my little leg in a small tub with walnut water and small hot towels."

The curious combination of being at once self-fascinated and outgoing that characterized Frida as an adult may have begun in the sick child's exacerbated awareness of the discrepancy between the inner world of daydreams and the outer world of social interchange. The dream of having an imaginary friend, a consoling confidante, never left her; explaining in her diary the origin of the double self-portrait called *The Two Fridas* (plate XIV), she wrote:

I must have been 6 years old when I experienced intensely an imaginary friendship with a little girl more or less the same age as me. On the glass window of what at that time was my room, and which gave onto Allende Street, I breathed vapor onto one of the first panes. I let out a breath and with a finger I drew a "door." . . . [Here Frida drew the window of her room.]

Full of great joy and urgency, I went out in my imagination, through this "door." I crossed the whole plain that I saw in front of me until I arrived at the dairy called "Pinzón." . . . I entered by the "O" of Pinzón and I went down in great haste into the *interior of the earth,* where "my imaginary friend" was always waiting for me. I do not remember her image or her color. But I do know that she was gay—she laughed a lot. Without sounds. She was agile and she danced as if she weighed nothing at all. I followed her in all her movements and while she danced I told her my secret problems. Which ones? I do not remember. But from my voice she knew everything about me. . . . When I returned to the window I entered through the same door drawn on the glass pane. When? For how long had I been with her? I do not know. It could have been a second or thousands of years. . . . I was happy. I blurred the "door" with my hand and it "disappeared." I ran with my *secret* and my joy as far as the furthermost corner of the patio of my house, and always in the same place under a cedar tree, I cried out and laughed, surprised at being *alone* with my great happiness and with the so vivid memory of *the little girl.* Thirty-four years have passed since I experienced this magic friendship and every time that I remember it, it revives and becomes larger and larger inside of my world.

When Frida was up and about again, a doctor recommended a program of physical exercise to strengthen her withered right limb, and Guillermo Kahlo, who had been unusually tender and concerned during his daughter's illness, made sure that she took up all kinds of sports, which were considered highly unusual for respectable young girls in Mexico at that time. She played soccer, boxed, wrestled, and became a champion swimmer. "My toys," she recalled, "were those of a boy: skates, bicycles." She liked to climb trees, row on the lakes of Chapultepec Park, and play ball.

Nevertheless, she said, "The leg remained very thin. When I was seven I wore little boots. In the beginning I supposed that the jokes [about my leg] did not injure me, but afterwards they did, and as time went on more intensely." Frida's childhood friend, the painter Aurora Reyes, says: "We were quite cruel about her leg. When she was riding her bicycle we would yell at her: *'Frida, pata de palo!'* [Frida, peg leg], and she would respond furiously with lots of curses." To hide the leg, she wore three or four socks on the thinner calf, and shoes with a built-up right heel. Other friends admired the fact that she never let her slight deformity keep her from physical activity.

They remember her, black bloomers showing, pedaling her bicycle like a demon around Centenario Park. "She was extremely well coordinated and graceful. When she walked, she made little jumps so that she seemed to float like a bird in flight."

But she was a wounded bird. And being wounded, she was different from the other children, and often lonely. Just at the age when she might have expanded her world beyond her family circle and made "best friends," she was forced to stay at home. When she recovered and returned to school, she was teased and left out. Her reaction was alternately to withdraw (she said she became an "introverted creature") and to overcompensate by becoming first a tomboy and later a "character."

As in the photograph in which she stood apart from the family gathering, so in the paintings in which she portrayed herself as a child, Frida is alone (even in her depiction of her family tree, she stands apart). Although this solitude has much to do with feelings she had at the time she produced the paintings, it is also certain that her painted memories contain much truth about the past: a lonely adult recalls earlier moments of loneliness.

In a 1938 painting inscribed with the words "They ask for airplanes and are given straw wings" (figure 4), Frida combined her recollection of a minor childhood disappointment with her memory of her freedom of movement being curtailed by polio and with her current frustration at being immobilized by surgery on her foot. Diego Rivera's biographer, Bertram D. Wolfe, said the painting recalls "the time when her parents dressed her in a white robe and wings to represent an angel (wings that caused a great unhappiness because they would not fly)." In it, Frida, who looks about seven, holds what she asked for and did not receive, a model airplane. The straw wings that she did receive are suspended by ribbons descending from the sky; clearly they cannot fly. To drive that point home, Frida has wound a ribbon around her skirt and nailed the bows at either end to the ground.

Another painting in which Frida shows herself as a solitary child is *Four Inhabitants of Mexico* (figure 5), from 1938. More ambiguous in its meaning than the self-portrait with straw wings, it at first looks like a harmless piece of Mexican folklore. It is, in fact, a forbidding image of a child confronting the emblems of her cultural heritage.

Unprotected by the walls of her family home, Frida sits on the dirt ground, sucking her middle finger, clutching the folds of her skirt, and impassively absorbing the comings and goings of the adult world. Flanking her are four odd characters: a pre-Columbian Nayarit idol, a Judas figure, a clay skeleton, and a straw horseman. Each of the four inhabitants was modeled after a Mexican artifact that the Riveras actually owned. The scene must be Coyoacán; La Rosita, a *pulque* bar near Frida's house, is visible in the background. The village square is "empty, with few people," Frida said, "because too much revolution has left Mexico empty." For all her love of her native land, Frida has painted a highly ambivalent view, identifying Mexico's sufferings with her own.

The young Frida stares at one of the four inhabitants, the pre-Columbian clay sculpture of a naked pregnant woman who is a symbol both of Mexico's Indian heritage and of the little girl's own future as a sexually mature woman. Like the adult Frida, the idol is broken; the fronts of its feet are missing and its head has been broken off and repaired. Frida told a friend that the idol is pregnant because, being dead, she has something alive inside, "which is the whole thing about Indians." And she is naked "because they have no shame about sex or stupid things like that."

The Judas figure, a large, mustachioed unshaven man wearing blue worker's overalls, gesticulates as if he were delivering a *pronunciamiento*, and holds one of the fuses in his network of explosives in a position that suggests an erect penis. He is the male counterpart of the passive pregnant idol, the leader-destroyer who is full of fury and sound and blows himself up. The long shadow that he casts on the earth goes right between the female idol's legs and lies next to her shadow, thus linking them as a couple. His shadow touches the little girl as well, so that she becomes, along with the Judas and the figurine, part of a family. Frida said she found more humor than menace in the Judas figure, explaining that the Judas was a pretext for joy, gaiety, and irresponsibility, and that it had nothing to do with religion. "It is burnt up," she said, ". . . it makes noise, it is beautiful, and because it goes to pieces it has color and form."

The grimacing skeleton, a large version of the small ones Mexican children like to dandle and bounce during the Day of the Dead, signifies "death: very gay, a joke," Frida said. Like the pregnant idol, the skeleton is in the child's line of vision; it, too, represents her future.

Behind the skeleton, in the middle distance, is the straw man, perhaps a revolutionary bandit like Pancho Villa, wearing a hat and a cartridge belt and riding a straw burro. He suggests a fragility and pathos in Mexican life, a poignant mixture of poverty, pride, and dreams. Frida said that she put him in her painting "because he is weak, and at the same time has such elegance and is so easy to destroy."

It is an odd vision of Mexico, for it suggests that the nation's inhabitants—made of papier-mâché, straw, and clay—are the ephemeral survivors of a terrible history. Yet these objects had a personal significance for the mature Frida; like the monkeys and other pets with which she surrounded herself, they were to her a kind of family; they offered familiar comfort in a world that often felt void. The four inhabitants, three of which reappear in *The Wounded Table*, 1940 (figure 55), were Frida's companions in a picturesque and sorrowful drama; in effect, as Frida created her Mexican persona, she herself became the fifth inhabitant of Mexico.

It took years for Frida to turn herself into that "fifth inhabitant." Polio was the beginning of the transformation. All her life she hated the withered leg that resulted from this illness, and she hid it with long Mexican skirts and compensated for it (and for her other wounds) by becoming the most Mexican of Mexicans.

Of his six children, Frida was the one to whom Guillermo Kahlo felt most attached. Rarely demonstrative, he would nonetheless murmur, *"Frida, lieber Frida,"* in a low voice when he came home to Coyoacán from his work in Mexico City. He recognized in her something of his own high-strung sensibility, his own introspection and restlessness. "Frida is the most intelligent of my daughters," Kahlo used to remark. "She is the most like me."

A man of fixed habits, he did not have much time for his children. He left home early in the morning for his studio at the corner of Madero and Motolina, above La Perla, the jewelry shop where he had once worked, in the center of Mexico City. Because of the distance from Coyoacán, he did not follow the Mexican custom of going home in the middle of the day to eat a large *comida*. Instead, Señora Kahlo prepared his lunch in a Mexican basket and sent it to him with a houseboy.

The studio, consisting of a small study and a darkroom, was his own private world, complete with the props necessary to portrait photography (Oriental rug, French chairs, backdrops with illusionistic landscapes), his big German cameras, his lenses and glass plates—and a scale-model locomotive with intricate parts that he painstakingly maintained. As befitted a cultured European of that period in Mexico, he also had a small but carefully selected library—mainly German books, including works by Schiller and Goethe, as well as numerous volumes of philosophy; he once sententiously informed his daughters that "philosophy makes men prudent and helps them to fulfill their responsibilities." Above his desk and dominating the room was a large portrait of a personal hero, Arthur Schopenhauer.

Every evening Guillermo Kahlo returned home at the same hour. Solemn, courteous, a little severe, he greeted his family, then went directly into the room that housed his German piano and shut himself in for an hour. His passions were Beethoven first, then Johann Strauss; the strains of the "Blue Danube" would be just audible through the thick walls. When he emerged, he ate alone, with his wife waiting on him in silence. After supper he played the piano again, and before retiring he always read.

Although Kahlo was not intimate with his children, he was attentive to his favorite. He stimulated Frida's intellectual adventurousness, lending her books from his library and encouraging her to share his curiosity about, and passion for, all manifestations of nature—stones, flowers, animals, birds, insects, shells. On occasion, Frida and her father would go to nearby parks, and while Kahlo (who was an amateur painter) painted watercolors, she spent hours collecting pebbles, insects, and rare plants along the river's edge. These she would take home to look up in books, to dissect, and to peer at under a microscope.

When she was old enough, her father shared with her his interest in Mexican archaeology and art and taught her to use a camera and to develop, retouch, and color photographs. Although the young Frida did not have much patience for the exacting work, something of her father's fastidiousness, his concern for minute surface detail, would later appear in her own paintings. Certainly the tiny brush strokes and the small scale that retouching photographs entails became second nature to Frida, and the stiff formality of her father's portraits affected her approach to portraiture. Acknowledging the link between his art and her own, Frida once said that her paintings were like the photographs that her father did for calendar illustrations, only instead of painting outer reality, she painted the calendars that were inside her head. And if Guillermo Kahlo's meticulously realistic paintings, mostly still lifes and sentimental farm scenes, did not influence Frida, the fact that he was a painter as well as a photographer did: Frida is yet another instance of a woman artist—other examples are Marietta Robusti (Tintoretto's daughter), Artemisia Gentileschi, Angelica Kaufman—with an artist father who encouraged her career.

After Frida's bout with polio, the two were drawn even closer to each other, bound by a shared experience of illness and loneliness. Frida recalled that her father's attacks frequently occurred at night, just before she went to bed. When she was a small child, she was hustled out of the way. Nothing was explained to her, and she would lie in bed in fright and wonder; in the morning she was equally perplexed to find her father acting perfectly normal, as if nothing had happened. He became, she said, a "kind of fearful mystery, for whom I also had pity." Later, she often accompanied him on photography outings, to be there when he needed her. "Many times when he went walking with his camera on his shoulder and me by the hand, he would suddenly fall. I learned to help him during his attacks in the middle of the street. On the one hand, I would make sure that he immediately breathed alcohol or ether, and on the other, I watched so that his camera would not be stolen."

Years later, Frida wrote in her diary: "My childhood was marvelous, because, although my father was a sick man (he had vertigos every month and a half), he was an immense example to me of tenderness, of work (photographer and also painter) and above all of understanding for all my problems."

Another testimony to her daughterly love is *Portrait of Don Guillermo Kahlo* (figure 7). It is based on a photograph that he probably took of himself, and was painted in 1952, eleven years after he had died of a heart attack, and only two years before her own death. Sober browns, grays, and black convey the seriousness of Herr Kahlo; the furrowed brow and the wild, haunted look in his overlarge eyes—eyes that are as round and shiny as his camera lens—hint at emotional imbalance. It is surprising that Frida once used the word "tranquil" to describe her father, for his surface calm came from control and taciturnity, not from any real feelings of peace. Similarly, Frida would choose to paint her own face always as an impassive mask to hide the disquiet within. Surrounding the man and his camera, and echoing the circular forms of eyes and lens, Frida has painted magnified cells containing dark nuclei afloat in a swarm of small dark marks that suggest sperm. Did she merely want to refer to the fact that he was her biological progenitor? Or does the background suggest that Frida saw a connection between her father and primal energy? Whatever their meaning, the effect of the staccato marks is to heighten the sense of Guillermo Kahlo's unrest.

The inscribed scroll below her father's bust reads: "I painted my father, Wilhelm Kahlo of Hungarian-German origin, artist-photographer by profession, in character generous, intelligent and fine, valiant because he suffered for sixty years with epilepsy, but he never stopped working and he fought against Hitler, with adoration. His daughter Frida Kahlo."

Chapter 3

The National Preparatory School

In 1922, FRIDA KAHLO entered what was undoubtedly the best educational institution in Mexico, the National Preparatory School. Out from under the thumbs of mother, sisters, aunts, away from the gentle, slow village life of Coyoacán, she was thrust into the heart of Mexico City, where modern Mexico was being invented and where students actually participated in that invention. Among her fellows were the cream of Mexico's youth, sons and daughters of professional people from the capital and from the provinces who wanted their children to prepare for the various graduate and professional schools of the National University. By the time their student days were over, not only had they helped to change both their school and their university; they were on their way to becoming leaders in the national community as well. It is no wonder that when Frida changed her birth date she chose to have been born the year of the outbreak of the Mexican Revolution. If the decision came in a flash of insight, the story behind it unfurled in her tumultuous years at the Preparatory School.

From its inception, the Preparatoria was impressive. It was founded in 1868, after the execution of Emperor Maximilian, when the Jesuit

College of San Ildefonso was transformed into part of the restored republic's system of free secular education set up by President Benito Juarez, and it was more like a college than a secondary school. Its first director, Gabino Barreda, described the curriculum as a ladder of knowledge, one step leading to the next, beginning with mathematics and culminating with logic. In between, students would take numerous courses in the physical and biological sciences; languages would be coordinated with the sequence of scientific study—first French, followed by English, in some cases German, and in the final two years, Latin. "The following," Barreda said, "will be our motto: liberty, order, progress; liberty as a means, order as a basis and progress as an end." His words were an interpretation of those carved in stone on the Preparatoria's escutcheon: "Love, Order and Progress."

In 1910, as the opening guns of the revolution were sounding in the provinces, Porfirio Díaz's last minister of instruction, Justa Sierra, created the National University of Mexico and made the Preparatoria an integral part of it; by the 1920s, attending the school meant being taught by the ablest minds of Mexico—biologist Isaac Ochoterena, for example; historian Daniel Cossio Villegas; philosophers Antonio Caso and Samuel Ramos; scholars of literature Erasmo Castellanos Quinto, Jaime Torres Bodet, and Narciso Bassols (then director of the National Law School), the last two of whom later served as education ministers. It also meant being caught up in a center of cultural and political ferment.

During the thirty-four-year dictatorship of Porfirio Díaz, the nation's course had been largely determined by a group of lawyers, accountants, and intellectuals known as the *científicos* ("scientific ones"; most of these men were students of the positivist philosophy of Auguste Comte). They had looked abroad to "modern" Europe for cultural and economic models, and they placed much of Mexico's industry and the exploitation of her natural resources in foreign—North American or European—hands. Indigenous Mexican culture was despised, and the Indians who created it were debased. Sophisticated Mexicans preferred imitations: paintings that looked like those of the Spanish masters Murillo or Zuloaga, avenues that copied the Champs-Élysées, and Beaux Arts buildings that resembled French neoclassic birthday cakes. Porfirio Díaz himself powdered his bronze skin to hide the fact that he was a Mixtec Indian with only a little Spanish blood.

It took a decade of revolution to return Mexico to the Mexicans, but by the 1920s the gains of the long battle were being consolidated. There were land and labor reforms, the power of the Catholic Church was severely curtailed, laws were passed decreeing the return of natural resources to the nation. As Mexicans began to forge a proud new identity, they rejected previously prized ideas and fashions borrowed from France and Spain, and they embraced native culture. "Idealists, persist in the salvation of the Republic," Antonio Caso exhorted his students. "Turn your eyes to the soil of Mexico, to our customs and our traditions, our hopes and our wishes, to what we in truth are!"

Upon his election in 1920, President Alvaro Obregón appointed as his minister of public education José Vasconcelos, a brilliant lawyer and philosopher of the post-*científico* generation, who had participated in the revolt against Díaz. Vasconcelos's aim was to make Mexican education truly Mexican: it was, he said, to be founded on "our blood, our language and our people." Launching a crusade to make Mexico literate, he ordered the construction of a thousand rural schools and then marshaled an army of teachers to take books (and the flag) into the hinterlands. He equipped libraries, constructed playgrounds and public swimming pools, and organized open-air art schools. He ordered classics like Plato's *Dialogues,* Dante's *Divine Comedy,* and Goethe's *Faust* to be published at prices the people could afford, and for those who could not read, he arranged free concerts and contracted with painters like Diego Rivera, José Clemente Orozco, and David Alfaro Siqueiros to work at masons' wages, decorating public walls with murals that glorified Mexican history and culture. Art, Vasconcelos believed, could inspire social change. His was a philosophy of intuition, opposed to the logic and empiricism that the *científicos* had revered. "Men are more malleable when approached through their senses," he said, "as happens when one contemplates beautiful forms and figures, or hears beautiful rhythms and melodies." His mystical belief in the greatness of Amerindian man was epitomized in his words: "The Spirit Shall Speak Through My Race."

This, then, was the mood of ardor and activism, anger and reformist zeal, that became Frida's matrix when she left the protective walls of her patio, broke with the familiar tempo of her barrio, and took the one-hour trolley ride into the city to go to her new school. "We do not speak of a time of lies nor of illusions, nor of daydreams," wrote Andrés Iduarte (director of the National Institute of Fine Arts in the early 1950s), who knew Frida at the Preparatoria. "That was a time of truth, of faith, of passion, of nobility, of progress, of celestial air and of very terrestrial steel. We were fortunate, together with Frida, we were fortunate, the young people, the boys, the children of my time: our vitality coincided with that of Mexico; we grew spiritually while the country grew in the moral realm."

The fortress-like colonial structure of reddish-brown volcanic stone that houses the Preparatory School stands only a few blocks from the Zócalo, Mexico's central plaza (said to be built over the great square and temples of the Aztecs), where the cathedral and government buildings, including the National Palace, are located. In Frida's day, this was also the university district, and near the Preparatoria were numerous stores, restaurants, public gardens, and movie houses, as well as various other schools, such as the Escuela Miguel Lerdo, outside which Preparatoria boys gathered each afternoon at five to wait for their girl friends to emerge. Street vendors found hungry customers for *carnitas* (broiled meat) or *nieve* (sherbet) or *churros* (fritters), and organ grinders filled romantic young ears with the sweet, sad tunes of Agustín Lara.

The Preparatoria's arcaded patios were a playground, a podium, and a battlefield. The gymnastics teacher would shout, "One, two; one, two!" as an army of feet jumped together and apart, and the walls resounded with the school's cry: "Shi . . . ts . . . púm/Jooya, Jooya,/Ca-chun, ca-chun, ra, ra,/Joooya, Joooya,/ PREPARATORIA!" In the patios, too, could be heard the earnest but passionate tones of youthful orators arguing for student rights or declaring their allegiances—right, left, center—while pranksters plotted mischief in dark stairways. The mood of ebullience sometimes spilled out of the school building into the streets; once during carnival season a boy dressed as Cupid hijacked a streetcar and drove the "madhouse on wheels" all over Mexico City. Sometimes bombs exploded, and firemen with hoses were summoned. Guns were fired; on one occasion, a shot blew off the fire chief's nose. "Formidable Affray at the Preparatory School!" ran the headline. "Aggression Against the Minister of Education!"

When Frida entered the Preparatoria, girls had just recently been admitted; not surprisingly, few attended, and Frida was one of thirty-five in a student body of some two thousand (one father allowed his daughter to enroll only on the condition that she promise not to talk to the boys). Probably Matilde Calderón de Kahlo resisted sending her daughter to such an unprotective place, but Guillermo Kahlo had no reservations. Having no son to fulfill his own disappointed scholarly ambitions, he pinned his hopes on his favorite child. Frida, like the most promising son in time-honored tradition, was to equip herself to enter a profession. That she passed the entrance examinations to the Preparatoria is an indication of her exceptional promise. She selected a course of studies that would lead her after five years to medical school.

At fourteen, Frida was slender and well proportioned—"a fragile adolescent" who radiated a strange vitality, a mixture of tenderness and willful spunk. She wore her thick black hair with bangs cut straight across her forehead (later she cropped it in a style that might have been "flapper" but for unruly curls). Full, sensuous lips, together with the dimple in her chin, gave her an impetuous, naughty look that was enhanced by shining dark eyes under heavy connecting eyebrows. She arrived at the school, where students wore no uniform, dressed like a German high school student, in a dark-blue pleated gabardine skirt, thick stockings, boots, and a broad-brimmed black straw hat with ribbons down the back. Alicia Galant, a friend (and portrait subject) who met Frida in 1924, remembers her in blue overalls with metal clasps bicycling in Coyoacán. This unconventional garb plus her boy's haircut made bourgeois mothers, who caught sight of her cycling with a group of boys, exclaim: *"Que niña tan fea!"* (What an ugly girl!) But her friends found her fascinating. Many of them recall that she always carried a schoolboy's knapsack amounting to "a little world on her back": texts, notebooks, drawings, butterflies and dried flowers, colors, and books printed in gothic script from the library of her father.

From the outset, the tomboy was seldom seen on the top floor of the Preparatory School's largest patio, where the girls' prefect, Dolores Angeles Castillo, held sway and where girls were expected to be when they were not in class. Frida considered most girls to be *cursi* (corny and vulgar), and irritated by their endless gossiping and pettiness, she called them *escuinclas* (pejoratively, "kids"; *escuincles* are hairless Mexican dogs). She preferred to romp in the school's corridors, participating in the activities of some of the many cliques that gave social life at the school its informal structure. There were groups that engaged in particular activities—sports, politics, journalism, literature, art, philosophy. There were debating groups, groups that went on excursions, and societies involved in social action. Some felt that Vasconcelos's popular reforms were the equivalent of a national rebirth. Others thought that the democratization of culture meant cultural debasement. Some read Marx; others were embittered by the reforms of the revolution. While radical students rejected religion, conservative ones defended the Catholic Church with zeal and violence. The various factions battled in the school's hallways and in the pages of innumerable school publications.

Frida had friends in several cliques at the Preparatoria. Among the Contemporáneos, a literary group, she knew the poet Salvador Novo and the essayist, poet, and novelist Xavier Villaurrutia. Later, she would become a close friend of the prominent poet Carlos Pellicer, and of course she knew the critic Jorge Cuesta (who married Diego Rivera's second wife, Lupe Marín). Known in the annals of Mexican literature as elitist, purist, and avant-garde in a Europeanizing way (they loved Gide, Cocteau, Pound, Eliot), the Contemporáneos were opposed to both social realism and the idealizing of indigenous culture. Another group whose company Frida enjoyed was the Maistros, which included two much-admired pro-Vasconcelos student orators: Salvador Azuela (son of the novelist Mariano Azuela, who wrote *The Underdogs,* the most prominent novel of the Mexican Revolution) and the radical leftist Germán de Campo.

But Frida's real *cuates* (pals) were the Cachuchas, named after the caps they all wore and famous at the Preparatoria for their brains and their mischief. This band of seven boys and two girls—Miguel N. Lira (whom Frida nicknamed "Chong Lee" because he was a respected scholar of Chinese poetry), José Gómez Robleda, Agustín Lira, Jesús Ríos y Valles (Frida called him Chucho Paisajes, "landscapes," because of his surname, "rivers and valleys"), Alfonso Villa, Manuel González Ramírez, and Alejandro Gómez Arias, along with Carmen Jaime and Frida—went on to become outstanding members of Mexico's professional class. Today, Alejandro Gómez Arias is a highly respected intellectual, a lawyer, and a political journalist; Miguel N. Lira became a lawyer and a poet; José Gómez Robleda was a professor of psychiatry at the university medical school, and Manuel González Ramírez was a historian, a writer, and a lawyer (he served both Frida and Diego on various occasions).

What united them in their school days was not so much an activity or a cause as an attitude of irreverence. Although they did not involve themselves with politics (they thought politicians acted out of narrow self-interest), they espoused a kind of romantic socialism mixed with nationalism. As followers of Vasconcelos they held high ideals for their country's future and agitated for reforms at the school. But at the same time they enjoyed creating anarchy in the classrooms, and their escapades were outrageous and sometimes terrible: once classrooms emptied when they rode a donkey through the halls; another time, they wove a web of fireworks around a dog, lit them, and sent the poor beast running and barking through the corridors. One of the group remembers that "it was the joking attitude we had toward people and things that drew Frida to us, not because she had the habit of laughing at other people but because it captivated her, and she began to learn it, and ended by becoming a master of pun and, when they were called for, of cutting witticisms." From the Cachuchas, Frida also learned a kind of comradely loyalty, a boyish way of handling friendship that she would keep all her life. In their company, her natural mischievousness deepened into a delight in subverting all authorities.

The Cachuchas' most outrageous "prank" involved Antonio Caso, one of the most revered of university professors, but from the Cachuchas' point of view an overly conservative thinker. "Linda," Frida explained to a school friend, "we can't take it anymore. He talks and talks, very beautifully, but without substance. We've had enough of Plato, Aristotle, Kant, Bergson, Comte, and he doesn't dare get mixed up with Hegel, Marx, and Engels. Something must be done!"

While the professor delivered a lecture on evolution in the Generalito, a large assembly hall that had once been a chapel, the Cachuchas placed a six-inch firecracker with a twenty-minute fuse outside the room, on top of the window above the pulpit. They tossed a coin to see who would light it. The lot fell to José Gómez Robleda. He remembers: "Gómez Arias, Miguel N. Lira, and Manuel González Ramírez left the school building. I stayed [and lit the fuse] and sat down in the Generalito next to the prefect of the girl students. After a while came the explosion. Baroom! The glass windowpanes broke, and a hail of glass and stones and gravel fell on Antonio Caso." The eloquent orator reacted with perfect aplomb. He casually smoothed down his mussed hair and went right on lecturing as if nothing had happened. As usual, the Cachuchas had prepared their alibis well—most of them had either left the building or were sitting innocently in the lecture hall—and thus escaped the fate of "bomb" makers who were caught: summary expulsion.

Legend has it that Frida was expelled once (the reason is unrecorded). Nothing daunted, she took her case directly to Vasconcelos, whose rivalrous animosity to the director of the Preparatoria, Lombardo Toledano, was well known; the minister ordered her reinstatement. "If you can't manage a little girl like that," he is reported to have said to the beleaguered Toledano, "you are not fit to be director of such an institution."

A favorite haunt of the Cachuchas was the Ibero American Library, only a short distance from the school. Although it was housed in the Old Church of the Incarnation, it was a warm and welcoming place, with a maze of low bookshelves to counter the grandeur of the tall, barrel-vaulted nave, which was decorated with murals by Roberto Montenegro and the bright silk flags of the Latin American countries. Two kindly librarians allowed the Cachuchas to use it almost as their private domain, and the "Ibero" became their meeting place. Each one had his or her particular corner. Here they argued, flirted, fought, wrote papers, drew pictures, and read books.

They read constantly—everything from Dumas to Mariano Azuela, from the Bible to Zozobra (published in 1919 by the poet Ramón López Velarde, whose work captured the spirit of the revolutionary years). They devoured the great works of Spanish and (in translation) Russian literature (Pushkin, Gogol, Andreyev, Tolstoy) and kept up with current Mexican fiction. Eventually Frida learned to read in three languages: Spanish, English, German. The imaginary biography of the fifteenth-century Florentine painter Paolo Uccello, which she read in a translation of Marcel Schwob's Imaginary Lives, moved her so deeply that she memorized it. Familiar with her father's collection of books on philosophy, she loved to talk as if Hegel and Kant were as easy to read as a comic strip. "Alejandro," she would cry, leaning out the window, "lend me your Spengler. I don't have anything to read on the bus!"

The Cachuchas and their friends had competitions to see who could discover a better book and who could finish it first, and they often dramatized what they read. Adelina Zendejas, one of the girls at the Preparatoria Frida did not consider cursi, recalls being part of a spellbound audience when Angel Salas (a Maistro), Frida, and Jesús Ríos y Valles recounted their imaginary voyages. Improvising on information gleaned from books they had read—H. G. Wells, Victor Hugo, Dostoyevsky, Jules Verne—they told of scaling the Himalayas, wandering through Russia and China, exploring the Amazon and the depths of the ocean. Their stories were full of realistic details: how they gathered the money for the trip, what they packed, how they selected their means of transportation. Angel Salas, who was to become a musicologist and composer, accompanied his inventions with Tarascan songs.

Boy companions, whether Cachuchas or not, Frida called *cuates* or *manis* (brothers); girls (except for the *escuinclas*) were *manas* (short for *hermanas,* or sisters). The *hermana* Frida mentions most often in letters is another high-spirited tomboy, Agustina Reyna (nicknamed "la Reyna" or "Reynita"). The two girls loved to loiter in the public gardens of the university district, where they would listen to the organ grinders and chat with truants and newsboys. From peddlers, Frida won sweets by the toss of a coin—she never lost—and acquired the savvy and argot of the street. Sometimes Angel Salas went with them to the Loreto Garden; there Frida would hold out her Cachucha cap, "begging" while Angel played his violin.

Frida enjoyed an endless battle of wits with the other female Cachucha, Carmen Jaime, who had read every philosophy book she could find (she grew up to become a scholar of seventeenth-century Spanish literature) and whose company must have been an education in itself. A truly eccentric young woman, she dressed sloppily in dark, masculine clothes, and earned the nickname "James," or even "vampire," by sporting a black cape when she went skating at dawn. The private language she invented she shared with the other Cachuchas, saying, for example, "Procedamos al comes"—"Let's proceed to the eat."

Although a voracious reader, Frida was not a dedicated student: she was interested in biology, literature, and art, but people fascinated her more. Fortunately, she was able to earn high marks without putting in much effort—she could read a text once and remember the contents. It was her right, she felt, not to attend lectures given by ill-prepared or boring teachers. Instead, she would sit just outside a class she had chosen to cut and read aloud to friends. When she did attend, she enlivened the proceedings. Once, bored by a psychology professor's exposition of his theory of sleep, she handed Adelina Zendejas a note: "Read it, turn it over, and pass it to Reyna. Don't laugh, because you'll be in trouble if you do and they'll probably expel you." On the other side of the paper was a caricature of the teacher as a sleeping elephant. Of course, none of the ninety students in the class could stifle his laughter as the drawing passed among them.

Her irreverence toward professors sometimes went as far as petitioning the director to remove them. "He is not a teacher," she would say. "[He] doesn't know what he's talking about since the text contradicts what he says, and when we ask him questions he is not capable of answering them. Let's eliminate him and renew the professorship."

The Cachuchas had no more respect for painters than they had for professors. When Vasconcelos, in 1921–1922, commissioned a number of artists to paint murals in the Preparatoria, the painters, perched on their scaffolds, became perfect targets. After a scaffold was built, for example, there would be wood shavings and scraps all over the floor. "We would set them on fire," said José Gómez Robleda, "and there the poor painter would be, amidst flames, and his paintings all ruined. The painters took to wearing huge pistols."

Of all the artists, Diego Rivera, commissioned to paint a mural in the Bolívar Amphitheater, the Preparatoria's auditorium, was the most colorful personality. He was thirty-six years old in 1922, world-famous, and fantastically fat. He loved to talk while he painted, and his charisma together with his frog-like appearance guaranteed him an audience. Another attraction—in those days when teachers and public servants wore black suits, stiff collars, and homburgs—was his characteristic dress: a Stetson hat, big black miner's shoes, and a wide leather belt (sometimes a cartridge belt), which could barely contain the baggy clothes that looked as if he had slept in them for a week.

Frida in particular was moved to mischief by Rivera. Although the amphitheater was off bounds to students while the artist was at work, she managed to slip in without being caught. She stole food out of his lunch basket. Once she soaped the stairway that descended from the amphitheater stage where he was painting, and then hid behind a pillar to watch. But Rivera's way of walking was slow and measured; placing one foot carefully before the other, he moved as if suspended in a liquid medium and never fell. The next day, however, Professor Antonio Caso tumbled down the same stairs.

A succession of beautiful models accompanied Rivera on the scaffold. One was his mistress, Lupe Marín (he married her in 1922). Another model was the well-known beauty Nahui Olín, who posed for the figure representing erotic poetry in the Preparatoria mural and was a painter herself. Frida liked to hide in the dark doorway, and if Lupe was on the scaffold, she would call out: "Hey, Diego, here comes Nahui!" Or when no one was with him and she saw Lupe arriving, she would whisper loudly, as if Diego were about to be caught in some compromising situation, "Watch out, Diego, Lupe's coming!"

It is part of Frida Kahlo's myth that she became infatuated with Diego Rivera during her Preparatoria years. Once when a group of girl students were discussing their life ambitions in an ice cream store, Frida reportedly came out with the astonishing statement: "My ambition is to have a child by Diego Rivera. And I'm going to tell him so someday." When Adelina Zendejas protested that Diego was a "pot-bellied, filthy, terrible-looking" old man, Frida retorted, "Diego is so gentle, so tender, so wise, so sweet. I'd bathe him and clean him." She would have his baby, she said, "just as soon as I convince him to cooperate." Frida herself recalled that while she taunted Diego with names like "Old Fatso," in her head she was always saying, "You'll see, *panzón* [fat-belly]; now you don't pay any attention to me, but one day I'll have a child by you."

In his autobiography, *My Art, My Life*, Rivera tells another story:

One night, as I was painting high on the scaffold and Lupe was sitting and weaving down below, there was a loud shouting and pushing against the auditorium door. All of a sudden the door flew open, and a girl who seemed to be no more than ten or twelve was propelled inside.

She was dressed like any other high school student but her manner immediately set her apart. She had unusual dignity and self-assurance, and there was a strange fire in her eyes. Her beauty was that of a child, yet her breasts were well developed.

She looked straight up at me. "Would it cause you any annoyance if I watched you at work?" she asked.

"No, young lady, I'd be charmed," I said.

She sat down and watched me silently, her eyes riveted on every move of my paint brush. After a few hours, Lupe's jealousy was aroused, and she began to insult the girl. But the girl paid no attention to her. This, of course, enraged Lupe the more. Hands on hips, Lupe walked toward the girl and confronted her belligerently. The girl merely stiffened and returned Lupe's stare without a word.

Visibly amazed, Lupe glared at her a long time, then smiled, and in a tone of grudging admiration, said to me, "Look at that girl! Small as she is, she does not fear a tall, strong woman like me. I really like her."

The girl stayed about three hours. When she left, she said only, "Good night." A year later I learned that she was the hidden owner of the voice that had come from behind the pillar and that her name was Frida Kahlo. But I had no idea that she would one day be my wife.

For all Frida's fascination with Rivera, she was, during her school years, the girl friend of the undisputed leader of the Cachuchas, Alejandro Gómez Arias. Known as a brilliant and charismatic orator, an amusing storyteller, an erudite scholar, and a good athlete, Alejandro was also handsome, with a high forehead, gentle dark eyes, an aristocratic nose, and delicately formed lips. His manner was sophisticated, a little *dégagé*. As he spoke of politics or Proust, painting or school gossip, his ideas flowed with all the ease of water; but to him, conversation was an art, and he orchestrated his silences with care, always keeping his audience's rapt attention.

His refined sensibility, his severe notion of self-discipline, and his critical acumen sometimes made him hard on his friends. He could play with words like a juggler, but the swift trident of his satire was devastating. He despised vulgarity, stupidity, venality, the misuse of power. He loved knowledge, moral probity, justice, and irony. The young orator's mellifluous voice, his graceful arms drawing arcs in space or briefly crossed upon his chest, his eyes full of passion, looking upward as if for inspiration, were captivating. "Optimism, sacrifice, purity, love, *alegría* are the orator's social mission," he would cry as he exhorted his fellows to dedicate themselves to their nation's "great destiny," to what he called "my Mexico."

Frida, who grew up to love great men, began by attaching herself to Alejandro. Having entered the Preparatoria in 1919, he was several classes ahead of her, and he became for a time her mentor, her *cuate*, and ultimately her boyfriend. Frida called him her *novio*, a term that in those days implied a romantic attachment that often ended in marriage (a *novio* is a fiancé, according to dictionary usage). But Gómez Arias feels that the terms *novio* and *novia* give an overly bourgeois notion of their relationship: he prefers to be called her "intimate friend" or her "young lover." The adolescent Frida, he says, "had a fresh, perhaps ingenuous and childlike manner, but at the same time she was quick and dramatic in her urge to discover life." Gentle and chivalrous, Alejandro wooed his "niña of the preparatoria," as she called herself, with flowers and witticisms. After school they used to be seen walking and talking without cease. They exchanged photographs and, whenever they were separated from each other, letters.

Frida's letters to Alejandro are still in his possession; they offer a picture of her life, and they vividly reveal her development from a child into an adolescent and finally into a woman. They also show her compulsion to tell about her life and her feelings, a need that would eventually impel her to paint mostly self-portraits. She wrote with an emotional candor that is surprising in an adolescent girl, and her characteristic impulsiveness is sustained in the momentum of her language: the flow of words is rarely measured by commas, periods, or paragraphs. It is, however, often enlivened with cartoon-like drawings. Frida illustrated things that happened to her—a fight, a kiss, herself sick in bed. She drew numerous smiling or crying faces and faces that did both at once (Alejandro sometimes called her *lagrimilla*, "crybaby"). She sketched modish beauties with long necks, bobbed hair, pencil-thin eyebrows, and pursed lips. Next to one of these she wrote in a mixture of Spanish and English, "One *tipo* ideal" (one ideal type) and the warning: "Don't tear her out because she is very pretty. . . . From the little doll above, you can see what progress I am making in drawing, isn't that so? Now you know that I am a prodigy in matters of art! So be very careful if the dogs should come near this admirable psychological and artistic study of one 'pay Checka' (one *tipo* ideal)."

Cachucha Manuel González Ramírez remembers that Frida developed a personal emblem that she used as a signature: an isosceles triangle with the point down that she sometimes transformed into a portrait by the addition of her features, the lower angle becoming a beard. Many of her letters to Alejandro are signed with a point-upward isosceles triangle, with no face.

In Frida's first letter to Alejandro, dated December 15, 1922, she sounds like a well-brought-up Catholic child; she has not yet found her own witty and intimate voice. The letter consoles Alejandro for some misfortune:

Alejandro: I was very sorry about what happened to you and really the biggest condolence came out of my heart.

The only thing that as a friend I advise you is to have enough strength of will to support such pains as God Our Father sends us as a test given the fact that we came into the world to suffer.

I have felt in my soul this pain and what I ask God is that he gives you the grace and sufficient strength to accept it.

Frieda

During the summer of 1923, Frida and Alejandro fell in love, and the letters become more personal, revealing her cajoling flirtatiousness and the intensely possessive nature of her attachment.

Coyoacán, August 10, 1923

Alex: I received your note yesterday at seven in the evening when I least expected that someone would remember me, and *least of all Dr. Alejandro,* but luckily, I was mistaken. . . . You don't know how delighted I was that you had confidence in me as if I were a *true friend* and you spoke to me as you had never spoken to me before, since you tell me with a little irony that *I am so superior* and *I am so far beyond you,* I will see the basis of those lines and not see what others would see in them . . . . . . and you ask my advice, something that I would give with all my heart, if the little experience of my 15 [sixteen] years is worth something, but if good intentions are enough for you not only is my humble advice yours but all of me is yours. . . .

Well Alex, write to me often and long, the longer the better, and meanwhile receive *all* the love of

Frieda

P.S.: Say hello to Chong Lee and to your little sister.

Since their relationship was not sanctioned by Frida's parents, the couple met clandestinely. Frida invented excuses for leaving the house, for returning late from school; because her mother was apt to ask to whom her daughter was writing, she often wrote in bed at night. Or she would dash off notes while standing in the post office. When she was sick she had to rely on Cristina, not always a cooperative accomplice, to mail her letters to Alejandro. So that she could receive his, she asked him to sign them Agustina Reyna. She promised to write to him every day as proof that she had not forgotten him. "Tell me if you don't love me anymore Alex, I love you even if you do not love me as much as a flea." To prove it, she filled her letters with kisses and expressions of affection. Sometimes she drew a circle near her signature, explaining, "Here is a kiss from your Friducha," or "My lips were here a long time." When she grew up and wore lipstick, she no longer needed the captions, but she kept circling the imprint of her lips on letters all her life.

During December 1923 and January 1924, Frida and Alejandro were separated not only by the inter-term vacation at the Preparatoria (which lasted from the end of final exams in mid-December to the beginning of the school year in mid-February) but also by the fact that on November 30, 1923, a rebellion against President Obregón broke out. By Christmas there was fighting in Mexico City. Vasconcelos resigned as minister of education in January to protest the ruthless suppression of the rebels, but he was persuaded to resume his post. The revolt lasted until March 1924, when it was finally put down, at a cost of seven thousand dead. But politics remained volatile, and in June, Vasconcelos resigned again (for the last time) in protest against the election (with the support of President Obregón and United States interests) of Plutarco Elías Calles as president of Mexico. When he was gone, conservative students in the Preparatoria turned their ire upon the walls the muralists had painted, scratching curses into the plaster and spitting on the motifs that offended them most.

Though the Cachuchas disdained politics and politicians, they must have participated in demonstrations in support of Vasconcelos. It is said that on Christmas Eve, 1923, some of them rode the trolley to the Desierto de los Leones (between Mexico City and Coyoacán) with the intention of entering the fray. (Either the flash of gunpowder in the distance or the sudden appearance of a full moon changed their minds; they boarded the next homeward-bound streetcar.) Much to her regret, Frida did not participate in these adventures, for her mother kept her at home whenever there was political agitation or the rumor of violence. Frida loathed being confined: "I am sad and bored in this town," she wrote in one note to Alejandro; "though very picturesque, [it] lacks a *no se quien* [I don't know who] who goes every day to the Ibero American." And on another occasion: "Tell me what's new in Mexico [City], about your life and about everything that you want to tell me since you know that here there is nothing but pasture and pasture, Indians and Indians, and huts and huts so that one can't get away and so that even if you don't believe it I am very bored with *b* of burro. . . . when you come for the love of God bring me something to read because each day I am becoming more ignorant. (Forgive me for being such a bum)"

December 16, 1923

Alex: I am very sorry that yesterday at four I didn't go to the University but my mother would not let me go to Mexico because they told her there was a *bola* [uprising]. What's more I did not register [for the next term] and now I don't know what to do. I beg you to forgive me since you will say I am very rude but it was not my fault, no matter what I did my mother took it into her head that she was not going to let me go out and there was nothing to be done, just put up with it.

Tomorrow, Monday, I am going to tell her that I have an exam in modeling [sculpture in clay] and I will spend the whole day in Mexico, it's not very certain since first I have to see what humor my mamacita is in and after that decide to tell this lie, if I go I'll see you at 11:30 at Leyes [the law school, a frequent rendezvous for Frida and Alejandro] so that you won't have to go to the University, please wait for me on the corner with the ice cream store. There is still going to be the *posada* [Christmas party] at Rouaix's house [the Rouaixes were family friends who lived in Coyoacán], the first that is to say now I am planning not to go but who knows when the hour arrives. . . .

But even if we are going to see each other I don't want you not to write me, because if you don't I am not going to write to you either, and if you have nothing to tell me send me 2 blank papers or tell me the same thing 50 times for that will show me that at least you remember me. . . .

Well receive many kisses and all my love.

Your
Frieda

Forgive the change of ink.

December 19, 1923

. . . I am upset because they punished me because of that idiot *escuincla* Cristina because I gave her a blow (because she took some of my things)—and she began to shriek for about half an hour and later they gave me a good thrashing, and they didn't let me go to yesterday's *posada* and they hardly let me go out in the street so that I can't write you a very long letter but I write you like this so that you will see that I always remember you even if I am sadder than anything since you can imagine, without seeing you, punished and the whole day without doing anything because I have a terrible temper. This afternoon I asked my mother if I could go to the plaza to buy some lace and I came to the post office so that I could write. . . .

Receive many kisses from your *chamaca* who misses you a lot. Say hello to Carmen James and Chong Lee (please)

Frieda.

December 22, 1923

Alex: Yesterday I did not write to you because it was very late at night when we returned home from the Navarros, but now I have lots of time to dedicate to you, the dance that night was OK; rather it was ugly but we still had a little fun. Tonight there is going to be a *posada* in Mrs. Roca's house and Cristina and I are going to eat there, I think it's going to be very pretty because lots of girls and boys are going and Mrs. Roca is very nice, tomorrow I'll tell you what it was like.

At the Navarros' dance I did not dance much because I was not very happy. I danced mostly with Rouaix, the rest of them were repulsive.

There is a *posada* now at the Rocha house but who knows if we are going. . . .

Write me don't be mean

Many kisses

Your Frieda

They lent me *The Picture of Dorian Gray*. Please send me Guevara's address so I can send him his Bible.

January 1, 1924

My Alex:

. . . Where did you spend New Year's Eve? I went to the Campos' house and it was as usual since we spent the whole time praying and afterward because I was so sleepy I went to sleep and did not dance at all. This morning I took communion and prayed to God for all of you. . . .

Imagine, yesterday I went to confession in the afternoon, and I forgot three sins and I took communion that way and the sins were big, now let's see, what shall I do, but the thing is that I have begun not to believe in confession and although I might want to, I cannot confess my sins well. I am very stupid, right?

Well *mi vida,* take note that I have written to you. I think that that must be because she doesn't love you at all your

Frieda

Forgive me for writing to you on this *cursi* paper but Cristina traded it for my white paper and though later I regretted it there was nothing to be done. (It's not so ugly, so ugly)

January 12, 1924

My Alex: . . . The thing of school registration is very green [bad] since a boy told me that it begins on the 15th of this month, and then there was a mess and my mother says that I am not going to register until things are well settled so that there is no hope of going to Mexico, and I have to accept staying in the town [Coyoacán]. What do you know about the revolt? Tell me something so that I am more or less informed about how things are going, since here, I am becoming more and more dumb. . . . I put it to you *chiquito* [little one] because it shames me. You will tell me to read the newspapers, but the trouble is that I am too lazy to read the newspapers and I start reading other things. I found very beautiful big books that have a lot of Oriental art and that is what your Friducha is reading now.

Well *mi lindo* [my handsome one], since I have run out of paper on which to write you and I am going to bore you with so many foolishnesses I say goodbye and I send you 1000000000000 kisses (with your permission) which can't be heard because otherwise the people of San Raphael [the district where Alejandro lived] would get agitated. Write me and tell me everything that happens to you.

Your Frieda

Give my love to la Reynilla [Agustina Reyna] if you see her. Forgive the indecent handwriting that I have made.

The next time Frida and Alejandro were separated was in April, when Frida went on a retreat. Despite her doubts about confession, she clearly had not yet lost her faith. "The exercises of the retreat were beautiful because the priest that directed them was very intelligent and almost a saint," she wrote on the 16th. "In the general communion they gave us the papal benediction and one gains many indulgences and you can ask for as many as you want, the one I prayed for most was Maty (Matilde) my sister and since the priest knows her he said he would pray a lot for her. I also prayed to God and to the Virgin that everything should go well for you and that you should love me always and I also prayed for your mother and your little sister. . . ."

In the second half of 1924 the tone of Frida's letters changed. The intensity of her love for Alejandro grows, and there is a hint of sadness and a certain insecurity in her need to be constantly reassured that he cares for her. Although she retains a girlish playfulness and candor, she also speaks of a plan to go with her boyfriend to the United States. (Once she mentions wanting to expand her world and change her life by traveling to San Francisco.) She was now Alejandro's "little woman," as well as his cuate. He recalls, "Frida was sexually precocious. To her, sex was a form of enjoying life, a kind of vital impulse."

Thursday, December 25, 1924

My Alex: Since I saw you I have loved you. What do you say? (?) Because it will probably be a few days before we see each other, I am going to beg you not to forget your pretty little woman eh? . . . sometimes at night I am very afraid and I would like you to be with me so that I should be less frightened and so that you can tell me that you love me as much as before; as much as last December, even if I am an "easy thing" right Alex? You must keep on liking easy things. . . . I would like to be even easier, a little tiny thing that you could just carry in your pocket always always. . . . Alex, write to me soon and even if it's not true, tell me that you love me very much and that you can't live without me. . . .

Your *chamaca, escuincla* or woman or whatever you want [Here Frida drew three little figures showing these three different types of females.]

Frieda

On Saturday I'll bring you your sweater and your books and lots of violets because there are lots at my house. . . .

answer   answer   answer   answer   answer   answer
  me   me   me   me   me   me
   "   "   "   "   "   "
   "   "   "   "   "   "
   "   "   "   "   "   "
   "   "   "   "   "   "

Do you know the news? [Here Frida drew a girl with corkscrew curls and a crown. Around her, like a veil, she wrote: "The *pelonas* are over with." By *pelonas*, she means "bobbed-hair flappers."]

My Alex: Today at 11 I picked up your letter, but I did not answer you until now because as you will understand, one can't write or do anything when one is surrounded by a crowd, but now that it's 10 at night, I find myself alone and it's the most propitious moment to tell you what I'm thinking. . . . Concerning what you tell me about Anita Reyna, naturally I would not get mad even as a joke, in the first place, because you are only telling the truth, which is that she is and always will be very pretty and very cute and in the second place, because I love all the people you love or have loved (?) for the very simple reason that you love them, nevertheless I did not much like the thing of the caresses because in spite of the fact that I understand that it is very true that she is *chulisima* [very cute], I feel something like . . . . . . well, how can I say it, like envy you know? but it is natural. The day you want to caress her even if it is a memory caress me and make believe that it is her eh? My Alex? . . . Listen little brother now in 1925 we are going to love each other a lot eh?* Forgive the repetition of the word "love." 5 times in one go but I am very gushy. Don't you think that we should keep on carefully planning the trip to the United States, I want you to tell me how you feel about going in December of this year, there is lots of time to arrange things do you agree? Tell me all the pros and cons and whether you really can go, because look Alex; it is good that we should do something in life don't you think so, since we'll be nothing but dopes if we spend our whole life in Mexico, because for me there is nothing more lovely than to travel, it is a real pain to think that I don't have sufficient willpower to do what I am telling you about, you will say no, that one needs not just willpower but also money power (dough) but one can gather it by working for a year and the rest is easier right? But since the truth is that I don't know much about these things, it's good for you to tell me the advantages and disadvantages and if truly the gringos are very disagreeable. Because you must see that all that I have written you from the asterisk to this line of writing, is full of castles in the air and it is good for me to be disillusioned right away. . . .

At 12 last night I thought of you my Alex and you? I think you thought of me, too because my left ear rang. Well since you already know that "New Year means new life" this year your little woman is not going to be a 7 kilo flapper kid but rather the sweetest and best thing that you have ever known so that you eat her up with nothing but kisses.

> Your *chamaca* adores you
> Friduchita

(a very happy new year to your mother and sister)

Frida said she could save money to go to the United States by working for a year; the truth was she had to earn money to contribute to the family income. Still, working during vacations and after school was less onerous than it might have been, because employment allowed her greater freedom. Many were the days when she dispatched a note to her mother saying that she would not be home until late, that she was going to help her father in the photography studio. Since the studio was in the middle of Mexico City, it was not too difficult sometimes to slip out for a rendezvous with Alejandro. "I do not know what to do to get some work," she wrote during one vacation, "since that is the only way that I will be able to see you daily the way I did before at school."

Work, other than helping her father, was not easy to find. For a brief period, Frida served as a cashier in a pharmacy, but she was inept; at the end of the day there was either too much or too little money in the till, and she frequently found herself putting her own earnings into the cash register in order to balance the books. Another time she followed up a want ad and took a job keeping accounts at a lumberyard for sixty pesos a month. In 1925, while she job-hunted, Frida studied shorthand and typing at the Oliver Academy. Excited about the prospect of employment at the Ministry of Education library,

Frida wrote, "They pay 4 or 4.50 and to me that doesn't seem bad at all, but the first thing I need is to know something about typing and charm. So just imagine how backward your pal is! . . ."

According to Alejandro Gómez Arias, it was during this period, when she was looking for work, that a woman employee of the Ministry of Education's library, whom Frida met while applying for the library job, seduced her. It is probably to this incident that Frida referred when, in 1938, she told a friend that her initiation into homosexual sex by one of her "schoolteachers" had been traumatic, especially so because her parents discovered the liaison and a scandal ensued. "I am full of the most terrible sadness," she wrote Alejandro on August 1, "but you know that not everything is as one would want it to be and what's the point of talking about it. . . ." At the end of the letter she drew a crying face.

In the same letter she told Alejandro, "I have been working in the factory, the one I told you about, during the day because there is nothing else to do while I look for something better, imagine how I'll be, but what do you want me to do, even though working there does not fascinate me in any way, there's nothing to be done about it, I have to bear it whether I want to or not." The factory job did not last long; her next one, a paid apprenticeship in engraving with a friend of her father's, the successful commercial printer Fernando Fernández, interested her more. Fernández taught Frida to draw by having her copy prints by the Swedish Impressionist Anders Zorn, and he discovered that she had, as he put it, "enormous talent." According to Alejandro Gómez Arias, Frida responded by having a brief affair with him.

At eighteen, Frida was clearly no longer the *niña de la Preparatoria*. The young girl who three years before had entered the National Preparatory School wearing pigtails and a German high school uniform was now a modern young woman, touched by the headlong buoyancy of the twenties, defiant of conventional morality, and unfazed by the raised eyebrows of her more conservative school friends.

The fierce originality of her new persona is visible in a series of photographs taken by Guillermo Kahlo on February 7, 1926. There is a formal portrait in which she carefully hides her thinner right leg behind her left one and wears a strange satin dress that has nothing to do with 1920s fashions. And there are several photographs taken the same day in which she stands out from her conventionally dressed family group by wearing a man's three-piece suit, complete with handkerchief and tie. She assumes a mannish posture, with one hand in her pocket and the other sporting a cane. She may have donned a man's clothes as a joke, but in any case, this young woman is no innocent child. In all the photographs, she looks straight out at us with a disconcertingly level glance, and in her gaze there is more than a hint of that mixture of sensuality and dark irony that will reappear in so many of her self-portraits.

PART 2

Chapter 4

Accident and Aftermath

IT WAS ONE of those accidents that make a person, even one separated by years from the actual fact, wince with horror. It involved a trolley car that plowed into a flimsy wooden bus, and it transformed Frida Kahlo's life.

Far from being a unique piece of bad luck, such accidents were common enough in those days in Mexico City to be depicted in numerous *retablos*.* Buses were relatively new to the city, and because of their novelty they were jammed with people while trolley cars went empty. Then, as now, they were driven with toreador bravado, as if the image of the Virgin of Guadalupe dangling near the front window made the driver invincible. The bus in which Frida was riding was new, and its fresh coat of paint made it look especially jaunty.

The accident occurred late in the afternoon on September 17, 1925, the day after Mexico had celebrated the anniversary of its independence from Spain. A light rain had just stopped; the grand gray govern-

---

* Small votive paintings offering thanks to a holy being, usually the Virgin, for misfortunes escaped. These works, which are also called ex-voto paintings, depict both the event and the holy agent of miraculous salvation.

ment buildings that border the Zócalo looked even grayer and more severe than usual. The bus to Coyoacán was nearly full, but Alejandro and Frida found seats together in the back. When they reached the corner of Cuahutemotzín and 5 de Mayo and were about to turn onto Calzada de Tlalpan, a trolley from Xochimilco approached. It was moving slowly but kept coming as if it had no brakes, as if it were purposely aiming at a crash. Frida remembered:

A little while after we got on the bus the collision began. Before that we had taken another bus, but since I had lost a little parasol, we got off to look for it and that was how we happened to get on the bus that destroyed me. The accident took place on a corner in front of the San Juan market, exactly in front. The streetcar went slowly, but our bus driver was a very nervous young man. When the trolley car went around the corner the bus was pushed against the wall.

I was an intelligent young girl, but impractical, in spite of all the freedom I had won. Perhaps for this reason, I did not assess the situation nor did I guess the kind of wounds I had. The first thing I thought of was a *balero* [Mexican toy] with pretty colors that I had bought that day and that I was carrying with me. I tried to look for it, thinking that what had happened would not have major consequences.

It is a lie that one is aware of the crash, a lie that one cries. In me there were no tears. The crash bounced us forward and a handrail pierced me the way a sword pierces a bull. A man saw me having a tremendous hemorrhage. He carried me and put me on a billiard table until the Red Cross came for me.

When Alejandro Gómez Arias describes the accident, his voice constricts to an almost inaudible monotone, as if he could avoid reliving the memory by speaking of it quietly:

"The electric train with two cars approached the bus slowly. It hit the bus in the middle. Slowly the train pushed the bus. The bus had a strange elasticity. It bent more and more, but for a time it did not break. It was a bus with long benches on either side. I remember that at one moment my knees touched the knees of the person sitting opposite me, I was sitting next to Frida. When the bus reached its maximal flexibility it burst into a thousand pieces, and the train kept moving. It ran over many people.

"I remained under the train. Not Frida. But among the iron rods of the train, the handrail broke and went through Frida from one side to the other at the level of the pelvis. When I was able to stand up I got out from under the train. I had no lesions, only contusions. Naturally the first thing that I did was to look for Frida.

"Something strange had happened. Frida was totally nude. The collision had unfastened her clothes. Someone in the bus, probably a house painter, had been carrying a packet of powdered gold. This package broke, and the gold fell all over the bleeding body of Frida. When people saw her they cried, '*La bailarina, la bailarina!*' With the gold on her red, bloody body, they thought she was a dancer.

"I picked her up—in those days I was a strong boy—and then I noticed with horror that Frida had a piece of iron in her body. A man said, 'We have to take it out!' He put his knee on Frida's body, and said, 'Let's take it out.' When he pulled it out, Frida screamed so loud that when the ambulance from the Red Cross arrived, her screaming was louder than the siren. Before the ambulance came, I picked up Frida and put her in the display window of a billiard room. I took off my coat and put it over her. I thought she was going to die. Two or three people did die at the scene of the accident, others died later.

"The ambulance came and took her to the Red Cross Hospital, which in those days was on San Jeronimo Street, a few blocks from where the accident took place. Frida's condition was so grave that the doctors did not think they could save her. They thought she would die on the operating table.

"Frida was operated on for the first time. During the first month it was not certain that she would live."

The girl whose wild dash through school corridors resembled a bird's flight, who jumped on and off streetcars and buses, preferably when they were moving, was now immobilized and enclosed in a series of plaster casts and other contraptions. "It was a strange collision," Frida said. "It was not violent but rather silent, slow, and it harmed everybody. And me most of all."

Her spinal column was broken in three places in the lumbar region. Her collarbone was broken, and her third and fourth ribs. Her right leg had eleven fractures and her right foot was dislocated and crushed. Her left shoulder was out of joint, her pelvis broken in three places. The steel handrail had literally skewered her body at the level of the abdomen; entering on the left side, it had come out through the vagina. "I lost my virginity," she said.

In the hospital, an old convent with dark, bare, high-ceilinged rooms, the doctors operated and shook their heads and deliberated: Would she live? Would she walk again? "They had to put her back together in sections as if they were making a photomontage," says one old friend. When she regained consciousness, Frida asked that her family be called. Neither of her parents was able to come. "My mother was speechless for a month because of the impression it made on her," Frida remembered. "It made my father so sad that he became ill, and I could not see him for over twenty days. There had never been deaths in my home." Adriana, who now lived with her husband Alberto Veraza near the blue house in Coyoacán, was so upset when she heard the news that she fainted; of Frida's family, only Matilde came at once. Still cut off from the others because her mother had not yet forgiven her elopement, she was glad to have the chance to help her younger sister. As soon as she read about the accident in a newspaper, she was by Frida's side, and since she lived closer to the hospital than her family, she was able to come every day. "They kept us in a kind of horrifying ward. . . . Only one nurse cared for twenty-five patients. It was Matilde who lifted my spirits; she told me jokes. She was fat and ugly, but she had a great sense of humor. She made everyone in the room howl with laughter. She knitted and she helped the nurse care for the patients." For a month Frida lay flat on her back, encased in a plaster cast and enclosed in a box-like structure that looked like a sarcophagus.

Besides Matilde, there were visits from the Cachuchas and other friends; but at night, when Matilde and her friends had gone home, Frida was haunted by the thought that she might have died, might die. Death was a memory of gold-speckled redness on naked flesh, of exclamations—*"La bailarina!"*—piercing the general wailing, of seeing, with that awesome and disengaged clarity that sometimes comes with shock, other victims crawling out from under the train and one woman running from the wreck holding her intestines in her hands. "In this hospital," Frida told Alejandro, "death dances around my bed at night."

As soon as she was able, Frida poured forth her feelings and thoughts in letters to Alejandro, who was confined at home with injuries more severe than his word "contusion" would indicate. She kept him informed of the progress of her recovery, writing with that mixture of literal detail, fantasy, and intensity of feeling that was to characterize the imagery in her paintings. There are notes of humor and *alegría*, but they never quite drown out a more somber refrain: *No hay remedio*—there is no recourse. "One must put up with it," she said. "I am beginning to grow accustomed to suffering." From the accident onward, pain and fortitude become central themes in her life.

Tuesday, October 13, 1925

Alex *de mi vida,* you more than anybody know how sad I have been in this piggy filthy hospital, since you can imagine it and also the boys must have told you about it. Everyone says I should not be so desperate, but they don't know what three months in bed means for me, which is what I need, having been a *callejera* [person who loves wandering about in the streets]. But what can one do, at least *la pelona* [the bald one, Frida's word for death—here she has drawn a small skull and crossbones] didn't take me away. Right?

Imagine how anguished I have been not knowing how you were, that day, and the next day. After they operated on me [Angel] Salas and Olmedo [Agustín Olmedo was a friend and, in 1928, a portrait subject of Frida's] arrived, it gave me pleasure to see them! especially Olmedo you have no idea, I asked them about you and they told me that what was the matter with you was painful but not serious and you don't know how I cried for you my Alex, at the same time that I cried for my pains, since I tell you that in the treatments, my hands became like paper and I sweated from the pain of the wound. . . . I was completely pierced through from the hip forward, for such a small thing I'll be a wreck for the rest of my life or else I'll die but now all that is past, one wound has already closed and the Dr. tells me that soon the other will close, they must already have told you what I have the matter with me, right? And it is all a question of how much time until the fracture I have in the pelvis closes and my elbow mends and other little wounds that I have in one foot heal. . . .

Concerning visits, a "mob of people" and a cloud of smoke have come to see me even Chucho Ríos y Valles asked after me several times by telephone and they say he came once but I didn't see him. . . . Fernández [Fernando Fernández, the printer] continues to give me *la moscota* [slang for money—"dough"] and now I have turned out to have even more aptitude for drawing than before since he says that when I am better he will pay me 60 a week, pure idle promises, but after all and all the boys from the town come every day to visit, Mr. Rouaix even cried (the father, eh, don't get the idea that I mean the son), well and you can imagine how many more. . . .

But I would give anything if instead of all the people from Coyoacán and the groups of old women who also came, you would come one day. I think that the day I see you Alex, I am going to kiss you, there's nothing to be done about it, now more than ever I have seen how much I love you with all my soul and I wouldn't exchange you for anyone, now you see that to suffer a little always serves a purpose.

Beyond feeling physically rather uncomfortable, although as I said to Salas I do not believe I was in very grave condition I have suffered a lot morally since you know how sick my mother was, and my father too, and to have given them this blow hurt me more than forty wounds, imagine, my poor little mother they say that she was as if crazy with tears for three days and my father who had been getting better got very sick, they have only brought my mother to see me twice since I have been here, which counting today is 25 days, which have seemed eternal to me and they have brought my father only once, so that I want to go home as soon as possible, but this will not be until my inflammation has completely died down, and all my wounds are healed so that there will not be any infection and I won't die, right? in any case not this week I think. . . . I'll wait for you counting the hours whenever it might be, here or at home because, seeing you the months in bed will pass much more quickly.

Listen Alex, if you can't come yet, write to me, you don't know how much your letter helped me to feel better, since I received it, I have read it, I think, twice a day and I always feel it is the first time.

I have a lot of things to tell you, but I can't write them to you because I am still very weak my head and eyes hurt when I read or write a lot but soon I'll tell them to you.

Speaking of something else I am wild with hunger, brother . . . and I cannot eat anything but the few revolting things that I told you about before, when you come bring me chocolate cake, candy drops and a *balero* like the one we lost the other day.

Get better soon. I will be another fifteen days in this hospital. Tell me how your pretty little mother and Alice [Alejandro's younger sister, Alicia] are.

your *cuate* who has become as thin as a thread. [Here Frida drew herself as a stick figure.] Friducha.

(I was very sad about [losing] the little parasol.) [Here she drew a crying "smile" face.] Life begins tomorrow! . . . . .

—I ADORE YOU—

Frida left the Red Cross Hospital on October 17, exactly one month after her accident. When she arrived home, she expected to be confined to her house for months, a prospect that horrified her almost more than the prospect of pain. Unlike the hospital, which was not far from the Preparatoria, Coyoacán was a long way from the center of Mexico City, and her school friends were unlikely to make the trip often. She also seems to have feared that at least some of them would be put off by her family's eccentricities: her mother's irritability, her father's silences. This, she said, "is one of the sadder houses that I have seen."

Tuesday, October 20, 1925

My Alex: At one o'clock on Saturday I arrived in the town, Salitas saw me leave the hospital and he must have told you how I got here, right? They brought me very slowly, but I still had two days of devilish inflammation but now I am happier because I am in my own house with my mother, now I am going to explain to you everything that is the matter with me without omitting any details as you asked me to do in your letter. According to Doctor Díaz Infante who looked after me in the Red Cross I am no longer in great danger and I am going to be more or less well . . . [but] we are already at the 20th and F. Luna [one of Frida's doctors; she used the name as a code word to signify her menstruation] has not come to see me and that is very grave. . . . [The doctor] doubts that I will be able to straighten my arm, because the articulation is good but the tendon is very contracted and it prevents me from moving my arm forward and if I am to be able to stretch it will be very slowly and with much massage and hot water baths, it hurts more than you can imagine, at every jerk that they give me I cry quarts of tears, in spite of the fact that they tell you not to believe in a dog's limp or a woman's tears, my foot also hurts a lot since as you must realize it is very smashed and also I have horrible shooting pains in the whole leg and I am very bothered as you can imagine but with rest they tell me that the bone will close soon and afterward little by little I will be able to walk.

And you, how are you doing and I likewise want to know exactly how you are since you see that there in the Hospital I could ask the boys everything and now it is much more difficult for me to see them, but I do not know whether they will want to come to my house, nor do you seem to want to come. . . . it is necessary for you not to be embarrassed in front of any of my family and least of all in front of my mother, ask Salas about what good people Adriana and Maty are, now Maty cannot come home often since every time she comes my mother disappears, poor little thing [Matilde] after she behaved so well toward me that time [in the hospital], but you know that each person's ideas are very different and there is no recourse one has to put up with it. Thus I tell you that it is not fair that you only write to me and you don't come to see me, since I will feel sadder about it than about anything in my life, you can come with all the boys one Sunday or any day you want, don't be bad, just put yourself in my place, five 5 months miserable and worse still very bored since if it is not a mass of old ladies that come to see me and the *escuincles* [boys] from around here who every now and then remember that I exist, I have to be alone and I suffer much more, look only Kity [Cristina], who you already know is with me, I will tell Maty to come on the day that you and the boys want to come and she already knows them and is a very good person. So is Adriana, el Güero [the blond one, Alberto Veraza] is not here, nor is my father, my mother won't object or say anything about it to me. I can't understand what you are ashamed of if you haven't done anything [wrong], every day they take me out to the corridor [in the patio] in my own bed because Pedro Calderas [her doctor] wants me to have air and sun so that I am no longer so enclosed as I was in that damned hospital. . . .

Well, my Alex, I'm boring you and I say goodbye with the hope that I will see you very soon eh? don't forget the *balero* and my candies—I warn you that I want something to eat because now I can eat more than before—

Say hello to the people in your neighborhood and please tell the boys not to be such nasty people as to forget me just because I'm at home.

Your *chamaca* Friducha [here she drew a smiling and weeping face]

Forgive my handwriting but I can hardly write.

Monday, October 26, 1925

Alex: I just received your letter today, and although I had expected it much before, it did a lot to take away the pains that I was having, since, imagine, yesterday Sunday at nine they chloroformed me for the third time to lower the tendon in my arm which as I already told you was contracted but since the chloroform has worn off which was at ten o'clock I was screaming until six in the afternoon when they gave me an injection of Sedol and it didn't do anything to me, since the pains continued although a little less intense, afterward they gave me cocaine and that was how the pains went away a little, but the attack of nausea (I don't know how to spell it) did not go away all day, afterward green green [Frida's expression for "horrible horrible"], the complete spleen, since imagine that the other day when Maty came to see me that is to say Saturday night my mother had an attack and I was the first to hear her shout and since I was asleep I forgot for a moment that I was sick and I wanted to get up I felt a horrible pain in my waist and an anguish more terrible than you can imagine Alex, since I wanted to stand up and I could not, finally I called Kity, and all that did me a lot of harm since I am very nervous, well I was telling you about yesterday, during the whole night I did nothing but vomit and I was horribly upset, poor [Cachucha Alfonso] Villa came to see me but they could not let him into my room since I was very bothered by those pains, Verastique [nickname for Adriana's husband] came, too, but I did not see him either. This morning I woke up with an inflammation where I have a fractured pelvis (How that word disgusts me) I didn't know what to do, so I drank water and I vomited it because of the same inflammation in my whole stomach which came from all the yelling I did yesterday. Now my head does not hurt anymore but I tell you that I am desperate from being in bed so much and in only one position, I wish that if only little by little, I could begin to sit, but there is no recourse for me except to endure it.

With respect to those who came to see me, which as I told you are not so few, but neither are they even a 3rd of the ones whom I like, a bunch of old ladies and girls who came more out of curiosity than out of affection, the boys that came are all those who you can imagine . . . but they don't even relieve my boredom in the moments they are with me, they search in all the drawers, they want to bring me a Victrola. Just think, the Blond Olaguibel brought me hers and on Saturday Lalo Ordóñez arrived from Canada bringing some rather terrific records with him from the U.S., but I can't stand more than one tune, since by the time I hear the second one my head hurts, the Galants come almost every day, the Campos, the Italians, the Canets etc., all the serious people of Coyoacán including Patiño and

Chava who brings me books like The [Three] Musketeers, etc., you can imagine how happy I will be, I already told my mother and Adriana that I want you to come, that is to say you and the boys (I forgot).
. . . Listen Alex I want you to tell me what day you are going to come so that if by chance a bunch of dimwits want to come the same day I will not receive them because I want to chat with you and that's all. Please tell Chong Lee (Prince of Manchuria) and Salas that I also very much want to see them that they should not be bad people who don't come see me etc. tell la Reyna the same, but I don't want her to come on the day that you come, because I don't want to have to be chatting with her and not be free to chat with you and the boys, but if it is easier to come with her, you already know that provided that I see you, it is all right if you come with the *puper* [Frida invented this word; the implication is derogatory] Dolores Angela. . . .

Alex come quickly, as quickly as you can, don't be so mean to your *chamaca* who loves you so much.

Frieda

But Alex did not come, at least not as often as Frida would have liked. Perhaps he had discovered her affair with Fernández. Whatever happened, Alejandro disapproved and felt betrayed. Fearing the loss of his love, Frida, with growing desperation, pleaded with him to come to see her.

November 5, 1925

Alex—You will say I have not written to you because I have forgotten you, but that's not so, the last time you came you told me that you would return very soon, one of these days, isn't that true? I have done nothing but wait for that day that has still not come. . . .

Pancho [Alfonso] Villa came Sunday—but F. Luna did not present himself, I am giving up hope— Now I am sitting in an armchair and surely on the 18th I will stand up, but I have no strength at all so that who knows how it will go—my arm is the same ([it moves] neither backward nor forward) I am full of desperation with *d* of dentist.

Come to see me don't be mean, man, it seems a lie that now that I most need you you vanish—tell Chong Lee that he should remember Jácopo Váldez who said so beautifully: "one knows who one's friends are when one is in bed or in jail" [for the words "bed" and "jail"

Frida substituted tiny pictures]—and tell him that I am still waiting for—YOU—

. . . if you don't come is it because you don't love me anymore at all eh? Meanwhile write me and receive all the love of your sister who adores you   Frieda

Thursday, November 26, 1925

My adored Alex: I cannot explain everything that is happening to me now, since, imagine, my mother had an attack and I was with her since Cristina ran off into the street, when you came and the wretched maid told you I was not home and I have an anger that you can't imagine, I wanted to see you for a little while alone, because it has been so long since we have been alone together, that I feel like saying all the insults I know to the miserable damned maid, afterwards I went out to call you from the balcony and I sent the maid to look for you but she did not find you, so that I had no recourse but to cry out of pure rage and suffering. . . .

Believe me Alex I want you to come, for I am ready to go to the devil and I have no recourse but to stand it since it is worse to get desperate don't you think? I want you to come and chat with me like before, for you to forget everything and for the love of your saintly mother come and see me and tell me that you love me even if it isn't true eh? (the pen doesn't write well in tears).

I would like to tell you so much Alex, but now I have a great desire to cry and I can't but tell me that you are going to come. . . . Forgive me, but it was not my fault that you came in vain my Alex.

Write to me soon

Your darling Friducha

On December 18, three months after the accident, Frida was well enough to go to Mexico City. It seemed a remarkable recovery. Her mother offered a mass of thanks that Frida had not died, and published in a newspaper a notice of the Kahlos' gratitude to the Red Cross Hospital for the care their daughter had received.

On December 26 Frida wrote, "Monday I begin work, that is to say Monday a week from today." Having missed her final examinations in the fall of 1925, she did not register for classes in the new year. Her medical expenses had been heavy, her family needed money, and it is probable that she continued to help her father in his studio and to take part-time jobs.

By this time, the rift between her and Alejandro had become a serious quarrel. From the following letter it is apparent that he has accused her of being "loose." In another, she admitted as much: "Although I have said I love you to many, and I have had dates with and kissed others, underneath it all I never loved anyone but you."

December 19, 1925

Alex: Yesterday I went to Mexico alone to walk around a bit, the first thing I did was go to your house (I don't know if that was a bad or good thing to do) but I went because I sincerely wanted to see you, I went at 10 and you weren't there, I waited until one-fifteen in the library and in the afternoon I returned to your house around four and you still weren't there, I don't know where you might have been, is your uncle still sick?

I went around with Agustina Reyna all day, according to what she says, she no longer wants to be with me much, because you told her that she was the same or worse than me, and that is a great disparagement for her, and I agree with her, since I am beginning to realize that "el Sr Olmedo" was telling the truth when he said that I am not worth a *"centavo,"* that is to say for all those who once called themselves my friends, because to myself, naturally I am worth much more than a *centavo* because I like myself the way I am.

She says that on various occasions you told her some of the things that I told you, details that I never told Reyna because there is no reason for her to know them and I cannot understand for what purpose you told them to her. The fact is that now no one wants to be my friend because I have *lost my reputation*, something that I cannot remedy. I will have to be friends with those who like me just the way I am. . . .

Lira brought up the false statement that I had given him a kiss and if I keep on enumerating things it will take whole pages; all this naturally worried me in the beginning, but later it began not to matter to me at all (this was exactly the bad thing) you know?

From all of them, Alex I would have taken it without giving it any importance, because it's what *Everyone* does do you understand? but I will never forget that you, whom I have loved as I love myself or more, saw me as a Nahui Olín [students considered the painter, Rivera's model, to be "fast" or "loose"] or even worse than she, who is an example of all of those women. Every time you have told me that you don't want to talk to me anymore you have done it as if to take a weight off yourself. And you had the gall Alex, to insult me, saying that I did certain things with someone else on the day that I did it for the first time in my life because I loved you as I love no one else.

And I am a liar because no one believes me, not even you, and thus little by little without feeling it, between all of you I am being driven crazy. Well, Alex, I would like to tell you everything, everything, because I do believe in you, but there is the misfortune that you do not believe in me, nor will you ever.

On Tuesday I am going, probably to Mexico if you want to see me I will be at the door of the Ministry of Education Library at 11. I will wait for you for an hour.

Yours Frieda

All her life Frida would use her intelligence, her magnetic charm, and her pain to firm her hold on those she loved, and in tear-spotted letters written during the long months of their quarrel, she tried to win her *novio* back. "For nothing in this life can I stop talking to you," she wrote on December 27, 1925. "I will not be your *novia*, but I will always talk to you even if you do not answer me . . . because I love you more than ever, now that you are leaving me." On February 19, 1926, she said that she was "prepared to make any sacrifice in order to do you good, since that way I will compensate a little for the bad that I did to you. . . . instead of everything that I could not or did not know how to give you, I will be yours, the day you want, so that at least this will serve as a proof to justify me a little."

Frida tried to persuade him that she was reforming her character. She would "remake" her life in order to be more like the girl he had fallen in love with three years before. Sometimes she was angry: "You told me on Wednesday that it was time to end everything and that I should go my own way," she wrote on March 13. "You think that that doesn't hurt me at all, because many circumstances make you believe that I do not have a drop of shame and that in the first place I am worth nothing and have nothing to lose anymore, but it seems to me that I told you once before that even if to you I am worth nothing, to myself I am worth more than many other girls, something that you will interpret as the pretension of being an exceptional girl (a title that you once gave me) (now I don't understand why) and for that reason I still take offense at what you so sincerely and with good intentions say to me."

A few days later, on March 17, she pleaded: "I waited for you until 6½ at the Convent and I would have waited a lifetime, but I had to get home on time. . . . Because you have been so good to me, since you are the only one who has loved me well, I beg you with all my soul not to leave me ever, remember that I cannot say that I count on my parents because you know perfectly how I am [situated], so that the only one who can look out for me is you, and you are leaving me because you imagined the worst, just to think about it pains me—you say you don't want to be my *novio* anymore. . . . What then do you want to do with me, where do you want me to go (it's a pity that what I imagined as a girl, that you would carry me in your pocket, can't come true) although you don't say it you know that no matter how many stupidities I have done . . . it will be a long time before we can forget, before we can be good *novios,* good spouses, don't tell me no for the love of God. . . . I will wait for you every day until 6 at Churubusco, maybe sometime you will pity and understand, as you understand yourself, your Frieda." On April 12 she promised, "If someday we get married, you will see how I am going to be full of 'good' almost made to order for you."

Frida's first *Self-Portrait*—indeed, her first serious painting (plate I)—was a gift for Alejandro. She began it sometime during the late summer of 1926, when she became ill again and was once more confined to the house in Coyoacán. By September 28, the portrait was almost finished; like so many of her self-portraits, it was a token by which she hoped to bind her loved one to her. "Within a few days the portrait will be in your house," she wrote. "Forgive me for sending it without a frame. I implore you to put it in a low place where you can see it as if you were looking at me."

The first *Self-Portrait* was thus a kind of visual entreaty, a love offering at a time when Frida felt that she had lost the person she most loved. It is a dark, melancholy work, in which she has succeeded in painting herself looking beautiful, fragile, and vibrant. She holds out her right hand as if she were asking for it to be held; no one, not even disaffected Alejandro, could resist taking that hand, one thinks. She is wearing a romantic wine-red velvet dress with what looks like a gold brocade collar and cuffs. Eschewing flapper styles, she stresses her femininity: a plunging neckline dramatically sets off her pale flesh, long neck, and breasts with prominent nipples. The tender depiction of her breasts seems a way of hinting at vulnerability without actually admitting it; by contrast, her facial expression remains cool and reserved. And instead of filling the width of her canvas with the portrait bust, Frida has left a strip of space on either side of the figure. Thus, as in Hans Memling's *Girl with a Pink*, the delicate, spiritual qualities of the sitter are emphasized, and the slender, elongated girl looks all the more alone against the dark ocean and the sky.

Perhaps the gift did, indeed, touch Alejandro's heart, for not long after he accepted it, he and Frida were reconciled. In subsequent letters to him, written while he was in Europe, she revealed how intensely she identified herself with her first *Self-Portrait*. She called it "Your Botticeli" [*sic*]. "Alex," she wrote on March 29, 1927, "your 'Botticeli' has also become very sad, but I told her that until you come back, she should be the 'sound asleep one,' in spite of this she remembers you always." On April 6: "Speaking of painters, your 'Botticeli' is well, but underneath it all one sees in her a certain sadness that she naturally cannot disguise, in the triangle . . . that you know is in the garden . . . the plants have grown, surely it must be because it is spring, but they will not flower except when you arrive—and so many other things wait for you." And on July 15, when she was expecting him to come home soon: "You cannot imagine how marvelous it is to wait for you, serenely as in the portrait."

The painting was like an alternate self, one that shared and reflected the artist's feelings, akin, in a way, to the little girl who befriended Frida in her childhood dreams. On the back of it are the words: "Frieda Kahlo at 17 years of age in September 1926. Coyoacán." (She was in fact nineteen.) A few inches below this, almost in defiance of the painting's tenebrous atmosphere, she wrote, in German, *Heute ist Immer Noch*—Today still goes on.

Chapter 5

The Broken Column

FRIDA'S LIFE from 1925 on was a grueling battle against slow decay. She had a continuous feeling of fatigue, and almost constant pain in her spine and right leg. There were periods when she felt more or less well and her limp was almost unnoticeable, but gradually her frame disintegrated. A lifelong friend, Olga Campos, who has Frida's medical records from childhood to 1951, says that Frida had at least thirty-two surgical operations, most of them on her spine and her right foot, before she succumbed twenty-nine years after the accident. "She lived dying," said writer Andrés Henestrosa, another close friend for many years.

The first relapse, evident in Frida's letters to Alejandro of September 1926, came about a year after the accident. A bone surgeon discovered that three vertebrae were out of place; she had to wear various plaster corsets that kept her immobilized for months as well as a special apparatus on her right foot. Apparently, at the time of the accident, the doctors at the Red Cross Hospital had neglected to check the condition of her spine before they presumed her to be mended and sent her home. Frida said, "no one paid any attention to me; what's more, they did not take X-rays." Her letters reveal that certain necessary medical treatments were not performed because her family could not afford to pay for them. When they could, the treatments were often ineffective. "The second plaster corset that they put on me doesn't work anymore," Frida wrote Alejandro during her relapse, "and for that they threw almost a hundred into the street, since they gave the pesos to a pair of thieves which is what most doctors are."

To heal her body after polio, Frida had forced herself to move and to become an athlete. To salvage what she could after the accident, she had to learn to keep still. Almost by chance, then, she turned to the occupation that would remake her life. "Since I was young," she said, "this misfortune did not at that time take on the character of a tragedy: I felt I had energies enough to do anything instead of studying to become a doctor. And without paying much attention, I began to paint."

Although she had flair, until her apprenticeship with Fernández there is no evidence that as a schoolgirl Frida had artistic ambitions. She took the required, highly academic art courses given at the Preparatoria—one in drawing and another in clay modeling (taught by Fidencio L. Naba, who had studied in Paris and won the Prix de Rome). In addition, she briefly entertained the idea that she might earn a living by making scientific drawings for medical books, and after looking at glass slides of biological tissue through a microscope, she practiced making such drawings at home. But aside from this, her schoolmates recall only that she was "interested in art," liked to watch the muralists at work, had an "artistic spirit," and never stopped drawing capricious interlaces in her schoolbooks. "Her passion," Manuel González Ramírez remembered, "was to make the lines meet among themselves and after two or three sinuous arcs, to make them meet again."

Whenever Frida herself told the story of her initiation into painting—and characteristically she found various ways to tell it—she was careful not to promote the familiar artists' myth of being born with a pencil in hand or to imply that "innate genius" had drawn her irresistibly to art from the age of three. To Julien Levy, at the time he was preparing her New York exhibition in 1938, she wrote (in English):

I never thought of painting until 1926, when I was in bed on account of an automobile accident. I was bored as hell in bed with a plaster cast (I had a fracture in the spine and several in other places), so I decided to do something. I stoled [sic] from my father some oil paints, and my mother ordered for me a special easel because I couldn't sit down [she means "sit up"], and I started to paint.

For her friend the art historian Antonio Rodríguez she embellished the story:

> My father had had for many years a box of oil colors and some paintbrushes in an old vase and a palette in a corner of his little photography workshop. Purely for pleasure he would go to paint at the river in Coyoacán, landscapes and figures and sometimes he copied chromos. Ever since I was a little girl, as the saying goes, I had been casting an eye in the direction of the box of colors. I could not explain why. Being so long in bed, I took advantage of the occasion and I asked my father for it. Like a little boy whose toy is taken away from him and given to a sick brother, he "lent" it to me. My mother asked a carpenter to make an easel, if that's what you would call a special apparatus that could be attached to my bed where I lay, because the plaster cast did not allow me to sit up. In this way I began to paint.

Her first subjects were those convenient to an invalid: she painted portraits of friends (two Cachuchas and two Coyoacán girl friends), of family (her sister Adriana), and of herself. Three of the paintings are known solely through photographs, and one, the 1927 portrait of Cachucha Jesús Ríos y Valles, was so bad, Frida thought, that she destroyed it. Though they are ambitious and promising, these paintings only begin to hint at the intricate, personal development that was to come. All are characterized by dark, gloomy tones, by stiff, rather amateurish drawing, and by an awkward handling of space that corresponds to no perceptual logic. Though the portrait of Adriana—she called it "la Boticelinda Adriana" (figure 12)—and those of Ruth Quintanilla and Alicia Galant have a certain stilted elegance, the painting of Miguel N. Lira, in which he appears surrounded by objects that must be symbolic of his efforts as a litterateur and poet, resembles, as she herself said, "a cardboard cutout." But there are sophisticated touches which prove that Frida did, as legend has it, spend hours poring over books on the history of art. The primary influence is clearly that of Italian Renaissance painting, especially that of Botticelli. In a letter to Alejandro she mentioned her admiration for the Italian mannerist Bronzino's portrait *Eleonora di Toledo,* and something of the poignant grace of that royal woman's hands is seen in Frida's delicate, aristocratic gesture in her *Self-Portrait.* There are traces as well of the linear elegance of the English Pre-Raphaelites, and of the sensuous elongated figures of Modigliani. Highly stylized motifs like spindly trees and scalloped clouds suggest such sources as medieval manuscript illumination or Art Nouveau illustrations; the spiral pattern that transforms the sea in the first *Self-Portrait* recalls Japanese screens and woodcuts.

Of the early paintings, however, only the first *Self-Portrait* hints at the intensely personal nature of Frida's future work. Perhaps this is because it was, like so many of her later self-portraits, a token of love, a kind of magic talisman that was crucial to the artist's well-being.

In reading Frida's letters to Alejandro from the period of her relapse of 1926–1927, one is struck, page after page, by the intensity of her appetite for life—her will not simply to endure but to enjoy. One is also struck by her plaintive loneliness and the omnipresence of pain, and the way she uses these to bind her lover to herself. "How much I would like to explain my suffering to you minute by minute," she wrote, knowing, as one friend put it, that "pity is stronger than love."

January 10, 1927

Alex: I want you to come, you don't know how I have needed you these days and how each day I love you more.

I am still sick, and you know how boring that is, I don't know what to do anymore since it has been more than a year that I've been this way and I'm fed up with so much sickness, like an old woman, I don't know how I'll be when I'm 30, you'll have to carry me all day wrapped in cotton. . . .

Listen tell me about your time in Oaxaca, and what kinds of terrific things you have seen, because I need to be told something new, because I was born to be a flowerpot and I never leave the dining room. . . . . . I am very very bored!!!!!! [Here she draws a weeping face.] . . . I dream about my bedroom every night and no matter how many times I go around and around it in my head, I don't know how to erase its image from my mind (what's more, every day it seems more of a bazaar). Well! What can we do, hope and hope. . . . . . The only one who has remembered me is Carmen James [Jaime] and she only once, she wrote me a letter and that's all—no one no one else————I who so many times dreamed of being a navigator and traveler! Patiño will answer me that it is one irony of life—ha ha ha ha! (don't laugh) But it is only 17 [actually nineteen] years that I have been stationed in my town— Surely later I will be able to say—I'm going on a trip—*I don't have time to talk to you*. . . . . [Here she writes a bar with seven notes of music.] Well after all to know China, Italy and other countries is secondary. The first thing is, when are you coming? . . . I hope it will be very very soon, not to offer you anything new but so that the same old Frieda can kiss you—

Listen see if among your acquaintances someone knows a good recipe to bleach hair—(don't forget).

And don't forget that with you in Oaxaca is your

Frieda

Alejandro left for Europe in March. He planned to be gone for four months, traveling and studying German; it has been said as well that his family sent him abroad "in order to cool off his close relationship with Frida." Perhaps Alejandro himself wanted to free himself from Frida's possessive and increasingly needful grip. Though he was deeply tied to his *novia*, and continued to care for her all her life, Frida's earlier promiscuity together with the horror of her present illness could have caused the young man to pull away.

Knowing how agonizing a farewell would be for both of them, Alejandro left Mexico without saying goodbye. Instead, he wrote that he had to be on hand when his aunt underwent surgery in Germany (recently he recalled that he invented this "operation" as a way of justifying his trip to Frida). He said that he would be back in July, but July came and went, and Frida kept writing to him overseas until he finally returned in November.

Sunday, March 27, 1927

My Alex: You cannot imagine with what pleasure I waited for you on Saturday, because I was sure that you would come, and that on Friday you had had something to do . . . at four in the afternoon I received your letter from Veracruz . . . imagine my sorrow, I don't know how to explain it to you. I don't want to torment you, and I want to be strong, above all to have as much faith as you, but I cannot console myself at all and now I am afraid that just as you did not tell me when you were leaving, you are deceiving me when you tell me that you are only going to be away for four months. . . . I cannot forget you even one minute, you are everywhere, in all my things, above all in my room, and in my books and my paintings. Not until today at 12 did I receive your first letter. Who knows when you will receive mine, but I am going to write to you twice a week and you will tell me if they get to you or to what address I can send them. . . .

Now, since you left I do nothing, not even read . . . because when you were with me, everything that I did was for you, it was for you to know about it, but now I don't want to do anything, nevertheless, I understand that I should not be that way, on the contrary I am going to study as much as I can and as soon as I feel better I am going to paint and do many things so that when you return I will be a little improved, it all depends on how long I am sick, I still have 18 days to go to make up a month of being in bed and who knows how much time I will be in that box, so that for the time being I do nothing, only cry and I hardly sleep because in the nights when I am alone and when I can think about you most freely, I go traveling with you. . . .

Listen Alex, surely you will be in Berlin on the 24th of April, and on that day it will be exactly a month since you left Mexico, I hope it won't be a Friday and you will spend it more or less happily. What a horrible thing to be so far away from you, I keep thinking that the mist carries you farther and farther from me, I feel such a desire to run and run until I reach you, but all these things that I feel and think, etc., I resolve like every other woman by crying and crying, what can I do, nothing. "I am full of *lagrimilla.*" Well Alex, on Wednesday when I write to you again I will say almost the same thing as in this letter, a little sadder and at the same time a little less sad, because three more days will have passed and that is three days less—and thus little by little suffering unspeakably the day in which I will see you again will come closer—and so yes, you'll never have to go to Berlin again.

Δ

Good Friday, April 22, 1927
My Alex: Alicia wrote me, but, since March 28, neither she nor anyone has had the least news of you. . . . There is nothing comparable to the desperation of not knowing anything about you for a month.

I continue to be sick and I am getting much thinner; and the doctor still is of the opinion that they should put the plaster corset on me for three or four months since the one with fluting, although a little less bothersome than this corset, gives worse results since as it is a thing of being in it for months, the patient grows attached to it, and it is more difficult to cure the sores than the sickness; with the corset I am going to suffer horribly since it needs to be irremovable and in order to put it on me they are going to have to hang me from the head and wait that way, until it dries, because otherwise it would be completely useless and by hanging me they are going to make my spine stay as straight as possible, but for all that which is not even half, you can imagine how I will be suffering. . . . The *old* doctor says that the corset gives very good results when it is well fitted, but that still remains to be seen, and if not, let the devil take me. They are going to put it on me Monday in the French Hospital. . . . The only advantage that this disgusting thing has is that I can walk. The advantage turns out to be counterproductive—what's more I am not going to go out in the street looking like that since they would surely take me to the madhouse. In the remote case that the corset does not give results they will have to operate, and the operation will consist—according to this doctor—in removing a piece of bone from one knee and putting it on my *espinazo* [Frida's word for spine], but before all that happens I will surely have eliminated myself from the planet. . . . Everything is reduced to this, I have nothing new to tell you; I am bored with *A* of Ay Ay Ay! My only hope is to see you. . . .   Write me

                                                      "

                                                      "

                                                      "

                                    and above all love me

                                                      "

                                                      "

                                                      "

                                                      "

                                                      "

                                                      Δ

                                          Saturday, June 4, 1927

Alex, *mi vida:* This afternoon I received your letter. . . . I have no hopes that you will be here in July, you are enchanted—in love with the Cologne Cathedral, and with so many things that you have seen! I on the other hand am counting the days until on that most unexpected day you return. . . . It makes me sad to think that you are going to find me still sick, since on Monday they are going to change the apparatus for the third time, this time to put it on me so that it is fixed, and so I will not be able to walk, for two or three months, until my spine knits perfectly, I don't know if afterward it will still be necessary to have an operation, in any case I'm already bored and many times I think that it would be preferable if the *tía de las muchachas* [aunt of the girls; she means death] would take me right away, don't you think? I'll never be able to do anything with this wretched sickness, and if this is true at 18 [nineteen] years of age I do not know how I will be later, every day I am thinner and you will see when you come how horrible I look with this huge worthless apparatus. [Here she draws herself in a plaster cast that covers her torso and shoulders.] Afterward I am going to be a thousand times worse, since imagine after having spent a month lying down (as you left me) another two with two different apparatuses, and now another two lying down, put into a sheath of plaster, later 6 more months with the little apparatus again in order to be able to walk, and with the magnificent hopes that they will operate on me and that I might end up in the operation . . . . . . like the bear. [Here she draws a bear walking along a path leading to the horizon—presumably she means to his death.] Isn't it enough to make a person desperate? Probably you'll tell me that I'm too pessimistic and *lagrimilla* and especially now that you are completely optimistic after having seen the Elbe? the Rifu, lots of Lucas Cranachs and Dürers and above all Bronzino and the Cathedrals, that way I could be entirely optimistic and always *niña*.

But if you come quickly, I promise you I will get better each day.

yours

Don't forget me—

Δ

July 22, 1927, Day of the Magdalene
My Alex: . . . In spite of so many sufferings I think I am getting better, it could be not true, but I *want to believe it,* anyway it is better, don't you think? These four months have been a continual pain for me, day after day, now I am almost ashamed not to have had faith, but it's that no one can imagine how I have suffered. Your poor *novia!*

You would have carried me, as I told you when I was little, in one of your pockets, like the golden nugget in the poem of [López] Velarde—but now I am so big! I have grown so much since then!

Listen my Alex: how marvelous the Louvre must be, how many things I am going to know when you come.

I had to look up Nice in the geography book because I couldn't remember where it was (I have always been "sometimes *brutilla*" [brutish, ignorant]) but now I'll never forget it—believe me.

Alex: I am going to confess something: there are moments when I think you are forgetting me, but it's not true, is it? You could not fall in love again with the Gioconda [*Mona Lisa*]. . . .

"News in my house":

—Maty now comes to this mansion. Peace has been made. (All the Catholic ladies [Veladora, Grandma, Pianista, etc.] will end their days for this chance anti-Catholic.)

—My father's studio is no longer at the "Perla" but rather at 51 Uruguay [street].

"Outside my house":

—Chelo Navarro had a little girl.

—Jack Dempsey beat Jack Sharkey in New York. Great sensation!

—The revolution in Mexico[1] reelectionists
                        anti-reelectionists*

"In my heart":

—Only you—

your

Frieda

[1] Interesting candidates: José Vasconcelos (?)
                        Luis Cabrera

July 23

My Alex: I just received your letter. . . . You tell me that later you will embark for Naples, and it is almost certain that you will also go to Switzerland, I want to ask you a favor, tell your aunt [Alejandro

---

* Frida refers to factions campaigning for presidential elections to take place early in 1928. With President Calles's support, former president Alvaro Obregón had had set aside the constitution's proviso forbidding any president to serve a second term, so that he could run for the office. A revolt against Obregón was violently suppressed.

traveled part of the time in the company of one of his aunts] that you want to go home, that you by no means want to stay there after August . . . you cannot imagine what it is like for me each day, each minute without you. . . .

Cristina is still just as pretty, but behaves in a completely worthless way with me and with my mother.

I painted Lira because he asked me to, but it is so bad that I don't even know how he can tell me that he likes it—totally horrible—I have not sent you the photograph because my father still does not have all the plates in order because of the change [of studios], but it's not worthwhile, it [the portrait] has a very overrefined background and he looks like a cardboard cutout, only one detail seems good to me (one angel in the background). You will see it soon, my father also took [a photograph of] the other one of Adriana, of Alicia [Galant] with the veil (very bad) and of the one that was supposed to be Ruth Quintanilla and that Salas liked. As soon as my father makes more copies I will send them to you. I only asked for one of each but Lira took them because he says he is going to publish them in a review that will come out in August (I already told you about it, didn't I?) It will be called "Panorama." In the first issue, amongst others, Diego, Montenegro (as a poet) and who knows how many more collaborated, I don't think that it will be very good.

I tore up the portrait of Ríos [Jesús Ríos y Valles], because you cannot imagine how it disgusted me, el Flaquer [Frida's nickname for a friend from Coyoacán, Octavio Bustamente] wanted the background (the woman and the trees) and the portrait ended its days like Joan of Arc.

Tomorrow is Cristina's saint's day, the boys are coming, and the children of Mr. Cabrera, they don't look like him (they are very ugly), and they hardly speak Spanish since they have spent twelve years in the U.S., and they only come to Mexico for vacations, the Galants also will come, la Pinocha [nickname for Frida's close friend Esperanza Ordóñez] etc., only Chelo Navarro is not coming because she is still in bed because of the baby, they say that it is really cute.

That's all that is happening in my house, but none of it interests me.

By tomorrow it will be a month and a half since I have been plastered up, and *four* months since I have seen you, I wish that . . . [soon] life would begin and I could kiss you. Will it be? Truly yes?

Your sister
Frieda

Alex: August begins— And I could say that *life* begins too, if I were sure that at the end of the month you would return. But yesterday Bustamente told me that you are probably going to Russia, and that will make you stay away longer. . . . Yesterday was Esperanza's saint's day and they gave a big dance at my house because they don't have a piano, the boys came (Salas, Mike [Lira], Flaquer), my sister Matilde, and other *mancebos y mancebas* [boys and girls]. They carried me into the living room on my little cart and I watched people dance and heard people sing, the *muchachos* were quite happy (I think) and Lira wrote a poem for la Pinocha and in the dining room the three boys talked, Miguel [Lira] quoted Heliodoro Valle—Tsiu Paŭ— López Velarde and various others. I think that the three of them rather like la Pinocha (aesthetically) and they have become very good friends.

I as always was *lagrimilla*. Although now every morning they take me out into the sun (4 hours) I do not notice that I'm getting much better, for the pains are always the same and I am quite thin, but in spite of this, as I told you in the other letter, I want to have faith. If there's enough money this month they will take another X-ray and I'll be more certain, but if not, in any case I am going to get up on the 9th or 10th of September and then I will know whether this apparatus has made me better or whether the operation is still necessary (I fear). But I still have to wait a long time to see if the absolute rest of these three months (I can almost say martyrdom) will give results or not.

According to what you tell me, the Mediterranean is marvelously blue. Will I know it someday? I think not, because I have very bad luck, and my greatest desire for a long time has been to travel—the only thing that will remain to me is the melancholy of those who have read travel books.

I'm not reading anything now—I don't want to—I don't study German nor do I do anything other than think about you. I believe myself to be surely full of wisdom—

And in the newspapers besides "Comings and Goings of Steamships," I only read "the editorial" and what's happening in Europe.

No one knows anything yet about the revolution here, now the one who seems to be strongest is Obregón, but no one knows anything.

Other than this nothing interesting. Alex did you learn a lot of French? Even though it isn't necessary to recommend it to you—attack it as much as you can eh?

What museums have you seen?

How are the girls in all the cities you have visited? and the boys? At the spas don't flirt much with the girls—those as exquisite as Botticellis and with good legs only in Mexico are they called "Medeas" and "Meches" [flames] and you can say to them: *Sorita,* do you want to be my *novia?* But not in France, nor Italy and definitely not in Russia where there are lots of *peladas communistas.* . . . You don't know with what pleasure I would give my whole life just to kiss you.

I think now that I have really suffered it is fair that I deserve it, no?

Will it be as you say in the month of August? Yes.

Your Frieda
(*I adore you*)

October 15, 1927

My Alex: The penultimate letter! Everything that I could tell you, you know.

Every winter we have been happy. Never like now. Life is ahead of us—of me—it is impossible to tell you what that means.

It is likely that I will be sick [when you return], but I don't know it anymore, in Coyoacán the nights are astonishingly beautiful as they were in 1923 and the sea, symbol in my portrait, synthesizes my life.

You have not forgotten me?

It would almost be unjust—don't you think?

Your Frieda

When Alejandro came back in November, he had not forgotten Frida. How could he? Even if the purpose of the trip was to separate the *novios,* the crescendo of pain and longing in her letters had kept her in his mind. But their relationship was diminished, and they gradually drifted apart, he caught up in university activities, she increasingly involved in art.

Almost everyone in Mexico who speaks of Frida's accident says that it was fated: she did not die because it was her destiny to survive, to live out a calvary of pain. Frida herself came to share this feeling that suffering—and death—is inevitable; since we each carry the burden of our fate, we must try to make light of it.

Later in life, she dressed cardboard skeletons in her own clothes and ordered a sugar skull with her name written on its forehead. She poked fun at *la pelona* the way a Catholic laughs at Catholicism or a Jew makes Jewish jokes—because death was her companion, her kin. Coquettishly, she defied her opponent: "I tease and laugh at death," she liked to say, "so that it won't get the better of me."

Though she painted death—her own metaphorically and that of others literally—Frida was not able to paint her accident. Years later, she said that she had wanted to, but couldn't, because to her, the accident was too "complicated" and "important" to reduce to a single comprehensible image. There is only an undated drawing, in the collection of Diego Rivera's son-in-law (figure 10). Its brusque, crude draftsmanship suggests the subject provoked so much distress that Frida could not control her line. Time and space are collapsed in a nightmare vision: two vehicles collide; injured victims are strewn on the ground; the Coyoacán house is there, and Frida appears twice—once lying on a stretcher encased in bandages and a plaster cast, and a second time simply as a large, childlike head, looking on, perhaps remembering a lost *balero*.

But if Frida did not paint her accident, it was the accident and its aftermath that led her eventually, as a mature painter, to chart her state of mind—to set down her discoveries—in terms of things done to her body: her face is always a mask; her body is often naked and wounded, like her feelings. Just as in her letters Frida told Alejandro that she wanted him to know her sufferings detail by detail, "minute by minute," in her paintings Frida was intent on making painful feelings known. She turned her body inside out, placing her heart in front of her breast and showing her broken spinal column as if her imagination had the power of X-ray vision or the cutting edge of a surgeon: if Frida's fantasy did not travel far from the confines of herself, she did probe deeply. The girl whose ambition was to study medicine turned to painting as a form of psychological surgery.

"I paint myself because I am so often alone," Frida said, "because I am the subject I know best." The confinement of invalidism made Frida see herself as a private world in much the same way that bedridden children see mountains and valleys in the shapes of their own limbs. Even when she painted fruit or flowers, it was with a vision seen through the filtering lens of herself. "I look like many people and many things," Frida said, and in her paintings, many things look like her. "From that time [of the accident]," she explained, "my obsession was to begin again, painting things just as I saw them with my own eyes and nothing more. . . . Thus, as the accident changed my path, many things prevented me from fulfilling the desires which everyone considers normal, and to me nothing seemed more normal than to paint what had not been fulfilled."

Painting was part of Frida Kahlo's battle for life. It was also very much a part of her self-creation: in her art, as in her life, a theatrical self-presentation was a means to control her world. As she recovered, relapsed, recovered again, she reinvented herself. She created a person who could be mobile and make mischief in her imagination rather than with her legs. "Frida is the only painter who gave birth to herself," says an intimate friend of Frida's, the photographer Lola Alvarez Bravo. In a sense, Alvarez Bravo explains, Frida did die during the accident. "The struggle of the two Fridas was in her always, the struggle between one dead Frida and one Frida that was alive." After the accident came a rebirth: "Her love for nature was renewed, the same as for animals, colors and fruits, anything beautiful and positive around her."

Frida, however, saw the change that the accident brought about in her not as a rebirth but as an accelerated process of aging. A year had passed since the accident when she wrote to Alejandro:

Why do you study so much? What secret are you looking for? Life will reveal it to you soon. I already know it all, without reading or writing. A little while ago, not much more than a few days ago, I was a child who went about in a world of colors, of hard and tangible forms. Everything was mysterious and something was hidden, guessing what it was was a game for me. If you knew how terrible it is to know suddenly, as if a bolt of lightning elucidated the earth. Now I live in a painful planet, transparent as ice; but it is as if I had learned everything at once in seconds. My friends, my companions became women slowly, I became old in instants and everything today is bland and lucid. I know that nothing lies behind, if there were something I would see it. . . .

What Frida described is the bleak, forbidding dream landscape that would reappear in many of her self-portraits: an outer expression of inner desolation. But she did not share her "painful planet" with many friends and she was forced to hide the intensity of her suffering from her family: "No one in my house believes that I am really sick, since I cannot even say so because my mother, who is the only one who grieves a little, gets sick, and they say that it was because of me, that I am very imprudent, so that I and no one but I am the one that suffers." The public Frida was gay and strong. Wanting to surround herself with people, she accentuated qualities she already possessed—vivaciousness, generosity, wit. Gradually, she became a famous personality. Aurora Reyes remembers that after her accident and during her relapse "she always acted happy; she gave her heart. She had an incredible richness, and though one went to see her to console her, one came away consoled."

"When we went to visit her when she was sick," Adelina Zendejas recalls, "she played, she laughed, she commented, she made caustic criticisms, witticisms, and wise opinions. If she cried, no one knew it." No one except Alejandro. After the accident, most of the caricatures she drew in her letters to him were weeping self-portraits.

Eventually the role of the heroic sufferer became an integral part of Frida: the mask became the face. And as the dramatization of pain became ever more central to her self-image, she exaggerated the painful facts of her past, claiming, for example, that she had spent not one but three months in the Red Cross Hospital. She created a self that would be strong enough to withstand the blows life dealt her; one who could survive—indeed transform—that bleak planet.

Both the strength and the emphasis on suffering pervade Frida's paintings. When she shows herself wounded and weeping, it is the equivalent to her letters' litany of moral and physical wounds, a cry for attention. Yet even the most painful of the self-portraits are never maudlin or self-pitying, and her dignity and determination to "put up with things" is evident in her queenly carriage, her stoic features. It is this blend of directness and artifice, of integrity and self-invention, that gives her self-portraits their peculiar urgency, their immediately recognizable steely strength.

Of all Frida's paintings, the one that most powerfully illustrates these qualities is *The Broken Column* (plate XXVIII), painted in 1944 soon after she had undergone surgery and when she was confined, as she had been in 1927, in an "apparatus." Here Frida's determined impassivity creates an almost unbearable tension, a feeling of paralysis. Anguish is made vivid by nails driven into her naked body. A gap resembling an earthquake fissure splits her torso, the two sides of which are held together by the steel orthopedic corset that is a symbol of the invalid's imprisonment. The opened body suggests surgery and Frida's feeling that without the steel corset she would literally fall apart. Inside her torso we see a cracked ionic column in the place of her own deteriorating spinal column; life is thus replaced by a crumbling ruin. The tapered column thrusts cruelly into the red crevasse of Frida's body, penetrating from her loins to her head, where a two-scrolled capital supports her chin. To some observers, the column is analogous to a phallus; the painting alludes to the link in Frida's mind between sex and pain, and it recalls the steel rod that pierced her vagina during the accident. A disjointed entry in her diary reads: "To hope with anguish retained, the broken column, and the immense look, without walking, in the vast path . . . moving my life created of steel."

The corset's white straps with metal buckles accentuate the delicate vulnerability of Frida's naked breasts, breasts whose perfect beauty makes the rough cut from neck to loins all the more ghastly. With her hips wrapped in a cloth suggestive of Christ's winding sheet, Frida displays her wounds like a Christian martyr; a Mexican Saint Sebastian, she uses physical pain, nakedness, and sexuality to bring home the message of her spiritual suffering.

Frida is no saint, however. She appraises her situation with truculent secularism, and instead of beseeching the heavens for solace, she stares straight ahead as if to challenge both herself (in the mirror) and her audience to face her predicament without flinching. Tears dot her cheeks, as they do the cheeks of so many depictions of the Madonna in Mexico, but her features refuse to cry. They are as mask-like as those of an Indian idol.

To convey the loneliness of physical and emotional suffering, Frida has painted herself isolated against an immense and barren plain. Ravines cut into the landscape are a metaphor for her injured body, like the desert deprived of the capacity to create life. In the far distance there is a strip of blue sea beneath a cloudless sky. When she painted her family tree Frida used the ocean to represent the fact that her paternal grandparents lived in Europe. In her first *Self-Portrait* it was, she said, the "synthesis of life." The sea in *The Broken Column* seems to represent the hope of other possibilities, but it is so far away, and Frida is so broken, that it is utterly beyond reach.

Chapter 6

Diego: The Frog Prince

WITHIN A FEW MONTHS of Alejandro's return from Europe, late in 1927, Frida had recuperated sufficiently to lead an almost normal, active life. Although she did not resume her studies—her leg still hurt and besides, she wanted to paint—she did rejoin her old school companions from the Preparatoria. Most of them were by this time students in the professional schools of the university, and firecrackers and water bombs had given way to national student congresses and protest demonstrations.

The principal causes for which they fought were two: José Vasconcelos's 1928–1929 campaign for the presidency against Calles's candidate, Pascual Ortíz Rubio, and the drive for university autonomy. The first was a lost cause; the second was won in 1929.

Former President Alvaro Obregón, having survived both an assassination attempt and a rebellion, won the presidency in January 1928. Six months later he was murdered. Emilio Portes Gil was appointed provisional president, and new elections were scheduled for the fall of 1929. Vasconcelos, who had concluded that the Calles regime was more corrupt and tyrannical than the dictatorship of Porfirio Díaz, decided to run against Ortíz Rubio as the candidate of the National Anti-Reelectionist party. He knew he had no hope of winning the election, but he and his supporters believed that the battle against *caudillaje* (rule by military chieftain) and for the rebirth of the democratic, Mexicanist spirit of the early twenties was a moral imperative.

The fight for university autonomy was not unrelated, for in part it too was a revolt against government oppression. It had begun essentially in 1912, when Justo Sierra declared that the university he had founded two years before should be free from government intervention. The institution's first rector, Joaquín Eguia Liz, went further: he said the university should be autonomous. Finally, on May 17, 1929, a nationwide student strike was triggered when the president of Mexico closed the law school after students rejected a proposed new system of examinations. The students massed, marched, held protest meetings, and painted propaganda signs. The government retaliated with mounted police, fire hoses, and guns. Alejandro Gómez Arias, elected president of the National Student Confederation in January 1929, was the battle's undisputed leader. "Samurai of my country," he called his fellow students in fiery speeches. "We will not be convinced by violence." In July, the law that established the National Autonomous University of Mexico was signed, approved by Congress, and handed ceremoniously to Alejandro.

Another student leader, one who channeled his passionate anti-militarism and anti-imperialism into numerous campaign speeches against the Callistas and for Vasconcelos, was Germán de Campo. During the long, lonely months of 1927, when Alejandro was away and Frida was trapped in one orthopedic corset after another, her friendship with "Germancito el Campirano," as she called him, had deepened. She adored the handsome young man's fun-loving spirit, his *alegría*, and his vehemence. An irrepressible dandy, he delivered the most fervent speeches wearing a boutonniere and an elegant felt hat and carrying a cane made of Indian bamboo. He was to die soon after the battle for university autonomy was won, silenced by a Callista bullet while giving a pro-Vasconcelos speech during a demonstration in San Fernando Park.

It was Germán de Campo who, sometime in the early months of 1928, introduced Frida into the circle of friends surrounding the exiled Cuban Communist revolutionary Julio Antonio Mella, who was, like Alejandro and de Campo, a student at the law school. Mella was editor of a student newspaper called *Tren Blindado* (The Blind Train) and of *El Liberador,* the Anti-Imperialist League's official organ, and he contributed to the Communist publication *El Machete.* Most important for Frida, however, he was also the lover of the Italian-born American photographer Tina Modotti, with whom he was walking on January 10, 1929, when he was assassinated by a gunman in the hire of the Cuban government.

Modotti had come to Mexico from California in 1923 as the great photographer Edward Weston's apprentice and companion, and she had stayed on after he left, becoming increasingly involved in communist politics, largely through her successive love affairs with the painter Xavier Guerrero and Mella. She was talented, beautiful, tempestuous, and sensitive, and exuded a vibrant strength, somehow managing to be earthy and otherworldly at the same time. Not surprisingly, she was adored by the Mexican art world of the 1920s, a circle that included the painters Jean Charlot, Roberto Montenegro, Best-Maugard, Nahui Olín, and Miguel and Rosa Covarrubias; the writer Anita Brenner; and the editor of *Mexican Folkways,* Frances Toor; and, of course, the major muralists, Orozco, Siqueiros, and Rivera. Frida and Modotti soon became fast friends, the younger woman—and neophyte painter—drawn naturally to the bohemian world of artists and communists that surrounded the photographer.

This was not Alejandro's world, though many of its members campaigned with him under the anti-Callista banner. By June 1928 his affair with Frida was over, ending finally when he fell in love with her friend Esperanza Ordóñez.

Frida did not let go easily. "Now as never before I feel that you do not love me anymore," she wrote to him. "But, I confess to you, I don't believe it, I have faith—it cannot be— Deep down, you understand me, you know I adore you! That you are not only a thing that is mine, but you are me myself!— Irreplaceable!" Nevertheless, two or three months later, through her friendship with Tina Modotti, Frida had joined the Communist party and had met Diego Rivera, replacing her old love with a new one.

Diego Rivera was forty-one years old when Frida came to know him, and he was Mexico's most famous—and infamous—artist. Certainly he had covered more walls than any other muralist.

He painted with such fluency and speed that it sometimes seemed he was driven by a telluric force. "I am not merely an 'artist,'" he said, "but a man performing his biological function of producing paintings, just as a tree produces flowers and fruit." Indeed, work was to him a kind of narcotic, and any impediment to it irritated him, whether it was the demands of politics, illness, or the petty details of daily life. Sometimes he labored without stopping for days at a time, taking his meals on the scaffold and, if necessary, sleeping there.

While he painted, he was surrounded by friends and onlookers whom he regaled with fictitious tales—of fighting in the Russian Revolution, for example, or experimenting with a diet of human flesh, especially young female flesh wrapped in a tortilla. "It's like the tenderest young pig," he said.

Despite his antics, and though the speed with which he painted made it appear that he was improvising, he was well trained, deliberate, a complete professional. He had been producing paintings since he was three, when his father, after watching him draw all over the walls, gave him a blackboard-lined room where he could draw to his heart's content.

Born in Guanajuato in 1887 to a schoolteacher (a Mason and freethinker) and his wife, a pious young woman who owned a candy store, Diego María de la Concepción Juan Nepomuceno Estanislao de la Rivera y Barrientos Acosta y Rodríguez was considered a prodigy from the beginning. At ten he demanded to be sent to art school, and while continuing his elementary education by day, he took night classes at the most prestigious art school in Mexico, the San Carlos Academy. He won prizes and scholarships, but by 1902 academic teaching seemed to him too limited, and he left school to work on his own.

In those days there was only one place for an aspiring art student, and Rivera, armed with a pension granted by the governor of Veracruz, sailed for Europe in 1907. After a year in Spain, he settled in Paris, where, except for various trips, he stayed until he returned to Mexico in 1921, leaving behind an adoring Russian common-law wife, Angelina Beloff, an illegitimate daughter by another Russian woman, and a host of friends from various, mostly bohemian coteries—Picasso and Gertrude Stein, for example, Guillaume Apollinaire and Elie Faure, Ilya Ehrenburg and Diaghilev.

His first job in Mexico City was to paint the mural entitled *Creation* in the amphitheater of the National Preparatory School. It is an odd work for a painter already fired with enthusiasm at the prospect of creating a revolutionary and specifically Mexican art. While its intellectual inspiration is clearly Vasconcelos's lay mysticism—it deploys idealized, monumental figures of theological virtues, and personifications of, for example, wisdom, strength, erotic poetry, tragedy, and science—it is virtually devoid of *Mexicanidad* in both style and content. Perhaps Rivera was still too enamored of European painting to find the forms and themes that would embody his ideals. Nevertheless, in *Creation*, he did discover his medium and his scale: the monumental mural. And if his subject matter here was universal and allegorical rather than native and real, it would not be long before the mythic muse with a classical body became Rivera's classic Mexican Indian mother.

Rivera's *Mexicanidad* first emerged in the Ministry of Public Education murals (1923–1928), which he began as soon as he finished the Preparatory School auditorium. In the ministry's three stories of open hallways surrounding a huge courtyard, he painted the Indians toiling in the fields and mines; being educated by saintly-looking Indian teachers in a rural, open-air school; holding a workers' meeting and dividing the lands restored to them by the revolution. He invented his own vocabulary for describing them: solid, brown, rounded bodies, round heads and an infinitude of hats—anonymous figures that came to be called (by his enemies) "Rivera's monkeys." His subject and his style eventually were so utterly merged that although influences (Giotto, Michelangelo) are obvious, his work does not look derivative: to some, Mexico itself, its folklore and folk, its cactuses and mountains, seems a "motif" invented by Diego Rivera. And whatever his specific subject, he portrayed the Indian valiantly struggling under continued oppression to gain new rights and liberties and a better life.

It was a grand and democratic theme, and Rivera and the other muralists embraced it with reformist zeal not only in their art but in their politics. In September 1923, taking their cue from the mushrooming of labor and peasant organizations in the postrevolutionary years, they gathered in Rivera's home to found the Syndicate of Technical Workers, Painters, and Sculptors; along with Rivera, David Alfaro Siqueiros, Fernando Leal, and Xavier Guerrero (then Tina Modotti's lover) formed the executive committee. In a manifesto, they declared their sympathy for the oppressed masses and their conviction that Mexican art "is great because it surges from the people; it is collective, and our own aesthetic aim is to socialize artistic expression, to destroy bourgeois individualism. We repudiate the so-called easel art and all such art which springs from ultra-intellectual circles, for it is essentially aristocratic. We hail the monumental expression of art because such art is public property. We proclaim that this being the moment of social transition from a decrepit to a new order, the makers of beauty must invest their greatest efforts in the aim of materializing an art valuable to the people, and our supreme objective in art, which is today an expression for individual pleasure, is to create beauty for all, beauty that enlightens and stirs to struggle."

With the reaction against positivism and the belief in the genius of intuition that were among the fruits of the revolution came a reevaluation of the art of the child, the peasant, and the Indian. Painters dared proclaim that "the art of the Mexican people is the greatest and the most healthy spiritual expression in the world." Pre-Columbian art, which had been spurned as alien and barbaric, now was seen as a reflection of something essentially, mysteriously—even nobly—Mexican. Rich Mexicans who in prerevolutionary days might have acquired works by the fashionable Spanish painter Ignacio Zuloaga now collected Toltec, Mayan, and Aztec idols. Popular artifacts were judged to be works of art, true expressions of "the people" rather than mere curios or junk. There was a revival of handicrafts, and urban Mexicans began to decorate their homes with bright objects from the market and cheap furniture made for *campesinos*. The regional costumes of Mexico were extolled, categorized, and even worn by cosmopolitan Mexican women. Mexican food replaced French cuisine at sophisticated tables. *Corridos* (ballads) were meticulously gleaned in all parts of the country, published, and sung in schools and concert halls. Modern Mexican composers Carlos Chávez and Silvestre Revueltas wove native rhythms and harmonies into their music, and Rivera's friend the U.S. composer Aaron Copland would write that "the principal imprint of the Indian personality—its deepest reflection in the music of our hemisphere— is to be found in the present-day school of Mexican composers."

The theater likewise took on a native color. *Tandas,* intimate theatrical reviews that followed old Spanish forms, were "Mexicanized," and parts were written for typically Mexican people, types that, as in the visual arts, were meant to symbolize aspects of the nation. Sophisticated urbanites flocked to see the *carpas*—street theaters set up in tents and showing satirical skits on the latest political fiascos—and people who used to enjoy only the classical ballet gathered in cities and towns to watch regional dances and learned to dance the *jarabe* and the *sandunga* at their own fiestas too. Gradually there developed a specifically Mexican style of modern dance, which adopted Indian themes and typical Indian movements such as, for women, grinding corn or carrying a baby in a *rebozo* (shawl), or, for men, planting and cutting in the fields. In 1919, Anna Pavlova danced a Mexican ballet, *La Fantasía Mexicana,* with properly indigenous music by Manuel Castro Padilla and sets and costumes based on native designs; it was so popular that extra performances were given in a bullring.

No matter what their bents or backgrounds, all but the most retrograde artists incorporated Mexican elements into their work. Even Europe-oriented easel painters blended bougainvillea pinks, Indian motifs, and intensities of feeling that are characteristically Mexican with imported ideas that ranged from Cubism, Dadaism, and Surrealism to German *Neue Sachlichkeit* and Picasso's neoclassicism of the 1920s. Others took a more purist approach to Mexicanism. Their nationalist fervor led them to believe that forging a truly noncolonial art meant rejecting foreign influences. They borrowed the simple forms and easily legible subject matter from Mexican popular art in hopes of creating a more direct and accessible style that would be free of the "elitist values" associated with European avant-garde painting; they resented Mexico's imitation of European modes, just as they resented ownership of Mexican oil deposits by foreign companies. Diego Rivera held precisely this nationalistic position. Even though he recognized in his more candid moments the need to merge European tradition with Mexican roots, he fulminated against the "false artists," the "lackeys of Europe" who copied European fashions and thus perpetuated the semi-colonial condition of Mexican culture.

Primitivism and the adoption of certain aspects of popular art in "high" art represented not only a rejection of bourgeois or European values but a romantic yearning for a primitive agrarian world where handmade artifacts flourished—a world that the artists must have felt was bound to disappear with the coming industrial age. Diego Rivera adored that past and sometimes painted it as an idyllic epoch, even though he devoutly believed that mankind's hope for the future lay in industrialization and communism. He and Frida surrounded themselves with Mexican popular art, and his collection of pre-Columbian sculpture is one of the best in Mexico.

In 1928, when Frida met him, Rivera was on the loose. He had gone to Russia in September 1927 as a member of the Mexican delega-tion of "workers and peasants" to attend the tenth anniversary of the October Revolution and to paint a fresco in the Red Army Club. He never completed the project, for there always seemed to be some bureaucratic obstruction or other, and in May 1928 he was precipitately called home by the Mexican Communist party, ostensibly to work in Vasconcelos's presidential campaign. (He later claimed he had been asked to run for president!)

By the time he reached Mexico in August, his marriage to the beauti-ful Lupe Marín had disintegrated. It had been a tumultuous marriage, passionately physical and physically violent: Rivera described Lupe as a spirited animal—"green eyes so transparent she seemed to be blind"; "animal teeth"; "tiger mouth"; hands like "eagle talons." The cause of the separation, according to Lupe, was Diego's affair with Tina Modotti. Tina had posed, along with Lupe, as a model for the splendid nudes in Rivera's mural at the National Agricultural School in Chapingo, and that had started the liaison. It was not Lupe's first encounter with Rivera's philandering. She had learned forbearance and occasionally vengeance: before an astonished group of guests, she once tore a rival's hair, ripped up a number of Rivera's drawings, and thrashed her husband with her fists; on another occasion she smashed some of Diego's pre-Columbian idols and served him a soup made of the shards. But Lupe could not tolerate the fact that she shared the spotlight in his Chapingo mural with another woman. Though Rivera's affair with Tina had ended before he left for Russia, the damage had been done.

As if he needed to fill the void in his life left by the departure of Lupe and their two small daughters, Diego had more love affairs during the period following his return from Russia than ever before or after. He had no trouble making conquests. Although he was undeniably ugly, he drew women to him with the natural ease of a magnet attract-ing iron filings. Indeed, part of his appeal was his monstrous appear-ance—his ugliness made a perfect foil for the type of woman who likes to play beauty to a beast—but the greater attraction was his per-sonality. He was a frog prince, an extraordinary man full of brilliant humor, vitality, and charm. He could be tender and was deeply sensu-ous. Most important, he was famous, and fame seems to be an irresistible lure for some women. It is said that women chased Rivera more than he chased them. He was pursued especially by certain young Americans who felt that a tryst with Diego Rivera was as much of a "must" as a trip to the pyramids of Teotihuacán.

Women, whether from Mexico or elsewhere, also liked to be with Diego simply because he liked to be with them. From his point of view, women were in many ways superior to men—more sensitive, more peace-loving, more civilized. In 1931, his voice dreamy, his eyes twinkling, his broad lips expanding into a languorous, Buddha-like smile, Rivera spoke to a New York reporter about his admiration for women: "Men are savages by nature. They still are savages today. History shows that the first progress was made by women. Men preferred to remain brutes who fought and hunted. Women remained at home and cultivated the arts. They founded industry. They were the first to contemplate the stars and to evolve poetry and art. . . . Show me any invention that did not originate in the desire [on the part of men] to serve women." Perhaps it was Rivera's years in Europe that made his approach to the opposite sex so different from that of the average *macho*. In any case, he enjoyed talking with women; he valued their minds, and such an attitude was, in those days in Mexico, or anywhere else, a rare delight for most women.

Rivera did, of course, appreciate their bodies too. He had a passion for beauty, a mammoth appetite for visual pleasure, and it is said that to model for Diego meant offering one's body to his flesh as well as to his eyes. What Frida thought of his reputation as a womanizer when she first met him is not recorded. Perhaps it attracted her; maybe she fell into that age-old, self-deceiving hope: I will be the one to capture and hold his love; he will love me in a different way. And of course she did and he did, but not without a struggle.

It is almost certain that Frida and Diego met for the first time at a party at Tina Modotti's home. First held in 1923 under Weston's aegis, the weekly gatherings Tina organized had done much to create in Mexico an artistic milieu, a bohemian ambience in which the latest ideas about art and revolution could be exchanged; they were, to put it mildly, lively affairs, with singing, dancing, spirited conversations, and whatever food and drink the hostess and her guests could afford. "The meeting [with Diego]," Frida said in 1954, "took place in the period when people carried pistols and went around shooting the street lamps on Madero Avenue and getting into mischief. During the night, they broke them all and went about spraying bullets, just for fun. Once at a party, given by Tina, Diego shot a phonograph and I began to be very interested in him in spite of the fear I had of him."

The probable truth of Frida and Diego's meeting at Tina Modotti's party—not a bad story in itself—has given way to a better tale. Indeed, there seem to be as many different versions as there are tellers, and Frida herself remembered the meeting in different ways at different times. The "official" version is that when she recuperated from her accident, she began to show her paintings to friends and acquaintances. One person who saw them was Orozco, and he liked them enormously. "He gave me an *abrazo* [a hug]," said Frida. She also took some canvases to a man she knew only by "sight." Frida remembered:

As soon as they gave me permission to walk and to go out in the street, I went, carrying my paintings, to see Diego Rivera, who at that time was painting the frescoes in the corridors of the Ministry of Education. I did not know him except by sight, but I admired him enormously. I was bold enough to call him so that he would come down from the scaffolding to see my paintings and to tell me sincerely whether or not they were worth anything. . . . Without more ado I said: "Diego, come down." And just the way he is, so humble, so amiable, he came down. "Look, I have not come to flirt or anything even if you are a woman-chaser. I have come to show you my painting. If you are interested in it, tell me so, if not, likewise, so that I will go to work at something else to help my parents." Then he said to me: "Look, in the first place, I am very interested in your painting, above all in this portrait of you, which is the most original. The other three seem to me to be influenced by what you have seen. Go home, paint a painting, and next Sunday I will come and see it and tell you what I think." This he did and he said: "You have talent."

Diego's version of the meeting, as told in *My Art, My Life,* is an example of his phenomenal memory and of his no less phenomenal imagination. He was a great storyteller, and if some of what he tells is embroidery on the facts, it also gives a largely accurate picture of his abiding fascination with Frida.

Just before I went to Cuernavaca, there occurred one of the happiest events in my life. I was at work on one of the uppermost frescoes of the Ministry of Education building one day, when I heard a girl shouting up to me, "Diego, please come down from there! I have something important to discuss with you!"

I turned my head and looked down from my scaffold. On the ground beneath me stood a girl of about eighteen. She had a fine nervous body, topped by a delicate face. Her hair was long; dark and thick eyebrows met above her nose. They seemed like the wings of a blackbird, their black arches framing two extraordinary brown eyes.

When I climbed down, she said, "I didn't come here for fun. I have to work to earn my livelihood. I have done some paintings which I want you to look over professionally. I want an absolutely straightforward opinion, because I cannot afford to go on just to appease my vanity. I want you to tell me whether you think I can become a good enough artist to make it worth my while to go on. I've brought three of my paintings here. Will you come and look at them?"

"Yes," I said, and followed her to a cubicle under a stairway where she had left her paintings. She turned each of them, leaning against the wall, to face me. They were all three portraits of women. As I looked at them, one by one, I was immediately impressed. The canvases revealed an unusual energy of expression, precise delineation of character, and true severity. They showed none of the tricks in the name of originality that usually mark the work of ambitious beginners. They had a fundamental plastic honesty, and an artistic personality of their own. They communicated a vital sensuality, complemented by a merciless yet sensitive power of observation. It was obvious to me that this girl was an authentic artist.

She undoubtedly noticed the enthusiasm in my face, for before I could say anything, she admonished me in a harshly defensive tone, "I have not come to you looking for compliments. I want the criticism of a serious man. I'm neither an art lover nor an amateur. I'm simply a girl who must work for her living."

I felt deeply moved by admiration for this girl. I had to restrain myself from praising her as much as I wanted to. Yet I could not be completely insincere. I was puzzled by her attitude. Why, I asked her, didn't she trust my judgment? Hadn't she come herself to ask for it?

"The trouble is," she replied, "that some of your good friends have advised me not to put too much stock in what you say. They say that if it's a girl who asks your opinion and she's not an absolute horror, you are ready to gush all over her. Well, I want you to tell me only one thing. Do you actually believe that I should continue to paint, or should I turn to some other sort of work?"

"In my opinion, no matter how difficult it is for you, you must continue to paint," I answered at once.

"Then I'll follow your advice. Now I'd like to ask you one more favor. I've done other paintings which I'd like you to see. Since you don't work on Sundays, could you come to my place next Sunday to see them? I live in Coyoacán, Avenida Londres, 126. My name is Frida Kahlo."

The moment I heard her name, I remembered that my friend, Lombardo Toledano, while Director of the National Preparatory School, had complained to me about the intractability of a girl of that name. She was the leader, he said, of a band of juvenile delinquents who raised such uproars in the school that Toledano had considered quitting his job on account of them. I recalled him once pointing her out to me after depositing her in the principal's office for a reprimand. Then another image popped into my mind, that of the twelve-year-old girl who had defied Lupe, seven years before, in the auditorium of the school where I had been painting murals.

I said, "But you are . . ."

She stopped me quickly, almost putting her hand on my mouth in her anxiety. Her eyes acquired a devilish brilliancy.

Threateningly, she said, "Yes, so what? I was the girl in the auditorium, but that has absolutely nothing to do with now. You still want to come Sunday?"

I had great difficulty not answering, "More than ever!" But if I showed my excitement she might not let me come at all. So I only answered, "Yes."

Then, after refusing my help in carrying her paintings, Frida departed, the big canvases jiggling under her arms.

Next Sunday found me in Coyoacán looking for Avenida Londres, 126. When I knocked on the door, I heard someone over my head, whistling "The Internationale." In the top of a high tree, I saw Frida in overalls, starting to climb down. Laughing gaily, she took my hand and ushered me through the house, which seemed to be empty, and into her room. Then she paraded all her paintings before me. These, her room, her sparkling presence, filled me with a wonderful joy.

I did not know it then, but Frida had already become the most important fact in my life. And she would continue to be, up to the moment she died, twenty-seven [twenty-six] years later.

A few days after this visit to Frida's home I kissed her for the first time. When I had completed my work in the Education building, I began courting her in earnest. Although she was but eighteen [twenty or twenty-one] and I more than twice her age, neither of us felt the least bit awkward. Her family, too, seemed to accept what was happening.

One day her father, Don Guillermo Kahlo, who was an excellent photographer, took me aside.

"I see you're interested in my daughter, eh?" he said.

"Yes," I replied. "Otherwise I would not be coming all the way out to Coyoacán to see her."

"She is a devil," he said.

"I know it."

"Well, I've warned you," he said, and he left.

Chapter 7

The Elephant
and the Dove

AFTER THEIR MEETING, however it occurred, Frida and Diego's courtship proceeded apace. Rivera visited Frida in Coyoacán on Sunday
afternoons, and Frida spent more and more time beside Diego on
the scaffold, watching him paint. Lupe, though separated from Diego,
was jealous:

> When I went to the Secretary of Education to leave his lunch—he was
> painting the murals in the Education Building—I was shocked to see the
> familiarity with which an impudent girl treated him. . . . She called him
> *"mi cuatacho"* [my big pal]. . . . This was Frida Kahlo. . . . Frankly I was
> jealous, but I didn't give it importance because Diego was susceptible to
> love like a weather vane. . . . But one day he said, "Let's go to Frida's
> house.". . . it struck me as very disagreeable to see this so-called youngster
> drink tequila like a real mariachi.

However disagreeable Frida may have seemed to Lupe, Diego's
attachment to her grew. Her candor disarmed him. Her odd mixture
of freshness and unmasked sexuality tempted him. That her spunk
and mischief appealed to his own boyish prankishness can be seen

in his fond recollection of a moment of mirth when, during a stroll in Coyoacán, they paused under a street lamp and were startled to see all the street lights in the neighborhood turn on. "On a sudden impulse, I stooped to kiss her. As our lips touched, the light nearest us went off and came on again when our lips parted." They kissed again and again under other street lamps with the same electrifying results.

Another attraction for Diego was Frida's quick, unconventional mind. Like Diego, she was easily bored. "He is irritated by only two things," Frida once wrote, "loss of time from work—and stupidity. He has said many times that he would rather have many intelligent enemies than one stupid friend." Frida and Diego did not bore each other. Each was delighted to have a companion who saw life with a similar mixture of irony, hilarity, and black humor. Both rejected bourgeois morality. Both talked about dialectical materialism and "social realism," yet for both realism was riddled with fantasy; as much as they admired a no-nonsense approach to life, they boosted the banal into the marvelous, and worshiped nonsense and imagination. Rivera used to complain: "The trouble with Frida is that she is too realistic. She has no illusions." And Frida used to bewail Rivera's lack of sentimentality; had he been more sentimental, however, she probably would have treated him as salt treats an oyster—one of Frida's sardonic, withering looks would have been enough to make a sentimental man shrivel.

Lupe said that when Frida first visited Diego on the scaffold, "her face was painted, she wore her hair Chinese style, her dress was décolleté a la 'flapper.'" Perhaps so. But before long, as a member of the Young Communist League, Frida was attending workers' rallies, taking part in clandestine meetings, making speeches. "She no longer wore white blouses," Alejandro Gómez Arias somewhat wistfully recalled. "Instead she wore black or red shirts and an enamel pin with a hammer and sickle." Not bothering with coquetry, she often also wore blue jeans and a leather jacket with patches—a worker among workers. Perhaps this, too, was attractive to Diego, who, when they met, was putting a great deal of energy into Communist party activities, as a delegate of the Mexican Peasant League, general secretary of the Anti-Imperialist League, and editor of *El Liberador*.

In 1928 he depicted Frida as a Communist militant in the *Insurrection* panel of his *Ballad of the Proletarian Revolution* mural series on the third floor of the Ministry of Education Building (figure 14). Flanked by Tina Modotti, Julio Antonio Mella, Siqueiros, and other fervent Communists, Frida appears as a grown-up tomboy, her hair cut short, her wiry body clad in a man's red work shirt with a red star on its pocket. With a charmingly eager and righteous expression on her face, she hands out rifles and bayonets—a political heroine and a fit companion for a Communist leader. While she modeled for her portrait, Rivera is said to have quipped, "You have a dog face." Not in the least put off, Frida retorted, "And you have the face of a frog!"

During their courtship Frida began to paint with new confidence and application. Diego was, she thought, the world's greatest painter, and the pleasure he took in her work made working worthwhile. Frida once said that when she first showed her paintings to Diego, "I was terribly anxious to paint frescoes." But when he saw them, he told her, "Your will must bring you to your own expression." For a brief period, however, Frida's will brought her to express herself in a Rivera-esque manner. "I began to paint things that he liked. From that time on he admired me and loved me."

Wisely, though he did advise, Rivera refrained from teaching Frida: he did not want to spoil her inborn talent. She, nevertheless, took him as a mentor; watching him, listening, she learned. As she developed, the Riveraesque style was to disappear, but other lessons remained with her. "Diego showed me the revolutionary sense of life and the true sense of color," she said to a journalist in 1950.

Rivera's influence can be seen in both the style and the substance of Frida's paintings from 1928 and 1929. *Portrait of Cristina Kahlo* (figure 13), painted early in 1928, follows the format of her first portraits: hard, slightly wooden outlines delineate forms, and a small stylized tree in the background contrasts with a larger branch in the foreground to define space in a naïve and rudimentary manner. Later in the same year, when she painted *Portrait of Agustín M. Olmedo,* Frida set her old school friend against an expanse of blue that, like many of Rivera's portrait backgrounds, is unbroken by motifs of any kind. She has borrowed as well Diego's way of painting the figure with broad, simplified areas of high-keyed color, a style that he had come to by overlaying his knowledge of European modernism with a thorough absorption of the values of Mexican popular and pre-Columbian art. Though Frida's paintings from this period are relatively large compared with most of her later work, they have very little detail of line or texture or modeling. It is as if she had extracted a figure from one of Diego's murals and placed it in the center of her canvas.

In the 1929 portraits *Niña* (figure 15) and *Portrait of a Girl*, the backgrounds are divided into two bright color zones: lavender and yellow in the case of *Niña*, blue-green and terra-cotta in the case of *Portrait of a Girl*. *Niña* wears an olive-green dress with red polka dots, the *Girl* wears pink. These are the festive yet astringent colors characteristic of Mexican popular art and indeed of Mexican life; they can be seen in kaleidoscopic movement on any market day.

Frida's color in these paintings departs from European tradition (which she had tried to adopt in her earliest works) even more than did that of Rivera, who had made a conscious decision to "Mexicanize" his color after he returned from Paris. It is as if, never having really mastered "classical" painting, she was freer to abandon its conventions. Similarly, in all her work, her drawing is more primitive than Diego's, and while in early paintings the adoption of the naïve folkloric manner served to camouflage the awkwardness that came from inexperience, later this primitivism, like the Mexican palette, became her stylistic choice.

Although Frida's early paintings of children cannot be called great paintings, they are touching and alive, especially because the childlike qualities of style, subject, and artist are perfectly meshed. Frida the inexperienced painter could adopt a naïve manner without affectation. Because of her own youthful spirit, she was able to gain children's confidence and thus to capture in her work their wistful freshness—that look in a child's eye that seems to combine the muteness of animals with the burden of wisdom. And whereas many of Rivera's paintings of children have a stereotypical cuteness—round cheeks and even rounder eyes, calculated to appeal to the tourist trade—Frida's are always particularized and authentic, filled, as most of his are not, with sharply observed details—big ears, skinny arms, bony elbows, strands of hair that won't stay put, underdrawers showing below the hem of a skirt. The large safety pin that holds together *Niña*'s best dress speaks volumes about the pride and poverty of children in Mexico.

Frida's intelligence worked in a different way from Diego's. Shunning theories and overviews, she penetrated into the particular, focusing on details of clothing, faces, trying to capture an individual life. Later, she would probe the insides of fruits and flowers, the organs hidden beneath wounded flesh, and the feelings hidden beneath stoic features. From his more distanced and abstract vantage point, Rivera encompassed the breadth of the visible world; he populated his murals with all of society and the pageant of history. Frida's subjects, by contrast, came from a world close at hand—friends, animals, still lifes, most of all from herself. Her true subjects were embodied states of mind, her own joys and sorrows. Always intimately connected with the events of her life, her images convey the immediacy of lived experience.

Immediacy and intimacy find their way even into *The Bus*, a 1929 painting in which Frida attempted to do, in her own way and on a tiny canvas, what Rivera did so often in his huge murals (figure 16). Stereotypes of Mexican society are all lined up on the bench of a rickety Mexican bus: a plump, lower-middle-class matron with a straw shopping basket; a worker holding a monkey wrench and dressed in blue denim overalls and a blue cap; in the center the heroine of the group, a barefoot, Madonna-like Indian mother suckling her infant, whom she swaddles in her yellow *rebozo;* next to her a small boy watching the world go by outside the window; an old man readily identified by his blue eyes and bulging money bag as a gringo (he recalls the fat capitalist in Rivera's Ministry of Education mural); a prissy young woman of the upper bourgeoisie (a fashionable scarf and a neat little pocketbook are her emblems). As a pair, the bourgeoise and the capitalist are contrasted with the housewife and the worker, for the two couples flank the central Indian mother in neat social symmetry. All in all, *The Bus* is a tongue-in-cheek Mexican version of Daumier's *Third-Class Carriage,* with the difference that in Frida's mildly Marxist message the figures range in social class, whereas in Daumier's realistic scene of third-class public transportation, everyone from top-hatted man to small boy, from woman with market basket to suckling mother is poor.

If the notion of painting a scene of social hierarchy is Riveraesque, the humor with which the social strata are portrayed in *The Bus* is pure Frida. She surely had a political conscience, but she also had a sharp sense of the ridiculous, even when the ridiculous came in the form of a baroque barrage of political theorizing from Diego. That she might have been gently pulling our (or Rivera's) leg when she painted *The Bus* is reinforced by certain details. The *pulquería* (bar) in the background is called La Risa (laughter), and the proletarian wears a necktie, plus a blue shirt with a white collar, a wry comment, perhaps, on the workers who are to inherit the earth in the best of all Marxist worlds.

In Frida's second *Self-Portrait* (plate II), the first she did after she became attached to Diego, the pale and melancholy Renaissance princess of the 1926 gift to Alejandro has vanished. Gone also are the spiraling Art Nouveau waves and other romantic accouterments with which the lovelorn teenager surrounded herself in her first *Self-Portrait*. Instead, we see a pink-cheeked contemporary girl framed by curtains—a prop adopted by folk artists from colonial portraiture and a device that served naïve painters (including Frida) well by eliminating the problem of setting the figure convincingly into surrounding space. Frida looks fresh in both senses of the word. She stares straight out at us with the unblinking intensity that caused one person who met her at this time to describe her as "bright as an eagle." Fierce enough to have commanded Rivera to come down from his scaffold, she is also fetching enough for him to have done so with alacrity.

When Frida went to Jesús Ríos y Valles and told him the news of her engagement to Diego, he replied, "Marry him, because you will be the wife of Diego Rivera, who is a genius." Other friends were astonished that Frida would leave Alejandro for an ugly old man like Rivera, but her school friend Baltasar Dromundo (who later wrote about Frida and Alejandro in his book on the Preparatory School) understood precisely why she did. "By the time she became involved with Rivera," he says, "her relationship with Alejandro was diluted. She was attracted to Diego's fame. Where Alejandro would cover Frida in flowers, Diego would have grabbed her and kissed her."

Whatever Guillermo Kahlo thought of the prospect of Diego Rivera as a son-in-law, his inability to provide his family with financial security, or even to pay Frida's medical expenses, which he knew would continue over the years, must have encouraged him to approve the proposal. Although Frida was by now the only unmarried daughter (Cristina was living with her husband by 1928; her daughter Isolda was born in 1929), the Kahlos' household expenses were still hard to meet. Neither of Frida's parents enjoyed good health, and Frida's accident had dashed their hopes that she would have a professional career. Whatever other drawbacks there might be to the union, if Frida married Diego Rivera, she would be marrying a man known to be both rich and generous, one who could be relied upon to support not only Frida but her family as well. (Indeed, soon after Diego married Frida, he paid off the mortgage on the Kahlos' Coyoacán house, which Frida's parents could no longer afford to keep, and allowed them to go on living there.)

It was Matilde Calderón de Kahlo, whom Frida once accused of stinginess, who could not accept her daughter's engagement to an ugly, fat, forty-two-year-old Communist and nonbeliever, even a rich one. She begged Alejandro Gómez Arias to do everything in his power to prevent the marriage. But everything in his power was very little, if anything. The wedding took place on August 21, 1929. Frida said:

> At seventeen [twenty] I fell in love with Diego, and my [parents] did not like this because Diego was a Communist and because they said that he looked like a fat, fat, fat Brueghel. They said that it was like marriage between an elephant and a dove.
>
> Nevertheless, I arranged everything in the court of Coyoacán so that we could be married the 21st of August, 1929. I asked the maid for skirts, the blouse and *rebozo* were also borrowed from the maid. I arranged my foot with the apparatus so that it couldn't be noticed and we got married.
>
> No one went to the wedding, only my father, who said to Diego, "Notice that my daughter is a sick person and all her life she will be sick; she is intelligent, but not pretty. Think it over if you want, and if you wish to get married, I give you my permission."

The couple were married in a civil ceremony in Coyoacán's ancient city hall by the town's mayor, who was, according to Diego, "a prominent *pulque* dealer." There were three witnesses: a hairdresser, a homeopathic doctor, and Judge Mondragón of Coyoacán. Rivera recalled that Frida's father was highly amused by his favorite daughter's wedding: "In the middle of the service, Don Guillermo Kahlo got up and declared, 'Gentlemen, is it not true that we are play-acting?' "

La Prensa (August 23, 1929), of Mexico City, reported:

> Diego Rivera got married—last Wednesday in the neighboring town of Coyoacán the *discutido pintor* ["much-discussed painter" was the almost inevitable prefix for Rivera's name when it appeared in the Mexican press] contracted marriage with Miss Frieda Kahlo, one of his disciples. The bride dressed, as you can see, in very simple street clothes, and the painter Rivera dressed *de Americana* [in a suit] and without a vest. The marriage service was unpretentious; it was celebrated in a very cordial atmosphere and with all modesty, without ostentation, and without pompous ceremonies. The

novios were warmly congratulated after the marriage by a few intimate friends.

A charming and funny photograph of the bride and groom accompanied this newspaper announcement. Looking tiny beside her huge husband, Frida stares at the photographer with her characteristic intensity. She makes no concessions to the solemnity of the occasion: in her right hand she holds a cigarette! It is easy to imagine her, just as Lupe Marín described her, drinking tequila "like a real mariachi."

Lupe Marín came to the wedding party, and by some accounts (she herself denied it) made a scene. Bertram Wolfe told the story:

> Pretending to be indifferent about Diego's love affairs, she hinted that she would be "broadminded" enough to attend his wedding. . . . Frida guilelessly invited Lupe to a party they gave afterwards for a few friends and relatives. She came, pretended to be very gay, then in the midst of the festivities, strode suddenly up to Frida, lifted high the new bride's skirt, and shouted to the assembled company: "You see these two sticks? These are the legs Diego has now instead of mine!" Then she marched out of the house in triumph.

Frida's account of the post-wedding festivities does not mention Lupe's affront: "That day they gave us a party in Roberto Montenegro's house. Diego went on such a terrifying drunken binge with tequila that he took out his pistol, he broke a man's little finger, and broke other things. Then we had a fight, and I left crying and went home. A few days passed and Diego came to fetch me and took me to the house at Reforma 104." As Andrés Henestrosa remembers the party, it took place on the roof of Tina Modotti's house. "There were items of lingerie hung on the roof to dry," Henestrosa recalls. "They made a good atmosphere for a wedding."

Chapter 8

Newlywed:
The Tehuana Frida

FRIDA AND DIEGO'S first home was a grand house built during the Díaz dictatorship, No. 104 on the elegant Paseo de la Reforma; demonstrating both his passion for nativism and his love of contradiction, Rivera had placed pre-Columbian figures in the entranceway of the French-gothic-style façade. Frida recalled that "as furniture we had a narrow bed, dining room furniture that Frances Toor had given us, a long black table, and a yellow kitchen table that my mother gave us and that we pushed into a corner for the collection of archaeological pieces." There was a live-in maid named Margarita Dupuy, and in addition, "they sent Siqueiros, his wife, Blanca Luz Bloom, and two other Communists to live in my house. There we all were, crowded together, under the table, in corners, in the bedrooms."

The Marxist ménage did not last long, for Diego—the general secretary of the Mexican Communist party—was under attack by Stalinist stalwarts. Many were the charges against him: his friendship with a certain government official, for instance, and the fact that he accepted commissions from a reactionary government. The Party felt these commissions were a kind of bribe: letting Rivera paint hammers and sickles in public buildings made the government look liberal and tolerant in the public eye. He was also rebuked for disagreeing with other Party leaders on issues such as the creation of specifically Communist trade unions and the likelihood that capitalist countries would attack Russia. His official connections with other leftist groups or individuals outside the Communist orthodoxy—Rivera befriended whom he befriended—were seen as a right-leaning deviation. Besides that, the muralist had always been unreliable as a Party functionary, never getting to meetings on time and when he got there trying to dominate them with his charismatic personality.

When the time came, he presided over his own expulsion from the Party, on October 3, 1929. Baltasar Dromundo describes the scene: "Diego arrived, sat down, and took out a large pistol and put it on a table. He then put a handkerchief over the pistol, and said: 'I, Diego Rivera, general secretary of the Mexican Communist party, accuse the painter Diego Rivera of collaborating with the petit-bourgeois government of Mexico and of having accepted a commission to paint the stairway of the National Palace of Mexico. This contradicts the politics of the Comintern and therefore the painter Diego Rivera should be expelled from the Communist party by the general secretary of the Communist party, Diego Rivera.' Diego declared himself expelled, and he stood up, removed the handkerchief, picked up the pistol, and broke it. It was made of clay."

Rivera remained a Communist; Marxist ideals continued to be the core of his subject matter in the very murals for which he was being chastised. But political activism had been almost as important to him as food, sleep, and painting, and now he was a political outsider. The Communist party press excoriated him; several of his old comrades broke with him. Tina Modotti, for example, whom only a few months before he had defended in court when she was wrongly accused of complicity in the murder of Julio Antonio Mella, found party loyalty a more powerful tie than friendship. She wrote to Edward Weston: "I think his going out of the party will do more harm to him than to the party. He will be considered a traitor. I need not add that I shall look upon him as one too, and from now on all my contacts with him will be limited to our photographic transactions." As Diego himself put it, years later: "I did not have a home—the Party having always been my home."

He worked harder than ever. In the same month that he married Frida, he had been appointed Director of the Academy of San Carlos, the art school he had attended as a boy, and he set out to revolutionize the school's curriculum and power structure. He devised a system of apprenticeship in which the school became a workshop instead of an academy. Teachers were, he said, to be subject to the appraisal of the students, and students were to think of themselves as artisans or technical workers. (Not surprisingly, opposition to Rivera's directorship grew, until less than a year after he had been hired, he was fired.)

He also painted prodigiously. By the end of 1929 he had finished the murals in the Ministry of Public Education; designed the scenes, props, and costumes for the ballet *H.P.* (Horse Power), composed by Carlos Chávez; finished a series of six large female nudes symbolizing Purity, Strength, Knowledge, Life, Moderation, and Health for the assembly hall of the Ministry of Health Building; and designed four stained-glass windows for the same building. Finally, he had begun his epic murals showing the Mexican people from the preconquest epoch to the present and even into the future on the walls of the main stairway of the National Palace. He was to work at the National Palace intermittently for six years, and not until the mid-1950s did he finish the panels of the upstairs corridor.

Frida did not paint much in the first months of her marriage. Being married to Diego was a full-time job. When he fell ill from strain, in September, she nursed him, carefully copying down the doctor's program for curing the collapse, and doing her best to make her husband follow orders. When he recovered, she was spiritually at his side for the absurd and humiliating Party trial, and she left the Party when he was expelled. Diego's almost superhuman work schedule (once when he was on a round-the-clock stint, he fell asleep on the scaffold and tumbled to the pavement below) did not inspire industry in Frida. Rather it taught her that the best way to see Rivera was to join him on the scaffold, where she was content to leave the role of genius to her husband, to play the great man's young wife. Oddly, she learned how to cater to his fancies from Lupe Marín, who arrived one day, took a good look around the house, whisked her off to La Merced market to buy pots and pans and other equipment, and then taught the young bride how to cook the foods Diego liked. In return, Frida painted Lupe's portrait.

From Lupe, too, Frida learned to take his midday meal to Diego in a basket decorated with flowers and covered by napkins embroidered with sayings like "I adore you." It was a custom adopted from Mexican *campesinas*, who carry their husbands' lunch to them in the fields.

If Diego was "homeless" as a result of his expulsion from the Party, he was unchastened: in December 1929 he accepted a commission from the American ambassador to Mexico, Dwight W. Morrow, to paint a mural in the Cortés Palace in Cuernavaca. The details were settled when Frida and Diego dined with the ambassador and his wife, the great personal charm of the four diners eclipsing what otherwise might have been perceived as a series of ironies. Here was an American capitalist—one who in 1928 had persuaded the government of President Plutarco Elías Calles to make an informal agreement to modify legislation dealing with Mexican oil rights in a way that favored U.S. investors—commissioning a Communist to paint a mural with an anti-imperialist subject: the fresco shows the brutalities of the Spanish conquest and the glories of the Mexican Revolution, with Zapata as hero, leading a white horse. At the same table was Diego Rivera, a vehement Marxist even if he had recently been ousted from the Party, accepting the commission—the same Diego Rivera who, acting as a member of the Anti-Imperialist League of the Americas, had, only months earlier, denounced the encroachment by Wall Street on Latin America and who, acting as a member of the Workers' and Peasants' Bloc, had headed a commission to free from jail the secretary of the Communist party together with many other Communist demonstrators detained for insulting Ambassador Morrow during a violent political demonstration.

Nor was the artist inclined to spurn the ambassador's further gesture of good will: when diplomatic duties took the Morrows to London in late December, they left their lovely rambling weekend house in Cuernavaca to Frida and Diego for the better part of the year it took to complete the murals. There, in the more clement weather and gentler atmosphere of the beautiful town on the low slope of a mountain some fifty miles from Mexico City, Frida and Diego had their honeymoon. While Diego worked, Frida wandered in terraced gardens, among fountains, oleander, and banana trees. From a small tower she could look north toward the village of Tres Marías and the mountains that divide the high plateau of Mexico City from the warm, fertile valley of Morelos; south toward the cathedral tower; and east toward the snow-topped volcanos Popocatepetl and Iztaccihuatl.

When Frida was not at home, she was most often at the Cortés Palace watching Diego paint. He valued her criticism, for she was as quick to detect falseness or pretension in art as in people, and as the years went on he came to depend more and more on her judgments. Frida was tactful; if she had something negative to say, she would soften the impact by making the suggestion with a certain tentativeness or by couching it in a question. Sometimes her comments were irritating, but Rivera paid attention, and sometimes he made changes. He loved, for example, to tell the story of Frida's reaction to his depiction of Zapata leading a white horse (Zapata's horse had been black) in the Cortés Palace mural. When she saw the sketch, she let out a shriek and said, "But, Diego, how can you paint Zapata's horse white?" Rivera argued that he should create beautiful things for "the people," and the horse remained white. But when Frida criticized the horse's heavy legs, Diego handed her his sketch and let her draw them the way she thought they should be. "I had to correct that white horse of Zapata," he chuckled, "according to Frida's wishes!"

The Riveras' "honeymoon" certainly lacked any of the usual languor. Art historian Luis Cardoza y Aragón, who visited the couple, described his days in Cuernavaca as a sleepless marathon of adventure and talk. Diego, he said, got up early and went to work. Frida and her guest slept late and enjoyed a large and leisurely breakfast together, after which they would make excursions to nearby towns—Taxco, Iguala, Tepoztlán, Cuautla. In the evenings they picked up Rivera, who inevitably would be taking advantage of the last rays of the sun or even painting by the dimmer light of a lamp. In spite of his long workday, he was always fresh and full of enthusiasm for the night's possibilities. The three friends would find a restaurant and straightaway order a bottle of tequila. Diego's stories began with the first glass. As they unfolded, the bottle emptied, and the episodes grew more and more extravagant. Once he got started, Diego did not want to stop, and the talk continued long after the party had returned home. Eventually Frida would abandon her weary but spellbound guest to the man he fondly called "the monster," and go to bed. After a week or so Cardoza fled, but his vivid memories stayed with him always. "Frida," he wrote, "was grace, energy, and talent united in one of the beings who has most stirred my imagination to enthusiasm. Diego and Frida were part of the spiritual landscape of Mexico, like Popocatepetl and Iztacci-huatl in the valley of Anahuac."

During the months in Cuernavaca, probably for the first time since her marriage, Frida painted. A lost canvas depicting a nude Indian woman from the waist up surrounded by tropical leaves must have been produced at this time, as must also Frida's portrait of Lupe Marín and several of the portraits of Indian children. Very likely Frida's third *Self-Portrait* (figure 18) comes from the Cuernavaca sojourn too.

There are subtle differences between the married woman depicted in the third *Self-Portrait* and the fiancée shown in the second, where Frida is Rivera's *niña bonita*—the pretty young girl whose freshness and candor he adored. Now instead of looking straight ahead with the undauntable directness of youth, Frida's face is turned at an angle, and her eyes seem to glisten with sadness. The mouth whose slightly upturned corners in the 1929 portrait made it look so insolent and firm, so ready to laugh, now looks melancholy. The change is a question of millimeters: the tiniest curve or shadow can completely alter facial expression.

Years later, Frida told a friend what happened in the months that intervened between these two self-portraits: "We could not have a child, and I cried inconsolably but I distracted myself by cooking, dusting the house, sometimes by painting, and every day going to accompany Diego on the scaffold. It gave him great pleasure when I arrived with the midday meal in a basket covered with flowers." After three months of pregnancy, Frida had an abortion because the fetus was in the wrong position. In a 1930 drawing of herself and Rivera, she drew, and then erased, a baby Diego seen as if by X-ray vision inside her stomach: the infant's head is up, his feet are down. *Frida ana the Caesarean Operation,* a curious and probably unfinished painting dated 1931, must likewise refer to the 1930 abortion. (She had never had a Caesarean operation, but she mentioned the possibility in a 1932 letter to a friend, saying a doctor had told her that in spite of her fractured pelvis and spine, she would be able to have a child by Caesarean section.) Besides her disappointment at not being able to bring her child to term, there were doubtless other unhappinesses in Frida's first year of marriage. It is said, for example, that Rivera had an affair with his young assistant Ione Robinson in 1930. Whatever the cause, Frida had to confront the fact that the misfortunes that marred her childhood would be equaled or surpassed by miseries in her adult life. "I suffered two grave accidents in my life," she once said. "One in which a streetcar knocked me down. . . . The other accident is Diego."

Their marriage was, to contemporary observers, a union of lions, their loves, battles, separations, and sufferings beyond petty censuring. Like saints or demigods, they needed no surnames: "Diego" and "Frida" were coin of the Mexican national treasure. Yet those who knew them best offer the most conflicting and contrasting appraisals of their life together.

Friends' insights, of course, depend on when they knew the Riveras. Still it can be said that almost everything that is "in" a marriage is there from the beginning, that all the characteristics and contradictions are present, suspended in a kind of psychological medium from which some aspects rise to the surface at one time, some at another, constantly separating and recombining in a thousand different ways. Thus we may say that from the beginning Frida loved Diego obsessively, or we may believe those who assert that she only grew to love him over time or that she sometimes hated him and wanted to free herself from his hold on her. Frida was in thrall to Diego's prodigal imagination—and bored by his endless fable-spinning. He was an unfaithful husband, of that there can be no doubt. But if Frida despaired at her husband's infidelities, there were times when she said she "couldn't care less" and was actually amused by Diego's affairs. Almost everyone agrees that Frida became a mother figure to Diego, yet the father-daughter relationship of the early years remained important until her death. Where is the truth? Surely it does not lie conveniently or neatly with one interpretation or another, but rather it twists and turns to take in all the contradictions.

There is no question that even when she hated him, Frida adored Diego, and that the pivot of her existence was her desire to be a good wife for him. This did not mean eclipsing herself: Rivera admired strong and independent women; he expected Frida to have her own ideas, her own friends, her own activities. He encouraged her painting and the development of her unique style. When he built a house for them, it was in fact two separate houses, linked only by a bridge. That she tried to earn her living so as not to depend on him for support and that she kept her maiden name pleased him. And if he did not open car doors for her, he opened worlds: he was the great maestro; she chose to be his admiring *compañera*. Being that brought into her life a palette of many colors, colors that were of a dazzling brightness, or somber with sorrow, but always combined in ways that were piercingly alive. Bertram Wolfe noted in his biography of Rivera:

> As is natural with two such strong characters, each totally directed from within, each wayward in an impulse and intense in sensibility, their life together was stormy. She subordinated her waywardness to his; otherwise life with Diego would have been impossible. She saw through his subterfuges and fantasies, laughed with and at his adventures, mocked at and enjoyed the color and wonder of his tall tales, forgave him his affairs with other women, his wounding stratagems, his cruelties. . . . Despite quarrels, brutality, deeds of spite, even a divorce, in the depths of their beings they continued to give first place to each other. Or rather, to him she came first after his painting and after his dramatizing of his life as a succession of legends, but to her he occupied first place, even before her art. To his great gifts, she held, great indulgence was in order. In any case, she told me once, with rueful laughter, that was how he was, and that was how she loved him. "I cannot love him for what he is not."

Gradually, Frida made herself into an essential pillar in the framework of Rivera's existence. Astute at discerning her husband's areas of vulnerability and need, she created in these areas ties to herself. In his autobiography, he called Frida "the most important fact in my life" (it should be noted, however, that the book's title, *My Art, My Life*, gives precedence to art).

Letters from Diego to Frida exhibited in the Frida Kahlo Museum reveal a tender solicitousness on the part of a man better known for his formidable thoughtlessness and for the brutal single-mindedness of his absorption in himself and his work. Often he signed his name by drawing his large lips and writing that they carried millions of kisses. A typical opening was: "Child of my eyes I leave you thousands of kisses." Or "To my beautiful little girl," or "For lovely Fisita, For the child of my eyes, life of my life." Such notes were paralleled by charming gestures—sometimes, like the notes themselves, intended to compensate for absences or neglect, as when one dawn, after a night on the town with lady tourists, he returned to Coyoacán with a cartload of flowers.

They demonstrated their tender feelings for each other in words and gestures. Mariana Morillo Safa, who knew them during the last decade of their time together, recalls how Frida used to listen for the sound of Rivera's homecoming each day. She would keep very still, and then, when she heard him at the door, she would whisper, "There's Diego!" He would kiss her fleetingly on the mouth. "How is my Fridita, my little child of my soul?" he would ask, as if he were talking to a child. "She treated him like a god," Mariana observes. "He treated her like a sweet thing."

Some observers feel that the affectionate nicknames they used for one another—"Frog-toad" or "Niña Fisita"—were all part of a charade, a gloss on the problems that persisted in their relationship, or another sign of their insistence on their Mexicanness, since diminutives of endearment are typical of Mexican as opposed to Castilian Spanish. Perhaps. But Cachucha Carmen Jaime remembers the "entranced" look on Rivera's face when he came home and stood on the threshold of Frida's room saying, "Chicuita" (a baby-talk version of *chiquita*, meaning "little one").

In Frida's first *Self-Portrait* she is dressed in a luxurious velvet Renaissance-style gown. In her second she presents herself as one of "the people" and, most emphatically, as a Mexican. Her lace-trimmed blouse is typical of the inexpensive clothes sold in Mexican market stalls, and her jewelry—colonial-style earrings and pre-Columbian jade beads—symbolizes the painter's identity as a *mestiza* (a person of mixed Indian and Spanish blood). "In another period I dressed like a boy with shaved hair, pants, boots, and a leather jacket," Frida said once. "But when I went to see Diego I put on a Tehuana costume."

Clearly, it was not bohemian casualness that had prompted Frida to choose for her wedding dress the borrowed clothes of an Indian maid. When she put on the Tehuana costume, she was choosing a new identity, and she did it with all the fervor of a nun taking the veil. Even when she was a girl, clothes were a kind of language for Frida, and from the moment of her marriage, the intricate links between dress and self-image, and between personal style and painting style, form one of the subplots in her unfolding drama.

The costume she favored was that of the women from the isthmus of Tehuantepec, and the legends surrounding them doubtless informed her choice: Tehuantepec women are famous for being stately, beautiful, sensuous, intelligent, brave, and strong. Folklore has it that theirs is a matriarchal society where women run the markets, handle fiscal matters, and dominate the men. And the costume is a lovely one: an embroidered blouse and a long skirt, usually of purple or red velvet, with a ruffle of white cotton at the hem. Accessories include long gold chains or necklaces of gold coins, which constitute a girl's hard-earned dowry, and for special occasions an elaborate headdress with starched lace pleats reminiscent of an outsized Elizabethan ruff.

Sometimes Frida wore costumes from other times and places; sometimes she mixed elements of different costumes in one carefully composed ensemble. She might wear Indian huaraches (sandals) or short leather boots of the type worn in the provinces in the beginning of the century as well as by the *soldaderas* who had fought alongside their men in the Mexican Revolution; sometimes, as when she posed for the photographer Imogen Cunningham, she wrapped her *rebozo* around her in the manner of a *soldadera*. Other times she wore an elaborately embroidered and fringed Spanish silk shawl. Layers of petticoats, their hems embroidered by Frida herself with ribald Mexican sayings, gave her walk a special grace and sway.

For Frida the elements of her dress were a kind of palette from which she selected each day the image of herself that she wished to present to the world. People who watched the ritual of her dressing recall the time and care she took, her perfectionism and precision. Frequently she tinkered with a needle before donning a blouse, adding lace here, a ribbon there. Deciding what belt would go with what skirt was a serious matter. "Does it work?" she would ask. "Is it good?" "Frida had an aesthetic attitude about her dress," painter Lucile Blanch remembered. "She was making a whole picture with colors and shapes."

To go with the exotic costumes, Frida arranged her hair in various styles, some typical of certain regions of Mexico, some her own invention. She would sweep it upward, sometimes pulling it so tightly at the temples that it hurt, and then braid into it bright woolen ribbons and decorate it with bows, clips, combs, or fresh bougainvillea blossoms. One friend observed that when she placed a comb in her hair, she pressed its prongs into her scalp with a "coquettish masochism." In later years, when she was weaker, she liked to have her sister, her niece, or close friends arrange it. "Comb my hair," she would say. "Arrange my hair with combs."

She adored jewelry, and from the first days of their marriage, Rivera bestowed it upon her as if he were offering gifts to an Indian princess. She wore everything from cheap glass beads to heavy pre-Columbian jade necklaces, from ornate colonial pendant earrings to a pair made in the shape of hands given her by Picasso in 1939. Her fingers displayed a constantly changing exhibition of rings, all of different styles and origins. People gave them to Frida, and with impulsive generosity, she just as often gave them away.

On one level, of course, Frida chose to dress as a Tehuana for the same reason that she adopted Mexicanism: to please Diego. Rivera liked the Tehuana costume; he traveled to the isthmus often in order to paint its people at work and play, and it is said that one of his various amours during his courtship of Frida had been a Tehuana beauty.

Rivera, who was of Spanish-Indian and Portuguese-Jewish descent (he sometimes claimed to have Dutch, Italian, Russian, and Chinese blood as well), liked to stress the Indian aspect of Frida's heritage, extolling her as authentic, unspoiled, and "primitive": "She is a person whose thoughts and feelings are unrestricted by any limitations forced on them by false necessities of bourgeois social conformity. She senses all experience deeply, because the sensitivity of her organism has not yet been dulled by overexertion along lines which lead to the dissolution of those innate faculties. . . . Frida despises mechanisms, and therefore has the resilience with which a primitive organism meets the stronger and always varied experiences of the life about him."

In fact, of course, Frida was a city girl, formed in a bourgeois, and later an "upper-bohemian," milieu that had nothing to do with the "simple" life of the Mexican Indian. And it is not improbable that for Frida, as for others in her set who dressed in Mexican costumes, donning peasant clothing had to do with the fashionable notion that the peasant or the Indian is more earthbound and thus more deeply sensual, more "real" than the urban sophisticate. By wearing native dress, women declared the primacy of their link with nature. The costume was a primitive mask, releasing them from the strictures of bourgeois mores. There was, of course, a political factor as well. Wearing indigenous dress was one more way of proclaiming allegiance to *la raza*. Certainly Rivera did not hestitate to make political mileage out of Frida's clothes. "The classic Mexican dress," he said, "has been created by people for people. The Mexican women who do not wear it do not belong to the people, but are mentally and emotionally dependent on a foreign class to which they wish to belong, i.e., the great American and French bureaucracy."

From the moment of their marriage, Frida and Diego began to play important roles in the theatrical scenario of each other's life. Wearing Tehuana costumes was part of Frida's self-creation as a legendary personality and the perfect companion and foil for Diego. Delicate, flamboyant, beautiful, she was the necessary ornament to her huge, ugly husband—the peacock feather in his Stetson hat. Yet while she happily played the role of Indian maiden for Diego, hers was an authentic artifice. She did not change her personality merely to suit Diego's ideal. Rather she invented a highly individualistic personal style to dramatize the personality that was already there and that she knew Diego admired. In the end, she was so extravagantly dashing that many people felt the peacock feather was more compelling (or more fetching) than the hat.

Indeed, Frida's Tehuana costume became so essential a part of her persona that several times she painted it devoid of its owner. The costume served as a stand-in for herself, a second skin never totally assimilated to the person hidden under it but so integral to her that even when it was taken off, it retained something of the wearer's being. It is a primitive, animistic approach to clothes that recalls the way a child senses his mother's presence in items of clothing that she might leave on a chair when dressing to go out. Clearly Frida knew this magic power of clothes to substitute for their owner; in her diary, she wrote that the Tehuana costume made "the absent portrait of only one person"—her absent self.

Always a form of social communication, as the years passed, Frida's costumes became an antidote to isolation; even at the end of her life, when she was very ill and received few visitors, she dressed every day as if she were preparing for a fiesta. As the self-portraits confirmed her existence, so did the costumes make the frail, often bedridden woman feel more magnetic and visible, more emphatically present as a physical object in space. Paradoxically, they were both a mask and a frame. Since they defined the wearer's identity in terms of appearances, they distracted her—and the onlooker—from inner pain. Frida said she wore them out of "coquetry"; she wanted to hide her scars and her limp. The elaborate packaging was an attempt to compensate for her body's deficiencies, for her sense of fragmentation, dissolution, and mortality. Ribbons, flowers, jewels, and sashes became more and more colorful and elaborate as her health declined. In a sense, Frida was like a Mexican piñata, a fragile vessel decorated with frills and ruffles, filled with sweets and surprises, but destined to be smashed. Just as blindfolded children swing at the piñata with a broomstick, life dealt Frida blow after blow. While the piñata dances and sways, the knowledge that it is about to be destroyed makes its bright beauty all the more poignant. In the same way, Frida's decoration was touching: it was at once an affirmation of her love of life and a signal of her awareness—and defiance—of pain and death.

Chapter 9

Gringolandia

EVEN BEFORE Plutarco Elías Calles took office in 1924, the euphoria of the first years of the Mexican mural renaissance had begun to sour. Conservative students at the Preparatoria had rioted, defacing their school's new murals; on the very day when the commissioner of those murals, Vasconcelos, resigned from his post as minister of education, Orozco and Siqueiros were barred from their scaffolds. In August, a presidential decree suspended most mural production in Mexico. The muralists began to disperse. Siqueiros abandoned painting for a while to become a labor leader in the state of Jalisco. In 1927, Orozco went to the United States and during the next six years painted murals at Pomona College in Claremont, California, at the New School for Social Research in Manhattan, and at Dartmouth College in Hanover, New Hampshire.

Rivera's situation was different. Although his work, too, was vandalized and threatened in 1924—the incoming head of the Department of Fine Arts proclaimed that his first official act would be to "whitewash those horrible frescoes"—somehow he managed to ingratiate himself with José Manuel Puig Casauranc, Calles's education minister, who called Rivera "the philosopher of the brush" and kept him on the government payroll for the next four years. (It was Diego's 1929 acceptance of the commission to paint a mural in the National Palace that was the immediate cause of his expulsion from the Communist party.) But the period from 1929 to 1934 was one of political repression. The military budget increased, and the attitude of tolerance toward leftists changed to virulent antagonism. Government support for labor unions ceased. Communists (Siqueiros, for example) were frequently jailed, deported, or murdered, or they simply "disappeared." By 1930–1931, anti-Communist hysteria in Mexico had brought forth the Gold Shirts, a fascist organization. The student riots that had led to the attacks on the Preparatoria murals in 1924 must have seemed sophomoric compared with the current mood of menace. For all Rivera's agility and stamina at keeping his fortunes afloat and his brush flowing, he could never be sure that a dark-suited government functionary might not appear one day as he perched on his scaffold at the National Palace and banish him from his work—after all, the vision of Mexico that he was painting was clearly that of a Marxist. If the Communists called him a "painter for millionaires" and a "government agent," the rightists called him an agent of the revolution. It was a good time for him to leave, and he did, joining Orozco in the United States. (When Siqueiros was expelled from Mexico in 1932, he too went to the United States, to Los Angeles to teach fresco technique.)

The situation was as full of ironies as the commission of Rivera by Ambassador Morrow to paint revolutionary murals in the Spanish conquistadores' palace. The Mexican mural renaissance had become renowned in the United States by the mid-twenties, and Rivera in particular had become a legend. No one seemed to pay much attention to the fact that he was a Communist whose murals were full of hammers and sickles, red stars, and unflattering portraits of Henry Ford, John D. Rockefeller, J. P. Morgan, and other robber barons. As critic Max Kozloff put it: "Nowhere else has avowedly proletarian art been so loftily sponsored by capitalist patronage." Like the reactionary Mexican government, the great leaders of U.S. capitalism could publicize their broad-mindedness by employing an artist like Rivera: anyone who footed the bill for Rivera's Marxist messages must have the public good rather than private gain in mind.

As for Rivera, if the accepting of commissions from the Mexican government and from U.S. capitalists earned him the disfavor of the

Communist party, it also gave him the chance to create public works for the glorification and edification of the industrial proletariat. After all, hadn't Lenin counseled revolutionaries to bore from within? And where better to do it than in the country that was both in the vanguard of the machine age and, at the outset of the Great Depression, apparently ripe for revolution?

Rivera made no secret of his revolutionary aims. Referring to his options after his expulsion from the Communist party, he told a New York reporter that there was only "one thing left for me, to prove that my theory [of revolutionary art] would be accepted in an industrial nation where capitalists rule. . . . I had to come [to the U.S.] as a spy, in disguise." His painting, he said, was intended to be Communist propaganda: "Art is like ham," he declared. "It nourishes people."

Perhaps even more important to Rivera was the fact that the capitalists of the United States were masters of the most marvelous technological achievements. The man who was nicknamed the "Lenin of Mexico" was as infatuated with the beauty of technology as he was with its revolutionary potential. With perhaps unintentional irony, he said of his fresco panel *Frozen Assets* (1931), in which a bank vault forms the substructure of a grim view of economic injustice in Manhattan in the Depression years: "There is so much beauty in the steel door of the safe vault. Perhaps future generations will recognize the machine as the art of our day."

Frida and Diego headed for San Francisco in the second week of November 1930, he armed with commissions to paint murals in the San Francisco Stock Exchange Luncheon Club and the California School of Fine Arts (now called the San Francisco Art Institute), secured for him through the efforts of the sculptor Ralph Stackpole, whom he had known in Paris, and William Gerstle, president of the San Francisco Art Commission. Diego remembered that on the night the invitation arrived, "Frida dreamed that she was waving goodbye to her family, on her way to this 'City of the World,' as she called San Francisco." En route she surprised Diego with a gift—a portrait of herself (now lost): "Its background was an unfamiliar city skyline. When we arrived in San Francisco, I was almost frightened to realize that her imagined city was the very one we were now seeing for the first time."

They arrived on November 10 and moved into Ralph Stackpole's large studio at 716 Montgomery Street, in the old artists' quarter. Lucile Blanch, who, with her husband, the painter Arnold Blanch, was visiting

San Francisco while he taught at the California School of Fine Arts, lived two flights below them. "Since they didn't have a phone, they used ours," she remembered. Mrs. Blanch said that "Frida did not set herself up as an artist," and was too shy about her paintings to ask her friend to look at them. "We were both painters, yet we did not talk about art," she recalled. "Frida and I felt like a couple of giggling girls. She scintillated in her talk, made fun of everything and everybody, laughing at things sportively and perhaps snobbishly. She was very critical if she thought something was pretentious, and often laughed at San Franciscans."

Rivera did not start painting his allegory of California at the Stock Exchange until January 17, over two months after his arrival. First he had to absorb the atmosphere and the look of his subject. Together with Frida, he explored San Francisco, its dramatic hills and bridges, its picturesque waterfront, its industrial outskirts, and drove into the environs to see orchards, oil derricks, a gold mine, and the wonderful burnt-sienna and ocher-orange land. He sketched the bread lines of wan, bleak-eyed, defeated men, and took note of the posh houses on Russian Hill, in front of which men in well-tailored suits and women in stylish, slinky dresses and pert little hats stepped into or out of gleaming automobiles.

Wanting to know the American people, he attended with Frida the annual Stanford-California football game. When asked by a newspaperman to comment on his impressions, he noted that the game was not tragic like a bullfight, but joyous: "Your game of football is splendid, thrilling, beautiful . . . a great living picture, spontaneous unconscious art. It is art in the mass, a new form of art." What Frida thought is not recorded; no one bothered to ask. At twenty-three, she had not yet developed the flamboyant personality that would in later years make her a center of attraction comparable with Diego, and reporters hardly noticed her except to comment, occasionally, on her youth and comeliness.

At one point in his preparations for the Stock Exchange mural, Rivera became obsessed with the figure of the tennis champion Helen Wills, and it was she, to the consternation of some, whom he chose to be "California's representative woman" in his allegory of California (it is said that she was also the model for the nude female whom he painted floating or flying on the ceiling). Years later Frida told a friend that while Rivera was making studies of Wills, following her to tennis courts and sketching her in action, he sometimes disappeared for days. When he did, Frida explored on her own, riding the trolley up and down the steep hills of the city. She brushed up on her English, visited museums, and wandered through Chinatown looking for Oriental silks with which to make long skirts. "The city and bay are overwhelming," she wrote to her childhood friend Isabel Campos. "What is especially fantastic is Chinatown. The Chinese are immensely sympathetic and never in my life have I seen such beautiful children as the Chinese ones. Yes, they are really extraordinary. I would love to steal one so that you could see for yourself. . . . it did make sense to come here, because it opened my eyes and I have seen an enormous number of new and beautiful things."

"We were feted at parties, dinners, receptions," Rivera recalled. "I gave lectures." Indeed, he not only lectured at such institutions as the San Francisco Society for Women Artists and the Pacific Art Association Convention, he was also offered (but did not accept) well-paid teaching jobs at the University of California and Mills College. Since his English was limited, he usually lectured in fluent French, with Emily Joseph, an art writer for the *San Francisco Chronicle* and wife of the painter Sidney Joseph, acting as translator at his side. Large audiences turned out to see and hear him discourse on art and social progress, passionate issues in the Depression years. In December the California Palace of the Legion of Honor gave Rivera a one-man show, and numerous California galleries exhibited his work; at one of his openings, the *Call-Bulletin* reported that the crowd consisted of "nearly everyone in San Francisco who has sung a song, represented his country as consul, crossed a desert on a camel, edited a magazine, or trod the boards."

When Rivera finally began painting he plunged in headlong, gathering about him a retinue of assistants, some salaried, others volunteer, who came from all over the world to apprentice with the legendary "maestro." There was, for example, the loyal and trusted Andrés Sánchez Flores, a young Mexican whom Rivera employed for years as his chemist. Expert at testing, grinding, and mixing pigments, Sánchez Flores also served Frida and Diego as chauffeur, for neither of them could drive. Rivera's chief assistant and plasterer in the United States was the artist Clifford Wight, a tall, powerfully built, and handsome man who had been a Canadian mounted policeman before traveling to Mexico to ask Rivera for work. Another helper, an eccentric one, was the painter Lord John Hastings, a radical Englishman who had been on his way from Tahiti to Mexico with the object of becoming Rivera's unpaid disciple when he met him by chance in San Francisco. Matthew Barnes, an artist and an actor, added a note of conviviality to the crew, and there were many others who joined the team for a while and then disappeared. Rivera's assistants and their wives befriended Frida, but though she was glad to have their company, she did not become close to any of them in San Francisco. Like many who feel shy and ill at ease in a new environment, she was a little disdainful of people she met, and that disdain sharpened into criticism. "I don't particularly like the gringo people," she wrote. "They are boring and they all have faces like unbaked rolls (especially the old women)."

Diego felt differently. He had a voracious appetite for new experience and sensation, thriving as much on good conversation as on good wine and food. He introduced Frida to his friends: Ralph Stackpole, of course, and his wife, Ginette; Emily and Sidney Joseph; Timothy Pflueger, architect of the new San Francisco Stock Exchange Building; and William Gerstle. She also renewed her acquaintance with the elderly insurance broker and art patron Albert M. Bender, who had visited Mexico and acquired a number of Rivera's paintings. Bender knew all the right people—it was he who had finally succeeded in obtaining permission for Rivera to enter the United States (as an avowed Communist, Rivera had been unable to get a visa)—and together with Stackpole he rounded up purchasers among them for Rivera's work.

In San Francisco, Frida met Edward Weston for the first time. She must have been curious to know him, for Tina Modotti surely would have spoken to her about him, and Rivera had great admiration for Weston's photographs. Although he looked like a quiet professor, Weston was a Whitmanesque volcano erupting with a sensuous and enraptured passion for life. "I am the adventurer on a voyage of discovery," he wrote of himself, "ready to receive fresh impressions, eager for fresh horizons . . . to identify myself in, and unify with whatever I am able to recognize as significantly part of me—the 'me' of universal rhythms." With Weston, as with Rivera, those "fresh horizons" were often women, and like Rivera, the photographer was irresistible. "Why this tide of women?" he asked, pleased but perplexed. "Why do they all come at once?"

Weston encountered the Riveras on December 14, 1930, and noted in his diary: "I met Diego! I stood beside a stone block, stepped out as he lumbered downstairs into Ralph's courtyard on Jessop Place—and he took me clear off my feet in an embrace. I photographed Diego again, his new wife—Frieda—too: she is in sharp contrast to Lupe, petite—a little doll alongside Diego, but a doll in size only, for she is strong and quite beautiful, shows very little of her father's German blood. Dressed in native costume even to huaraches, she causes much excitement on the streets of San Francisco. People stop in their tracks to look in wonder. We ate at a little Italian restaurant where many of the artists gather, recalled the old days in Mexico, with promises of meeting soon again in Carmel."

In one of the photographs, probably taken in Stackpole's studio, an elephantine Diego gazes lovingly at his bride dressed up in her Mexican costume and wearing three necklaces of heavy pre-Columbian beads. She does not look at her spouse. Instead, she looks out at the photographer with—and this is unusual for a woman who rarely smiled at the camera—flirtatious, quizzical amusement.

While in San Francisco, Frida also became friends with Leo Eloesser, a famous thoracic surgeon who specialized as well in bone surgery and whom Rivera had met in Mexico in 1926. For the rest of her life, it was his medical advice she trusted above that of any other doctor, and her letters to him are full of questions about her various ills. In December 1930, when she consulted him for the first time, he diagnosed a congenital deformation of her spine (scoliosis) and a missing vertebral disk. Beyond that, soon after she arrived in San Francisco her right foot had begun to turn out more pronouncedly, and its tendons became so strained that walking was difficult.

At the age of forty-nine, Dr. Eloesser was chief of service at the San Francisco General Hospital as well as clinical professor of surgery at the Stanford University School of Medicine. But the demands of his profession did not keep him from the company of people he loved, and the short, dark-haired man with intense, intelligent eyes that often twinkled was loved in turn by everyone who knew him, including Frida. In the years to come, he was to follow his strong social (but not especially political) conscience, undertaking humanitarian missions to Russia, South America, and China, and in 1938 serving as a doctor with the Spanish Republican Army. From his "retirement" in 1952 until his death in 1976 at the age of ninety-five, he concerned himself with community medicine in a remote *ranchería* near the village of Tacámbaro in Michoacán, Mexico.

He was a complete nonconformist whose odd, endearing habits amused his friends. At midnight he used to leave his office, rig his thirty-two-foot sloop, and sail up the bay to Red Rock Island. At dawn, after breakfast on board, he would sail back to the city and to work. On occasion he would cut short his midnight cruise to appear around three in the morning at the bedside of patients on the critical list. He was also an excellent musician, and the weekly chamber music gatherings at his apartment on Leavenworth Street were famous, drawing such musician friends as Isaac Stern, Joseph Szigeti, and Pierre Monteux. Once he boarded a train to go to a medical convention on the east coast carrying nothing but his viola and his toothbrush. En route, he spent his nights fiddling and writing the paper that he was to deliver at the convention. No one knew when the doctor slept.

As a gesture of love and gratitude, perhaps also as a form of payment for his medical attentions, Frida painted *Portrait of Dr. Leo Eloesser* (figure 21) and inscribed it "For Dr. Leo Eloesser with all love, Frieda Kahlo. San Francisco Cal. 1931." Dressed in a somber suit and a white shirt with an impeccably starched high collar, he stands stiffly, one hand resting on a table upon which his identifying object—a model sailboat inscribed *Los Tres Amigos* (The Three Friends)—is placed. Another identifying object is the drawing signed "D. Rivera" that hangs on the bare wall, for Eloesser was a patron of the arts. The pose is standard for full-length portraits of men in eighteenth- and nineteenth-century Mexico, and the extreme primitivism of the style suggests that Frida had in mind a naïve portrait, like that of Secundino Gonzáles by the well-known nineteenth-century primitive painter José María Estrada, whom she admired. In *Portrait of Dr. Leo Eloesser,* she has substituted Mexico's naïve provincial portraiture (which she and Diego collected) for Rivera's murals and portraits as her chief source of inspiration.

"A few notes on the painting may not be amiss," Dr. Eloesser wrote on January 10, 1968, when the portrait was about to be donated to the Medical School of the University of California by the San Francisco Hospital: "Frida Kahlo de Rivera painted it at my home at 2152 Leavenworth St., during the Riveras' first visit to San Francisco. . . . It is one of her early, early works. Mainly grey and black in tone, it represents me standing alongside a model for a sailing ship. Frida had never seen a sailing ship. She asked Diego about the rigging of the sails, but he would give her no satisfaction. He told her to paint the sails as she thought they should look. Which is what she did."

During her half year in San Francisco, especially when she was confined by her foot problem, Frida painted several other portraits. As always, her subjects were friends, and as always, the personal link between artist and patron or subject affected the look and meaning of her work: Frida's portraits echo her style of sociability, which was direct, unpretentious, witty, and astute in its judgments of others. One careful pencil drawing captures much of the aristocratic hauteur and sophistication of Milan-born, Oxford-educated Lady Cristina Hastings, whose swings between states of boredom and explosive anger or humor Frida found congenial and amusing. Another friend, a black American whose identity is unknown, appears in *Portrait of Eva Frederick* (figure 19) and in a contemporaneous drawing of a nude. Whoever she is, Eva Frederick is clearly a woman of intelligence and heart, one for whom Frida had great sympathy. Equally clearly, Frida had little rapport with the sitter for *Portrait of Mrs. Jean Wight*, dated January 1931, which shows the wife of Rivera's chief assistant seated before a window that gives out onto a view of San Francisco (figure 20). It is a bland, conventional portrait. Years later, when Jean Wight stayed with the Riveras in Mexico, Frida wrote of her exasperation with her guest: "She has the enormous defect of completely believing that she is very ill, she does nothing but talk of her sicknesses and of vitamins, but she makes no effort to study something or to work. . . . Jean has nothing in her head but idiocies, such as how to have new dresses made, how to paint her face, how to comb her hair so that she looks better, and she talks all day of 'fashions' and of stupidities that don't amount to anything, and not only that, but in addition she does it with a pretentiousness that leaves one cold."

By mid-February, Diego had completed his allegory of California, less than a month after he began it. Not surprisingly, he had worked himself and his assistants to the point of exhaustion. To recuperate, he and Frida left San Francisco for the home of Mrs. Sigmund Stern, a friend of Albert Bender's and a prominent art patron, who lived in the country at Atherton. What was to have been a restful ten-day vacation lasted six weeks, during three of which Diego painted a pastoral mural in Mrs. Stern's dining room.

Very likely it was here that Frida painted *Luther Burbank,* her portrait of the California horticulturist known for his work in creating hybrid vegetables and fruits (figure 22). (The creator not of new machines but of new plants also appealed to Diego, who had put him in his allegory of California.)

Frida has turned Burbank into a hybrid himself—half tree, half man. He is dwarfed by the huge green leaves of an uprooted plant that he has "mated" or is about to "mate" with another plant, but instead of planting the hybrid, he himself is planted: he stands in a hole, and his brown-trousered legs become a tree trunk. A kind of X-ray vision allows Frida to show the continuation of the tree-man under the earth, where his roots are entangled with a human skeleton. Burbank, with his two feet (turned tree trunk) quite literally in the grave, is the first instance in Frida's painting of what would become a favorite theme: life-death duality and the fertilization of life by death. She was still following Rivera's vision: at Chapingo, he transformed the lower part of Tina Modotti's nude body into a tree trunk to show the continuity between plant and human life, and death nurturing life.

Luther Burbank is also the first indication that Frida Kahlo was to become a painter of fantasy rather than a painter of straightforward, relatively realistic portraits. What prompted the change we do not know. Possibly she saw some Surrealist art in San Francisco, or perhaps something in her own life made her recall the imaginative forays in Rivera's Mexican murals (like those at Chapingo) or in Mexican popular art. In any case, with its mixture of invention, wit, and miniaturist detail, and with its blustering blue sky and bare green hills (plantless except for Burbank's two fruit trees), the painting points forward to such works of mingled realism and imagination as *My Grandparents, My Parents and I.*

When Frida and Diego returned to San Francisco on April 23, Rivera finally proceeded to fulfill his long-standing commission from William Gerstle for the fresco at the California School of Fine Arts. And Frida turned her hand to *Frida and Diego Rivera,* a sort of wedding portrait painted a year and a half after the wedding (plate III). Like the portraits of Jean Wight and Eva Frederick, it has an informative inscription written on a ribbon, a device used by both Riveras that derives from Mexican colonial painting. The message is as ingenuous in tone as the painting is naïve and folkloric in style: "Here you see us, Me Frieda Kahlo, with my beloved husband Diego Rivera. I painted these portraits in the beautiful city of San Francisco California for our friend Mr. Albert Bender, and it was in the month of April in the year 1931." If Frida did indeed paint *Luther Burbank* in Atherton, and if we are to believe that she painted the wedding portrait "in the beautiful city of San Francisco . . . in the month of April," then she must have been working almost as hard as her husband, contradicting Lucile Blanch's memory that "she did not paint much" and that "she did not set herself up as an artist" in San Francisco. Judging from the leap in quality between *Portrait of Mrs. Jean Wight,* painted in January, and the wedding portrait, Frida was secretly taking her métier quite seriously. In May she wrote to Isabel Campos: "I spend most of my time painting. I expect to have an exhibition in September (my first) in New York. I have not had enough time here, I could only sell a few paintings."

In the double portrait, she shows herself and Diego the way San Franciscans saw them, as newlyweds. Diego looks immense next to his bride. (He was over six feet tall and, in 1931, weighed three hundred pounds. Frida was five feet three and weighed about ninety-eight pounds.) Her depiction of him coincides with her description of his appearance in the long essay "Portrait of Diego" that she wrote years later for the catalogue of a Rivera retrospective: "His enormous stomach, drawn tight and smooth as a sphere, rests upon his strong legs, beautiful columns, that end in large feet pointing outward at an obtuse angle as if to embrace all the world and to support himself invincibly on the earth like an antediluvian being from which emerges, from the waist up, an example of future humanity, distant from us by two or three thousand years."

Rivera is portrayed as the great artist wielding his palette and brushes; Frida in the role she loved best, the genius's adoring wife. Diego stands with his feet as solidly planted as the cornerstones of a triumphal arch; her dainty beslippered feet do not look substantial enough to support her, and they appear barely to brush the ground. She floats in the air like a china doll, sustained by the grip of her monumental mate. Yet Frida's penetrating gaze has a note of demonic humor and gritty strength, and for all the solicitousness and "femininity" of her pose and dress, she is self-possessed. The portrait depicts a young woman presenting—perhaps with a certain becoming diffidence but also with pride in her "catch"—her new mate to the world. It evokes a type familiar in Mexico: the wife who willingly assumes the submissive role but who in fact runs the household and manages her husband with a deft and delicate dominance.

The wedding portrait is revealing in another way as well. In it, Diego turns his head slightly away from his bride, and both his arms hug his sides. Her head inclines toward his shoulder, and her arms move in his direction; the couple's clasped hands are placed in the center of the canvas, suggesting the importance, to Frida, of the marriage bond. From the beginning, the painting implies, Frida knew that Diego was unpossessable, that his first passion in life was his art, that though he might love her, his real devotion was to beauty, Mexico, Marxism, "the people," women (many of them), plants, the earth. "Diego is beyond all limited and precise personal relations," Frida wrote. "He does not have friends, he has allies: he is very affectionate, but he never surrenders himself." She wanted, she said, to be his best ally.

In San Francisco, Frida learned that one of the ways to be Rivera's best ally, to hold him with even the light grip that she displays in the wedding portrait, was to be diverting. At a dinner attended by numerous art world people, for example, she noticed that a young woman seated next to Diego was eagerly vamping him; he was beaming. Frida sipped her wine and began her counterattack; quietly at first, she began singing and acting out humorous, off-color Mexican songs. As the wine took effect, she grew sassier until she had the whole table in the palm of her hand; with Diego's amused, affectionate eyes resting upon her, she had triumphed. The sauciness and the determination to be "Rivera's woman" are unmistakable in Frida's wedding portrait; surely it was with a secret twinkle that she gave the general outline of herself and Diego the same shape as the initial carved on Diego's belt buckle—the letter *D*.

While Frida presented her husband to the spectator as a standing figure facing politely forward, he was busy at the California School of Fine Arts, presenting himself seated with his back to his audience. His mural is a monumental trompe l'oeil joke: Diego and his assistants appear on an illusionistically depicted scaffold, engaged in painting a fresco of a worker on what appears to be the actual wall of the room. Like so many images of workers in that decade when there was little available work, Rivera's helmeted hero looks like a cross between Goliath and G.I. Joe, as he clutches the control levers of a future into which his eyes gaze with that meaningful earnestness that typifies 1930s images of the representative man. Shown discussing the art school's architectural plans beneath the scaffold are Timothy Pflueger, William Gerstle, and Arthur Brown, Jr., the school's architect, all three dressed in suits and hats that distinguish them from the shirt-sleeved artists and the worker. Right in the center of *The Making of a Fresco* Rivera's ample derriere droops over the edge of the scaffold as he contemplates his painting of the firmer and fitter man to whom the future belongs. Thus tongue in cheek does Rivera instruct art students on the relation between art and revolution! If his arrival in San Francisco to paint the Stock Exchange murals was heralded by some public indignation—"Rivera for Mexico City; San Francisco's best for San Francisco" ran one headline—his exit was accompanied by a blast of controversy. Painter Kenneth Callahan's complaint was typical. "Many San Franciscans," he said, "choose to see in this gesture [Rivera's rear view] a direct insult, premeditated as it appears to be. If it is a joke, it is a rather amusing one, but in bad taste." Rivera's social messages did not exactly foment social revolution in the U.S., but they did cause considerable commotion.

On June 8, 1931, five days after he finished the fresco, Frida and Diego flew to Mexico, where he had been summoned by letters and telegrams from President Ortíz Rubio, who was anxious for Rivera to complete the mural he had begun on the stairway of the National Palace. They stayed in the blue house in Coyoacán while, with the money he had earned from American patrons, Rivera began to build their new home in the San Angel section of Mexico City, the home that was to be two houses linked by a bridge. (A 1931 photograph shows the Riveras together with the Russian filmmaker Sergei Eisenstein, who was in Mexico making his epic film *Que Viva Mexico!*, standing on the steps of the patio in Coyoacán.)

A week after their return, Frida wrote to Dr. Eloesser:

Coyoacán, June 14, 1931

Dear Doctor:

You cannot imagine the pain that not seeing you before coming here gave us, but it was impossible. I telephoned your office three times without finding you since no one answered, so I left word with Clifford [Wight] asking him to do me the favor of giving you an explanation. Also, imagine, Diego was painting until twelve the night before the day we left San Francisco and we had no time for anything, so that this letter serves first of all to ask you a thousand pardons and to tell you also that we arrived safely in this country of enchiladas and fried beans—Diego is already working in the Palace. He has had something the matter with his mouth and what's more he is very tired. I would like, if you write to him, that you tell him that it is necessary for his health for him to rest a little, since if he keeps on working like this he is going to die, don't tell him that I told you that he is working so much, but tell him that you know about it and that it is absolutely necessary for him to rest a little. I would be most grateful to you.

Diego is not happy here since he misses the friendliness of the people of San Francisco as well as the city itself, now he wants nothing other than to return to the United States to paint. I arrived feeling very well, skinny as always and bored with everything, but I feel much better. I do not know with what to pay you for my treatment and for all the favors that you did for me and Diego. I know that the worst way would be with money, but no matter how great my gratitude it would never compensate for your kindness so that I implore and beg you to be good enough to let me know how much I owe you since you cannot imagine how much pain it caused me to leave without having given you anything equivalent to your kindness. In your answer to my letter tell me how you are, what you are doing, everything, and please say hello to all the friends, especially to Ralph and Ginette [Stackpole].

Mexico is as always, disorganized and gone to the devil, the only thing that it retains is the immense beauty of the land and of the Indians. Each day the United States' ugliness steals away a piece of it, it is a sad thing but people must eat and it can't be helped that the big fish eats the little one. Diego sends many greetings. Receive the affection that you know is held for you by

                                                            Frieda

The Riveras were not to be in Mexico for long: in July, Frances Flynn Paine, a New York art dealer, art adviser to the Rockefellers, and a member of the board of directors of the Mexican Arts Association, came to Mexico to invite Diego to have a retrospective exhibition at New York's fledgling Museum of Modern Art.

During the conservative regimes of Calles and his successors, enthusiasm for cultural exchange had gone hand in hand with improved United States–Mexico relations. One of the results was the Mexican Arts Association, hatched at the Manhattan home of John D. Rockefeller, Jr., to "promote friendship between the people of Mexico and the United States by encouraging cultural relations and the interchange of fine and applied arts." Rockefeller contributed the initial funding; his brother-in-law, the New York banker Winthrop W. Aldrich, was the association's president (it is probably not a coincidence that both the Rockefeller and the Aldrich families had enormous holdings in Latin America). If Rivera was good enough for the Calles administration, the association decided, he was good enough for capitalism: "Diego's very spinal column is painting, not politics," argued Mrs. Paine in her essay for the catalogue of Rivera's show.

Certainly Diego could not resist the honor of a retrospective at the Museum of Modern Art—a show that would be the museum's second one-man show (the first was Matisse's) and its fourteenth exhibition. Once again he left his National Palace murals unfinished, and at dawn on a mid-November day, he and Frida, accompanied by Mrs. Paine and by Rivera's faithful plasterer, Ramón Alva, sailed into New York harbor aboard the *Morro Castle*. Diego was on deck, full of his usual ebullience. He waved his arms, pointing out the beauty of the lights in Manhattan skyscrapers, the glories of the fog, the rising sun, tugboats, ferries, riveters at work on a dock. A stream of smoke rose from his seven-inch cigar and curled over the broad brim of his tan sombrero. His smile was, as always, genial, his manner courteous. The newcomer announced to the *New York Herald Tribune* reporter who had come on board to interview him: "There is no reason in the world why any person born on our two continents should go to Europe for inspiration or study. Here it is—the might, the power, the energy, the sadness, the glory, the youthfulness of our lands"; and admiring the Equitable Building (1914) in lower Manhattan, a behemoth that rises forty stories straight up from the building line (it was one of the buildings that caused the city to write the zoning law of 1916, requiring setbacks for skyscrapers), he pronounced: "There we are on our own earth, for whether the architects knew it or not, they were inspired in that design by the same feeling which prompted the ancient people of Yucatan in the building of their temples." Rivera played to the hilt the role of cultural ambassador from the South. The peoples of North

6. Self-portrait by Guillermo Kahlo, c. 1907.

7. *Portrait of Don Guillermo Kahlo, 1952.*

8. Frida as a schoolgirl, 1923.

9. Alejandro Gómez Arias, c. 1928.

10. Frida's drawing of her accident.

11. Frida (standing, left, wearing a man's suit) with members of her family. Back row, from left: her aunt, her sister Adriana, Adriana's husband Alberta Veraza; middle row: her uncle, her mother, her cousin Carmen; front row: Carlos Veraza, Cristina. Photograph by Guillermo Kahlo, 1926.

12. *Portrait of Adriana*, 1927.

13. *Portrait of Cristina Kahlo*, 1928.

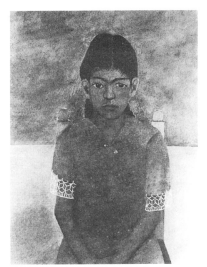

14. Diego Rivera's portrait of Frida distributing arms, in his Ministry of Education mural, 1928.

15. *Niña*, 1929.

16. *The Bus*, 1929.

17. Frida and Diego on their wedding day, August 21, 1929.

18. *Self-Portrait*, 1930.

19. *Portrait of Eva Frederick*, 1931.

20. *Portrait of Mrs. Jean Wight*, 1931.

21. *Portrait of Dr. Leo Eloesser*, 1931.

22. *Luther Burbank*, 1931.

23. Frida and Diego at the Rouge plant of the Ford Motor Company, Detroit, 1932.

24. On the scaffold at the Detroit Institute of Arts, 1932.

25. With (from left to right) Lucienne Bloch, Arthur Niendorff and Jean Wight, on the roof of the Detroit Institute of Arts, watching the solar eclipse, August 31, 1932.

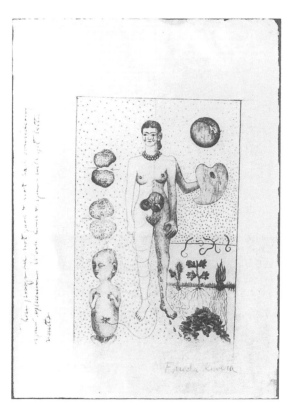

26. *Frida and the Abortion*, lithograph, 1932.

27. After the death of her mother. Photograph by Guillermo Kahlo, 1932.

28. *Self-Portrait on the Borderline Between Mexico and the United States*, 1932.

29. Painting
*Self-Portrait on
the Borderline.*

30. *Self-Portrait*, 1933.

31. Rivera's Rockefeller Center mural as repainted in the Palace of Fine Arts, Mexico City, 1934.

32. With Diego and an unidentified friend at the New Worker's School, New York City, 1933.

33. With Nelson Rockefeller and Rosa Covarrubias in 1939.

34. *My Dress Hangs There*, 1933.

36. With Ella Wolfe in New York, 1935.

35. Rivera's portrait of Frida, Cristina and Cristina's children, in his mural at the National Palace, 1935.

37. *Self-Portrait*, 1935.

38. Isamu Noguchi. Photograph by Edward Weston, 1935.

39. *Memory*, 1937.

40. *Remembrance of an
Open Wound*, 1938.

41. With her niece and nephew, Isolda and Antonia Kahlo.

42. With Diego in front of the organ cactus fence at San Angel.

43. The Riveras' linked houses in San Angel.

sleep, that is what has most impressed me here, it is terrifying to see the rich having parties day and night while thousands and thousands of people are dying of hunger. . . .

Although I am very interested in all the industrial and mechanical development of the United States, I find that Americans completely lack sensibility and good taste.

They live as if in an enormous chicken coop that is dirty and uncomfortable. The houses look like bread ovens and all the comfort that they talk about is a myth. I don't know if I am mistaken but I'm only telling you what I feel.

Shyness and her dislike of gringo society made Frida stick close by Rivera's side at his Museum of Modern Art opening on December 22, despite the presence of friends such as Lucienne Bloch and Anita Brenner. The vernissage was a major social event, a gathering of Manhattan's elite, among them John D. and Abby Rockefeller, art world sophisticates like Frank Crowninshield, and of course, museum officials. The guests merrily drank and chattered against the backdrop of Rivera's painted pageant of Mexico, their social glitter and sartorial swank in sharp contrast with the exhibition's pièce de résistance, the group of newly completed fresco panels showing Rivera's Marxist view of Mexico: *Agrarian Leader Zapata, Liberation of the Peon,* and *Sugar Cane,* which depicts workers oppressed by landowners. (The three other panels, depicting his view of the urban proletariat, including *Frozen Assets,* were not finished in time for the opening, and they were added to the show a few days later.) In equally sharp contrast with the assembled art patrons and patronesses, decked out in black tie and pale, floor-length evening gowns, was Frida Kahlo—olive-skinned, almost swarthy, and strikingly exotic in her bright Tehuana finery—standing quietly next to the protective bulk of her garrulous husband.

Rivera's show not only received critical acclaim, it also drew the highest attendance of any exhibition at the Museum of Modern Art to that time. By January 27, 1932, when it closed, 56,575 people had paid admission to see it, and the dean of New York art critics, Henry McBride, had described the artist in the *New York Sun* (December 26, 1931) as "the most talked about man on this side of the Atlantic."

No doubt the success of Rivera's show made Frida's life in New York more amusing. She met many people, and with her new friends, she explored Manhattan, enjoyed leisurely lunches, and went to the movies—preferably horror movies and the comedies of the Marx Brothers, Laurel and Hardy, and the Three Stooges. "We had lunch with Frieda at Reuben's and laughed a lot together," Lucienne Bloch wrote in her diary. "Then went to see *Frankenstein,* which Frieda wanted to see again." Something else that made her days more fun was the fact that Rivera was no longer working against a deadline and could spend more time with her. "Had a delicious meal at the speakeasy with Diego Rivera and wife," Lucienne wrote, and she went on to note that "Frieda can't stand the Hotel Barbizon-Plaza because the elevator boys snub her because they can see she is no rich person. The other day she called one of them a son of a bitch and she asked us if it was the correct term."

By the time the Riveras' stay in Manhattan was nearing its end, Frida was no longer the shy, reclusive creature she had been when she arrived. Though she still complained about many aspects of Gringolandia, she was now caught up in an active and glamorous life. On March 31, for example, the Riveras, along with a Pullman-car load of culture-hungry New Yorkers, traveled to Philadelphia to attend the premiere of the Mexican ballet *H.P.,* which was conducted by Leopold Stokowski. Frida's reaction was at once forthright and impudent. A month or so later she set down in a letter to Dr. Eloesser what she did not hesitate to say at the time: "As concerns what you asked me about the Ballet by Carlos Chávez and Diego. It turned out to be a *porquería* [disgusting mess] with a *P* of . . . . . not because of the music or the decorations but because of the choreography, since there was a crowd of insipid blonds pretending they were Indians from Tehuantepec and when they had to dance the Zandunga they looked as if they had lead instead of blood. To sum up, a pure and total *cochinada* [piggery]."

Chapter 10

Detroit:
Henry Ford Hospital

To DIEGO Rivera, Detroit was the heart of American industry, the home of the American proletariat. Thus when William Valentiner, director of the Detroit Institute of Arts, and art historian Edgar P. Richardson, also on the staff of the institute, met Rivera in San Francisco and proposed that he come to Detroit to paint murals on the theme of modern industry, Rivera was delighted. The Detroit Arts Commission, then headed by the president of the Ford Motor Company, Edsel Ford, approved, and when Ford agreed to pay ten thousand dollars for the large murals celebrating Detroit industry—in particular the automotive industry, and even more particularly the Ford Motor Company—the deal was made. In April 1932, the most famous painter in the world dispatched his assistants to oversee the preparation of the walls and the lime plaster. At noon on April 21, he and his wife stepped off the train in the city that Diego felt would be the proper place to paint "the great Saga of the machine and of steel."

They were met at the station by a welcoming party that included Valentiner, the Mexican vice-consul, some twenty members of a Mexican cultural club, Diego's assistants and their wives, and the press.

Frida, according to the *Detroit News*, wore a black silk brocade dress with corded shirrings at the round neck, a long dark-green embroidered silk shawl, high spindle-heeled slippers, heavy dark uncut amber beads, and a jadeite necklace with carved pendants. In his awkward English, Rivera introduced her: "His name is Carmen," he said (with the rise of Nazism, he did not like to use her German name). Frida, in response to a photographer's request that she wave, "ended the little upward flourish of her hand with a lightning-like comic salute," before dashing down the steps of the train to embrace friends and to thrust a ukulele she was carrying into the hands of Clifford Wight. When asked if she, too, was a painter, she replied in fluent English, "Yes, the greatest in the world."

Frida and Diego went directly from the station to their new lodgings, a characterless but convenient one-bedroom furnished apartment in the Wardell, a mammoth residential hotel at 15 Kirby East and Woodward Avenue, just across the street from the Detroit Institute of Arts. On its letterhead, the Wardell called itself "the best home address in Detroit." What that meant, the Riveras discovered after a few weeks, was that the hotel did not take in Jews. "But Frida and I have Jewish blood!" Diego shouted. "We are going to have to leave!" Anxious to keep their business, a hotel official protested, "Oh, no! We don't mean it that way!" and offered to lower the rent. Rivera retorted, "I won't stay here no matter how much you lower the price, unless you remove the restriction." Desperate for customers, the management promised to comply and also reduced the rent from $185 to $100 a month.

Not long after settling in at the Wardell, Frida and Diego met Edsel Ford and the other members of the Detroit Arts Commission, and Rivera began to prepare his mural studies for their approval. Sometimes, with Frida at his side, he toured the Ford Motor Company's River Rouge complex in Dearborn, and other factories around Detroit, tirelessly sketching machinery, assembly lines, and laboratories. He was as excited by the prospect of painting machines as he had been by the prospect of painting agrarian Mexico after his return from Europe in 1921. "I now placed the collective hero, man-and-machine, higher than the old traditional heroes of art and legend," he wrote in his autobiography.

On May 23 the Arts Commission approved his sketches for two large panels on the north and south walls of the Detroit Institute of Arts' glass-roofed Garden Court. Though the court's Italian baroque design—

with its walls complicated by arches, grillwork, Doric pilasters, and relief plaques of Etruscan motifs—displeased him (he called the huge stepped fountain *"horrorosa"* and "a symbol of the way that we have clung to the old culture"), the artist had great ambitions. He would pour "a new wine into the old bottles," he said, "and paint the story of the new race of the age of steel." He felt, however, that for this great theme, two walls were not enough, so he asked to decorate all twenty-seven panels around the court. The commission enthusiastically agreed, and Diego prepared more sketches, envisioning "a wonderful symphony," a vast depiction of Henry Ford's industrial empire that would contain the composer's admiration for Henry Ford and his accomplishments and Marxist principles as well. "Marx made theory," said Rivera. "Lenin applied it with his sense of large-scale social organization. . . . And Henry Ford made the work of the socialist state possible."

Meanwhile, as they had been in New York, the Riveras were wooed by the wealthy supporters of culture and entertained by the "right" people, but with less happy results. People found Frida and her Mexican costumes bizarre, and she retaliated against the narrow snobbism of Grosse Pointe matrons by being outrageous, deliberately shocking the haute bourgeoisie. Invited to tea at the home of Henry Ford's sister, she talked enthusiastically about communism; in a Catholic household, she made sarcastic comments about the Church. Coming home from one or another lunch or tea organized by various committees of society women, she would shrug her shoulders and, trying to make up for a dull day with a lively recounting of it, would tell how she had used four-letter words and expressions such as "Shit on you!" while pretending not to know their meaning. "What I did to those old biddies!" she would say, laughing with evident satisfaction. Once, when Frida and Diego returned after spending an evening at the home of Henry Ford, whom Frida knew to be an avowed anti-Semite, Diego burst into the apartment chortling heartily. Pointing to Frida, he cried, "What a girl! Do you know what she said when there was a quiet moment at the dining room table? She turned to Henry Ford, and she said, 'Mr. Ford, are you Jewish?' "

"This city seems to me like a shabby old village," Frida wrote to Dr. Eloesser on May 26. "I don't like it at all, but I am happy because Diego is working very happily here, and he has found a lot of material for his frescoes that he will do in the museum. He is enchanted with the factories, the machines, etc., like a child with a new toy. The industrial part of Detroit is really most interesting, the rest is, as in all of the United States, ugly and stupid." Everything about Detroit seemed inferior to Mexico. In Mexico, Frida said, there was more sparkle and a greater contrast between light and shade. There, even the poorest huts were tended with a certain love of beauty and order, while the dilapidated houses in Detroit were dirty and neglected.

Then there was the matter of food. Frida had no use for the bland American cuisine, though she finally developed a taste for three native concoctions: malted milk, applesauce, and American cheese. She ate quantities of hard candies or sticky sweets like taffy and nougat that reminded her of *cajeta,* the caramelized goat's milk from Mexico. Even after she discovered several small grocery stores that catered to the Mexican population of Detroit, and managed to cook Mexican meals, the electric stove she was forced to use seemed to her perversely intractable.

If Frida had some compunctions about being welcomed into the houses of the elite and enjoying lavish parties in the midst of the Depression, Rivera, who never worried about embracing contradictions, did not. When Frida chastised him once for being a Communist but dressing like a capitalist in a tuxedo, he felt no chagrin. "A Communist must dress like the best," he said. And he was proud of the attention his wife received, recalling her success at a folk dancing party given by Henry Ford with as much delight as he remembered her caustic remarks: "Frida, looking lovely in her Mexican costume, soon became the center of attraction. Ford danced with her several times."

In Diego's version of the denouement of this evening (with the details rearranged to make himself appear in the best light), Henry Ford escorted him and Frida outside, where a new Lincoln, complete with chauffeur at the wheel, was waiting. "Ford told Frida that the chauffeur had already been paid and that both he and the car were at Frida's disposal for the time she remained in Detroit. I was embarrassed for us both and thanked Ford but declared that neither Frida nor I could possibly accept such a lavish gift. This car, I said, was too rich for our blood. Ford took my refusal with gracious understanding. Then, without our knowledge, he got his son Edsel to design a special small Ford car, which he presented to Frida a short time later."

In the last year of her life, Frida told the story differently: "When we went to Detroit, Henry Ford met me and he gave a party for his workers; and even though I was lame, they fixed me up with an apparatus, and I danced a heel and toe with Ford, and the next day he asked me if he could ask Diego for permission to give me a Ford. Diego said yes, and it was in that Ford that we returned to Mexico, and that Ford was a salvation for Diego because he exchanged it for a station wagon and it was very useful; later he exchanged this car for another one called 'The Frog' and an Opel."

Actually, the car was a trade: hating to be obliged to anyone, Rivera insisted on paying for it with a portrait of Edsel Ford. In the end, he thought he'd been "taken," for what Sánchez Flores brought home to his boss was not the latest model Lincoln, which Rivera had expected to receive, but a simple four-door sedan worth much less than the portrait. "I'll never drive that damn thing!" Rivera said.

Frida's dislike of Detroit and Detroit society may have had much to do with her physical condition: when she wrote to Dr. Eloesser on May 26, she was two months pregnant. Though her "consultation" with him is characteristically matter-of-fact, its oblique beginning and restless exploration of alternatives reveal her anxiety—and her hope:

Of myself, I have much to tell you although it is not very pleasant as we say. In the first place my health is not at all good. I would like to talk to you about everything except this, since I understand that you must already be bored with hearing everyone's complaints, bored with sick people but I would like to think that my case will be a little different because we are friends, and Diego like me loves you very much. This you know well.

I will begin by telling you that I went to see Dr. Pratt because you recommended him to the Hastings. The first time I had to go because my foot continues to be sick and this is as a result of the toe that is naturally in worse condition than when you saw me since two years have already gone by. I am not worried very much about this matter because I know perfectly well that there isn't any remedy for it and it does no good to cry. In the Ford Hospital, which is where Dr. Pratt is, I don't remember which doctor diagnosed that it was a "trophic ulcer." What is that? When I knew that I had such a thing in my foot, I was dumfounded. The most important question now, and this is what I would like to consult with you about before consulting with anyone else, is that I am two months pregnant; for this reason I saw Dr. Pratt again, he told me that he knew my general condition, because he had talked with you about me in New Orleans, and that I did not need to explain to him again the question of the accident, heredity, etc., etc. Given the state of my health, I thought that it would be better to abort, I told him so, and he gave me a dose of "quinine" and a very strong purge of castor oil. The day after I took this I had a very light hemorrhage almost nothing. During five or six days I have had a bit of blood, but very little. In any case I thought I had aborted and I went to see Dr. Pratt again. He examined me and he told me that no, that he is completely sure that I did not abort and that his opinion is that it would be much better if instead of making me abort with an operation I should keep the baby and that in spite of the bad condition of my organism, bearing in mind the little fracture of the pelvis, spine, etc., etc. I could have a child with a Caesarean operation without great difficulties. He says that if we stay in Detroit for the next seven months of the pregnancy, he will take good care of me. I want you to tell me your opinion in complete confidence since I do not know what to do in this case. Naturally I am willing to do what you think is best for my health, and Diego says the same. Do you think that it would be more dangerous to abort than to have a child? Two years ago I had an abortion with an operation in Mexico, when I was more or less in the same condition as now, with a three months pregnancy. Now I am only two months pregnant and I think it would be easier, but I do not know why Dr. Pratt thinks that it would be better for me to have the child. You better than anyone know what condition I am in. In the first place with this heredity in my blood I do not think that the child could come out very healthy. [Frida probably refers to her father's epilepsy.] In the second place I am not strong and the pregnancy will weaken me more. What's more, at this moment the situation for me is rather difficult since I do not know exactly how long Diego will need to finish the fresco and if, as I calculate, he finishes in September, the child would be born in December and I would have to go to Mexico three months before it was born. If Diego finishes later it would be best if I waited for the child to be born here, and anyway, afterward there would be terrible difficulties in traveling with a newborn child. Here I have no one in my family who could take care of me during and after the pregnancy, since poor little Diego, no matter how much he wants to take care of me, he cannot, since he has in addition the problem of work and thousands of things. So that I would not count on him for anything. The only thing I could do in this case would be to go to Mexico in August or September and have the child there. I do not think that Diego would be very interested in having a child since what preoccupies him most is his work and he is absolutely right. Children would take fourth place. From my point of view, I do not know whether it would be good or not to have a child, since Diego is continually traveling and for no reason would I want to leave him alone and stay behind in Mexico, there would only be difficulties and problems for both of us, don't you think? But if like Dr. Pratt you really think that it is much better for my health not to abort and to have the baby, all these difficulties can be somehow overlooked. What I want to know is your opinion more than anyone else's since in the first place you know my situation and I would thank you from my heart if you would tell me clearly what you think would be best. In case the operation to abort were the best thing, I beg you to write to Dr. Pratt, since probably he is not very aware of all the circumstances and since it is against the law to abort, perhaps he is afraid or something and later it will already be impossible to have the operation.

If on the contrary, you think that I could get better by having the child in that case I want you to tell me if it would be preferable for me to go to Mexico in August and to have it there with my mother and my sisters or to wait until it is born here. I do not want to bother you anymore, you do not know, Doctorcito, how much it pains me to bother you with these things, but I talk to you as to the best of my friends rather than just as a doctor, and your opinion will help me more than you can imagine. For I do not count on anyone here. Diego as always is very good to me but I do not want to distract him with such things now that he is burdened with all the work and more than anything else he needs tranquillity and calm. I do not have enough confidence in Jean Wight and Cristina Hastings to consult with them about things like this which have an enormous importance and which because of one false move can take me to the grave! [Here Frida has drawn a skull and crossbones.] For this reason now that I am at the right time I want to know what you think and to do what would be best for my health which I think is the only thing that interests Diego since I know that he loves me, and I will do everything I can on my part to give him pleasure in everything. I do not eat at all well, I have no appetite, and with much effort I drink two glasses of cream a day and a little meat and vegetables. But now with the bothersome pregnancy, I want to vomit all the time and I am fed up. I get tired from everything since my spine hurts and I am also rather bothered by the thing of the foot since I cannot exercise and as a result my digestion is not functioning! Nevertheless I have the will to do many things and I never feel "disappointed by life" as in Russian novels. I understand perfectly my situation and I am more or less happy, in the first place because I have Diego and my mother and father whom I love so much. I think that that is enough and I don't ask miracles of life or anything close to it. Of my friends you are the one I love most and for this reason I dare to bother you with such foolishness. Forgive me and when you answer this letter tell me how you have been and receive from Diego and from me our affection and a hug from

Frieda

If you think I should have the operation immediately I would be grateful if you sent me a telegram telling me in a veiled form so as not to compromise yourself in any way. A thousand thanks and my best regards. F.

By the time Dr. Eloesser had responded to this letter, enclosing a note for Dr. Pratt, Frida had decided against the abortion, hoping against hope that Dr. Pratt was right. Neither Diego's concern for her health nor the fact that he did not want another child could make her change her mind once it was made up. Nor could Rivera make Frida obey the doctor's orders and stay quietly in the apartment. She was lonely, sick, bored. He was fired with enthusiasm for his work and had no intention of staying home to look after his wife. So when Lucienne Bloch came to Detroit in June, he insisted that the young artist move in. "Frida has nothing to do," he told Lucienne. "She has no friends. She's very lonely." He hoped that Lucienne would encourage Frida to paint, but Frida had other ideas. She was, Lucienne recalls, learning to drive instead.

Lucienne slept in the living room on a Murphy bed that she would push out of sight in the morning before her hosts awoke so that they would not feel crowded. While Diego was away, Frida sketched or painted desultorily in the living room, and Lucienne worked at the dining room table, designing small figurines for a Dutch glassworks. As the end of June approached and the summer heat made the small apartment stifling, Frida began to spot, her uterus "hurt," and she suffered prolonged attacks of nausea. Nothing, however, could shake her optimism. Lucienne recalls: "She was just hoping to be pregnant, so I said, 'Have you seen the doctor?' and she said, 'Yes, I have a doctor, but he tells me I can't do this, I can't do that, and that's a lot of bunk.' She did not visit him the way she should have."

Frida lost her child on July 4, 1932.

Lucienne's diary for the next day tells the story: "Sunday evening. Frieda was so blue and menstruating so. She went to bed and the doctor came and told her, as usual, that it was nothing, that she must be quiet. In the night I heard the worst cries of despair, but thinking that Diego would call me if I could help, I only dozed and had nightmares. At five, Diego rushed into the room all disheveled and pale and asked me to call the doctor. He came at six with an ambulance and got her, in the agonies of birth . . . out of the pool of blood she had made and . . . the huge clots of blood she kept losing. She looked so tiny, twelve years old. Her tresses were wet with tears."

Frida was rushed in the ambulance to the Henry Ford Hospital. Lucienne and Diego followed in a taxi. As orderlies wheeled Frida through a cement corridor in the hospital's basement, she looked up between painful contractions and saw a maze of different-colored pipes near the ceiling. "Look, Diego! *Qué precioso!* How beautiful!" she cried.

Rivera was distraught while he waited for news of Frida's condition. "Diego was tired all day," Lucienne's diary records. "Hastings tried to cheer him up by going with all of us to the fourth of July parade. In my mind, there was all the time the big chunks of blood and Frida's screaming. Diego thought the same. He thinks that a woman, to stand such pain, is far superior to a man who never could stand the pain of childbirth."

Frida's thirteen days in the hospital were grim. A man lay dying in the next room. She felt like escaping but she was too sick to move, and the heat enervated her even more. She kept bleeding and weeping. Seized by fits of despair at the thought that she might never have children, at not really knowing what was wrong with her, why her fetus had not taken form but had "disintegrated" in her womb, she would cry, "I wish I were dead! I don't know why I have to go on living like this." Rivera was appalled at her suffering and was full of premonitions of disaster. When they extracted liquid from her spine, he became convinced that she had meningitis.

But five days after her miscarriage, she took up a pencil and drew a bust-length *Self-Portrait*. In it she wears a kimono and a hair net, and her face is swollen from tears. And even in the midst of misery she could find laughter. When Lucienne brought her a parody of a condolence telegram that she had composed and signed "Mrs. Henry Ford," Frida laughed so hard, Lucienne recalls, that what was left of the decomposed fetus was delivered, and she bled profusely.

Frida wanted to draw her lost child, wanted to see him exactly as he should have looked at the moment when he was miscarried. The second day in the hospital, she begged a doctor to let her have medical books with illustrations on the subject, but the doctor refused; the hospital did not allow patients to have books on medicine because the images in them might be upsetting. Frida was furious. Diego interceded, telling the doctor, "You are not dealing with an average person. Frida will do something with it. She will do an artwork." Finally Diego himself provided Frida with a medical book, and she made a careful pencil study of a male fetus. Two other pencil drawings that probably come from this same moment, and that are more surrealistic and fanciful than anything she had done before, show Frida asleep in bed surrounded by strange images that represent her dreams, or perhaps the fleeting visions seen under anesthesia, and are attached to her head by long, looping lines. Apparently done using the Surrealist technique of "automatism," the images seem to have sprung into being through free association—a hand with roots, a foot that is like a tuber, city buildings, Diego's face. In one of the drawings, Frida lies naked on top of the bedcovers. Her long hair flows over the edge of the bed and metamorphoses into a network of roots that creep along the floor.

On July 17, Lucienne and Diego brought Frida home from the hospital. On July 25, Rivera began painting at the Detroit Institute of Arts. On July 29, twenty-five days after her miscarriage and twelve days after she was released from the hospital, Frida wrote again to Dr. Eloesser.

Doctorcito querido:

I have wanted to write you for a longer time than you can imagine, but so many things happened to me that until today I have not been able to sit down calmly, take the pen and write you these lines:

In the first place I want to thank you for your kind note and telegram. At that time I was enthusiastic about having the child after having thought of all the difficulties that it would cause me, but surely it was rather a biological thing since I felt the need to give myself over to the child. When your letter arrived I was still more encouraged since you thought it possible for me to have the child and I did not deliver the letter that you sent me to Dr. Pratt, being almost sure that I could withstand the pregnancy, go to Mexico in good time and have the child there. Almost two months had gone by and I had not felt any discomfort, I was almost in a continuous rest taking care of myself as well as I could. But about two weeks before July 4th I began to notice that almost every day a kind of *sanguaza* [contaminated blood] came out of me, I became alarmed, saw Dr. Pratt and he told me all this was natural and that he thought that I could easily have the child with a Caesarean operation. I continued like that until the fourth of July when without knowing why I miscarried in a wink of the eye. . . . The fetus did not take form since it came out all disintegrated in spite of my being already three and one half months pregnant. Dr. Pratt did not tell me what the cause of this was or anything, and he only assured me that another time I could have another baby. Until now I do not know why I miscarried and for what reason the fetus did not take form, so that who knows what the devil is going on inside me, for it is very strange, don't you think? I had such hope to have a little Dieguito who would cry a lot, but now that it has happened there is nothing to do but put up with it. . . . In the end there are thousands of things that always remain in complete mystery. In any case I have a cat's luck since I do not die so easily and that's always something! . . .

Give yourself a little escape and come to see us! We have a lot to chat about with you and with good friends one forgets that one is in this very mulish country! Write to me and don't forget your friends who love you very much.

Diego and Frieda

"There is nothing to do but put up with it," Frida wrote. "I have a cat's luck." Her indomitable will had begun to triumph over despair and apathy.

Henry Ford Hospital (plate IV) is dated simply July 1932. It is the first of the series of bloody and terrifying self-portraits that were to make Frida Kahlo one of the most original painters of her time; in quality and expressive power it far surpasses anything she had done before. Rivera noted the change: speaking of her painting after the miscarriage, he said, "Frida began work on a series of masterpieces which had no precedent in the history of art—paintings which exalted the feminine qualities of endurance of truth, reality, cruelty, and suffering. Never before had a woman put such agonized poetry on canvas as Frida did at this time in Detroit."

In *Henry Ford Hospital,* Frida lies naked in her hospital bed, hemorrhaging onto a single sheet. A large tear runs down her cheek, her stomach is still swollen from pregnancy. The unflattering depiction of her body is typical of Frida: this is clearly a nude perceived by a woman, rather than one idealized by a man.

Against her swollen stomach, she holds six vein-like red ribbons from the ends of which float a series of objects symbolic of her emotions at the time of the miscarriage. One is a fetus, and the ribbon that links it with Frida is continuous with, and obviously meant to represent, the child's umbilical cord. She has placed it directly above the pool of blood from her miscarriage and given it the male genitals of the "little Diego" she had hoped it would be.

All the floating symbols of maternal failure, including the fetus, are in the same large scale in relation to Frida regardless of their actual size. The salmon-pink torso on a pedestal is "my idea of explaining the insides of a woman," Frida said; several sperm-like organisms, presumably an X-ray view of the drama of conception, appear on the torso's surface, and two spinal columns, also drawn there, refer to her injured backbone or possibly to the congenital scoliosis of the spine diagnosed by Dr. Eloesser in 1930. Wanting to get things right, Frida copied medical illustrations of pelvic bones to paint what she said was the principal cause of her miscarriage.

The snail, Frida once explained, refers to the slowness of the miscarriage, which, like a snail, was "soft, covered and at the same time, open." The meaning of the strange piece of machinery below the bed is ambiguous. According to Lucienne Bloch, it represents Frida's hips, which seems likely, since all the other symbols are intimately connected with the female body. Bertram Wolfe thought the machine was an "iron vise suggesting the wracking grip of pain," and given Frida's statement that after her experience in Detroit, "anything mechanical" always meant bad luck and pain, this interpretation seems plausible as well. Frida herself told one friend that the machine was meant to remind her of Diego, and to another she said that she had "invented [it] to explain the mechanical part of the whole business."

The lurid lavender orchid, with its projecting stem, looks like an extracted uterus. "Diego gave it to me in the hospital," Frida said. "When I painted it, I had the idea of a sexual thing mixed with the sentimental."

Frida's hospital bed floats beneath a blue sky in an immense, barren plain; she said that she painted the ground beneath the bed earth color because she was trying to express solitude and loneliness. But, she added in a seeming contradiction, "Earth to me is Mexico, people around, and everything, so it was a help to me, when I had nothing, to put the earth around me." Clearly visible on the horizon is the Rouge River complex, with its coke ovens, conveyors, smokestacks, and water towers. It suggests Frida's distance from Diego, who, when she was hospitalized, seemed to be so far from her, caught up as he was with sketching the Rouge. The faraway buildings also evoke the patient's perception of the outer world's indifference to her plight, her feeling of separation from everyday life. The world outside the hospital functions cleanly and efficiently; Frida, on the other hand, is a wreck. Her desolation is underscored by the disjunctive scale—she looks tiny in relation to the bed—and by the way the bed is tipped up and drawn in an intentionally incorrect perspective. The absence of a top sheet and the placement of the bed out of doors make vivid the feeling of helpless exposure that many hospital patients experience. Frida is floating, disconnected, empty, unprotected.

To help her combat depression, Lucienne and Diego conspired to keep Frida occupied, and as soon as she was strong enough, to get her away from the apartment. To this end, soon after her return from the hospital, Rivera secured permission for her and Lucienne to use a lithography workshop in a local arts-and-crafts guild. With the help of technical advice from a workshop assistant, and after consulting a book on lithography, the two women began drawing on the lithographer's stones.

Despite her poor health and the torrid summer weather, Frida went with Lucienne to the workshop every day from eight o'clock till three. Frida was "like the wildest animal when anyone came into the studio to see us 'fool around,'" Lucienne wrote in her diary. "They didn't realize how serious we were in the work. Frieda would be so cross, she would swear each time a fly came settling on her arm."

When they printed Frida's stone, however, they were "horribly disappointed," Lucienne wrote. "The worst streaks appeared on the stone and wouldn't come out. All Frieda's work gone kaput. Diego came to see in the evening which was sweet of him because he had been working all day in the museum. . . . Frieda decided to try the same sketch all over again, so we worked again the next day. No one dares come and watch, we are so ferociously at work. . . . Seeing Diego start over and over again the thing he hasn't done well gives us courage."

Finally, they produced a few prints that seemed technically satisfactory, and Rivera suggested they send some of them to George Muller, a New York lithography expert, in order to get his advice. He sent Frida back her print with his comments: "These proofs are not good and not bad considering your experience. Work hard and you will get better results." It was a message as bland as an aphorism in a fortune cookie. Frida, who in any case preferred the directness, immediacy, and privacy of oil painting, returned to her easel. But the lithograph—called *Frida and the Abortion*—remains, a powerful and heartrending image (figure 26). In it, Frida stands naked and as passive as a paper doll, submitting to the various stages of her pregnancy. A male fetus is attached to her by a long winding vein, and a much less developed embryo is curled within her womb. Cells in two different moments of division show an earlier stage in the development of her lost child. Two tears fall on her cheeks, and the hemorrhage that ended her pregnancy is depicted in droplets of blood that run down the inside of her leg and into an earth that is both a grave and a garden. In contrast to Frida, the earth is fertile: its plants, nourished by Frida's blood, have grown into shapes that echo the eyes, hands, and genitals of her male fetus.

Frida's body is divided into light and dark halves, as if to reveal the light and dark halves of her psyche, the presence within her of life and death. On her dark side is a weeping moon, and a third arm which holds a palette shaped rather like the fetus, implying, perhaps, that painting is an antidote to maternal failure, that for Frida, making art must take the place of making children.

Three more times (according to Rivera's count) Frida was to try to have a child. Even though she knew her husband did not want another offspring, she was convinced that having his baby would strengthen her hold on him. Rivera recalled that it was because of the danger to Frida that he "forbade her to conceive again," but her close friend

Ella Wolfe, Bertram Wolfe's wife, believes that Frida could have had a baby if she had stayed in bed for five or six months, and that the problem lay with his refusal to sire another child. "Diego was very cruel to Frida about having a child. She was dying to have a baby by him. That's the way Diego was."

Mute testimony to Frida's longing is found in the blue house at Coyoacán: in her collection of books on parturition; in the human fetus in a jar of formaldehyde that was a gift from Dr. Eloesser in 1941 and that she, typically, kept in her bedroom; and most poignantly, in her large collection of dolls and dollhouse furnishings. Frida had all kinds of dolls: old-fashioned ones, foreign dolls, cheap Mexican dolls made of rags or of papier-mâché. Chinese dolls are propped on a shelf near her pillow. Beside her bed is an empty doll bed where she once kept a favored doll, and three little dolls are enclosed with Rivera's baptism dress in a vitrine in her bedroom. One that she treasured, a boy doll, had been given to her by a Cachucha (probably Alejandro) shortly after her accident, when she was hospitalized. Among Frida's notes to Alejandro from 1926 is this doll's baptismal certificate, written in careful Art Deco capitals to make it look official and adorned with a charming drawing of a winged turtle. The certificate reads:

LEONARDO

He was born in the Red Cross in the year of grace, 1925 in the month of September and he was baptized in the town of Coyoacán in August of the following year—

> His mother was
> Frieda Kahlo
> His Godparents
> Isabel Campos
> and Alejandro Gómez Arias

Frida was a good "mother." Displayed in Rivera's bedroom is a list of tasks to be accomplished: certain dolls were to be taken to the doll hospital; some needed new bodies, one needed a wig. "But don't lose them," she warned. When friends took leave of her, she would often say, "Bring me a doll." They often did.

Frida transferred her yearnings for a baby to other people's children—especially (after she returned to Mexico) to Diego and Lupe Marín's daughters Lupe and Ruth and Cristina's two, Isolda and Antonio, who were in and out of their aunt's house as if it were their own and whom she delighted in spoiling. She lavished a different but equally warm attention on her numerous pets—a pack of *escuincle* dogs, various monkeys, cats, parrots, doves, an eagle, and a deer. When the monkeys and parrots accompany Frida in self-portraits, they often seem a substitute for children. And she tended the plants in her garden as if they were as needy as infants. Flowers and fruit she painted so that they look alive, projecting upon them the full force of her obsession with fertility.

Many of her paintings express this fascination with procreation, and some directly reflect her despair at not having children. One of the most moving of the latter is *Me and My Doll,* painted in 1937, a year in which, from the evidence of the number of paintings on this theme, she must have had another miscarriage (figure 48). In it Frida and a large naked baby doll sit side by side on a child's bed, as if posing for a formal photograph; the doll is lifeless and wears a dumb, fixed smile that forms a bitter contrast with Frida's sober demeanor. Instead of a conventional image of a mother cooing over her infant, we see a woman sitting bolt upright, facing not toward the "child" but straight ahead. She is smoking, and she is very much alone.

A disjointed passage from Frida's journal of 1944 reveals that her sadness over not having a child lasted even after she had found other things to fill her life. "I sell everything for nothing. . . . I do not believe in illusion . . . the great vacillator. Nothing has a name. I do not look at forms . . . drowned spiders. Lives in alcohol. Children are the days and here is where I end." Painting was the best antidote to Frida's pervasive sense of barrenness—that barrenness that is seen in the desert backgrounds of so many of her self-portraits. The year she died, she told a friend: "My painting carries within it the message of pain. . . . Painting completed by life. I lost three children. . . . Paintings substituted for all of this. I believe that work is the best thing."

The shock of the miscarriage and the slower realization that she would never bear children made Frida say she wanted to die. Yet her grasp on life was too strong, her rootedness too resilient, for her to succumb to grief. When she was strong enough, she would go every day to the art institute at lunchtime, carrying Diego's lunch in her big Mexican basket. Since Diego was on a rigorous diet, she conscientiously made the basket's contents less bountiful than was her wont, or Diego's desire. Still, she only picked at the food, and there was always some left over. José de Jesús Alfaro, an unemployed Mexican dancer who, like a number of other men out of work, spent much of his time watching Rivera paint, remembers: "Frida came in every day at about eleven-thirty. Diego looked down and then descended from the scaffold. There were Coca-Cola boxes on the floor and he and Frida would sit on them and he'd say, 'Sit down, *muchachos,* sit down.' The Mexican-style food was always delicious. I went to the institute to get something to eat."

After lunch Frida would draw, knit, read, or simply watch Rivera paint. During their breaks from work she loved to get Rivera's assistants to expand on their life stories; all of them remember her great capacity for human feeling, compared with Rivera's more abstract, less personal interest in his fellowman. If Rivera was gruff, she would intercede for them: when, for example, Stephen Dimitroff tried to charm his way into Rivera's employ by speaking Bulgarian, he was dismissed with a shout from the maestro: "No more assistants!" "Help the *pobrecito,*" Frida cried. "He just wants to watch you work." And Rivera did.

Occasionally she left the courtyard to wander slowly through the institute's galleries with Dr. Valentiner. The museum director was astonished at her critical discernment. She would stop suddenly and say, "That's a fake!" or "That's beautiful!" What appealed to her had nothing to do with the pieties of connoisseurship. She loved Rembrandt and Italian primitives, and had an extraordinary eye for lesser-known treasures.

At home, with Lucienne, she made a schedule to study biology, anatomy, and history, and she gave Lucienne Spanish lessons. The two women bought a blackboard, and Lucienne borrowed books from the library, encouraging Frida to read them by reading them herself. But "Frieda has great difficulty doing things regularly," Lucienne wrote in her diary. "She wants schedules and to do things like in school. By the time she must get into action, something always happens and she feels her day broken up." Although Frida inherited her father's fastidiousness and need for order, she did not inherit his rigorously disciplined work habits. If friends dropped in, she let them interrupt her, and even if the visitor was Jean Wight, who she knew would bore her by chatting about fashion, she did not feel capable of telling her guest that she was busy.

When Frida was painting, however, she put in long hours, starting early in the morning and working until it was time to take Diego's lunch to the institute. A good day's work made her exuberant. She painted four of the five paintings from the Detroit period in one burst of energy that began with the lithograph and *Henry Ford Hospital.* Shortly thereafter, she produced *Showcase in Detroit,* and then on August 30 she began *Self-Portrait on the Borderline Between Mexico and the United States.*

It was here, in Detroit, that she adopted a certain posture as a painter, a pose that was at once serious and mocking. She pretended not to consider her work important, and as if to emphasize her "amateur" status, she did not don the masculine workers' attire of so many women artists. Instead, she wore frilly Mexican costumes under a ruffled apron more appropriate to a fiesta than to painting with oils. Yet when she finally settled down to work, she worked with concentration. "My paintings are well painted," she once said, "not with speed, but with patience. . . . I think that at least [they] will interest a few people." And she cared enough about her particular painting methods to invent a painting stand that facilitated them. It consisted of an aluminum pipe that went from floor to ceiling, with a support attached to it that could slide up and down according to which part of the painting was in progress—or whether the artist could stand or had to sit. She and Lucienne were convinced that the pipe could also be used for the display of paintings. Why, they asked, should paintings always be displayed on walls?

At Rivera's suggestion Frida began to paint on metal, to make her works seem more like Mexican ex-votos, or *retablos.* After preparing the small panels of sheet aluminum with an undercoating to form a binder between metal and pigment, she would proceed as if she were painting a fresco rather than an oil, first drawing the general outlines of her image in pencil or ink, and then, starting in the upper left corner, working with slow, patient concentration across and from the top downward, completing each area as she went along. Compared to the method of a painter who works on a canvas a little bit all over, loosely brushing in color areas and gradually refining the image, her method was primitive—almost a coloring-book approach—but it was effective. (In later years, she would block in broad areas of color before bringing the image, section by section, to a high degree of verisimilitude.)

Henry Ford Hospital is the first painting Frida did on sheet metal, the first work from her hand that is clearly modeled on Mexican votive paintings in style, subject, and scale. It may have been Rivera's idea, too, that she record her miscarriage in the same way that a *retablo* (plate V) records a disaster the victim has survived. In any case, starting in 1932, *retablos* form the single most important source for Frida's primitivizing style, and even as her paintings became less primitive and more realistic, *retablos* continued to be a principal model.

In most *retablos,* the holy image—Virgin, Christ, or saint—that saves the sick, wounded, or otherwise endangered person appears in the sky surrounded by an aureole of cloud puffs. A dedicatory inscription tells the story of the trouble, complete with name, date, and place, describes the miraculous intervention, and offers the donor's thanks. But although Frida's *"retablo"* contains none of these elements (as Rivera once wrote: "Frida's *retablos* do not look like *retablos,* or like anyone or anything else . . . [for] she paints at the same time the exterior and interior of herself and of the world") and although it substitutes floating symbolic objects for the usual holy image, the combination of fact and fantasy in this and in many other of Frida Kahlo's paintings is very like that in *retablos.* As in *retablos,* the drawing is naïvely painstaking, the color choices are odd, the perspective is awkward, space is reduced to a rudimentary stage, and action is condensed to highlights. Adherence to appearances is less important than the dramatization of the ghastly event or the miraculous encounter between the victim and the resplendent holy image. Both Frida's paintings and *retablos* record the facts of physical distress in detail, without squeamishness. Both evince a kind of deadpan, reportorial directness; since salvation has already been granted, there is no need for the rhetoric of entreaty. The tale is told not to elicit pity but to settle accounts with God. The narration must be accurate, legible, and dramatic, for a *retablo* is both a visual receipt, or thank-you note, for the delivery of heavenly mercy, and a hedge against future dangers, an assurance of blessings.

As her pain subsided and other facets of life in Detroit came into focus, Frida's renewed interest in the world around her appeared, along with her grief, in her art. *Showcase in Detroit* depicts the display window of a shop where street decorations were manufactured, all decked out with garlands of red, white, and blue and other symbols of Americana in anticipation of Independence Day. Frida probably saw and sketched the window just before her miscarriage, but she painted it after she finished *Henry Ford Hospital.* The timing of its conception would explain the painting's lighthearted mood, so different from the more intense and unhappy works that followed the loss of her child. Lucienne Bloch remembers how the painting came to be. She and Frida were shopping for sheet metal. "We were walking together on John R., and we saw one of those old musty-looking stores in a poor neighborhood. It was so extraordinary— all these camp things that had no connection—that Frida stopped in front and said, 'Ah, that's lovely, that's beautiful!' " To Frida, the window display was like Mexican folk art, thus more genuine than elitist modern art; when she told Rivera about the window, he quickly understood her enthusiasm and suggested, "Why don't you paint it!"

On August 31, sweltering in the ninety-nine-degree heat, Frida, Lucienne, Diego, Rivera's assistant Arthur Niendorff, and Edsel Ford stood on the roof of the Detroit Institute of Arts and watched a solar eclipse through pieces of smoked glass. "Frieda seemed totally disgusted with the eclipse and when it was at its fullest, she said it was not beautiful at all, [no better than] 'a cloudy day when the full business was showing itself.' " Lucienne's diary also notes that Frida started a new painting that day—a full-length self-portrait in which she stands on a gray stone pedestal that is inscribed "Carmen Rivera painted her portrait in the year 1932," and that marks the border between the U.S. and Mexico.

Showcase in Detroit is an affectionate spoof of American taste and mores; *Self-Portrait on the Borderline Between Mexico and the United States* (figure 28) reveals Frida in a more critical mood; her wit, while no less evident, has an edge to it. She is clad, for example, in a long pink dress and old-fashioned lacy gloves, "proper" attire for a Grosse Pointe evening; in her left hand, defying propriety, is a cigarette, in her right a small Mexican flag.

Perhaps inspired by the solar eclipse, Frida has, for the first time in her paintings, placed the sun and the moon together in the sky. Their juxtaposition became one of the most powerful symbols in her work. It represents the unity of cosmic and terrestrial forces, the Aztec notion of an eternal war between light and dark, the preoccupation in Mexican culture with the idea of duality: life-death, light-dark, past-present, day-night, male-female. Discussing the coexistence of the sun and the moon in Rivera's art, Bertram Wolfe explained: "In most nature religions, as in ancient Mexican mythology, the lords of the heavens are the Sun and the Moon: the Sun being the masculine principle, the fertilizer and life-giver, and the Moon (or in some Mexican traditions the Earth) the feminine principle, the mother of gods and men." The juxtaposed sun and moon also refer to the idea that all nature mourns Christ's death. They can signify as well the darkness that fell upon the earth during the crucifixion, or the solar elipse which astronomers say happened about the time when Jesus was crucified. The sun and moon often flank the cross in medieval crucifixion scenes, and their joint presence in depictions of Christ's sacrifice is a tradition that continued in the Renaissance, in colonial Mexico, and in Mexican popular art. Frida knew this Christian symbolism and combined it with pagan meanings to heighten the dramatic intensity of her imagery.

In *Self-Portrait on the Borderline Between Mexico and the United States,* both the sun and the moon are on the left (Mexican) side of the painting. As for the U.S. portion, an American flag floats in a cloud of industrial smoke, and the scene is dominated by the modern world of skyscrapers, bleak brick factories, and machines, all of which contrast sharply with Frida's vision of ancient agrarian Mexico. Diego was forever comparing the beauty of American machines and skyscrapers with the splendor of pre-Columbian artifacts. When Frida, on the other hand, painted smokestacks (labeled "Ford"), they belched smoke, and her windowless skyscrapers look like tombstones. In the middle ground she has placed four industrial chimney stacks that resemble automatons; they derive from the automatons that Rivera put in his California School of Fine Arts mural or from the chimney-automatons he designed for *H.P.*, where he showed a ship docked at "Machine City," and they are meant to be seen in opposition to the pre-Columbian idols on the Mexican side of the border. In the foreground, on the U.S. side, instead of rooted plants we see three round machines, two of which radiate rays of light and energy (as contrasted with the radiant Mexican sun), and all of which have electric cords (as opposed to their counterparts, the Mexican flowers, which have roots). Frida has cleverly depicted a cord, which extends from one of the machines, transforming itself into the roots of one of the Mexican plants. The machine's other cord is plugged into an outlet on Frida's pedestal.

It was a machine that had mowed Frida down in her 1925 accident; it was in "Motor City" that she lost her child, and it was machinery that took Diego away from her for so many hours while she was in Detroit. Agrarian Mexico, on the other hand, meant life, human connectedness, beauty, and she longed to return to it. "To tell you the truth," she had written to Dr. Eloesser in July, *"no me hallo!* [I am not happy here!] as the kitchen maids would say, but I have to pluck up my courage and stay because I cannot leave Diego."

Her yearning for Mexico, for the comforting embrace of her family and her barrio, was to be heartbreakingly fulfilled: on September 3 she received a telegram informing her that her mother, who had developed breast cancer six months before, was desperately ill, perhaps dying. For three hours Frida tried to reach one of her sisters in Mexico by telephone, but she could not get a line. She asked Lucienne to investigate flights. Discovering there were none, she became hysterical. "Here they talk about all this progress," she ranted. "Why can't we go by plane? What's the matter with all these 'modern conveniences'?" Lucienne went to fetch Diego from the Detroit Institute of Arts; they returned to find Frida in "torrents of tears."

The next day Diego put Frida and Lucienne on the train for Mexico. "Frieda cried in the dark compartment," Lucienne wrote in her diary. "This time it was for leaving Diego and not knowing how her mother is, either. Frieda [was] all shaking like a little child."

The train took them through Indiana and Missouri. At Saint Louis, they got off and had lunch on the roof of the Hotel Statler, where they watched airplanes fly by. Frida was hemorrhaging again, and felt too weak to walk, so they went to the movies. In a newspaper, they read that the Rio Grande was flooded—this explained why the telephone lines to Mexico had been out. The following night, in Laredo, Texas, they awoke to find the train moving very slowly through floodwater. Because the bridges were out of commission, they had to wait twelve hours at the border. Finally, they took a bus across the least damaged bridge to Nuevo Laredo, which was brimming with excitement—vendors hawking food, families saying passionate goodbyes, people standing around just enjoying the spectacle. Before boarding the train once more, Frida bought *cajeta,* scooping the sticky caramel up with her fingers, as she had as a girl.

The passage through northern Mexico was beautiful, for it was the rainy season, and the desert was full of rivulets and glistening cacti. Frida did not see it. "[She] got more and more hectic," Lucienne wrote, "and the last hours were agony for her. We arrived in Mexico City at 10 P.M., Thursday, September 8th. There were sisters, cousins and men to meet her, all crying and hysterical. We even forgot the valises."

They stayed at Matilde's house in the Doctores district of Mexico City. The following morning Frida, accompanied by Lucienne, went to see her mother in Coyoacán. Matilde Calderón de Kahlo was in critical condition. "She can't seem to want to give herself any philosophy, but cries and cries and looks deadly pale," Lucienne wrote, adding, "Her father is a dear, very fussy, deaf and shabby and Schopenhauerish."

On September 10, Frida wrote a letter to Diego telling him all the details of her mother's illness. Then her thoughts turned, as if for solace, to her love and need for her husband:

Although you tell me that you see yourself as very ugly, with your short hair when you look in the mirror, I don't believe it, I know how handsome you are anyway and the only thing that I regret is not to be there to kiss you and take care of you and even if I would sometimes bother you with my grumbling. I adore you my Diego. I feel as though I left my child with no one and that you need me. . . . I cannot live without my *chiquito lindo* [handsome little one]. . . . The house without you is nothing. Everything without you seems horrible to me. I am in love with you more than ever and at each moment more and more.

> I send you all my love
> Your *niña chicuititita*

Niñita Chiquitita preciosa [little tiny pretty girl], Diego wrote in reply,

I include this [letter] only to accompany the papers with many kisses and love [for] my beautiful Friduchita. I am very sad here without you, like you I can't even sleep and I hardly take my head away from work. I don't even know what to do without being able to see you, I was sure that I had not loved any woman as I love the *chiquita* but not until now that she has left me did I know how much I really love her, she already knows that she is more than my life, now I know, because really without you this life does not matter to me more than approximately two peanuts at most.

I already finished six more panels since you left, working always with the fixed idea that you should see the things when you return. I'm not telling you anything because I want to see what a face the *chicua* will make when she sees them. Tomorrow I am going at last to the factory of chemical products. They didn't want to let me in because of such secrets and dangers. How stupid and shocking, it was necessary for Edsel to write in order for them to give me permission.

On September 15, one week after Frida's arrival, and two days after having 160 gallstones removed, Matilde Calderón de Kahlo died. Lucienne wrote in her diary: "Her sisters all came wrapped in dark [shawls] and red in eyes. Frieda sobbed and sobbed. It was terribly sad for her. They didn't tell their father until the next morning. He was almost crazy about the idea sometimes, and would lose his memory and ask why his wife wasn't there." A photographic portrait of Frida taken at this time by her father shows her dressed in black and wearing an expression that is new in her photographs: she looks as if grief had sucked all the concavities of her face inward. There is a darkness in her eyes, the unmistakable darkness of sorrow.

During the remaining five weeks of her stay in Mexico, Frida devoted most of·her time to her family. She and Lucienne took Guillermo Kahlo for walks in a nearby park. Stopping to gaze at what Lucienne thought were "very *pompier*" scenes, he exclaimed over their beauty. "He is still a romantic." He was still an eccentric too. "Sometimes," she noted, "he gets into fits of bad character and yells with a knife."

They also spent hours chatting with Frida's sisters, Adriana and Cristina, who lived in Coyoacán, and with Matilde, whose bourgeois home with its flowery wallpaper, fake Louis XVI rugs, and lace curtains surprised Lucienne, who was used to Frida and Diego's *Mexicanista* taste. Frida took perverse delight in *objets* such as white porcelain ashtrays shaped like shells, decked with gold and violets, each displaying· a nude woman painted to look as though she were lying on the shell's side. "It's so horrible it's beautiful!" she would cry.

On one occasion Frida and Lucienne went to San Angel to check the progress of the linked modern houses, designed by the architect and painter Juan O'Gorman. Frida liked the idea of having two separate houses. "I can work," she told Lucienne, "and he can work."

In mid-October, the painter and cartoonist Miguel Covarrubias and his wife, the American-born dancer and painter Rosa Rolando, produced a delicious Mexican farewell dinner. Frida was both gay and sad. The next day, a crowd of at least twenty people came to the train station to say goodbye—Lupe Marín with one of her sisters, Frida's father, her sisters, and many others. When the train left the station, Frida cried for a while, then went silently to bed.

It was a cold, forbidding dawn on October 21 when they arrived back in Detroit. Diego, wearing a suit belonging to Clifford Wight because, after his diet, his own clothes were too big for him, was on the platform to meet them. "Frida returned to Detroit," he wrote in his autobiography. "She had been watching her mother die, and was spent with grief. Added to this, she was horrified by my appearance. At first she could not recognize me. In her absence, I had dieted and worked so hard that I had lost a great deal of weight. . . . The moment I saw her, I called out, 'It's me.' Finally acknowledging my identity, she embraced me and began to cry."

The painting entitled *My Birth* (plate VI) was probably conceived and even begun before Frida's trip to Mexico, but she finished it after her return to Detroit. The first of the series suggested by Diego that records the years of her life, it shows, as Frida put it, "how I imagined I was born." It is one of the most awesome images of childbirth ever made.

We see the infant's large head emerging between the mother's spread legs from the doctor's vantage point. Heavy, joined eyebrows identify the child as Frida. Blood covers the inert, drooping head and skinny neck. The baby looks dead.

A sheet covering the woman's head and chest, as if she had died in childbirth, emphasizes the total exposure of delivery. As a substitute for the mother's head, on the wall directly above her is a painting of another grieving mother, the Virgin of Sorrows pierced by swords, bleeding and weeping. Frida said that she included the Virgin of Sorrows in *My Birth* as "part of a memory image, not for symbolic reasons." It is a detail of furnishings remembered from childhood—just the kind of object her devoutly Catholic mother would have cherished. The bed, said Frida, was her mother's bed; both she and her sister Cristina were born in it. Possibly the pink lace border on the pillowcase and the sweet pastel walls that contrast so markedly with the ghastliness of the scene are childhood memories too. Less fanciful than *Henry Ford Hospital*, *My Birth* is like a *retablo* in both style and content; indeed, there is a scroll set aside for an inscription along the painting's lower edge. But the requisite information was never filled in. Perhaps Frida felt it would be superfluous to tell the story again in words. Or perhaps she wanted to say that here no miraculous salvation had occurred. *My Birth* depicts a calamity, not a close call, not a disaster averted by divine intercession for which thanks should be given: the icon of the Virgin gazes ineffectually upon a scene of double death.

The stripped-down image of pain in *My Birth* also recalls a famous Aztec stone sculpture of parturition (c. 1500) that depicts a squatting woman giving birth to a full-grown man's head, her face set in a forbidding grimace of pain (plate VII). The woman in childbirth is, in Aztec religion, the equivalent of a warrior capturing a sacrificial victim; she represents the birth of an era. Frida surely knew the sculpture, and it is likely that she also knew its meanings; for her, as for the Aztecs, the idea of birth was full of portent. Rivera wrote of Frida's *My Birth:* "The mother's face is that of the *mater dolorosa,* with her seven daggers of pain which make possible the opening from which the child Frida emerges, the only human force since the marvelous Aztec master . . . who has given plasticity to the actual phenomenon of birth."

Although *My Birth* depicts Frida's own birth, it also refers to the recent death of her unborn child. It is thus a picture of Frida giving birth to herself. "I wanted to make a series of pictures of every year of my life," Frida said of the painting. "My head is covered because, coincidentally with the painting of the picture, my mother died." "My head," she said, indicating that it is her own head that is covered. Years later, she wrote in her diary next to several small drawings of herself: "The one who gave birth to herself . . . who wrote the most wonderful poem of her life."

As the Detroit winter grew bitter and bleak, Frida bought a fur coat to keep out the gales, but foul weather was within as well as without. Not only did she have to absorb her double loss, progenitor and progeny, she also had to deal with Rivera's irascibility. His weight loss had played havoc with his health and spirits. Lucienne wrote in her diary: "I feel *de trop* at the Wardell, and when Diego said he couldn't sleep at night because of the winter and kept Frieda awake, I at once looked for a room. . . . Frieda gets so moody and cries so often and needs comfort. Diego is nervous and seems to feel even irritated at Frieda's presence." Many times in Detroit, Frida would cry on Lucienne's shoulder, telling her friend about the "hardships of her life with Diego, how irregular and different [he was] from what she was used to." If she "held her own," Frida explained, Rivera would say, "You don't love me," which put her in an even more helpless position.

Rivera was wearing himself out, working against time. He had to finish the Detroit murals quickly, because he had other projects planned. In October 1932 he had been selected to paint a mural in Rockefeller Center in New York, and in January 1933 he received a commission to do a mural on the theme of "machinery and industry" at the 1933 World's Fair in Chicago. His schedule was such that it was difficult for Frida even to join him at work. Often he would begin at midnight, after his assistants had prepared a section of wall with fresh plaster, and after it had dried just enough to have the right consistency so that the paint could sink in and become part of the wall. He would start by blocking in the drawing and modeling the highlights in grays and blacks; then, by the first light of dawn, he applied color, often painting until lunchtime. What little free time he had was not necessarily spent with Frida, for he was active in Detroit's Mexican community, organizing and financing trains to take back to Mexico people who had come to the United States to work in the glory days of the 1920s and were hard hit by the Depression.

In spite of all her problems, Frida gradually detached herself from mourning and reattached herself to life. By February, when she was interviewed and photographed, at the Wardell, for the *Detroit News,* she was working on a bust-length *Self-Portrait* painted on a small metal panel (figure 30). It shows her dressed in a white blouse with lace trim around the scoop neckline and a string of pre-Columbian jade beads; the color of jade is echoed in the wool that holds back her braids and in the painting's pale-green background. She looks fresh and lovely, less girlish than in her 1929 and 1930 self-portraits, more self-assured, ready to amuse and be amused. Her restored spirits are revealed as well in the *Detroit News* article, which appeared in Florence Davies's "Girls of Yesterday: Visiting Homes of Interesting People" column under the headline "Wife of the Master Mural Painter Gleefully Dabbles in Works of Art." Even if she was called a "dabbler," at least attention was being accorded to her art and personality, and compared with the shy girl of the previous year, she had acquired a definite social aplomb. Davies wrote:

Carmen Frieda Kahlo Rivera . . . is a painter in her own right, though very few people know it. "No," she explains, "I didn't study with Diego. I didn't study with anyone. I just started to paint." Then her eyes begin to twinkle. "Of course," she explains, "he does pretty well for a little boy, but it is I who am the big artist." Then the twinkles in both black eyes fairly explode into a rippling laugh. And that is all that you can coax out of her about the matter. When you grow serious, she mocks you and laughs again. But Señora Rivera's painting is by no means a joke. . . .

In Detroit she paints only because time hangs heavily upon her hands during the long hours while her husband is at work in the court. So thus far she has finished only a few panels. . . . "But it's beautifully done," you exclaim. "Diego had better look out." "Of course," she cries, "he's probably badly frightened right now"; but the laughter in her eyes tells you that she's only spoofing you—and you begin to suspect that Frede [*sic*] believes that Diego can really paint.

Chapter 11

Revolutionaries in the Temple of Finance

WHILE RIVERA labored to finish his frescoes at the Detroit Institute of Arts so that he could move on to Rockefeller Center, a publicity campaign against his murals was building. No sooner had they been finished and officially unveiled on March 13, 1933, than a storm of disapproval burst forth. Churchmen found them sacrilegious, conservatives saw them as Communistic, and prudes thought they were obscene. The murals were called a "heartless hoax on his capitalist employers," and a "travesty on the spirit of Detroit." Some civic-minded citizens threatened to wash them from the walls. Others organized committees to defend them. The debate was broadcast in newspapers and on the radio. Thousands of people came to see the murals, and popular support grew. Edsel Ford rose to Rivera's defense: "I admire Rivera's spirit," he said. "I really believe he was trying to express his idea of the spirit of Detroit." When a large group of industrial workers took it upon themselves to guard the murals, Rivera was euphoric. This, he said, was "the beginning of the realization of my life's dream." The Riveras left Detroit a week after the unveiling, confident that the "art form of the industrial society of the future" had had a splendid overture.

It was bitterly cold in the third week of March when Frida and Diego, accompanied by assistants Ernst Halberstadt and Andrés Sánchez Flores arrived in Grand Central Station. In less than two days, the Riveras had installed themselves in a two-bedroom suite on a high floor of the Barbizon-Plaza, and Diego was at work in the RCA Building. The lunches and dinners Frida brought him grew cold on the scaffold beside him as he painted or stood motionless before his fresco, looking and looking, silently appraising what he had accomplished and planning his next day's stint.

Rivera at work was one of the liveliest shows in town, and tickets were issued to a public willing to pay to watch him. Frida herself went to the RCA Building two or three times a week, often in the evening, when the paying audience had gone. She would spend a few hours beneath the scaffold, sucking hard candies, talking to friends who came by, teaching Mexican ballads to Lucienne Bloch and Stephen Dimitroff in the privacy of the temporary shack that served as a center of operations for the project. She was delighted to be back in cosmopolitan Manhattan, where she had many friends in the art world as well as in "high society" and where she felt more at home. It was, unlike Detroit, a port city; water offered the hope of escape. When she was homesick, she could dream of taking the next boat back to Mexico.

But as she had in Detroit, Frida spent most of her time at home. She did not paint regularly; if in Detroit she had painted "only because time [hung] heavily on her hands," now that time hung more lightly, she hardly worked at all. During her eight-and-a-half-month stay in Manhattan she produced only one painting, and that one was still not finished when she left. Instead of painting, she read, took care of the apartment, saw friends, went to the movies, and shopped. Another pastime was the game of *cadavre exquis*, an old parlor game adopted by the Surrealists as a technique to explore the mystique of accident. The first player starts by drawing the top of a body and then folds the paper so that the next player draws the next section without seeing how the figure has been begun. When Frida was a player, the resulting monsters were hilarious. She had a lurid imagination, and her fascination with sexual organs, also seen in the drawings in her journal and in a number of her paintings, burst forth in the "exquisite corpses." "Frida did all the worst ones," Lucienne Bloch recalls. "Some of them made me blush, and I do not blush easily. She would show an enormous penis dripping with semen. And we found out later when we unfolded the paper that it was a woman all dressed up with big bosoms, and all that, until it got to the penis. Diego laughed and said, 'You know that women are far more pornographic than men.' "

Frida's "pornography" and her new, mischievous self-assurance are also evident in her mode of teasing the New York press. For one interview she received reporters while lying in bed, sucking a long stick of candy. "She stuck it under the bedcovers and she raised it slowly," says Suzanne Bloch, who witnessed the scene. Keeping a straight face and without a pause in the flow of her talk, Frida secretly delighted in the reporters' embarrassment. Another time, a journalist asked, "What does Mr. Rivera do in his spare time?" and without hesitating, Frida replied, "Make love."

She adored department stores, shops in Chinatown, and dime stores. "Frida went through dime stores like a tornado," Lucienne recalls. "Suddenly she would stop and buy something immediately. She had an extraordinary eye for the genuine and the beautiful. She'd find cheap costume jewelry and she'd make it look fantastic." Sometimes, swift as an eagle, she would pocket some trinket that entranced her, and once outside the store, give it to a friend. When an acquaintance suggested that she buy herself some stylish clothes, Frida briefly gave up her long native skirts for the amusement of wearing chic Manhattan modes—even hats—and twitching her hips along the Manhattan sidewalks in a parody of the confident strut of a Manhattan socialite. She poked fun at everything that struck her as funny, and that was a lot. American drugstores, for example, were a fantasy world. Once when she was passing a pharmacy in a taxi, the word "Pharmaceuticals" written on the outside struck her as so ponderous that she composed a song called "Pharmaceuticals" and, much to the driver's mirth, sang it loudly during the remainder of the ride.

Diego asked friends to escort Frida to films and other events. The sculptor David Margolis, then Rivera's assistant, remembers taking her to see Jean Cocteau's *The Blood of a Poet*, which they liked so much that they saw it again the same day with Diego. Completely lacking in intellectual pretension, Frida openly admitted that she thought the theater dull and preferred to go to Brooklyn to see Tarzan films. To her, gorilla movies were hilarious and surreal. Both Frida and Diego were, Lucienne recalls, "bored to tears" by classical music; during one performance of Lucienne's father's *Sacred Service*, Diego fell asleep. On another occasion, while listening to Tchaikovsky, Lucienne and Frida "acted like the worst mischiefs, making drawings and paper birds and giggling awfully—this in Carnegie Hall!"

Bored or not, it is scarcely surprising that Diego fell asleep during concerts. Working fourteen to fifteen hours per day, he was determined to unveil his new mural by May Day, the workers' holiday. But as the unveiling approached, trouble began to brew. While Diego had made no secret of his politics when accepting the commission, neither had he made any concessions to the mural's location, opposite the main entrance to the RCA Building in Rockefeller Center. The painting's left side showed the United States, with Wall Street businessmen on a binge, unemployed workers and protesters bullied by mounted police, and the dehumanization of war. The right half displayed a Marxist utopia, with workers, peasants, soldiers, athletes, teachers, and child-toting mothers united in the effort to build a better world.

Apparently the thought that capitalists might do well not to hire an avowed Communist to decorate one of the world's truly great urban complexes, a monument to capitalist success, had not occurred to the young Nelson Rockefeller, who, as executive vice-president of Rockefeller Center, had signed the contract. He had himself set the murals' grandiloquent theme: "Men at the Crossroads looking with Hope and High Vision to the Choosing of a New and Better Future." His representatives had approved the sketches. He had publicly supported Rivera's Detroit frescoes, and he had brimmed with enthusiasm whenever he came to see the progress of the murals, ignoring misgivings voiced by Frances Flynn Paine, who had served as Rivera's agent for the mural commission, and others connected with the RCA Building or with the Rockefellers.

Then on April 24, when the fresco was two-thirds finished, the *New York World-Telegram* saw enough of it to publish an article under the headline "Rivera Paints Scenes of Communist Activity and John D. Jr. Foots Bill." The mural's "dominant color is red" noted the *World-Telegram*, "red headdress, red flag, waves of red in a victorious onsweep." Suddenly the atmosphere at Rockefeller Center grew hostile. Overnight the heavy scaffolding was replaced with a flimsier, movable structure. The number of guards was increased. They picked fights with Rivera's assistants; one threatened to "brain" an assistant if he tried to take a snapshot of the mural, and when Rivera himself brought someone to photograph it, the guards sent the man away. Frida told Lucienne that "something could happen anytime now," and Lucienne, familiar with Frida's imperturbability, thought: "Things are getting very serious if *she* says it." The next day, after Rivera had screened the scaffold from public view with large sheets of tracing paper, Lucienne photographed the fresco with a camera she had brought in hidden beneath her skirt.

By the first of May, Diego had transformed a sketch of a "labor leader" into an unmistakable portrait of Lenin. On May 4, Nelson Rockefeller wrote to him asking him to substitute the face of an unknown man for that of Lenin. Lenin's portrait, he argued, would "seriously offend a great many people." Rivera declared that to remove the head of Lenin would be to destroy the entire conception of the mural. He offered a compromise: he would balance the head of Lenin with the head of Abraham Lincoln. The answer came on May 9, at a time when most of Diego's assistants were having lunch in a nearby restaurant. Rockefeller's rental manager, followed by twelve uniformed security guards, stalked into the RCA Building and ordered the artist to stop working. Slowly Rivera laid down his big brushes and the kitchen plate he used as a palette, and climbed down from the scaffold. He was handed a check for the full amount owed to him (the remaining $14,000 due on a $21,000 contract) and a letter that told him he was fired.

Rivera was stunned. He, who usually moved with a fat man's liquid grace, walked woodenly to the work shack and changed out of his overalls. More guards appeared and pushed the movable scaffold away from the wall. Within half an hour Radio City personnel had covered the mural with tar paper and a wooden screen.

When they heard the news, Diego's assistants rushed like avenging angels back to the RCA Building to help him, but there was nothing, beyond protest, to be done. Lucienne Bloch did manage to scrape white paint off two second-story windows to form the words "Workers Unite! Help Protect Rivera M—" Guards stopped her before she could finish the word "Murals."

Once again, Rivera was at the center of public outcry. As mounted police looked on, ready to move at the first sign of violence, his defenders picketed Rockefeller Center and Nelson Rockefeller's home, waving banners that read: "Save Rivera's Painting" and yelling: "We want Rockefeller with a rope around his neck! Freedom in art! Reveal Rivera's murals!" A group of artists and intellectuals that included Walter Pach, George Biddle, Rockwell Kent, Boardman Robinson, Waldo

Pierce, H. L. Mencken, and Lewis Mumford petitioned Nelson Rockefeller to reconsider his decision. Wittier comment came in the form
of E. B. White's poem "I Paint What I See," published in *The New
Yorker*. An imaginary conversation between Rockefeller and Rivera,
it ends with a standoff:

> "It's not good taste in a man like me,"
> > Said John D.'s grandson Nelson,
> "To question an artist's integrity
> "Or mention a practical thing like a fee,
> "But I know what I like to a large degree,
> > "Though art I hate to hamper;
> "For twenty-one thousand conservative bucks
> "You painted a radical. I say shucks,
> > "I never could rent the offices—
> > "The capitalistic offices.
> "For this, as you know, is a public hall
> "And people want doves, or a tree in fall,
> "And though your art I dislike to hamper,
> "I owe a *little* to God and Gramper,
> > "And after all,
> > "It's *my* wall . . ."
>
> *"We'll see if it is," said Rivera.*

But there was no reconsideration, and it turned out to be Rockefeller's wall in the end. Nine months later, after the Riveras had left
New York, the mural was chipped off and thrown away. (Perhaps Rivera
had the last word after all. When he repainted the Rockefeller Center
mural in Mexico City's Palace of Fine Arts in 1934, he placed John
D. Rockefeller, Sr., among the revelers on the capitalist side of the
mural, in close proximity to the syphilis spirochetes that swarm on
the propeller.)

Rivera's disappointment at not being allowed to finish his mural
was compounded by attacks from the Communist party, which continued to excoriate him for accepting commissions from millionaires: to
Joseph Freeman, editor of *New Masses*, the Rockefeller Center mural
was "reactionary" and "counterrevolutionary." Finally, on May 12,
Diego received a telegram from his friend Albert Kahn, architect for
the General Motors Building at the Chicago World's Fair (and the
designer of the Detroit Institute of Arts as well), saying that his commission to paint the "Forge and Foundry" mural at the fair, for which

sketches had already been drawn, had been canceled. It was a terrible blow to Rivera's dream of painting murals for modern industrial society.

Frida was, of course, caught up in the fracas. She attended protest meetings—her personal protest was a return to wearing Mexican costumes after her experiment with conventional clothes—and she typed countless letters dictated to her by Diego. Doing whatever she could to shore up the pro-Rivera ranks, she was her husband's most loyal defender. A few months after Rivera was fired, Nelson Rockefeller came up to her at the opening of Sergei Eisenstein's film *Que Viva Mexico!* "How are you, Frida?" he politely inquired. Frida turned on her heels, flipping her long skirts and petticoats, and marched off. (She was a realist, however. A photograph taken in the fall of 1939, when Rockefeller was in Mexico helping with the arrangements for the exhibition entitled "Twenty Centuries of Mexican Art," put on at the Museum of Modern Art in 1940, shows Frida sitting beside him at a buffet lunch.) A newspaper reporter who interviewed Frida shortly after the showdown wrote:

Señora Diego Rivera, the comely young wife of the artist whose fresco has been ordered covered—perhaps permanently—because of its Communistic viewpoint, is grieved, but not perturbed. . . .

A girlish Spanish type, olive skinned, doe-eyed, lithe and slender, she sat down on the edge of her bed in a room filled with friends and sympathizers, and associates of her husband, closed her ears to their excited conversations and told us just how she feels about it. . . .

She believes that the Rockefellers have acted so "because they were afraid of public opinion," and she feels very certain that "Mrs. Rockefeller probably feels badly about it." They saw the preliminary sketches with Lenin's portrait, more prominent there than in the painting, she said, and they approved.

"The Rockefellers knew quite well the murals were to depict the revolutionary point of view—that they were going to be revolutionary paintings," she said quietly. "They seemed very nice and understanding about it and always very interested, especially Mrs. Rockefeller.

"We were their guests at dinner two or three times, and we discussed the revolutionary movement at great length.

"Mrs. Rockefeller was very nice to us always. She was lovely. She seemed very interested in radical ideas—asked us many questions. You know she helped Mr. Rivera at the Museum of Modern Art and really battled for him."

When Rivera was ordered off the scaffold at Rockefeller Center, he announced that he would use what was left of Rockefeller's fee "to paint in any suitable building that is offered, an exact reproduction of the buried mural—I will paint free of charge except for the actual cost of materials." No suitable site was offered him, and he finally chose to paint instead the history of the United States, as seen from a revolutionary perspective, on twenty-one movable panels in a dilapidated, soon-to-be-razed building at 51 West Fourteenth Street that housed a Lovestonite organization called the New Workers' School.*

On June 3, one month after the beginning of the Rockefeller Center battle, Frida and Diego moved downtown to a two-room flat at 8 West Thirteenth Street so that Rivera could be nearer to his work. Diego let it be known that the new apartment was more expensive than the Barbizon-Plaza suite; in his pride, he did not want to admit that Rockefeller had hurt him financially. In September they moved again, to an apartment on the fourteenth floor of the Hotel Brevoort, on Fifth Avenue at Eighth Street.

Between May 9, when he was thrown out of Rockefeller Center, and July 15, when he started work at the New Workers' School, Rivera was too demoralized, bitter, and angry to paint. Friends noted that Frida's eyes were often red from weeping. But though he did not paint, Rivera was not idle. He and Bertram Wolfe did research on American history in preparation for the New Workers' School fresco cycle. He gave numerous lectures about art and politics, and he made public appearances not only to defend his position on the RCA Building mural but also to support other causes, such as the Scottsboro Defense Fund. On May 15 he addressed fifteen hundred Columbia University students who were protesting the dismissal of Donald Henderson, an economics instructor and an avowed Communist. Frida, who tended to be rather distant at these manifestations—she saw them as theater rather than as history—was at his side, sitting in her usual bolt-upright position, looking like an Aztec princess. During the five-hour demonstration there were fist and water fights, the university president was burned in effigy, and the statue of Alma Mater was blindfolded and a black-draped coffin labeled "Here lies academic freedom" placed at her feet. *The New York Times* reported: "Diego Rivera, Mexican artist dismissed recently from Rockefeller Center, and his wife, Car-

* The Lovestonites were an anti-Stalinist Communist group headed by Rivera's friend and biographer Bertram D. Wolfe.

men, addressed the students in front of the sundial, where he urged the students to 'wrest control of the university from Dr. Nicholas Murray Butler.' "

When Rivera began to paint again, he became his old expansive self. Louise Nevelson, who had taken an apartment with Marjorie Eaton on the ground floor of the Thirteenth Street building, recalled that the Riveras' "house was always open in the evening, and anyone who wanted to would come. They were very serious about people; they didn't make distinctions. I was never in a home like Diego's. Princesses and queens . . . one lady richer than God. And workmen, laborers. He made no distinction, and all were treated like one body of people. It was very simple. Diego and Frieda liked it so much because at the other place uptown they had had a doorman, and of course Frieda and he did not believe in that. They were delighted to find a place where they could come in and not be bothered. So every night people came, and then he'd take the gang to a little Italian restaurant on 14th Street."

Both Nevelson and Eaton were aspiring young artists, and they were happy to be in the company of the great Rivera, even though, in order to enjoy that company, they had to put up with a certain amount of "bohemian" unreliability. Having been asked to come to the Riveras' apartment at six, they would find Diego resting and Frida not dressed. Frida would try on various skirts and blouses, asking for Rivera's opinion. Then she would disappear for half an hour, returning in a new costume. When she was finally dressed, it was Rivera's turn to disappear. After a long bath he would suddenly announce, "We will go to dinner," and he would escort the three young women to some Chinatown or Greenwich Village restaurant, where they would be joined at a long table by other friends.

At one such dinner, there were among the diners Frida and Diego, Nevelson, Eaton, the modern dancer Ellen Kearns and the sculptor John Flanagan, who worshiped Rivera and liked to sit and watch him paint for hours. "We used to carry on," Nevelson recalled. "There'd be a white tablecloth and we'd put, say, powdered sugar on it. One person would start the composition, then another would add to it, spilling wine, shaking pepper, moving things around until the tablecloth was a whole landscape. Diego was great for having fun."

Indeed he was. Louise Nevelson was a beautiful, vivacious, strong-willed divorcée in her early thirties, a passionate devotee of art and of men. Before long she had joined the ranks of Rivera's assistants and had painted an expressionistic portrait of the maestro looking ugly, as he told her he thought he was, but unmistakably a genius. He showed his gratitude by taking her to an Indian shop, asking her what she liked, and buying the necklace she admired.

Soon all the assistants were aware that Rivera was spending a lot of time with Louise. A July entry in Lucienne's diary reports that Diego did not appear at work at all that day, and that Sánchez Flores told the other assistants that Rivera very much liked "the girl that sticks around Diego." Lucienne was indignant; "Frieda is too perfect a person," she wrote, "for anyone to have the strength to take her place." When Rivera did not turn up at the New Workers' School a second time, Sánchez Flores told the others that Rivera was in Louise's company again. "I felt so bad for Frieda," wrote Lucienne on that day.

Frida no longer went every day to the scaffold. She was not well—her right foot felt paralyzed, and she had to keep it raised as much as possible—and she was lonely. Lupe Marín, who came to stay for a week on her way back to Mexico from Europe, recalled that "Frida did not go out. She spent the whole day in the bathtub. It was too hot to go out in the streets."

Often Diego did not come home until dawn. Frida would call Suzanne Bloch and say, "Oh, I hate to be alone!" or "I'm feeling blue. Please come and see me." Once when Suzanne spent the night with Frida, Frida whiled away the evening cooking a battalion of little puddings for Diego to eat when he returned.

Rivera did show some concern for Frida, asking Lucienne and Stephen Dimitroff to persuade her to paint, though it was, Lucienne thought, merely because "he wanted to be independent of her." Noting that Frida admired a small fresco panel that Lucienne had just finished, Rivera encouraged his wife to try the medium herself. After a display of recalcitrance, Frida did, but the bust-length *Self-Portrait* she produced was horrible, she thought. When the figure was finished, she wrote all around the head (mostly in English): "Absolutely rotten, *No sirve* [It doesn't work]. Oh! boy very ugly, Frieda." In disgust, she dropped the panel—it cracked but did not break—and threw it away. Lucienne and Stephen, who thought it was beautiful, retrieved it from the garbage can and took it home. Later, during a move, the edges broke off, but the main section remains intact, and it is not "rotten" but full of charm. The face that stares out of the plaster has the intense physical presence of a Faiyum mummy portrait. Even in this experimental work, Frida's self-presentation is startlingly alive.

The strain between Frida and Diego was exacerbated by another conflict. Frida was desperate to go back to Mexico, at least for a visit. After four years of living almost continuously in the United States, she still felt alienated by Gringolandia and its way of life. In a letter to Dr. Eloesser written some years later, when she was happily back in her native country, she expressed her feelings about the relative merits of the U.S. and Mexico, admitting that in Mexico, "one always has to go around with ones thorns sharp . . . to defend oneself from all the *cabrones* [bastards] . . . who get into hot arguments wanting always to get ahead and to screw the next person." In the U.S., on the other hand, one could relax because "there people are dumber and more malleable."

What's more [she continued] in relation to Diego's work the people here [in Mexico] always respond with obscenities and dirty tricks, and that is what makes him most desperate since he has only to arrive and they start attacking him in the newspapers, they have such envy for him that they would like to make him disappear as if by enchantment. On the other hand in Gringolandia it was different, even in the case of the Rockefellers, one could fight against them without being stabbed in the back. In California everyone treated him very well, also they respect the work of anyone, here he does no more than finish a fresco and the next week it is already scratched or spat upon with phlegm. This as you must understand would disillusion anyone above all when one works like Diego, using all the effort and energy of which he is capable, without taking into consideration that art is "sacred" and all that series of *pendejadas* [stupidities], but on the contrary, toiling like any bricklayer. On the other hand, and this in my personal opinion, in spite of the fact that I understand the advantages that the United States have for any work or activity, I don't like the gringos with all their qualities and their defects which are very great, their manner of being, their disgusting puritanism, their Protestant sermons their endless pretension, the way that for everything one must be "very decent" and "very proper" seems to me rather stupid. I know that the people here are thieves, *hijos de la chingada, cabrones,* etc. etc. but I don't know why, they do even the most horrible things with a little sense of humor, while the gringos are *"sangrones"* [dullards] by birth, although they are very respectful and decent(?). Also their system of living seems to be the most repugnant, those damned parties, in which everything from the sale of a painting to a declaration of war is resolved after swallowing many little cocktails (they don't even know how to get drunk in a spicy way) they always take into account that the seller of the painting or the declarer of war is an "important" personage, otherwise they don't give one even a nickel's worth of attention. In the U.S. they only suck up to the "important people" it doesn't matter to them that they are *unos hijos de su* mother [Frida wrote "mother" in English] and like this I can give you a few other little opinions of those gringo types. You might tell me that you can also live there without little cocktails and without "parties," but without them one never amounts to anything, and it is irritating that the most important thing for everyone in Gringolandia is to have ambition, to succeed in becoming "somebody," and frankly I no longer have even the least ambition to be anybody, I despise the conceit and being the *gran caca* does not interest me in any way.

Unlike Frida, Rivera liked the United States and its citizens; he liked the adulation the Manhattan art world gave him, and he was determined to stay in New York until the New Workers' School panels were completed. Moreover, to him, going back to Mexico was going backward in time. He was convinced that the world revolution would happen in an industrialized country, and he wanted to be there, at least on the ideological barricades, fighting with images as ammunition. He said that he and Frida should sacrifice their comforts and their love of home for the great Communist cause. Frida did not agree. She thought all this was a lot of "bunk."

On November 16, 1933, Frida wrote to her friend Isabel Campos that she spent her time in Gringolandia "dreaming about my return to Mexico."

New York is very pretty [she went on] and I feel better here than in Detroit, but in spite of this I am longing for Mexico. . . . Yesterday we had snow for the first time, and soon it will be so cold that . . . the aunt of the little girls [death] will come and take them away. Then there will be nothing to do but dress in woolen underwear and put up with snow. I do not feel the cold so much because of my famous long skirts but sometimes I feel a cold draft that could not even be prevented by twenty skirts. I still run around like crazy and I am getting used to these old clothes. Meanwhile some of the gringa-women are imitating me and trying to dress *a la Mexicana*, but the poor souls only look like cabbages and to tell you the naked truth they look absolutely impossible. That doesn't mean that I look good in them either, but still I get by (don't laugh). . . .

Tell me what you want me to bring you from here, because there are so many really adorable things that I don't know what would be good to bring you, but if you have a special taste for something, just tell me and I'll bring it.

As soon as I arrive you must make me a banquet of *pulque* and *quesadillas* [fritters] made of squash blossoms, because just thinking about it makes my mouth water. Don't think I'm forcing this on you and that already from here I am begging you to give me a banquet. It's just that I am reminding you, so that you don't look wide-eyed when I arrive.

What do you know about the Rubés and all the people who used to be our friends? Tell me some gossip, because here no one chats with me about anything and from time to time gossip is very pleasant to the ear . . . here come a thousand tons of kisses for you to share and keep most of them for yourself. . . .

Frida ends her letter with a drawing of herself in front of Manhattan skyscrapers. She weeps, and a comic strip balloon says, "Don't forget me." Above her is a sad-faced sun. In the middle of the drawing is a boat moving through the ocean in the direction of Mexico. There, the sun smiles.

Frida's longing to absent herself from New York, to return home, is visible in her painting called *My Dress Hangs There* (figure 34), which is signed on the back in chalk and inscribed: "I painted this in New York when Diego was painting the mural in Rockefeller Center." Since it was finished after she returned to Mexico, and because it shows the influence of Rivera's Radio City mural, she no doubt continued working on it until her departure.

Directly in the middle of a composite image that shows Manhattan as the capital of capitalism as well as a center of poverty and protest in the Depression years hangs Frida's Tehuana costume. Flanked by cold, anonymous skyscrapers with endless blank windows in regular rows, and hanging on a powder-blue hanger hooked over a powder-blue ribbon, the embroidered maroon blouse and pea-green skirt with pink ribbons and white ruffles looks exotic, intimate, and feminine. By absenting herself from her dress, Frida is saying that her dress may hang in Manhattan, but she is elsewhere; she does not want any part of "Gringolandia." Though empty clothing in this painting is not yet the anguished symbol it was to become in later works, the clothes exert a powerful presence nonetheless; Frida already knew the emotional reverberations of empty dresses.

The message is delivered with a light touch, a leftist view of Manhattan in the guise of a charming folkloric parody. Frida mocks the North American obsession with efficient plumbing and the national preoccupation with competitive sports by setting upon pedestals a monumental toilet and a golden golf trophy. Business, religion, and the drastic eclecticism of U.S. taste are targets too. Snaking around the cross in the stained-glass window of Trinity Church is a large red *S* that turns the crucifix into a dollar sign; a red ribbon links the church's gothic tower with a Wall Street Doric temple, Federal Hall; and instead of Federal Hall's marble steps, Frida has pasted on her canvas a graph showing "Weekly Sales in Millions": in July 1933, big business appeared to be doing fine, but the masses—tiny, swarming figures at the bottom of the painting—were not the beneficiaries. An outsize telephone perched on top of an apartment building is the city's heart; its black wire loops in and out of windows like an immense circulatory system, connecting everything.

Thus Frida laughs at America. But she has something serious to say as well about human waste and wasted human beings in a capitalist society: a garbage pail overflows with a hot-water bottle, daisies, a stuffed toy rabbit, a liquor bottle—and a frilly cloth smeared with blood, a bone, globs of entrails, an object that looks like a human heart, and most horrific of all, a bloody human hand.

One curious thing about the cast of characters in Frida's view of Manhattan is that none of the leading actors is alive. The artist's empty dress takes center stage. Automatons are her opposite. On the steps of Federal Hall stands the statue of George Washington, a reminder of the revolutionary idealism of the past. The billboard showing Mae West plays a different kind of role. At the time that Frida was at work on this painting, Rivera, in a conversation about his view of the American ideal of beauty ("the George Washington Bridge, a trimotor, a good automobile, or any efficient machine"), said that as for human beauties, Mae West "is the most wonderful machine for living I have ever known—unfortunately on the screen only." Frida did not see it that way. She has placed Mae West next to the church with its dollar-sign window, because the film star, too, represents false values—in her case, vanity, luxury, the worship of glamour. Her sumptuousness is ephemeral: the edges of the billboard on which she appears are peeling away from the frame, and the buildings below it are burning.

In the lower part of the painting Frida has rendered "the masses" as pointillist multitudes of minute heads and hats constituting bread lines, crowds of demonstrators, soldiers on parade, and the audience at a baseball game. Over twenty fragments of photographs and other bits of cut-up paper have been chosen and glued on the canvas with great deliberation, in terms of composition as well as of meaning. Several have a pattern of swarming spots that look like microscopic life. Juxtaposed with the masses of hats, they suggest the idea of microcosm/macrocosm, the great continuum of life so dear to both Frida and Diego.

To top it all off, the Statue of Liberty raises high her torch, a satirical reminder of what the United States was meant to stand for in better days. The only thing that does not belong here is Frida's dress, and it may be that the collaged steamship puffing painted smoke in the harbor was a stroke of wishful thinking. Frida would have liked to be on it.

Through the shortening days of autumn, Frida and Diego argued about whether to stay in New York or return to Mexico. On one occasion Lucienne Bloch and Stephen Dimitroff found them in such a heated argument that Rivera picked up one of his paintings—an oil depicting desert cacti that resembled grasping hands—and shouted: "I don't want to go back to that!" Frida retorted: "*I* want to go back to that!" Diego grabbed a kitchen knife and, as his wife and friends looked on in horror, ripped his painting to shreds. When Lucienne tried to stop him, Frida held her back. "Don't!" she cried. "He'll kill you!" Stuffing the tattered bits of canvas into his pockets, Diego stalked out of the apartment, impervious to a bombardment of imprecations in Lucienne's native French. "Frieda trembled all day," Lucienne wrote in her diary. "[She] couldn't get over the loss of the canvas. She said it was a gesture of hate towards Mexico. He feels he must go back there for Frieda's sake, because she is sick of New York. . . . She has to accept the fact that she is to blame."

Finally, early in December, the frescoes in the New Workers' School were finished. On December 5 a farewell reception was given. On December 8, 9, and 10 there were public showings of the completed murals, with a lecture given by Rivera every evening at eight. But Rivera had not yet, as he had promised he would do, spent every penny of Rockefeller's fee painting revolutionary frescoes in the United States. Not until he had completed two small panels in the Union Square headquarters of the New York Trotskyites was he broke and ready to leave.

On December 20, 1933, Frida and Diego boarded the *Oriente*, bound first for Havana and then for Veracruz. "We got together a group," Louise Nevelson said, "put the money together, and bought tickets for them. Took them bodily onto the boat and saw that they left."

PART 4

Chapter 12

A Few Small Nips

WHEN THE RIVERAS returned to Mexico from the United States at
the end of 1933, they moved into their new home on the corner of
Palmas and Altavista in San Angel: two sleek international-modern
cubic shapes "Mexicanized" by their colors (pink for Diego's house;
blue for Frida's) and by the wall of organ cactus that surrounded them.
Ella Wolfe says that Diego wanted two separate houses because "it
seemed, from a bohemian point of view, the 'interesting' or 'arresting'
thing to do." A Mexican newspaper put it another way: "[Diego's]
architectural theories are based on the Mormon concept of life, that
is to say, the objective and subjective interrelationships that exist between the *casa grande* and the *casa chica!*" ("Big house" in Mexico
refers to a man's home; "little house" is an apartment for a mistress.)
And indeed, the new houses were separate but unequal. Rivera's, of
course, was bigger. It contained a large high-ceilinged studio, really
a semipublic place where he entertained and sold paintings, and a
spacious kitchen; most meals were eaten there. Frida's blue house
was more private and compact. It had three stories: a garage at ground
level; a living room/dining room and small kitchen above it; and on

the top floor, reached by a spiral staircase, a bedroom/studio with a huge picture window, plus a bath. Its flat roof was made into a terrace by the addition of a metal railing: from here the bridge led to Diego's studio.

Home at last from Gringolandia, occupied with fixing up the two houses, the kind of task she loved, Frida should have been happy, but the evidence of her paintings in the next two years shows that she was not. In 1934 she produced no paintings at all. The following year she completed only two: the astoundingly gruesome *A Few Small Nips* (plate VIII) and a *Self-Portrait* (figure 37) in which her short, curly "poodle" haircut gives her a totally different look from the Frida with smoothly pulled back hair who appears in the small panel she painted shortly before leaving Detroit in 1933.

A Few Small Nips is based on a newspaper account of a drunken man who threw his girl friend on a cot and stabbed her twenty times; brought before the law, he innocently protested, "But I only gave her a few small nips!" In the painting, we are presented with the immediate aftermath of the murder: the killer, holding a bloodied dagger, looms over his dead victim, who lies sprawled on a bed, her naked flesh covered with bloody gashes. As in some depictions of the dead Christ descended from the Cross, one of the woman's lifeless arms hangs downward, her wounded and bleeding palm open toward us. Streams of blood flow from the fingers and splash onto the acrid, greenish-yellow floor (yellow, Frida later said, stood for "insanity, sickness, fear"). As if the small sheet of tin cannot contain the horror, splotches of blood continue out onto the painting's frame, becoming life-size red splashes. The impact on the viewer is immediate, almost physical. We feel that someone in our actual space—perhaps ourself— has committed this violence. The transition from fiction to reality is made by a trail of blood.

Hand in pocket, fedora set at a jaunty tilt, the murderer looks as brutal as the woman looks brutalized. Indeed, the painting presents stereotypes, the *macho* and the *chingada,* his victim. *Chingada,* literally the "screwed one," is Mexico's most familiar curse and a word used frequently by Frida. "The verb [*chingar,* to screw]," Octavio Paz said, "denotes violence, an emergence from oneself to penetrate another by force. . . . The verb is masculine, active, cruel: it stings, wounds, gashes, stains and it provokes a bitter, resentful satisfaction. The person who suffers this action is passive, inert and open, in contrast to the active, aggressive and closed person who inflicts it." Frida told a friend that she painted the murderer as he appears here "because in Mexico killing is quite satisfactory and natural." She added that she had needed to paint this scene because she felt a sympathy with the murdered woman, since she herself had come close to being "murdered by life."

"Murdered by life": within a few months of the Riveras' return to Mexico, Frida felt that all her hopes for setting up a new and harmonious existence had been extinguished. Diego had embarked upon a love affair with her younger sister, Cristina. In her anguish, Frida cut off the long hair Diego loved and stopped wearing Tehuana costumes. And as if the immediate pain was too great to record, she painted *A Few Small Nips*, depicting not her own experience but her suffering projected onto another woman's calamity.

No one knows when the affair began (probably in the summer of 1934), or how and when it ended, or indeed, if it stopped and began again. We do know that Rivera was not pleased to be back in Mexico, and like a sulky child, he blamed Frida for making him return. Though he had been invited to paint murals in the Mexico City Medical School and soon secured the commission to repaint his Rockefeller Center fresco on a large wall on the third floor of the Palace of Fine Arts, he felt angry and apathetic and he did not work. Poor health added to his misery. Despite all the puddings and pistachio ice cream he had consumed in Manhattan, his drastic diet in Detroit had left him shrunken and saggy, prey to glandular disorders, hypochondria, and extreme irritability. (Finally, in 1936, a doctor treating him for an infection of the tear duct of his right eye ordered him to be "reinflated.") He was "weak, thin, yellow, and morally exhausted," Frida wrote to Ella Wolfe in July:

Because he doesn't feel well he has not begun painting, this has made me sadder than ever, since if I don't see him happy, I can never be tranquil, and his health worries me more than my own. I tell you that if it was not that I do not want to mortify him more, I would not be able to stand the very great pain I have from seeing him like this, but I know that if I say that it grieves me to see him like that, he worries more and it is worse. . . . he thinks that everything that is happening to him is my fault, because I made him come to Mexico . . . and that this is the cause of his being the way he is. I do everything possible to encourage him, and to arrange things in a way that is easier for him, but I have still not succeeded in anything, since you cannot imagine how changed he is compared to the way you saw him in New York, he does not want to do anything and he has absolutely no interest in painting here, I agree with him completely, because I know the reasons he has for being like this, with the people from around here who are the most mulish in the world, and the most uncomprehending without changing what needs to be changed in the world which is full of that type of bastards . . . he says that he no longer likes *anything* of what he has done, that his painting done in Mexico and part of that in the United States is *horrible,* and that he has wasted his life miserably that he no longer wants to do anything.

Frida's own health was not much better than Diego's. She was in the hospital at least three times in 1934: once to have her appendix removed, once for an abortion performed after three months of pregnancy, and a third time because the foot problems that had troubled her in New York grew worse. "My [right] foot continues to be bad," she wrote to Dr. Eloesser, "but it can't be helped and one day I am going to decide that they should cut it off so that it won't annoy me so much anymore." The foot was operated on for the first time; the healing process was very slow. To make matters worse, since Diego's depression and inertia kept him from working, funds were low. With all these troubles, it was natural that Frida should have turned for solace to her sister Cristina, who had been deserted by her husband not long after the birth of her son, Antonio, in 1930, and was living with her children (and Guillermo Kahlo) in the blue house in Coyoacán.

In many ways the sisters complemented one another. Frida was the brilliant one who had made the brilliant marriage, a gifted artist with the celebrity that came with being Rivera's wife; Cristina, on the other hand, was blessed with motherhood. She was lively, generous, and beguilingly feminine. In Rivera's depiction of her in his 1929 Health Building mural (at Frida's suggestion, Cristina had posed for one of the allegorical nudes), she is the essence of voluptuous sexuality, a plump Eve holding a flower (that looks like a vagina), while a seductive serpent whispers in her ear. ". . . She lives a little bit in the . . . ether," Frida wrote of her some time later. "She still keeps on asking . . . who is Fuente Obejuna [a play by Spanish writer Lope Félix de Vega]? and if she goes to see a movie she always asks, well, but who is the informer? who is the assassin? who is the girl?, in sum, she does not understand either the beginning or the end, and in the middle of the movie she usually delivers herself to the arms of Morpheus."

Surely it was not malice that made Cristina betray her sister, though perhaps a touch of rivalry did play a part. More likely she was overwhelmed. Rivera was the great maestro, and a genius who is a charmer is hard to resist. Probably he persuaded his sister-in-law that he desperately needed her. No doubt he thought he did, for after her abortion, Frida had been told by her doctors to refrain from sexual intercourse. Still, it was an unconscionable affair, embarked upon as casually as his earlier flings and perhaps with intentional cruelty. "If I loved a woman," Rivera wrote in his autobiography, "the more I loved her, the more I wanted to hurt her. Frida was only the most obvious victim of this disgusting trait."

"I have suffered so much in these months that it is going to be difficult for me to feel completely well soon," Frida wrote to Dr. Eloesser on October 24, "but I have done everything I can to forget what [has] happened between Diego and me and to live again as before. I do not think that I will succeed completely since there are things that are stronger than one's will, but I can no longer continue in the very great state of sadness that I was in, because I was heading with large strides toward a neurasthenia of that horrible type that makes women turn into idiots and *antipáticas* [nasty people] and I am even happy to see that I was able to control the state of semi-idiocy that I was in."

And on November 13: "I believe that by working I will forget the sorrows and I will be able to be a little happier. . . . I hope my stupid neurasthenia will soon go away and my life will be more normal again—but you know it is rather difficult and I will need much willpower to manage even to be enthusiastic about painting or about doing anything. Today was Diego's saint's day and we were happy and it is to be hoped there will be many days of this kind in my life."

On November 26 she wrote again, apologizing because she had not sent the doctor a drawing she had promised him:

I made various, they all turned out to be frightful and I decided to tear them up before sending you *porquerías* [junk]. Then I fell into bed with influenza and only got up two days ago and naturally the first thing I did was to start making the drawing, but I do not know what happens to me so that *I can't do it*. It all comes out less than what I want, and I even began to shriek with rage but without managing to produce anything good. Thus I decided in the end to tell you this and to ask you to be good enough to forgive me such rudeness, do not think that I do it because of lack of desire to make the drawing, but rather because I am in such a state of sadness, boredom, etc. etc. that I can't even do a drawing. The situation with Diego is worse each day. I know that much of the fault for what has happened has been mine because of not having understood what he wanted from the beginning and because of having opposed something that could no longer be helped. Now, after many months of real torment for me, I forgave my sister and I thought that with this things would change a little, but it was just the opposite. Perhaps for Diego the troublesome situation has improved, but for me it is terrible. It has left me in a state of such unhappiness and discouragement that I do not know what I am going to do. I know that Diego is for the moment more interested in her than in me, and I should understand that it is not his fault and that I am the one who should compromise if I want him to be happy. But it costs me so much to go through this that you can't have any idea of what I suffer. It is so complicated that I don't know how to explain it to you. I know that you will understand it anyway and you will help me not to let myself be carried away by idiotic prejudices, but nevertheless I wanted so much to be able to tell you all the details of what is happening to me in order to lighten my pain a little. . . .

I believe that soon this state of unspeakable troubles will pass and someday I will be able to be the same as I was before. . . .

Write me when you can. Your letters give me great pleasure. . . .

Now we can no longer do what we said we would do, destroy all of humanity and let only Diego, you, and me remain—since now Diego would no longer be happy.

While Frida tried desperately not to be "carried away by idiotic prejudices" and clung to the hope that her "unspeakable troubles" would pass, Diego was, she told Dr. Eloesser, "busy day and night." Sometime in early November, he had begun his *Modern Mexico* mural on the left wall of the National Palace stairway (figure 35). Once more Cristina posed for him, this time accompanied by her two children and holding a political document instead of a flower. Nevertheless, she looks seductively round in face and body, and her golden eyes have that blank, orgasmic expression that Rivera reserved for women with whom he was sexually infatuated. Lovingly, he has made Cristina's dainty feet in their high-heeled sandals a pivot for his whole composition. Frida, who sits behind Cristina holding a book with a political text for a boy to read, plays the role of eager young activist more convincingly than her sister; for one thing, she wears the right costume: denim skirt, blue work shirt, and cropped hair. She also wears a pendant bearing a red star emblazoned with a hammer and sickle.

It seems likely that Diego's affair with Cristina lasted longer than is generally thought. *A Few Small Nips* is one indication that the affair continued into 1935. And early that year Frida abruptly moved out of her San Angel house and, taking her favorite spider monkey with her, went to live in a small modern apartment in the center of Mexico City at Avenida Insurgentes 432.

It was to be the first of many separations (Frida actually consulted a lawyer, her friend and fellow Cachucha Manuel González Ramírez, about a divorce), and it set a curious pattern. Even though they lived apart, Frida and Diego saw each other constantly. He kept some of his clothes in her apartment, and wanting to be fair to both sisters, he bought Frida a set of blue leatherette and chromium 1930s "moderne" furniture just like the red set he had already purchased in order to furnish a flat for Cristina on fashionable Florencia Street.

Perhaps Frida took the apartment as much to create a life of her own as to get away from Diego. After all, her friends the painter María Izquierdo (Rufino Tamayo's mistress) and the photographer Lola Alvarez Bravo (Manuel Alvarez Bravo's wife) had recently rented an apartment together and tried to make a living on their own; why couldn't Frida do the same?

Certainly she put on a brave front, acting gay and delighting others with her sardonic humor, so that though a few close friends knew what she was going through, new acquaintances, such as Mary Schapiro, who met Frida while traveling in Mexico, did not suspect the extent of her unhappiness. But Alejandro Gómez Arias, who went to see her at the flat, remembers the time Frida flew into a rage upon spotting Cristina at a gasoline station across the street. "Look!" she cried. "Come here! Why does she come and fill up her car in front of my house?" And *A Few Small Nips* remains as the proof of Frida's hurt.

Finally, in early July, Frida packed and flew to New York with Anita Brenner and Mary Schapiro. The trip was both a desperate fleeing and a madcap flight. On the spur of the moment, the women decided to travel not by train but in a private Stinson plane flown by a pilot they had happened to meet the night before at a lively dinner party given by Diego. The grueling six-day journey included many forced landings. To escape her terror, Frida slept in the back seat. Eventually the women abandoned the plane and traveled to Manhattan by train. There, Mary (recently separated from her husband) and Frida stayed together at the Holly Hotel near Washington Square, and after confiding her troubles to Lucienne Bloch and to Bertram and Ella Wolfe, Frida came to a resolution. "As the flames of resentment died down within her," Bertram Wolfe wrote, "she knew it was Diego she loved and that he meant more to her than the things that seemed to stand between them." Reconciling herself to a marriage of mutual "independence," she wrote to her husband on July 23, 1935:

[I know now that] all these letters, liaisons with petticoats, lady teachers of "English," gypsy models, assistants with "good intentions," "plenipotentiary emissaries from distant places," only represent *flirtations,* and that at bottom *you and I* love each other dearly, and thus go through adventures without number, beatings on doors, imprecations, insults, international claims—yet we will always love each other. . . .

All these things have been repeated throughout the seven years that we have lived together, and all the rages I have gone through have served only to make me understand in the end that I love you more than my own skin, and that, though you may not love me in the same way, still you love me somewhat. Isn't that so? . . . I shall always hope that that continues, and with that I am content.

As for Rivera, though he knew he would keep on deceiving her, he regretted wounding her. And one thing was certain: if he had had to choose between the two sisters, he would have chosen Frida. In his autobiography, he tells of an incident that took place sometime after Frida's return from New York in 1935. Assassins hired by the German ambassador fired two shots into his studio (the reason, according to Rivera, was that as a Communist and outspoken antifascist, he was persona non grata with the Germans). The killers apparently aimed at a "typist" who was posing for him in the chair where Frida habitually sat and chatted with Diego while he worked. He identified the "typist" as Cristina Kahlo. "Afterward it occurred to me," said Diego, "that the would-be assassins had thought that by killing Frida they could hurt me infinitely more than if they struck at me. In this respect, they were absolutely right." Keeping Cristina as a "secretary" can have done nothing to heal Frida's wound, but his words reveal the depth of Rivera's love for his wife.

If in *A Few Small Nips* Frida made it graphically clear that her wound had not closed, she also made it obvious that she was not going to allow herself to be maudlin about her woes. She had made up her mind not to be a wretched *"antipática,"* but instead to be the wise, calm, amused, forgiving woman who appears in the *Self-Portrait* with curly hair. She would turn life's "nips" into a joke. Thus the truly devastating violence of the subject matter in *A Few Small Nips* is mitigated not only by Frida's primitivistic style but also by a strong note of caricature seen in sly, incongruous details—the delicate lace trim on the pillowcase, the festive pink-and-blue walls, the pink, be-flowered garter and the rolled-down stocking on the dead woman's leg that suggest she was a whore. Most incongruous of all is the pair of doves, one black, one white, that hold in their beaks a pale blue ribbon inscribed with the painting's title. They belong in a valentine, not a massacre. Frida said they stood for good and evil.

Frida's black humor, a characteristically Mexican kind that relishes horror and laughs at death, is nowhere more vivid than in *A Few Small Nips*. The viewer's response is twofold—and uncomfortable; it combines a kind of convulsed outrage and laughter. Examples of this brand of mordant wit abound in Mexico's popular culture. One thinks, for instance, of the little clay hospital scenes sold for a few pennies in the markets of Guadalajara, showing doctors and nurses gleefully brandishing the severed head or leg, the extracted heart of the patient who lies on the operating table. On the toys' bases appear captions such as *"Por un Amor!"* (For a Love), *"Ultima Lucha!"* (Last Battle), or *"Ni Modo Cuate!"* (Too Bad, Pal). Or one thinks of the sugar coffins with tiny skeletons that are made as edible treats for the Day of the Dead; jokes such as the one that goes: "He was lucky: of the three bullets that hit him, only one killed him," or stories like the one that tells of a man who cured his friend of a hangover headache by emptying his pistol into his head.

Retablos and anonymous paintings of the dead or flagellated Christ are also recalled in *A Few Small Nips*. So are genre scenes like the one that hangs in Frida's dining room and that shows one man threatening another with a knife outside a *pulquería*. But the principal source for *A Few Small Nips* is certainly the satiric graphics of José Guadalupe Posada (1851–1913), whose chapbook and song illustrations, penny broadsides showing sensational horror scenes (plate IX), and *calavera* (skeleton) prints, in which skeletons act out the foibles of human life, Frida adored. Indeed, Frida's tiny panel could be called a painted broadside.

Even at their most violent, Posada's prints contain an element of humor that undoubtedly appealed to Frida. Years later in her diary, she wrote: "Nothing is worth more than *laughter*. It is strength to laugh and to abandon oneself, to be light. *Tragedy* is the most ridiculous thing." By the end of 1935, she had forced herself to dismiss the Cristina-Diego affair. She shrugged her shoulders and steeled her psyche, and let out that deep, infectious laugh. *A Few Small Nips* was Frida's *carcajada*, a burst of laughter so explosive that it could blow away pain. Humor, like hope, was a mainstay that helped her to survive her embattled life.

But if Frida dismissed the affair, she did not forget, and two and three years later she gave testimony to its lingering impact in *Memory*, 1937, and in *Remembrance of an Open Wound*, 1938. Whereas in *A Few Small Nips* and in earlier works like the bloody Detroit paintings, Frida depicted the female body (usually her own) in actual physical pain or death, in *Memory* and *Remembrance* she has begun to use physical wounds as symbols for psychic injury. And she is no longer the passive female, recumbent and submitting to her fate; instead, she is an upright woman staring out at the viewer, conscious of, and insisting that the viewer be conscious of, her personal suffering.

In *Memory* (figure 39), which also may refer to her transformation from child to woman after the accident, Frida appears with cropped hair, and she is wearing non-Mexican clothes—a skirt and a cowskin bolero that she actually owned, and that she wore when Lucienne Bloch photographed her during her trip to New York in 1935. She is flanked by her alternate identities—schoolgirl clothes and Tehuana costume, both linked to her by red ribbons (veins or bloodlines) and both hanging on red hangers that are suspended by ribbons from the sky. Each set of clothing has one stiff, paper-doll-like arm. The central

Frida is armless (and thus helpless). One bandaged foot refers to the operation on her right foot in 1934, when Rivera fell in love with Cristina; the bandage is wrapped in such a way that the foot looks like a sailboat, and it stands in the ocean while the normal one stands on the shore. Perhaps the boat foot is a symbol of separation from Diego; the sea very likely is a symbol of suffering—an "ocean of tears," like the pools of water Frida drew under weeping self-portraits in her letters to Alejandro.

Memory is an excruciatingly accurate rendering of pain in love, as simple and straightforward as a valentine heart shot through by an arrow. One is convinced that Frida knew all too well that the trite expression "broken heart" has a basis in a real, physical sensation— an ache or a sense of fracture in the chest—a feeling that a sword turns and twists in an ever-expanding wound. In Frida's painting, her broken heart has been yanked out of her chest, leaving a gaping hole pierced by a shaft which recalls the handrail that impaled her body during her accident. On the ends of the metal rod sit two tiny cupids, blithely ignoring the agony that each up and down movement of their seesaw causes the human fulcrum. Frida's huge heart lies at her feet, an imposing monument to the immensity of her pain. Her heart is a fountain; its severed valves pump rivers of blood into the bleak landscape. Blood flows up into the distant mountains and down toward the sea, where a red delta opens into blue water. The image has something of the brutality of an Aztec sacrifice in which the live victim's beating heart was torn from him, and blood ran in rivulets down the stone temple steps to the ground, where his arms and legs were sold as meat. Indeed, the red river gushing from Frida's extracted heart captures the poetry of blood that pervades so much of Latin American culture. One thinks not only of pre-Columbian and colonial art, but also of bullfights and of fighting cocks stabbing each other with their sharp spurs. In *One Hundred Years of Solitude,* Gabriel García Márquez wrote of a thread of blood that began in the murdered José Arcadio's ear, traveled all through the town of Macondo, and returned to its source. Similarly, Frida combined concrete realism and fantasy when she took the insides of her body out, and presented them as symbols of feeling.

Frida's literal, ferocious use of the extracted heart as a symbol for pain in love in *Memory* and in other works is not so grotesque when understood in the context of Mexican culture. It is, for example, as naïvely straightforward as the manner in which pain is symbolized in such Mexican colonial paintings as the famous *Polyptych of Death*, in which an anonymous painter illustrated the verse "God will not despise a penitent and humble heart" by showing clerics grinding their own extracted hearts in a huge mortar, and pictured the command "crush your heart and bear upon it" with an angel squashing a human heart in a press. In modern Mexico, as in colonial times, the Sacred Heart, often girdled with a crown of thorns or otherwise wounded and bleeding, appears in myriad forms, from the silver hearts that are pinned on the velvet skirts of wooden Christs, to red silk cushions in the shape of hearts, to paintings in which the Sacred Heart is laced with veins, crowned with thorns, and sometimes either bursts with flames symbolizing religious fervor or sprouts foliage from the severed artery at the top. Frida herself had a pillowcase embroidered with cupids holding a sacred heart and the words "Wake Up Sleeping Heart," and these are exactly the kinds of images she drew upon for *Memory*, where her heart is broken, her body is armless, and her psyche is divided into three people, none of whom is complete.

When in the following year Frida painted the similarly bloody self-portrait called *Remembrance of an Open Wound*, her wounds were still not healed, but her attitude toward them had changed (figure 40; *Remembrance* was destroyed in a fire, but it is recorded in a black-and-white photograph). As in *A Few Small Nips*, sex and painful wounds are linked with humor—Edgar Kaufmann, Jr., who purchased the painting for his father, remembers that it had "lyrical bright Mexican colors: pink, red, orange, black; you somehow felt that pain and joy were indistinguishable." As in *Memory*, physical wounds allude to psychological ones. But now Frida seems almost brazen and perverse in the way she sits with her legs apart and pulls up the white ruffle of her Tehuana skirt in order to display two wounds, one her bandaged foot propped on a stool, the other a long gash on her inner thigh. This "open" wound—an invented one—drips blood onto the white petticoat. Next to the gash lies a leafy plant, possibly a reference to the link Frida saw between her own blood and wounds and the idea of fertility, a connection first set forth in *Frida and the Abortion*. The thigh wound is intended as an allusion to her genitals conceived as a sexual wound or as the real wound in her vagina caused by the metal rod that pierced her pelvic region during the accident. She candidly told male friends that the way she placed her right hand beneath her skirt and near her sex in the painting was meant to show that she was masturbating. Even so, Frida looks straight out at the spectator, totally unabashed.

The period when she painted *Memory* and *Remembrance* was a relatively happy one for Frida. But she had had to be the conquistador of happiness, slaying pain and trampling troubles that lay in her path. While *Memory* reveals how the hurt of Diego and Cristina's affair led eventually to the emergence of a more independent, stronger woman—one who gained strength by stating her vulnerability—*Remembrance* shows that Frida transformed the "open wound" of jealousy and betrayal into a different kind of openness. She is the sexually free woman, a dauntless flirt, and for all her apparent intentness—her insistence on her suffering—she is a little insouciant. As she stares at us, nearly smiling, it is as if she were about to wink.

Chapter 13

Trotsky

JUST AS THE ACCIDENT transformed Frida from a madcap girl into a young woman with a deep vein of melancholy as well as a ferocious will to combat sadness, Rivera's affair with Cristina changed her from an adoring bride into a more complex woman, one who could no longer even pretend to be a pretty appendage to her more "important" spouse; she had to learn to be—or to pretend to be—her own source, autonomous. Of course, she kept on shining and reflecting in the dazzle and glow of Diego's orbit, making her husband happy; but more and more, the light that attracted people to Frida was her own.

The Riveras' curious relationship of independence and interdependence was symbolized by the two houses in which they lived, and by the bridge that linked the dwellings to each other. Both houses belonged to Diego. But when Frida was angry at him, she could lock the door on her end of the bridge, forcing him to go downstairs, cross the yard, and knock on her front door. There, as often as not, he would be told by a servant that his wife refused to receive him. Huffing and puffing, Rivera would climb his stairs, cross the bridge again, and through Frida's closed door, plead for forgiveness.

Diego provided the money; Frida managed it. Rivera took no interest in finances, leaving large checks in payment to him in unopened letters for years. When reprimanded, he would counter, *"Demasiado moles-tia"* (Too much bother). He spent money when he felt like it, and though his and Frida's life style was relatively modest, their expenses were enormous. A river of money flowed out in payment for the pre-Columbian idols Diego kept adding to his collection. "Frida used to scold me sometimes for not keeping enough money to buy such prosaic things as underwear," Diego said, but, he added, collecting was "worth it." Rivera also was generous in his support of leftist political organizations, and of his own and his wife's families. Another great expense, of course, was Frida's medical bills. "There were times," Diego once complained, when her medical expenses "virtually bankrupted me."

Frida did her best to keep costs down, scrupulously recording expenditures in an account book, which is now displayed in the Frida Kahlo Museum. She was responsible for all the household expenses, including items like house paint, plaster, and servants' wages. It was never easy. Cash came and went in mysterious ways, and she was often flat broke. From 1935 to 1946 she kept an account with Alberto Misrachi, a charming and literate man who owned one of the best bookshops in Mexico City and whom she painted in 1937. He and his wife, Anita, were good friends; he served as the Riveras' dealer, their accountant, and their banker as well. A typical message from Frida reads: "Albertito, I am going to ask you the favor of advancing me next week's money, because I have none left from this week." Or:

I am going to ask you the favor of advancing me next week's money, since from this week not one penny remains, since I paid you the 50 that I owed you, 50 to Adriana, 25 that I gave to Diego for Sunday's outing and 50 to Cristi, and I ended up like the bear. [She refers to bears trained to dance with tambourines to earn a few coins for their masters.]

I did not ask Diego for the check because it pained me to bother him since he is very irritated about money but since in any case you would have to give me the week's money on Saturday, I preferred to ask you for it, and you will not give me money on Saturday but instead not until the following week. Do you agree? Of the $200.00 please take the 10 that I owe Anita and pay them to her for me, since she lent them to me on Friday at Santa Anita. (Don't forget to give them to her, since she'll say that I am very ratty if I don't pay them back.)

Thank you for the favor and lots of love.

In other notes she said she needed money for a hospital bill, for rent, for Diego's expenses, for masons, for house paint, for the moving of Diego's idols, for the materials used in the construction of the little pyramid that served as a pedestal for pre-Columbian sculptures in the garden at Coyoacán. Another time she wanted to buy two parakeets, and once she had to pay for a Tehuana costume. "Albertito," she wrote, "The carrier of this note is a lady who sold Diego a Tehuana dress for me. Diego was supposed to pay for it today, but since he went to Metepec with . . . some *Gringachos* [a slightly more pejorative version of "Gringos"], I forgot to ask him for the pennies early enough and he left me without a dime. In a word, it is a question of paying this lady $100.00 (one hundred pesos) and putting them on the account of Diego, keeping this letter as a receipt." The arrangement with Misrachi may have been casual, but it worked.

When all was well between Frida and Diego, the day usually began with a long, late breakfast in Frida's house, during which they read the mail and sorted out their plans—who would need the chauffeur, which meals they would eat together, who was expected for lunch. After breakfast, Diego would go to his studio; occasionally he would disappear on sketching trips to the countryside, from which he would not return until late at night. (Sometimes such trips were Diego's way of showing his boundless hospitality to female tourists who were "fascinated" to see the environs of Mexico City in the company of the great Mexican master.)

Occasionally after breakfast, Frida would go upstairs to her studio, but she did not paint consistently, and weeks went by when she did not work at all; in 1936 she completed, as far as we know, only two paintings, *My Parents, My Grandparents and I* and a self-portrait (now lost) that was to have been a gift for Dr. Eloesser. More often, once the affairs of the household had been settled, the chauffeur would drive her into the center of Mexico City to spend the day with a friend. Or she might join a friend for an excursion, as she put it, "to some little village where there is nothing but Indians, tortillas and beans and lots of flowers and plants and rivers."

Frida frequently visited with her sisters Adriana and Matilde but it was Cristina whom she saw most often. By the time in 1935 when she returned to San Angel, Frida had forgiven Cristina, as perhaps she would never totally forgive Diego, for their liaison, and her younger sister became once more her chief companion, her ally in adventure and solace in pain. When Frida needed a confidante or an alibi, Cristina was ready; when Frida was to undergo surgery, she always insisted on holding Cristina's hand while the chloroform mask was placed on her face.

Together with her offspring, Cristina became so much a part of the Rivera household that her daughter Isolda's recollection is that "Always, from the age of four on, I lived with Diego and Frida." Frida was the perfect aunt, showering her niece and nephew with love and presents and helping to pay for schools as well as music and dancing lessons. They returned her love. In 1940, Frida placed Isolda and Antonio among her closest companions in *The Wounded Table* (figure 55), and when she was away they wrote her loving letters full of little drawings of lovebirds labeled "Frida" and "Diego" and hearts pierced by arrows and bleeding into a chalice. Isolda's letters are particularly coquettish. "Frida. How are you, I want you to tell me the truth do you love me or not, answer me please. . . . one never forgets in all one's life a person as pretty as you, precious, lovely, enchanting, my life my love I give to you."

Indeed, Cristina and Cristina's children came to represent for Frida both family and the familiar world of her own childhood. Whereas the adolescent Frida had complained that Coyoacán was a sleepy, boring "village" with nothing to offer except "pasture and pasture, Indians and Indians and huts and huts," the adult Frida now saw that world as a refuge from the demands of Diego and his high-powered entourage. At least, that is the way she painted it in *My Parents, My Grandparents and I.* At twenty-eight or nine, Frida clearly relished her familial roots and the remembered contentment of being enclosed in the patio of her Coyoacán home.

The Riveras' home in San Angel was, by contrast, a mecca for the international intelligentsia. Writers, painters, photographers, musicians, actors, refugees, political activists, and people with money to spend on art all found their way to the pink and blue houses on the corner of Palmas and Altavista. John Dos Passos and Waldo Frank were among the foreign visitors who sought out the Riveras. Among their fellow countrymen, they could count as friends such people as

President Lázaro Cárdenas, the photographer Manuel Alvarez Bravo, and the beautiful film star Dolores del Rio. Although Rivera's fame made some of Mexico's other celebrities jealous, most of them delight in their memories of Diego and Frida, who, in her Tehuana finery, presided over the heterogeneous but generally bohemian milieu. Often there was a festive midday *comida* which took place in Rivera's pink house at a long table covered with flowers, fruit, and earthenware crockery. Marjorie Eaton, who went to Mexico at the Riveras' invitation in the fall of 1934, remembers: "I came for lunch, and a spider monkey promptly sat on my head and took the banana out of my hand. I had to balance the monkey, whose tail was around my neck, as I was show-ing my sketches."

The bold spider monkey, probably Fulang-Chang (meaning "any old monkey"), a great favorite of Diego's, was remembered by another frequent luncheon guest, Ella Wolfe, who had come to Mexico with her husband while he was working on *Portrait of Mexico* (a collabora-tion with Rivera) and on his biography of the muralist. The monkey, its long tail held high for equilibrium, would leap through an open window, jump on the dining table, pick out a piece of fruit from the bowl, and as if he thought his softhearted masters might try to repossess his loot, flee into the garden to hide and feast. Sometimes the Riveras' monkeys were not so nice. One had a crush on Rivera, and when a famous movie actress came to lunch she discovered, to her dismay, that monkeys are jealous creatures and are apt to bite their rivals. Rivera, ever pleased to be the recipient of love, thought the spat be-tween monkey and beauty queen hilarious.

In the evenings, Frida often went with friends to night spots in the center of the city, and her taste for the culture of *la raza* came out in her enthusiasm for the circus, street theater, movies, and boxing matches. Jean van Heijenoort, who became an intimate friend of Frida's in 1937, remembers that "some evenings, Frida and Cristina and I would go dancing at the Salón México, a popular working-class dancing place. I would dance with Cristina. Frida watched." Frida would sit and smile that mysterious, seductive half-smile, her feline eyes ab-sorbed in the sway and swirl of couples, the sweat of courtships, the thump, bounce, and cry of the popular music that inspired Aaron Cop-land's symphonic piece *El Salón México*.

Despite Lupe Marín's "memory" that, as a girl, Frida "drank tequila like a mariachi," it was probably at this time that she began to carry a little flask of cognac in her purse or hidden in her petticoats. Sometimes she carried liquor in a perfume bottle, which she whisked out from inside her blouse as if she wanted to douse herself with cologne, downing a swig so quickly that most people did not notice what she was doing. It was generally held that "Frida could drink any man under the table," and various of Dr. Eloesser's letters to her contain affectionate admonitions to cut down on alcohol. She had given up her "cocktailitos," she would reply, and was drinking only a daily beer. To Ella Wolfe, who believes her to have been an alcoholic, she wrote (in 1938): "You can tell Boit [Bert], that I am now behaving reasonably well in the sense that I do not drink so many *copiosas* [copious ones, huge goblets] . . . tears . . . of Cognac, Tequila, etc. . . . this I consider to be another advance toward the liberation of . . . the oppressed classes. I drank, because I wanted to drown my sorrows, but now the damned things have learned to swim, and now decency and good behavior weary me!"

As Frida drank, her behavior became more and more "indecent," and less and less bourgeois. She adopted the mannerisms of what she saw as the true people of Mexico, the *pelados* (penniless Indians or city bums), peppering her speech with popularisms and four-letter words—*groserías*—that she picked up in the marketplace. She was not unique in this: Mexican women from the art or literary world bent on being as colloquially Mexican as possible often use foul language. But Frida used it with a special exuberance and biting wit. And, as with many of her compatriots, wild conviviality and laughter frequently carried a flip side of loneliness and the fatalistic acknowledgment of poverty and death: expressions that burst frequently from her lips, like *hijo de la madre chingada,* or *pendejo* or *cabrón,* have a kind of violence to them, a mixture of joy and despair, and a defiant affirmation of the curser's pride in being Mexican.

Increasingly during the months that followed her return to San Angel, Frida became Diego's *compañera* and his helpmeet. She indulged him, nursed him when he was ill, fought with him, punished him, and loved him. He supported her, took pride in her accomplishments, respected her opinions, loved her—and continued to philander. And now, increasingly, so did she. As often as not, when Frida took the car for the day, it was to keep a rendezvous with a lover, male or female.

Frida's homosexuality, which had caused a trauma when it began during her last year at the National Preparatory School, had reemerged after she entered Diego's bohemian, freethinking world, where love affairs between women were common and condoned. Men had their *casa chica,* women had each other. In these circumstances, Frida felt no shame about her bisexuality. Neither did Diego. Lucienne Bloch remembers the morning in Detroit when, dawdling over Sunday breakfast, Rivera suddenly astonished Lucienne by pointing to Frida and saying, "You know Frida is homosexual, don't you?" The only one who was embarrassed was Lucienne. Frida just laughed as Diego went on to tell how she had teased and flirted with Georgia O'Keeffe at Stieglitz's gallery and how he believed that "women were more civilized and sensitive than men because men were simpler sexually." Men's sexual organ was "just in one place," said Rivera. Women's, on the other hand, was "all over the body, and therefore two women together would have a much more extraordinary experience."

"Frida had many girl friends and lesbian friends," recalls Jean van Heijenoort. "Her lesbianism did not make her masculine. She was a kind of ephebe, boyish and emphatically feminine at the same time."

As does everything else in her intimate life, Frida's lesbianism appears in her art. But not overtly. Along with self-love and psychic duality, it is suggested in her double self-portraits, and it emerges in many of her paintings as a kind of atmosphere, a sensuality so deep that it was stripped of the conventional sexual polarities, a hunger for intimacy so urgent that it ignored gender. Like Picasso, who is reported to have said that the intensity of his friendship with the poet Max Jacob made him able to imagine making love to him in order to know him more completely, Frida, when she loved someone, wanted the absolute connection of physical union. Thus when, in 1939, she painted a pair of loving women in *Two Nudes in a Forest* (figure 53)— the same light- and dark-skinned women who ride a sponge in the 1938 painting *What the Water Gave Me* (figure 50)—they could easily represent herself and a woman she loved. She has placed them outside the realms of time, space, and convention, bordered on one side by a lush jungle from which they are watched by a spider monkey (symbol of lust) whose tail wraps around coiling, twisting branches, and on the other by a precipice where roots protrude from the earth as if from a freshly dug grave. In such inhospitable terrain the women cling to each other. One is a seated guardian figure; she wears a red shawl as if she were an Indian Madonna. According to Dolores del Rio, to whom the painting was a gift, "the indigenous nude is solacing the white nude. The dark one is stronger." Yet it is from the tip of the dark woman's red shawl that drops of blood (symbol of the woman's or her people's suffering) fall into the fissured Mexican earth.

Rivera actually encouraged Frida's homosexual affairs, some say because he knew that as an older man he could not (or did not want to) satisfy his much younger wife. Others say he wanted to keep her occupied so that he could be free. Jean van Heijenoort surmises that "he considered Frida's lesbian affairs a sort of safety valve." He adds: "Frida did not tell me if Diego fulfilled her sexually. She talked about their relationship, but not about that. But there is no question that she had very strong sexual needs. Once she told me that her view of life was 'Make love, take a bath, make love again.' It was in her nature."

Frida's powerful sexual appetite—both homo- and heterosexual—expressed itself in an unmistakable aura that fairly radiates from the surfaces of all of her paintings. It permeates the more visceral of her still lifes, and is the principal subject of works like the 1944 panel *Flower of Life* (figure 64) and another, from 1947, *Sun and Life* (plate XXXII). It is, of course, difficult to locate the precise source of this sexual energy; it resides, perhaps, in the paintings' strange, dense atmosphere, in their vibrancy and magnetism. Even her most innocent self-portraits have a peculiar electric charge that makes viewers pause in front of them in the same way that passersby were attracted to Frida's vital presence. Another part of the sexual charge lies in Frida's face—her penetrating, devouring glance beneath those hairy eyebrows, her carnal lips beneath a slight mustache. And, friends have noted, Frida's most passionate love affair was with herself. Indeed there is a strong element of self-fascinated autoeroticism in her display of wounds in paintings like *Remembrance of an Open Wound* and in later wounded self-portraits.

Until late in her life, when her physical frailty made heterosexual intercourse difficult, Frida in fact preferred men to women, and she took many as lovers. But although Rivera believed in free love for himself and was cavalier about the openness with which he carried on, he did not, in spite of his general lack of *macho* attitudes and his great admiration for women, tolerate his wife's heterosexual affairs. Those she had to hide, carefully locking the door to the bridge that led to Diego's house, or arranging a tryst at Cristina's home in Coyoacán. Her husband, she warned her lovers, was perfectly capable of murder.

One of the intrepid men who ignored the warnings and fell in love with Frida at this time was the sculptor Isamu Noguchi, whose great talents were even then recognized in New York art circles. Ebullient, charming, exceptionally handsome, he came to Mexico in 1935 with the help of a Guggenheim grant, the loan of Buckminster Fuller's car (a Hudson), and the prospect of a commission to do a relief mural at the Abelardo L. Rodríguez Market in Mexico City—a site where a number of other muralists were at work on other walls. Eight months later, he had completed a mural in polychrome cement and carved brick.

Given the small size of the Mexican art world in those days, it was inevitable that Noguchi and Frida would meet. When they did, Noguchi was immediately enchanted. "I loved her very much," he said. "She was a lovely person, absolutely marvelous person. Since Diego was well known to be a lady chaser, she cannot be blamed if she saw some men. . . . In those days we all sort of, more or less, horsed around, and Diego did and so did Frida. It wasn't quite acceptable to him, however. I used to have assignations with her here and there. One of the places was her sister Cristina's place, the blue house in Coyoacán.

"Cristina I liked very much. She was smaller than Frida and had charming green eyes. She was more sort of normal. Cristina hadn't got that fire of Frida. We got along very well, all three of us. I knew Frida well during an eight-month period. We went dancing all the time. Frida loved to dance. That was her passion, you know, everything that she couldn't do she loved to do. It made her absolutely furious to be unable to do things."

Noguchi and Frida's romance sometimes smacked of a French bedroom farce. The two were planning, says Marjorie Eaton, to take an apartment together as a rendezvous spot. The lovers even ordered a set of furniture for the place, but it did not arrive, because the man who was supposed to deliver it assumed that the furniture was for Frida and Diego, and took it upon himself to go to San Angel to present Rivera with the bill. "That," says Marjorie Eaton, "was the end of the romance between Frida and Noguchi."

Others say the affair had a different, equally comic end. When Rivera discovered it, he was so enraged that he sped to the Coyoacán house, where the lovers were in bed. Frida's *mozo* (houseboy), Chucho, warned his mistress of Diego's arrival. Noguchi threw on his clothes, but one of the hairless dogs pounced upon a sock and ran off with it.

Noguchi, deciding that the better part of valor was discretion, abandoned the sock, scrambled up the orange tree in the patio, and fled over the roof. Of course, Diego found the sock and did what Mexican *machos* are supposed to do under such circumstances. As Noguchi tells it: "Diego came by with a gun. He always carried a gun. The second time he displayed his gun to me was in the hospital. Frida was ill for some reason, and I went there, and he showed me his gun and said: 'Next time I see you, I'm going to shoot you!' "

Those days, Rivera often used his gun as a sort of emotional equalizer, brandishing it in defense not only of his *macho* pride but of his political ego as well. Although the political climate in Mexico had swung to the left with the election of Lázaro Cárdenas in 1934 (Cárdenas ejected Calles from Mexico in April 1936, set Mexico back on the road to land and labor reforms, and in 1938 nationalized the oil industry, expropriating numerous foreign investments), Rivera was still under attack by the Communist party. If anything, the attacks had become even more intense, for as early as 1933, when Leon Trotsky, having become convinced that it was impossible to stay in the same international as Stalin, began to form the Fourth International, Diego had declared his sympathies with the Trotskyite movement. And although he did not officially join the Mexican section of Trotsky's party until 1936, he had painted Trotsky's portrait in New York City's Trotskyite headquarters, and had added a portrait of him to the second version of the Rockefeller Center mural at the Palace of Fine Arts. (Trotsky helps to support a banner inscribed with the words: "Workers of the world/ Unite in the IVth International!") Rivera came to agree with Trotsky that the rise of bureaucracy in the Soviet Union was harmful, and like Trotsky he was a champion of revolutionary internationalism as opposed to Stalin's doctrine of "socialism in a single country." No doubt, he had a special sympathy for the heroic figure of the exiled leader because he himself felt exiled from and outraged by the pro-Stalin Mexican Communist party.

The conflict between Trotskyites and Stalinists in Mexico—as everywhere else in the Western world—was virulent and violent. Battles between politicized artists were the talk of the town. Orthodox Communists not only reviled Rivera for his Trotskyism; since it was political, they stepped up their "criticism" of his art as well. He painted in palaces and he painted for gringo tourists: What kind of revolutionary, they asked, was that?

Rivera decided to tell his side of the story at a conference on progressive education at the Palace of Fine Arts that began on August 26, 1935. His lecture, entitled "The Arts and Their Revolutionary Role in Culture," was well received. The following afternoon, Siqueiros, passionately committed to Stalin's version of communism, read a paper on the Mexican mural movement, including a scathing attack on Rivera's role in it. Siqueiros's vehemence demanded no less from Diego. He leaped to his feet and shouted his denial of all Siqueiros's accusations. The congress's chairman, also at that time head of the Department of Fine Arts, reprimanded Diego; this was a conference, he said, not a debate. But Rivera pulled his pistol from his hip pocket, waved it in the air, and demanded equal time. The chairman conceded; a duel of words between Rivera and Siqueiros was scheduled for the following afternoon.

The next day, theatrically late, Rivera pressed through the crowd that had come to hear the debate and joined Siqueiros on a balcony overlooking the stage. Surveying the audience battling for seats, he requested and was given a larger hall. Once again the crowds scrambled for seats. When the adversaries finally spoke, the event quickly became dull and bland; it terminated with a tedious discussion of what percentage of his work each artist sold to tourists. By this time, the audience was restless. People snickered, harumphed, and yawned. Frida, furious with anyone she thought behaved with disrespect toward Diego, kept whirling around in her seat and glaring at offenders.

After the last of the audience had straggled out, there was a final confrontation, which was recorded (slightly sanitized) for posterity in the Communist journal *New Masses* by the "victim," Emanuel Eisenberg. According to Eisenberg, Frida stormed up to him and enigmatically shrieked: "See a crowd?" Eisenberg was bewildered, all the more so when she slapped him across the mouth. "He's been laughing at me all evening!" she screamed. "Every time I turn my head! These bastard gringos come down from that ——— country for nothing else than to make fun of us here!" Rivera, seizing the occasion for chivalry and revenge, tore up the stairs and swung twice at the writer's jaw. Friends dragged him away and he left, shouting, "He's a son-of-a-bitch Stalinist!" But at least this time he did not pull a gun.

Although Frida shared Diego's enthusiasm for Trotsky, she never became a member of the Trotskyite party; in Mexico, it consisted of a few intellectuals and people involved in trade union life and was too small and too poor to be something one could join without working actively for it. But the Spanish Civil War, which broke out on July 18, 1936, mobilized her political conscience. In her view, the Spanish Republic's struggle against Franco's revolt signified "the liveliest and strongest hope to smash fascism in the world." Together with other Loyalist sympathizers, she and Diego formed a committee to raise money for a group of Spanish militiamen who had come to Mexico seeking economic aid. She herself was part of the "Commission of the Exterior"; it was her job to contact people and organizations outside Mexico in order to raise funds. "What I would like to do," she wrote to Dr. Eloesser on December 17, 1936,

would be to go to Spain, since I believe that it is now the center of all the most interesting things that are happening in the world. . . . The welcome that all the Mexican workers organizations gave this group of young militiamen has been the most enthusiastic thing. They have succeeded in getting many of them to vote to give one day's salary to help the Spanish comrades, and you cannot imagine the emotion it causes to see the sincerity and enthusiasm with which the poorest organizations of *campesinos* and workers, making a true sacrifice (since you very well know the miserable conditions in which these people live in the little towns), have given nevertheless a whole day's wages for those who are now fighting in Spain against the fascist bandits. . . . I have already written to New York, and to other places, and I think I will obtain help, which, even if it is small, will mean at least food or clothing for some children of workers who are fighting on the front at this moment. I would like to ask you to do whatever possible to make propaganda among friends in San Francisco.

Frida's engagement in the political ferment both focused her energies and brought her closer to Diego. And he needed her help. In 1936 and 1937, eye and kidney problems kept him hospitalized for weeks at a time, while her health, except for her foot (she had another operation on it in 1936), was good. When she wrote to thank Dr. Eloesser for his support of her cause on January 5, 1937, she wrote from the sanatorium where she was staying to keep Diego company: "I try to help him as best I can but nevertheless, no matter how much good will I have about trying to partially alleviate his problems, my help is not enough. . . . I would like to write you a long letter with personal things about me and Diego, but you can't imagine how much time I spend [she refers to her work for the Spanish militiamen], one could almost say that it's a miracle if we succeed in sleeping four or five hours." In her next letter to Eloesser (January 30, 1937), she said: "I have worked very hard and tried to help him [Diego] in every way I could while he is in bed, but as you know he is desperate when he doesn't work and nothing makes him adjust to it."

By December 19, 1936, when Leon and Natalia Trotsky boarded the oil tanker *Ruth* in Oslo, bound for Mexico, Trotsky had spent nine long years in exile. Expelled from Moscow by decision of the Fifteenth Congress of the Bolshevik Party, he had lived in Alma-Ata, a city in eastern Soviet Central Asia, until 1929, when he was deported from Russia. He had moved to the island of Prinkipo, off the coast of Turkey, then in 1933 to France and finally to Norway. During all those years, he had never lost faith in the idea that he was destined to change the world, and he had worked tirelessly toward that goal. But when Norway, too, under economic pressure from the Soviet Union (the Russians threatened to cancel their large imports of Norwegian herring), decided to send him on his way, and as country after country rejected his petition for asylum, he and Trotskyites everywhere came close to despair.

So it was that on November 21, Rivera, who had joined the Mexican section of the (Trotskyite) International Communist League in September, received an urgent cable from Anita Brenner in New York saying that it was a matter of life or death to know immediately whether the Mexican government would grant Trotsky asylum. The political bureau of the Mexican section of the league met at once. Rivera and Octavio Fernández, a leader of the Mexican Trotskyite group, were secretly dispatched to see President Cárdenas, who was at the moment in the north of Mexico overseeing his land distribution program at La Laguna. When they arrived at Torreón, Rivera presented the petition for Trotsky's asylum in his own name, and Cárdenas granted it, provided that Trotsky would pledge not to interfere in the internal affairs of Mexico.

The *Ruth* arrived in the harbor of Tampico on the morning of January 9, 1937. Natalia Trotsky, made wary from months of being surrounded by guards and years of living with the constant threat of assassination by Stalin's agents, was afraid to leave the boat. Trotsky told the police that he and his wife would not disembark unless they saw the faces of friends. Just as they were about to be forcibly deposited on shore, a government cutter approached carrying a welcoming party consisting of some familiar faces—Max Shachtman (a founder of the American Trotskyite movement) and George Novak (secretary of the American Committee for the Defense of Leon Trotsky)—as well as local and federal authorities, Mexican and foreign journalists, and Frida Kahlo. Frida had come to represent her husband, who to his fury missed the Russian revolutionary's arrival because he was still hospitalized. It would have been a moment of triumph for Rivera; as Trotsky was to acknowledge: "It was to him above all that we were indebted for our liberation from captivity in Norway." Satisfied that they were in safe hands, Trotsky and Natalia walked down the wooden pier to freedom. He, wearing tweed knickerbockers and a cap, and carrying a briefcase and a cane, walked with his chin held high, his stride that of a proud soldier. She, a little dowdy in a suit and looking worn and worried, watched her feet so as not to trip on the rough planks of the narrow dock. Just behind them walked Frida, lithe and exotic in her *rebozo* and long skirt. "After four months of imprisonment and isolation," Trotsky wrote, "this meeting with friends was especially cordial."

A special train called "El Hidalgo" (the nobleman) was sent by Cárdenas to carry the party to the capital. To protect Trotsky from GPU agents, it left Tampico in secrecy at ten at night, and on January 11 arrived at Lechería, a small station on the outskirts of Mexico City. In the predawn darkness, at a nearby restaurant, Rivera (temporarily released from the hospital for the occasion) and other members of the Mexican Trotskyite group joined forces with various government officials and police to form a welcoming party. Meanwhile at the Riveras' San Angel home, a number of people gathered to give the impression that Trotsky was expected to arrive there, and at Mexico City's main railroad station, fake welcomers milled about with ostentatious expectancy.

The retinue at Lechería station had a long wait before a column of smoke appeared in the distance, and the rumble of the oncoming train was heard. In spite of all the red herrings, reporters and photographers, including Agustín Victor Casasola (1874–1938), the great photojournalist of the Mexican Revolution (or one of his associates in the family-run business), were there to catch the moment when Trotsky,

Natalia, and Frida descended from the train. Trotsky embraced Rivera, and together with Natalia was driven quickly by way of side streets to the blue house in Coyoacán, where he was to live rent-free for the next two years. (Cristina had recently moved a few blocks away to a house on Aguayo Street, probably purchased for her by Rivera. Guillermo Kahlo went to live with Adriana, keeping a room in the house he had built in which to store his photographic equipment.) The Trotsky party arrived at noon. Already the house was surrounded by a police guard.

One hour later Jean van Heijenoort found his way to Coyoacán. The tall, blond Frenchman, trained as a mathematician, had served as Trotsky's secretary since 1932, and after learning that Mexico would grant his mentor asylum, had come to Mexico City by way of New York. Inside the blue house he found Frida and Diego busy installing their guests. Rivera, always thrilled by danger, whether real or imagined, was solicitous about the details of Trotsky's safety. Since neither Trotsky nor Natalia spoke Spanish, Frida was to be their principal adviser and escort; Cristina would sometimes serve as chauffeur. Trustworthy servants were essential, and Frida had arranged for several of her own to serve her guests. As a security measure, the windows of the house that looked out on the street were filled in with adobe bricks, and Trotskyite party members were to do their bit by spelling the police guard and standing vigil at night. Later, when there was suspicion that the house might be attacked from the house next door, Diego did not hesitate or fuss about ways to strengthen the wall that divided his and his neighbor's gardens. In a typically grand and generous gesture, he simply purchased the adjacent lot, evicted the neighbor, and hired workmen to connect the two properties—a move that made it possible, in the 1940s, to expand the garden of the Coyoacán house and to add a new wing with a studio for Frida.

The Trotskys were in high spirits, relieved to be out of immediate danger, pleased with the blue house, the patio filled with plants, the spacious, airy rooms decorated with popular and pre-Columbian art and numerous paintings. "We were on a new planet in Rivera's house," Natalia wrote.

The house must have seemed a "new planet" to Guillermo Kahlo too. "Who are these people?" he asked his daughter. "Who is Trotsky?" Frida told him that Trotsky was the creator of the Russian army, the man who had made the October Revolution, the companion of Lenin.

"Ah," said Kahlo. "How strange!" Later, he called Frida over and said, "You esteem this person, don't you? I want to talk to him. I want to advise him not to get involved with politics. Politics are very bad."

Bad or not, Trotsky did not let up the pace of his political activity. He went to work immediately, and on January 25, two weeks after his arrival, *Time* magazine could print: "At latest reports, Host Diego Rivera had had to return to a hospital with a kidney ailment; Mrs. Trotsky had gone to bed with what seemed to be a recurrence of her malaria; Guest Trotsky respectfully watched and waited on by dark-eyed young Hostess Rivera, had resumed dictation to his secretaries of his monumental Biography of Lenin begun nearly two years ago." Trotsky also asked for the formation of an international commission to examine the evidence used against him at the Moscow trials, and worked furiously to prepare his deposition.

The commission consisted of six Americans, one Frenchman, two Germans, an Italian, and a Mexican. The American educator and philosopher John Dewey served as chairman. To make ready for the hearings, the Coyoacán house was transformed. A six-foot barricade of bricks and sandbags was built overnight to further protect the largest room in the house, where the sessions were to be held. Forty seats were arranged for journalists and invited guests. A long table was set up, behind which sat Trotsky, Natalia, Trotsky's secretary, and members of the commission. Supplementary police watched for assassins and saboteurs.

The first of the Dewey Commission's thirteen sessions took place on April 10, 1937, and the "trial" lasted a week. Diego Rivera attended wearing a wide-brimmed hat decked with a peacock feather. Frida, arrayed in Tarascan jewelry and Indian costumes, sat as close as possible to Trotsky, who answered his interrogators with his usual precision and with a sure command of the enormous amount of information that he had gathered to discredit his accusers. At the end, exhausted but exhilarated, he closed his defense with this flourish: "The experience of my life, in which there has been no lack either of success or of failures, has not only not destroyed my faith in the clear, bright future of mankind, but, on the contrary, has given it an indestructible temper. This faith in reason, in truth, in human solidarity, which at the age of eighteen I took with me into the workers' quarters of the provincial Russian town of Nikolayev—this faith I have preserved fully and completely. It has become more mature, but not less ardent."

Dewey's response was exactly right: "Anything I can say will be an anticlimax." In September the commission handed down its verdict: Trotsky had demonstrated his innocence beyond the least suspicion of a doubt.

During the months following the "trial," the Riveras and their guests saw much of each other. Although both Rivera and Trotsky were obsessive workers, with little time for social life, the two couples ate together often, and they went on picnics and excursions to places near Mexico City, Trotsky collecting different species of cactus that he found in the countryside and carrying enormous specimens, roots and all, home with him in Rivera's car. He was given the use of a house in Taxco, an extravagantly picturesque silver mining town high in the mountains south of Cuernavaca, and every so often he and his entourage went there for a week or so. Exhilarated with the freedom, Trotsky would ride his horse furiously over the steep rocky terrain, worrying his companions, who could not keep up. When Frida and Diego visited him there, Diego spent his days painting tree trunks shaped like women, a rather forced attempt to inject surrealism into his vision of Mexico. Because of her *"maldita pata"* (damned paw), Frida spent her time chatting and drinking cognac while watching the hubbub of balloon and ice cream vendors, children and old women, in the central plaza.

No matter how long or well he knew a person, Trotsky always kept a certain guarded formality. Yet with the Riveras he was unusually friendly and relaxed. Diego was the one person who could visit Trotsky at any time without making an appointment, and he was one of the few people whom Trotsky received without having a third person present. A highly methodical man, Trotsky apportioned certain activities to certain hours during each day. Rivera was the opposite, and for a period of time, the Russian's relationship with him broke the confines of his rigidity. For his part, Diego admired Trotsky's courage and moral authority, and respected his discipline and commitment. In Trotsky's presence, he tried to bridle his compulsion to fantasize, and made an effort to rein in his anarchical ways.

"If they were together," Jean van Heijenoort recalls, "Diego might dominate the talk, and then Trotsky would take the floor. They would talk mostly about Mexican politicians, and Diego had a very penetrating mind for people, for what a person really was. That was a bit different from Trotsky, who always interpreted things in terms of tendencies, left-right, all that—abstract concepts. Trotsky enjoyed this side of Diego, and Diego's insights were helpful to Trotsky." In addition, Trotsky was pleased to have the world-famous muralist within the ranks of the Fourth International. In a *Partisan Review* article entitled "Arts and Politics" (published in August–September 1938), he extolled Rivera as the "greatest interpreter" of the October Revolution. A mural by Rivera was, Trotsky wrote, "not simply a 'painting,' an object of passive aesthetic contemplation, but a living part of the class struggle."

For all his years, the Russian's physical presence was impressive. He carried himself like a hero. His gestures were dynamic, his stride military. Piercing blue eyes behind round tortoise-shell glasses and a firmly set jaw transmitted intellectual fervor and tenacity, and although he had humor, there was about him a certain commanding severity. He was a man used to getting his way.

He was also a man with a vigorous interest in sex. Around women, Trotsky became especially animated and witty, and though his opportunities were few, his success seems to have been considerable. His was not a romantic or sentimental approach; it was direct and sometimes even crude. He would fondle a woman's knee under the table, or make an unabashedly forthright proposition. At one point, his lust for Cristina led him to plan a kind of fire drill, a practice escape over the garden wall at night plus a dash to Cristina's house on Aguayo Street. Only the expressed misgivings of his entourage and possibly Cristina's own fond but firm disinterest finally dissuaded him from this reckless adventure.

While his mane of white hair and his even whiter beard made her nickname him "Piochitas" (little goatee) and refer to him as *"el viejo"* (the old man), Trotsky's reputation as a revolutionary hero, his intellectual brilliance and force of character, attracted Frida. No doubt Rivera's obvious admiration for him fanned the flames: an affair with her husband's friend and political idol would be the perfect retaliation for Rivera's affair with her sister. In any case, Frida deployed all her considerable seductive powers to attract Trotsky, enhancing intimacy by speaking to him in English, which Natalia did not understand. "Frida did not hesitate to use the word 'love,'" Jean van Heijenoort recalls. "'All my love' were the words she used when she said goodbye to Trotsky."

Frida hardly needed to invent ploys to attract Trotsky. At twenty-nine, she was at that perfect moment when youthful prettiness merges with character to define a more compelling loveliness. What Trotsky saw when he met Frida was the woman she herself depicted in the March, 1937, self-portrait *Fulang-Chang and I* (plate XIII) and in *Escuincle Dog with Me* from the following year (figure 49; the painting is lost, but is documented in a photograph): a seductive young woman with a full face and sensuous lips. Her eyes are appraising, appealing, and wise, without the wariness that would fill them in later self-portraits. There is, however, a note of explosive but contained emotion, a mood of slightly perverse, even insolent, amusement in the way, for example, in *Fulang-Chang and I,* Frida's features "match" those of her pet—Frida always maintained that her paintings were full of humor, for those with the wit to see. Surely, as in both Western and Mayan tradition, the monkey is a symbol of lust or promiscuity. And in *Escuincle Dog with Me,* as in *Remembrance of an Open Wound,* Frida's pose, cigarette in hand, is deliberately provocative; there is something naked and yet absolutely self-contained in the unblinking, undeviating directness of her gaze; like the regard of certain animals and children, it makes the viewer feel naked too. From the evidence of these self-portraits it is perfectly clear that Frida is a woman who has loved and been loved by men.

Trotsky began writing letters and slipping them into books he had recommended to Frida. Then, often in the presence of Natalia and Rivera, he would hand Frida the book as she left the house. A few weeks after the end of the Dewey Commission sessions, the coy flirtation had become a full-fledged love affair. The couple met at Cristina's house on Aguayo Street.

Fortunately, Rivera was unaware of the liaison, but by the end of June, Natalia was jealous and deeply depressed. She had been married to Trotsky for thirty-five of her fifty-five years, and they had left their imprint: her wonderfully warm, intelligent face was creased by deep lines. Pathetically, she wrote in a note to her husband: "I saw myself in a mirror at Rita's, and found I look much older. Our inner state has an enormous importance in old age; it makes us look younger, it also makes us look older." Trotsky's entourage feared that if the affair was exposed, the scandal would discredit the Russian in the eyes of the world.

On July 7, Trotsky left the Coyoacán house and went to stay at a farm that was part of a large hacienda near San Miguel Regla, approximately eighty miles northeast of Mexico City. On July 11, Frida went with Lupe Marín's brother, Federico, to the hacienda to visit him. When Natalia learned about the trip, she wrote her husband a letter in which her injured feelings cry out between the lines. It seems that she herself had hoped to go as well, but thanks to deliberately poor communications between herself and the Riveras, she had been left behind. A few days later she received Trotsky's distinctly underplayed report on Frida's visit. He told her that he had just come back from fishing when

all of a sudden visitors arrived. Frida in the company of Marín and the aforementioned Gómez [nephew of the hacienda's owner]. Frida said you "could not" come. . . . The visitors (all three) had lunch with me, while drinking quite a bit and carrying on a lively conversation in Spanish (I took part whenever I could). After the meal Gómez took us all to see some old mines and the main farmhouse (state chambers, flower beds—a splendor!), on the way over we took a look at a basaltic canyon. . . . No conversations worthy of note took place, except what I was told about you. After a hastily drunk coffee, Frida and Marín left, to get back before dark (the road is bad). . . . Frida spoke "well" of you to me—she mentioned the concert, the movie; she was perhaps too "optimistic" in order to reassure me, nonetheless it seemed to me you are doing slightly better.

When Trotsky joined Natalia in Coyoacán for three days on July 15, he saw Frida and Diego as well, and immediately upon his return to the hacienda, he wrote to his wife:

Now, let me tell you about the visit. I was received by F. D. was in his studio, where a photographer was taking pictures of his paintings.
   The first thing I did was to ask permission to call you on the telephone. Meanwhile, F. sent for D. No sooner had I sat down, the telephone rang; it was Marín's wife, asking F. when she could find you at home (she wants to bring you flowers). . . . I was surprised how unpleasantly F. spoke with her. While we were waiting for D., F. told me that she was planning to go away. "Not to New York?" "No, I have no money for that; somewhere around Veracruz."
   D. arrived with a parrot on his head. We spoke standing up, because D. was anxious to leave. F. said something to D., who translated for

me with a smile: "She says if it were not so late she would accompany you as far as Pachuca and come back by bus." She had said nothing of the kind during the three minutes we were waiting for D. Why did she tell him that? He translated her words for me in a very friendly way. Excuse me for writing you all these details, but maybe they will interest you, at least a little.

Clearly Trotsky's affair with Frida was over. The next day Trotsky wrote: "I remembered that yesterday I did not even thank F. for her intention to accompany me and generally I behaved in a thoughtless manner. Today I wrote her and D. a few affable words." In this letter, and in others, he expressed the flood of love for Natalia that came over him after his break with Frida. "I love you so much, Nata, my only one, my eternal, my faithful, my love and my victim!"

Ella Wolfe believes that it was Frida, not Trotsky, who ended the affair, and that she probably did so during her visit to San Miguel Regla. From there, Trotsky wrote Frida a nine-page letter begging her not to break relations with him, and telling her how much she had meant to him during the weeks that they had been together. "It was a plea, the kind of plea that a young lover at the age of seventeen would make to somebody he loved, instead of a man in his sixties. He was truly infatuated with Frida, and she meant a great deal to him." Frida sent the letter to Ella, because, she said, it was so beautiful. Nevertheless, she ordered her friend to tear it up after reading it, and Ella did as she was told. *"Estoy muy cansada del viejo,"* Frida wrote. "I am very tired of the old man."

Flattered to be loved by the great Russian, fascinated by his mind, and moved by his desire, Frida was delighted to have an affair with Trotsky; but she did not love him. In the end, both of them retreated from what could only have led to disaster. "It was impossible to go on without committing themselves completely or without an incident with Natalia, Diego, or the GPU," says Jean van Heijenoort.

After Trotsky returned from the hacienda to Coyoacán on July 26, life in the blue house more or less returned to normal. But the delicate chemistry of relationships between the two couples had been subtly altered. Frida no longer flirted so flagrantly with Trotsky. There were no *sous-entendus,* no secret letters. The word "love" no longer was heard in their farewells. Trotsky and Frida became simply close friends. But lovers that become close friends always retain a little frisson of intimacy. In a film showing Trotsky, Natalia, Frida, Diego, Jean van Heijenoort, and others, taken in Coyoacán in 1938, Frida cuddles in Rivera's lap in such a kittenish way that one suspects her of trying to excite her former lover's jealousy. On her lips is the provocative half smile she wears in *Remembrance of an Open Wound.*

Months after their affair was over, on November 7, 1937, the anniversary of the Russian Revolution and also Trotsky's birthday, Frida gave her ex-lover a present. The gift was one of her most charming self-portraits (plate XII). Curiously, she presents herself to the revolutionary leader in the form of a colonial-style bourgeois or an aristocratic woman rather than as a Tehuana or a political activist. She stands like a prima donna between two curtains with all the poise of a Creole maiden, holding in her primly clasped hands a bouquet of flowers and a sheet of paper inscribed with the words: "For Leon Trotsky with all love I dedicate this painting on the 7th of November, 1937. Frida Kahlo in San Angel, Mexico."

She is dressed "fit to kill" in colonial jewelry and with a purple carnation and a red ribbon in her hair. Her lips are crimson, her cheeks are pink, and her nails are painted red. She has chosen the colors of her clothing with consummate skill—a salmon-pink skirt, an ocher *rebozo,* and a wine-colored blouse, all beautifully set off by the painting's olive-green background. The highly original mixture of colors suggests that Frida's color sense, like her subject matter, comes straight out of her life—out of the colors she actually wore. Indeed, her aesthetic finesse in art was part of the same impulse that made her take great care with clothing, interior decoration—even the laying of her table. The pink and green velvet frame that she chose for this self-portrait, for example, compliments the painting in the same way that her yellow shawl is becoming to Frida. It underscores her idea that there is no great division between a charming or pretty object and a work of art.

In her first *Self-Portrait,* offered to her first love when he rejected her, a winsome and pure Frida entreats him to return; the seductive, worldly Frida of the Trotsky portrait, having rejected her lover, now teases him by giving herself back to him in the form of a portrait. "I have for long admired the self-portrait by Frida Kahlo de Rivera that hangs on a wall of Trotsky's study," wrote the French Surrealist poet and essayist André Breton the following year. "She has painted herself dressed in a robe of wings gilded with butterflies, and it is exactly in this guise that she draws aside the mental curtain. We are privileged to be present, as in the most glorious days of German romanticism, at the entry of a young woman endowed with all the gifts of seduction, one accustomed to the society of men of genius." Thus Frida appears not only in the self-portrait dedicated to Trotsky but also in the more or less contemporaneous *Fulang-Chang and I, Escuincle Dog with Me,* and *Remembrance of an Open Wound.* Breton could have been describing these self-portraits when he wrote: "There is no art more exclusively feminine, in the sense that, in order to be as seductive as possible, it is only too willing to play alternately at being absolutely pure and absolutely pernicious. The art of Frida Kahlo is a ribbon about a bomb."

Chapter 14

A Painter in Her Own Right

AFTER FRIDA'S AFFAIR with Trotsky ended, the Riveras' life resumed the pattern, more or less settled and accepted, of shared activities and mutual autonomy. Both Frida and Diego worked and played hard. Their love affairs became more casual. Frida laughed at Diego's escapades, and pursued her own in secret. She began as well to take her professional life more seriously, painting in a more disciplined way and greatly improving her technical skills; between 1937 and 1938, she produced more paintings than she had done in all her previous eight years of marriage. Perhaps recognizing these changes, she confided to Lucienne Bloch in a letter dated February 14, 1938, that Trotsky's coming to Mexico was the best thing that ever happened in her life.

"Ella Darling," she wrote to Ella Wolfe (in Spanish) in the spring,

I have wanted to write to you for centuries, but as always, I do not know what messes I get into so that I never answer letters nor do I behave myself like the proper people. . . . Well, *niña*, permit me to thank you for your letter and for your kindness in asking me about Diego's shirts, I am sorry not to be able to give you the measurements that you asked me for, since no matter how much I search in their collars, I don't find even a trace of what could be called a number indicating the thickness of the neck of Don Diego Rivera y Barrientos. Thus I think the best thing to do would be, in case this letter arrives on time, which I doubt very much, to tell Martin please to buy me six of the biggest shirts that exist in Nueva Yores, those shirts that are so large it seems incredible that they could be for a person, that is to say the biggest on the planet, commonly called earth. I think that you can buy them in stores for sailors, over there on one of New York's shores, which one . . . I can't remember, in order to describe it to you as I should. In sum, if you don't find them, well . . . *ni modo!* [It doesn't matter.] Anyway, I am grateful for your attention and he is too. [Martin Temple was a manufacturer and a leftist who, during the rise of Nazism, formed an organization in Mexico City, of which the Riveras were members, that collected funds to help people escape from Hitler's Germany; Temple had a seven-year love affair with Frida's half-sister Margarita, and when he did not marry her, she entered a nunnery.]

Listen, *niña,* a few days ago Diego received a note from Boit, he says to say thank you for him, and that he should please send the *mosca* [dough] from Covichi [*sic;* Covici, Friede, Inc., was the publisher of Wolfe and Rivera's 1938 *Portrait of Mexico*] and the *mosca* from the man who bought the drawing or watercolor from him. Tell him that in fact he has lost various letters and the reason that Boit gives in his letter is precisely the correct one. So that it would be good if whatever has to do with the powerful and never very well pondered *mosca* should be sent in a special form in order to avoid that the *rupas se la avancen.* [In popular usage, *rupas* means "thieves" and *se la avancen* means "steal it."] As you can see, my lexicon is becoming more florid every day, and you can understand the importance of such a cultural acquisition within my extensive and immense culture! Diego says to say hello to Boit, the same to Jay [the Wolfes' son], Jim [Ella's brother] and to all the *cuatezones* [great pals].

If you want to know something about my singular person, here goes: Since you left this beautiful country, I have had a sick hoof, that is to say, foot. With the last operation that they did (precisely a month ago), I am healing and they have hacked me up four times. As you will understand, I feel truly "poifect" and I feel like getting even with the doctors, and all their progenitors, beginning with our good parents, in general terms, Adam and Eve. But since that would not be enough to console me, nor to let me rest, having had my revenge on those bastards, I abstain from such punishments, and here I am, turned into a true "saint" with patience and everything that characterizes that special fauna. . . . What's more, other more or less disagreeable things have happened to me which are the center of my misfortune, things which I will not tell you because they are of insignificant worth. The rest, daily life, etc., is exactly the same as you know it to be, with the exception of all the natural changes due to the lamentable state in which the world now finds itself, what philosophy, and what comprehension!

Besides illnesses, political messes, visits from gringa tourists, losses of letters, Riveraesque arguments, preoccupations of the sentimental sort, etc., my life is, like the poem of López Velarde, . . . the same as its daily mirror. [Frida is quoting a line from Velarde's *"La Suave Patria": "Fiel a tu espejo diario . . ."*] Diego too has been sick, but now he is almost well, he continues working as always, a lot and well, he is fatter, just as garrulous and greedy, he sleeps in the bathtub, he reads the newspapers in the WC and he amuses himself for hours playing with Don Fulang-Chang (the little monkey) for whom a consort was obtained, but unfortunately it turned out that the lady in question was a little hunchbacked, and she didn't please the gentleman enough for the hoped-for marriage to be consummated, so that there still are no descendants. Diego still loses all the letters that reach his hands, he leaves his papers everywhere, . . . he gets very cross when one calls him for a meal, he pays compliments to all the pretty girls, and sometimes . . . he makes an *ojo de hormiga* [to make an "ant eye" is a popular expression for disappearing or hiding] with some city girls who arrive unexpectedly, on the pretext of "showing them" his frescoes, he takes them for a day or two . . . to see the different landscapes . . . . for a change, he no longer fights as he did before with the people who bother him when he is working, his fountain pens go dry, his clock stops and every fifteen days it has to be sent to be fixed, he keeps wearing those huge miner's shoes (he has used the same ones for three years). He gets furious when he loses the keys of the car, and usually they appear in his own pocket, he does not take any exercise nor does he ever sunbathe, he writes articles for newspapers that generally cause a terrific uproar, he defends the

IVth International with cloak and sword, and he is enchanted that Trotsky is here. Now I have more or less told you the principal details.

. . . As you can observe, I have painted. Which is already something, since I have spent my life up until now loving Diego and being a good-for-nothing with respect to work, but now I continue loving Diego, and what's more I have begun to paint monkeys seriously. Concerns of the sentimental and amorous order . . . there have been a few, but without going beyond mere flings. . . . Cristi was very sick, they operated on her gall bladder and she was in very critical condition, we thought she would die, fortunately she survived the operation very well, and now although she does not feel very well, she is much better. . . . The little ones are adorable, el Tonito (the philosopher) [Antonio Kahlo] is more intelligent each day and he builds many things with the "mechanism." Isoldita is in third grade, she is very naughty and very cute. Adriana my sister and the little blond Veraza, her husband (they were the ones that went with us to Ixtapalapa) always remember you and Boit, and they send you greetings. . . .

Well pretty one, I hope that with this exceptional letter, you will at least love me a little bit again, and thus little by little until you love me as much as before . . . answer my love by writing me a powerful letter-missive that will fill with *alegría* this very sad heart that beats for you from here TIC-TAC!!! Literature is terrible for representing and giving the volume of interior noises, so it's not my fault if instead of sounding like a heart, I sound like a broken clock, but . . . you know what I mean, my dear children! And let me tell you, it's a pleasure. Lots of kisses for both of you, lots of hugs, all my heart, and if there's a little left over divide it between Jay, Jim, Lucienne, Dimy [Stephen Dimitroff] and all my soul *cuates.* Give lots of love to your mother and father and to the little baby who loved me so much.

Your loved and multifarious *chicua,*
Friduchín

"As you can observe, I have painted," she wrote, and indeed, she had. From 1937, in addition to *Fulang-Chang and I,* the *Self-Portrait* she made for Trotsky, and *Memory,* come *My Nurse and I, The Deceased Dimas,* and the still life called *I Belong to My Owner.* The list for 1938 includes not only *Remembrance of an Open Wound* and *Esquincle Dog with Me,* but such works as *Four Inhabitants of Mexico,*

They Asked for Planes and Only Got Straw Wings, Girl with a Death Mask, Me and My Doll, What the Water Gave Me, and three more still lifes, *Tunas, Pitahayas,* and *Fruits of the Earth.* Beyond that, Frida was not only more productive; she was also becoming more adept at making her art correspond to her evolving persona. In sophisticated ways her paintings now portrayed not merely "incidents" in her life but glimpses of her inner being and the way she perceived its relation to the world. As we have seen, *Fulang-Chang and I,* the *Self-Portrait* dedicated to Trotsky, and *Remembrance of an Open Wound* clearly show her new confidence in her female attractiveness. Others, such as *Memory, My Nurse and I,* and especially *What the Water Gave Me,* are equally clear indications of her development toward greater psychological complexity and technical sophistication.

Several works from this period suggest that Frida continued to feel the sorrow of childlessness; very likely she had another miscarriage or abortion in 1937. *My Nurse and I, The Deceased Dimas, Four Inhabitants of Mexico, They Asked for Planes and Only Got Straw Wings,* and *Girl with Death Mask* all show children in unhappy situations; in all but *The Deceased Dimas* (and possibly *Girl with Death Mask*), the child is Frida. This nostalgia for her own childhood reflects, I think, current maternal longings—Frida is identifying herself as the child she could not have. *Me and My Doll* is an even more emphatic statement of her frustrated desire for motherhood.

Two of these paintings—*My Nurse and I* and *Four Inhabitants of Mexico*—evince as well Frida's preoccupation with her roots in Mexico's past, a passion for her heritage that may have been heightened by the renewed realization that she would leave no progeny to link her with future generations. More and more in these years, the ethic of *Mexicanidad* pervaded Frida's existence on many levels: it was a style, a political stance, and a psychological support. It expressed itself in her behavior and her appearance, in the decoration of her home, and in her art.

Frida rightly judged *My Nurse and I,* in which she has painted herself as an infant with an adult's head, suckling in her dark Indian nurse's arms, to be one of her best paintings (plate X). It is a declaration of her faith in the continuity of Mexican culture, in the idea that Mexico's ancient heritage is reborn in each new generation, and that Frida, as an adult artist, continues to be nourished by her Indian ancestry. In it she has literally placed her being within the bosom of her Indian past, melding her feeling about her own life with pre-Columbian culture's stress on magic and ritual, its cyclical view of time, its idea of cosmic and biological forces working together, and the importance it gave to fertility. The painting recalls the ritualistic dignity of a well-known Olmec stone sculpture called *Señor de las Limas,* in which a child with an adult's face is held in the arms of an adult male. It also brings to mind ceramic sculptures like those from Jalisco (c. 100 B.C.– A.D. 250) that depict a mother holding her suckling child, and in which, as in *My Nurse and I,* the ducts and glands of the lactating breasts are revealed in a plant-like pattern on the breasts' surface. Massive and brown, Frida's nurse is a concretization of Mexico's Indian heritage and of the Mexican earth, plants, and sky. As if in sympathy with the nursing mother, milk-white veins in a huge leaf in the background are engorged. The raindrops in the sky are "milk from the Virgin"; thus had Frida's own Indian nurse explained to her the phenomenon of rain. The engorged leaf and the "Virgin's milk," the praying mantis and the metamorphosing caterpillar/butterfly that are camouflaged against the stems and leaves of plants, all express Frida's faith in the interconnectedness of every aspect of the natural world and in her own participation in that world.

"I appear with the face of an adult woman and the body of a baby girl, in the arms of my nana," Frida said of *My Nurse and I.* "From her nipples falls milk as from the sky. . . . I came out looking like such a little girl and she so strong and so saturated with providence, that it made me long to sleep." She also said that she painted the nurse's face as a mask because she could not remember how her nana looked. But the matter is more complicated than that. For although Frida might have intended the nurse to be a sanguine, reassuring image, one that could lull her to sleep, there is little that is comforting in the nurse's aspect. The fearsome Teotihuacán stone mask with its blank staring eyes could hardly be more chilling as a mother image; a funerary mask, it evokes the ritual savagery of the Mexican past, and suggests that that past encompasses the present and threatens Frida's life. Frida appears to be simultaneously protected by the nurse and offered as a sacrificial victim.

Nor does Frida look like a sleepy, satisfied, cuddled infant. The piercing look she gives the viewer seems to say that along with the milk, which she described as "saturated with providence," she also imbibes a terrible knowledge of her own fate. That tragic sense of destiny might have Christian overtones as well: the painting makes an obvious analogy with the motif of the "Madonna Caritas" in which the Virgin suckles the infant Christ, and it can also be compared to a Pietà.

It may be that there is yet another dimension to *My Nurse and I.* The frightening nurse has loose black hair and eyebrows that meet, a sign that she is the baby's ancestor or perhaps another side of Frida. Indeed, *My Nurse and I* may be, like *My Birth,* a double self-portrait; in it one aspect of Frida nurtures the other, becoming the life-sustaining half in the central duality of Frida's adult self.

As the child in *Four Inhabitants of Mexico* sees her destiny in the skeleton in the square, so does *Girl with Death Mask* combine Frida's and Mexico's preoccupation with death. The child—who may well be Frida, for she looks like the little girl in *My Grandparents, My Parents and I*—stands in a barren landscape holding a *zempazúchil,* the yellow flower that in Mexico since Aztec times has been associated with death and is used to decorate graves on the Day of the Dead. Her fate, her mortality, is clapped upon her face in the form of a white skull mask. The tiny painting, no bigger than a hand, was a gift to Dolores del Rio, who says that it represents the child Frida never had, and that it was prompted by a conversation between herself and Frida about Frida's unhappiness at not being able to bear Diego a child.

The Deceased Dimas (plate XI) is identified on an inscribed ribbon that reads: "The *difuntito* Dimas Rosas at three years of age, 1937." (In Mexico, the Day of the Dead is a fiesta that lasts several days, and one day is devoted to dead children, or *difuntitos.*) Dimas Rosas was an Indian child, probably one of several siblings belonging to a family in Ixtapalapa whom Rivera used as models and to whom the artist was a *compadre.* (A *compadre* is a person related to another person as a result of a religious ceremony; Rivera and Dimas's father became *compadres* when Dimas was baptized and Rivera was chosen as godfather.) Despite Diego's scientific arguments, the father of this family persisted in consulting witch doctors rather than medical doctors, with the result that his children kept dying. In this situation, as in her painting, Frida would have responded with a kind of fatalistic sorrow rather than shock or sentimental compassion. Like so many who witness poverty and death frequently, she would have known how helpless she was to change the outcome.

The painting follows a Mexican tradition of postmortem portraiture that stretches back to colonial times, and that in turn derives from a

European tradition beginning in the Middle Ages. At first, in Nueva España, such portraits served the moralistic function of honoring a person considered to be exemplary. Later, they served as mementos for the family of the deceased. One such memorial hangs above the head of Frida's bed in the Frida Kahlo Museum. It shows a dead child crowned with flowers, his body and the bed on which he lies strewn with blossoms. Like Dimas, this child holds flowers in his lifeless hands, and his head rests on a sausage-shaped pillow, but there is an obvious difference. Dimas's parents could not have afforded to commission such a souvenir. His portrait records a traditional child's lying in state: garbed like a saint or a holy personage, Dimas wears a cardboard crown and the silk mantle of the Magi who came to adore the infant Christ. But Dimas's tiny brown feet are bare, and he lies on a humble straw *petate,* the mat that serves as the standard bed of Mexico's poor. Like corn, the straw mat is so fundamental to Mexican peasant life that there are many idiomatic expressions based on the word. One of these turns the noun into a verb: *se petateó* means "he has taken himself and his *petate* for eternal sleep." *De petate a petate* means "from birth to death."

Just as in *Henry Ford Hospital* and *My Birth* Frida transformed her source in *retablos,* and in *My Nurse and I* began with another well-known type, the Madonna Caritas, so in *Dimas* she has altered a traditional mode in subtle ways so that the convention amplifies her originality. Dimas is not seen in the side view typical of postmortem portraits. Instead, the soles of his feet face us, at once bringing to mind Andrea Mantegna's dramatic "feet first" *Dead Christ.* Like the Italian Renaissance master, Frida has raised the dead person's head on a pillow so that the spectator stares straight into death's pallor. The intention is to extract the maximum dramatic intensity from the scene. By having Christ's feet seem to stick out at the viewer, Mantegna forces one to become almost physically engaged with Christ's wounds and to dwell upon the significance of his death. In Frida's *Dimas,* the "feet first" perspective thrusts the viewer headlong into the position of a mourner leaning over the body of the dead child, and then forces him to recognize death in its most factual and physical—not to say pedestrian—aspects. Frida is unsparing. She does not cosmeticize death. Drops of blood dribble from the corner of Dimas's mouth, and his slightly open, unfocused eyes are both haunting and horrible. There is a note of pathos in the little postcard image of Christ's flagellation that has been placed on Dimas's pillow, evidence of the simple faith of the child's family. But what Frida has painted is an atheist's view of death—literal and nontranscendent. Dimas will be rolled in his *petate* and put into the ground, one more victim of Mexico's high rate of child mortality. The sardonic quality of Frida's conception is revealed in the title she gave this painting when she showed it in New York in 1938: *Dressed Up for Paradise.*

It was not provincialism that made Frida borrow folk art modes. She was knowledgeable about art and she knew artists, critics, and art historians. When asked whom she admired, she mentioned Grünewald and Piero della Francesca, Bosch and Clouet, Blake and Klee. She loved the primitivism and fantasy of Gauguin and Rousseau, yet hers was distinct from theirs because it stemmed from Mexican popular tradition.

The adoption of primitivism as an approach to style and imagery had several advantages for Frida. Besides reaffirming her commitment to Mexico's indigenous culture, it was, in a sense, a leftist political statement, for it expressed her feeling of solidarity with the masses. Adapting a popular art style also coincided with Frida's finely wrought self-image. Like her costumes, Mexican popular art is full of festive color and *alegría,* and like her life, it is often theatrical and bloody. Being a painter of such charming, if offputting, folkloric pictures added to Frida's self-creation as a fabulous, exotic creature. It offered another advantage as well. Primitivism reveals and conceals. Were it not for their small scale and *retablo*-like style, paintings like *A Few Small Nips* or *My Birth* would be unbearable to look at. With fantasy, bright color, and charmingly naïve drawing, Frida distanced both the viewer and the artist from her painting's painful content. The popular art manner undercuts, and simultaneously underscores, the impact of horrific images—images that the example of popular art emboldened her to present. Works such as *Dimas* and *Henry Ford Hospital* are thus ingeniously ingenuous, and Frida's primitivism is an ironic stance. It allowed her both to display, and to mask and mock, the intimate torments of the self.

Frida's still lifes are curious assortments of fruits and flowers into which she projected all kinds of personal feelings—her fascination with fecundity and death, for example, and her *Mexicanidad. I Belong to My Owner,* known only from a photograph, depicts a bunch of peculiarly animate desert flowers whose toothy pods and snake-like blossoms allude both to sexual organs and to Frida's love of her native land; an earthenware vase is inscribed with the painting's title and with "VIVA MEXICO." What did Frida mean by the contrast between the vase full of dry, prickly-looking Mexican wild flowers (which she adored and used to decorate her table) and the single cut rose lying on a table with no water, so that it certainly will die? Perhaps the painting refers to the period when her love was divided between Diego and Trotsky, and the title is a pun on an emotional truth: that Frida, for all her "flings," would always belong to Diego.

The three other still lifes from this period are similarly *Mexicanista*. Frida deliberately chose exotic Mexican fruits that have none of the neutrality of apples and oranges, and that often look decidedly bizarre. *Tunas,* for example, shows the fruit of a prickly pear cactus, which Frida associated with Mexico; in letters she speaks of her native country as "Mexicalpán de las Tunas." On a tablecloth whose undulations she has transformed into a landscape and a cloudy sky are three *tunas* shown in different states of ripeness—a life cycle that ends with a maroon-red fruit split open to form a vaginal shape, but even more emphatically suggesting an extracted heart; no doubt, the splotches of red on the plate and the tablecloth are allusions to blood.

Like *Tunas, Pitahayas* (now lost) and *Fruits of the Earth* (figure 66) allude to the cycle of life—to sex and death. In the latter, corn cobs, two sheathed, the third stripped of its husk and with half its kernels gone, suggest time's passage, and the stem of an upside-down mushroom thrusts upward like a phallus or a bone. In *Pitahayas* a toy skeleton sits on a lava rock holding its scythe over a pile of the pomegranate-type fruits of the night-blooming cereus; most of the fruits are split open to reveal the juicy pulp within. André Breton, who was as quick as Frida to descry the sexual nature of this fruit, said: "I never imagined that world of fruits which encompasses such a marvel as the *pitahaya,* whose coiled pulp is like the colour of rose petals, whose skin is grey, and which tastes like a kiss blended of love and desire."

Frida's imperfect fruits look as if they have struggled to survive in the parched Mexican earth. As survivors, they reminded Frida of herself, and her still lifes are thus a kind of self-portrait: far from being meaningless volumes of a certain color and shape, they are symbols of a larger drama; they are placed not on a conventional tabletop, but in a mountain landscape and beneath the tumultuous Mexican sky.

When Frida was in one of her bouts of work, she would retire to her studio and paint with complete concentration. But like a surf rider losing a wave, she easily lost her momentum. Diego did what he could to encourage her. "She's working now," he would say to friends—meaning she could not be interrupted. "Diego always wants me to paint and do nothing else but that," Frida wrote in a letter to art dealer Julien Levy. "But I am lazy and I paint very little." She was not really lazy; rather she was so modest about her work that she professed a lackadaisical attitude toward it, and was reluctant to show it to anyone.

Thus it was at Diego's urging that she participated in a group show at the small University Gallery in Mexico City early in 1938. "Since I came back from New York [in 1935] I have painted about twelve paintings, all small and unimportant, with the same personal subjects that only appeal to myself and nobody else," she wrote (in English) in her February 14 letter to Lucienne Bloch. "I send four of them to a gallery, which is a small and rotten place, but the only one which admits any kind of stuff, so I send them there without any enthusiasm, four or five people told me they were swell, the rest think they are too crazy."

Among the "four or five people" who thought Frida's work was "swell" was Julien Levy, who owned a small, elegant surrealist-oriented gallery on East Fifty-seventh Street in Manhattan. "To my surprise," she went on in her letter to Lucienne, "Julian [sic] Levy wrote me a letter, saying that somebody talked to him about my paintings, and that he was very much interested in having an exhibition in his gallery, I answered sending few photographs of my last things, and he send another letter very enthusiastic about the photos, and asking me for an exhibition of thirty things on October of this year."

Although she told Lucienne, "I don't know what they see in my work. Why do they want me to have a show?" she accepted Levy's invitation.

Frida's attitude toward her work was both a pose and more than a pose: it was part of her character. No matter how much admiration and encouragement she received, and even when, later on, she needed money, she did not think in careerist terms—she never pushed for exhibitions, patrons, or reviews. If someone bought a picture she would say she felt sorry for the purchaser: "For that price they could buy something better," or "It must be because he's in love with me." Having a recognized genius for a husband provided her with a protective buffer; she could pretend that she played at art, making tiny private paintings while Diego made huge public ones, even when she was painting seriously and even though art was a mainstay in her life. The folkloric character of her work, and her decision to present it in popular art frames made of tin, shells, mirrors, velvet, or sometimes plaster painted with Talavera tile patterns, were part of the stance of being an amateur—as if, deliberately, she chose to relegate her art to the realm of the "charming" and "exotic," safe from serious criticism and competition. She preferred to be seen as a beguiling personality rather than to be judged as a painter. Her paintings expressed, in the most vivid and direct way possible, her reality; making them was only part of, and no more important than, making and being Frida Kahlo.

As Rivera had encouraged her to exhibit her work, so it was he who, in the summer of 1938, arranged, almost surreptitiously, her first major sale. The purchaser was the film star Edward G. Robinson. Like everyone else with an interest in art and the money to acquire it who visited Mexico, he, with his wife, Gladys, had come to Rivera's studio. "I kept about twenty-eight paintings hidden," Frida remembered. "While I was on the roof terrace with Mrs. Robinson, Diego showed him my paintings and Robinson bought four of them from me for two hundred dollars each. For me it was such a surprise that I marveled and said: 'This way I am going to be able to be free, I'll be able to travel and do what I want without asking Diego for money.' "

It was in April 1938 that the Surrealist poet and essayist André Breton first saw Frida's work. Breton was in his heyday. Noble and leonine in appearance, articulate, world famous, he was the "pope of Surrealism," a movement he more than anyone else had created. He had been sent to Mexico by the French Ministry of Foreign Affairs to give some lectures. Pleased to leave France at a time when war seemed imminent, he wanted to make contact with Trotsky (Breton had joined the Communist party briefly in 1928 and then attacked it publicly after he broke with it in the early 1930s), but what was foremost in his mind was to explore a land that he discovered to be, as he had predicted, the "Surrealist place *par excellence.*" The following year, he wrote: "I find the Surrealist Mexico in its relief, in its flora, in its dynamism conferred on it by the mixture of its races, as also in its highest aspiration." He observed all this *sur-réalité* on trips with the Riveras to the environs of Mexico City, to Guadalajara (June 1938),

XIV   The Two Fridas, 1939

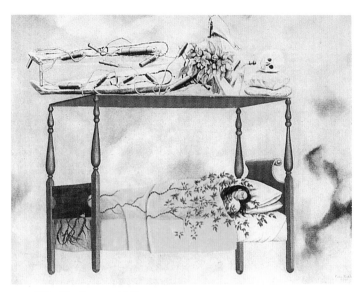

XV   The Dream, 1940

XVI   Self-Portrait, 1940

and to churches in the vicinity of the capital. (Trotsky occasionally accompanied him. On one trip, he became incensed when Breton stole *retablos* from a church wall. To the Frenchman, these ex-votos were Surrealist treasures. To the Russian, for all his Marxist ideology, they were religious icons.)

Breton and his strikingly beautiful wife, Jacqueline, stayed first with Lupe Marín and then, for their remaining months in Mexico, with the Riveras at San Angel. Although Frida had anticipated his arrival with excitement—Jean van Heijenoort had told her how handsome he was—she did not take to him. His theorizing and manifesto making seemed to her pretentious, feckless, and boring, and she was put off by his vanity and arrogance. But Jacqueline, who was a painter like herself, had a more sprightly intelligence, which amused and delighted Frida; they became intimate friends.

In July, the Bretons, the Riveras, and the Trotskys traveled to Pátzcuaro in Michoacán, a graceful town of cobblestone streets, large plazas, and low white houses with carved wooden pillars and tiled roofs. Their intention was to make excursions to the little villages around Lake Pátzcuaro during the day and to have conversations about art and politics in the evenings. They planned to publish these talks under the title "Conversations in Pátzcuaro." (During the first evening of "conversation," Trotsky dominated, expounding his theory that in the Communist society of the future, there would be no division between art and life. People would decorate their own houses, but there would be no professional easel painters catering to the tastes of private patrons.)

Not surprisingly, Frida and Jacqueline were not participants in these discussions. Frida was glad to be excluded; she hated official or organized talks and found politics on the plane of abstract theory wearisome. At Pátzcuaro, the two women sat in a corner and played games— such Surrealist games as *cadavre exquis* and the rather more innocent Mexican hand games Frida remembered from her childhood. "We acted like two pupils of a school," says Jacqueline Breton, "because Trotsky was very strict. For example, we could not smoke. He told us that women shouldn't smoke. Frida lit a cigarette anyway. She knew he would say something, so we left the room to smoke outside. We both loved Trotsky. He exaggerated and was very old-fashioned."

Though Frida scorned Breton, Breton was entranced by Frida, and his pleasure increased when he saw her paintings. He not only offered to organize an exhibition for her in Paris, following her New York debut; he also wrote a flattering, if somewhat rhetorical, essay for the brochure of the Julien Levy show. In it, he proclaimed Frida to be a self-created Surrealist:

> My surprise and joy were unbounded when I discovered, on my arrival in Mexico, that her work had blossomed forth, in her latest paintings, into pure surreality, despite the fact that it had been conceived without any prior knowledge whatsoever of the ideas motivating the activities of my friends and myself. Yet at this present point in the development of Mexican painting, which since the beginning of the nineteenth century has remained largely free from foreign influence and profoundly attached to its own resources, I was witnessing here, at the other end of the earth, a spontaneous outpouring of our own questioning spirit: what irrational laws do we obey, what subjective signals allow us to establish the right direction at any moment, which symbols and myths predominate in a particular conjunction of objects or web of happenings, what meaning can be ascribed to the eye's capacity to pass from visual power to visionary power? . . .
>
> This art even contains that drop of cruelty and humor uniquely capable of blending the rare effective powers that compound together to form the philtre which is Mexico's secret. The power of inspiration here is nourished by the strange ecstasies of puberty and the mysteries of generation, and, far from considering these to be the mind's private preserves, as in some colder climates, she displays them proudly with a mixture of candour and insolence. . . .

Early in October, after an exuberant going-away party, Frida left for New York in high spirits. Her forthcoming show and the recent sale of the four paintings to Edward G. Robinson bolstered her self-assurance and independence. She was "feeling her oats." Indeed, she led friends like Noguchi and Julien Levy to believe that she was separated from Diego, that she was "fed up" with him and was "living her own life." Levy, who was one of the various men to fall under Frida's spell at this time, remembered that "she acted as a free agent vis-à-vis other men. She professed not to care about Diego's other girl friends, and used to tell me dispassionately about a girl friend of Diego's who was also a friend of hers. She wanted to give me the impression that she missed Diego, but didn't love him anymore. Sometimes she'd talk about him in a sort of masochistic way, and sometimes as if he were her darling slave whom she couldn't abide. 'That old fat pig—he'd do anything for me,' she said. 'I'll tell him what to do, but he's so repulsive.' And at other times she'd say, 'He's just a doll.

I'm so lonesome for him. In a funny way, I just adore him.' It was all double talk, depending on her own mixed feelings."

Whatever the state of her marriage, there is no question that Frida was worried about leaving Diego alone in Mexico, and he was concerned that everything should go well for her in New York. He gave her advice and letters of introduction to important people—among them Clare Boothe Luce, then managing editor of *Vanity Fair* and hostess to a sophisticated circle of artists and intellectuals. In a letter to Frida dated December 3, 1938, he wrote: "You ought to do a portrait of Mrs. Luce even if she doesn't order it from you. Ask her to pose for you and you will get a chance to speak with her. Read her plays—it seems that they are very interesting—it may be that they will suggest to you a composition for her portrait. I think it would be a very interesting subject. Her life . . . is extremely curious; it would interest you." Rivera also wrote about Frida's forthcoming exhibition to his friend Sam A. Lewisohn, a collector and the author of *Painters and Personality*, which included an essay on Rivera: "I recommend her to you, not as a husband but as an enthusiastic admirer of her work, acid and tender, hard as steel and delicate and fine as a butterfly's wing, loveable as a beautiful smile, and profound and cruel as the bitterness of life."

Among Frida's papers is a handwritten list, drawn up by or with Diego, of potential guests to invite to her opening. The names are those of old friends as well as powerful or famous acquaintances. They include artists, dealers, collectors, museum people, critics, writers, publishers, political activists, and millionaires: Ben Shahn, Walter and Magda Pach, Pascal Covici, Sam A. Lewisohn, Mrs. Charles Liebman, Peggy Bacon, A. S. Baylinson, Alfred Stieglitz, Lewis Mumford, Meyer Schapiro, Suzanne Lafollette, Niles Spencer, George Biddle, Stuart Chase, Van Wyck Brooks, John Sloan, Gaston Lachaise, Holger Cahill, Dorothy Miller, Alfred H. Barr, Jr., Miss Adelaide Milton de Groot, Mrs. Edith G. Halpert, Henry R. Luce, Mr. and Mrs. William Paley, E. Weyhe, Carl Zigrosser, Dr. Christian Brinton, and George Grosz. Mr. and Mrs. Nelson A. Rockefeller and Mr. and Mrs. John D. Rockefeller are on the list too. Clearly Rivera saw fit to forgive his old antagonist and so did Frida.

"A painter in her own right" became Frida's suffix in New York—just as Diego was invariably referred to as *el muy distinguido pintor* in Mexico. Yet there is no question that being the wife of Diego Rivera added to the sensation of Frida's show. Even Breton's catalogue essay introduced Frida as the beautiful and pernicious butterfly who accompanied her monstrous Marxist husband. Nor did the gallery hesitate to make mileage out of her link with Rivera. The press release, for example, said:

An exhibition of paintings by Frida Kahlo (FRIDA RIVERA) opens Tuesday, November 1st, at the JULIEN LEVY GALLERY, 15 East 57th St. Frida Kahlo is the wife of Diego Rivera, but in this, her first exhibition, she proves herself a significant and intriguing painter in her own right. Frida Kahlo was born in Coyoacara [sic] (a suburb of Mexico City) in 1910. In 1926 she was the victim of a serious motor accident (the psychological effects of which may be noted in her subsequent painting). Bedridden for some time, she started to paint with a primitive but meticulous technique, both her transient and her most personal thoughts of the moment. In 1929 she became the third wife of Diego Rivera who encouraged her subsequent painting, and last year she met the surrealist, André Breton, who enthusiastically praised her work. She herself writes, "I never knew I was a Surrealist until André Breton came to Mexico and told me I was one. I myself still don't know what I am."

As an actual fact, her paintings combine a native Mexican quality which is naive, an unusual, female frankness and intimacy, and a sophistication which is the surrealist element. The paintings are in the Mexican tradition, painted on metal, and framed in charming Mexican peasant frames of glass and tin. The work of this newcomer is decidedly important and threatens even the laurels of her distinguished husband. The exhibition will continue for two weeks until November 15th.

At her opening, Frida looked spectacular in her Mexican costume—a perfect complement to the paintings decked out in folkloric frames. The crowd was large and animated, for in those days there were few art galleries and even fewer avant-garde galleries, and an opening like Frida's was a great event. Levy remembers that Noguchi and Clare Luce were full of excitement about the show, and that Georgia O'Keeffe and many other art world luminaries were there. None of them had ever seen anything quite like the group of twenty-five paintings on display.

The catalogue listed these titles:

1. Between the Curtains (Self-Portrait dedicated to Trotsky)
2. Fulang Chang and Myself
3. The Square Is Theirs (Four Inhabitants of Mexico)

On the whole, the press was delighted with the paintings and with their creator. *Time* magazine reported in its Art section that the "flutter of the week in Manhattan was caused by the first exhibition of paintings by famed muralist Diego Rivera's German-Mexican wife, Frida Kahlo. Too shy to show her work before, black-browed little Frida has been painting since 1926, when an automobile smashup put her in a plaster cast, 'bored as hell.' " The *Time* reviewer found Breton's description of Frida's work as "a ribbon around a bomb" to be a "fairly exact, if flattering figure. Little Frida's pictures, mostly painted in oil on copper, had the daintiness of miniatures, the vivid reds and yellows of Mexican tradition and the playfully bloody fancy of an unsentimental child."

The patronizing tone—"little Frida"!—was implicit in other criticisms as well. A few were unfavorable. Howard Devree of *The New York Times* (probably referring to *My Birth* and *Henry Ford Hospital*) complained that some of Frida's subjects were "more obstetrical than aesthetic." Another critic quibbled about the pretentiousness of printing Breton's essay in the brochure in the original French rather than in translation, and carped at the way "Mrs. Diego Rivera . . . should

A Painter in Her Own Right   231

insist on using her maiden name, Frida Kahlo (and then put her husband's name beside it in parenthesis)." Actually, we know from Bertram Wolfe that Frida used her maiden name precisely because she did not wish to ride on Rivera's fame; surely it was Levy and Breton who "insisted" on the parentheses.

Frida herself had no complaints about the exhibition and she was pleased by the attention. The day of her opening she wrote to Alejandro Gómez Arias:

On the very day of my exhibition I want to chat with you even if only this little bit.

Everything was arranged *a las mil maravillas* [marvelously] and I really have terrific luck. The crowd here treats me with great affection and they are all very kind. Levy did not want to translate A. Breton's preface and that is the only thing that seems to me to be a little unfortunate since it seems rather pretentious, but now there is nothing to be done about it! How does it seem to you? The gallery is terrific, and they arranged the paintings very well. Did you see *Vogue?* There are three reproductions, one in color—the one that seemed the best. Write to me if you remember me sometime. I will be here two or three weeks more. I love you very much.

Frida later said that her show sold out. She exaggerated. The truth is that only about half the paintings sold, which was impressive enough, considering that these were Depression years. (Sold before the opening, of course, were the four paintings owned by Edward G. Robinson, who lent them to Levy for the exhibit. The *Self-Portrait* dedicated to Trotsky belonged to Trotsky. Levy may have exhibited other privately owned paintings as well.) The gallery records have been misplaced, but Levy recalled that a psychiatrist, the late Dr. Allan Roos, purchased *My Grandparents, My Parents and I* out of the show. Sam Lewisohn bought a still life—almost certainly *I Belong to My Owner.* Frida sold a few works without Levy's help—possibly, Levy believed, one to the great collector Chester Dale, who adored Frida, and played the role of "grandpa or good daddy" toward her, paying for at least one of her operations and delighting in the way she teased him. Mary Schapiro (who by this time had married Solomon Sklar) bought *Tunas* from the exhibition, and Frida gave her *Fulang-Chang and I.* Photographer Nickolas Muray bought *What the Water Gave Me. Remembrance of an Open Wound* was acquired by the prominent industrialist Edgar J. Kaufmann, Sr., commissioner of Frank Lloyd Wright's recently completed, and soon to be famous, house called Fallingwater, at Bear Run, Pennsylvania. Frida said that art critic Walter Pach (an old friend of the Riveras), purchased a painting from the show. And if some paintings remained unsold, the show did stimulate future sales. Clare Boothe Luce did not, as Rivera had hoped, commission Frida to paint her portrait, but she did commission a commemorative portrait of her friend the actress Dorothy Hale, who had just committed suicide, and in 1940 she purchased the *Self-Portrait* dedicated to Trotsky. It is said that Frida received a commission to do a portrait of the famous actress Katharine Cornell at this time, but she never did it. Conger Goodyear fell in love with *Fulang-Chang and I;* since it already belonged to Mary Sklar, he commissioned Frida to paint a similar self-portrait, which he said he would give to the Museum of Modern Art but instead kept until his death, when it formed part of his bequest to the Albright Knox Museum. She sat in her hotel room at the Barbizon-Plaza, and within a week produced *Self-Portrait with Monkey* for him.

Frida was indifferent to being lionized, but it must have been gratifying to be swept up in a social whirl even though she was unaccompanied by her celebrated spouse. A personality to reckon with, she did not need to move in Diego's broad, bubbling wake, and it was exhilarating to deploy her considerable—if eccentric—social graces on her own, to see how many people she could charm.

Manhattan was a carnival. She did not do much painting, though she had a sketchbook in which she sometimes drew (or planned to draw) things that caught her attention. "I did that . . ." or "I will do that in my sketchbook," she would say. Nor did she frequent museums. Julien Levy recalled that someone took her to the Museum of Modern Art, but she complained about the difficulty of walking. She wrote to Alejandro Gómez Arias: "In a private collection of painting I saw two marvels, a Piero della Francesca that seemed to me to be the most fantastic in the world and a little El Greco, the smallest that I have seen, but the most wonderful of all. I will send you reproductions." What she loved to do was sit in the Hotel Saint Moritz's sidewalk café and watch people pass by against the backdrop of Central Park. Store windows held her enthralled. And she delighted in the varied street life of New York—the exoticism of Chinatown, Little Italy, Broadway, Harlem. Wherever she went she caused a sensation. Julien Levy remembered a visit to the Central Hanover Bank on Fifth Avenue: "Arriving inside the bank with her, I found we were surrounded by a flock of children who had followed us, despite all protests of the doorman. 'Where is the circus?' they were calling. 'Fiesta' would have been more accurate. Frida was dressed in full Mexican costume. She was beautiful and picturesque but sadly she did not wear bouffant-skirted native costumes for effect. 'I must have full skirts and long [she said], now that my sick leg is so ugly.'"

Through Levy, Frida was introduced to a lively and intelligent group of people, for he was urbane, articulate, and handsome, and he loved adventure and surprise. One of the Surrealists Frida met through him was Pavel Tchelitchew, whose painting exhibition "Phenomena" preceded Frida's at the gallery. "I like this guy," Frida said. "I like his work because it has freaks in it." And the Surrealists adored Frida, for she was possessed, as Breton had remarked, of that necessary Surrealist asset *"la beauté du diable."* An accomplished raconteur, she had a way of speaking directly to whoever was at her side, giving him the full force of her personality. Her voice was soft, warm, and low, somewhat masculine, and she did not try to improve upon her colorful English or her foreign accent, for she knew that these enhanced her magnetism. The Surrealist critic Nicolas Calas remembers that she "fit completely the Surrealist ideal of woman. She had a theatrical quality, a high eccentricity. She was always very consciously playing a role and her exoticism immediately attracted attention."

Only her health held her back. Julien Levy wanted to take Frida bar-hopping in Harlem, but, he recalled: "She didn't jump to it, possibly because she was tired, and she couldn't enjoy herself late at night. Bar-hopping is not easy to do if you are not light on your legs. She couldn't overcome invalidism. After walking three blocks, her face would get drawn, and she'd begin to hang on your arm a little bit. If you kept walking, that would force her to say, 'We must get a cab.' She didn't like to say that." Frida had reason not to want to walk long distances. Her right foot was still giving her problems. She had developed warts on the sole of one foot, and her spine continued to ache. After her show closed, she fell seriously ill and visited numerous doctors, orthopedists and specialists. Finally, Anita Brenner's husband and Frida's good friend, Dr. David Glusker, succeeded in closing the trophic ulcer that Frida had had on her foot for years. In addition, symptoms that suggested that she was suffering from syphilis prompted her doctors to administer a Wassermann and Kahn test. The result was negative.

If her health prevented Frida from enjoying museums and bar-hopping, it did not stop her from enjoying freedom from Diego. Far beyond the range of her husband's pistol, she made the most of her seductive powers, relishing, quite openly, the effect she had on men. Levy saw Frida as a kind of "mythical creature, not of this world—proud and absolutely sure of herself, yet terribly soft and manly as an orchid." Her self-fascination fascinated men, including Levy, who took a series of photographs of her naked to the waist, arranging and rearranging her long black hair. "She used to do her hair with things in it. When she unbraided it, she'd put these things in a certain order on her dressing table and then braid them back in. The hair preparation was a fantastic liturgy. I wrote a poem to her about it, and sent her a Joseph Cornell box. I gave Cornell a lock of Frida's hair, my poem, and a photograph of Frida, and he put together a box with blue glass and mirrors and the presence of Frida."

Once Levy took Frida to Pennsylvania to visit his client and friend Edgar Kaufmann, Sr., who, Levy said, wanted to be Frida's patron. The train ride was everything train rides are supposed to be—a slow but inexorable buildup of erotic anticipation. When they arrived, however, Frida flirted not just with Levy, but with their elderly host and his son as well. She was "very cavalier with her men," Levy recalled. She liked to play one off against the other, and she would pretend to one suitor that she thought the other was a nuisance or "a bore." At bedtime, Levy and the senior Kaufmann tried to wait each other out so as to spend the last moments of the evening in romantic solitude with Frida. When she retired, Fallingwater's complicated double stairway served as the stage for the evening's drama. After biding his time until he thought everyone was peacefully asleep, Levy emerged from his room and started up one side of the staircase. Much to his astonishment, he found his host climbing the stairs on the other side. Both retreated. The same confrontation took place several times. In the end, Levy gave up. But when he returned to his bedroom, there was Frida—waiting for him!

A more serious suitor by far was Hungarian-born Nickolas Muray. The son of a post office employee, Muray had arrived in the United States in 1913; he was twenty-one years old and had twenty-five dollars in his pocket. By the end of the 1920s he had become one of America's most successful portrait photographers. His portraits of celebrities appeared in *Harper's Bazaar* and *Vanity Fair*—one of his numerous photographs of Frida was published in *Coronet* in 1939—and he was active in commercial photography as well. A man of many parts, he also wrote criticism for *Dance* magazine, flew airplanes, was a champion fencer (he won the United States Olympic Saber title in 1927 and 1928 as well as foil and épée team championships), had had by the time he died in 1965 four wives—he was single when Frida met him—and four children, and was a generous patron of the arts, who frequently bought paintings to help a friend in need of money. In the 1920s, the Wednesday evening gatherings at his Macdougal Street studio attracted such notables as Martha Graham, Ruth St. Denis, Sinclair Lewis, Carl Van Vechten, Edna St. Vincent Millay, Eugene O'Neill, Jean Cocteau, T. S. Eliot, Gertrude Vanderbilt Whitney, and Walter Lippmann. Yet Muray possessed not only energy and charm, glamour and sophistication; he also retained an unspoiled simplicity and kindness, a capacity for tenderness and intimacy, that must have appealed to Frida. His handsome face and lean, graceful body surely charmed her too. She had met him in Mexico (probably through Miguel Covarrubias, who, like Muray, contributed to *Vanity Fair*), and he had helped Frida with the planning of her exhibition, photographing her work, arranging things like shipping and later unpacking and checking the condition of the paintings when they arrived in New York. He also advised her on the printing of the catalogue. Probably Frida's liaison with him had begun in Mexico, but in New York, away from Rivera's jealous scrutiny, the affair flourished.

Their relationship was volatile—Frida quarreled with him at the opening of her show—but the intensity of their love is revealed in the letters Frida wrote (in English) from Paris. "My adorable Nick, Mi niño," she wrote on February 16, 1939:

. . . your telegram arrived this morning, and I cried very much—of happiness, and because I miss you with all my heart and my blood. Your letter, my sweet, came yesterday, it is so beautiful, so tender, that I have no words to tell you what a joy it gave me. I adore you my love, believe me, like I never loved anyone—only Diego will be in my heart as close as you—always. . . . I miss every movement of your being, your voice, your eyes, your hands, your beautiful mouth, your laugh so clear and honest. *YOU*. I love you my Nick. I am so happy to think I love you—to think you wait for me—you love me.

My darling give many kisses to Mam on my name. I never forget her. [Mam is unidentified; Muray's daughter Mimi thinks she was Muray's studio assistant.] Kiss also Aria and Lea [Muray's daughters]. For you, my heart full of tenderness and caresses. one special kiss on you neck. your

Xochitl

On February 27, 1939:

My adorable Nick—

This morning after so many days of waiting—your letter arrived. I felt so happy that before starting to read it I began to weep. My child, I really shouldn't complain about any thing that happens to me in life, as long as you love me and I love you. It is so real and beautiful, that makes me forget all pains and troubles, makes me forget even distance. Your words made me feel so close to you that I can feel near me your laugh. That laugh so clean and honest that only *you* have. I am just counting the days to go back. A month more! And we will be together again. . . .

My darling, I must tell you, that you are a bad boy. Why did you send me that check of 400 bucks? Your friend "Smith" is an imaginary one—very sweet indeed, but tell *him,* that I will keep *his check untouched* until I come back to New York, and there we will talk things over. My Nick, you are the sweetest person I have ever known. But listen darling, I don't really need that money now. I got some from Mexico, and I am a real rich bitch, you know? I have enough to stay here a month more. I have my return ticket. *Everything is under controll* so realy, my love, it is not fair that you should spend any thing extra. . . . Any way, you can not imagine how much I appreciated your desire of helping me. I have not words to tell you what joy it gives me to think that you were willing to make me happy and to know how good hearted and adorable you are. —My lover, my sweetest, mi Nick—mi vida—mi niño, te adoro.

I got thinner with the illness, so when I will be with you, you will only blow, and . . . up she goes! the five floors of the La Salle Hotel. Listen Kid, do you touch every day the fire "whachamaycallit" which hangs on the corridor of our staircase? Don't forget to do it every day. Don't forget either to sleep on your tiny cushion, because I love it. Don't kiss anybody else while reading the signs and names on the streets. Don't take any body else for a ride to our Central Park. It belongs only to Nick and Xochitl. —Don't kiss anybody on the couch of your office. Only Blanche Heys [a good friend of Muray's] can give you a masage on your neck. You can only kiss as much as you want, Mam. Don't make love with anybody, if you can help it. Only if you find a real F.W. [fucking wonder] but *don't love her.* Play with your electric train once in while if you don't come home very tired. How is Joe Jinks? How is the man who massages you twice a week? I hate him a little, because he took *you* away from me many hours. Have you fence a lot? How is Georgio?

Why do you say that your trip to Hollywood was only half successful? Tell me about it. My darling, don't work so hard if you can help it. Because you get tired on your neck and on your back. Tell Mam to take care of yourself, and to make you rest when you feel tired. Tell her that I am much more in love with you, that you are my darling and my lover, and that while I am away she must love you more than ever to make you happy.

Does your neck bother you very much? I am sending you here millions of kisses for you beautiful neck to make it feel better. All my tenderness and all my caresses to your body, from your head to your feet. Every inch of it I kiss from the distance.

Play very often Maxine Sullivan's disc on the gramophone. I will be *there with you* listening to her voice. I can see you lying on the blue couch with your white cape. I see you shooting at the sculpture near the fire place, I see clearly, the spring jumping on the air, and I can hear your laugh—just like a child's laugh, when you got it right. Oh my darling Nick I adore you so much. I need you so, that my heart hurts. . . .

For all the ardor Frida felt toward Muray, however, neither he nor any of his rivals could compete with the deep attachment Frida felt for Diego. And she knew he loved her too. When illness and her anxiety at leaving him for such a long period made her reluctant to travel to Paris for the show Breton was organizing, Diego tried to allay her doubts.

December 3

Mi niñita chiquitita:

You have kept me so many days without news of you and I was uneasy. I am pleased that you feel a little better and that Eugenia is taking care of you; give her my thanks and keep her with you while you are there. And I am glad you have a comfortable apartment and place to paint. Don't hurry with your pictures and portraits, it is very important that they turn out *retesuaves* [extra scrumptious], for they will complement the success of your exhibit and may give you a chance to do more portraits. . . .

What will you give me for good news that you surely must know already? Dolores the marvelous is going to spend Christmas in New York. . . . Have you written to Lola [pet name for Dolores del Rio]? I suppose it's silly of me to ask you.

I am pleased with the commission of your portrait for the Modern Museum [he most likely refers to the Conger Goodyear commission]; it will be magnificent, your entering there from your very first exhibit. That will be the culmination of your success in New York. Spit on your little hands and make something that will put in the shade everything around it, and make Fridita the Grand Dragon [*la mera dientona*]. . . .

Don't be silly. I don't want you for my sake to lose the opportunity to go to Paris. TAKE FROM LIFE ALL WHICH SHE GIVES YOU, WHATEVER IT MAY BE, PROVIDED IT IS INTERESTING AND CAN GIVE YOU SOME PLEASURE. When one is old, one knows what it is to have lost what offered itseif when one did not know enough to take it. If you really want to please me, know that nothing can give me more pleasure than to know you have it. And you, my *chiquita,* deserve everything. . . . I don't blame them for liking Frida, because I like her too, more than anything. . . .

> *Tu principal sapo-Rana* [Your No. 1 toad-frog]
> Diego

In her diary Frida inserted a draft of what might have been her reply to Diego's letter. It was written on his birthday, December 8, 1938. She addressed Diego as *"Niño mio—de la gran ocultadora"* (My child of the great occultist—i.e., herself).

> It is six in the morning
> and the turkeys are singing,
> heat of human tenderness
> Solitude accompanied—
> Never in all my life
> will I forget your presence
> You picked me up when I was destroyed

and you made me whole again
In this small earth
Where will I direct my glance?
So immense so profound!
There is no longer any time, There is no longer anything.
distance. There is only *reality*
What was, was forever!
What exists are roots
that appear transparent
transformed
In the eternal fruit tree
Your fruits give off their aromas
your flowers give their color
growing with the joy
of the winds and the blossoms.
Do not stop giving thirst
to the tree of which you are the sun, the tree
that treasured your seed
"Diego" is the name of love.

Chapter 15

This Pinchisimo Paris

IN JANUARY 1939, when Frida sailed for France, Europe was in a state of uneasy peace. Hitler had been "appeased" at Munich, and the Spanish Civil War was drawing to a close: on February 27, Britain and France recognized the Franco regime. In the world capital of culture, fascists and Trotskyites, Communists and capitalists, liberals and conservatives, waged verbal battle, debating the fine points of theory while the first of what was to be a flood of refugees awaited an uncertain fate.

Frida stayed first with André and Jacqueline Breton in their small apartment at 42 Rue Fontaine (the intersection of Surrealist and Trotskyite circles in Paris), but it was not a happy visit. In the first place, the exhibit Breton had supposedly organized was delayed: "The question of the exhibition is all a damn mess," Frida wrote Nickolas Muray on February 16:

Until I came the paintings were still in the custom house, because the s. of a b. of Breton didn't take the trouble to get them out. The photographs which you sent *ages ago, he never received*—so he says—

the gallery was not arranged for the exhibit *at all* and Breton has no gallery of his own long ago. So I had to wait days and days just like an idiot till I met Marcel Duchamp (marvelous painter) who is the only one who has his feet on the earth, among all this bunch of coocoo lunatic sons of bitches of the surrealists. He immediately got my paintings out and tried to find a gallery. Finally there was a gallery called "Pierre Colle" which accepted the damn exhibition. Now Breton wants to exhibit together with my paintings, 14 portraits of the XIX century (Mexican), about 32 photographs of Alvarez Bravo, and lots of popular objects which he bought on the markets of Mexico—*all this junk,* can you beat that? For the 15th of March the gallery suppose to be ready. But . . . . . . the 14 oils of the XIX century must be *restored* and the damn restoration takes a whole month. I had to lend to Breton 200 bucks (Dlls) for the restoration because he doesn't have a penny. (I sent a cable to Diego telling him the situation and telling that I lended to Breton that money—he was furious, but now is *done* and I have nothing to do about it.) I still have money to stay here till the beginning of March so I don't have to worry so much.

Well, after things were more or less settled as I told you, few days ago Breton told me that the associated of Pierre Colle, an old bastard and son of a bitch, saw my paintings and found that only *two* were possible to be shown, because the rest are too *"shocking"* for the public!! I could of kill that guy and eat it afterwards, but I am so sick and tired of the whole affair that I have decided to send every thing to hell, and scram from this rotten Paris before I get nuts myself.

In the second place, Frida was ill; her February 16 letter was written from her bed in the American Hospital. Fed up with Breton, and inconvenienced by having had to share a cramped room with the Bretons' small daughter Aube, she had moved at the end of January to the Hotel Regina on the Place des Pyramides, whence she was taken by ambulance to the hospital "because I couldn't even walk." She had contracted a colibacterial inflammation of the kidneys. To Muray on February 27 she wrote:

I feel rather weak after so many days of fever because the damn infection of collibacili makes you feel rotten. The doctor tells me I must of eaten something which wasn't well cleaned (salad or raw fruits) I bet you my boots, that in Breton's house was where I got the lousy collibacili. You don't have any idea of the dirt those people live in, and the kind of food they eat. Its something incredible. I never seen anything like it before in my damn life. For a reason that I ignore, the infection went from the intestines to the bladder and the kidneys, so for two days I couldn't make pipi and I felt like if I were going to explode any minute. Fortunately everything *its OK now,* and the only thing I must do is to rest and to have a special diet.

She elaborated in a letter to Ella and Bertram Wolfe:

You see, I had my belly full of anarchists and every one of them would have put a bomb in some corner of my poor intestines. I felt that until this moment the situation was hopeless since I was sure that *la pelona* [death] was going to take me away. Between the belly pains and the sadness of finding myself alone in this *pinchisimo* [vile] Paris, which seems to me like a kick in the navel, I assure you that I would have preferred that with one tug the devil had taken me. But when I found myself in the American Hospital where I could "bark" in English and explain my situation, I began to feel a little better. [Frida's inability to speak French doubtless contributed to her low opinion of Paris.] At least I could say: "Pardon me I burped!!" (Of course that was not the case, since to be precise, I could not even complain or curse by burping.) Not until four days ago could I have the pleasure of letting out the first "burp" and from that happy day until now I feel better. The reason for the anarchist uprising in my belly was that it was full of *colis,* and those wretches, wanted to transgress the decent limit for their activity, and it occurred to them to go out on a spree promenading through my bladder and kidneys, and frankly it began to burn me up, since they played the devil in my kidneys and they were now sending me to the morgue. In a word, I was only counting my days until my fever went down so that I could catch a boat and escape to the United States, since here they did not understand my situation nor did anyone give a damn about me. Little by little, I began to bounce back.

She did not "go back to the damn hotel because I couldn't stay all alone." Instead, Mary Reynolds, "a marvelous American woman who lives with Marcel Duchamp invited me to stay at her house and I accepted gladly because she is really a nice person and doesn't have anything to do with the stinking 'artists' of the group of Breton. She is very kind to me and takes care of me wonderfully."

By this time, the question of the exhibition was finally settled, and she told Muray:

Marcel Duchamp has help me a lot and he is the only one among this rotten people who is a real guy. The show will open *the 10th of March* in a gallery called "Pierre Colle." They say its one of the best here. That guy Colle is the dealer of Dali and some other big shots of the surrealism. It will last two weeks—but I already made arrangements to take out my paintings on the 23rd in order to have time to packed them and take them with me on the 25th. The catalogues are already in the printing shop, so it seems that everything is going on alright. I wanted to leave on the "Isle de France" the 8th of March, but I cable Diego and he wants me to wait till my things are shown, because he doesn't trust any of this guys to ship them back. He is right in a way because after all I came here *only* for the damn exhibition and would be stupid to leave two days before it opens. Don't you think so?

Despite her miseries, Frida did participate in the "surrealistic" pleasures of Paris. She got to know such luminaries of Surrealist circles as the poet Paul Eluard and Max Ernst, whose intense blue eyes, white hair, and beaky nose appealed to her, and whose painting she liked, but whose personality she found a little inaccessible—like dry ice. Her new friends escorted her to artists' cafés and to nightclubs like the Boeuf-sur-le-Toit, where she listened to jazz (she came to love the music of the black American pianist Garland Wilson) and where, as usual, she watched other people dance. Already proficient at the *cadavre exquis*, she now became an expert at other Surrealist games. Breton's favorite—and he took it very seriously, becoming irate if anyone spoke out of turn—was the *jeux de la vérité* (truth or consequences). People who refused to tell the truth were asked to do things like crawl into the room blindfolded and on all fours and then guess who it was who had kissed them. On one occasion Frida refused to answer the question "What's your age?" and the punishment was: "You must make love to the armchair." "Frida sat on the floor and did it beautifully," one player remembers. "She caressed the armchair as if it were a beautiful creature."

The world of haute couture embraced her too. Schiaparelli was so taken with her Tehuana costumes that she designed a *robe Madame Rivera* for fashionable Parisians, and Frida's beringed hand appeared on the cover of *Vogue*.

When she was able, she visited Chartres and a chateau or two on the Loire, and spent some time in the Louvre. She also went to the "thieves market" and bought

lots of junk, which is one of the things [she wrote Muray] I like best. I don't have to buy dresses or stuff like that because being a "tehuana" I don't even wear pants, nor stockings either. The only things I bought here were two old fashioned dolls, very beautiful ones. One is blond with blue eyes, the most wonderful eyes that you can imagine. She is dressed as a bride. Her dress was full of dust and dirt, but I washed it, and now it looks much better. Her head is not very well adjusted to her body because the elastic which holds it, is already very old, but you and me will fix it in New York. The other one is less beautiful, but very charming. Has blond hair and very black eyes, I haven't wash her dress yet and is dirty as hell. She only have one shoe, the other one she lost it in the market. Both are lovely, even with their heads a little bit loose. Perhaps that it is which gives them so much tenderness and charm. For years I wanted to have a doll like that, because somebody broke one that I had when I was a child, and I couldn't find it again. So I am very happy having two now. I have a little bed in Mexico, which will be marvelous for the bigger one. Think of two nice hungarian names to baptize them. The two of them cost me about two dollars and a half.

But for all the amusements, and even after she had left the Bretons' house and recovered her health, Frida found Paris decadent; most of all she hated what she saw as the empty posturing of the *Bohème*.

You have no idea the kind of bitches these people are. They make me vomit. They are so damn "intellectual" and rotten that I can't stand them any more. It is really too much for my character. I rather sit on the floor in the market of Toluca and sell tortillas, than to have any thing to do with those "artistic" bitches of Paris. They sit for hours on the "cafes" warming their precious behinds, and talk without stopping about "culture" "art" "revolution" and so on and so forth, thinking themselves the gods of the world, dreaming the most fantastic nonsenses, and poisoning the air with theories and theories that never come true. Next morning—they don't have any thing to eat in their houses because *none of them work* and they live as parasites of the bunch of rich bitches who admire their "genius" of "artists." *shit* and only *shit* is what they are. I never seen Diego or you [Muray], wasting their time on stupid gossip and "intellectual" discussions. that is why you are real *men* and not lousy "artists." —Gee weez! It was worthwhile to come here only to see why Europe is rottening, why all this people—good for nothing—are the cause of all the Hitlers and Mussolinis. I bet you my life I will hate this place and its people as long as I live. There is something so false and unreal about them that they drive me nuts.

She despaired over the Loyalist defeat in the Spanish Civil War and she saw firsthand the suffering of Spanish refugees. With Diego's help, she arranged for the departure of four hundred of them for Mexico.

If you knew in what conditions those poor people who have succeeded in escaping from concentration camps exist it would break your heart. Manolo Martínez, the *compañero* of Rebull [Daniel Rebull was one of the Spanish militiamen whom Frida met in Mexico in 1936 or 1937] has been around. He tells me that Rebull was the only one who had to stay on the other side since he could not leave his wife who was dying. Perhaps now that I am writing this to you they will have shot the poor man. These French mules have behaved like hogs with all the refugees, they are a bunch of bastards of the worst kind that I have ever known. I am nauseated by all these rotten people in Europe—and these fucking "democracies" are not worth even a crumb.

Although Frida represented Mexico at one or more Trotskyite meetings and continued to consort with the group until she left Paris—indeed, she had a brief affair with one of them, staying with him for a week in Mary Reynolds's Montparnasse home—she was ready to support Diego when she learned, not long after she reached Paris, that he had broken with Trotsky. "Diego has now fought with the IVth [International] and told piochitas (Trotsky) to go to hell in a very serious manner," she wrote to Ella and Bertram Wolfe. ". . . *Diego is completely right.*"

Personal and political conflicts had begun to erode the Rivera-Trotsky friendship at about the time Frida left Mexico in October to attend her New York exhibition. Her absence made Rivera feel dejected and a little lost. In this irritable mood, it was inevitable that Trotsky's didactic manner would get on his nerves. In turn, Rivera's unpredictability and his self-indulgent fablemaking irked Trotsky. One incident points to the differences in temperament. On November 2, 1938, the Day of the Dead in Mexico, Rivera appeared at the Coyoacán house brimming with mischief and presented Trotsky with a large purple sugar skull with "Stalin" spelled out in white sugar on its brow. Trotsky did not acknowledge the humor or the gift, and as soon as Diego left the house, he told Jean van Heijenoort to destroy it.

Before long, political arguments that both men would previously have kept below the simmering point came to a boil. They disagreed about the class nature of the Soviet state, Rivera's involvement with trade union groups, and Rivera's support of Francisco Mújica (whom Trotsky considered to be the bourgeois candidate) in the current presidential election campaign. The real problem was that Rivera's Trotskyism was neither consistent nor profound. He would say things like: "You know, I'm a bit of an anarchist," and behind Trotsky's back he would accuse him of being a Stalinist. With his anarchic attitude toward any dogmas or systems other than his own, Rivera was incapable of staying obediently under Trotsky's ideological wing or serving as a reliable party functionary. Also, like many intellectuals in the period just before World War II, he became disillusioned with Trotsky's Fourth International, seeing it as a futile and "vainglorious gesture." He was displeased when Trotsky, after trying to persuade him that he could serve the cause better through his art than through administrative work, took steps to limit his influence within the Mexican Trotskyite party. In late December, he wrote Breton a letter criticizing Trotsky's methods, and Trotsky asked him to rewrite it, eliminating two untrue statements. Rivera agreed, but never made the alterations.

Early in the new year, Rivera resigned from the Fourth International. On January 11, Trotsky stated to the Mexican press that he no longer felt any "moral solidarity" with Rivera, and that henceforth he could not accept Rivera's hospitality. Yet on January 12, Trotsky was still hoping to bring Rivera back into the fold, for he wrote to Frida about the conflict, soliciting her help. Beneath the letter's detailed explanations and political arguments—he told Frida about Diego's trade union work and the letter to Breton—there is a note of passionate urgency that suggests how much the loss of Rivera as a friend and political comrade meant to Trotsky. "Dear Frida," he wrote:

We here are all very happy, and even proud of your success in New York, because we consider you as an artistic ambassador not only from San Angel, but also from Coyoacán. Even Bill Lander, objective representative of the American press, informed us that, according to press notices, you had a genuine success in the States. Our heartiest congratulations. . . .

However . . . I wish to communicate to you some complications with Diego, which are very painful to me and to Natalia and to the whole household. It is very difficult for me to find the real source of Diego's discontent. Twice I tried to provoke a frank discussion on the matter, but he was very general in his answers. The only thing I could extract from him was his indignation at my reluctance to recognize those characteristics in him which would make for a good revolutionary functionary. I insisted that he should never accept a bureaucratic position in the organization, because a "secretary" who never writes, never answers letters, never comes to meetings on time and always makes the opposite of the common decision is not a good secretary. And I ask you, why should Diego be a "secretary"? That he is an authentic revolutionary needs no proof, but he is a revolutionary multiplied by a great artist and it is even this "multiplication" which makes him absolutely unfit for routine work in the party. . . .

A few days ago Diego resigned from the 4th International. I hope his resignation will not be accepted. For my part, I will do everything possible to settle at least the political matter, even if I am not successful in settling the personal question. However, I believe your help is essential in this crisis. Diego's break with us would signify not only a heavy blow to the 4th International, but—I am afraid to say—it would mean the moral death of Diego himself. Apart from the 4th International and its sympathizers I doubt whether he would be able to find a milieu of understanding and sympathy not only as an artist but as a revolutionary and as a person.

Now, dear Frida, you know the situation here. I cannot believe that it is hopeless. In any case, I would be the last to abandon the effort to reestablish the political and personal friendship and I sincerely hope that you will collaborate with me in that direction.

Natalia and I wish you the best of health and artistic success and we embrace you as our good and true friend.

After the break, Trotsky tried to persuade Rivera to accept money for rent while he looked for another place to live. Rivera refused. Finally, in April 1939, Trotsky moved with his entourage to a house on Avenida Viena in Coyoacán, within walking distance of the blue house on Avenida Londres. He left behind, among other mementos, the *Self-Portrait* Frida had given him, and a pen that had also been a gift from her. She had bought it from Misrachi's book store, and she had gone to the trouble of getting a sample of Trotsky's signature without his knowledge in order to have it engraved on the pen's barrel.

Although Frida went along with Diego's move away from Trotsky, she retained a fondness for him, even after his death. In 1946, for example, she denied Rivera's demand that she lend him the pen she had given Trotsky so that he could use it to sign his application for readmission to the Communist party. She was endlessly indulgent of Diego's political caprices, yet some part of her continued to respect her old friend's memory. In the end, however, in connection with her own readmission to the Communist party, she too denounced Trotsky, describing his January 1939 letter to her as "absolutely impossible." She also recalled meeting his murderer, Ramón Mercader, alias Jacques Mornard, during her stay in France:

In Paris I had met Mornard, the one who killed him, and he went around insinuating to me that I should take him to Trotsky's house. "Not me, because I am quarreling with the old Trotsky," I told him. "I only ask you, please, to find me a house near there." "Well look for it yourself, because I am too sick to look for houses for anyone, and I cannot give you lodging in my house, nor can I introduce you to Trotsky, I never will introduce him to you." But the girlfriend [Sylvia Ageloff] came and introduced him.

While Mercader, a GPU agent who posed as a Trotskyite, was courting Sylvia Ageloff, an American Trotskyite visiting Paris at the same time as Frida, he apparently also pursued Frida, without success. A friend of Sylvia Ageloff, Maria Craipeau, wanting to explain Sylvia's role in the assassination, wrote an article in which she repeats the story "Mornard" told her about his meeting with Frida Kahlo, a story the young man found so hilarious it made him laugh till he cried. "I'm going to tell you something funny," "Mornard" began. "Really I have never in my life been so ridiculed. Listen: I learned about the arrival in Paris of Frida Kahlo, the wife of Diego Rivera. I bought an enormous bouquet and went in search of her." "Mornard" followed Frida from one place to another, armed with his gigantic floral offering, which he finally attempted to bestow on her at an exhibition opening. When Frida rejected both the flowers and the man, he went out in the street and offered the bouquet to the first woman he saw. She fled in terror, and the flowers ended up in a gutter. Asked by Maria Craipeau why he had been so intent on meeting Frida Kahlo, the agent said merely, "It would have amused me to meet her," and left the room.

By the time it finally opened, Frida told Muray, she no longer cared "if the show will be a successful one or not. . . . People in general are scared to death of war and all the exhibitions have been a failure, because the rich bitches don't want to buy anything." (She canceled a London exhibition that was to have been held at Guggenheim Jeune, Peggy Guggenheim's Cork Street Gallery, in the spring. "So what is the use," she asked rhetorically, "of making any effort to go to London to waste time only?")

The show was called "Mexique," and if it was not exactly a one-woman exhibition (Breton did indeed surround Frida's paintings with pre-Columbian sculptures, paintings from the eighteenth and nineteenth centuries, photographs by Manuel Alvarez Bravo, and his own collection of what Frida had called "all that junk"—toys, a ceramic candelabrum, a huge sugar skull, ex-votos, and other popular art objects that he had acquired in Mexico), Frida was the main feature. Jacqueline Breton recalls that the opening was a lively affair, but that during most of it, Frida stayed in the corner; since her French was limited, she may well have felt left out. And as she had feared, the exhibition was not a financial success. The French were too nationalistic, says Jacqueline Breton, to be very interested in the work of an unknown foreigner. Besides that, "Women were still undervalued. It was very hard to be a woman painter. Frida said, 'Men are kings. They direct the world.' "

Frida's work did, however, receive a favorable review in *La Flèche*. The critic, L. P. Foucaud, said that each of the seventeen paintings exhibited was a "door opened on the infinite and on the continuity of art." He called Frida's color "pure" and her drawing "perfect," and praised the "authenticity" and "sincerity" of her work, saying that in a period when "guile and swindle are in style, the striking probity and exactitude of Frida Kahlo de Rivera spare us many strokes of genius." And the Louvre saw fit to purchase *The Frame*, a charming portrait of Frida with her hair done up with a yellow-green ribbon and topped with a huge yellow flower, which is now in the collection of the Musée National d'Art Moderne, Centre Georges Pompidou.

Of all Frida's admirers, Diego, naturally, had the most to say about her Paris triumph. Within weeks of her arrival, he wrote, his wife had won the hearts of the Paris art world: "The more rigorous the critics, the greater their enthusiasm. . . . Kandinsky was so moved by Frida's paintings, that, right before everyone in the exhibition room, he lifted her in his arms, and kissed her cheeks and brow while tears of sheer emotion ran down his face. Even Picasso, the most difficult of difficults, sang the praises of Frida's artistic and personal qualities. From the moment he met her until the day she left for home, Picasso was under her spell."

As a token of his affection for her, Picasso gave Frida a pair of earrings in the form of tiny tortoise-shell hands with gold cuffs. He also taught her a Spanish song, *"El Huérfano,"* which begins: *"Yo no tengo ni madre ni padre que sufren mi pena,/Huérfano soy."* (I have neither mother nor father to suffer my pain,/I am an orphan.) It became one of her favorites and in later years she often sang it for Diego and for friends.

On March 17, Frida summarized her impressions for Ella and Bertram Wolfe:

Ella linda and Boitito *my real cuates:*
After two months I write to you. I already know that you are going to say the same thing as always—that "chicua" is a mule! but this time believe me that it was not so much mulishness but rather that bandit luck. Here go the powerful explanations: a) since I arrived I have been in a frightful mess. I have been cross as hell since my exhibition had not been arranged. My paintings were waiting for me very calmly at the customs house because Breton hadn't even collected

them. You do not have even the slightest idea of the kind of old cockroach Breton and almost all the surrealist group are. In a word, they are perfect sons of . . . their mother. I will tell you the whole story of said exhibition in detail when we see each other's faces again since it is long and sad. But in a summarized synthesis the thing was delayed by a month and a half before the date etc. etc. of the famous exhibition was completely sure.

All of this happened with the accompaniment of quarrels, insults, arguing, gossip, much anger and annoyances of the worst kind. Finally, Marcel Duchamp (the only one amongst the painters and artists from here that has his feet on the ground and his brains in their place) was able to succeed in arranging the exhibition with Breton. It opened on the 10th of this month in the *Pierre Colle* gallery which according to what they tell me is one of the best here. There were a lot of people on the day of the opening, great congratulations to the "chicua," amongst them a big hug from *Juan Miró* and great praises for my painting from *Kandinsky*, congratulations from *Picasso* and *Tanguy*, from Paalen and from other "big cacas" of Surrealism. In sum I can say that it was a success, and taking into account the quality of the taffy (that is to say the crowd of congratulators) I believe that the thing went well enough. . . .

Soon we will talk about everything at length. Meanwhile I want to tell you: that I have missed you very much—that I love you more and more—that I have behaved myself well—that I have not had adventures nor lovers, nor anything of the kind, that I miss Mexico more than ever—that I adore Diego more than my own life—that once in a while I also miss Nick [Muray] a lot, that I am becoming a serious person, and that to sum up, until I see you again I want to send you both lots of kisses. Divide some of them equitably among Jay, Mack, Sheila and all the *cuates*. And if you have a small moment see Nick and give him a little kiss also and another for Mary Sklar.

Your *chicua* who never forgets you

Frida

A week after writing to the Wolfes, Frida was finally able to leave that "rottening" Europe. She sailed from Le Havre on March 25, bound for New York. Not all her memories of Paris were negative. She made good friends there, even among the "big cacas" of Surrealism, and she was entranced by the city's beauty. Back in Mexico, she wrote this wistful letter (in Spanish) to a woman friend in Paris (probably Jacqueline Breton, because the name "Aube" appears in the margin of the copy she later inserted in her diary, where she speaks of the woman's daughter).

Since you wrote to me, on that day so clear and so far away, I have wanted to explain to you, that I cannot escape the days, nor return in time to the other time. I have not forgotten you—the nights are long and difficult. The water. The boat and the pier and the departure, that was making you so small, to my eyes, imprisoned in that round window, that you looked at in order to keep me in your heart All this is intact. Later came the days, new days of you. Today I would like my sun to touch you. I tell you that your daughter is my daughter, the puppet people arranged in your large room full of glass, are both of ours.

The *huipil* with reddish-purple ribbons is yours. Mine, the old plazas of your Paris, above all the marvelous Place des Vosges, so forgotten and firm. The snails and the bride doll are yours too, that is to say you are you. Her dress is the same one that she did not want to take off on the day of the wedding with no one, when we found her almost asleep on the dirty floor of a street. My skirts with ruffles of lace, and the old blouse . . . make the absent portrait of only one person. But the color of your skin, of your eyes and your hair changes with the wind of Mexico. You also *know* that everything that my eyes see and everything that I touch with my own self, from all the distances, is Diego. The caress of cloth, the color of color, the wires, the nerves, the pencils, sheets of paper, dust, cells, war and the sun, all that lives in the minutes of the no-clocks and the no-calendars and the no-empty glances, is *him*— You felt it, for that reason you allowed the boat to carry me from Le Havre, where you never said goodbye to me.

I will always continue writing to you with my eyes. Kiss the little girl.

Chapter 16

What the Water Gave Me

FRIDA'S RESPONSE to being welcomed into the Surrealist pantheon by its founding spirit was a show of innocent dismay. "I never knew I was a Surrealist," she had said, "till André Breton came to Mexico and told me I was. The only thing I know is that I paint because I need to, and I paint always whatever passes through my head, without any other consideration."

There may have been some cunning mixed with her naïveté. Frida Kahlo wanted to be perceived as an original, one whose personal fantasy was nourished in a general way by Mexican popular tradition rather than by any foreign "isms." This is precisely how Breton and Rivera wanted to see her too, and it is true that her art is striking in its inventiveness and candor, its apparent freedom from the influences of European art movements. But Frida was much too sophisticated, much too well informed about the art of the past and the present, to have been a perfectly pure, self-generated artist, if such a thing exists. In fact, her emphatic disclaimer sounds suspiciously similar to Breton's definition of Surrealism: "Pure psychic automatism by which one intends to express verbally, in writing or by other method, the real functioning of the mind. Dictation by thought, in the absence of any control exercised by reason, and beyond any esthetic or moral preoccupation."

Breton's theories had surely preceded him to Mexico, and Frida certainly was not ignorant of them. Moreover, she knew that the Surrealist tag would help bring her critical acclaim, and she was happy to be accepted in Surrealist circles, first in New York, where Julien Levy's gallery was a focal point for the movement, and then in Paris. Had she objected to the label, her friend Miguel Covarrubias would not have categorized her as a Surrealist in the catalogue of the "Twenty Centuries of Mexican Art" exhibition at New York's Museum of Modern Art. On the other hand, Frida made sure that it was not *she* who gave herself that label. Art historian Antonio Rodríguez quotes her as saying: "I adore surprise and the unexpected. I like to go beyond realism. For this reason, I would like to see lions come out of that bookshelf and not books. My painting naturally reflects these predilections and also my state of mind. And it is doubtless true that in many ways my painting is related to that of the Surrealists. But I never had the intention of creating a work that could be considered to fit in that classification."

There was no doubt about what was the most fashionable movement in international art circles in 1940. When the "International Exhibition of Surrealism" opened on January 17 at Inés Amor's Galería de Arte Mexicano in Mexico City, it was the season's great cultural and social event. The exhibition had already traveled from Paris to London; it had been organized by André Breton together with the Peruvian poet César Moro and the Surrealist painter Wolfgang Paalen, who had emigrated to Mexico in 1939 with his wife, Frida's good friend Alice Rahon, also a Surrealist painter and poet. The guest list for the show's opening, published in the newspaper, included "all Mexico."

The catalogue promised "Clairvoyant Watches," "Perfume of the Fifth Dimension," "Radioactive Frames," and "Burnt Invitations." (If the show did not fulfill all these promises it at least made good on the last one—the invitations sent to a select few were elegantly singed along their edges.) Most of the men were in formal attire, and the women wore the latest modes from Paris. Lupe Marín's sister Isabel fluttered about in a white tunic as the "Apparition of the Great Sphinx of the Night," an enormous butterfly on her head all but hiding her pretty face. Undersecretary of the Treasury Eduardo Villaseñor gave a suitably inscrutable inaugural speech while Mexico's social and cultural elite sipped fine whiskeys and cognacs and ate the gourmet supper offered by Inés Amor. When the party broke up, many of the guests went on to dance at El Patio, a popular cabaret.

Most of the reviews were positive. One critic, however, said the inaugural fiesta "had the character of a very correct visit to Surrealism, but not of a deep-felt or fiery encounter." In fact, he said, Surrealism had lost its enemies, become fashionable, and was dead. Thoughtful reviewers noticed that with few exceptions, the Mexican participants in the show were really not Surrealists at all. Frida, for example, was disqualified from the movement because of her "spiritual ingenuousness." She herself commented in a letter to Nickolas Muray that everyone in Mexico was becoming a Surrealist just to be in the show, but she sent two paintings anyway: *The Two Fridas*, 1939, and *The Wounded Table*, 1940, the only large-scale canvases she ever produced, and paintings upon which she had worked with special urgency, partly because she wanted them to be ready for the show.

Although the "International Exhibition of Surrealism" was important as Mexico's first direct contact with European Surrealist art, its effect on Mexican art was less dramatic than the organizers had hoped. They had seen Mexico as fertile ground for Surrealism, yet Mexicans were not especially receptive. One obstacle was the dominance of the muralist movement, with its commitment to realism. Another impediment, this one harder to circumvent, lay in the fact that Mexico had its own magic and myths and thus did not need foreign notions of fantasy. The self-conscious search for subconscious truths that may have provided European Surrealists with some release from the confines of the rational world and ordinary bourgeois life offered little enchantment in a country where reality and dreams are perceived to merge and miracles are thought to be daily occurrences.

But if the "International Exhibition of Surrealism" and the presence of a number of European Surrealist refugees did not produce a Surrealist movement in Mexico, they did play an important role in stimulating the development of fantastic realism during the 1940s, a time when a number of Mexican artists rejected the hegemony of the muralist movement. Frida was surely one for whom contact with Surrealism served to reinforce both a personal and a cultural inclination toward fantasy. Though she was a Surrealist discovery rather than a Surrealist, there is a definite change in her work after her direct contact with Surrealism in 1938. Paintings from the early 1930s like *Luther Burbank* or *Henry Ford Hospital* display a naïve style and fantasy based on Mexican popular art. After 1938 her paintings became more complex, more penetrating, more disturbingly intense. As the lines that delineated Frida's personality gained strength and the shadows filled with ambiguity, the mischievous impetuosity of her 1929 *Self-Portrait* and the devilish, feminine charm of the *Self-Portrait* she dedicated to Trotsky gave way to a new mystery and magnetism, a greater depth of self-awareness. And if this feeling has much to do with Frida's cumulative years of suffering, the example of Surrealism's stress on the subconscious as the source of artistic content cannot be overlooked, either. Certainly Breton's theories affected the enigma and the psychological innuendo of her most Surrealist work, *What the Water Gave Me* (figure 50), a painting she said had special importance to her. It shows a bathtub reverie in which images of apprehension and recollection, sexuality, pain, and death float on the bathwater above the bather's submerged legs. The mood is elusive and subdued. Memories are glimpsed, not grasped. This feeling of insubstantiality is sustained in the overall transparent gray-blue tonality and the unusually thin paint application. Daliesque in its plethora of minute and irrationally juxtaposed detail, but also recalling Frida's admiration for Bosch and Brueghel, this canvas is the most complex and deliberately enigmatic of all Frida's works.

Frida has painted her own legs from the bather's viewpoint, partially obscured by bathwater. The tips of her feet, protruding from the water, are grotesquely doubled by reflection so that they look like fleshy crabs. The big toe of the deformed right foot is cracked open—a reference to her accident and to later operations. Like something in a horror movie, a twisted, severed vein creeps out of one of the holes in the drain next to her injured toe and drips blood into the water. (Frida's fascination with blood revealed itself in her paintings beginning in 1932, but in the late 1930s it took on a more subtle sexual and sadomasochistic intensity as she observed the intricate dynamics of blood's trickle and flow.) Also bringing to mind a scene from a horror film is the parade of insects, plus a snake and a tiny dancer, that moves across a tightrope held up by a rock/phallus, a mountain peak, and a masked seminude man. The rope lassos the neck and waist of a drowned Frida, who has blood spurting from her mouth and whose naked flesh has turned an ugly shade of gray. A final, blood-curdling detail is the daddy longlegs, several of whose legs reach down from the tightrope to touch Frida's face.

Not surprisingly, *What the Water Gave Me* was the painting with which André Breton chose to illustrate his essay on Frida when it was reprinted in his book *Surrealism and Painting*. He said that when he was in Mexico, Frida was just finishing this work: "*What the Water Yields Me* illustrated, unbeknown to her, the phrase I had once heard from the lips of Nadja [the heroine of Breton's Surrealist novel *Nadja*]: 'I am the thought of bathing in the mirrorless room.' " In a mirrorless room one perceives oneself only from the chest down. The mind can turn inward, and the body, uninhibited by reflections, can play any games it wants.

One can easily see why so many people have called Frida a Surrealist. Her self-mortifying portraits have a surrealistic emphasis on pain and a definite undercurrent of suppressed eroticism. Her use of hybrid figures (part animal, part plant, part human) is familiar from Surrealist iconography, where human limbs sprout branches, and a figure may have the head of a bird or a bull. Frida's frequent opening up or severing of portions of the human body recalls the severed heads and hands or the hollow torsos seen so often in Surrealist painting. Her placement of scenes of dramatic inaction in immeasurably large, open spaces—spaces that are disconnected from everyday reality—can also be construed as a Surrealist device to disassociate the spectator from the rational world. Even her closed-in, claustrophobic spaces might have a Surrealist source: Frida's walls of omnivorous-looking tropical leaves crawling with camouflaged insects recall Max Ernst's lush jungle landscapes.

But Frida's outlook was vastly different from that of the Surrealists. Her art was not the product of a disillusioned European culture searching for an escape from the limits of logic by plumbing the subsconscious. Instead, her fantasy was a product of her temperament, life, and place; it was a way of coming to terms with reality, not of passing beyond reality into another realm. Her symbolism was almost always autobiographical and relatively simple. Although Frida's paintings served a private function, they were meant, like murals, to be accessible in their meaning. The magic in Frida's art is not the magic of melting watches. It is the magic of her longing for her images to have, like ex-votos, a certain efficacy: they were supposed to affect life. Frida explored the surprise and the enigma of immediate experience and real sensations.

The Surrealists invented images of threatened sexuality. Frida made images of her own ruined reproductive system. When in *Roots*, 1943, she joined her own body with a green vine (plate XXVII), she was communicating a specific personal feeling—a childless woman's longing for fertility. Her emotion is utterly clear. Eroticism ran more in Frida's veins than in her head—for her, sex was less Freudian mystification than a fact of life. Similarly, she did not need the tutoring of de Sade to depict with a frankness that verged on ferocity the drama of physical suffering. When Frida paints a stabbed naked woman, a stabbed Virgin of Sorrows or her own stabbed flesh, it is not an anonymous image of pain, nor a Freudian symbol like the punctured finger protruding from a window in Max Ernst's *Oedipus Rex*. When she splits open her torso to reveal a ruined classical column in place of her spinal column, it is not make-believe; she is reporting on her own physical condition. When she paints herself twice in *Tree of Hope*, 1946, once seated and once recumbent (plate XXX), this has nothing to do with irrational juxtaposition for the purpose of creating a "sur-reality." It is not that paradigm of Surrealism described by the French poet Lautréamont, the "chance encounter of a sewing machine and an umbrella on a dissection table." It is a particular surgical patient anesthetized on a hospital trolley and watched over by the part of her being that was strengthened by hope and by will. This bluntness contrasts in the strongest fashion with Surrealist indirection and ellipses.

Even *What the Water Gave Me* is, in fact, more real than surreal. For while the accumulation of small and fantastic details makes this painting appear to be less coherent and less grounded in earthy reality than other works, all its images are closely tied to events or feelings in Frida's life, and the scene taken as a whole is perfectly plausible as a "real" depiction of the dreamer and her dream.

Julien Levy said that Frida rarely talked about her work, but did talk to him about *What the Water Gave Me*. "It's quite explicit," Levy explained. "It is an image of passing time. She indicated, for one thing, that it was about time and childhood games and the sadness of what had happened to her in the course of her life. Dreams, as Frida grew older, were all of them sad. The child's dreams were happy. As a child she played with toys in the bathtub. She had dreams about them. The painting's images relate to her bathtub games. And now she looks at herself in the bathtub, and, as with backward dreaming, all her dreams have turned to a sad ending. She also used to talk a lot about masturbating in the bathtub. And then, she talked about the perspective of herself that is shown in this painting. Philosophically her idea was about the image of yourself that you have because you do not see your own head. The head is something that is looking, but not seen. It is what one carries around to look at life with."

What water offered Frida was a soothing suspension of the objective world so that she could immerse her fantasy in a constellation of fleeting images of the type that cross the inner eye when consciousness is ebbing away. Yet even in this, the most fantastic of her paintings, Frida is down to earth. She has, in fact, depicted "real" images in the most literal, straightforward way. We may not know what each detail means, but she did. Frida's poetry is not one of subtle nuances. Nothing is amorphous or blurry. She draws her lines and is utterly concrete.

Perceiving this, and knowing that realism and Marxism go hand in hand, Diego argued that Frida was a "realist." In a 1943 article called "Frida Kahlo and Mexican Art," he wrote:

> In the panorama of Mexican painting of the last twenty years, the work of Frida Kahlo shines like a diamond in the midst of many inferior jewels; clear and hard, with precisely defined facets. . . .
>
> Recurring self-portraits which are never alike and which increasingly resemble Frida, are everchanging and permanent like a universal dialectic. Monumental realism is brilliantly apparent in Frida's work. Occult materialism is present in the severed heart, the blood flowing on tables, the bathtubs, the plants, the flowers, and the arteries closed by the hemostatic forceps of the painter.
>
> Monumental realism is expressed to the smallest dimensions; tiny heads are sculpted as if they were colossal. So they appear when the magic of a projector magnifies them to the size of a wall. When the photomicroscope enlarges the background of Frida's paintings, reality becomes apparent. The web of veins and the network of cells are distinct, although they lack some elements, giving a new dimension to the art of painting. . . .
>
> Frida's art is individual-collective. Her realism is so monumental that everything has "n" dimensions. Consequently, she paints at the same time the exterior and interior of herself and the world. . . .
>
> In a sky composed of oxygen plus hydrogen plus carbon, and the prime mover electricity, the spirits of space, Huarakan, Kukulkan and Gukamatz are alone with parents and grandparents, and she is in the earth and in

matter, thunder, lightning and the light rays, which in their conversion finally created man. But for Frida, that which is tangible is the mother, the center of all, the mother-sea, tempest, nebula, woman.

If what is described here hardly sounds like the kind of realism that is accessible to the masses and moves them to think of social reform, it is nevertheless realism in the context of Rivera's thought. Frida's paintings, like Rivera's murals, and indeed, much of Mexican art from *retablos* to Posada's engravings, interweave fact and fantasy as if the two were inseparable and equally real.

Frida's humor, too, differs from the sophisticated and disenchanted urge to paradox of European Surrealism. "Surrealism," said Frida, "is the magical surprise of finding a lion in a wardrobe, where you were 'sure' of finding shirts." Her idea of Surrealism was playful: "I use Surrealism as a means of poking fun at others without their realizing it, and of making friends with those who do realize it." Frida's Surrealism was the fun of surprising people by putting a skeleton Judas on top of her bed's canopy, or decorating her plaster casts with iodine and thumbtacks, or making *cadavres exquis*. For her own amusement and to give away as presents, Frida liked to assemble fanciful objects out of an assortment of curios. Probably she got the idea from Breton, Miró, and Dali's Surrealist "assemblages," or from Marcel Duchamp or Joseph Cornell, each of whom paid tribute to Frida by making her a box containing irrationally juxtaposed objects. In Mexico, she could have been inspired by her intimate friend Machila Armida, who made bizarre concoctions of objects like the one in which she incorporated a butterfly, an alligator, a snake, a mask, and barbed wire in order to menace what must be the bride doll that Frida found in Paris in 1939 (and included in her 1943 still life *The Bride Frightened at Seeing Life Opened*).

In the Frida Kahlo Museum beneath a protective glass ball is an assemblage of small objects—an equestrian cowboy on top of a skull, tin soldiers, dice, toy angels, all on pedestals—that might be one of Frida's works. A piece that was surely hers, a gift for Alejandro Gómez Arias, was a world globe that Frida covered with butterflies and flowers. In a later year, when she was sick and unhappy, she asked for it back and covered the butterflies and flowers with red paint to symbolize both her politics and her pain.

Frida made these collage objects in the same spirit in which she arranged her furnishings or her clothes. Unlike the Surrealists, she did not think that her incongruous juxtapositions held a profound significance. For her, ambiguity was a game. Less complex and ironic, more fatalistic and earthily sardonic than Surrealist humor, Frida's humor was a jest at pain and death. By contrast, Surrealist humor is deadly serious. "The trouble with *El Señor* Breton," Frida said once, "is that he takes himself so seriously."

A few discerning critics (besides Rivera) recognized the differences between Frida's art and orthodox Surrealism. In his article "Rise of Another Rivera," published in *Vogue* on the occasion of Frida's Julien Levy exhibition, Bertram Wolfe said: "Though André Breton, who will sponsor her show in Paris, told her she was a *surrealiste,* she did not attain her style by following the methods of that school. . . . Quite free, also, from the Freudian symbols and philosophy that obsess the official Surrealist painters, hers is a sort of 'naive' Surrealism, which she invented for herself. . . . While official Surrealism concerns itself mostly with the stuff of dreams, nightmares, and neurotic symbols, in Madame Rivera's brand of it, wit and humor predominate."

After visiting Frida in Mexico in 1939 to take notes for a projected article, the art historian Parker Lesley wrote her that the main point of his article would be to define her painting as an example of "conscious, purposeful, and useful symbolic painting in opposition to the unconscious, totally obscure cabalistic productions of ingenious frauds such as Dali. You know clearly what you have painted, he admits that he has not the vaguest idea of the meaning of his work. Consequently, the differences, aesthetic and psychological, between honesty and charlatanism should be made available to a reading public."

And in a series of articles on Frida written over the years, Antonio Rodríguez stated his view that Frida was not a Surrealist but rather a "painter deeply rooted in reality . . . an extraordinarily realistic painter." Although it seems connected with that of the Surrealists, he said, "Frida's work, instead of wanderings in the world of oneirocritical sensations, is a bleeding memory of what she has experienced, a kind of autobiography."

In later years, Frida vehemently denied that she was a Surrealist. Surrealism's loss of vogue in the 1940s may have had something to do with this. As Julien Levy said, "the cock was crowing. Practically everyone, when the cock crowed, denied that he was a Surrealist, because it wasn't chic." Many artists who had once been infatuated with Surrealism came to see it as decadent and European. After the war, Paris was no longer the cultural capital of the world; Americans felt that New York was the place where vital new art was being invented, and Mexicans continued to take pride in their native culture. But there were other reasons for Frida's defection as well. Breton's ardent Trotskyism must have exasperated Frida after she and Diego broke with Trotsky; certainly her and Diego's decision in the 1940s to attempt to rejoin the Communist party would have made them both denounce the art movement. Around 1952, Frida put some of her thoughts on the subject in a letter to Antonio Rodríguez:

Some critics have tried to classify me as a Surrealist; but I do not consider myself to be a Surrealist. . . . Really I do not know whether my paintings are Surrealist or not, but I do know that they are the frankest expression of myself. . . . I detest Surrealism. To me it seems to be a decadent manifestation of bourgeois art. A deviation from the true art that the people hope for from the artist. . . . I wish to be worthy, with my painting, of the people to whom I belong and to the ideas that strengthen me. . . . I want my work to be a contribution to the struggle of the people for peace and liberty.

It is interesting that perhaps Frida's most Surrealist work is the diary that she kept from around 1944 to the time of her death. The red leather volume with the initials "J.K." imprinted in gold on the cover (it was said to have belonged to John Keats) was purchased in a rare-book store in New York City by a friend and given to Frida with the hope that filling it might offer her some solace at a time when she was sick and lonely. Into its pages (now there are only 161, because at the end of her life friends tore out sections of it) Frida poured a moving and poetic soliloquy made up of images and words. Since the journal is private and thus did not need to be accessible in its meaning, the grounding in realism to which Frida was committed in her paintings is absent here. The drawings were produced in a playful, improvisatory way, like the assemblage objects or the decorations on her plaster casts. The fact that what she drew or wrote in her journal was intended only for her—or Diego's—eyes freed her to be truly surrealistic if she wished.

Images and words flow with a freedom that must have come from her knowledge of Surrealist "automatism." There are pages of seemingly unconnected words or phrases, and there are lists of words that start with the same letter, occasionally arranged as if they were poems. Perhaps Frida simply liked the words' sound. She wrote, for example (in Spanish):

Now he comes, my hand, my red vision. larger. more yours. martyr of glass. The great unreason. Columns and valleys. the fingers of the wind. bleeding children. the micron mica. I do not know what my joking dream thinks. The ink, the spot. the form. the color. I am a bird. I am everything, without more confusion. All the bells, the rules. The lands. the great grove. the greatest tenderness. the immense tide. garbage. bathtub. letters of cardboard. dice, fingers duets weak hope of making construction. the cloths. the kings. so stupid. my nails. the thread and the hair. the playful nerve I'm going now with myself. An absent minute. You've been stolen from me and I'm leaving crying. He is a *vacilón*.

The diary included love messages to Diego, pages of autobiography, declarations of political faith, expressions of anxiety, loneliness, pain, and thoughts about death. Frida loved nonsense, and the journal is full of it. There are areas of obsessive visual patterning where repeated marks are like lists of meaningless words. She invents fantastic forms and creatures, bizarre people, wild ceremonies. Two of her odder characters are the "strange couple from the country of the dot and the dash." They are "One-eye," a naked man, and "Neferisis," a nude woman holding a fetus. "One-eye," she says, "married the beautiful 'Neferisis' (the immensely wise) in a hot and vital month. To them was born a son with a strange face called Neferunico, he being the founder of the city commonly called 'Lokura' [madness]."

The drawings in the journal are done in bright colored inks, pencils, and crayon handled in a manner that is, if one takes into account the meticulousness of Frida's oil painting style, astonishingly free and painterly. They often have the look of having been made in a trance or by someone drugged. Color bursts wildly out of outlines, lines hurtle or meander as if she were doodling. Figures are fragmented and distorted. Faces are often grotesque masks, and some have multiple profiles that show the influence of Picasso, whose exhibition at Mexico City's Museum of Modern Art Frida admired in the summer of 1944. There are pages full of bodies and parts of bodies that have no logical relationship to each other. The starting point for many images was a drop of ink. Or sometimes Frida began a drawing by putting a spot of color on a page and then, while the color was still wet, closing

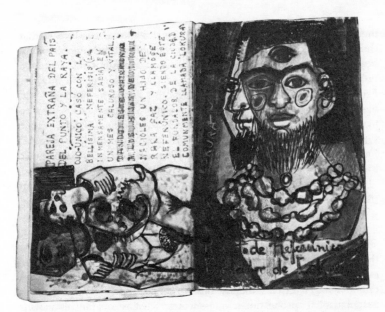

Diary pages.

the diary, so that the spot changed shape and was doubled. Using these shapes as points of departure, she elaborated on them, inventing beasts or dragons like the "horrendous Ojosauro primitivo."

Of such surrealistic procedures for incorporating accident into art, Frida wrote: "Who would say that spots live and help one live?! Ink, blood smell. I do not know what ink I would use that would want to leave its track in such forms. I respect its wishes and I will do what I can to flee from myself worlds, Inked worlds—land free and mine. Far away suns that call me because I form a part of their nucleus. Foolishness . . . What would I do without the absurd and the fleeting?"

The idea of using line and form to capture fantastic images from the unconscious occurs also in several drawings, done on small, loose sheets of paper in the 1940s. Several of these comprise highly intricate networks of lines in which images such as faces, breasts, feet, veins, and eyes seem to be metamorphosed out of the very substance of the lines' energy and momentum. Frida's webs and doodles appear as obsessive as lunatics' drawings. Yet they sometimes look intentionally crazy. It is as if Frida self-consciously used the technique of Surrealist automatism to probe her own neuroses; what she came up with is not pure emotional authenticity (if there is such a thing). Her result is as full of artifice as any art.

And paradoxically, there is a kind of "realism" even in these drawings and diary sketches in which Frida tries to tap the spontaneous process of thought through free-flowing color and form. For an often bedridden invalid, the adventures of the unconscious mind and its ever-changing encounters at the crossroads of consciousness are, after all, a principal reality, just as "real" as daydreams. In the end, Frida was right when she said: "They thought I was a Surrealist, but I wasn't. I never painted dreams. I painted my own reality."

PART 5

Chapter 17

A Necklace of Thorns

In New York, after her Paris sojourn, Frida stayed briefly with her friend the pianist Ella Paresce; she left precipitately for Mexico before the end of April. Her affair with Nickolas Muray had come to an end.

"Dear, Dear Frida," Muray wrote in the middle of May:

I should have written you long ago. It is a difficult world you and I live in.

It has been pretty desperate for you but so no less for me when I left you in N.Y. and I heard from Ella P. [Paresce] everything about your departure.

I was not shocked or angry. I knew how unhappy you were, how much you needed your familiar surroundings, your friends, Diego, your own house and habits.

I knew N.Y. only filled the bill as a temporary substitute and I hope you found your haven intact on your return. Of the three of us there was only two of you. I always felt that. Your tears told me that when you heard his voice. The one of me is eternally grateful for the Happiness that the half of you so generously gave. My Dearest Frida—

like you I've been starved for true affection. When you left I knew it was all over. Your instinct guided you so wisely. You have done the only logical thing for I could not transplant Mexico to N.Y. for you and I've learned how essential that was for your happiness. . . .

My affection for you curiously has not changed, nor ever will. I hope you'll understand that. I should like a chance to prove that. Your painting is a joy to me. Very soon I shall mail you your color portrait I promised you. It is on exhibition in Los Angeles Art Center. I want to know everything you want me to know.

Affectionately Nick

If Frida went home because she needed her "familiar surroundings," it is also clear that Muray hurt her deeply, probably by an involvement with the woman who became his wife in June. One friend recalls that when Frida returned to Mexico, she was unhappy because a "handsome American man" had jilted her, and for a cruel reason: her physical ailments hindered the free physical expression of sexual love. The handsome man could well have been Muray. Certainly the closing paragraph of Muray's May letter is fond rather than ardent.

In her despair, Frida telephoned him from Mexico, and he wrote:

Darling you must pull yourself together and lift yourself by your own bootstraps. You have at your fingertips a gift that love God or gossip cannot take away from you. You must work work paint paint work work. You must believe in yourself and in your own power. I also want you to believe that I will be your friend no matter what happens to you or me. You must know I mean this. I am self conscious writing to you of love and heart, because, because I am not sure if you won't misconstrue what I say. . . .

Caring for you will never end. It can't! I just as well get rid of my right arm my ear or my brain. You understand that don't you. Frida you are a great person a great painter. I know you'll live up to this. I also know I've hurt you. I will try to heal this hurt with a Friendship that I hope will be as important to you as yours to me is

Your Nick

On June 13 she replied with a farewell that has some of the poignancy of her first *Self-Portrait,* and none of the buoyancy of her other letters to Muray or of the saucy self-portraits from the previous year.

Nick darling, I got my wonderful picture you send to me, I find it even more beautiful than in New York. Diego says that it is as marvelous as a Piero de la Francesca. To me [it] is more than that, it is a treasure, and besides, it will always remind me that morning we had breakfast together in the Barbizon Plaza Drug Store, and afterwards we went to your shop to take photos. This one was one of them. And now I have it near me. You will always be inside the magenta *rebozo* (on the left side). Thanks million times for sending it.

When I received your letter, few days ago, I didn't know what to do. I must tell you that I couldn't help weeping. I felt that something was in my throat, just as if I had swallowed the whole world. I don't know yet if I was sad, jealous or angry, but the sensation I felt was in first place of a great despair. I have read your letter many times, too many I think, and now I realize things that I couldn't see at first. Now, I understand every thing perfectly clearly, and the only thing I want, is to tell you with my best words, that you deserve in life the best, the very best, because you are one of the few people in this lousy world who are honest to themselves, and that is the only thing that really counts. I don't know why I could feel hurt one minute because you are happy, it is so silly the way mexican wenches (like myself) see life sometimes! But you know that, and I am sure you will forgive me for behaving so stupidly. Nevertheless you have to understand that no matter what happens to us in life, you will always be, for myself, the same Nick I met one morning in New York in 18 E. 48th St. I told Diego that you were going to marry soon. He said that to Rose and Miguel [Covarrubias], the other day when they came to visit us, so I had to tell them that it was true. I am terribly sorry to have said it before asking you if it was O.K., but now it's done, and I beg you to forgive my indiscretion.

I want to ask from you a great favor, please, send by mail the little *cushion*, I don't want anybody else to have it. I promise to make another one for you, but I want that one you have now on the couch downstairs, near the window. Another favor: Don't let "her" touch the fire signals on the stairs (you know which ones). If you can, and it isn't too much trouble, don't go to Coney Island, specially to the *Half Moon*, with her. Take down the photo of myself which was on the fire place, and put it in Mam's room in the shop, I am sure she still likes me as much as she did before. Besides it is not so nice for the other lady to see my portrait in your house. I wish I could tell you many things but I think it is no use to bother you. I hope you will understand without words all my wishes. . . .

About my letters to you, if they are in the way, just give them to Mam and she will mail them back to me. I don't want to be a trouble in your life in any case.

Please forgive me for acting just like an old fashion sweet heart asking you to give me back my letters, it is ridiculous on my part, but I do it for you, not for me, because I imagine that you don't have any interest in having those papers with you.

While I was writing this letter Rose telephoned and told me that you got married already. I have nothing to say about what I felt. I hope you will be happy, very happy.

If you find time once in a while, please write to me just a few words telling me how you are, will you do it? . . .

Thanks for the magnificent photo, again and again. Thanks for your last letter, and for all the treasures you gave me.

Love
Frida

Please forgive me for having phoned to you that evening. I won't do it any more.

Losing Nickolas Muray's love and being replaced by another woman was heartbreaking for Frida, not only because her affair with him had been more than casual, but because, even as Muray wrote, "Of the three of us there was only two of you," she and Diego were separating. By midsummer she had moved into her own blue house in Coyoacán, leaving Diego in San Angel. By September 19 they had begun divorce proceedings, and by mid-October they had petitioned for a divorce by mutual consent before the court of Coyoacán. Frida's old friend Manuel González Ramírez served as her lawyer. By the end of the year, the divorce came through.

Friends have several explanations for the separation and divorce, none of which is entirely convincing. Possibly Rivera learned of Frida's affair with Nickolas Muray; certainly the real passion she felt for the dashing Hungarian would have made him even more jealous than usual. Some say that the source of the Riveras' problem was sexual—Frida's physical fragility or her lack of desire made her either unable or unwilling to satisfy Rivera's sexual needs. Others say that Rivera was impotent. Frida once blamed Lupe Marín for breaking up her marriage. It is true that Rivera always retained an attraction to his ex-wife, and he was tied to her as the mother of his children. "When Frida was good for nothing anymore, he came singing at my windows," Lupe said. His admiration for her beauty certainly shows in his 1938 *Portrait of Lupe Marín*, but Lupe also remembered that he painted the portrait at Frida's urging, and that Frida was not at all jealous of Rivera's attentions to his former wife. Another theory is that Rivera divorced Frida to protect her from reprisals as a result of his political activities. Jean van Heijenoort thinks he might have found out about Frida's affair with Trotsky.

When the divorce proceedings were initiated, there was a rumor that Rivera was planning to marry the pretty Hungarian painter Irene Bohus; but though she became one of his assistants after the decree was final, and though Frida was certainly jealous of her, eventually the two women became such close friends that her name is one of those that decorate the wall of Frida's bedroom. Perhaps there was a triangle: a photograph (published in October 1939) shows Bohus and Diego in Rivera's San Angel studio; both artists are painting the famous American movie star Paulette Goddard. Rivera is widely believed to have been romantically involved with Paulette Goddard, who had taken up residence at the luxurious San Angel Inn, just across the street from Rivera's studio. The press made much of this affair, and so did Diego. But though Frida was displeased by Rivera's infatuation, she and Paulette, too, became friends, and in 1941 Frida painted *The Flower Basket*, a charming still life tondo for her ex-rival.

In October, the press reported that Frida and Diego said divorce was the only way to preserve their friendship. New York's *Herald Tribune* noted that Frida and Diego had been parted for five months, and that Rivera had called the divorce just a matter of "legal convenience." In *Time* magazine he elaborated: "There is no change in the magnificent relations between us. We are doing it in order to improve Frida's legal position . . . purely a matter of legal convenience in the spirit of modern times."

Some newspapers said that "artistic differences"—of all things!—had led to the separation, that it would help Frida to "paint more freely."

At a party he gave to celebrate his divorce, Rivera proffered still another reason. Bertram Wolfe's *Diego Rivera: His Life and Times* had just been published, and in it Wolfe had said: "This is the tenth year of their marriage, and Diego grows more and more dependent upon his wife's judgment and comradeship. If he should lose her now, the solitude which besets him would be much heavier than it is." At the party, Diego asked a friend to "tell Bert that I have divorced Frida to prove that my biographer was wrong."

The separation had been accomplished with "no trouble, no fuss," Diego told a reporter at San Angel. "There are no sentimental, artistic, or economic questions involved. It is really in the nature of a precaution." His esteem for Frida, he continued, was higher than ever. "Nevertheless, I believe that with my decision I am helping Frida's life to develop in the best possible way. She is young and beautiful. She has had much success in the most demanding art centers. She has every possibility that life can offer her, while I am already old and no longer have much to offer her. I count her among the five or six most prominent modernist painters."

When the same journalist interviewed Frida in Coyoacán, she had little to say. "We have been separated for five months. Our difficulties began after my return to Mexico from Paris and New York. We were not getting along well." She added that she had no intention of marrying again, and cited "intimate reasons, personal causes, difficult to explain" as the motive for the divorce.

Like the rift over Diego's affair with Cristina in 1934 and 1935, the Riveras' separation was unconventional. They saw each other often, and their lives remained intricately intertwined. Frida continued to look after Diego's well-being, handling his correspondence and helping with his business transactions. When the American engineer Sigmund Firestone commissioned a pair of life-size self-portraits by Frida and Diego as a memento of their hospitality to him and his daughters, it was Frida who served as intermediary. On January 9, 1940, just after the divorce came through, Firestone wrote to Diego from the U.S.: "I trust that by this time you and Frida are busy painting yourselves for my benefit. Please make them both on the same size canvas as I intend to always keep them together in memory of our pleasant acquaintanceship. You remember my telling you of my talk with Frida, at the Reforma, and of having advised her that the total cost will be $500.00 to be divided between you two for the two paintings." On February 15, Frida responded (in English) on Diego's behalf, because, she wrote, "his English is lousy and he is ashamed to write." She said that she had had "some troubles," but that her portrait was finished

XVII   Self-Portrait with Monkey, 1940

XVIII   Self-Portrait with Cropped Hair, 1940

XIX   Self-Portrait, 1940

XX   Self-Portrait with Monkeys, 1943

XXI   Self-Portrait as a Tehuana, 1943

XXII   Thinking About Death, 1943

XXIII   Self-Portrait with Small Monkey, 1945

XXIV   Self-Portrait, 1947

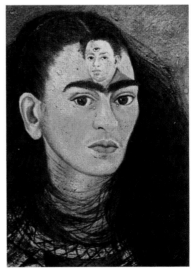

XXV   Self-Portrait, 1948

XXVI   Diego and I, 1949

XXVII   Roots, 1943

XXVIII   The Broken Column, 1944

XXIX   Without Hope, 1945

XXX   Tree of Hope, 1946

XXXI   The Little Deer, 1946

XXXII   Sun and Life, 1947

XXXIII The Love Embrace of the Universe, the Earth (Mexico), Diego, Me and Señor Xolotl, 1949

XXXIV Self-Portrait with the Portrait of Doctor Farill, 1951

XXXV Viva la Vida, 1954

and she would send it as soon as Diego finished his. Frida then described in the most understated way possible what her "troubles" were:

Diego is happier now than when you saw him. He eats well and sleeps well and work with great energy. I see him very often but he doesn't want to live in the same house with me anymore because he likes to be alone and he says I always want to have his papers and other things in order, and he likes them in disorder. Well anyway I take care of him the best I can from the distance, and I will love him all my life even if he wouldn't want me to.

Frida signed her letter, as she was wont to do, with magenta-pink lipstick kisses, and she enclosed (as also was her wont) bright pink feathers as a token of her affection.

Diego and Frida continued to entertain and make public appearances together as well. Friends remembered the commotion the divorcees made arriving, always late, at Rivera's box in the concert hall of the Palace of Fine Arts accompanied by his daughters, a current mistress, and either Cristina Kahlo or Lupe Marín. Parker Lesley recalls one such occasion: "No one paid any attention to the dance performance by Carmen Amaya. Everyone stared at Frida, who wore her Tehuana dress and all Diego's gold jewelry, and clanked like a knight in armor. She had the Byzantine opulence of the Empress Theodora, a combination of barbarism and elegance. She had two gold incisors and when she was all gussied up she would take off the plain gold caps and put on gold caps with rose diamonds in front, so that her smile really sparkled." Frida was pleased with the company of the art historian because Lesley not only was entranced with Frida's person, he also admired her work. "For her, this was better than love," he says. When the dancers broke for intermission, Frida took the attractive young American by the hand, giving it a squeeze, and led him to the bar. Crowds parted before them as if she were a queen.

Frida was openly seductive. She "loved the minuet of flirtation" and danced it well. But even as she dallied with others, her real interest remained focused on Diego. Just as her Tehuana costume hid her physical ailments, her diamond-studded smile and her flamboyant flirtatiousness hid the pain of rejection. In public she was vibrant, devil-may-care; defiantly she embarked on love affairs, one in particular with a Spanish refugee, Ricardo Arias Viñas, whom she probably met during her work for the Spanish Republican cause. In private, she confided her anguish to a few close friends—and to her art.

"Nick Darling," she wrote to Nickolas Muray on October 13, "I couldn't write to you before, since you left [Muray had been in Mexico in September], my situation with Diego was worse and worse, till came to an end. Two weeks ago we began the divorce. I have no words to tell you how much I been suffering and knowing how much I love Diego you must understand that this troubles will never end in my life, but after the last fight I had with him (by phone) because it is almost a month that I don't see him, I understood that for him it is much better to leave me. . . . Now I feel so rotten and lonely that it seems to me that nobody in the world has suffer the way I do, but of course it will be different I hope in a few months."

All during the fall of 1939 and winter of 1940 Frida was depressed and ill. She had a fungus infection on the fingers of her right hand that sometimes prevented her from working, and worse still, terrible pains in her spine. Some of the doctors she consulted recommended an operation; others opposed it. Dr. Juan Farill told her she needed complete rest, and he ordered an apparatus with a twenty-kilogram weight to stretch her spine. A photograph taken by Nickolas Muray shows her trapped in this device; her expression, though forbearant, cries out with the agony of being unable to move. By the end of 1939, she was so desperate that she was drinking a full bottle of brandy each day.

Although she was lonely, she avoided company, especially friends she had in common with Diego. In her October letter to Muray she said she had not seen the Covarrubiases or Juan O'Gorman, because "I don't want to see anyone that is near Diego," and to Wolfgang Paalen she wrote that she had refused to see him and Alice Rahon because her current situation was the hardest thing she had ever been through; given her state of mind, the best thing she could do for her friends, she said, was not to see them. In January, she wrote to Muray: "I don't see anybody. I am almost all day in my house. Diego came the other day to try to *convince* me that nobody in the world is like *me!* Lots of crap kid. I *can't* forgive him, and that is all—"

Years later, in his autobiography, Rivera recollected his and Frida's divorce with a Riveraesque mixture of self-deprecation and self-congratulation. At least in retrospect, he was aware of Frida's suffering:

I never was . . . a faithful husband, even with Frida. As with Angelina and Lupe, I indulged my caprices and had affairs. Now, moved by the extremity of Frida's condition [he refers to her ill health], I began taking stock of myself as a marriage partner. I found very little which could be said in my favor. And yet I knew that I could not change.

Once, on discovering that I was having an affair with her best friend [he refers to Cristina], Frida left me, only to return with somewhat diminished pride but undiminished love. I loved her too much to want to cause her suffering, and to spare her further torments, I decided to separate from her.

In the beginning, I only hinted at the idea of a divorce, but when the hints brought no response, I made the suggestion openly. Frida, who had by now recovered her health, responded calmly that she would prefer to endure anything rather than lose me completely.

The situation between us grew worse and worse. One evening, entirely on impulse, I telephoned her to plead for her consent to a divorce, and in my anxiety, fabricated a stupid and vulgar pretext. I dreaded a long, heart-wrenching discussion so much that I impulsively seized on the quickest way to my end.

It worked. Frida declared that she too wanted an immediate divorce. My "victory" quickly changed to gall in my heart. We had been married for 13 [actually ten] years. We still loved each other. I simply wanted to be free to carry on with any woman who caught my fancy. Yet Frida did not object to my infidelity as such. What she could not understand was my choosing women who were either unworthy of me or inferior to her. She took it as a personal humiliation to be abandoned for sluts. To let her draw any line, however, was this not to circumscribe my freedom? Or was I simply the depraved victim of my own appetites? And wasn't it merely a consoling lie to think that a divorce would put an end to Frida's suffering? Wouldn't Frida suffer even more?

During the two years we lived apart, Frida turned out some of her best work, sublimating her anguish in her painting.

On the day the divorce papers came through, Frida had nearly finished what is probably her best-known painting, *The Two Fridas* (plate XIV). American art historian MacKinley Helm was there:

I had tea with Frida Kahlo de Rivera . . . on the December day in 1939 when there was handed into the studio a set of papers announcing the final settlement of her divorce from Rivera. Frida was decidedly melancholy. It was not she who had ordained the dissolution of the marriage, she said; Rivera himself had insisted upon it. He had told her that separation would be better for them both, and had persuaded her to leave him. But he had by no means convinced her that she would be happy, or that her career would prosper, apart from him.

She was working then on her first big picture, a huge canvas called *Las Dos Fridas*. . . . There are two full-length self-portraits in it. One of them is the Frida that Diego had loved . . . the second Frida, the woman whom Diego no longer loves. There the artery is ruptured. The Frida scorned tries to stay the flow of blood, momentarily, with a pair of surgeon's forceps. When the divorce papers arrived, while we were looking at the picture, I half expected her to seize the dripping instrument and fling it across the room.

"I began painting it three months ago and I finished it yesterday," Frida said to reporters a few days later. "That's all I can tell you." *The Two Fridas* sit side by side on a bench, their hands joined in a stiff but poignant clasp. The Frida Diego no longer loves wears a white Victorian dress; the other wears a Tehuana skirt and blouse, and her face is perhaps just a shade darker than that of her more Spanish companion, suggesting (like the contemporaneous *Two Nudes in a Forest*) Frida's dual heritage—part Mexican Indian and part European. Both Fridas have their hearts exposed—the same unashamedly literal device to show pain in love that Frida used in *Memory*. The unloved Frida's lace bodice is torn to reveal her breast and her broken heart. The other Frida's heart is whole.

Each Frida has one hand placed near her sexual organs. The unloved woman holds surgical pincers, the Tehuana Frida a miniature portrait of Diego Rivera as a child, taken from an old photograph that is now among the memorabilia in the Frida Kahlo Museum. From the crimson frame of the oval-shaped miniature springs a long red vein that also resembles an umbilical cord emerging from a placenta. Diego's egg-shaped portrait thus seems to stand for both a lost baby and a lost lover. To Frida, Diego was both.

The vein winds around the Tehuana Frida's arm, continues through her heart, then leaps across space to the other Frida, circling her neck, entering her broken heart, and finally ending on her lap, where she shuts off its flow with the surgical pincers. A note to Diego in Frida's journal says: "My blood is the miracle that travels in the veins of the air from my heart to yours." In anger and despair at the divorce, she cuts off this magical flow with surgical pincers. But the blood continues to drip, and in her white lap it forms a pool that overflows to make another puddle. Below, stains on her skirt echo red embroidered flowers. The striking image of blood on white cloth makes one think of martyrdom, of miscarriage, of sheets besmirched with blood in several of Frida's paintings. But even in the face of tragedy, Frida is sardonic: some of the small embroidered flowers are slyly transformed into dripping splotches of blood.

The two Fridas' willfully impassive faces are profiled against a gray-and-white sky as turbulent as the one El Greco painted above the hilltop at Toledo: dark rents in the jagged clouds at once reflect the figures' inner turmoil and heighten the disturbing paralysis of pose and demeanor. As often in her full-length self-portraits, Frida is alone in an endless, flat, empty space. (In bust-length self-portraits, walls of vegetation often close off space directly behind the figure.) Except for the Mexican bench on which she sits, she is completely disconnected from any solid objects that might provide the comfort of familiarity. All her powers of observation are fixed instead on her own image—a focus that makes the self-contained image all the more explosive.

And all the more alone: Frida's only companion is herself. The doubling of her self deepens the chill of loneliness. Abandoned by Diego, she holds her own hand, and links her two selves with a blood vein. Her world is thus self-enclosed, a dead end. Frida once said that *The Two Fridas* showed the "duality of her personality." Like those other self-portraits that show her twice (*Two Nudes in a Forest* and *Tree of Hope*), *The Two Fridas* is an image of self-nurture: Frida comforts, guards, or fortifies herself.

There are other kinds of duality at work here too. The long hours spent scrutinizing her reflection in the mirror and reproducing that reflection must have accentuated Frida's sense of having two identities: the observer and the observed, the self as it is felt from within and the self as it appears from without. Thus Frida not only depicted herself twice, here and in other self-portraits; she approached the body and face schismatically. Her body, either nude or dressed in ruffles and ribbons, she painted as a subject for the artist's scrutiny; the female in the passive role of pretty object, victim of pain, or participant in nature's cycles of fecundity. By contrast, looking at her face in the mirror, she perceived herself as depictor, not as object depicted. She thus became both active artist and passive model, dispassionate investigator of what it feels like to be a woman and passionate respository of feminine emotions. Rivera recognized this dichotomy as male-female when he called Frida *"la pintora mas pintor"*—using both the feminine and the masculine terms.

In her January 1940 letter to Nickolas Muray, Frida mentioned that she was "working like hell" to finish a big painting for the Surrealist show, and on February 6 she said she intended to send this same painting to Julien Levy, and that she was working hard for the exhibition Levy had offered her in October or November. (The exhibition was never held because, Levy said, the war in Europe made it impossible.) The work to which she referred is *The Wounded Table*—yet another painting full of dripping blood (figure 55). Like *The Two Fridas*, it is a dramatization of loneliness. In the double self-portrait Frida accompanied herself. Here she is accompanied by her niece and nephew, Isolda and Antonio Kahlo, by her pet fawn, El Granizo (meaning "hail," presumably because his spots resembled hailstones), and by a Judas, a pre-Columbian idol, and a skeleton, but their presence is not consoling.

Behind a long table, Frida and her three inanimate companions face us like a tribunal. The brutish, overalls-clad Judas embraces her, his network of phallic fuses seeming to ensnare her as well. The elongated arm of the Nayarit idol (based on a sculpture of an embracing seated couple now in the Frida Kahlo Museum) is painted in such a way that it appears both to hug Frida and to be a continuation of her right arm. Equally intimate with her, the grinning clay skeleton fondles a lock of her hair, entangling it in the coiled spring that forms its forearm. The Judas's chest and right foot are bleeding, the idol has peg legs, and the skeleton has a broken right foot (like Frida). Even the table is wounded. Blood oozing from its knots drips onto the floor, onto the Judas's and the skeleton's feet, and onto the ruffle of Frida's Tehuana skirt; each of its legs is a flayed human leg like that of an *écorché*. As a symbol of domesticity, the wounded table must stand for Frida's broken marriage.

Frida has staged this painting carefully. Two heavy fringed curtains are pulled back to reveal a wooden platform in front of a backdrop that consists of a stormy sky and predatory jungle plants. The characters are in a moment of suspended animation, like actors just after the curtain is raised. Their stasis is that of the storm's eye: they seem frozen by the heroine's panicked loneliness. Probably the play being performed was a way of sending a message to Diego: the actors sit in judgment, and the judgment they hand down as they stare at the viewer is clearly an angry one.

Frida's preoccupation with death at the time of her divorce is revealed again in *The Dream*, 1940, where she sleeps in her four-poster bed floating in the lavender, cloud-filled sky of her dream—a sky that appears to be a continuation of the lavender shadows on the rumpled white garment that envelops her (plate XV). Once again, she pairs herself with a skeleton, this time one in the form of the Judas that she actually did keep on top of her bed's canopy, and that she explained to frightened or bewildered visitors as an amusing reminder of her own mortality. While Frida sleeps, the plant embroidered on her bright yellow bedspread (she did, in fact, have a bedspread embroidered with flowers) springs to life, becoming a thorny vine that bursts into foliage around her face and grows away from the bedspread and into the air as though it were a real plant, not just stitches of embroidery thread. It is as if Frida were dreaming of a time, long after death, when plants would sprout from her grave.

Like Frida, the skeleton rests its head on two pillows, but instead of a vine, it is entwined with wires and explosives, and it holds a bouquet of lavender flowers. Unlike Frida, whose face is calm in sleep, the skeleton stares and grimaces. At any moment, one feels, it could explode, making Frida's dream of death a reality. The skeleton is Frida's "lover," as Diego once teasingly said. It is her other half.

In almost all the self-portraits from the year of her divorce, Frida gives herself companions—skeletons, a Judas, her niece and nephew, her own alternate self, and her pets. The most intriguing of these are her monkeys, who often embrace her like intimate friends.

In her first self-portrait with a monkey, the 1937 painting *Fulang-Chang and I*, Frida's companion is primarily a symbol of promiscuity. But it is also her offspring and her ancestor (in *Moses*, 1945, she put a male and a female ape next to the original man and woman): Frida draws a parallel between her pet's simian features and her own and then goes on to emphasize her feeling of connectedness to the animal by wrapping a lavender silk ribbon around its neck and hers. All of this is done in the spirit of affection and humor. When, on the other hand, in the 1940 *Self-Portrait with Monkey* (plate XVII) she winds a blood-red ribbon around her own neck four times and then uses it as a metaphoric bloodline to tie herself to her monkey, the feeling is one of desperation; and the way the animal wraps its arm around her so that its paw merges with, or seems to be an extension of, her braided hair is sinister.

After the divorce, Frida's monkeys, and especially the spider monkey called Caimito de Guayabal (meaning guava-patch fruit), which Diego had brought her upon his return from a trip to southern Mexico, helped to fill some of the place vacated by her great mischievous, jealous child, Diego; they also took the place of the children she would now surely never have. Thus in her art, monkeys play a more complex and subtle role. Beginning in 1939, when she portrayed herself in bust-length self-portraits with things like ribbons, veins, vines, thorny branches, monkeys' paws, or strands of her own hair encircling her neck, one feels that these "connectors" threaten to choke her, and they heighten the sense of claustrophobia created by walls of inter-twining jungle plants that close off space directly behind her. And though they console her and provide company, the monkeys under-score her terror at being alone. Their physical proximity is disturbing. For all their child-like innocence, spider monkeys are emphatically not children; they are wild jungle animals. In Frida's paintings their animal restlessness heightens the tension of her regal calm, and hints at a bestial wildness hidden beneath her skin.

In another 1940 *Self-Portrait,* which Frida sold to Nickolas Muray, she is accompanied by Caimito de Guayabal and a black cat, and from her necklace of thorns dangles a dead hummingbird (plate XVI). The monkey combines what appears to be an almost human capacity for empathy toward his abandoned mistress with simian unpredictability. As he gingerly fingers Frida's necklace of thorns, the viewer feels that with one ill-considered tug, he could deepen her wounds. The cat is a menace too. Poised to pounce, his ears forward, he fixes his eyes on the hummingbird, which hangs against Frida's bare, already bleed-ing flesh. Since the hummingbird not only represents a species with which Frida felt closely associated (she turned her eyebrows into a bird in a 1946 drawing and people said she moved with the swift lightness of a hummingbird), its lifeless body probably refers to the fact that once again Frida felt "murdered by life." It has another mean-ing as well: in Mexico, hummingbirds are used as magic charms to bring luck in love.

Frida wears Christ's crown of thorns as a necklace again in yet an-other bust-length *Self-Portrait* from the same year, one in which a hand-shaped brooch holds a ribbon on which she has written: "I painted my portrait in the year 1940 for Dr. Eloesser, my doctor and my best friend. With all love, Frida Kahlo" (plate XIX). As in the Muray *Self-Portrait,* and in *The Broken Column*—indeed, in many of her self-portraits—Frida has amplified her personal misery by giving it Christian significance. She presents herself as a martyr; the thorns draw blood. Although she had rejected religion, Christian imagery, especially the theatrically bloody martyrdoms familiar in Mexican art, pervades Frida's work. The bloodiness and self-mortification goes back, of course, to Aztec tradition, for the Aztecs not only practiced human sacrifice, they also pricked their own skin and punctured their ears to draw blood so that crops would flourish. But it was Christianity that brought to colonial Mexico the depiction of pain in realistic and human terms, with the result that almost every Mexican church has a frighteningly veristic sculpture of Christ, either whipped at the post, dragging his cross, or dead, his body always full of bloody, suppurating wounds. Frida, who owned a particularly stomach-turning painting of Christ on the road to Calvary, used the same extreme pain and realism to get her private message across; if she borrowed the rhetoric of Catholicism, it was because her paintings were, in their own way, about salvation.

Although she was at this time trying to accelerate production in order to be able to make a living from her work, and although there are similarities in the various bust-length self-portraits' formats, Frida did not use a formula. To be sure, the angle at which her head is turned is often the same; this was clearly the angle that minimized the movement involved in turning back and forth between canvas and mirror. But each painting is treated as a separate self-confrontation. Acute attention to details, like the way the hummingbird is tied to the necklace of thorns, the choice and placement of plants (white buds next to dried brown twigs in the Eloesser *Self-Portrait*, for example), or the precise rhythm and tightness of an encircling ribbon, makes each portrait marvelously distinct. In all of them, Frida appears grave, her head held high with her characteristic hauteur. Her face is older, tenser, and more wary than it was in self-portraits done before her separation from Diego. One feels a charge of emotion behind the mask of control as Frida braces herself against her own vulnerability, and at the same time makes sure that the viewer recognizes her suffering. Her elaborate self-mythologizing performance provides psychological distance from what might otherwise be overwhelming grief. Calling perhaps upon the pieties of her Catholic childhood, she turns herself into an icon that she—and others—can worship, thus transcending pain.

The self-portraits from 1940 also show clearly the degree to which Frida had by this time grasped the power of color to communicate emotion. To eyes accustomed to the French tradition in the visual arts, Frida's color choices—olive, orange, purple, many earthy tones, and a hallucinatory yellow—are jarring. Although her bizarre palette reflects her love of the untutored color combinations in Mexican popular art, Frida cunningly makes color set off psychological drama. Pink is often used in ironic contrast to violence or death; in several self-portraits a yellow olive accentuates the feeling of claustrophobic oppression; the gray blue of Frida's skies and the lavender or burnt sienna of her earth give an edge to the expression of alienation and despair. Since not much black is used to model forms, her paintings often have a visionary brilliance.

In her diary in the mid-1940s, Frida explained the meaning of colors in a sort of prose poem: "I will try," she wrote, to use "the pencils that are sharpened to the infinite point that always locks forward." There follows a list of hues, some of them designated by small patches of colored lines arranged in patterns, others identified by name:

GREEN: warm and good light
REDDISH PURPLE: Aztec. Tlapali [Aztec word for "color" used for painting and drawing]. Old blood of prickly pear. The most alive and oldest.
BROWN: color of *mole*, of the leaf that goes. Earth.
YELLOW: madness, sickness, fear. Part of the sun and of joy.
COBALT BLUE: electricity and purity. Love.
BLACK: nothing is black, really *nothing*.
LEAF GREEN: leaves, sadness, science. The whole of Germany is this color.
GREENISH YELLOW: more madness and mystery. All the phantoms wear suits of this color. . . . . . or at least underclothes.
DARK GREEN: color of bad news and good business.
NAVY BLUE: *distance*. Also tenderness can be of this blue.
MAGENTA: Blood? Well, who knows!

The Eloesser *Self-Portrait* has lurid colors—pink, greenish ocher, yellow, the bright red of Frida's lips and blood. Its baroque opulence and the predominance of an opalescent pink contrasts in the strongest way with the painful image of Frida's bleeding neck. One is reminded of the lacerated Christ figures in Mexican churches, where gruesome wounds are surrounded by pretty flowers, luxurious laces, velvets, and gold. By contrast, *Self-Portrait with Monkey* is dark and austere; black in the interstices between leaves in the foliage wall suggests that the time is night; the nocturnal gloom is only intensified by the blood-red ribbon circling and recircling Frida's neck. In the *Self-Portrait* (figure 56) commissioned by Sigmund Firestone, on the other hand, the combination of a bright yellow-green background with purple ribbons in black hair, plus jade beads and the lavender embroidery on the white *huipil* (shirt or blouse), sets the viewer's teeth on edge, as Frida surely knew it would. If yellow and greenish yellow meant madness, Frida must have been feeling crazy, for she used a lot of yellow in the paintings produced during her divorce from Diego.

Frida painted another self-portrait in 1940 in which color's unnerving bite transmits her distress at being separated from Diego. *Self-Portrait with Cropped Hair* shows the artist sitting on a bright yellow Mexican chair in the midst of a large expanse of reddish-brown earth that is covered with strands of her shorn black hair (plate XVIII). The sky is full of pinkish, nacreous clouds that should be soft and lovely, but are instead airless and oppressive, like the clouds in the *Self-Portrait* dedicated to Dr. Eloesser. The chair is gay and folkloric, but the way Frida has made it the only bright object in the painting accentuates the feeling of desolation.

A month after her divorce came through, Frida did what she had done in 1934 in response to Rivera's affair with Cristina: she cropped her hair. On February 6, she wrote to Nickolas Muray: "I have to give you bad news: I cut my hair, and look just like a ferry [fairy]. Well, it will grow again, I hope!" One story has it that Frida warned Diego that she would cut off her long hair, which he adored, if he persisted in his current liaison (perhaps with Paulette Goddard). He persisted, and she carried out her threat. Whether the story is true or not, it is certainly typical of Frida. A mood of angry retaliation is expressed in *Self-Portrait with Cropped Hair,* in which she has also stripped herself of the Tehuana costume Diego liked her to wear. Instead, she is dressed in a man's suit that is so large it must be Diego's. She sits with her legs apart like a man, and she wears men's black lace-up shoes and a man's shirt. Earrings are her only vestige of femininity.

By destroying attributes of female sexuality, Frida has committed a vengeful act that serves to heighten her loneliness. A lock of hair hangs between her legs like a murdered animal. She holds the scissors that did the cropping poised near her genitals, in exactly the position of the surgical pincers that cut the vein connecting her with Diego's miniature portrait in *The Two Fridas*. In both paintings one senses that some macabre act has been performed—a violent rejection of femininity, or a desire to excise the part of herself that possesses the capacity to love. The symbolic cutting away of vulnerability and attachment does not, of course, arrest the malignancy of sorrow. In *The Two Fridas*, blood keeps on dripping from the cut vein. In *Self-Portrait with Cropped Hair*, Frida is surrounded by sinisterly animate strands of her hair that spread all over the earth and entwine themselves like vines or snakes in the rungs of her yellow chair. Because these black locks do not diminish in size as they recede in space, they seem to float in the air, thus recalling the veins, vines, roots, and ribbons that in other self-portraits are symbols of Frida's feeling of being (or desire to be) linked with realities beyond herself. Here, as in *The Two Fridas*, anger and pain join forces to sever Frida's connections with the outside world—and most specifically, with Diego. Frida is utterly alone in a vast, empty plain beneath a sunless sky. At the top of the painting are the words of a song: "Look if I loved you, it was for your hair. Now that you are bald, I don't love you anymore." Frida makes a rueful jest of her feckless retaliation: cutting off a sign of femininity becomes nothing more than the illustration of a popular song. Defiant, alone, surrounded by a testimony to her vengeance that is as gruesome as the drips and splotches of blood in other paintings, Frida is an unforgettable image of anger and of injured sexuality.

Rivera's observation that Frida turned out some of her best work during their divorce was well taken. She worked hard because she was determined not to accept money from Diego. In her October 13, 1939, letter to Muray she had said: "Darling, I must tell you that I am not sending the painting with Miguel [Covarrubias]. Last week I had to sell it to somebody thru Misrachi because I needed the money to see a lawyer. Since I came back from New York I don't accept a damn cent from Diego, the reasons you must understand. I will never accept money from any man till I die. I want to beg you to forgive me for doing that with a painting that was done for you. But I will keep my promise and paint another one as soon as I feel better. It is a cinch." (The painting was probably a self-portrait. To replace it, she painted the *Self-Portrait* in which a hummingbird hangs from her necklace of thorns.)

She tried to live off her paintings, making more efforts than ever before to sell them, sending them in small groups to Julien Levy. Her friends rallied around and were there when she needed them. Conger Goodyear, for example, wrote to Frida on March 3, 1940: "I think you are quite right to take nothing from [Diego]. If you really need money let me know and I will send you some. I want another picture of yours anyway. Will you give me first choice of those you are sending [to Julien Levy]?" Anita Brenner wrote to offer help with medical expenses, and said that Dr. Valentiner wanted to know if Frida needed money. Mary Sklar and Nickolas Muray sent her money every month. "Nick darling," she wrote Muray on December 18, 1939, "You will say that I am a complete bastard and a s. of a b.! I asked you [for] money and didn't even thank you for it. That is really the limit Kid! Please forgive me. I was sick two weeks. My foot again and grippe. Now I thank you a million times for your kind favor and about the paying back I want you to be so sweet to wait till January. The Arensberg from Los Angeles will buy a picture. [Walter G. Arensberg was a well-known collector who fell in love with Cubism at the time of the Armory Show in 1913 and later expanded his taste to include Surrealism.] I am sure I will have the bucks next year and immediately I will send you back your hundred bucks. It is OK with you? In case you need them before, I could arrange something else. In any case I want to tell you that it was really sweet of you to lend me that money, I needed it so much . . . I think that little by little I'll be able to solve my problems and survive!!" To raise money, she thought of renting her house to tourists, but the scheme came to nothing: "to fix the house would of cost a lot of money which I didn't have and Misrachi didn't lend me," she told Muray, "and in second place because my sister wasn't exactly the person indicated to run such a business. She doesn't speak a damn word of English and would of been impossible for her to get along well. So now I am hoping only in my own work."

Friends encouraged her to enter the Guggenheim Foundation's 1940 Inter-American competition, in hopes that she would get a grant. Mary Sklar's brother, the critic and art historian Meyer Schapiro, and Carlos Chávez were two of her sponsors. Others who wrote letters of reference were William Valentiner, Walter Pach, Conger Goodyear, André Breton, Marcel Duchamp, and Diego Rivera. Schapiro said: "She is an excellent painter, of real originality, one of the most interesting Mexican artists I know. Her work looks well beside the best pictures of Orozco and Rivera; in some ways it is more natively Mexican than theirs. If she hasn't their heroic and tragic sentiment she is nearer to common Mexican tradition and feeling for decorative form."

Frida's own statements (in Spanish) in her application are a model of modesty (and misspelling); perhaps she would have done better to sound more complex and self-important, for she was not awarded the fellowship.

PROFESSIONAL ANTECEDENTS:

I began to paint twelve years ago, during convalescence from an automobile accident that forced me to stay in bed for almost a year. During all these years I have worked with the spontaneous impulse of my feeling. I have never followed any school or anyone's influence, I have not expected to get from my work more than the satisfaction of the fact of painting itself and of saying what I could not say in any other way.

WORK:

I have done portraits, figure compositions, also subjects in which landscape and still life take on great importance. I have been able to find, without being forced by any prejudice, a personal expression in painting. For twelve years my work consisted of eliminating everything that did not come from the internal lyrical motives that impelled me to paint.

Since my subjects have always been my sensations, my states of mind and the profound reactions that life has been producing in me, I have frequently objectified all this in figures of myself, which were the most sincere and real thing that I could do in order to express what I felt inside and outside of myself.

EXHIBITIONS AND PAINTING SALES:

I did not exhibit until last year (1938) in the Julien Levy Gallery in New York. I took twenty-five paintings. Twelve were sold to the following people:

Conger Goodyear	New York
Mrs. Sam Lewison	New York
Mrs. Claire Luce	New York
Mrs. Salomon Sklar	New York
Edward G. Robinson	Los Angeles (Hollywood)

Walter Pach	New York
Edgard Kauffman	Pittsburgh
Nicholas Murray	New York
Dr. Roose	New York

and two other people whose names I do not remember, but that Julien Levy can identify. The exhibit took place from the 1st to the 15th of November, 1938.

Afterward I had an exhibition in Paris, organized by André Breton in the Renou et Colle Gallery, from the 1st to the 15th of March, 1939. My work interested the critics and artists of Paris. The Louvre Museum (Jeux de Paume) acquired one of my paintings.

Although Frida wanted to live off her paintings, she did not compromise her art in any way in order to make it salable. Only friends would purchase such painful and bloody works as the *Self-Portrait* sold to Muray. And on those rare occasions when a painting was commissioned, she did not necessarily produce what the patron expected, but rather turned the commission into another opportunity to transmit her private despair. Even when the commission was a portrait of someone other than herself, Frida could not help but make it a personal statement— one intimately connected with events in her own life.

This is certainly the case with one of the paintings Frida completed during her separation from Diego, *Suicide of Dorothy Hale* (figure 54), a work so gory it recalls the horror of *A Few Small Nips*. The suicide is shown in three successive stages. First there is the tiny upright figure close to the high window of the Hampshire House, from which Dorothy Hale jumped on October 21, 1938. Next we see a much larger upside-down falling figure, eyes wide open and looking at us. Cottony clouds partially obscure her, making her plunge through space all the more palpable. Finally there is a large figure lying stiff as a china doll on the ground in a pool of blood. Blood trickles out of her ear, mouth, and nose, curiously accentuating the beauty of her face. Her eyes are still open, and they look at us with all the plaintive calm of a wounded animal.

Clare Boothe Luce, who commissioned the portrait at the opening of Frida's New York exhibition, says that Frida had known Dorothy in Mexico and New York. She was part of a small coterie of friends connected with *Vanity Fair* (of which Mrs. Luce was managing editor), a group that included Miguel and Rosa Covarrubias, Muray, and Noguchi.

"She was a very beautiful girl," Noguchi recalls. "All of my girls are beautiful. I went to London with her in 1933. Bucky [Buckminster Fuller] and I were there the night before she did it. I remember very well, she said, 'Well, that's the end of the vodka. There isn't any more.' Just like that, you know. I wouldn't have thought of it much, except afterward I realized that that's what she was talking about. Dorothy was very pretty, and she traveled in this false world. She didn't want to be second to anybody, and she must have thought she was slipping."

In her own words, Mrs. Luce tells the story of the portrait: "Dorothy Donovan Hale was one of the most beautiful women I have ever known. Not even the young Elizabeth Taylor, whom she resembled, was more beautiful. A former Ziegfeld showgirl, she was the wife of Gardiner Hale, a fashionable New York portrait painter. The young Hales had many friends, not only in society, where Hale garnered his portrait commissions, but among the artists of the period, including Diego Rivera and Frida Kahlo.

"Hale was killed in an automobile accident on the West Coast in the mid-thirties, leaving Dorothy with very little money. When she flunked out on Hollywood screen tests, she returned to New York, where friends—among them myself—gave her enough money from time to time to go on living in the style to which her life with Gardiner had accustomed her.

"We all believed that a girl of such extraordinary beauty and charm could not be long in either developing a career or finding another husband. Unhappily, Dorothy had very little talent and no luck.

"As I remember, it was in the spring of 1938 that she joyfully confided in me that she had met 'the great love of her life'—Harry Hopkins, President Franklin D. Roosevelt's most trusted political adviser and closest personal confidant. The engagement, she said, would soon be announced. She and Hopkins would be married 'from the White House.' But meanwhile, well, she needed money to pay the rent on her suite at the Hampshire House.

"Items about her engagement to Hopkins appeared in some of the gossip columns. But other gossip columnists quoted 'White House sources' as denying that the Hopkins-Hale affair would end at the altar. The marriage never came off. Those in the know in Washington said that FDR had ordered Harry Hopkins to end his affair with Dorothy, and to marry instead Lou Macy, a close friend of the Roosevelts, which Hopkins did. Most of the gossip columnists made it brutally clear that Dorothy had been jilted.

"So once again, poor Dorothy needed money to pay her rent. And once again I said OK. But this time, I also said, 'What you badly need, Dorothy, is a job.' We decided that she could easily handle a job as hostess in the American Art Pavilion at the World's Fair. Bernard Baruch, a good friend of mine, was a good friend of Bob Moses, the head honcho at the fair. So I set up an appointment for Dorothy to meet Baruch and get a letter of introduction to Moses.

"Some days later, I was fitting a dress in the made-to-order department of Bergdorf Goodman. A model pirouetted in, wearing a really gorgeous evening gown. I asked the price. It was about five hundred to six hundred dollars—an enormous price for one dress forty years ago. I said, 'Too expensive for me.' The saleswoman said, 'Mrs. Gardiner Hale has just ordered it.' I thought angrily: So that's how she spends the money she says she needs so badly for the rent!

"When she telephoned a few days later, I was so annoyed with her I hardly listened to what she said. This was that she had decided to go on a very long trip. For the time being, she wanted to keep her destination a secret, but as she would be gone for a long time, she was giving herself a farewell cocktail party, and was inviting only her dearest friends. So would I come, and 'Darling, what do you think I should wear at my farewell party?'

"It was on the tip of my tongue to say, 'How about that gorgeous Bergdorf dress you bought with the rent money I gave you?' But I didn't. If she really was going on a long trip, the wretched rent-money story was ended anyway. What I said, rather coldly, was: 'I'm sorry I can't make your party. The thing you look best in is your old Madame X black velvet. Hope the trip lives up to your expectations.' And hung up.

"In the early morning of the day after the party, the police telephoned. At about 6:00 A.M., Dorothy Hale had jumped out of the window of her top-story suite in the Hampshire House. As the cocktail party had ended sometime before midnight, she had had a long time to think.

"She was wearing my favorite—her black velvet 'femme fatale' dress, and a corsage of small yellow roses, which Isamu Noguchi, it turned out, had sent to her.

"The only message she had left in the apartment was a note addressed to me. She thanked me for my friendship and asked me to see that her mother, who lived in upstate New York, was notified so that arrangements could be made to have her buried in the family plot.

"It was such a waste. Dorothy was so beautiful. And so vulnerable. Bernie Baruch telephoned the minute he read the news in the papers. He told me that when Dorothy had asked him to use his influence with Bob Moses to get her a job, he had told her that it was too late in life for her to try to get a job that would provide her with the kind of life she was used to. What she needed to get was not a job, but a husband. The best way to do that, he told her, was to go out to parties, looking as beautiful as possible. So he said he gave her a thousand dollars, but only on one condition—that she would use it to buy the most beautiful dress she could find in New York.

"A short while after that, I went to a gallery exhibition of Frida Kahlo's paintings. The exhibition was crowded. Frida Kahlo came up to me through the crowd and at once began talking about Dorothy's suicide. I didn't want to talk about it, as my conscience was still bothering me because I had been accusing Dorothy falsely—in my thoughts—of taking advantage of me. Kahlo wasted no time suggesting that she do a *recuerdo* of Dorothy. I did not speak enough Spanish to understand what the word *recuerdo* meant. I thought it meant a portrait done from memory. I thought Kahlo would paint a portrait of Dorothy in the style of her own *Self-Portrait* [dedicated to Trotsky], which I bought in Mexico (and still own).

"Suddenly it came to me that a portrait of Dorothy by a famous painter friend might be something her poor mother might like to have. I said so, and Kahlo thought so too. I asked the price, Kahlo told me, and I said, 'Go ahead. Send the portrait to me when it is finished. I will then send it on to Dorothy's mother.'

"I will always remember the shock I had when I pulled the painting out of the crate. I felt really physically *sick*. What was I going to do with this gruesome painting of the smashed corpse of my friend, and her blood dripping down all over the frame? I could not return it—across the top of the painting there was an angel waving an unfurled banner which proclaimed in Spanish that this was 'The Suicide of Dorothy Hale, painted at the request of Clare Boothe Luce, for the mother of Dorothy.' I would not have requested such a gory picture of my worst enemy, much less of my unfortunate friend.

"Among Dorothy's many ardent admirers were Constantin Alajalov, a well-known *New Yorker* cover artist, and Isamu Noguchi, the sculptor. I don't remember now which one I telephoned, asking him to come to see me on an urgent matter about Dorothy. In any event, I told whichever one arrived that I was going to destroy the painting with a pair of library scissors, and I wanted a witness to this act. In the end, however, I agreed not to destroy the painting, if the banner proclaiming I had commissioned it could be scrubbed off, and painted over. So Dorothy's admirer took the painting away and wiped out the offensive legend."

Frida's memorial to Dorothy Hale turned out to be more like a *retablo* than a *recuerdo*, inasmuch as it shows the disaster taking place (as well as the protagonist's death) and there was, as Mrs. Luce points out, an angel in the sky. A gray strip along the lower edge of the portrait has a legend written in blood-red script: "In the city of New York on the 21st of the month of October, 1938, at six in the morning, Mrs. DOROTHY HALE committed suicide by throwing herself out of a very high window of the Hampshire House building. In her memory, [now comes a blank space where the words have been painted out] this *retablo*, having executed it FRIDA KAHLO." At the right side of the inscription, under the words "committed suicide" and above the word "KAHLO," is a patch of red from which blood dribbles downward. And as in *A Few Small Nips*, blood, painted illusionistically and in the viewer's scale, besmirches the painting's frame. It seems that in her two most terrifying images of women's violent deaths—both of them, significantly, painted during periods when Diego was causing her great pain—Frida felt compelled to extend the painting's space out into the real space of the spectator, bringing the horror of the subject home. She has enhanced this feeling of immediacy by painting one of Dorothy Hale's shoeless, stockinged feet so that it appears to protrude into our space. The trompe l'oeil foot casts a shadow on the word "HALE" in the painting's inscription.

The bleak unreality of the space in which the suicide takes place is characteristic of Frida's paintings where the true subject is loneliness or despair. The dead Dorothy Hale lies on the empty, brown ground. Not a city street, not the sidewalk in front of Hampshire House, this anonymous space is simply a stage, unconnected in terms of scale or perspective with the skyscraper looming behind it. In this space, no concrete objects give us our bearings in the "real," normal world.

Nothing is available to touch, to confirm sanity. Everything looks insubstantial and unfamiliar, as in a bad dream.

For all the gruesomeness, *Suicide of Dorothy Hale* has a curiously gentle, lyric aspect to it, too. The dead woman's delicate, fresh beauty is intact even after the fall. So are the signals of Dorothy's feminine charms—the Madame X "femme fatale" dress, the corsage of yellow roses that had been a token of a man's admiration. Perhaps Dorothy Hale was the victim of a set of values that Frida Kahlo did not share, but Frida's compassion for her fall—literal and figurative—and her identification with her dead friend's plight gives *Suicide of Dorothy Hale* a peculiar intensity. Abandoned by Diego, Frida could easily understand why the jilted woman might give a farewell party, and then, clad in her most beautiful dress, plunge to her death. In the months of separation from Diego, Frida often thought, as she had after her accident, that it might be preferable if *la pelona* would take her away. But Frida was a survivor: *"No hay remedio,* one has to put up with it." She wrote to Nickolas Muray: "Let me tell you kid, that this time has been the worst in my whole life and I am surprised that one can live through it." But of course, she did.

Chapter 18

Remarriage

ON MAY 24, 1940, Trotsky's bedroom was machine-gunned by a group of Stalinists that included the painter David Alfaro Siqueiros. The assassination attempt failed—Trotsky and Natalia rolled behind their bed to escape the bullets. "They acted like firecracker makers," said Frida of the assassins. "They killed a gringo called Shelton Harte, they buried him in the Desierto de los Leones, and they fled. Naturally the police caught them; they put Siqueiros in jail but Cárdenas was his *cuate*." (Siqueiros was released less than a year later on the condition that he leave the country. He went to Chile to paint murals.)

Because of his much publicized falling-out with Trotsky, Rivera immediately came under suspicion, and not long after the assassination attempt, Paulette Goddard watched from her hotel window as the police assembled to cordon off the San Angel studio. She telephoned Rivera to warn him, and Irene Bohus, who was with him at the time, stuffed Diego onto the floor of her car, covered him with canvases, and drove right past Police Colonel de la Rosa and his thirty men. During his weeks in hiding, Paulette Goddard was, Rivera said, the only person (besides Irene) who knew his whereabouts. "[She] brought delicacies and wines on frequent visits. Her lovely presence alone was enough to make my retreat a delight." Like Siqueiros, Rivera had his friends among government officials. Two of them discovered his hiding place and, as he told it, came to warn him that he was in danger and to give him a passport prepared for entry into the United States. "I quietly slipped out of Mexico and headed for San Francisco." Actually, it was not such a quiet departure. Rivera left Mexico from the Mexico City airport, and he went with a regular passport and with the promise of a commission to paint a mural for the library of San Francisco Junior College—to paint it, in fact, in public, at Treasure Island, as part of the Golden Gate International Exposition's "Art in Action" show.

Soon he was installed with Irene Bohus in a studio apartment at 49 Calhoun Street on Telegraph Hill. (He planned to put Bohus in his mural—she was to symbolize the woman artist—but she left his employ and his studio before his portrait of her was finished, because, it is said, her mother objected to her cohabiting with the artist without benefit of judge or clergy. Rivera substituted a portrait of Emmy Lou Packard, another assistant—one who did not inhabit his studio.)

With its theme of Pan-American Unity, the Treasure Island mural expressed Rivera's current approach to politics. Though he had split from Trotsky, he remained (for a few years) an ardent anti-Stalinist, and after the Stalin-Hitler pact in 1939, he became an impassioned advocate of inter-American solidarity in opposition to totalitarianism. His real political aim, he told Sigmund Firestone in a letter dated January 30, 1941, was to establish "a common citizenship" for everybody in the Americas and to destroy the leading totalitarians of the era: Hitler, Mussolini, and Stalin. He wanted to create a single democratic intercontinental culture, a union, he said, of the ancient traditions of the South and the industrial activity of the North.

In his mural, he painted his personal form of pan-Americanism: Rivera and Paulette Goddard hold each other's hands while also embracing the tree of love and life. Her blue eyes and his brown ones are amorously interlocked, and her virginal white dress is pulled up to show her lovely legs. She represents "American girlhood," Rivera explained in his autobiography, ". . . shown in friendly contact with a Mexican man." Rivera's back is turned to Frida, who stands alone with brush and palette in hand, looking out into space with a gaze that is as abstract as that of the Statue of Liberty. She is "Frida Kahlo, [the]

Mexican artist with [a] sophisticated European background who has turned to native plastic tradition for inspiration; she personifies the cultural union of the Americas for the South."

Frida became severely ill after the attempt on Trotsky's life and Rivera's subsequent departure for the U.S. When, three months later, Ramón Mercader, who had finally succeeded in gaining Frida's confidence and friendship, murdered Trotsky by plunging an ice ax into his skull, she was distraught. She called Diego in San Francisco to give him the news. "They killed old Trotsky this morning," she cried. *"Estúpido!* It's your fault that they killed him. Why did you bring him?"

Because she had met the assassin while in Paris, and had invited him to her house in Coyoacán to dine, Frida was under suspicion. The police picked her up and interrogated her for twelve hours. "They sacked Diego's house," she remembered. "They stole a magnificent clock that I had given him, drawings, watercolors, paintings, paints, suits—they looted the house through and through. There were thirty-seven policemen here prying into everything in the house. I had known that they would come, and I arranged the papers and threw all political papers into the cellar of the big house under the kitchen. Then they brought the police and we—my sister and I—cried for two days in jail. And meanwhile, this house was left empty, and my sister's little children had been left alone, without food, and we begged a policeman: 'Be good enough to just go and give the children something to eat.' After two days they freed us because we were not guilty either of the assassination or of the shooting [Siqueiros's assassination attempt]."

After the war, in his efforts to be readmitted to the Communist party, Rivera proudly claimed that he had secured Trotsky's asylum with the purpose of having him assassinated, and some people have argued that Diego and Frida might in fact have had a part in the plot to kill Trotsky. This seems farfetched: the Riveras may not have subscribed to conventional morality, but they were not amoral, and they loved life too passionately to be capable of murder, no matter what the dictates of the Comintern. Rivera's boast was typical of his clownish political opportunism, similar to his saying that he fought alongside Zapata or Lenin or, as he told the Chilean poet Pablo Neruda, who visited Mexico in 1940, that he was part Jewish and was the real father of the Nazi general Rommel (he told others that Pancho Villa was Rommel's father), a "fact" that he warned Neruda must be kept secret for fear that its disclosure would have disastrous international consequences. Politically Diego was a weather vane. When, in the 1950s, he heard the news of the murder of Beria, chief of the Soviet GPU, he turned to his friend the art critic Raquel Tibol and said: "Raquelito, we must open a bottle of vodka to toast the return of the Trotskyites to power in the Soviet Union." What he thought about the long-range political implications of Trotsky's murder at the time, he kept to himself. But the short-range, personal implication was clear: he ordered an armed guard to protect him while he was painting on Treasure Island, for he was convinced there would be reprisals against him.

If Diego did not spend many hours mourning his ex-comrade, he was profoundly upset when he heard about Frida's arrest and her worsening illness. He went to Dr. Eloesser for medical advice on her behalf. The doctor recommended that Frida come to San Francisco, and he telephoned her to tell her that he did not approve of the medical treatment she was receiving in Mexico. In his view, her problem was a "crisis of nerves" for which surgery, recommended by her Mexican doctors, was no remedy.

Diego loves you very much [Dr. Eloesser wrote], and you love him. It is also the case, and you know it better than I, that besides you, he has two great loves— 1) Painting 2) Women in general. He has never been, nor ever will be, monogamous, something that is imbecilic and anti-biological.

Reflect, Frida, on this basis. What do you want to do?

If you think that you could accept the facts the way they are, could live with him under these conditions, and in order to live more or less peacefully could submerge your natural jealousy in a fervor of work, painting, working as a school teacher, whatever it might be . . . and absorb yourself until you go to bed each night exhausted by work [then marry him].

One or the other. Reflect, dear Frida, and decide.

Frida decided. Early in September she flew to San Francisco, where Diego and Dr. Eloesser met her at the airport. After spending a few days with Diego in his apartment, she was admitted to Saint Luke's Hospital, where Dr. Eloesser rejected the grave diagnoses of the Mexican doctors and prescribed rest and abstention from alcohol. He also recommended electro and calcium therapy. Her health and spirits were soon restored. "I was very ill in Mexico," she wrote Sigmund Firestone in November from New York City, where she had gone to arrange with Julien Levy the proposed 1941 exhibition and to testify in the suit that Lupe Marín had brought against Bertram Wolfe and his publisher for maligning her in various ways in his biography of Rivera. Frida went on (in English):

Three months I was lying in an awful apparatus on my chin which made me suffer like hell. All the doctors in Mexico thought I had to be operated on my spine. They all agreed that I had tuberculosis on the bones due to the old fracture I suffered years ago in an automobile accident. I spend all the money I could afford to see every specialist on bones there, and all told me the same story. I got so scared that I was sure I was going to die. Besides, I felt so worried for Diego, because before he left Mexico I didn't even know where he was for ten days, shortly after [before] he could finally leave, Trotsky's first attempt of assassination took place, and after, they killed him. So the whole situation for me, physically and morally was something I can not describe to you. In three months I lost 15 pounds of weight and felt lousy all together.

Finally I decided to come to the States and not to pay any attention to Mexican doctors. So I came to San Francisco. There I was in the hospital for more than a month. They made every possible examination and found *no* tuberculosis, and *no* need for an operation. You can imagine how happy I was, and how releved [*sic*]. Besides, I saw Diego, and that helped more than any thing else. . . .

They found that I have an infection in the kidneys which causes the tremendous irritation of the nerves which go through the right leg and a strong anemia. My explanation doesn't sound very scientific, but that is what I gathered from what the doctors told me. Anyhow I feel a little better and I am painting a little bit. I will go back to San Francisco and marry Diego again. (He wants me to do so because he says he loves me more than any other girl.) I am very happy. . . . We will [be] together again, and you will have us together in your home [she refers to the pair of self-portraits Firestone had commissioned].

Frida announced the remarriage matter-of-factly, but the final decision had not been that simple. Among the complications was her love affair with the young Heinz Berggruen, now a much respected art dealer and collector, then a twenty-five-year-old refugee from Nazi Germany. In his capacity as public relations officer for the Golden Gate International Exposition, he had met Diego Rivera, and the two men had become good friends. One day Rivera mentioned that Frida had come to San Francisco to have her leg examined by Dr. Eloesser. "He took me to the hospital," Berggruen recalls, "and I will never forget the way he looked at me when, just before we went into Frida's room, he said, 'You are going to be very much taken by Frida.' He said it in a pointed way. Diego was extremely perceptive and intuitive; he knew what would happen. Perhaps he even wanted it to happen. There was something diabolical in him. He led me on. He took me by the hand."

When the slender youth with large seductive eyes, a fragile poetic beauty, and an almost feminine, romantic sensibility entered Frida's room, "there was a click," says Berggruen. "She was stunning, just as beautiful as in her paintings. I stayed and Rivera went away. I visited Frida every day for the month that she was hospitalized."

They had little privacy—it was a hospital rule that patients could not lock themselves in, and the room had a swinging door—but "the risk of discovery," says Berggruen, "only heightened the intensity of our being together. For rather wild young people—and Frida was a very wild, passionate person—danger gave an added incentive."

When Frida went to New York, Heinz Berggruen traveled with her, departing discreetly one day ahead, then waiting for her at a stop along the route. The couple spent nearly two months together at the Barbizon-Plaza Hotel. "We were very happy. Frida was a tremendous revelation to me. She dragged me to parties. In Julien Levy's milieu, there were lots of parties. Although her leg hurt, she could move around very easily."

They shared a ready sense of humor and a foreigner's perception of the oddities of the U.S.A. In the mornings, for example, when they read newspapers, Frida would burst into laughter over the little photographs of columnists that accompanied their texts. "Look at those crazy heads!" she would say. She could not imagine why the newspaper bothered to print photographs of these often unattractive faces. "It's not possible. They must be crazy in this country!" she cried. Something else that Frida found uproariously funny was the hotel room's automatic breakfast chute. After placing an order, one pushed a button and, Berggruen explains, "Wham. A thermos of coffee and a plate of toast dropped into the trap!"

"God, these Americans," Frida exclaimed. "Everything in this country is mechanized, even breakfast!" But as the weeks passed, there were violent fights. "Frida was a tempestuous woman. I was impressionable and immature." Partings were followed by reconciliations. Not so completely in love as her companion, and older than he by eight years, Frida was perhaps a little cavalier. "She took the relationship more casually than I did," says Berggruen. "There was much misery in it for me. But it is possible, also, that she was asking for more from me than I could give. I was not adult enough to guide her. I wanted to get ahead in my own life, and I sensed that with Frida there could be immense complications and hindrances. She was in such agonies. Her relationship with Diego was extremely difficult. Things didn't click anymore. She was deeply unhappy with him. On the other hand, she felt she needed someone strong to lean on. He was a heavy man physically; in a way he was a huge animal, and she was so fragile both physically and mentally. He gave her something solid to lean on."

The New York idyll ended painfully. Frida accepted Rivera's remarriage proposal, and Berggruen returned to San Francisco before she did. They never saw each other again.

Actually, Diego had asked for her hand several times, with Dr. Eloesser acting as go-between, warning her that Rivera would not reform, telling Rivera that the separation had exacerbated Frida's illness and that by marrying her again he could help her stay well. Diego knew that Frida's health was deteriorating. "I'm going to marry her," he said to Emmy Lou Packard, "because she really needs me." But the truth was he needed her too. The separation, he said, "was having a bad effect upon both of us."

Frida received advice from other friends as well. Anita Brenner wrote to her of Diego's "foolishness," and speaking from the point of view of a woman who truly knew what independence was, as well as a woman with keen insight into human nature, she said (in Spanish):

He is basically a sad person. He looks for warmth and a certain air which are always in the exact center of the universe. Naturally he looks for you. Although I am not sure if he knows that you are the only one of all of them that really loved him. (Possibly Angelina [Beloff], too.) It's natural to want to return to him, but I wouldn't do it, since what attracts Diego to you is what he doesn't have, and if he doesn't have you tied down completely, he will keep on looking for and needing you. One wants, of course, to be near him and to help him, take care of him, accompany him, but this is what he is unable to tolerate. Every time he turns a corner he is moonstruck. And you would be the moon if you were in this elusive position. . . . it seems to me that for you it would be best to be coquettish. Don't let yourself be tied down completely; do something with your own life; for that is what cushions us when the blows and falls come. Above all, inside, the blow is not as strong if there is something which allows one to say: Here I am, I am worth something. I am not so completely identified as someone else's shadow that when I cannot be in their shadow I am nothing, and I feel that they have insulted and humiliated me until I can't stand it any longer. Basically what I am saying is that one depends only on oneself, and from there must come everything that is needed to be able to put up with things and to do things, for good humor, for everything.

Despite Brenner's advice Frida cabled Dr. Eloesser from New York on November 23, 1940, telling him that she would arrive in San Francisco on November 28 and asking him to reserve her a room in a "not very elegant" hotel. Her weeks in Manhattan had "lifted her spirits." She had seen old friends and even managed to finish a few paintings. She asked him not to tell anyone of her arrival: "I want to escape from going to the inauguration of the fresco. I do not want to meet Paulette and other dames." The doctor replied that Frida should send her luggage directly to his house, which was at her disposal.

There were, according to Rivera, certain conditions on which Frida agreed to remarry him (perhaps Anita Brenner's advice had had some effect after all):

. . . she would provide for herself financially from the proceeds of her own work; that I would pay half of our household expenses—nothing more; and that we would have no sexual intercourse. In explaining this last stipulation, she said that, with the images of all my other women flashing through her mind, she couldn't possibly make love with me, for a psychological barrier would spring up as soon as I made advances.

I was so happy to have Frida back that I assented to everything.

On December 8, 1940, Diego's fifty-fourth birthday, Frida and he were married for the second time. The ceremony was brief. They had applied for a license on December 5. The county clerk brought the marriage papers to the courtroom, which was opened specially for the Sunday wedding. The marriage was performed by Municipal Judge George Schoenfeld, with only two friends, Rivera's assistant Arthur Niendorff and his wife, Alice, present. Frida wore a Spanish costume with a long green-and-white skirt and a brown shawl. Her face looked beautiful but was ravaged by months of suffering. There was no reception. In fact, Rivera, always in love with painting, went off to work at Treasure Island on the very day of his wedding. There, before an audience of appreciative assistants and the public that came to watch the "Art in Action" section of the fair, he stripped off his shirt to show his undershirt, covered with the imprints of his wife's magenta lipstick.

After the wedding Frida and Diego were together for nearly two weeks in California before she returned to Mexico in time for Christmas with her family. *"Emilucha linda,"* she wrote to Emmy Lou Packard (in Spanish) from Coyoacán:

I received your two short letters, many thanks *compañera*. I'm anxious that you finish all the work so both of you will come to Mexicalpán de las Tunas. What I would give to be just around the corner so I could visit you today but it's no use, I'll have to put up with the wait, sister.

I miss both of you very much. . . . Don't forget me. I entrust the big-child [Diego] to you with all my heart, and you don't know how thankful I am that you are concerned and taking care of him for me. Tell him not to have so many tantrums and to behave himself.

Now I only count the hours and the days before I will have both of you here. . . . Be sure that Diego sees the oculist in Los Angeles. And that he doesn't eat too many spaghettis so he won't get too fat. . . .

In February the Treasure Island mural and a few other painting commissions were finished. Trotsky's assassin had been captured and had not accused Rivera of being an accomplice. Diego packed his things and went home to Frida in Mexico, where he moved into the blue house on Londres Street, keeping San Angel as his studio.

Frida had prepared his bedroom in Coyoacán with loving care. It had a dark wooden bed wide enough to encompass his bulk and pillows gaily embroidered (perhaps by Frida) with flowers and "sweet nothings." On the wall she placed an old-fashioned coatrack in the hope that he would hang his overalls, Stetson hat, and other garments on hooks instead of dropping them on the floor. And there were shelves for his pre-Columbian idols, a bureau to house his huge shirts, and a table where he could write. (Of course, he kept a bedroom in San Angel for himself as well: on those occasions when he escorted gringas to "see the sights" of Mexico and captured them with his glistening, hyperthyroid gaze and genial, Buddha-like smile, he needed a place to which to take them when they returned to the city.)

The Riveras' reconciliation soon settled into a comfortable, reasonably happy pattern, a pattern that was no longer determined mainly by Diego, but rather by mutual agreement or compromise; from now on, the terms on which Frida lived her life would be more or less her own. Having gained in confidence and independence through her exhibitions and through her insistence on financial and sexual autonomy, she became more maternal toward Diego, an attitude immediately evident in her letter to Dr. Eloesser dated March 15, 1941:

Queridisimo [Dearest] Doctorcito:

You are right to think that I am a mule because I didn't even write to you when we arrived in Mexicalpán de las Tunas, but you must realize that it was not pure laziness on my part but rather that when I arrived I had a lot of things to arrange in Diego's house, and you must have an idea of how he needs to be taken care of and how he absorbs time, since as always when he arrives in Mexico he is in a devilish bad humor until he acclimatizes himself once again to the rhythm of this country of craziness. This time the bad mood lasted more than two weeks, until they brought him some marvelous idols from Nayarit and seeing them he began to like Mexico again. Also, the other day, he ate a very delicious duck *mole,* and this also helped to give him back his pleasure in life. He stuffed himself with duck *mole* that I thought would give him indigestion, but as you know he has a resistance that can be put to any test. After those two events, the idols from Nayarit and the duck *mole,* he decided to go out to paint water colors in Xochimilco, and little by little he got himself into a better humor.

Frida went on to tell the doctor about her life and her difficulties with her guest Jean Wight, who had accompanied her to Mexico. Jean Wight's defects, as Frida saw them, were indiscretion, sloth, and Stalinism:

It is not that I am boasting, but if she is sick, I am worse off than she, and nevertheless, dragging my foot as best I can, I do something, or I try to fulfill as best I can my obligation to take care of Diego, I try to paint my little monkeys or to have the house at least in order, knowing that this means to diminish many difficulties for Diego and to make his life less tiresome since he works like a burro in order to give one something to swallow. . . .

I gave myself the intention that although I am lame, it is preferable not to pay much attention to sickness, because in any case one can kick the bucket simply by stumbling against a banana peel. Tell me what you are doing, try not to work so many hours, have more fun, since the way the world is going we are all on death's door and it is not worth while to leave this world without having had a little fun in life. . . .

According to Emmy Lou Packard, who came to Mexico with Rivera to continue working as his assistant, and who lived in the blue house in San Angel for almost a year, a typical day in the Rivera household began with a leisurely breakfast during which Frida or Emmy Lou would read the morning paper, full of news of the war, aloud to Diego, who was having trouble with his eyes and did not want to tax them. After breakfast, Rivera would turn his attention to his work. He and Emmy Lou went to his studio in San Angel around ten or eleven. At 1:30 or 2:00 P.M. they returned to the Coyoacán house for lunch, bringing, on days when Rivera had spent the morning drawing in the local marketplace, Indian foods such as *huitlacoche* (a fungus that forms on ears of corn) for the cook to prepare. Lunch was usually a simple meat or chicken dish; there was always guacamole to spoon onto tortillas, and Frida drank several *copitas,* which made her animated and gay. Because he was worried about his health at this time, Rivera abstained. (In addition to the trouble with his eyes, he had thyroid problems and bouts of hypochondria that convinced him he was dying.)

If Frida had been painting in the morning, she would sometimes appear, not in her usual flowing skirts, but in work clothes—denim pants and a Western-style workman's jacket—and would invite Diego and Emmy Lou into her studio before lunch to see what she had done. "He always seemed to be somewhat in awe of her work. He never said anything negative. He was constantly amazed at her imagination,"

Emmy Lou recalls. "He'd say, 'She is a better painter than I am.'"

If Frida had not been painting during the morning, she might well have gone to the market with a friend or with one of her sisters to buy flowers, household items, or any objects that struck her fancy. She knew the artisans and shopkeepers; one of her favorites was Carmen Caballero Sevilla, who sold extraordinary Judas figures, as well as other handicrafts, such as toys or piñatas, that she made. Diego also made purchases, but Señora Caballero remembers that "The *niña* Fridita was the one who spoiled me most; she paid a little more than the maestro did. She did not like to see me toothless. Once a man hit me and I lost my teeth, well, it was a time when I did some very pretty work for her, and she gave me as a present these gold teeth that I now wear. I am grateful to her. I gave her only the skeleton and she dressed it and even put a hat on it." Señora Caballero was not the only person Frida assisted. Driving to and from the market, she would recognize the poor people who came to beg for a few centavos when her car stopped in traffic, and even if there were six or seven of them, she gave each one something. "She loved them and she spoke to them in a way that was a gift better than money," says Jacqueline Breton, who visited Mexico a second time in the mid-forties.

Frida also enjoyed domestic duties: making her house attractive for Diego was not a chore but a delight, and Rivera frequently took part in household decisions; when she remodeled the kitchen, covering the walls with blue, white, and yellow tiles as in a traditional provincial kitchen, she consulted with Diego first. Of course, he approved: the kitchen was emphatically *Mexicanista*, with its big clay pots set out on the tiled range, and the multitude of tiny earthenware mugs hooked on the wall in a pattern that spelled "Frida and Diego."

The dining room, too, was decorated in a way that showed the Riveras' allegiance to Mexico's *campesino* culture. Its walls were hung with naïve still lifes, masks, and other popular art objects, and its pinewood floors were painted with *polvo de congo*, the yellow paint used in peasant homes, and covered with straw *petates*. As in the houses of the poor, the lights were bare electric bulbs dangling from their cords, and Frida usually placed a simple Mexican oilcloth printed with myriad small flowers on the unpainted rough wood of the table. Guests would sit there for hours, drinking out of red clay cups and eating off earthenware plates; that "bourgeois" invention the living room was seldom used.

Emmy Lou Packard remembers that "every day Frida made the table into a still life for Diego," arranging dishes and fruit and six or seven huge bouquets of flowers that she brought back from the morning's shopping expedition and simply plunked into clay jars, often leaving their wrappings around them. Diego always sat at the end of the table to get the best view, with Frida and Emmy Lou on either side.

Frida liked to enliven this tableau with animals—a chipmunk in a cage, or, on the loose, her little parrot, Bonito, who was then her favorite pet and used to nestle under the blankets when she rested in bed. During lunch, Bonito chattered, cocked his head, and gave people his quizzical round-eyed look before bestowing beaky kisses upon them. His favorite dish was butter; watching him make his pigeon-toed way around an obstacle course of clay pots and bowls set up by Frida and Diego, and then delve into his buttery reward, kept guests in fits of laughter. Meanwhile, outside in the patio, a large male parrot, which drank quantities of beer or tequila, cursed and squawked: *"No me pasa la cruda!"* (I can't get over this hangover!) If his cage was open, he would put his head down and make a beeline for some unsuspecting guest's appetizing ankle.

After the *comida*, Frida would sometimes lie in the sun in the patio, spreading her Tehuana skirts over the warm clay tiles and listening to the birds. Or she might stroll around the garden paths with Emmy Lou, noticing with loving attention each little flower as it came into bloom, playing with her pack of bald Aztec dogs, holding out her hand as a perch for tame doves or for her pet eagle (an osprey), which she named "Gertrude Caca Blanca," because the bird dropped white excrement all over the steps. Most entertaining of all were the two gray turkeys, which lived in the garden. "The male would do a *macho* dance in front of the female, who paid no attention," Emmy Lou remembers. "When he'd start drumming his feet on the ground loudly, she would begin to pay attention. Finally, she would lower herself to the ground and spread her wings. He'd jump on her back and drum with his wings outspread. Then it was all over. It was these ordinary things of life—animals, children, flowers, the countryside—that most interested Frida. The animals were to her like children." (On December 15, 1941, after Emmy Lou had returned to California, Frida wrote to her: "Imagine, the little parrot 'Bonito' died. I made a little burial for him and everything, and I cried for him a lot since, you remember, that he was marvelous. Diego also felt very sad about it. The little monkey 'El Caimito' got pneumonia and he too was about to drop dead, but 'sulphanilamide' made him better. Your little parrot is very well—he is with me here.")

In the afternoon, after Emmy Lou and Diego returned to the San Angel studio, Frida sometimes rested. She might then visit a friend, take care of her own or Diego's business, or paint. Some afternoons she went to the movies or, occasionally, to a boxing match. Diego liked the symphony, but Frida did not, so she would dress Emmy Lou in her clothes and send her in her stead. She preferred the concerts of mariachi bands that she heard in the Garibaldi Plaza, where she could feast on tacos and, for a few pesos, request her favorite songs to be sung by groups of itinerant musicians who competed to see who could sing more movingly and who could be more dashing in tight pants, bright scarves, and huge, ornate hats.

In the evenings Diego came home for a late supper of hot chocolate and *pan dulce*—sweet rolls and pastries that were served on a large platter and were made in a multitude of different shapes, some of which referred humorously (and sometimes pornographically) to parts of the human body. Frida and Diego would amuse themselves by drawing *cadavres exquis* or singing *corridos*. Although Diego couldn't carry a tune, he loved to sing, and he took pleasure in listening to Frida, for she sang with great spirit, and could handle the falsetto breaks in songs like "La Malagueña" beautifully. Diego also delighted in Frida's ability to cut straight through pretension to truth and in the shuttlecocks of her repartee—so much so that he sometimes teased her in ways that hurt, just to get a response. He would, for example, taunt her about his affair with Cristina, saying to a guest, "Frida composed the Mexican song called 'El Petate' because there's a line in it that says, 'I don't love you, I love your sister.'" Such jibes occasionally left Frida impassive, but more often she retaliated. One day at lunch she gave Diego a schoolmarm lecture about one of Rivera's models, who Frida thought had huge, ugly breasts. "They're not so big," Diego countered. Frida came back with, "That's because you always see them when she's lying down!"

The Riveras' instinctive compatibility is evident in another of Emmy Lou's stories: Once, when the three were to meet at a movie theater to attend a film about the German invasion of Russia, Diego and Emmy Lou could not find Frida in the crowds milling about outside. Diego whistled the first bar of the *Internationale*. From somewhere in the crowd came the second; it was unmistakably Frida. The whistling continued until the couple found each other and all three went in to take their seats.

The calm, assured mood of Frida's March 15 letter to Dr. Eloesser had changed by July 18, when she wrote to him again. In the interim, her father had died and her health had worsened. Nevertheless, she spoke of misfortune in a spirited, headlong tone: even with a friend as close as Dr. Eloesser, she tried to hide grief and pain behind a façade of *alegría*.

Dearest doctorcito,

What will you say of me—that I am more like saxophone music than like a jazz band. Not even thanks for your letters, nor for the baby boy [the fetus that Dr. Eloesser had sent her as a gift] that gave me such joy—not even one word in months and months. You are totally right if you send me to hell. But you know that if I don't write you, it doesn't mean I remember you any less. You know that I have the great defect of being lazy as only I can be lazy with regard to that thing of writing letters. But believe me I have thought a lot about you and always with the same affection. . . .

My hoof, paw or foot is better. But my general state is rather fu . . . I think that this is because I don't eat enough—I smoke a lot—and something strange! I drink *no* cockteltitos or cocktelazos anymore. I feel something in my tummy that hurts and I have a continuous desire to burp. (Pardon me—burpted!!) My digestion is that of the *vil tiznada* [the dastardly tippler]. My mood abominable. Every day I'm becoming more ill-tempered (in the Mexican sense of the word) non-valorous (Academic Spanish style of the language) that is to say *very grouchy.* If there is any remedy in medicine which improves the humor of people like me—proceed to advise me about it so that I can swallow it immediately, to see what effect it has. . . .

The remarriage functions well. A small quantity of quarrels—better mutual understanding and on my part, fewer investigations of the tedious kind, with respect to the other women, who frequently occupy a preponderant place in his heart. Thus you can understand that at last—I have learned that *life is this way* and the rest is painted bread [just an illusion]. If I felt better healthwise one could say that I am happy—but this thing of feeling such a wreck from head to toe sometimes upsets my brain and makes me have bitter moments. Listen, aren't you going to come to the International Medical Congress that will be held in this beautiful city—so called—of the Palaces? Take heart and grab a steel bird and [fly to] Zócalo Mexico. What will it be? Yes or Yes? Bring me lots of Lucky and Chesterfield cigarettes because here they are a luxury my friend. And I can't afford daily dough for nothing but smoke.

Tell me about your life. Something that proves to me that you still think that in this land of Indians and gringo tourists there exists for you a girl who is your real true friend.

Ricardo [probably Ricardo Arias Viñas, Frida's Spanish-refugee lover] became a little jealous of you because he says that I speak to you in the familiar *tu* but I explained to him everything that is explicable. I love him very much and I told him that you know this.

I am going now—because I have to go to Mexico [City] to buy paintbrushes and colors for tomorrow and it is getting late.

Let's see when you write me a very long letter. Say hello to Stack and Ginette [Ralph and Ginette Stackpole] and to the St. Lukes [Hospital] nurses. Above all to the one that was so good to me—you know which one—I can't remember her name right now. It begins with M. Goodbye Doctorcito *Chulo* [cute]. Don't forget me.

Lots of love and kisses from

Frida

The death of my father was something terrible for me. I think that it's owing to this that I became much less well and I grew rather thin again. You remember how handsome he was and how good?

Poor health and her father's death depressed Frida; the war in Europe intensified her distress. She shared Diego's anguish over the people, places, and political values that were being threatened or destroyed, an anguish that deepened after the invasion of Russia in June.

Diego had always loved Russia and Russians. In his Paris years he had learned to speak Russian with Angelina Beloff and his numerous Russian friends, and the ideals of the Russian Revolution had filled his heart and mind through all the intervening years—not less because he considered these ideals to have been betrayed by Stalin. "At least the revolutionary masses are on the march in Russia," he wrote to

Emmy Lou Packard after her return to the United States. "I am in despair because I can't be with them."

His despair was compounded by the fact that, having left the Trotskyite movement, and still under attack by the Communist party, he had no organizational base through which to channel his feelings into action. Thus, though his pro-Russian fervor was not immediately accompanied by a reappraisal of Stalin—it was some time before "the executioner" would be transformed into "Uncle Joe"—he began during this period to reconsider his attitude toward both the Soviet leader and the Communist party. If his pact with Hitler had made Stalin look like a traitor, the valiant defense of the Russian homeland made him look like a hero. And moral outrage at the Soviet purges changed to surprise when numerous people presumed to be dead reappeared, freed from prison camps so they could fight at the front. Emmy Lou Packard recalls that when she read the newspaper to him, "all Rivera wanted to hear about was news of the Russian front. I would read the name of some Russian general, and Diego would say, 'So it wasn't true that they killed all those people that were on the list of the people who were purged!' "

Frida, though her politics were less intense than Diego's, understood his feelings. *"Pobrecito!"* she said of him to Emmy Lou. "Poor thing! He is lonely now that he is not in the Communist party and not in the midst of the movement."

On New Year's Eve, 1942, Frida wrote to Dr. Eloesser from her bed, where she was confined by grippe, angina, and "all the other troubles": "I believe the war will continue in its apogee for the whole of this year that will just be born tomorrow and we cannot hope for very happy days. . . . I don't have much to tell you because I live the simplest life you can imagine. Diego is working in the Palace, and I stay home painting *moninches* [Frida's word for monkeys] or scratching my belly, now and then I go to a movie in the afternoon and there's nothing more to tell you. Every day I dislike more the 'right' people and parties and the shitty bourgeois fiestas, so that I flee from all this as much as I can."

Frida's somberness was reflected most eloquently, of course, in her paintings. *Self-Portrait with Braid,* 1941, is one of the first bust-length self-portraits that she produced after her return to Mexico from San Francisco (figure 57). It can be seen as a comment on her remarriage—

as a counterpart to *Self-Portrait with Cropped Hair,* from the period of her divorce. One imagines that the hair strewn all over the ground in the earlier self-portrait has been gathered, braided, and shaped into the pretzel on top of Frida's head. Putting back her hair is a reaffirmation of the femininity she had denied, but the affirmation is not joyous. Unruly strands seem as disconcertingly alive as the hair she had cropped and painted the year before; they are nerve ends of an anxious psyche. No less disquieting are the huge predatory jungle leaves with sharp, serrated edges that hide Frida's nakedness. Their swirling rhythm suggests a turmoil held in check behind her calm features. Thick stems, recalling the blood vessel in *The Two Fridas,* encircle her chest, preventing free movement. Oppressiveness is reinforced by the heavy choker of pre-Columbian beads and the painting's muted colors add to the mood of melancholy. Though her remarriage might, as she put it, "function well," it will not be roses without thorns.

In *Self-Portrait with Bonito,* 1941, Frida is dressed uncharacteristically in a simple dark blouse that suggests mourning—for her father, for the victims of war, and perhaps also for the death of Bonito, who perches on her shoulder. The foliage that surrounds her face literally crawls with life. Caterpillars have eaten holes in several leaves; life's perishability is the message here. One caterpillar is trapped in a spider's web spun between Frida's hair and a leaf, a link—albeit a spooky one—between Frida and the world. When she was unhappy, Frida always sought ways to reaffirm her grip on life. One way that was to become more and more important as the years went on and her life became increasingly confined was to make her connectedness with nature not just a matter of habit—adoring her pets, tending her flowers, arranging bowls of fruit, etc.—but a matter of faith.

Perhaps it was to reaffirm that faith and to build something permanent in a world gripped by death and destruction that the Riveras in 1942 began building Anahuacalli, a bizarre, gloomy temple-museum on a lava bed in the Pedregal district—*pedregal* means "stony ground"—near Coyoacán. "Frida and I started a strange kind of ranch," Rivera said. "Here we planned to raise our own food staples, milk, honey, and vegetables, while we prepared to build our museum. In the first weeks, we erected a stable for our animals. . . . During the war, this building was 'home' for Frida and me. After the war, it was converted exclusively into a home for my idols." Building a "home" together helped to cement their remarriage and it was a project that allowed them to "flee" from bourgeois society and the war-torn world by putting down their roots in the Mexican earth.

In the end, what was built was an anthropological museum (it opened to the public in 1964) that serves as a monument to one man's passion for his native culture. In a style he described as a composite of Aztec, Mayan, and "Rivera Traditional" (the same style in which he built the new wing to the Coyoacán house), Rivera constructed, out of the gray volcanic rock of the surrounding fields, a building that is both brutal and elegant. Because of its ceremonial grandeur, Anahuacalli has been alternately called Diego's "pyramid" or his "mausoleum," and he poured into it every penny he could spare. Frida did what she could to help. She gave her husband title to a piece of land that she had bought with her own money in order to house a Spanish refugee and his family, and sold her apartment on Insurgentes. On February 14, 1943, she wrote to her friend, patron, and portrait subject Marte R. Gómez, a prominent agricultural engineer who then headed Mexico's Ministry of Agriculture:

I have been worried about Diego for a long time. First for his health, and for economic difficulties which, as a consequence of the war, he begins to have, precisely in the moment when I would have wanted him to feel calm and sure in order to paint and to do what he wants after an untiring life of work. It is not exactly the immediate problem of getting enough to live on more or less normally that worries me. It is a question of something that for Diego has enormous importance, and that I don't know how to help him solve. As you know, after painting, what interests him most in life, and the only thing that really gives him joy and enthusiasm, is his idols. For more than 15 years he has spent most of what he earns by means of his incessant work on forming his magnificent collection of archaeological pieces. I don't think there is a better collection in Mexico, and even in the national museum certain pieces that are so very important do not exist. Diego has always had the idea of constructing a house for his idols, and a year ago he found a place that truly merits the "house of idols," in the Pedregal of Coyoacán. He bought a piece of land in a little town called San Pablo Tepetlapa. He began to build the house just eight months ago. You cannot imagine with what love and enthusiasm he made the plans, working whole nights after painting all day. Believe me, no one has seen anyone build something with the joy and affection Diego Rivera has when dealing with what he likes and admires most. Beyond that, the piece of land is marvelous for what he wants to do, and the landscape which you can see from this place is the most magnificent that you can imagine, with the Ajusco [mountain] in the background. I would like you to see it with your own eyes because I cannot describe it.

The fact is, that with the war, and all the circumstances that you know about, Diego does not have the money to finish the construction which is barely finished up to half of the first floor. I have no words to tell you the tragedy that this means for Diego, and the pain that I have in being impotent to help him in anything. The only thing I can do, and I already have done it, was to sell a little house that I had on Insurgentes in order to lessen expenses, but naturally this was only a partial solution.

Frida went on to ask if the government might be willing to help by financing an archaeological museum for Rivera's collection. She proposed that the museum should be the property of Mexico, with the condition that until his death, Diego could live and work near his idols in his own study at the top of the pyramid. Such a museum, Frida argued, "would be the pride of the present civilization. . . . You know how much I love him, and can understand how it pains me to see him suffer by not having something that he so deserves, because what he asks is nothing in comparison with what he has given."

Six years later, when she wrote her "Portrait of Diego," Frida had not lost her enthusiasm: "The stupendous work that he is constructing . . . grows in the incredibly beautiful Pedregal landscape like an enormous cactus that looks at the Ajusco, sober and elegant, strong and refined, ancient and perennial; from its entrails of volcanic rock it cries out with voices of centuries and days: Mexico is alive! Like Coatlicue, it contains life and death; like the magnificent terrain on which it is built, it embraces the earth with the firmness of a living and permanent plant."

So, too, does Frida embrace the stony earth in *Roots* (plate XXVII), which expresses her and Diego's love for the vast sea of volcanic rock where they built Anahuacalli, and which was, in fact, entitled *El Pedregal* when in 1953 she sent it and four other works to the British Arts Council's Mexican art exhibition at the Tate Gallery in London. Indeed, starting in 1943, the Pedregal with its rough gray crevassed rock appears in the backgrounds of many of her self-portraits. Whether the Riveras ever did carry out their plan to cultivate vegetables in their terrain in the Pedregal is not certain, but in *Roots,* Frida plants her own body there. By rooting herself in the land Diego loved, she was able to attach herself more closely to him. That this brought her relative contentment is evident in this small panel which is one of her least tormented self-portraits.

Roots gives brilliant evidence of Frida's growing desire to become deeply embedded in nature. In her diary in 1944, she wrote of the "vegetable miracle of my body's landscape." Her wish for fertility transformed itself into an almost religious belief that everything under the sun was intimately linked and that she could partake in the flow of the universe. *Roots* is like a reversal of (or counterpart to) *My Nurse and I.* In the 1937 painting, Frida was an infant suckling at an earth mother's plant-like breast. In *Roots,* it is Frida who nourishes nature by giving birth to a vine.

With her elbow propped on a bed pillow, Frida dreams that her body extends over a large expanse of desert terrain. Her solitary presence in the wilderness is as mysteriously dream-like—and as natural—as that of Rousseau's *Sleeping Gypsy,* a painting that Frida surely knew and loved. A window in her torso opens to reveal not broken bones or barren womb, but the rocky landscape beyond. From this mystic womb the pliant green vine emerges and spreads luxuriantly along the desert floor. Frida's blood courses through its arteries, and continues in red vesicles that extend like creeping roots beyond the edges of its leaves. Thus does Frida become a source of life rooted in the parched Mexican earth. *Roots* may also allude to the idea of the body fertilizing nature's cycles after death: in front of Frida the earth cracks open to form a dark ravine, and a grave-like cavern lies at her feet. Frida's suspension over these precipices depends on the continuance of her dream.

Just as Frida grows into the earth, so Diego's temple, with "its entrails of volcanic rock," was to "grow like an enormous cactus," embracing life and death as well as the soil of Mexico like "a living and permanent plant." To gain immortality, Diego constructed; Frida, in *Roots,* linked her very body with the chain of life.

Chapter 19

Patrons, Politics, Public Recognition

IN THE 1940s, perhaps as a result of the acclaim that came from her exhibitions abroad, and from her participation in the big International Exhibition of Surrealism in Mexico City, Frida's career took on momentum. Recognition brought patrons, commissions, a teaching job, a prize, a fellowship, participation in cultural organizations, conferences, art projects, and even the occasional invitation to write for periodicals. All this must have been an incentive for her to take herself more seriously as an artist. Besides, she was determined to earn her keep, and therefore worked more diligently than ever before.

The paintings she produced were generally larger-scale than those she had done in the 1930s, and they appear to have been aimed at a broader audience, to be less like private talismans or votive images intended for her own needs or for Diego's personal pleasure. As her technical proficiency grew, her realism became more meticulous in terms of texture and modeling, her imagery more sophisticated, less full of girlish charm. She painted more of the highly detailed, bust-length (and relatively salable) self-portraits than the narrative portraits such as *The Broken Column* and *Tree of Hope*, in which her figure appears in fantastical, always painful situations and which relate more to the *retablo*-like paintings of the early 1930s. Nevertheless, painting remained first and foremost a vehicle of personal expression. "Since the accident changed my path, and many other things," she told Antonio Rodríguez, "I was not permitted to fulfill the desires which the whole world considers normal, and nothing seemed more natural than to paint what had not been fulfilled. . . . my paintings are . . . the most frank expression of myself, without taking into consideration either judgments or prejudices of anyone. I have painted little, and without the least desire for glory or ambition, but with the conviction that, before anything else, I want to give myself pleasure and then, that I want to be able to earn my living with my craft. . . . many lives would not be enough to paint the way I would wish and all that I would like."

She continued to be self-deprecating about her art. "As far as painting goes, I keep at it," she wrote to Dr. Eloesser on July 18, 1941. "I paint little but I feel that I am learning something." And she still needed prodding of various sorts in order to motivate herself to paint. Rivera helped, often by praise, sometimes by withholding money, but her erratic work habits, together with her physical disabilities, prevented her from producing paintings quickly, and hence from amassing enough salable works for another one-woman exhibition in a commercial gallery. She nonetheless did exhibit in a number of important group shows. In 1940, besides participating in the Surrealist show in Mexico City and in the Golden Gate International Exhibition in San Francisco, she sent *The Two Fridas* to the Museum of Modern Art's "Twenty Centuries of Mexican Art," prompting Frank Crowninshield to write in *Vogue* that "the most recent of Rivera's ex-wives" was "a painter apparently obsessed by an interest in blood." In 1941 her *Frida and Diego Rivera* was exhibited in the Boston Institute of Contemporary Arts "Modern Mexican Painters" exhibition, which traveled to five other U.S. museums, and in 1942, *Self-Portrait with Braid* was included in "20th Century Portraits," organized by Monroe Wheeler for the Museum of Modern Art. *The Two Fridas, What the Water Gave Me,* and the 1940 *Self-Portrait* in which she wears a thorn necklace and is accompanied by a monkey and a cat were shown in 1943 in "Mexican Art Today" at the Philadelphia Museum of Art, and in the same year a 1940 *Self-Portrait* was included in "Women Artists" at Peggy Guggenheim's Art of This Century gallery. (Some years later, in her *Confessions of an Art Addict*, Guggenheim commented that while she hated the enormous frescoes of Rivera, Orozco, and Siqueiros, she very much liked the work of Frida Kahlo, "having included her in my women's shows, realizing how gifted she was in the true Surrealist tradition.")

Because the exposure her art was given in Mexico came later and was, during her lifetime, less prestigious, Frida always acknowledged that her value as an artist was first recognized in the United States. Nevertheless, her reputation in Mexico was growing. In January and February of 1943, she participated in an exhibition of a hundred years of Mexican portraiture at the Benjamin Franklin Library, an English-language institution on the Paseo de la Reforma. The following year the library presented another historical survey, "The Child in Mexican Painting," and Frida contributed a painting called *The Sun and the Moon* (now lost). In 1944, works by Frida and Diego inaugurated a new (but short-lived) gallery called Galería de Arte Maupassant at 128 Paseo de la Reforma. An undated exhibition announcement from the Galería Orozco-Rivera (situated at the same address) says the gallery will present work by Orozco, Rivera, and Kahlo, as well as sculpture by María Teresa Pinto.

Frida was also invited to participate in the "Salon de la Flor," an exhibition of flower paintings that was part of an annual flower show in Mexico City. The invitation to paint flowers must have been welcome; Frida's special kinship with the natural world grew more intense as the years went on and as her childlessness became an undeniable fact of life. She sent *Flower of Life* (figure 64) to the "Salon de la Flor," and it is likely that *Magnolias*, 1945, and *Sun and Life* (plate XXXII) were intended for that show as well. One can imagine how surprising the overt sexual symbolism of the 1944 and 1947 paintings must have been to the flower-loving public of Mexico City: in both *Flower of Life* and *Sun and Life* Frida transforms tropical-looking plants into male and female genitals.

In both paintings, cosmic and sexual forces are linked. The sun is clearly a force for fertility. An explosion of life-starting sperm from a phallus in *Flower of Life* (originally titled *Flame Flower*) can also be seen as rays of holy light descending on a fetus that emerges from a womb. A flash of lightning heightens the drama. In *Sun and Life*, the drops of seminal fluid that spurt from various phallic plants are echoed in the sun's tears and in a weeping fetus that is enclosed in a leafy womb. The tears indicate that for Frida, nature's fecundity was sometimes a painful reminder of her own thwarted procreative urge. And indeed, about the time she painted *Sun and Life* she had another miscarriage; this time it was a lover's child, not Rivera's. Three concerns impelled her to make art, she told a critic in 1944: her vivid memory of her own blood flowing during her childhood accident; her thoughts about birth, death, and the "conducting threads" of life; and her desire to be a mother.

By the second half of the decade, Frida's work was well enough regarded in her native country to be included in most major group exhibitions. And the Mexican "art scene" was changing as well. Although the muralists were still painting their social-realist frescoes, they no longer overshadowed either modernist or surrealizing easel painting. Rufino Tamayo, whose work had formerly been scorned as being too European, now led the avant-garde. Foreign influences were less suspect, and more was known about art developments in other countries. Whereas Inés Amor's Galería de Arte Mexicano had once been the only important art gallery, now many new ones were opening up. Galleries need portable paintings to show and sell, so the easel painting, which had been considered an emblem of bourgeois decadence, became the painter's most frequent and popular production. Frida, of course, had been painting little easel paintings all along.

One sign of Frida's growing reputation was her selection in 1942 to be a founding member of the Seminario de Cultura Mexicana, an organization (under the auspices of the education ministry) that at first comprised some twenty-five artists and intellectuals, and whose purpose was to promote the spread of Mexican culture through lectures, exhibitions, and publications. (When Alejandro Gómez Arias nominated Frida to be one of the founding members of the more prestigious Colegio Nacional, an institution comparable to the Académie Française, the nomination was opposed. As Gómez Arias recalls, "The education minister asked me to help found the Colegio Nacional in 1942, and I proposed two women—one a famous biologist who had written a classic volume on cacti, and Frida. Both were rejected, Frida because there were already two painters in the Colegio Nacional—Orozco and Rivera—and the biologist because her teacher was already a member." Or so the other committee members said. Gómez Arias implies that they were rejected because they were women.)

The Seminario de Cultura Mexicana published a scholarly journal, the second issue of which included Rivera's "Frida Kahlo and Mexican Art." And Frida was asked by her old friend and fellow Cachucha Miguel N. Lira, who headed the Seminario, to contribute one or two articles each month for the radio or the press. In 1943, as part of her work for this organization, she helped to arrange the first of the jury-free exhibitions called "Salon Libre 20 de Noviembre" (to celebrate the day when the Mexican Revolution began) that took place in the Palace of Fine Arts. In addition, she helped arrange a National Painting Fair in the Alameda Park, and in 1944 she was invited to participate in a conference on popular mural painting sponsored by the Ministry of Education.

Frida was selected as one of six artists to receive a government fellowship in 1946, but the greatest honor came in September of that year, at the annual National Exhibition at the Palace of Fine Arts. Orozco was awarded the National Prize of Arts and Sciences for his Hospital de Jesús murals in Mexico City, but a special agreement between the President and the Minister of Education made it possible to give out four other painting prizes, of five thousand pesos each. These went to Frida (for her *Moses*), and to Doctor Atl, Julio Castellanos, and Francisco Goitia. Though encased in a plaster cast after an operation on her spine, she appeared at the opening reception dressed like a princess and received her prize.

There were government commissions as well. In 1941 she was asked to paint a series of portraits of "The five Mexican women who have most distinguished themselves in the history of the 'pueblo,'" as she put it, for the dining room of the National Palace. "Now they've got me trying to find out what kind of cockroaches those women were," she wrote to Dr. Eloesser,

what kind of faces they had, and what kind of psychology oppressed them, so that at the hour when I daub them the public will know how to distinguish them from the vulgar and common females of Mexico—who I will tell you, in my opinion, would include more interesting and more terrific women than the group of ladies in question. If among your curiosities you find some fat book that speaks of Doña Josefa Ortiz de Domínguez—of Doña Leona Vicario [both women were connected with the movement for independence]—of Doña [illegible] Xochitl [during the reign of the Toltec king, Xochitl popularized the intoxicating drink named *pulque*, made from the fermented juice of the maguey]—of Sor Juana Inés de la Cruz [the great Mexican poet-nun (1651–1695)]—do me the huge favor of sending me a few facts or photographs, engravings—etc. of the epoch and of their very prudent effigies. With this job I am going to earn a few bucks which I will dedicate to the purchase of some billy goats that give pleasure to my eye, smell and touch—and to the purchase of some very lovely tall flowerpots that I saw the other day in the market.

Unfortunately, the portraits of notable women were never completed. A second, smaller government commission was, but the painting, an extraordinary tondo still life Frida produced in 1942 for President Manuel Avila Camacho's dining room, was rejected. Perhaps Señora Avila Camacho found it too full of fruits, vegetables, and flowers that hinted disquietingly at human anatomy.

Frida thus continued to have a hard time finding and satisfying clients. Diego often sent the Americans who flocked to his studio over to Coyoacán to look at her work, but for the most part, there were bites, not buyers. Walter Arensberg, for example, was still dithering two years after Frida told Nickolas Muray that he would "buy a picture." On December 15, 1941, she wrote to Emmy Lou Packard:

From what you tell me about the Arensbergs I want you to tell them that Kaufmann has the painting of the "Birth." I would like them to buy the one of "Me Suckling" [*My Nurse and I*] since they would give me a nice pile. Above all, now that I am going about like a complete wretch. If you have the opportunity go to bat for me with them, but do it as though it came from you. Tell them that it is a painting that I painted at the same time as "the birth" and that you and Diego like it very much. You already know which one it is, right? The one where I am with my nurse suckling *puritita leche* [pure milk]. Do you remember? I hope you will encourage them to buy it from me, since you cannot imagine how much I need the bucks now (Tell them it is worth 250 dollars)—I'll send you the photo so that you will tell them lots of nice things and you will promote their interest in that "work of art." OK kid! Also tell them about the one with "the bed" [*The Dream*] that is in New York, it could be that they will be interested in that one—it is the one with the skeleton on top, do you remember? That one is worth 300 bucks. Let's see if you can give me a little push, sweetie, for I tell you that truly I urgently need dough.

Emmy Lou wrote back, predicting the final outcome: "I am going to battle for you. Who knows what the results will be. It appears to me that Arensberg only wants the painting of birth—as a document—he is spending all his dough now on trying to show that Bacon wrote the works of Shakespeare. Stendahl [a Los Angeles art dealer] says that he does not buy any paintings now."

Far from courting patrons, Frida made neither herself nor her paintings ingratiating. "I did not feel so sad about the death of Albert Bender," she wrote to Dr. Eloesser, "because I don't like Art Collectors, I don't know why, but now each day art in general gives me less of a kick, and above all those people that exploit the fact of being 'connoisseurs of art' in order to boast of being 'chosen by God,' many times I get on better with carpenters, shoemakers, etc. than with all that crowd of stupid, so-called civilized, chatterboxes, called 'cultivated people.' "

Even when sales picked up, in the mid-1940s, earning a living was not easy. A 1947 entry in Frida's account book, for example, shows that she sold *The Two Fridas* to Mexico City's Museum of Modern Art for four thousand pesos; it was purchased, according to the museum's director, Fernando Gamboa, because Frida desperately needed money and no one else wanted to buy it. By that time, however, Frida did have several enthusiastic patrons, who competed sporadically to purchase her work. Chief among them was Eduardo Morillo Safa, an agricultural engineer and a diplomat, who bought, over the years, some thirty Kahlos and in 1944 commissioned portraits of his two daughters, Mariana and Lupita, of his mother, Doña Rosita Morillo, of his wife and son and of himself.

Frida's portraits of others are almost always less vibrant and original than her subject paintings and self-portraits—perhaps because, in painting a specific individual, she did not feel free to project all her complex fantasy and feeling—her "own reality"—onto the image.

There is, however, one major exception. Certainly the most extraordinary portrait of a friend that Frida ever produced is that of Doña Rosita Morillo, and here she did not hesitate to make the painting an expression of deep personal emotion (figure 68). Although Frida's style did not develop in a linear way—in the same year, she could paint portraits with meticulous realism or with primitivistic simplification—*Doña Rosita Morillo* shows her general move toward an extremely refined, miniaturistic realism that is a far cry from the broader handling of the mural-style Mexicanist portraits of 1929–1930 or the naïve portraits of 1931 which are based on a folk limner tradition.

Wise but judging, powerful but worn, Doña Rosita embodies the essence of grandmotherliness. She seems the concretization of a basic human longing for such familial values as comfort, communion, and continuity. Like Van Gogh's *La Berceuse,* who holds a rope that leads out of the painting to an unseen cradle she is rocking, Doña Rosita holds her knitting, and from it a length of wool leads our eye out of the painting to the very space in which we stand. Knowing the way Frida used ribbons and other such connectors to establish emotional linkage, we can assume that the length of wool was meant to offer the viewer a concrete tie to the portrait subject. Doña Rosita's consoling bulk fills the canvas from side to side; pushed up close to the picture plane, she is as solid as a bulwark.

The tangle of vegetation that closes off space just behind the old woman reflects what she is. Darkness in the gaps between leaves shows that the time is night, which to Frida meant the end of life. Other signals of old age and death are brown leaves, and five desiccated, gray, leafless sticks. But as always, Frida presents death as part of the cycle of life: the dead sticks form props for a tangle of live, green, prickly flowering plants that loop and snake across the surface of the painting. In her own way, Doña Rosita is prickly-looking too. For all the wisdom and compassion in her eyes, the set of her mouth suggests that she possesses the critical cantankerousness of old women who watch successive generations making all the predictable errors.

Frida has given unusually close attention to specific textures in this painting, building up the image with heavy layers of pigment, and painting each detail with a different touch. The woolliness of Doña Rosita's sweater and shawl, like the hairy texture of the flowering plant, is carefully painted with numerous tiny strokes. The old woman's soft white hairs are picked out one by one. Indeed, the richness of surface detail is almost obsessive; it is as though Frida wanted Doña Rosita herself to materialize. Frida is the opposite of the kind of artist who abbreviates or synthesizes the visual world, conjuring up verisimilitude with broad bravura brush strokes. Instead, she paints every iota of what she sees, bit by bit, centimeter by centimeter, stroke by stroke. Essentially hers is an urge to recreate the world as a solid, palpable reality on the canvas.

The portrait of Mariana Morillo Safa, Doña Rosita's granddaughter, displays the same focus on minute detail and the same peculiar intensity that reflects Frida's fondness for her subject (figure 67). With her fawn-like gaze, and her huge pink bow, this child has all the qualities that oil painting was invented to create; she looks so real that we feel we could reach out and pinch her cheek or tickle her chin. Like a dewy peach in a Dutch seventeenth-century still life, she is an object of desire.

Frida adored children. She treated them as equals, and both in her art and in life she allowed them their own special dignity. As early as 1928, when Rivera, knowing she needed money, found her a job teaching art to children, her approach to her pupils was both that of a child among peers and that of an adult not wanting to "spoil" youthful creativity. Like Rivera, who wrote an elegy to children's art, Frida felt that before children were "turned into idiots by schools or by their mamas," they possessed purer creative powers than adults. "Diego got me a job as a drawing teacher," Frida said, "and I lay on the floor on my stomach with all the boys on their bellies too. And we drew, and I said to them, 'Don't copy anymore, paint your houses, your mothers, your brothers, the bus, things that happen.' We played marbles and spun tops and I became a better and better friend of theirs."

Later in life Frida may no longer have been able to play marbles on the floor, but her attitudes had changed not a whit. Her second cousin Roberto BeHar remembers visiting Frida during the 1940s, when he was attending a Catholic boarding school. Noticing one day that he was wearing a scapulary, she cried, "What's that?" He explained that if you wore it and you happened to die, you would go straight to heaven. "Who gave it to you?" Frida asked. A nun, Roberto replied. "*Dile a la madrecita que vaya chingar a su madre pero no a ti!*" she shrieked. "Go tell the little nun to screw her mother but not you!" Another time, Roberto showed Frida a map he had traced for home-work. "What?!" Frida cried in disapproval. "You must paint it free-hand." Roberto did, reluctantly, because he was afraid that the contours of the countries would not be accurate. He was right—his teacher gave him a zero. On his next visit with Frida, he showed her this result. She put a number one in front of the zero, and announced, "I am the teacher!"

Frida needed to be (and was) an important person in all "her" children's lives. Not long ago Mariana Morillo Safa reminisced about posing for Frida. "I loved her, and she loved me and petted me all the time. I am sure that because she did not have children of her own, she loved me and my sister more. My father said to us: 'Be affectionate with Frida. She does not have children and she loves you very much.' "

Mariana's parents would drop their youngest daughter at Frida's house on Saturday mornings and return to fetch her in the late afternoon. Since Frida could not paint for much more than an hour at a stretch, and rested for several hours in between, the portrait took two or three months to complete.

Frida would sit her model on a little chair that she had bought especially for her, and which Mariana took home when the portrait was done. "She kept me very quiet and still. I got tired, but she talked to me all the time and told me funny stories. She would tell me to keep a straight face, which I couldn't do. She was always so tender."

Frida loved to give Mariana presents. She had a Tehuana dress specially made for her, and another time, when Mariana won in a game, she gave her a red coin purse shaped like a boot. When Eduardo Morillo Safa came to fetch his daughter, he told her that she was badly brought up to accept the gift. Frida was angry. *"Metiche* [meddler]!" she cried. "This is a game between Mariana and me!" and Mariana kept the purse.

Frida's affection for Mariana continued over the years. From 1946 to 1948, the Morillo Safa family lived in Caracas, where the engineer served as Mexican ambassador to Venezuela. Frida was recuperating from one of her many spinal surgeries when she received a letter from Mariana that so delighted her that she answered her *"Cachita, changa, maranga"* with a note and a long poem, a sample of which follows:

> From Coyoacán, so sad
> oh, Cachita of my life,
> I send you these mushy verses
> from your real pal, Frida.
>
> Don't think that I'm playing "dead,"
> and that I'm not writing to you,
> since singing with all my love I
> send this ballad to you.

You went to Caracas
in a powerful airplane,
and from here I miss you
with all my heart. . . .

Don't forget your Mexico,
it is the root of your life,
and always keep in mind that with songs
your pal Frida awaits you.

Besides Morillo Safa, another of Frida's favorite patrons was the engi-neer José Domingo Lavin, who commissioned a circular portrait of his wife in 1942, and in 1945 commissioned *Moses* (figure 69). The painting was the result of a chance conversation that took place at lunch at the Lavins' house. Her host showed Frida his recently pur-chased copy of Freud's *Moses and Monotheism*. She read a few pages and asked him to lend it to her. She was fascinated, and when she had finished the book, he suggested that she try to put her ideas about the book into a painting. Within three months *Moses* was finished. Two years later, Frida gave an informal lecture about it to a gathering in Domingo Lavin's home.

The opening paragraphs of Frida's explanation are interesting for what they reveal of the candid and completely unpretentious way in which she approached her art:

As this is the first time in my life that I have tried to "explain" one of my paintings to a group of more than three people, you will forgive me if I get a little mixed up and a little dusty. . . .

I read [Freud's *Moses*] only once, and I began to paint the picture with the first impression it gave me. Yesterday, as I wrote these words for you, I reread it, and I must confess to you that I find the painting very incomplete and rather different from what the interpretation should be of what Freud analyzes so marvelously in his *Moses*. But now, there is nothing to be done, neither to take away from it nor to add to it, so I'll tell about what I painted just as it is and about what you can see here in the painting. Of course, the main theme is "MOSES" or the birth of the HERO. But I generalized in my way (a very confused way) the deeds or images that impressed me the most as I read the book. As for what is there "on my account," you can tell me whether I put my foot in it or not.

Because of its broad theme and its multitude of tiny figures, many viewers have compared Frida's *Moses* to a mural. But it is far from

"public" art. By handling her historical subject in such a freely individualistic manner, Frida managed to turn it into an expression of her
personal preoccupation with procreation as part of the cycle of life.
Even the painting's composition suggests procreation: Frida combined
a naïvely additive method of organizing forms (seen in the painting's
various sections) with an overall coherence based on bilateral symmetry
and recalling the anatomy of the female pelvic region. Moses' birth
is situated, quite appropriately, in the middle.

The child is born beneath a huge red sun emitting rays that end
in hands. As a device, of course, this image has its origins in Egyptian
reliefs of the Amarna period, but a more direct source for Frida's
conception is Rivera's Preparatory School mural where hands at the
ends of rays of light signify, according to Diego, "Solar energy, the
life source of all." In a similar vein, Frida explained in her essay on
Moses that the sun in her painting was conceived as "the center of
all religions, as First GOD and as creator and reproducer of LIFE."

Moses' birth stands for the birth of all heroes. On either side of
the central natal event is a group of historical heroes that range from
Christ to Lenin, from Buddha to Hitler—the "big wigs" Frida called
them. Above them are gods; below them are the masses seething in
the wars that make history. In the lower left corner is, Frida said,
"the first man the constructor, in four colors (four races) accompanied
by his near ancestor, the ape." In the lower right corner is "the mother,
the creator with the child in arms" accompanied by a female monkey,
likewise holding her offspring. Between the heaven crammed with
gods and the one arrayed with heroes are a human and an animal
skeleton plus, for good measure, a devil. Large embracing fingers represent the earth opening its hands to protect and receive the dead, "generously and without distinctions"—just the kind of monumental, embracing hands Rivera sometimes depicted in his murals.

"On either side of the child," Frida explained, "I put the elements
of his creation, the fertilized ovum and cellular division." A scattering
of raindrops accompanies birth's breaking of water, and (as in *Flower
of Life*) fallopian tubes that look both like flowers and like human
hands reach out from the central womb.

Dividing the central birth scene from the lateral historical sections
are two ancient tree trunks, Frida's favorite symbol for the life-death
cycle. The decaying wood bursts forth with new green-leafed shoots,
and old broken branches are made to resemble the fallopian tubes.

New life, she said, always sprouts from "the trunk of age." In the center foreground, entwined in a tracery of vein-like roots, a snail shell spurting fluid into a conch symbolizes "love."

Moses reveals Frida's urge to encompass all time and all space in one vision. Like *Roots,* it is an expression of her religion, a vitalistic form of pantheism which she shared, to a great extent, with Diego. Frida's faith was an all-embracing view of the universe as an elaborate web of "conducting threads," a *"harmony* of form and *color"* in which "everything moves according to only one law—life. No one is apart from anyone. No one fights for himself. All is all and one. Anguish and pain, pleasure and death are nothing but a *process* in order to *exist."* Her diary (this passage was written in 1950) continues:

No one is more than a functioning or part of the total function. . . . We direct ourselves toward *our own* selves through millions of beings—stones— bird creatures—star beings—microbe beings—fountain beings to ourselves. Variety of the *one* incapacity to escape the *two,* the three, the etcetera of always—in order to return to the *one.* But not to the *sum* (sometimes called *god,* sometimes *liberty,* sometimes *love)—* No— We have always been hate-love-mother-child-plant-earth-light-lightning-etc.-world giver of worlds—universes and universal cells.

"La Esmeralda" does not refer to an emerald or a jewelry store in Mexico City. Rather it is the Ministry of Public Education's School of Painting and Sculpture, renamed by its students after the street where it was first located. When the school opened, in 1942, there were more faculty than students, for the director, Antonio Ruiz, a painter of diminutive works full of humor and fantasy, started by hiring an impressive staff of twenty-two. By 1943 these included such prominent artists as Jesús Guerrero Galván, Carlos Orozco Romero, Agustín Lazo, Manuel Rodríguez Lozano, Francisco Zúñiga, María Izquierdo, Diego Rivera (who taught composition), and Frida Kahlo. Frida's starting pay was 252 pesos for twelve hours of teaching, three days a week. Although her employment after the first three years was informal, to say the least, she was registered as a teacher for a decade.

Not all the instructors were Mexican—the French-born Surrealist poet Benjamin Péret taught French, for example—but their spirit was emphatically *Mexicanista.* Though the school's plant was shabby and primitive, consisting of one large classroom and a patio where the students painted (when it rained, the patio flooded and the students had to walk about on planks), to the teachers at La Esmeralda, all Mexico was a studio. Instead of asking their students to draw from plaster casts or to copy European models, they sent them out into the streets and fields, to work from nature. Their aim was not to produce artists, but to "prepare individuals whose creative personality [would] later express itself in the arts"; the five-year program included courses in mathematics, Spanish, history, art history, and French. Each student's initiative was to be kindled by direct contact with teachers. Since the students were mostly poor, tuition and art materials were free.

One of the first students, the painter Guillermo Monroy, recalls that "in the beginning there were only about ten students. Then from my barrio came a gang of about twenty-two boys. When I entered the school, I didn't know anything about art, because I was a worker from a family of carpenters. I had only had six years of school, and I didn't even know that art schools existed. I was a furniture varnisher and upholsterer. Later I wanted to learn to carve wood, because I worked in a colonial furniture shop. So, as a worker, I went to La Esmeralda."

Frida's arrival at La Esmeralda made a great impression. Some students were admiring; others, like Fanny Rabel (then called Fanny Rabinovich), were skeptical at first:

"It is an old vice of women not to have confidence in women. So, in the beginning, when they told me that I was going to have a woman teacher, I did not like the idea. I had only had male teachers and male companions. Almost everything in Mexico was managed by the masculine gender, and there were very few girls in the school. My landscape teacher, Feliciano Peña, had told me, 'Well, I have seen this Frida Kahlo in the office, and she looked at me and asked me, "Are you a teacher here?" and I said, "Yes." Then Frida said, "What's this about teaching? I don't know anything about teaching." ' Peña was very angry and said to me, 'How can she be a teacher if she doesn't know anything about teaching?'

"But the moment that I met Frida I was fascinated because she had a gift to fascinate people. She was unique. She had enormous *alegría*, humor and love of life. She had invented her own language, her own way of speaking Spanish, full of vitality and accompanied by gestures, mimicry, laughter, jokes, and a great sense of irony. The first thing she did when I met her was to say, 'Oh, you are one of the *muchachitas* here! You are going to be my student! Listen, how do you do this thing of giving classes? I don't know. What's it about?

I don't have the slightest idea how to teach. But I think it's going to be all right.' This disarmed me. She was very friendly, and her relationship with all her students began on the familiar *tu a tu* basis of equality. She became like a big sister, like a mother watching her *muchachitos.*"

As Guillermo Monroy remembers it, Frida was "brotherly, an extraordinary teacher, a comrade. She was like a walking flower. She told us to draw what we had in our houses—clay jars, popular art, furniture, toys, Judases—so we didn't feel like strangers in the school."

If Frida was a "walking flower," her pupil Monroy retains something of what she taught: he is a writer of florid grace. Among his several impassioned articles about his beloved *maestra* is this description of Frida's first day of teaching at La Esmeralda:

I remember her entering the school of Painting and Sculpture, "La Esmeralda," for the first time. She appeared there all of a sudden like a stupendous flowering branch because of her joyfulness, kindness, and enchantment. This was owed, surely, to the Tehuana dress that she wore, and that she always wore with such grace. The young people who were going to be her students . . . received her with true enthusiasm and emotion. She chatted with us briefly after greeting us very affectionately, and then immediately told us in a very animated way: "Well, kids, let's go to work; I will be your so-called teacher, I am not any such thing, I only want to be your friend, I never have been a painting teacher, nor do I think I ever will be, since I am always learning. It is certain that to paint is the most terrific thing that there is, but to do it well is very difficult, it is necessary to do it, to learn the skill very well, to have very strict self-discipline and above all to have love, to feel a great love for painting. Once and for all I am going to tell you that if the little experience that I have had as a painter is helpful to you in any way, you will tell me so, and that with me you will paint everything you want and feel. I will try to understand you the best I can. From time to time I will permit myself to make a few observations about your work, but also, I ask you, as the *cuates* that we are, that when I show you my work, you will do the same. I will never take the pencil from you in order to correct you; I want you to know, dear children, that there does not exist in the whole world a single teacher who is capable of teaching art. To do that is truly impossible. We will surely talk a lot about some theoretical question or another, of the different techniques used in the plastic arts, of form and content in art, and of all those things that are intimately related to our work. I hope you will not be bored with me, and when I seem a bore to you, I ask you, please, not to keep quiet, all right?" These simple and rather pure words were pronounced in a way that was without affectation or posing, completely lacking in pedantry.

After a brief silence, *la maestra* Frida asked all her students what we wanted to paint. On hearing this very direct question, the entire group became disconcerted for a few moments, and looking at each other, we didn't know what to answer right away, but I, seeing how pretty she was, asked her with great frankness to pose for us. She, visibly moved and with a slight smile of acceptance that blossomed on her lips, asked for a chair. As soon as she sat down, she was surrounded by easels and students.

Frida Kahlo was there before us; gravely, astonishingly quiet, keeping a silence so deep and so impressive that no one, none of us, dared to interrupt. . . .

Her students agree that Frida's teaching was completely unprogrammatic. She did not impose her ideas on them; rather she let their talents develop according to their temperaments, and taught them to be self-critical. Her remarks were penetrating, but never unkind, and she mitigated both praise and blame by making it clear that what she said was only a personal view, which could be wrong. "It seems to me that this should be a little stronger in color," she would say. "This should be in balance with that; this part is not very well done. I would do it this way, but I am me, and you are you. It's an opinion and I could be mistaken. If it's helpful to you, take it, and if not, leave it."

"The only help she gave us was to stimulate us, nothing more," says another of her pupils, Arturo García Bustos. "She did not say even half a word about how we should paint, or anything about style, as the maestro Diego did. She did not pretend to explain theoretical things. But she was enthusiastic about us. She'd say, 'How well you painted this!' or 'This part came out very ugly.' What she taught us, fundamentally, was love of the people, and a taste for popular art. She'd say, for example, 'Look at that Judas! How marvelous! Look at those proportions! How Picasso would like to succeed in painting something with that expressiveness, with that force!' "

Fanny Rabel believes that "Frida's great teaching was to see through artist's eyes, to open our eyes to see the world, to see Mexico. She did not influence us through her way of painting, but through her way of living, of looking at the world and at people and at art. She made us feel and understand a certain kind of beauty in Mexico that we would not have realized by ourselves. She did not transmit this sensibility verbally. We were very young, simple and malleable—one of us was only fourteen years old, another was a peasant. We were not intellectual. She did not impose anything. Frida would say, 'Paint what you see, what you want.' We all painted differently, followed our own routes. We did not paint like her. There was lots of chatting, jokes, conviviality. She was not giving us a lesson. Diego, on the other hand, could make a theory about anything in a minute. But she was instinctive, spontaneous. She would become happy in front of any beautiful thing."

"Muchachos," she would announce, "locked up here in school we can't do anything. Let's go into the street. Let's go and paint the life in the street." And to the markets, slums, colonial convents and baroque churches, to neighboring towns like Puebla, to the pyramids of Teotihuacán they went. Once, on crutches, she escorted them to Xochimilco to visit Francisco Goitia, who years before had been commissioned by the government to paint the types and customs of the Indians, and who, having all but abandoned painting, continued to live in a primitive hut, teaching village children.

On the way to and from their destinations Frida taught her students *corridos* and revolutionary Mexican songs, and they taught her the songs they were learning in the Communist Youth Organization. Often they stopped in *pulquerías,* where balladeers sang the songs of *la raza* for a few pesos. Painter Hector Xavier, who was enrolled at La Esmeralda but not in Frida's class, went along on one of her trips to Teotihuacán. "When we were leaving to return to the city," he remembered, "the truck stopped in front of a *pulquería.* Frida was riding in front next to the driver—partly because she had discovered that he had a very interesting face and partly because it was more comfortable than the back. She called me to get down from the back of the truck. 'All the *muchachos,*' she said, 'to the *pulquería!* As for me, I will stay with this gentleman who takes the wheel.' So we got down and she gave us a little purse with money. We entered the *pulquería,* and for the first time I saw the calabash cups for *pulque,* and it seemed to me, also, that we could invite all the people there for a drink. Well, Frida was paying. Finally, Frida said, 'Everybody up,' and we climbed back on the truck. She continued chatting with the driver, who was telling her very good anecdotes. Two blocks from the school, the truck stopped, and Frida said, 'Whoever feels in good enough shape to continue the trip and to go to school, come with us, and whoever does not, get down.' So we arrived at the school with a smaller group, but very happy with the whole experience in Teotihuacán and the *pulque* in the *pulquería* and the spirit of Frida."

After a few months, Frida found the long commute between Coyoacán and La Esmeralda taxing to her health. She did not, however, want to give up teaching, so she asked her students to come to her home. At first, a large group commuted to Coyoacán, but most eventually dropped out of her class, discouraged by the long bus ride. In the lives of the four who remained—Arturo García Bustos, Guillermo Monroy, Arturo Estrada and Fanny Rabel, Frida became as central a person as she was in the lives of Mariana Morillo Safa and Roberto BeHar. "We got so used to Frida, and liked her so much, that it was as if she had been there always," Fanny recalled. "Everybody loved her in a strange way. It was as if her life was always so close to those around her that you were tied up with her, as if you couldn't live without her." They were to stay with her for years, even after they had finished school. Just as Rivera's students were called "Los Dieguitos," Frida's came to be called "Los Fridos."

When they first arrived at her house, Frida would say to them, "The whole garden is ours. Let's go paint. This is your room to store your work things. I am going to work in my studio. I will not come out every day to see your work." Indeed, her schedule was unpredictable. She gave critiques as seldom as once every two weeks and as often as three times a week, with Rivera sometimes present and commenting on the work as well. The occasions were like parties: Frida served food and drink, and sometimes afterward took her students to the movies. "I remember particularly one occasion when she came down into the garden dressed in black carrying a cane and with her hair adorned with an infinity of flowers," says García Bustos. "We were all in love with Frida. She had a special grace and attraction. She was so *alegre* that she made poetry around her." On another morning, in June 1944, Monroy was equally bewitched. A light fog inundated the garden, and he, having arrived early, was busy painting a maguey plant near a little fish pool. Full of pleasure in trying to capture what he saw, he burst into song. And then, he recalls, "I began to feel a strange, disquieting sensation on my shoulders, a light chill, afterward heat, later soft electric charges; I felt that my shoulder was split into blue streaks of lightning. . . . [I turned to find] nothing less than Frida Kahlo . . . who, full of smiles and coupling her eyes with mine, said: 'Continue singing, Monroycito, you know that I also like to sing. . . .

How wonderful your painting is turning out, take lots of pleasure and thrill in that little maguey. How moving it is to paint, don't you think? What a beautiful plant!'" Then Frida smiled softly, kissed Monroy on the left cheek, and as she took leave of him, advised, "Keep on working, continue painting, don't ever stop singing."

For her pupils, Frida's Coyoacán house was an education in itself. Their models were anything close at hand—monkeys, dogs, cats, frogs and fish, all the plants in the garden, all the art in the house. Frida tried to give them an aesthetic approach to everyday life by means of such games as arranging and rearranging the fruit, flowers, and earthenware plates on the dining room table to see who could make the most striking composition. "[She] constantly renewed the scenography of objects around her," remembers Fanny Rabel. "She would wear twenty rings one day and twenty other rings another day. Her milieu was full of things, and they were always kept in order."

Frida made her pupils into a family—her family—and her house an exotic home for them, one in which they encountered a whole new world. "When she was ill and staying home, there were always people around," Fanny Rabel says. "That was one of the things that impressed me very much—all those people, crazy people like Jacqueline Breton, Leonora Carrington [English-born Surrealist painter, who has lived in Mexico since 1947], Esteban Frances [Spanish-born Surrealist painter], Benjamin Péret, artists and collectors and all kinds of friends. I looked at them with huge eyes, and Frida used to wink at me, because I was so impressed. And I remember after many years I used to tell her that I thought I was never going to be an artist, because I was too normal, and one must have to have a great personality to be a great artist. Then Frida would say, 'You know why they do all those crazy things? Because they don't have any personality. They must make it up. You are going to be an artist because you have talent. You are an artist, so you don't have to do all those things.'"

As much as Frida advocated direct contact between art and life, she also wanted her students to read (Walt Whitman and Mayakovsky, for example), and to learn from art history, by sketching pre-Columbian sculptures in the anthropology museum and colonial art in other museums. Pre-Hispanic art she called the "root of our modern art," and besides the anonymous *retablo* painters, her favorite artists were José María Estrada, Hermenegildo Bustos, José María Velasco, Julio Ruelas, Saturnino Herrán, Goitia, Posada, Doctor Atl, and of course, Diego. She showed her pupils books with reproductions of paintings by such

Europeans as Rousseau and Brueghel. Picasso, she told them, was a "great and many-sided painter." She also conveyed to them her interest in biology, showing them slides under a microscope and talking about microorganisms as well as plants and animals. Eager to share her own fascination with the formation of life, she did not hesitate to include sex education in her curriculum. She lent them books illustrating the development of the human fetus as well as books on erotic art, which she loved.

Some of Frida's students had studied mural painting with Rivera at La Esmeralda, and knowing their interest, Frida arranged for them to paint various murals. Near her house, on the corner of Londres Street, just next door to the home of the dethroned King Carol of Rumania, there was a *pulquería* called La Rosita. Along with those of most other *pulquerías* in Mexico, the government had whitewashed its mural decoration for reasons of health and high-mindedness. Frida obtained permission for her students to paint new murals on the two exterior walls facing the street, and soon three of the four "Fridos" plus several other student artists between the ages of fourteen and nineteen were working there free of charge with brushes and paint supplied by Frida and Diego. *El maestro* and *la maestra* came to watch the work progress and gave advice, but they did not participate in the actual painting.

The project was conceived and executed in the spirit of fun. No one presumed that a great work of art would be produced. The style combined the broad, simplified realism of Rivera with the awkward primitivism of the *pulquería* mural tradition. The subjects—town and country scenes based on the bar's name (The Little Rose) and on the theme of *pulque*—were delegated according to each student's predilection. Fanny Rabel recalls that her job was to paint a little girl. She also put roses in the pasture. (In those days, children were deemed a suitable subject for women artists, and not surprisingly, Fanny later became a specialist in painting children.)

The fiesta to inaugurate La Rosita was announced by an illustrated, tongue-in-cheek Posada-like broadside distributed in the plazas, markets, and streets of Coyoacán:

The spectator! with his chitchat on the news of the day! Kind radio listeners: Saturday, the 19th of June, 1943, at 11 in the morning Grand Premiere of the Decorative Paintings of the Great *Pulquería* La Rosita on the corner of Aguayo and Londres, Coyoacán, D.F. The paintings that adorn this house were painted by: Fanny Rabinovich, Lidia Huerta, María de los Angeles Ramos, Tomás Cabrera, Arturo Estrada, Ramón Victoria, Erasmo V. Landechy and Guillermo Monroy under the direction of Frida Kahlo, professor of the School of Painting and Sculpture of the Ministry of Public Education. Acting as sponsors and as guests of honor: Don Antonio Ruiz and Doña Concha Michel, who offer to all the distinguished clientele of this house a succulent lunch consisting of an exquisite Barbecue imported directly from Texcoco, which they sprinkled with the supreme *pulques* from the best haciendas that produce the delicious national nectar. Add to the charm of this festival a band of Mariachis with the best of their singers from the lowlands, sky rockets, firecrackers, thunder-making fireworks, invisible balloons, parachutists made of maguey leaves, and whoever wants to be a bullfighter may throw himself into the ring on Saturday afternoon, since there also will be a little bull for the *aficionados.* Exquisite *pulques,* lavish prizes, pretty gifts, superior quality, painstaking attention.

"All Mexico" came to the opening—famous personalities of the worlds of art, literature, film, music, plus students from La Esmeralda and the people of Coyoacán. It was a spectacular occasion that delivered almost as much as the announcement promised. There were fireworks, balloons, and a parade of celebrities. The folksinger Concha Michel, Frida, and the girls among the art students all came dressed as Tehuanas. The *pulquería* and the streets were decorated with brightly colored tissue-paper cutouts, and confetti fell like rain. Filmmakers scurried about; their film of the opening was later projected in all the theaters belonging to the distributors, Cine Mexico. Press photographers and reporters were there in abundance. Mariachi bands played loudly, and Frida and Concha Michel sang *corridos,* to much applause. Among the songs were *corridos* written for the occasion that told about Frida, about the La Rosita murals, and about *pulquería* painting in general. The verses were printed up like Posada's ballad illustrations on cheap colored paper and handed out to assembled guests.

At the height of the festivities Guillermo Monroy sang the fifteen verses of his *corrido,* of which here are six:

> The barrio of Coyoacán
> formerly was so sad!
> And that was because it lacked
> something to be happy about.

To paint La Rosita
took a lot of work!
The people had already forgotten
the art of the *pulquería.*

Doña Frida de Rivera,
our beloved teacher,
says to us: Come, boys,
I will show you life.

We will paint *pulquerías,*
also the façades of schools—
art begins to die
if it stays in the academy.

Neighborhood friends,
I want to advise you
not to take so much *pulque*
because you can get bloated.

Think of the fact that you have wives
and dear little children!
It's one thing to be gay
and another to lose one's senses!

Arturo Estrada's *corrido* spoke of the past and present of *pulquería*
murals:

Formerly it looked so bad,
that we could not deny;
when it began to be painted,
it began to be a *pulquería*

with street kid language
the drunkards criticized.
Some said: How pretty!
and others said: Ay, how disgusting.

In spite of this, sirs,
the people are getting excited
and they are very interested
in doing it the honors.

Along with the music, there was dancing in the street. Sombrero
on head and hands clasped behind his back, Rivera was photographed

dancing a Yucatecan *jarana* with Concha Michel. Frida, the pain in her back and foot dulled by excitement and tequila, danced *jaranas*, *danzones*, and *zapateados* with Diego. And of course, there was some tipsy clowning. On a dare, Hector Xavier stole a friend's hat, put it on his own head, then dipped his hand in the *mole* sauce and drew brown stripes on the other man's face. "But," says Xavier, "the greatest thing of that afternoon was when I told Diego: 'Maestro, the French teacher [Benjamin Péret], who is over there, wants to dance a *zapateado* with you,' and Diego, nimble and quick, with that body that moved and swayed, went toward the guy and coldly said to him, 'Let's dance.' The guy said, 'No, I don't dance. I don't know how to dance a *zapateado*.' He had only recently arrived from Europe. The strangest thing in Diego's attitude of being the great figure as an artist was the frolicking and the menace. When the man said no, he couldn't dance the *zapateado*, Diego took out his pistol and said, 'I'll teach you,' and the French teacher did the *zapateado* with Diego. One had to see Diego move, an upright elephant, slow, graceful."

All the dignitaries made speeches, few of them in celebration of La Rosita. Concha Michel spoke passionately about the current state of the Mexican Revolution, which, she said, had done nothing but enthrone the reactionaries in power so that the people of Mexico took refuge more and more in *pulque*. Diego went further: another revolution was needed, he said. Then he softened this thought, adding that it was up to the artists to make the revolution by painting murals on all the *pulquerías*, "so that the people can express their complaints, their needs, and see their ideal, or their right to a better world, given shape." Finally, the poet Salvador Novo addressed himself to the murals being celebrated. He congratulated the artists and Frida, who, he said, had renewed the approach to art instruction in Mexico. More congratulations came to Frida from Dolores del Rio, for "this cultural work which will create true art and make art available to our people, who do not enter the palaces and who cannot help seeing art if it is on *pulquerías*."

Justifiably the student artists were thrilled with their success. The people of the parish liked the murals so much, according to *La Prensa*, that several commissions for other *pulquería* murals were offered. And having interviewed Frida at the opening fiesta, the reporter noted: "Frida Kahlo, satisfied with her work, said to us that she hoped this crusade in favor of art would result in a resurgence of spontaneity and of pure art, since the disciples will paint in the open air and in an atmosphere where sincere criticisms will cause them to improve their styles. Frida intends that they should decorate all the *pulquerías* of Mexico, so typical and so beautiful, with Mexican motifs." Another newspaper took a more skeptical view of Frida's goals: "In the end, there is a tendency to resuscitate what is Mexican—each in his own way."

Thanks to the success of the La Rosita murals, Frida obtained another project for the "Fridos" in 1944. An old friend of the Riveras had built the Posada del Sol, a luxury hotel, and he wanted Diego and Frida to paint murals in the hall for wedding banquets. Although Rivera was not interested, and Frida's physical condition by then made it impossible for her to take on such a commission, they did not reject the offer. They said they would do it on the condition that the "Fridos" assist them with the job. The hotel owner set the theme: great loves from world literature. The young artists presented their sketches and went to work. But since they considered the assigned subject to be trite and old-fashioned, they disregarded it, and instead painted motifs related to love in Mexico—for example, courtship in the midst of a fiesta or the desperate passions of soldiers during the revolution. The owner was not amused. He canceled the contract and had the work destroyed.

A more appropriate mural project was secured for the "Fridos" in 1945. In order to improve the working conditions of laundresses— mainly widows and unwed mothers who took in wash in order to survive and who often did their washing in muddy streams—President Cárdenas had sponsored the building of several public laundries. The one in Coyoacán comprised several small houses: one for ironing, another for a nursery, another for dining, and the last a meeting room for public and social functions. It was here that "Los Fridos" painted their murals.

Well indoctrinated after two years of contact with Frida and Diego, the young artists were delighted to have a project that would serve the public good. Frida gave them paints and brushes, and the laundresses contributed enough money to pay for the painters' refreshments. After planning the mural around a chosen theme, they worked independently on their individual designs. "Later, at the moment of definitive selection, with the help of *la maestra* Frida's clear vision, we formed a single plan, taking the best and most positive from each one, giving unity to the theme and to the ensemble."

García Bustos remembers that they presented their various projects to Frida, and then to a large group of washerwomen. "My particular project moved these washerwomen very deeply. They wept when they examined it, because they said that it reminded them of the sorrows of their lives. They asked us whether we could veil the misery a little, since some of them were going to appear as portraits in the mural. Monroy's project was the one that was finally chosen, because it was less painful in subject matter." Each painter took responsibility for the subject and wall that he or she had drawn, and each participated in the execution of all the panels, respecting the pictorial personality of its designer.

The group worked with enthusiasm, except for Fanny Rabel, who says she felt like a "dog without a master" because her design for the nursery (again she chose to involve herself with the theme of children) had to be abandoned for lack of funds. But, she says, the experience was "beautiful, because all day long we had those women around and we made sketches of them." The "Fridos" included the laundresses' portraits in the scenes of washing, ironing, sewing, and eating. A photograph of the preparatory drawings on the walls (the mural, executed in tempera on dry walls, did not last) shows a style that is more skillful and sophisticated than that of the La Rosita murals. Large, simplified volumes are depicted in a few succinct lines—a Riveraesque version of the kind of spare, elliptical line drawing that Picasso and Matisse made popular in the 1920s.

When the mural was done, a rather formal invitation went out for the inauguration: "The group of young people Fanny Rabinovich, Guillermo Monroy, Arturo Estrada and Arturo García Bustos, of the School of Painting and Sculpture of the Ministry of Public Education, invite you to see the mural painting that they executed in the House of Women "Josefina Ortiz de Domínguez" situated in Coyoacán, D.F., No. 1 Tepalcatitla Street (Barrio del Niño Jesús)." The invitation told of the financial sacrifices the laundresses had made in order to build the laundry and said: "Considering that our effort was made by the people and for the people, we think it will interest you, given your civic and social sense, to accept our invitation, and if you find our work valid, you will be a collaborator in the labor that with modesty, but with firm resolve, we have undertaken, for the planting and growth in our time of the marvelous tradition of Mexican art of the past, when everything from the most humble household utensil to the collective temple was a work of art."

On March 8, Women's Day in Mexico, the students and teachers of La Esmeralda joined the laundresses for the opening. Fanny Rabel says that there were numerous speeches, and it was more like a political meeting than a fiesta. But there was also music, leaflets printed with a *corrido* to sing, and platters of tacos filled with nopal cactus, cooked by the laundresses.

Frida did other things to further her students' careers. She helped them to find jobs as artists' assistants and to exhibit their work. As early as June 1943, when they had only just begun to study with her, they had a show, and in 1944, together with other students at La Esmeralda, they showed their work at the Palace of Fine Arts. In February 1945, they had another joint exhibition, at the Gallery of Plastic Arts on Palma Avenue, which was run by a friend of Frida's.

The "Fridos" contribution to the 1945 "Exposición de Arte Libre 20 de Noviembre," a huge tempera painting that Estrada, García Bustos, and Monroy had worked on together in Frida's garden, was full of revolutionary fervor. Inflammatorily entitled *Who Exploits Us and How They Exploit Us*, it drew a lot of attention, not all of it favorable. First someone threw sulfuric acid on it. Then a storm of public protest broke out when authorities in the Department of Fine Arts withdrew the painting. Calm was restored after one of Diego's assistants repaired the maligned work, and it was purchased for nine hundred pesos by a well-known collector.

The political controversy was hardly surprising. Frida had always seen her students as "comrades," and Rivera was not exaggerating the political impetus his wife gave to her students when he wrote: "She encouraged the development of a personalized style of painting, and urged her followers to hold firm political and social views. Most of her adherents are members of the Communist party." Frida inculcated leftist theory in her pupils by her own and Diego's example. By 1946, Rivera had applied for readmission to the Party, and Frida, though she dragged her feet for a while, ended by following in his political footsteps. As one friend put it, "If Diego had said, 'I am the Pope,' Frida would have become a papist." Frida put it even better. Among her papers is a scribbled rhyme: *"Yo creí a D.R./Con el burgués una fiera;/pero adoro sus ideas/porque no escoge a las feas."* (I believed in Diego Rivera/Devil take the bourgeoisie;/but I adore his ideas/ because he does not choose the ugly ones.) Ironically, Diego's several applications were rejected until 1954; Frida, possibly because she had never officially become a Trotskyite, was welcomed back into the Communist fold in 1948, after undergoing the usual humiliating ritual of "self-criticism" that orthodoxy required.

Although there is no question about where her sympathies lay, the intensity of Frida's politics remains a subject of some controversy. Some people see her as a leftist heroine; others see her as basically apolitical. The heat or coolness of her concern seemed to depend on the political bias of the person to whom she was talking, and, of course, on Diego's current views. Thus, leftists tend to perceive Frida as a vehement Communist, while those who are either naïve about, or indifferent to, politics, or those who disapprove of Frida's communism, tend to see her as a nonpolitical creature. (Interestingly, it is her male students who portray her as a political being; her one female disciple, Fanny Rabel, does not remember her taking political stances: "She was a humanist, not a politicized woman.") What can be said with certainty is that at least beginning in the 1940s, Frida stressed social content in art and took an interest in the political development of her young protégés, recommending Marxist literature and involving them in political discussions between herself and Diego. Painting, she said, should play a role in society. Quick to admit that she was incapable of making political paintings, she nevertheless encouraged her students to follow the Riveraesque tradition of socially conscious and "Mexicanist"realism rather than to attach themselves to the current of European-inspired, modernist easel painting.

Eventually the "Fridos" formed an organization of left-wing painters who shared their ideal of bringing art to the people. Known as the Young Revolutionary Artists, the group grew to include forty-seven members, and held various ambulatory exhibitions on market days in different working-class sections of Mexico City. To this day, they credit Frida with their political formation. Years after her death, Arturo Estrada eulogized Frida at the opening of a retrospective exhibition of her work: "Her roots in the tradition of our people made her always alert to problems of the majority, attending humanely also to the particular problems of her neighbors, the humble women of the district of El Carmen in Coyoacán, where women young and old found in Frida a friend who spiritually and economically gave help to their pains, calling her affectionately, 'niña Fridita.' . . . Her active political militancy made of the *maestra* Frida Kahlo an authentic daughter of the people, with whom she was identified in all their manifestations."

The four original disciples of Frida Kahlo maintain their solidarity even today. To them, being called "Los Fridos" is a matter of pride. Yet they never modeled their art on their teacher's, and each works in a distinct style. What unites them is their sympathy for the Mexican poor and their love for Mexican culture. When the "Fridos" finished the course of studies at La Esmeralda, Frida said to them, "I'm going to be very sad, because you are not going to be here anymore." Rivera knew just how to reassure his wife: "It is the moment in which they are going to walk alone," he told her. "Even though they go their own ways, they will come and visit us as always, because they are our comrades."

Chapter 20

The Little Deer

IN ONE of Frida's most stoic images, *Self-Portrait with Small Monkey*, painted in 1945, a spider monkey holds a ribbon that starts by circling Frida's signature, winds around the neck of a pre-Columbian idol, then proceeds to form a noose-like loop around Frida's neck, enlaces both her dog's and her monkey's neck, and finally loops around a sharp, illusionistically painted nail that is driven into the painting's background (plate XXIII). The ribbon, always for Frida a symbol of connectedness, is here, like the nail, sinister and threatening. Silky and yellow (yellow for illness and madness), it hints at some psychic asphyxiation, while the nail evokes the martyrdom of physical pain.

When Frida reduced her teaching schedule in 1944, it was because of steadily worsening health. The pain in her spine and foot was increasing. A bone surgeon, Dr. Alejandro Zimbrón, prescribed complete rest, and he ordered a steel corset (she wears it in *The Broken Column*), which for a while somewhat lessened her suffering. Without its support she felt that she could not sit or stand. She had no appetite, and she lost thirteen pounds in six months. Fainting spells and a slight fever confined her to bed. Then, after yet another battery of tests, Dr. Ramíriz Moreno pronounced that she had syphilis and prescribed a series of blood transfusions, sunbaths, and a treatment with bismuth. Other doctors did other examinations, including X-rays and spinal taps. Dr. Zimbrón said her spine needed to be reinforced, and he recommended an operation, but none was performed. On June 24, when Frida wrote to Dr. Eloesser from her bed, because her spine hurt too much for her to sit in a chair, she had been wearing Dr. Zimbrón's apparatus for five months.

Each day I am worse. . . . In the beginning it was hard for me to get accustomed to it, since it is a hell of a thing to put up with this type of apparatus but you cannot imagine how badly I felt before putting it on. I could no longer really work because no matter how insignificant they were, all movements exhausted me. I got a little better with the corset but now I feel just as sick again, and I am now very desperate because I cannot find anything to improve the condition of my spine. The doctors tell me that my meninges are inflamed, but I can't understand what's going on because if the reason is that the spine should be immobilized to avoid irritation of the nerves, how is it that with all this and the corset I again feel the same pains and the same annoyances?

Listen, *Lindo*, this time when you come, for the love of God, explain to me what kind of screw up I have and if it has any remedy or if *la tostada* [death] is going to take me one way or the other. Some doctors again insist on operating on me but I will not allow myself to be operated on unless, if it is indeed absolutely necessary, *you* were to do it.

At one point in 1945 Frida was encased in a new plaster corset ordered by Dr. Zimbrón, but the pains in her spine and leg worsened, and the device was removed after two days. Her medical record says that she was injected with Lipidol (for a spinal tap), and that the Lipidol was not "removed." The result was an increase in "pressure" in her brain and constant headaches. (Alejandro Gómez Arias recalls that the Lipidol, instead of going down into the area of Frida's spine, traveled up into her brain, where it could be seen in X-rays.) As the months wore on, her spine hurt more than ever, especially when she was excited.

Toward the end of her life Frida described the succession of orthopedic corsets she wore after 1944 and the treatments that went with them as "punishment." There were twenty-eight corsets in all—

one made of steel, three of leather, and the rest of plaster. One in particular, she said, allowed her neither to sit nor to recline. It made her so angry that she took it off, and used a sash to tie her torso to the back of a chair in order to support her spine. There was a time when she spent three months in a nearly vertical position with sacks of sand attached to her feet to straighten out her spinal column. Another time Adelina Zendejas, visiting her in the hospital after an operation, found her hanging from steel rings with her feet just able to touch the ground. Her easel was in front of her. "We were horrified," Zendejas recalls. "She was painting and telling jokes and funny stories. When she got too tired and couldn't stand it any longer they came and lowered her with an apparatus and laid her in bed, but again with the rings so that her spine would not contract and so that the vertebrae would not get stuck together."

Yet another gruesome tale comes from Frida's friend the pianist Ella Paresce. A Spanish doctor friend who knew nothing about orthopedics put a plaster corset on Frida. "It was very exciting, and we laughed a lot about the thing. Then during the night the corset began to harden, as it was supposed to do. I happened to be spending the night there in the next room, and about half past four or five in the morning, I heard a crying, nearly shrieks. I jumped out of the bed and went in, and there was Frida saying she couldn't breathe! She couldn't breathe! The corset had hardened, but it hardened so much that it pressed her lungs. It made pleats all around her body. So I tried to get a doctor. Nobody would pay any attention at that hour in the morning, so finally I took a razor blade and knelt on the bed over Frida. I began slowly, slowly cutting that corset right over her breast. I made about a two-inch cut so that she could breathe, and then we waited until a doctor appeared, and he did all the rest. Afterward we laughed to tears over this thing, and she painted the corset, which is still visible in the museum in Coyoacán."

Though publicly she made light of it, Frida was obsessed by her suffering. She wanted to find out everything she could about her physical condition, and kept herself informed (but confused) about her ailments by reading articles and medical books, and consulting numerous doctors. An invalid can be pardoned for hypochondria. In Frida's case, of course, there also was an element of narcissism. Indeed, it is possible to argue that invalidism was essential to her self-image, and that if Frida's physical problems had been as grave as she made out, she would never have been able to translate them into art. No less an authority than Dr. Eloesser believed that most of Frida's surgical operations were unnecessary, that she was caught in a familiar psychological syndrome that impels patients to want surgery. After all, an operation is a way of getting attention. Many people believe that Rivera would have left Frida had she not been so sick, and Frida was quite capable of consenting to an unnecessary operation if it would strengthen her hold on Diego.

In addition, a surgical incision is a sure thing: it provides a kind of certainty to people whose grip on reality, whose sense of actually being alive and connected with the world, is faltering. It also allows the patient to be passive, to make no decisions, and yet to have something concrete and real happen. Surgical intervention has a sexual aspect as well. Ultimately it can be an expression of hope—the next doctor, the next diagnosis, the next operation, will bring salvation.

Frida's wounded self-portraits were a form of silent crying. In images of herself footless, headless, cracked open, bleeding, she turned pain into the most dramatic image possible in order to impress on others the intensity of her suffering. And by projecting pain outward and onto the canvas, she also extracted it from her own body. Self-portraits were fixed, immutable replicas of her mirror image, and neither reflections nor canvases feel pain.

As antidotes to pain, the wounded self-portraits may have served in another way. One thinks of the experience of catching a glimpse of one's reflection in a mirror at a moment of physical or emotional anguish. The image in the mirror is astonishing—it looks like us, but it does not share our pain. The disjunction between our sense of ourselves in pain (perceived from the inside out) and the surface evidence, offered by the mirror, of an apparently pain-free self (seen from the outside in) can function as a steadying influence. The reflected image recalls to us our familiar physical self, providing a feeling of continuity. If Frida was drawn to mirrors because they comforted her in this way, painting the image she saw in the mirror was a way of making that reassuring image permanent. Thus self-portraits could serve as aids to objectivity or dissociation. Also, by looking at her wounded self in her paintings, Frida could sustain the illusion of being the strong, objective onlooker to her own misfortune.

In *Without Hope*, 1945, Frida stages her drama in that vast, heaving sea of volcanic rock the Pedregal (plate XXIX). The faults and fissures of the land symbolize the violence done to her body. Dramatic action is not clear, but the horror is unequivocal. Frida lies weeping in bed. Between her lips she holds the tip of a huge, membranous funnel—a cornucopia of gore containing a pig, a chicken, brains, a turkey, beef, sausage, and a fish, plus a sugar-candy skull with "Frida" written on its forehead. These she may be vomiting onto the easel that straddles her bed, making the carnage the source of her art. Or the image could refer to those pre-Columbian speech symbols that look like comic strip balloons, with the funnel of butchery symbolizing a scream of rage and horror.

Another explanation is that Frida painted *Without Hope* after convalescing from an operation, and that the funnel depicts her disgust when her doctor, full of the best bedside-manner cheer, announced: "Now you can eat anything!" Since she was so thin, the doctors made her eat puréed food every two hours. On the back of the painting's frame Frida wrote a rhyme: *"A mí no me queda ya ni la menor esperanza. . . . Todo se mueve al compás de lo que encierra la panza."* (Not the least hope remains to me. . . . Everything moves in time with what the belly contains.)

The sheet that covers Frida's naked body is dotted with round microscopic organisms that look like cells with nuclei or perhaps eggs waiting to be fertilized. Their form is echoed in the blood-red sun and pale moon that appear together in the sky. Thus Frida once again extends the meaning of her body's misadventures into the opposite worlds of the microscope and the solar system. It could also be that she set the funnel of horror in *Without Hope* between cells and celestial orbs in order not to aggrandize but rather to minimize, by contrast with the great span of things, her own personal miseries.

Very likely, too, the simultaneous presence of the sun and the moon refers, as in some of Frida's other paintings, to the Aztec notion of an eternal war between light and dark, or to Christ's crucifixion, where the sun and moon together indicate the sorrow of all creation at the death of the savior. Thus, whether the funnel is a hemorrhage, a miscarried child, a scream, or a force-fed meal, the gore gushing from (or to) Frida's mouth and onto (or from) an easel that evokes a cross can be seen as a ritualistic offering, a personal and imaginary rite that redeems or renews through suffering.

"Lovely Ella and Dear Boit," Frida wrote to the Wolfes on February 15, 1946:

Here the comet appears again! Doña Frida Kahlo, although you won't believe it!! I write to you from my bed, because for *four* months I have been in bad shape with my crooked spine, and after having seen numerous doctors from this country, I have decided to go to New York to see one who they say is absolutely terrific. . . . Everyone here, the "bone men" or orthopedes, feel that I should have an operation that I think is very dangerous, since I am very thin, worn out and completely going to hell, and, in this state, I do not want to let myself be operated on without first consulting with some high up doctor of Gringolandia. Thus I want to ask you a very great favor, which consists in the following:

I enclose here a copy of my clinical history that will serve to make you realize all that I have suffered in this damned life, but also if possible, you will show it to Dr. Wilson who is the one I want to consult with there. It is a question of a doctor specialist in bones whose complete name is Dr. Philip Wilson, 321 East 42nd Street, N.Y.C.

What I am interested in is knowing these points:

1) I could go to the U.S.A. more or less in the beginning of April. Will Dr. Wilson be in New York then? Or if not, when could I meet him?

2) After he more or less knows about my case through the clinical history that you could show him, would he be willing to receive me to make a serious study of me and to give me his opinion?

3) In case he accepts, does he think it necessary that I should go directly to *a hospital* or might I live in another place, and only go several times to his office?

(All this is extremely important for me to know because I have to calculate the dough which is now meager.) You know what I mean kids?

4) You can give him the following information, for greater clarity: I have been in bed *4* months and I feel very weak and tired. I would make the trip by plane to avoid worse disturbances. They would put a *corset* on me to help me to stand the discomforts. (An orthopedic corset or one of plaster.) How long does he think it will take him to do the diagnosis taking into account that I have X-rays, analyses and all kinds of things of that type. 25 X-rays from 1945 of the spine, leg and foot. (If it is necessary to take new ones there, I am at his disposal for whatever . . . !)

5) Try to explain to him that I am not a "millionairess" or anything

close to it. Rather the question of dough is a little "grey-green" shading into the color of the wing of a yellow cricket.

6) VERY IMPORTANT

That I put myself in his magnificent hands because besides knowing his great reputation through the doctors, he was personally recommended to me in Mexico by a man who was his client and who is called ARCADY BOYTLER who admires him and adores him because he relieved him of something that was also in the dorsal spine. Tell him that Boytler and his wife spoke with great enthusiasm about him and that I am absolutely delighted to see him since I know that the Boytlers adore him and they esteem me enough to send me to him.

7) If you think of other practical things (remember what kind of a mule I am) I would be grateful to you with all my little heart, adored children.

8) In order to consult with Dr. Wilson, I will send you the dough that you indicate.

9) You can tell him more or less what kind of a ranch-style cockroach your *cuate* Frida Kahlo *pata de palo* is. I leave you in complete liberty to give him any kind of explanations and you even may describe me (if it is necessary ask Nick for a photo so that he should know what I look like).

10) If he wants some other information, proceed swiftly to write me so that everything will be in order before putting my foot in it (thin or fat).

11) Tell him that as a sick person I am rather stoic, but that now it is a little hard for me because in this f . . . ing life, one suffers but one learns, and that in addition the pile of years has made me more *pen. . . .sadora* [thoughtful, but she probably was going to say *pendeja*, which is a swear word meaning "stupid"].

Here are other facts for you, not for *el* Doctorcito Wilsonito,
1st, you are going to find me a bit changed.

grey hairs bother me. So does skinniness.

I am a little bit gloomy because of this trouble.
2nd, married life goes very well. . . .

Many kisses and thanks from your *cuatacha*
Frida

Say hello to all the friends

On May 10 she cabled Ella to say that she would fly to New York on the twenty-first of that month to be operated on by Dr. Wilson. Since she refused to be anesthetized unless she could hold her sister's hand, Cristina would accompany her.

The operation was performed in June at the Hospital for Special Surgery. Four vertebrae were fused with a piece of bone extracted from her pelvis and with a metal rod fifteen centimeters long. Frida's recovery was good. During her recuperation (over two months in the hospital) she was in high spirits. Ordered not to paint, at first she drew instead. But before long, she disobeyed doctors' orders and produced, in the hospital, a painting (unidentified) which she later sent to the "Salon del Paisaje," a landscape exhibition in Mexico City.

Among the many friends who visited Frida in the hospital was Noguchi. It was to be the last time he saw her. "She was there with Cristina," he remembers, "and we talked for a long while about things. She was older. She was so full of life, her spirit was so admirable." Noguchi gave Frida a glass-covered box full of butterflies, which she hung over her hospital door and later placed on the underside of the canopy of one of her two four-poster beds.

On June 30, she wrote to Alejandro Gómez Arias (her letter is full of invented words interspersed with numerous English words, which here are in italics):

Alex darling,

They do not allow one to write very much, but this is only to tell you that *the big* operation already took place. Three *weeks* ago they proceeded to the cutting and cutting of bones. And he is so marvelous this doctor, and my body is so full of vitality, that they already proceeded to have me stand on my *"puper" feet* for two little minutes, but I myself do not *believe* it. The first two weeks were full of great suffering and tears so that I do not wish my pains on anybody. They are very strident and evil, but now, this week, my yelling diminished and with the help of pills I have survived more or less well. I have two huge scars on my back in this form. [Here she drew her naked body with two long scars with the marks of surgical stitches. One scar runs from her waist straight down to below the coccyx, the other is on the right buttock.] From here [an arrow points to the scar on her buttock] they proceeded to the pulling out of a slice of the pelvis in order to graft it onto the column, that is where my scar ended up being less hair-raising and straighter. Five vertebrae were damaged and now they are going to be like a rifle [in popular usage, "in terrific shape"]. The bother is that the bone takes a long time to grow and to readjust itself and I still have to spend six weeks in bed before they release me and I will be able to flee from this terrifying *city* to my beloved Coyoacán. How are you *please* write to me and send me *one* book please don't forget me. How is your mamacita? Alex, don't abandon me alone in this evil hospital and write me. Cristi is very very bored and we are burning up with the heat. It is enormously hot and we no longer know what to do. What's happening in Mexico. What's happening with "la raza" there.

Tell me things about everybody and above all about you.

Your F.

I send you lots of affection and many kisses. I received your letter which cheered me so much! Don't forget me.

By October, Frida was back in Coyoacán and full of plans. On the eleventh she wrote to her patron Eduardo Morillo Safa in Caracas:

My dear Engineer,

Today I received your letter, thank you for being just as kind to me as you always are, and for your congratulations for said prize [the prize she was awarded for *Moses* by the Ministry of Public Education]. (I still have not received it) . . . you know how they are, those retarded bastards! Along with your letter, that is to say, in the same moment, I received one from Dr. Wilson who was the one who operated on me. It made me feel like an automatic rifle! He says that I can now paint *two hours* a day. Before I received his orders I had already started to paint, and I can stand up to *three* hours dedicated to painting and painting. I have almost finished your first painting [*Tree of Hope*] which is of course nothing but the result of the damned operation! . . .

Your letter enchanted me, but I continue to feel that you find yourself pretty much alone and unconnected, among those people who live in such an old fashioned and fu. . .ed-up world! Nevertheless it will help you to cast an *ojo avisor* [sharp eye] on South America in general and later you can write the pure, bald truth, striking a comparison with what Mexico has achieved in spite of its misfortunes. I am very interested in knowing something about the painters in Venezuela. Can you send me photos or magazines with reproductions? Are there Indian painters? Or only *mestizo*?

Listen, young man, with all my love I will paint you a miniature of Doña Rosita [Morillo Safa's mother, whose portrait Frida had painted in 1944]. I shall have photographs made of the paintings and from a photograph of the large portrait I can paint the little one, what do you think? I will also paint the altar with the virgin of sorrows, and the little pots with green wheat, barley, etc. since my mother arranged this kind of altar every year, and as soon as I finish this first painting which I told you is almost ready, I will begin yours, the idea of painting the bald one [death] with the woman with a shawl also seems wonderful to me, I will do what I can so that the above-mentioned paintings turn out somewhat *piochas* [terrific]. As you asked me to do, I will deliver them to your house, to your aunt Julia. Sending you a photo of each one as I finish them, the color you will have to imagine, my friend, because it is not difficult for you to guess since you already have so many Fridas. You know sometimes I tire of daubing, especially when I have shooting pains, and I continue more than three hours, but I hope that within a few months I will be less worn out. In this damned life one suffers a lot, brother, and although one learns, one resents it very much, in the long run, no matter how much I do to play the strong one, there are times when I would like to throw in the sponge. I'm not kidding! Listen, I don't like to feel that you are sad, now you see that there are in this world people like me who are worse off than you, who keep on plugging, so that you should not undervalue yourself and as soon as you can, return to Mexicalpán of the *Pulque* and you already know that here life is hard, but tasty, and you deserve many good things because the real truth is that you are super terrific, compañero. You know that I say this from the heart, your soul mate.

Now I really cannot tell you any gossip from these parts, because I spend my life cloistered in this stupid mansion of forgetfulness, dedicated supposedly to recuperating and to painting, in my leisure moments, I see no class or *raza* neither high nor proletariat, nor do I go to my "literary-musical" reunions. At most I listen to the odious radio, that is a punishment worse than being purged, I read the *dailies*, which are just as bad. I am reading a fat book by Tolstoy that is called *War and Peace* that I think is terrific. Novels of love and counter-love don't give me any pleasure, and only from time to time do detective stories fall into my hands. Each day I like more the poems of Carlos Pellicer, and of one or another poet like Walt Whitman. Outside of that, I don't get involved with literature. I want you to tell me what you like to read so that I can send it to you. Naturally you will have heard about the death of Doña Estercita Gómez, the mother of Marte [the engineer Marte R. Gómez]. I did not see him personally, but I sent him a letter with Diego. Diego tells me that it was very difficult for him and that he is very sad. Write to him.

Thank you sweety for the offer to send me things from there, whatever it is that you give me will be a remembrance that I will keep with deepest love. I received a letter from Marianita and it pleased me immensely, I will answer her, give Licha and all *Chamacos* my love.

To you, as you already know, I send a kiss and the sincere affection of your *cuate*.

Frida

Thank you because you are going to send me dough and I'm rather needing it.

Frida mentioned "shooting pains." The truth was that the spinal fusion did not permanently alleviate her back problems. When she was released from the hospital and returned to Mexico, she was first bedridden and then enclosed in a steel corset for eight months. Dr. Wilson had ordered her to lead a quiet life with frequent rests, but Frida did not follow his orders, and her health deteriorated. The pain in her spine grew worse, she lost weight, developed anemia, and the fungus infection on her right hand recurred.

Alejandro Gómez Arias believes that Dr. Wilson fused the wrong vertebrae. One of Frida's doctors, Dr. Guillermo Velasco y Polo, an assistant to the surgeon Dr. Juan Farill, who performed other spinal fusions a few years later in Mexico, also holds this opinion. He says that the metal plate Dr. Wilson inserted "was not put in the right place, because it was just below the sick vertebrae. Perhaps it was for this reason that Frida then put herself in the hands of Dr. Farill. Here in the English Hospital, it was a question of removing the piece of metal that Dr. Wilson had inserted and trying to do a spinal fusion with a bone graft." Cristina maintained that the operation performed in New York was so painful that Frida was given extremely large doses of morphine, and she began to hallucinate and to see animals in the hospital room. Afterward, she could not shake her drug addiction. It is true that Frida's handwriting became larger and less controlled around this time, and her journal often sounds frenetic and euphoric.

Hindsight, no doubt, made Frida's spinal fusion look like a failure. But Frida herself said the surgeon was "marvelous" and that she felt terrific. It may be that she subverted her own recovery. Lupe Marín recalled that "Dr. Wilson's operation left Frida perfectly well, they thought, but during a night of desperation—possibly Diego did not come home, or something—Frida attacked herself and opened all her wounds. So there was nothing to do with her, absolutely nothing." A similar story has it that sometime after the spinal fusion, Frida threw herself on the ground in a rage, and the fusion came "unfused." Unfortunately, the precise medical data are unavailable, but she is said as well to have had osteomyelitis, an inflammation of the bone marrow that causes progressive deterioration of the bones and that certainly the spinal fusion could not cure.

Tree of Hope, 1946, which in her letter to Morillo Safa Frida called "nothing but the result of the damned operation," shows a weeping Frida, clothed in a red Tehuana costume, sitting guard over a Frida who lies naked but partially covered with a sheet on a hospital trolley (plate XXX). The recumbent Frida appears to be still anesthetized after an operation that has left deep incisions on her back—the same scars she drew in her letter to Alejandro Gómez Arias, except that here they are open and bleeding. The seated Frida proudly holds an orthopedic corset painted—with an irony typical of Frida—bright pink with a crimson buckle: her trophy for her medical marathon. That she also wears another corset is evident from the two braces that support her chest. It is not, however, the back brace that really buttresses Frida; rather, a flag in her right hand does—a green flag emblazoned in red with words that Frida often repeated to friends: "Tree of Hope, keep firm." It is the first line of a song from Veracruz she liked to sing. The song continues: "Don't let your eyes cry when I say goodbye," suggesting that the tree of hope is a metaphor for a person, and in the particular case of this painting, for the guardian Frida who weeps with compassion but sits firmly upright. The notion of making paintings based on songs came from Rivera's frescoes on the third floor of the Ministry of Education, as well as from Posada's ballad sheets. Frida, however, always used the songs only as a starting point for images of personal drama. "Tree of Hope, keep firm" was her rallying cry and motto.

But Frida's tree of hope grows from her pain: in the painting, the flag's red tassels are analogous to the blood dripping from the patient's wound, and the flagpole's red pointed tip suggests the bloody sharp end of a surgical instrument. The two Fridas are bounded on one side by a precipice (where a clump of "hopeful" grass sprouts in the volcanic rock) and on the other by a rectangular grave or trench, which is a more ominous version of the dark ravines that streak across the barren land and that serve as a metaphor for Frida's wounded flesh. But despite all the horror and danger, this painting is an act of faith, like a *retablo*. Here Frida's faith is in herself, not in a holy image; the guardian Frida resplendent in her Tehuana dress is her own miracle worker.

"The landscape is day and night," Frida said of *Tree of Hope* in her letter to Morillo Safa. "And there is a skeleton (or death) that flees terrified in the face of *my will to live*. You can imagine it, more or less, since my description is clumsy. As you can see, I possess neither the language of Cervantes, nor the aptitude of a poetic or descriptive genius, but you are quick-witted enough to understand my language which is a little bit 'relaxed.' " In the painting as it now stands, although the will to live is perfectly evident, the fleeing skeleton has been painted out. Death is present only metaphorically, in the grave-like trench and in the dialectic of light and dark (sun and moon) that accompanies the living and the nearly dead Fridas. Oddly, the Frida that holds hope sits beneath the moon, while the daylight sun reveals the devastated surgical patient. One might speculate that this is because the sun, here a huge reddish orb, is nourished, according to Aztec belief, by human blood.

Another 1946 painting that records the spinal fusion is *The Little Deer*, a self-portrait in which Frida presents herself with the body of a young stag (Granizo, her model, was male), her human head crowned with antlers (plate XXXI). Originally it was owned by Arcady Boytler, the man who recommended Dr. Wilson to Frida, and who, as Frida mentioned in her letter to Ella Wolfe, had spinal problems of his own. Like *The Broken Column*, *The Little Deer* uses simple metaphors to show that Frida is prey to suffering. Running through a glade, the deer is pierced by nine arrows that will slowly kill him; surely this must refer to Frida's own journey through life, persecuted by the injuries that gradually destroyed her. The little deer's arrow wounds bleed, but Frida's face is calm.

The painting points to psychological sufferings as well. Indeed, in her life as in her art, Frida's physical and psychic suffering were interconnected. Starting with the divorce, and probably even before that, her illnesses coincided so often with periods of spiritual trauma that one can surmise she "used" them to hold onto or to win back Diego. Ella Wolfe says that *The Little Deer* relates to "the agony of living with Diego." Another close friend says that the arrows signify Frida's suffering due to male oppression, which would make them analogous to the knife wounds in *A Few Small Nips.*

In *The Little Deer* Frida once again used flawed objects to refer to her injuries, both physical and psychological. Massive tree trunks of dry, cracked wood with broken branches signify decay and death, and the knots and gashes in the bark echo the wounds in the deer's flank. Beneath its hooves is a slender, leafy green branch that has broken off a young tree, a symbol of the artist's (and the deer's) broken youth. The branch also points to Frida's general sympathy for damaged things. Once when a gardener brought her an old chair, asking if he should throw it away, she requested him to give her the broken leg, and she carved her own lips on it to make a gift for a man she loved. The branch may also have another meaning: Antonio Rodríguez says that "in the pre-Hispanic world, in order to enter paradise, one put a dry branch [on the dead person's grave], and resurrection was the resurrection of the dry branch into a green branch."

By painting herself as a deer, Frida expressed again her feeling of oneness with all living things. It is a feeling that has a source in Aztec culture. As Anita Brenner explained in *Idols Behind Altars,* there is a pervasive Indian attitude underlying much of Mexican culture which assumes that human beings "participate of the same stuff of being, with other lives not human." For this reason, pre-Columbian artists produced abstract, composite creatures, half human and half animal, to symbolize the idea of continuance and rebirth. Pre-Columbian gods were not specific beings, but dynamic complexes with many changing forms and attributes. "Worship," wrote Anita Brenner, "was a longing, not to acquire god's character and mode of life (which was never defined), but rather an identification with some attribute or function of divinity. Thus an Aztec worshipper could pray, 'I am the flower, I am the feather, I am the drum and mirror of the gods. I am the song. I rain flowers, I rain songs.' " This, of course, sounds like Frida speaking of herself as a mountain or a tree or saying in her diary that human beings are part of a single current and that they direct themselves to themselves "through millions of stone beings, bird beings, star beings, microbe beings, fountain beings. . . ." To the Aztecs, certain animals had peculiar meanings. The parrot, for instance, because it could talk, was looked upon as a supernatural creature and symbolized as a man-headed bird. The Aztecs also believed that a newborn human has an animal counterpart; a person's fate was tied to that of the animal that represented the calendrical sign of the day of his or her birth. Similarly, Frida perceived herself as a creature with metamorphic potential. Her head could be flowers, her arms could become wings, her body could transform itself into a deer. Certainly Surrealism had something to do with this, but the magical approach to life that is an ancient part of Mexican culture is its real source.

The Little Deer comes out of Mexican folklore and poetry too. There is a popular song that begins:

> I am a poor little deer that lives in the mountains.
> Since I am not very tame, I don't come down to drink water during the day.
> At night, little by little, I come to your arms, my love.

And in her "Verses Expressing the Feelings of a Lover," Sor Juana Inés de la Cruz wrote:

> If thou seest the wounded stag
> that hastens down
>   the mountainside,
> seeking, stricken, in icy stream
> ease for its hurt,
> and thirsting plunges in
>   the crystal waters,
> not in ease, in pain it mirrors
>   me.

Although its drama is imaginary, Frida's self-portrait as *The Little Deer* refers to her own life: the idea of a wounded victim being like a deer is expressed in a 1953 entry in her diary. Mourning the untimely death of a close friend, the painter Isabel (Chabela) Villaseñor (who played the beautiful young Indian wife in Eisenstein's *Que Viva Mex-*

ico!), she drew a portrait of herself holding a dove and with her body crisscrossed by long lines that look like lances. "Chabela Villaseñor," she wrote. "Until I leave, Until I travel your path—Have a good trip Chabela! Crimson, Crimson, Crimson, Life death." On the next page there is a memorial poem to her lost friend:

> You left us, Chabela Villaseñor
> But your voice
> your electricity
> your enormous talent
> your poetry
> your light
> your mystery
> your Olinka
>
> all of you, you remain alive
>
> Isabel Villaseñor painter poet singer.
>
> Crimson
> Crimson
> Crimson
> Crimson
> like the blood
> that runs
> when they kill
> a deer.

Chapter 21

Portraits of a Marriage

YEARS AFTER Frida and Diego died, friends remembered them as "sacred monsters." Their escapades and eccentricities were beyond the petty censurings of ordinary morality; not simply condoned, they were treasured and mythologized. As for being "monsters," the Riveras could harbor Trotsky, paint paeans to Stalin, build pagan temples, wave pistols, boast of eating human flesh, and carry on in their marriage with the vast imperiousness of Olympian deities. By the 1940s, Diego, of course, was an ancient myth. Frida, on the other hand, was new to mythic stature, and during this decade their myths meshed.

After the remarriage, while the bond between Frida and Diego deepened, so did their mutual autonomy. Even when they lived together, Diego's absences were frequent and long. Both had love affairs: his were open, hers (with men) she continued to keep secret because of his wild jealousy. Not surprisingly, their life was full of violent battles followed by bitter separations and tender reconciliations.

Starting with the "wedding portrait" of 1931, Frida recorded the vicissitudes of her marriage. The various paintings that show her and Diego together, or that include Diego only by implication—for example, in tears on Frida's cheeks—reveal the extent to which the Riveras' relationship changed with the years even while certain underlying realities remained constant. *Frida and Diego Rivera,* 1931; *Self-Portrait as a Tehuana,* 1943; *Diego and Frida 1929–1944,* 1944; *Diego and I* and *The Love Embrace of the Universe, the Earth (Mexico), Diego, Me and Señor Xolotl,* both 1949, all express Frida's great love and need for Rivera. Tellingly, he connects with her in a different way in each painting. In the earliest, the wedding portrait, their relationship is a little stiff. Like figures in a double portrait by a folk limner, they face forward, rather than toward each other. This, together with the large sliver of space between them and the light clasp of their hands, makes the couple appear like new partners who have not yet learned the elaborate, interlocking steps of the marriage dance. By contrast, in the 1943 *Self-Portrait as a Tehuana,* Frida's obsessive love for her unpossessable husband has made her trap his image in her forehead in the form of a "thought" (plate XXI). One year later, in *Diego and Frida 1929–1944* (figure 62), she has intertwined herself so closely with Diego that their faces form a single head—a symbiotic state that is clearly not a comfortable, harmonious union. In *Diego and I,* Frida's despair over Rivera's philandering is almost hysterical; his portrait is lodged in her forehead, but he himself is elsewhere, and Frida seems to be strangling in the swirl of her own hair—a woman drowning in solitude (plate XXVI). When she painted *The Love Embrace,* she still wept, but the relationship appears to have found some resolution; Frida holds Diego in an embrace rather than a stranglehold (plate XXXIII). Whereas in the 1931 marriage portrait Frida played a daughterly role, and in 1944 the couple seem to have achieved, if not mutuality, at least a more or less matched battle, in *The Love Embrace* Frida finally possesses Diego in the way that presumably worked out best for them both—he is a big baby lying contentedly in her maternal lap.

The Riveras had much in common: humor, intelligence, Mexicanism, social conscience, a bohemian approach to life. But the greatest bond may have been their enormous respect for each other's art. Rivera took pride in his wife's professional successes and he admired her growing artistic mastery. He would tell people that before he or any of his colleagues had had a painting hung in the Louvre, Frida had had that honor, and he loved to show her off to friends. One visitor recalls that the first thing Rivera did when she met him was to say that she must meet Frida. "There is no artist in Mexico that can compare with her!" Rivera said, beaming. "He immediately told me that when he was in Paris, Picasso had taken a drawing by Frida, looked at it for a long time, and then said: 'Look at those eyes: neither you nor I are capable of anything like it.' I noticed that in telling me this his own bulging eyes were shining with tears."

Expounding on Frida's genius, Rivera would say, "We are all clods next to Frida. Frida is the best painter of her epoch." In his 1943 article "Frida Kahlo and Mexican Art," he wrote: "In the panorama of Mexican painting of the last twenty years, the work of Frida Kahlo shines like a diamond in the midst of many inferior jewels; clear and hard, with precisely defined facets." Frida was, he said, "the greatest proof of the renaissance of the art of Mexico."

Frida reflected the compliment back to Diego. To her, Diego was the "architect of life." She listened to his stories and theories with amused skepticism, sometimes interjecting, "Diego—it's a lie," or bursting out with her contagious belly laugh. When he talked she often made odd little movements with her hands. These were signals to let his listeners know what was true and what was false in his conversation. In her "Portrait of Diego," she wrote:

His supposed mythomania is in direct relation to his tremendous imagination. That is to say, he is as much of a liar as the poets or as the children who have not yet been turned into idiots by school or mothers. I have heard him tell all kinds of lies: from the most innocent, to the most complicated stories about people whom his imagination combined in fantastic situations and actions, always with a great sense of humor and a marvelous critical sense; but I have never heard him say a single stupid or banal lie. Lying, or playing at lying, he unmasks many people, he learns the interior mechanism of others, who are much more ingenuously liars than he, and the most curious thing of the supposed lies of Diego, is that in the long and short of it, those who are involved in the imaginary combination become angry, not because of the lie, but rather because of the truth contained in the lie, that always comes to the surface.

. . . Being the eternally curious one, he is at the same time the eternal conversationalist. He can paint hours and days without resting, chatting while he works. He talks and argues about everything, absolutely everything, like Walt Whitman, enjoying talking with everyone who wants to listen to him. His conversation is always interesting. It has sentences that astonish, that sometimes wound; others are moving, but never do they leave the listener with an impression of uselessness or emptiness. His words disturb terribly because they are alive and true.

Frida tolerated and even indulged Rivera's egocentric idiosyncrasies, and was extremely protective of him, coming to his defense, for example, when he was under attack for making art for millionaires, or when people accused him of being a millionaire himself. In "Portrait of Diego," she challenged his critics with rhetoric that seems to flare at the nostrils.

Against the cowardly attacks that are made on him, Diego always reacts with firmness and with a great sense of humor. He never compromises or yields: he faces his enemies openly, the majority of them are sneaky, and a few are brave. He counts always on reality, never on elements of "illusion" or of "the ideal." This intransigence and rebelliousness are fundamental in Diego, they complement his portrait.

Among the many things that are said of Diego, these are the most common: they call him mythmaker, publicity-seeker, and the most ridiculous, millionaire. . . . It is unbelievable, surely, that the lowest, most cowardly and stupidest insults to Diego have been vomited in his own house: Mexico. By means of the press, by means of barbaric and vandalous acts in which they have tried to destroy his work, using everything from the innocent umbrellas of "decent" señoras who scratch his paintings hypocritically, and as if they were doing it in passing, to acids and table knives, not forgetting common ordinary spit, worthy of the possessors of so much saliva and so little brains; by means of groups of "well-brought-up" youths who stone his house and his studio, destroying irreplaceable works of pre-Cortesian Mexican art—which form part of Diego's collection—those who run away after having their laugh by means of anonymous letters (it is useless to speak of the valor of their senders) or by means of the neutral and Pilate-like silence of people in power, charged with guarding or importing culture for the good name of the country, not giving any importance to these attacks on the work of a man who, with all his genius, his unique creative effort, only tries to defend liberty of expression not only for himself, but also for all. . . .

But the insults and the attacks do not change Diego. They form part of the social phenomena of a world in decadence, and nothing more. The whole of life continues to interest, to amaze him, with its changeability, and everything surprises him with its beauty, but nothing disappoints or intimidates him because he knows the dialectical mechanism of phenomena and of events.

Frida was prepared to defend her husband physically as well as with words. Once, in a restaurant, a drunk at the next table picked a fight with him, calling him a damned Trotskyite. Diego knocked the man down, but one of his companions pulled a gun. Furious, Frida jumped in front of him, yelling insults. She was felled by a blow to her stomach. Fortunately, waiters intervened, but in any case, Frida had drawn so much attention that the assailants fled.

If *Roots* suggests a moment of matrimonial calm and contentment, the small painting entitled *Diego and Frida 1929–1944* indicates that it came to an end in 1944. Indeed, the Riveras were separated for much of this year. As usual, they continued to see each other frequently, and in spite of the separation they celebrated their fifteenth wedding anniversary with a big fiesta and an exchange of gifts. *Diego and Frida 1929–1944* was Frida's anniversary gift to her husband. Encapsulating her urge to unite with—literally to be—Diego, she painted herself and her husband as a single head divided vertically into two halves. A necklace consisting of a tree trunk with spiky branches enlaces their common neck. Clearly, the fragility of the marital bond made Frida all the more anxious to possess Diego by merging her identity with his.

The spouses' names and the dates of their married years are inscribed in the tiny clam shells that decorate the painting's lily-shaped frame, the swelling sides and curved volutes of which recall the womb-like *Flower of Life,* also painted in 1944. Whether Frida intended this double portrait's frame to suggest a flower or a womb—she was, she said, the embryo that "engendered him"—she surely intended the tiny pink and red shells and the pearly snail shells glued to its surface to have a sexual reference. To Frida, shells were symbols of birth, fecundity, and love: in the painting itself, a scallop and a conch intertwined by roots that extend from the necklace tree represent, Frida said (referring to similar shells in *Moses*), "the two sexes who are wrapped by roots, always new and alive."

The male-female duality is seen as well in the simultaneous presence of the sun and the moon, and in the divided portrait head itself. Indeed, the notion of showing duality by dividing a head down the middle was probably taken from pre-Columbian art (Frida often wore a brooch with a Tlatilco head that is two faces joined in one with a single eyebrow) or from the Mexican depictions of the Trinity as three bearded heads merged in one.

As a token of love, *Diego and Frida 1929–1944* is a little jarring. Oppressively convoluted shapes seem an outward manifestation of inner convolutions. The spouses' faces are dissimilar in size and conformation, so that though they are joined, parts do not line up; the disjunction suggests the explosive instability of Frida's marriage. To hold herself and Diego together, she has bound the single head with the necklace tree, whose branches are leafless, just as the Riveras' union was childless. The intertwined branches look like Christ's crown of thorns—the marriage bond is a martyrdom.

Three months later, they were still living apart when on Christmas Day Rivera wrote a note addressed "To the celebrated painter and distinguished lady Doña Frida Kahlo de Rivera with affection, devotion and profound respect from your unconditional *milagro* [miracle]." On the other side of the paper he said: "My dear niña fisita don't let the fight make you angry. Know my affection and my desire that we should see the world once more together as we did last year and that I will see you smile again and know that you are happy. Give your Cupid back his foundation and let this friendship and this affection last forever."

They did rejoin, and their love, in the deepest sense, did "last forever." So did the pain. Most of the thorny moments in Frida's marriage to Diego came from his erratic and self-indulgent behavior. He would be enthralled with someone or something, and after possessing and enjoying that person or object, would discard it the way a child discards an old toy. When his doctor pronounced him unfit for fidelity, Rivera happily followed the prescription.

Some people say that Frida enjoyed hearing Diego recount his amorous adventures, and it is true that she often joked about her husband's incorrigible philandering. In public she scoffed: "Being the wife of Diego is the most marvelous thing in the world. . . . I let him play matrimony with other women. Diego is not anybody's husband and never will be, but he is a great *camarada.*" In her "Portrait of Diego" she explained this attitude further:

I will not speak of Diego as "my husband" because it would be ridiculous, Diego never has been and never will be anyone's "husband." Nor will I speak of him as a lover, because to me he transcends the domain of sex, and if I speak of him as a son I will have done nothing but describe or paint my own emotions, almost my self-portrait, not the portrait of Diego. . . . Probably some people expect of me a very personal, "feminine," anecdotal, diverting portrait, full of complaints and even a certain amount of gossip, the type of gossip that is "decent," interpretable or usable, according to the morbidity of the reader. Perhaps they hope to hear from me laments about "how much one suffers," living with a man like Diego. But I do not believe that the banks of a river suffer for letting the water run, or that the earth suffers because it rains, or the atom suffers discharging its energy . . . for me everything has a natural compensation. Within my difficult and obscure role of ally of an extraordinary being, I have the same reward as a green dot within a quantity of red: I have the reward of "equilibrium." The pains or joys that regularize life in this society, rotten with lies, in which I live are not mine. If I have prejudices and if the actions of others, even the actions of Diego Rivera, wound me, I make myself responsible for my inability to see with clarity, and if I do not have such prejudices, I should admit that it is natural for the red corpuscles to fight against the white ones without the slightest prejudice, and that this phenomenon only signifies health.

This broad-minded attitude may well have been true of Frida late in life and in cases where the affair was trivial. Yet to her most intimate friends, she bewailed the difficulties of her marriage.

"When I was alone with her," Ella Wolfe remembers, "she would tell me how sad her life was with Diego. She never got used to his loves. Each time the wound was new, and she kept on suffering till the day she died. Diego never cared. He said having sex is like urinating. He couldn't understand why people take it so seriously. But he *was* jealous of Frida—a double standard, *'el gran macho.'* "

That she "kept on suffering" is evident in her self-portraits, and it is especially poignant in the two in which she wears the festive Tehuana headdress. In both *Self-Portrait as a Tehuana,* from 1943, and the 1948 *Self-Portrait* (plates XXI and XXV), Frida's face, with its penetrating gaze beneath dark, connecting eyebrows, its carnal red lips and faint mustache, looks perverse, even demonic. In the 1948 work she is forty years old, and the contours of her face are fuller, coarser, less oval; the five years that elapsed between these two portraits took their toll. But Frida confronts the depredations of age without the comforting cosmetics of self-delusion.

There is something sinister about the way Frida expresses her longing to possess Diego in the earlier painting. She is as devouring as a carnivorous tropical flower. Intertwined with the white threads that radiate from the vegetable pattern of the lace ruffle are black roots that actually are continuations of the veins of leaves that adorn her hair. This live network of tentacles seems an extension of Frida, paths of energy and feeling for one who despaired at her solitude and confinement and who wished to extend her vitality beyond the limits of her body. Like a female spider peering out from the center of her web, Frida traps Diego's image in her forehead; she seems to have consumed her prey and lodged the thought of him within her own being in the form of a miniature portrait within a portrait.

Frida handles thwarted love differently in the 1948 *Self-Portrait*. Except for a hint of tension around the mouth and a glistening sadness in her eyes, Frida's face is, as always, determinedly composed. Yet furious emotions thrash beneath her skin. At the top of the painting, on a leaf, she signed her name and the year in the same color as the leaf's veins—blood red. Three bright teardrops on her dark skin suggest her fascination with her own appearance in grief, the narcissism of sorrow. One feels that in a moment of despair, with hot, wet tears running down her cheeks, she has turned to the mirror for solace and communion, to find another person, the strong, alternative Frida, and to paint her. Such self-consciousness deadened feeling, while doubling it. By painting both the griever and the observer, Frida became the voyeur of her own emotions.

The peculiarly charged, disjunctive relationship between Frida and her Tehuana costume in this painting, the way her face seems quite separate from the lace that frames it, underscores the psychological duality of the weeping Frida, the sense of simultaneously feeling and perceiving oneself to feel. The split seems particularly painful because one can easily imagine why she decked herself out in the bride-like frills and veil—these self-portraits are a plea for Diego's love. But pretty plumage was a mask as well as a magnet; it told of beauty and love while it hid uglier feelings—rejection, jealousy, rage, fear of abandonment. Thus it was that the greater the menace of loss, the more elaborate and desperately festive Frida's self-decoration.

If arraying herself in ruffles and lace was a device to win Diego back, another was to make him realize that her sufferings might prove fatal. In *Thinking About Death*, painted the same year as *Self-Portrait as a Tehuana*, an opening in Frida's forehead shows a skull and crossbones in a landscape (plate XXII). The same type of large leaves that ran with the sap of Frida's life in *Roots* are gathered here into a thick, succulent wall behind her head. In front of and intertwined with these leaves are brown branches with cruel red thorns. Frida looks out at us with a sage and sober gaze that is almost Egyptian in its imperturbability; indeed, her dress and features in this self-portrait recall the famous bust of the unflappable Nefertiti, whom Frida admired. She once spoke of "the marvelous Nefertiti, wife of Akhenaten, I imagine that besides having been extraordinarily beautiful, she must have been 'a wild one' and a most intelligent collaborator with her husband."

No doubt *The Mask*, 1945, in which Frida holds a purple mask with orange hair and dopey, doll-like features over her face, was painted during another period in which she was being betrayed by Diego. Her tears fall onto the mask, and her own black eyes peer through two holes torn in the mask's eyes, which are painted to look like actual holes in the canvas. The displacement of the tears from the weeper to the weeper's mask could hardly be more disturbing. Frida is clearly commenting on the inability of a mask to hide emotions when the wearer is under severe stress. The feeling of hysteria that this painting communicates is augmented by the heavy, grayish-green wall of ugly leaves and prickly cacti that press in on Frida from behind.

Two drawings from the 1940s reveal Frida's continuing anguish. She weeps in the 1946 *Self-Portrait* (figure 63), and in *Ruin*, a gift for Diego in 1947, she spells out her misery with the words "Avenida Engaño" (Deceit Avenue). A cracked head, labeled "RUIN" and depicting what may be an amalgam of Frida and Diego, interlocks with an architectural structure, part of which is a tree with its branches chopped off. Twenty projections from this structure are numbered; they are said to refer to Rivera's extramarital affairs. On the right, what looks like a commemorative monument is inscribed with the words: "Ruin/House for birds/Nest for love/All for nothing."

As we have seen, Frida was by no means the passive victim of Diego's ambient lusts, and she countered his infidelity with numerous casual, and some not so casual, extramarital affairs. Though her fragility, her illnesses, her numerous operations, meant that there were many periods in which she could not lead an active sex life, she had none of the passivity associated (at least in literature) with the stereotypical "long-suffering" Mexican woman. One of her lovers recalls that her physical ailments were no hindrance at all: "I've never seen anyone sturdier in the expression of affection than Frida!" Nor did she have compunctions about pursuing any man she wanted. She believed that what she called *la raza*—a people unspoiled by the hypocritical demands of civilization—was less inhibited about sexuality, and since she wanted to be primitivistic in her behavior, she made a point of being outspoken about matters of sex (although she did not talk about the details of her own sex life). She had sex on her mind often, a fact that is evident in her paintings and drawings, as well as in her diary.

Frida's longest and deepest affair was with a Spanish-refugee painter who wishes to remain anonymous, and who lived in Mexico. He says that he actually lived in the Coyoacán house and that Rivera accepted this arrangement with equanimity, but Frida's letters reveal that she tried to conceal the liaison from Diego. In October 1946, for example, after she had been with her lover in New York earlier that year, she wrote to Ella Wolfe to ask her to serve as mail drop while he was in the U.S.:

Ella darling of my heart,

It will surprise you that this lazy and shameless girl writes to you, but you know that one way or the other, with or without letters, I love you very very much. Over here there is no important news, I am better, I am already painting (an idiotic painting) but something is something, better than nothing. . . .

I want to ask you a huge favor as big as the pyramid of Teotihuacán. Will you do it for me? I am going to write to B—— at your house so that you will forward the letters to where he is, or perhaps you will keep them to deliver them to him in your own hand when he passes through New York. For the love of God, don't let them out of your hands unless it is *directly into his.* You know what I mean kid! I would not even want Boit to know anything if you can avoid it, since it is better that only you keep my secret, do you understand? Here *no one* knows anything, only Cristi, Enrique—*you* and me and the boy in question know what it's about. If you want to ask me anything about him in your letters, ask me with the name of SONJA. Understood? I beg you to tell me how he is, what he's doing, if he is happy, if he takes care of himself etc. Not even Sylvia [probably Sylvia Ageloff] knows a single detail, so don't chatter with *anyone* about this subject please. To you I can say that I truly love him and that he makes me feel the desire to live again. Speak well of me to him, so that he should be happy, and so that he knows that I am a person who is, if not very good, at least *Regularcita* [OK].

I send you thousands of kisses and all my love.

Frida

Don't forget to *tear up* this letter in case of future misunderstandings—
Promise?

To this day Frida's lover continues to be passionately devoted to
her, treasuring the tiny oval *Self-Portrait*—a miniature about two
inches high—that she made for him around 1946. He keeps it in a
box together with other relics—a pink hair ribbon, an earring, a few
drawings, and the Tlatilco head mounted on a silver backing to form
a brooch. The liaison lasted until 1952, but increasingly as the years
went on and her physical frailties made relations with the opposite
sex more difficult, Frida turned to women, often to women with whom
Diego was having an affair. As Raquel Tibol put it, "she consoled herself
by cultivating the friendship of women with whom Diego had amorous
relations."

That Frida's masculine side became more pronounced in the late
forties is apparent in her self-portraits: she gave her features an ever
more masculine cast, making her mustache even darker than it actually
was. But there was always a definite androgynous aspect to both Frida
and Diego; both were attracted to what they saw of their own gender
in their mate. Rivera loved Frida's boyishness as he loved her "Zapata"
mustache—he was furious once when she shaved it off. She loved his
soft, vulnerable quality as she loved his fat man's breasts; it was the
part of Diego that she knew ensured his need for her. She wrote:
"Of his chest it must be said that if he had disembarked on the island
governed by Sappho, he would not have been executed by the female
warriors. The sensitivity of his marvelous breasts would have made
him admissible. Even so, his virility, specific and strange, makes him
desirable also in the dominions of empresses avid for masculine love."

One of the "empresses" was film star María Félix, whose liaison
with Diego became a public scandal. The trouble began when Diego
was preparing for his huge retrospective at the Palace of Fine Arts.
He planned to make the portrait of María Félix on which he was working the exhibition's centerpiece; naturally, it caused a stir even before
it was finished. The press posed the question: During the forty modeling
sessions to which no witnesses were admitted, was María posing naked
for Rivera? Her diaphanous dress, they noted, hardly concealed the
contours of her body. Photographs were published showing Rivera
gazing amorously into his model's eyes. (In the end, María Félix refused
to lend her portrait to the show, and Rivera replaced it with an equally

44. With the Trotskys on their arrival at Tampico, 1937.

45. Frida and Trotsky, 1937.

47. A gathering in Lupe, Marín's apartment in 1938. From left, Luis Cardoza y Aragón, Frida, Jacqueline and André Breton, Lupe, Diego, and Lya Cardoza.

46. With, from left, Trotsky (seated), Diego, Natalia Trotsky Reba Hansen, André Breton, and Jean van Heijenoort, on an outing near Mexico City, June 1938.

48. *Me and My Doll*, 1937.

49. *Escuincle Dog with
Me*, c. 1938

50. *What the Water Gave Me*, 1938.

52. With Nickolas Muray.
Photograph by Nickolas Muray,
c. 1938.

51. At her New York exhibition,
1938.

53. *Two Nudes in a Forest*, 1939.

64. *Flower of Life*, 1944.

65. *Still Life*, 1942.

66. *Fruits of the Earth*, 1938.

67. *Portrait of Mariana Morillo Safa*, 1944

68. *Doña Rosita Morillo*, 1944.

69. *Moses*, 1945.

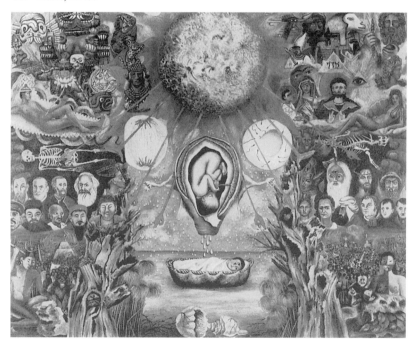

70. With Granizo ("the little deer") when he was a fawn, c. 1939. Photograph by Nickolas Muray.

71. With Diego at a political rally, c. 1946.

72. With three of her students, c. 1946. From left, Fanny Rabel, Arturo Estrada and Arturo García Bustos.

73. Frida, c. 1947.

74. Detail from Rivera's 1947-1948 Hotel del Prado mural, in which he depicted himself as a boy; Frida's hand rests protectively on his shoulder.

75. Diego with María Félix, 1949.

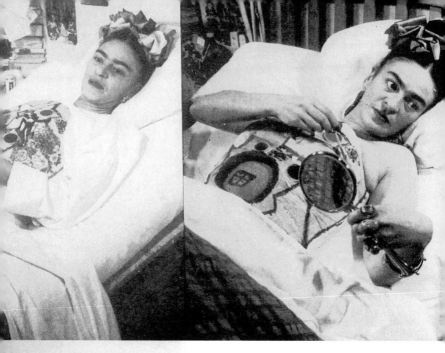

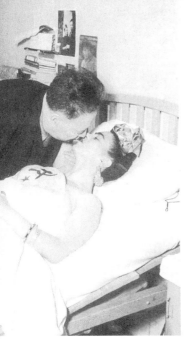

76. Frida's last year in the hospital, 1950-1951. Above left, holding a sugar skull with her name on it; above right, painting one of the succession of plaster corsets she endured; left, with Diego.

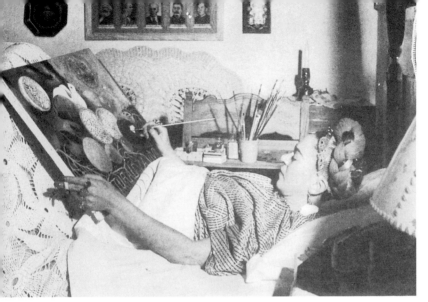

77.   Painting *Naturaleza Viva*, at home, 1952.

78.   With her servants, c. 1952.

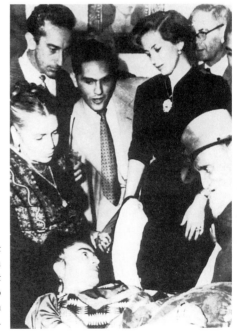

79.   Being carried into the gallery at the opening of the Homage to Frida Kahlo in 1953. Looking on are (left to right) Concha Michel, Antonio Peláez, Dr. Roberto Garza, Carmen Farell, and (lower right) Doctor Atl.

80. *Marxism Will Give Health to the Sick*, 1954.

81. Frida's studio, the unfinished portrait of Stalin on the easel.

82. Protesting the ouster of Guatemalan president Jacobo Arbenz Guzmán by the CIA in July 1954. Juan O'Gorman is beside Frida, Diego behind her.

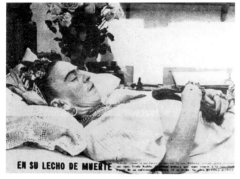

83. On her deathbed.

84. Diego flanked by Lázaro Cárdenas (left) and Andrés Iduarte following the hearse to the crematorium.

85. Frida's bed, Frida Kahlo museum.

provocative one, a life-size nude of another beauty, the poet Pita Amor.)

Disregarding Rivera's disclaimers, the press also reported that the *muy distinguido pintor* planned to marry the actress just as soon as he could get a divorce. Three leading papers published the "news" that María Félix had accepted Diego's proposal on condition that she could bring her twenty-two-year-old girl friend, a beautiful Spanish refugee who had served Frida as nurse and companion, into the marriage as part of a sort of ménage à trois. Rivera claimed that his romance with María Félix had nothing to do with his intention, which he did not deny, to divorce Frida. "I adore Frida," he said smoothly, "but I think my presence is very bad for her health." He admitted his infatuation with María Félix: "like hundreds of thousands of Mexicans," he was in love with her.

Memories of the affair are almost as numerous as rememberers. Most people say that Rivera was infatuated but not deeply in love with María Félix, and that she never really wanted to marry him, but liked the attention she got from the scandal. Some say that in order to be independent from Diego at this time, Frida took an apartment for a few months in the center of Mexico City near the Revolution Monument. Perhaps it was her near-death there in a fire—a candle she left burning on a table set her skirt ablaze and she was saved by a building employee who heard her screams—that convinced Diego to return to her. Others say that Frida was amused by the affair, that Rivera kept her informed about the progress of his courtship by telling her every detail and every problem and by sending her drawings and notes saying things like: "This is from your enamored Frog-toad," or captioning a drawing of himself as a weeping toad, "This is how your Toad-frog is crying." Frida pretended she did not mind. She even wrote María Félix a note offering to give her Diego as a present (María turned down the offer).

It is typical of Frida that her own relationship with María Félix continued during this period and after. Indeed, Frida, María , and Pita Amor—with whom, it is said, Rivera also had an affair—were all intimate friends. (Pita Amor's photograph was one of those Frida lovingly affixed to her bed's headboard, and María Félix is the first name on the list that adorns Frida's bedroom in Coyoacán.)

Adelina Zendejas tells of the time when, as a reporter for the magazine *Tiempo,* she was sent to interview Diego about his affair with María. She asked him, "Are you going to get a divorce?" and he said,

"From whom?" Zendejas said, "From Frida, because you are going to marry your goddess María Félix." Diego said, "If you want, you can telephone right now and you will see that María and Frida are chatting together." Adelina countered that she had heard that Diego had already petitioned for a divorce. Diego said, "Look, that must be a FUF." Adelina was perplexed. FUF, Diego explained, was the *Frente Unido de las Feas* (United Front of Ugly Women), because, said Diego, "they are jealous of the beauty of both Frida and María." Adelina, whose informant about the divorce had been the beautiful Lupe Marín, said, "It was not only the ugly women who told me." "Then," said Diego, "it's the FUA." Again Adelina was perplexed. FUA was the *Frente Unido de las Abandonadas* (United Front of Abandoned Women), Rivera explained. "That's who must have said it." Diego was referring to Lupe Marín, but when Adelina went back to her original source, Lupe said, "Frida is an imbecile who is letting María get into her house and steal Diego from her. Diego is infamous, but the idiot is Frida."

Yet perhaps Frida was not such an "idiot" after all, for she lost neither the friendship of María Félix nor her husband. Rivera, in his autobiography, recounted the dénouement with uncharacteristic succinctness. When María Félix refused to marry him, he said, he returned to Frida, who was "miserable and hurt. Within a short space of time, however, everything was well again. I got over my rejection by María. Frida was happy to have me back, and I was grateful to be married to her still."

None of the stories of Diego's affair with María Félix and Frida's reaction to it (whether true or not) can negate the anger and sorrow that are manifest in the weeping self-portraits of 1948 and 1949. *Diego and I* was just a sketch, showing Frida with flowers adorning her braided hairdo, when the photographer and writer Florence Arquin and her husband, Samuel A. Williams, purchased it in Mexico; the portrait that arrived in the United States showed her crying (in this painting even her features seem to weep), with a mass of loose hair swirling around her neck as if it were going to choke her. As in *Self-Portrait as a Tehuana,* a small portrait of Diego rests on her eyebrows— Diego was the constant intruder in her thoughts. No matter what she said, no matter how she shrugged her shoulders and laughed in public, *Diego and I* remains a painted record of Frida's lonely passion for her husband, and of her despair at the possibility of losing him.

That record appears in her journal as well. Many of its pages form what might best be described as a prose poem addressed to Diego. His name is everywhere. "I love Diego—no one else," she wrote. In a moment of loneliness she exclaimed: "Diego, I am alone." Then, a few pages later: "DIEGO," and finally, days, months, or possibly years later (Frida did not usually date diary entries, and she sometimes added a page written in an earlier period): "My Diego. I am no longer alone. You accompany me. You put me to sleep and you revive me." Elsewhere, following a page full of nonsense words and phrases spun out in stream-of-consciousness fashion, there is a notation that seems to refer to Frida's loneliness at Rivera's absence. "I am going with myself," she wrote. "An absent moment. You have been stolen from me and I am weeping as I go. He is a *vacilón* [joker or philanderer]."

Many people say that the Riveras never had a sexual bond, that they were mainly companions. And to be sure, camaraderie was a strong part of Frida's attitude toward her husband. But she did also retain an unmistakable, strong erotic love for him, even when his physical desire for her subsided after the first few years of marriage, and even though she stipulated that her bond with him be celibate after their remarriage. Her carnal love for Diego gives much of her journal the quality of an erotic love letter: "Diego: Nothing is comparable to your hands and nothing is equal to the gold-green of your eyes. My body fills itself with you for days and days. You are the mirror of the night. The violent light of lightning. The dampness of the earth. Your armpit is my refuge. My fingertips touch your blood. All my joy is to feel your life shoot forth from your fountain-flower which mine keeps in order to fill all the paths of my nerves which belong to you." Or, a few pages later:

My Diego:
    Mirror of the night.
    Your green sword eyes inside my flesh. Waves between our hands. All you in the space full of sounds—in shade and in light. You will be called AUXOCROMO—the one that attracts color. I CROMOFORO—the one that gives color. You are all the combinations of number. life. My desire is to understand line form movement. You fill and I receive. Your word crosses all the space and reaches my cells that are my stars of many years retained in our body. Enchained words that we could not say except in the lips of sleep. Everything was surrounded by the vegetal miracle of the landscape of your body. Upon your form, at my touch the cilia of flowers, the sounds

of rivers respond. All the fruits were in the juice of your lips, the blood of the pomegranate . . . of the mammee and pure pineapple. I pressed you against my breast and the prodigy of your form penetrated through all my blood through the tips of my fingers. Odor of essence of oak, of the memory of walnut, of the green breath of ash. Horizons and landscapes— that I crossed with a kiss. A forgetfulness of words will form the exact idiom to understand the glances of our closed eyes.

You are present, intangible and you are all the universe that I form in the space of my room. Your absence shoots forth trembling in the sound of the clock, in the pulse of light; your breath through the mirror. From you to my hands I go over all your body, and I am with you a minute and I am with you a moment, and my blood is the miracle that travels in the veins of the air from my heart to yours.

THE WOMAN

THE MAN

The vegetal miracle of my body's landscape is in you the whole of nature. I traverse it in a flight that with my fingers caresses the round hills, the . . . valleys, longing for possession and the embrace of the soft green fresh branches covers me. I penetrate the sex of the whole earth, its heat embraces me and in my body everything feels like the freshness of tender leaves. Its dew is the sweat of an always new lover. It is not love, nor tenderness, nor affection, it is the whole of life, mine that I found when I saw it in your hands, in your mouth and in your breasts. In my mouth I have the almond taste of your lips. Our words have never gone outside. Only a mountain knows the insides of another mountain. At times your presence floats continuously as if wrapping all my being in an anxious wait for morning. And I notice that I am with you. In this moment still full of sensations, my hands are plunged in oranges, and my body feels surrounded by you.

Given the intensity of Frida's carnal love for Diego, it is not surprising that his sexual infidelities hurt. To protect herself, she took the stance of the indulgent mother—a relationship which was just as sensual as that of being his mate, but in a different way. Instead of feeling Diego's "green sword eyes inside [her] flesh," instead of her body feeling "surrounded" and "penetrated" by the "prodigy" of Diego's form, she was the one who held him in her lap, bathed him, cared for him like a mother. Indeed, this mother-son bond was so physical that Frida announced in her diary her desire to "give birth" to Diego: "I am the embryo, the germ, the first cell that—in potency—engendered him— I am *him* from the most primitive and the most ancient cells, which with 'time' became him," she wrote in 1947. Another time, she confided: "At every moment he is my child, my child born every moment, diary, from myself." And in "Portrait of Diego" she said: "Women . . . amongst them I—always would want to hold him in their arms like a newborn baby."

That is exactly what she does in *The Love Embrace of the Universe, the Earth (Mexico), Diego, Me and Señor Xolotl*, painted at about the same time as *Diego and I*. Here Frida is a kind of Mexican earth mother, and Diego is her baby. A bright red crevasse cracks open her neck and chest, and a magical fountain of milk sprays forth from where her breast and heart would be, food for the large, pale baby Diego lying in her lap. He holds a maguey plant painted in fiery orange, yellow, and gray—an emblem of his "fountain-flower," which was Frida's metaphor for his sex. Tears make Frida a weeping Madonna, a Madonna who has lost, or fears she will lose, her child.

In "Portrait of Diego," written during the year she painted *The Love Embrace*, Frida described the Diego she had painted with all the keen physicality of a doting mother:

His form: with his Asiatic-type head upon which grows dark hair so thin and fine that it seems to float in the air, Diego is an immense baby with an amiable face and a slightly sad glance. . . . and very seldom does an ironic and tender smile, the flower of his image, disappear from his Buddha-ish mouth with its fleshy lips.

Seeing him nude, you immediately think of a boy frog standing on his hind legs. His skin is greenish white like that of an aquatic animal. Only his hands and face are darker, because the sun burned them. His infantile shoulders, narrow and round, flow without angles into feminine arms that end in marvelous hands, small and delicate in design, sensitive and subtle like antennae that communicate with the whole universe. It is amazing that these hands have served to paint so much and that they still work indefatigably.

Fussing over Diego was Frida's pleasure. She would laugh about having his enormous underclothes made in cheap cottons, preferably in bright Mexican pink. (He was too fat to fit into ready-made underwear.) Or she would grumble affectionately: "Oh, that boy, already he has spoiled his shirt." When Rivera dropped his clothes on the floor, Frida would scold him gently. His response, even when she was really angry, was to hang his head in silence like a guilty child, relishing the attention.

Rivera liked being babied. That there was much of the little boy in him, he himself showed in his Hotel del Prado mural (figure 74), where, in 1947–1948, he painted himself as a fat, devilish boy in knee pants (a frog in one pocket and a snake in the other), standing in front of Frida, depicted as a mature woman with one hand resting protectively on his shoulder. One of the happier moments in the day was his bath. As a schoolgirl, Frida had told her friend Adelina how much she liked Rivera, how much she would love to "bathe him and clean him!" Her wish was granted, for like his earlier wives, she discovered that he needed encouragement to take a bath. She bought various toys to float in the bathwater, and scrubbing her husband with sponges and brushes became a household ritual.

Like any child, when Diego did not get what he wanted he made a fuss. Antonio Rodríguez remembers an occasion when he went to see Frida, accompanied by his youngest son, "whom she treated with great affection." Diego was not there. Frida gave the child a toy, "one of those tanks that arrived in Mexico during the war, saying 'keep it hidden, because if Diego comes and sees you playing with it, he will get angry or take it away.' My son did not pay attention to her, and he kept on playing with it. When Diego arrived, and saw my son with the toy, he made a face like a little boy almost crying, and said to Frida: 'Why do you give me things and later take them away?' Frida said, 'I'll give you another one. I'll buy another.' But Diego left the room murmuring, 'I don't want anything anymore.' He was almost in tears. It was as if he were really a child."

Frida wrote of Diego's infantile egocentricity in "Portrait of Diego":

The images and ideas flow in his brain with a rhythm that is different from the common one, and because of this, his intensity of fixation and his desire to do always more are uncontainable. This mechanism makes him indecisive. His indecision is superficial, because finally he succeeds in doing whatever he wants with a sure and well-planned will. Nothing better illustrates this modality of his character than what his aunt Cesarita, his mother's sister, once told me. She remembered that when Diego was a very small child he entered a store, one of those little variety shops full of magic and surprise that we all remember with affection, and standing in front of the counter, with a few centavos in his hand, he looked at and surveyed again and again the whole universe contained within the store, while he desperately and furiously screamed: "What do I want!" The store was called "The Future," and this indecision of Diego's has lasted his whole life. But although he seldom arrives at a decision to choose, he carries inside him a vector line that goes directly to the center of his will and his desire.

To accommodate the "vector line" of Diego's will and desire, Frida was at once protective and abnegating. "No one will ever know how I love Diego," she wrote in her diary. "I don't want anything to wound him, nothing should bother him or take away the energy that he needs to *live*—to live the way he wishes, to paint, see, love, eat, sleep, to feel himself alone, to feel himself accompanied—but I would like to give *all* to him. If I had health I would like to give it *all* to him. If I had youth he could take it all."

Frida would not thus sacrifice herself for a love that was merely romantic or maternal. She did so for Diego because even in his willful "childishness" she saw evidence of his superiority. To Frida, Diego was a man whose vision, impelled by the unerring vector of his desire, embraced the universe even as, in *The Love Embrace*, the universe embraces him. To show this in the painting, she placed a third eye in the middle of his forehead and she called this the eye of "supervisibility" or the *ojo avisor* (informing eye). And in "Portrait of Diego" she wrote: "His large, dark, and extremely intelligent bulging eyes—almost out of their orbits—are held in place with difficulty by eyelids that are swollen and protuberant, like those of a frog. They are very much more separate from each other than other eyes. They enable his vision to embrace a much wider visual field, as if they were constructed especially for a painter of spaces and multitudes. Between those eyes, so distant one from the other, one divines the invisible eye of Oriental wisdom."

Frida holds Diego, and she in turn is held by an earth goddess who represents Mexico and resembles a pre-Columbian idol. The idol is actually a cone-shaped mountain, a reference perhaps to mountain-pyramid symbolism in pre-Columbian religion, or to Frida's characterization (in her diary) of herself and Diego as mountains. Its slopes are half green and half brown, perhaps to show that it comprises both the earth of Mexico and the plants that grow there, or perhaps to indicate the contrast of Mexico's desert and jungle terrain or the alternation of the dry and rainy seasons. Like Frida, the idol-mountain has long loose hair, not black, but made of cactus. And the chest, like Frida's, is cracked open in a *barranca*. Near this wound sprouts a patch of green grass—Frida's way of saying that nature alternates between cycles of destruction and rebirth, life and death. The gash goes all the way to the earth goddess's nipple, from which one drop of milk falls, like a tear.

As always in Frida's paintings, the concrete, specific connection of *The Love Embrace* with an actual event (the María Félix affair) is not the whole truth: although Frida is wounded and weeping, she is also caught up in a series of love embraces, set one inside the other, that not only expresses her belief in the interrelatedness of all things in the universe, but also forms the matrix that joins and sustains herself and her spouse. Plucked from the earth, the mountain floats in the sky so that the roots from the cacti growing up and down its slopes dangle in space. These roots, some red as if they were veins, are, like all the roots in Frida's paintings, strangely alive. Frida once drew her notion of love as a tangle of red roots growing downward, and in *The Love Embrace* the dangling but live roots symbolize the hardiness of her and Diego's love.

In Frida's extraordinary cosmology, the idol-mountain (earth, Mexico) is, in turn, embraced by a larger divinity, a pre-Columbian-looking goddess of the universe, divided into light and dark and still only partly concretized out of the half-night, half-daytime sky. Frida and Diego are thus doubly encompassed by universal love and by their ancient progenitors, once on the earthbound and once on the celestial level. *The Love Embrace* can be seen as a fantastic Assumption of the Virgin in which Mother and Son are rejoined in a pre-Columbian heaven. But the image, with its familiar Mexican plants, its homely and humorous inclusion of Frida's favorite *escuincle* dog, Xolotl (modeled on a pre-Columbian ceramic dog from Colima that Frida owned), curled up on the universe's arm, is a concrete expression of a particular time when Frida's sense of the fragility of her hold on Rivera as a husband made her all the more determined to hold on to him as a child.

In the end Frida kept her husband. She was the woman Diego loved more than any other. "If I had died without knowing her," Rivera once confided to Carmen Jaime, "I would have died without knowing what a real woman was!" On another occasion, Carmen Jaime heard Frida say to Diego: "What do I live for? For what purpose?" and he answered: "So that I live!" And to Frida, Diego was—everything. She wrote in her diary:

Diego. *beginning*
Diego. *constructor*
Diego. *my baby*
Diego. *my boyfriend*
Diego. *painter*
Diego. *my lover*
Diego. *"my husband"*
Diego. *my friend*
Diego. my mother
Diego. me
Diego, universe
Diversity in *unity*

Why do I call him *My* Diego? He never was nor ever will be mine. He belongs to himself.

PART 6

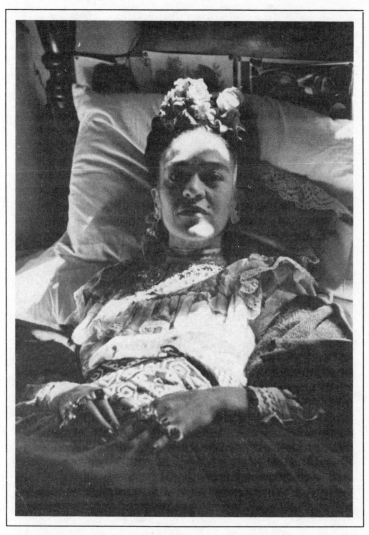

Chapter 22

Naturaleza Viva:
Alive Still Life

THE ARROWS that pierced the flanks of *The Little Deer* struck deep and did not fall out. For all the vitality that was left in the young deer's body, he would not find his way out of the thick forest enclosure to the blue sea and sky beyond. The spinal fusion of 1946, wrote Cachucha Miguel N. Lira, began "the calvary that would lead to the end." By early 1950, Frida was so sick that she had to go to a hospital in Mexico City. She was to remain there for a year.

During a brief trip to Mexico, Dr. Eloesser saw her before she was hospitalized, and on January 26, 1950, he scribbled some notes about her condition. On the third of January, he wrote, Frida "awoke to find the four toes of her right foot black on the ends. The night before on retiring the toes were OK. Dr. came that day and sent her to the hospital. For the past year has been eating very little—lost . . . weight. In last 3 years has been taking much Seconal. No alcohol 3 years." Dr. Eloesser mentions that Frida had been painting up to three months prior to his visit, that she had headaches, and that for a period of time she had had a continuous fever. Her leg, he said, was in constant pain. The rest is illegible except for the word "gangrene."

On January 12, in a letter to her dentist, Dr. Fastlich, about a broken dental bridge, Frida said: "Forgive the trouble that I'm giving you. I am still in the hospital since 'for a change' they operated on my spine again and I can't leave until tomorrow, Saturday, to go to my neighborhood Coyoacán. Still in a corset and rather screwed up! But I am not discouraged and I will try to start painting as soon as I can." Besides these troubles, Frida was suffering from poor circulation in her right leg, which would explain the black toes and "gangrene." On February 11, from Coyoacán, she wrote to Dr. Eloesser that she had seen five doctors, including Dr. Juan Farill. She trusted him, she said, for he seemed the most "serious"; he recommended that her foot be amputated, leaving only the heel.

My dearest Doctorcito:

I received your letter and the book, a thousand thanks for all your marvelous tenderness and your immense generosity with me.

How are you? What are your plans? I am in the same state I was in when you left me the last night that I saw you.

Dr. Glusker brought a Dr. Puig, a Catalan bone surgeon educated in the U.S. to see me. His opinion is like yours, to amputate the toes, but he thinks it would be better to amputate up to the metatarsus in order to obtain a less slow and less dangerous cicatrization.

Until now the five opinions that I have had are the same—amputation. Only the place of the amputation varies. I do not know Dr. Puig well, and I do not know what to decide to do, since it is so important for me, this operation, that I am afraid of doing something stupid. I want to beg you to give me your sincere opinion of what I should do in this case. For the reasons that you know, it is impossible for me to go to the U.S. and also because it means a great quantity of money because I know that at this moment it represents a much larger effort for him [Diego] since the peso is worth shit. If the operation in itself is not something out of this world, do you think that these people could do it for me? Or should I wait until you can come, or should I get the dough and do it there with you? I am desperate since if it really has to be done, the best thing would be to confront the problem as soon as possible, don't you think?

Here in bed, I feel that I am vegetating like a cabbage and at the same time I think that the case must be studied in order to attain a positive result from the purely mechanical view. That is to say: to be able to walk, to be able to work. But they tell me that since the leg is in such bad shape, the cicatrization will be slow and I will spend a few months unable to walk.

A young doctor, Dr. Julio Zimbrón, proposes to me a strange treatment that I want to ask you about, because I do not know up to what point it might be a good idea. He says that he guarantees that the gangrene will disappear. It is a question of some subcutaneous injection of light gases, helium-hydrogen and oxygen. . . . What is your immediate impression, do you think there is truth in all this? Couldn't embolisms form? I am rather afraid of it. He says that he thinks that with his treatment I will not need the amputation. Do you think that is true?

They are driving me crazy and making me desperate. What should I do? It is as if I am being turned into an idiot and I am very tired of this fucking foot and I would like to be painting and not worrying about so many problems. But, it can't be helped, I have to be miserable until the situation is resolved. . . .

Please, *Lindisimo* be good enough to advise me what you think I should do.

The book by Stilwell seemed fantastic to me, I hope you will get me more on Tao, and the books of Agnes Smedley on China.

When will I see you again? It does me such good to know that you really love me and that no matter where you go, you watch over me (from the sky). I feel that this time I only saw you a few hours. If I were healthy I would go with you to help you to make people turn into beings that are truly useful to others. But the way I am, I am useless even as a gutter cap.

I adore you

Frida

Not long after writing to Dr. Eloesser, Frida went back to the English Hospital and put herself under the care of Dr. Juan Farill. She had already been operated on twice when, in mid-April, her sister Matilde wrote to Dr. Eloesser on her behalf:

Today I answer your letter directed to Frida in the Hospital and in the name of Frida I thank you for all the affection and good wishes that your letters show towards Frida. She wants me to tell you everything that has to do with her operation and I do it with pleasure, in spite of the fact that the telling of it carries horrors suffered and that until today no progress has been seen.

She has been through a real Calvary and I don't know how this thing will go, since as I told you in my first letter they fused three vertebrae with a bone of I don't know who and the first 11 days were something terrifying for her. Her intestines became paralyzed, she has had a temperature of 39 and 39½ [degrees centigrade] every day since the day after they operated on her, constant vomiting and constant pains in her spine and when the corset was put on her body and she lay on the place where the incision was, thus began this process and to calm her the doctors gave her a double injection of Demerol . . . and other things with the exception of morphine, because she cannot tolerate morphine. Her temperature continued and she began, this way, to suffer with pains in her sick leg and although they were of the opinion that it was phlebitis, they did not inject for phlebitis but from that moment on there was a Council of the Indies pricking her with injections and medicines. The fever did not stop and then I noticed that she was emitting a very bad odor from her back, I pointed it out to the Doctor and the next day they . . . opened up the corset and they found an abscess or tumor, all infected, in the wound and they had to operate on her once more. She suffered another time the paralysis of her intestines, horrible pains and instead of progress, other horrible problems. They put on another new plaster corset and this one took something like four or five days to dry and they left a duct to drain out all the secretion.

They gave her Chloromycetin every four hours and her temperature began to drop a little but that's the way it has been since the 4th of April when they operated for the second time and now the corset is dirty as a pigsty since she is secreting through her back, it smells like a dead dog and these "señores" say that the wound is not closing and the poor child is their victim. This time she will need another corset and another operation or treatment in order to get rid of all the illness. I do not know why, Dr. Eloesser, but I think, without Frida's knowing it, that the infection is not superficial, but rather, I think, that the grafted bone has not stuck on the vertebrae and this has infected everything. Of course I do not say this to her, because the poor thing is in torment and she deserves compassion. I do not understand how she could have decided to have this stupid operation without being in good health, since they did a blood test when she had the fever and had already been operated on and she had only 3 thousand hemoglobin and this has been a real setback for her. Thus she doesn't get well nourished, she is worn out and tired of staying in one position and she says all the time that she feels that she is lying on broken glass. The way I see her suffering, I would like to give her my life, but those "señores" say all the time that it is going well and it will come out well. But, I hesitate to say it to you Dr. Eloesser, but, without knowing anything about medicine, I know that Frida is not well. It is necessary to wait until they do the third operation or treatment and we will see once more how she will be. The stitches do not heal over and the wound does not look as though it is closing. She does not know this, since what she is suffering is already enough. It would have been preferable to stay the way she was, since the gangrene has gone down and the black ends have fallen off.

We have suffered along with her, because all of us her sisters adore her and it pains us so much that she suffers this way. She is worthy of admiration for she is so abnegating and strong and thanks to this she puts up with her misfortune. I would have wanted to write to you before, but I could not, Dr., since with these anxieties that we have I do not have time for anything. Today she is eating better and they have given her three plasmas of 500 or ½ a liter and quantities of sucrose and with this her spirits are a little better. They give her lots of vitamins and thus she is surviving. She sends you loving greetings and regards and she says that you should read my letters as if they were from her, because she cannot write. Diego sends you greetings also, he has behaved very well this time and she is tranquil.

Frida says to send you many kisses much love and that you should not forget her. . . . All my sisters send our greetings and we remember you often, since Frida speaks of you all the time and for all of us you are her good friend.

On my part many regards for you dear Dr.

Matilde

During Frida's year in the English Hospital, Rivera took a small room next to hers so that he could spend the night near his wife. During some periods he slept in the hospital every night except Tuesdays, which were reserved for his work at Anahuacalli, or so he said.

Diego could be extraordinarily tender, rocking Frida to sleep in his arms as if she were a little girl, reading poetry by her bedside, or, once when she had a terrible headache, distracting her by dancing around her bed brandishing a tambourine and pretending to be a bear. Other times, he was less attentive. According to Dr. Velasco y Polo, part of the reason Frida was hospitalized was that it was convenient for Diego, who wanted his freedom. "And the highs and lows of Frida while she was in the hospital depended on how Diego behaved." If he was attentive, she was happy and her pains vanished. If he stayed away, she cried and her pains increased. She knew that if she was ill enough, he would be by her side. As Velasco y Polo puts it: "She couldn't offer her pain to the Virgin so she offered it to Diego. He was her god."

Frida was no ordinary patient. The nurses adored her for her gaiety (and her generous tips); the doctors liked her because, says Velasco y Polo, "she never complained. She never said this is badly done. She stood it all a little bit *a la Mexicana,* suffering, but without protesting." Frida clung to her sense of the ridiculous; she loved to play, and on days when her natural exuberance won out against pain, she created a stage from the semicircular metal contraption designed to keep her right leg raised, and produced puppet shows with her feet. When the bone bank sent a bone extracted from a cadaver in a jar labeled with the name of the donor, Francisco Villa, Frida felt as vital and as rebellious as the revolutionary bandit hero Pancho Villa. "With my new bone," she cried, "I feel like shooting my way out of this hospital and starting my own revolution." Because of a fungus infection contracted from one of the bone grafts, Frida's back was injected each morning (she was the first person in Mexico to take the antibiotic Terramycin), and when her doctors removed the drain, she would exclaim over the beautiful shade of green. She also liked to let friends peek through a hole in her plaster cast at the raw, unhealing wound.

Frida's room was almost as exceptional as its occupant. It was decorated with candy skulls, brightly painted candelabra from Matamoros shaped like the tree of life, white doves made of wax with paper wings that to Frida signified peace, and the Russian flag. On her bedside table were towering piles of books and neat little pots of paint and a jar of brushes. Sheets of paper were pinned to the wall, and she persuaded her visitors—among them Miguel Covarrubias, Lombardo Toledano, Eulalia Guzmán, and other well-known Communists—to sign their names there in support of the Stockholm Peace Congress. (In 1952, Diego made Frida, sitting in her wheelchair and holding out a copy of the Stockholm Peace Petition for her compatriots to sign, the heroine of his mural *The Nightmare of War and the Dream of Peace*. The hero, larger and more lofty by far, was Stalin.)

Visitors also signed their names on Frida's various plaster corsets, and decorated them with feathers, mirrors, decalcomanias, photographs, pebbles, and ink. When her doctors ordered her paints removed, Frida painted her current cast with lipstick and iodine. There is a photograph of Rivera watching as his bedridden wife carefully paints a hammer and sickle on a corset that covers her entire torso.

Something else Frida produced while confined to her hospital bed was a series of so-called emotional drawings. These were part of an experiment conducted by her friend Olga Campos, who was studying psychology at the university at the time, and who had plans to write a book on the relationship between human emotions and line, form, and color. The twelve pairs of drawings that resulted reveal Frida and Diego's spontaneous pictorial responses to the idea of pain, love, joy, hate, laughter, jealousy, anger, fear, anguish, panic, worry, and peace. Composed of numerous lines, Frida's drawings show her fascination with intricate webs and root-like forms. Diego's, by contrast, capture his reactions to the different emotions in a few broad, swift strokes.

When she felt well enough, and the doctors permitted it, Frida painted, using a special easel that attached to her hospital bed so she could work while lying on her back. By early November, after six operations, she was able to paint approximately four or five hours a day. She worked on *My Family*, begun years before and never finished, in which she once again gathered her forebears around her, this time adding her sisters and her niece and nephew. It was as though painting genealogical ties consoled her for the fact that she was literally falling apart. The very act of painting had become a source of spiritual support. "When I leave the hospital two months from now," she said, "there are three things I want to do: paint, paint, paint."

Frida's hospital room was always full of visitors. Dr. Velasco y Polo recalls her fear of solitude and boredom. What she liked was gaiety, spicy gossip, and dirty jokes. Volatile by habit, she would, says the doctor, "get very excited and say, 'Listen to that son of a bitch, please throw him out of here. Send him to the devil.' When she saw me with a pretty girl, she'd cry, 'Lend her to me! I'll smoke that one myself!' She liked to talk about medicine, politics, her father, Diego, sex, free love, the evils of Catholicism."

Part of Frida's appeal was her ability to listen. Elena Vásquez Gómez, an intimate friend from Frida's last years, says, "We healthy people who went to visit her came away comforted, morally fortified. We all needed her."

Fanny Rabel's memory is similar: "She did not concentrate on herself. One did not feel her miseries and conflicts when one was with her. She was full of interest in others and in the outside world. She would say, 'Tell me things. Tell me about your childhood.' Frida said that she liked this better than the movies. She would become very moved, and sometimes she cried when people talked. She could listen for hours. Once when I went to the hospital, Frida was coming out of anesthesia. When she saw me and my son through the glass window, she said she wanted to see us. Another time she was talking about the other patients in the hospital. She was very worried, because they seemed to be really sick. It was as if she herself were on a vacation."

Visits from children gave Frida a special delight. She had a little disciple, a nine-year-old Indian boy from Oaxaca named Vidal Nicolas, who came to see her often. He would stand by her bedside wearing his serape, and with his huge adoring eyes, watch her paint. "He has great talent," she said, "and I am going to pay for all his education and send him to the San Carlos Academy." Frida died before Vidal could prove his talent, but the incident illustrates her impulse to throw her energies into great plans. Most of the schemes, whether trips to Europe or the education of this child, remained enthusiasms, for by 1950 Frida was too sick to realize her hopes.

Another form of entertainment was movies. Rivera borrowed a projector and every week he rented different films. Frida especially loved Laurel and Hardy, Charlie Chaplin, and the movies directed by El Indio Fernández. When she had seen the whole series of their films, she watched them over again. Her sisters and friends would keep her company. Olga Campos recalls that "Cristina brought a big basket full of all kinds of foods, and a large group of us had lunch with Frida every day—*enchiladas, moles.* We'd see the latest movies. There was always a bottle of tequila. There was a party on in Frida's room every day."

That is how Frida described her year in the hospital too: "I never lost my spirit. I always spent my time painting because they kept me going with Demerol, and this animated me and it made me feel happy. I painted my plaster corsets and paintings, I joked around, I wrote, they brought me movies. I passed three years [again, Frida exaggerates] in the hospital as if it was a fiesta. I cannot complain."

In spite of what seems like a hit-or-miss medical history, Frida had the best care available at the time. Dr. Wilson was a pioneer in orthopedic surgery and a well-known specialist in spinal fusion. Dr. Farill was one of the most prominent surgeons in Mexico, founder of a hospital for lame children where he charged no fee to those too poor to pay. He handled his patients with just the right mixture of authority and gentle sympathy. Always informal with her doctors, Frida called him *"chulito"* (cutie), and she followed his advice so faithfully that Rivera even took to asking the doctor to persuade Frida to do things that he himself could not convince her to do. Even when she was well enough to go home, she continued to see him almost daily. Perhaps she was especially attached to him because he was, like herself, lame (his leg and foot had been operated upon, and for years he walked with crutches and then with an orthopedic apparatus).

Frida gave Dr. Farill two paintings, a 1953 *Still Life* with a peace dove and a Mexican flag, inscribed *"Viva la Vida* and Dr. Farill and I painted this with love Frida Kahlo," and in 1951 the extraordinary *Self-Portrait with the Portrait of Doctor Farill* (plate XXXIV), in which she shows herself painting him. Done while Frida was convalescing at home from the series of bone grafts on her spinal column that he had performed, it is a secular *retablo,* with Frida the saved victim of a narrowly escaped danger and Dr. Farill taking the place of the holy image. Its strange, suffused intensity convinces us that it was, like an ex-voto, vital to the artist's well-being; it records a real-life event not as a plea for compassion but as a confirmation of faith.

In the painting, Frida is seated in her wheelchair, working on a portrait of Dr. Farill. Except for her jewels, she is dressed almost as soberly as a nun. She wears her favorite *huipil* from Yalalag—the one with the lavender silk tassel—and a full black skirt. She sits rigidly straight; her loose blouse conceals the bulky orthopedic corset. Bare surroundings underscore the great austerity and dignity of this woman. They delineate loneliness too, for though friends were attentive, Frida was, as an invalid, very much alone. Like the vast, open desert that is her backdrop in other paintings, the blank, confining walls of the room in this one reverberate with her solitude. A wide blue band along the lower part of the wall is almost the only bright color in the painting, but the muted tones are poignant, not dull. A person who has been close to death does not need magenta to feel alive; for that person, even beige, brown, black, and gray are vibrant.

Frida's diary describes her frame of mind:

I have been sick a year. . . . Dr. Farill saved me. He gave me back the joy of life. I am still in a wheelchair and I do not know if soon I will be able to walk again. I have a plaster cast, which, in spite of being a frightful bore, helps my spine feel better. I do not have pains. Only a weariness . . . and as is natural, often desperation. A desperation that no words can describe. Nevertheless, I want to live. I already have begun to paint the little painting that I am going to give to doctor Farill and that I am doing with all my affection for him.

Frida has placed her extracted heart, laced with red and blue veins, on her heart-shaped palette; it is the very pigment with which she creates art. She offers the doctor her heart-palette both as a token of affection and as a testimony to her suffering. In her other hand she holds a bunch of paintbrushes with pointed tips. They drip red paint, immediately reminding the viewer of surgical instruments. Painting for Frida was, after all, a form of psychological surgery; she cut and probed into her very spirit. When her brush dipped into the palette of her heart, it came out red.

"I do not have pains," she had written. "Only a weariness . . . and as is natural, often desperation. A desperation that no words can describe." Home from the hospital, she continued to deteriorate, and although her doctors tried, nothing could be done to improve her health for long. Mostly she remained in her house, a prisoner of monotony and, despite her brave words, of pain. She could propel herself in her wheelchair, but when she tired of sitting, she could walk only short distances, and this with a cane or crutches, as well as the help of painkillers injected by her nurse—first an Indian woman, Señora Mayet, and then, in 1953, a Costa Rican named Judith Ferreto. To be sure, the general pall was illuminated by visitors and stints of work, but these distractions were all too brief and could not dispel for long the pervasive gray blur of invalidism.

Like the adolescent who, after the bus accident, wrote to her boyfriend that she was lonely and "bored with a *b* of burro" and that she wished *la pelona* would take her away, Frida was often lonely, oppressed by tedium, and suicidal. She was, of course, sustained by the mythic persona that she had built up over the years. But now her defiant *alegría* took on an edge of desperation; the flamboyant mask was becoming brittle and paper-thin.

Her day began with tea brought to her in bed by her nurse. After a light breakfast, she would paint, usually in bed, or if she was able, in the studio or outside in the sunshine of the patio. In the afternoons, she received visitors. María Félix and Dolores del Rio and her husband, the famous film actor and singer Jorge Negrete, came often, and artists and writers, and such political associates as Teresa Proenza (an intimate friend who served as secretary to Cárdenas) and Elena Vásquez Gómez (who was at that time working for the Ministry of Foreign Relations). Her sisters Matilde and Adriana visited her frequently; Cristina came every day, and her children once or twice a week. In the last year of her life, it was Cristina who looked after her day and night, spelling the nurse so that her sister would never be alone. When she came, Frida would greet her tenderly: *"Chaparrita* [chubby one], what are you up to?" And Cristina, just as tender, braided flowers into Frida's hair and assured her that various household matters would be attended to properly.

When she was sufficiently strong, Frida entertained in the living room or the dining room. Otherwise, friends ate on a little table in her bedroom. Elena Martínez, Frida's cook from 1951 to 1953, especially remembers the visits of María Félix. The film star loved Frida's company because with her she could let down her hair; instead of playing prima donna, she could play court jester, dancing and singing for the invalid, making her laugh. "María Félix was very intimate, and she would lie on the bed next to Frida for a little while to rest."

There were occasional outings, excursions to places near Mexico City. Sometimes Dr. Velasco y Polo would pick her up in his Lincoln Continental convertible, and Frida would revel in the sense of speed and openness the wind gave, and in being able to see all around. Sometimes they would get out of the car, walk only a few yards, sit down to rest. "Give me a double tequila," she would say. Occasionally she was able to go with her nurse to spend a day or so in nearby towns such as Puebla or Cuernavaca, where, if she could walk without too much discomfort, they browsed among the stands in the plazas at which popular art objects were sold. Wherever she went, "in one moment you would see a multitude following her," Judith Ferreto remembers. "Whenever we would go to the movies, there were shoeshine boys and boys selling newspapers . . . [and she would say] 'they always like to go to the movies. I know, because I was one of them, so please bring them with us, and buy some cigarettes for them.' They were very young, but she knew that they all smoked. . . . You could see in the faces of the people how they liked her."

Sometimes when she was strong enough to go out at night, Diego would gather a group of friends—the photographer Bernice Kolko, Dolores del Rio, Maria Asúnsulo (a great beauty whose features are recorded in portraits by various Mexican painters), poets Carlos Pellicer and Salvador Novo—and take her to a restaurant. "We'd dance and sing and drink and eat and be gay," Bernice Kolko recalls, "and we'd sit her down at the table and Diego used to dance with me or with someone else, and she used to be so happy. She always liked gaiety."

Frida's staff at Coyoacán adored her, for when she was well enough she worked in the kitchen alongside them, and she treated servants like family. The *mozo* Chucho, who had worked for her for almost twenty years, was almost in love with her. He liked to drink, and so did she, so they often enjoyed a *copita* together. "I love him for many things," said Frida, "but first because he makes the most beautiful baskets that you will ever see." Chucho bathed her when she was too weak to take care of herself. He would undress her very tenderly and carry her to the bathtub. When she was washed and dried, he would dress her and arrange her hair and carry her back to bed as if she were a baby.

As Frida's health declined, her attachments—to things, to politics, to painting, to friends, and to Diego—grew more and more intense. Abhorring solitude, as if having no one there or nothing to do would leave a void into which terror would flow, she clung to her connections with the world. "I very much love things, life, people," she told a friend in 1953.

A cabinet and a dressing table in her bedroom are crammed with her collection of little things—dolls, dollhouse furniture, toys, miniature glass animals, pre-Columbian idols, jewelry, all kinds of baskets and boxes. She loved to arrange and rearrange them, and she used to say, "I'm going to be a little old woman and go around my house fixing up my things." She received gifts like a young child, impetuously ripping open the wrappings, exclaiming her pleasure in the contents.

"Because she was immobile," says Fanny Rabel, "the world came to her. The boxes full of toys were very clean and well arranged. She knew where everything was."

Just as compulsively as she solicited gifts, she gave things away. "If one refused to accept a present, she would get very angry, so you had to accept," says Jesús Ríos y Valles. If receiving gifts was a way of bringing the world to her, giving was a way of extending herself out into it, and of confirming her relation to other people.

Politics was another way, and during her last years Frida's allegiance to the Communist party, to a system that claimed to explain the past and encompass the future of mankind, became devotion. Her diary reveals that her faith in the interconnectedness of all things grew more and more fervent as her body disintegrated and that this faith was now mediated by the Party: "The revolution is harmony of form and of color and everything exists and moves beneath only one law—life," she wrote. And later, on November 4, 1952:

Today as never before I am accompanied (25 years) I am now a Communist being. . . . I have read the history of my country and of almost all the nations. I know their class conflicts and economics. I understand clearly the materialistic dialectic of Marx, Engels, Lenin, Stalin and Mao Tse. I love them as the pillars of the new Communist world. . . . I am only one cell of the complex revolutionary mechanism of the people for peace and of the new Soviet—Chinese—Czechoslovakian—Polish people who are bound by blood to my own person and to the indigenous peoples of Mexico. Amongst these large multitudes of Asiatic people there will always be my own faces—Mexican faces—of dark skin and beautiful form, limitless elegance, also the blacks will be liberated, they are so beautiful and brave.

On March 4, 1953: "I lost equilibrium with the loss (the passing) of STALIN— I always wanted to know him personally but now it doesn't matter— Nothing stays everything is revolutionized." Interspersed with such statements are chaotic drawings—Frida divided in two, half dark, half light, and much of her figure scratched out; a globe with a hammer and sickle; Frida holding a peace dove while long lance-like lines entrap her smudged head. Some are accompanied by exclamations: "Peace, revolution," "Viva Stalin, Viva Diego," or "Engels, Marx, Lenin, Stalin, Mao." (Photographic portraits of these five men still hang in a row at the foot of Frida's bed.)

Always in the past Frida's politics had bound her more closely to Diego. But now that she was enfolded once more within the bosom of the Party and he was not, her position was more complicated. She turned on Trotsky like a cat with her claws out, accusing the dead leader of any number of sins, from cowardice to theft, and stated that only her sense of hospitality had prevented her from refusing to accede when Diego invited him to stay in her house. "One day," she said in an interview published in Mexico's leading newspaper, *Excelsior*,

Diego said to me: "I am going to send for Trotsky," and I said to him: "Look, Diego, you are going to make a tremendous political error." He gave me his reasons and I accepted. My house had just been fixed up. *El viejo* Trotsky and *la vieja* Trotsky arrived with four gringos, they put adobe bricks in all the doors and windows [of my house]. He went out very little because he was a coward. He irritated me from the time that he arrived with his pretentiousness, his pedantry because he thought he was a big deal. . . .

When I was in Paris, the crazy Trotsky once wrote to me, and he said to me, "Diego is a very undisciplined individual who does not like to work for peace, only for war. Be good enough to convince him to return to his party." I told him: "I can't influence Diego at all. Because Diego is separate from me, he does whatever he wants and so do I, what's more, you robbed me, you broke my house and you stole from me fourteen beds, fourteen machine guns and fourteen of everything." He only left me his pen, he even stole the lamp, he stole everything.

And to a friend, journalist Rosa Castro, she declared:

I was a member of the Party before I met Diego and I think I am a better Communist than he is or ever will be. They kicked Diego out of the party in 1929, at the time of our marriage, because he was in an opposition. I had only just begun to know about politics. I followed him personally. My political error. And not until ten years ago [actually five years] did they restore my carnet. Unfortunately I have not been an active member because of my illness; but I have not failed to pay a single fee, nor have I failed to inform myself of every detail of the revolution and of the counter-revolution in the entire world. I continue to be a Communist, absolutely, and now, anti-imperialist, because our line is that of peace.

Painting, too, was a way of confirming her connection with the world, and she felt better and happier when she was painting. "Many things in this life now bore me," she said, "[and] I am always afraid I will get tired of painting. But this is the truth: I am still passionate about it." Confined to her house and often bedridden, she painted mostly still lifes—the fruits of her garden or the local market, which could be placed on a table by her bed. Because the fruits are painted larger in relationship to the background than they were in the still lifes from the 1930s and 1940s, one feels that she has literally drawn close to her subject, pressing her eyes and nose near the objects of her love and desire. In the close world of the bedridden, the truly real objects are those within arm's reach. Significantly, though her fruits are ripe and tempting, they are also sometimes bruised. Even as she enjoyed their vitality and sensuous beauty and delighted in the oneness with nature that she felt in painting them, she recognized their transience.

As always when painting objects other than herself, Frida made her fruits look like her. Her melons and pomegranates are cut open, revealing juicy, pulpy centers with seeds, making us remember her wounded self-portraits and her association of sex with pain. Sometimes she peels off just a little of a fruit's skin. Or she jabs a tiny flagpole into the flesh, recalling the arrows, thorns, and nails that torture her own flesh in self-portraits. In one 1951 *Still Life* (now lost), the flagpole's pointed tip emerges inside the halved fruit's soft, dark interior; in another, the wound brings forth three drops of juice, like the three tears on Frida's cheeks in several self-portraits. Near the melon in this painting, Frida has placed one of her pre-Columbian ceramic dogs from Colima, and though he is only made of clay, his wistful eyes glisten. In a number of late still lifes, coconuts have faces with round, simian eyes weeping tears; the artist's identification with nature was so strong that the fruits she laid out to paint wept with her.

As her devotion to communism intensified, the personal quality of her painting began to trouble her. "I am very worried about my painting," she wrote in her diary in 1951. "Above all to transform it, so that it will be something useful, since until now I have not painted anything but the honest expression of my own self, but absolutely distant from what my painting could do to serve the Party. I should struggle with all my strength for the little that is positive that my health allows me to do in the direction of helping the Revolution. The only real reason to live."

Frida tried to politicize her still lifes by inserting flags, political inscriptions, and peace doves nesting among the fruits. (In these years Rivera, too, used the dove as a symbol; Stalin, for example, holds a peace dove in *The Nightmare of War and the Dream of Peace*.) By the fall of 1952, she felt she had progressed along the road toward socialist art. "For the first time in my life my painting tries to help the line traced by the party. REVOLUTIONARY REALISM," she wrote in her diary. But the truth is, Frida's still lifes are a hymn to nature and to life. She acknowledged their peculiar animation when she titled one of them (painted in 1952) *Naturaleza Viva*, meaning "alive nature," as opposed to the usual Spanish term for still life, which is *naturaleza muerta*, or "dead nature." Not only are the fruits and the way they are painted restless; even the title, written across the bottom of this painting, pulsates with life: the words are formed out of creeping tendrils.

The still lifes Frida painted in 1951 and earlier are neat and precise in technique, full of refined detail and sly, suggestive wit. By 1952 her style had changed radically; the late still lifes are not just animate but agitated. They have a kind of wild intensity, as if Frida were flailing about in search of something solid, a raft in a heavy sea of impermanence. Brushwork becomes looser; she has lost the exquisite precision of the miniaturist. Her characteristic small, slow, affectionate strokes give way to messy, frenetic handling. Colors are no longer clear and vibrant, but strident and grating. Modeling and surface texture are so summary that oranges lose their firm, appealing roundness; watermelons no longer look succulent. In several earlier still lifes Frida's pet parrots perched amid the fruits. Looking out at the spectator quizzically, they gave the paintings a special kind of charm. Now parrots are replaced by peace doves daubed in the roughest, most slapdash manner.

The contents of the late still lifes seem as agitated as the style. Fruit is no longer neatly piled on a tabletop; instead it is most often spread on the earth or beneath an open sky. Several still lifes are divided into day and night, with the sun and the moon echoing the shape of the fruits. The choice of still life as a subject does not communicate a feeling of domestic plenty or well-being. Nor does Frida, like so many artists, paint fruit because it is one of the most abstract of subjects, its emotionally neutral shapes and colors lending themselves to formal manipulation more freely than, say, landscape or portrait subjects. On the contrary, Frida's still lifes take on an apocalyptic note. Suns have faces, full moons have an embryonic rabbit-like creature drawn on their surfaces, a creature closely resembling a well-known carved stone representation of an Aztec *pulque* god, which Rivera inscribed in the moon in his *Tlazolteotle, God of Creation* mural at the Hospital de la Raza (1952–1954).

Pulque, that ambrosia of delirium so loved by the suffering Mexican poor, had long been (with tequila and brandy) Frida's anodyne. Now to kill pain she took larger and larger doses of drugs as well. The hasty brushwork and the deterioration of her artistic control were symptoms of this. "The style of her last paintings shows anxiety," Dr. Velasco y Polo says, "with states of excitation of the type that come from drug addiction." Always a fastidious painter, she now got her hands and clothes covered with pigment, and this, said Judith Ferreto, made her desperate.

Her style also suffered because Frida was in a hurry. She was in a hurry because she needed to complete a commission in order to get money for drugs or to help Diego financially. (Once, when Diego was so broke that he was about to sell a present María Félix had given him, Frida, though she was extremely sick at the time, announced to her nurse: "I must paint tomorrow. I don't know how I am going to do it. . . . I have to make money. Diego doesn't have any dough.") Or she was in a hurry because she could only paint for a short while before succumbing to pain or to the stupor that came from too many painkillers. Most of all, she was in a hurry because she knew her death was close.

But even as her paintings became ever more clumsy and chaotic, Frida kept on straining for balance and order in her art. In her diary for 1953 there are two studies for still lifes in which she tried to achieve harmony by applying the golden section. Feeling control slip from her fingers, she was looking for a controlling absolute.

Frida's most intense friendships during this time were with women: María Félix, Teresa Proenza, Elena Vásquez Gómez, and the artist Machila Armida. These are the women whose names, together with the names of Diego and of Irene Bohus, are painted in pink on her bedroom wall. Her house, Frida said, was theirs. Though she still had devoted men friends—Carlos Pellicer, for example, came to see her often, and so did some of the Cachuchas—she was too much of an invalid to go out and seek men's company.

Several among her old friends were put off by the coterie of intimates that surrounded Frida like a queen's guard. Yet there is something poignant and archetypal in this gathering of women around Frida's bedside during her final years. Just as women are the bearers of life, they are also the traditional attendants to death.

Diego now cajoled his women friends into becoming intimate with her, asking them to visit her, to pass the night with her. Sometimes she was quite aggressive about her lesbianism. One friend was so shocked when Frida kissed her goodbye on the lips that she pushed her away, and Frida fell backward onto the ground. Raquel Tibol recalls Frida's fury when she rejected Frida's advances; Raquel, who had been living with the Riveras at Coyoacán, had to go live in the San Angel studio, thus giving Frida another reason to be upset. Made jealous by the affair she suspected Diego was having with Tibol, she tried to hang herself from her bed's canopy, and would have died had not her nurse found her and taken her down in time.

Tibol also tells of the suicide of a brain-damaged girl (she had a trephination of the cranium) who was the sister of one of Frida's patrons, and whose advances Frida spurned: "The girl had a strong fixation on Frida. Frida was repelled by her. When I returned to the San Angel studio, the girl took advantage of my absence, and like an animal, went into the house to see if she could have some physical contact with Frida. An obsessive lesbian, the girl said, 'If you don't pay attention to me I'll kill myself.' She went down to the little dining room, took poison, went upstairs, and fell dead at the foot of Frida's bed. Chucho was the one who called Diego, who laughed uncontrollably and then arranged for the body to be removed and for the story not to come out in the press. It never appeared in the newspaper that someone had killed herself in Frida's room."

Other than Cristina, Judith Ferreto was probably the woman closest to Frida during these last years. Alejandro Gómez Arias remembers her as a tall, good-looking, dark-haired woman who underscored her masculinity by wearing high black boots. But she was tender. Like many private nurses, Judith came to feel a proprietary love for Frida. She was convinced that she knew what was best for her patient and that doctors, friends, Diego—even Frida herself—did not. Her devotion was sometimes tyrannical. Sometimes Frida rebelled. "You are like a fascist general imposing things on me," she would protest. And from time to time, she became so thoroughly exasperated with her nurse that she would scream at her or kick her. Several times she threw Judith out of the house, only to call her back again, saying, "You are the only one that can help me." Judith noticed that usually when Frida sent her away it was because her condition was growing rapidly worse.

As with other people she loved, Frida was determined to bind her nurse to her, but when she had accomplished this, she felt suffocated and guilty. "I think I have cultivated your feelings for my own advantage, to use them in a good way for myself," she said to Judith. "I would like you to love me, to take care of me the way you do, but not to suffer so much. . . . Many of my good friends know I've been suffering all my life, but nobody shares the suffering, not even Diego. Diego knows how much I suffer, but to know is different from suffering *with* me." Her nurse became almost a part of Frida, another way to extend herself out into the world and to pull the world into her being.

"I started working with her during the night as well as during the day," Judith remembered, "because she was very lonesome, constantly, but especially during the night, even when a lot of people were around. . . . In my hands she was like a child. Many times I felt that she was like my child, because she behaved that way. She liked to fall asleep the way babies do. As if she were a baby, you were supposed to sing a song or tell a tale, or to read something. Our beds were in the same room. You could not behave like a nurse with Frida; a nurse would not lie down with a patient or sit on a patient's bed. But with Frida and Diego it was different. So I always lay down beside her as a support for her back and she called me her 'little prop.' And sometimes I sang to her, and to Diego too. In that way, she would start falling asleep. She always slept with some medications that the doctor prescribed. Sometimes they would not take effect for two hours, depending on her condition, of course. All this time, before she fell asleep, I was beside her. She would ask me for another cigarette, and at the very last moment she would always have a cigarette in her hand. When I could see that her hand was no longer able to hold it and that its direction was not right for her mouth, I would ask her if she wanted me to take it away. She would say 'No' with a movement because she couldn't speak, though she could understand. She was still enjoying the cigarette. I would watch until the moment when I could take it away and she wouldn't know it. That meant she was sleeping.

"She always asked me, 'Please don't leave me immediately when I fall asleep. I need you nearby, and I feel it even after I am asleep, so don't go away immediately.' I would remain beside her bed for an hour or more until I thought she wouldn't know that I had left her. At that moment I would put her back in the right position on her side, and put special pillows behind her back to support her. I tried to make the pillow under her head neat and smooth, because everything was so painful in her body. I would always hear when her breathing changed, and when she woke up she would sometimes be furious and say, 'You don't sleep just in order to listen to me!' But I think this made her happy."

Of necessity, Frida's life and Diego's were quite separate. They kept different hours. He left for work at eight and came home late, usually after Frida had eaten supper. They slept in different parts of the house, Frida upstairs in the modern wing, Diego downstairs in a room that, suitably, gave onto the dining room. "They lived together, but apart," Ferreto said.

As an invalid, there was little Frida could do for Diego. Once she had been able to mother him, to cook for him and cater to his whims, to care for him when he was ill; now she could not help him (in 1952, he had cancer of the penis, which was arrested with X-ray therapy when he refused amputation), and had only her suffering to bind him to her. Her several suicide attempts were perhaps more than anything else a way of showing him how much she suffered. But being a man with a passionate appetite for all aspects of living, he could not limit himself to a life in which caring for Frida was his chief preoccupation. Sometimes tender, sometimes callous, he was always unreliable. There were terrible fights and periods of separation, and though she often said to friends that she no longer minded his love affairs because "he needs someone to take care of him," and though she asked her women friends to look after Diego, even implying that they should give him romantic attention, when he was not with her, Frida cried out to him in anguish in her diary:

If only I had his caress near me the way the air caresses the earth. The reality of his person would make me happier. It would distance me from the feeling that fills me full of gray. Nothing would then be so deep in me, so final. But how do I explain to him my enormous need for tenderness! My loneliness of many years. My structure ill adapted because it is inharmonious. I think it is better to go, to go, *to escape.* Let everything pass in a second, *Ojalá* [God grant].

"I love Diego more than ever," she told her journalist friend Bambi not long before her death, "and I hope to be of use to him in something and to keep on painting with all *alegría* and I hope nothing will ever happen to Diego, because the day that he dies I am going with him no matter what. They'll bury us both. I have already said 'don't count on me after Diego goes.' I am not going to live without Diego, nor can I. For me he is my child, my son, my mother, my father, my lover, my husband, my everything."

The isolation and pain that filled Frida "full of gray" was brightened in December 1952 by her participation in the repainting of La Rosita. Noting that her students' earlier murals had faded, she decided that they should be replaced. This time, the participating artists included two of the "Fridos" (García Bustos and Estrada), plus a group of Rivera's assistants and protégés. The students drew studies and, with Frida's help, selected the best designs. She directed the project, walking on crutches out to the bar to watch her disciples work.

The walls were repainted in fresco in a single day and with new subjects, this time including much-publicized sentimental events and current celebrities. María Félix was portrayed twice. On one panel she was seated on a cloud above a group of upside-down men who illustrated the panel's title: *El mundo de cabeza por la belleza* (The world head over heels in love with beauty). Another section showed Frida dressed as a Tehuana next to Arcady Boytler. She holds a peace dove, and below her is a scroll with the words: "We love peace." Frida herself chose the grouping that included Rivera flanked by María Félix and Pita Amor.

Although Frida said the murals were painted "for pure pleasure, for pure *alegría*, and for the people of Coyoacán," and that they were intended to resuscitate the "intentionally Mexican and critical spirit that has encouraged the best of our painters and engravers in the first quarter of the century, among them, José Guadalupe Posada and Saturnino Herrán," the new decorations of La Rosita (lost when the bar was razed) were much less authentically popular and Mexican than the 1943 versions. The subjects were sophisticated in-jokes and famous personalities, close friends of the Riveras, instead of anonymous *campesinos* symbolizing the themes of *pulque* and the rose; there was even talk of changing the *pulquería's* name to something like "The loves of María Félix." Thus the repainting of La Rosita was more of a social event for cultured people than an effort to renew the culture of "the people." It was as if Frida and Diego were amusing themselves by borrowing a popular tradition and turning a working-class bar into a celebration of upper bohemia.

The inauguration of the new murals was timed to coincide with

Rivera's sixty-sixth birthday, on December 8. Frida wanted to have a traditional Christmas *posada* with a parade of guests singing as they walked through the streets to the open doors of the blue house; the festivities were to become an even more celebrated event than the first opening of La Rosita. Rosa Castro recalled the dazzling but grotesque afternoon. Frida was talking to Rosa about the misery of being enclosed in orthopedic corsets, when suddenly, at dusk, she cried, "No more!" She ripped off her corset and sallied out to join the festivities, leaving Rosa Castro behind to watch the guests milling about the house. Rosa remembers especially the scene in Frida's bedroom. There, hanging from the rafters—those same rafters from which Frida herself had hung while waiting for one of her plaster corsets to dry—was a multitude of Judases, dressed by Frida in her own and Diego's clothes. They swung and twirled, their cardboard bones jostled by the continuous flow of people moving in and out of the room.

Shouting in the street outside called Rosa Castro to the door. There was Frida, her hair loose and flowing over her shoulders, her face wild with excitement that must have been partly the result of drugs taken so that she could endure the pain of walking without the support of her corset. She staggered toward her house, arms raised above her head, her voice joining in the general uproar of the crowd that followed her. In the dim evening light, a cloud of dust billowed up around the celebrants. And above the noise of the singing, laughing, whistling crowd, Frida's voice could be heard. "Never again!" she cried triumphantly, referring to her imprisonment in corsets. "Never again, no matter what happens! Never again!"

Chapter 23

Homage to Frida Kahlo

A FEW MONTHS after the second opening of La Rosita, in the spring of 1953, Lola Alvarez Bravo decided to organize an exhibition of Frida's paintings in her Galería Arte Contemporaneo at Amberes 12, in the city's fashionable Pink Zone. "They had just performed a bone transplant, and unfortunately, the bone was diseased and they had to remove it again," she recalled. "I realized that Frida's death was quite near. I think that honors should be given to people while they are still alive to enjoy them, not when they are dead." She proposed the idea to Diego. He was enthusiastic, and together they told Frida. "It was a very joyful announcement for her, and her health actually improved for a few days while she was planning and thinking about it. The doctors thought that she could not get any worse and that this might give her a boost."

The show was to be Frida Kahlo's first one-person exhibition in her native land, and to Frida, devastated by illness, it was a triumph. She sent out charming folkloric invitations—little booklets printed on colored paper, which she strung together with bright woolen ribbons. The message was in the form of a ballad written in Frida's hand:

With friendship and love
born from the heart
I have the pleasure of inviting you
to my humble exhibition.

At eight in the evening
—since, after all, you have a watch—
I'll wait for you in the gallery
of that Lola Alvarez Bravo.

It is at Amberes twelve
and its doors open on the street
so that you won't get lost
because that's all I'm going to say.

All I want is for you to tell me
your good and sincere opinion.
You are a learned person
your knowledge is first-class.

These paintings
I painted with my own hands
and they wait on the walls
to give pleasure to my brothers.

Well, my dear *cuate*,
with true friendship
I thank you for this with all my heart
Frida Kahlo de Rivera.

The gallery also printed a brochure in which Lola Alvarez Bravo called Frida a "great woman and artist," and stated the obvious truth that Frida had deserved this homage for a long time.

When the night of the opening approached, Frida was in such poor health that the doctors forbade her to move. But she did not want to miss her vernissage. And somehow her attendance was becoming, of its own momentum, an event. The phones at the gallery kept ringing: Would Frida be there? Was she too sick to come? Art reporters in Mexico and abroad called to ask about the show. The day before the exhibition opened, Lola Alvarez Bravo learned that Frida had taken a turn for the worse, but still insisted on coming to the inauguration. She would send her bed so that she could attend lying down. A few hours later, the huge four-poster arrived, and the gallery staff set about rearranging the paintings so as to include the bed as part of the show.

The day of the opening, tension mounted. The staff bustled about straightening paintings, checking labels, primping flowers, seeing that the bar was stocked, with the glasses in neat rows and the ice ready. As was the gallery's custom, a short while before the appointed hour the staff closed the doors to give themselves a moment of peace in which to make sure the place was clean and well-arranged. It was at this point, Lola Alvarez Bravo recalls, that a crowd of hundreds of people gathered on the street: "There was a traffic jam outside, and people were even pushing at the door, because they insisted on getting into the gallery immediately. I didn't want them to come in until Frida arrived, because it would be very hard for her to get in once the gallery was jammed with people." Finally, the gallery was forced to open its door for fear that the restive crowd would break it down.

Minutes after the guests poured into the gallery, sirens were heard outside. People rushed to the door and were astonished to see an ambulance accompanied by a motorcycle escort and Frida Kahlo being carried from it into her exhibition on a hospital stretcher. "The photographers and reporters were so surprised," says Lola Alvarez Bravo, "that they were almost in shock. They abandoned their cameras on the floor. They were incapable of taking any pictures of the event."

Someone did, fortunately, have the presence of mind to take a photograph of this extraordinary moment in Frida's life. It shows her dressed in native costume and jewelry, lying on the stretcher. As she is carried into the gallery, she is being greeted by friends. Old, lame, white-bearded Doctor Atl, the legendary painter, revolutionary, and volcanologist, looks down at her with an expression of intense feeling. Frida's wide, staring eyes dominate her ravaged face; undoubtedly she had had to be heavily drugged.

She was placed in her bed in the middle of the gallery. A grinning skeleton Judas affixed to the underside of her bed's mirror-lined canopy lay face down as if he were watching her. Three smaller Judas figures dangled from the canopy, and the four-poster's headboard was covered with pictures of Frida's political heroes, photographs of family, friends, and Diego. One of her paintings hung on the footboard. The bed was to remain in the exhibition even after the opening, its embroidered pillows scented with Schiaparelli's "Shocking" perfume.

Like one of those lavishly gowned saints that recline on satin sheets and are cherished in Mexican churches, Frida held court. "We asked people to keep walking," said Lola Alvarez Bravo, "to greet her and then to concentrate on the exhibition itself, because we were afraid the crowd might suffocate her. There was really a mob—not only the art world, the critics, and her friends, but quite a lot of unexpected people came that night. There was a moment when we had to take Frida's bed out to the narrow terrace in the open air, because she could hardly breathe anymore."

Carlos Pellicer acted as traffic policeman, dispersing the crowd when it gathered too closely around Frida, insisting that guests form a line in order to congratulate the artist one by one. When the "Fridos" came up to her bed, Frida said, "Stay with me a little while, *chamacos,*" but they could not linger, because other well-wishers pressed them on.

Liquor flowed. The hum of talk was pierced by brays of laughter as people enjoying themselves cracked jokes and greeted friends. It was one of those parties where excitement reaches a feverish intensity. Everyone recognized it as a major event. Carlos Pellicer had tears in his eyes when he read aloud a poem he had written about Frida, who drank and sang *corridos* with her guests. She asked the writer Andrés Henestrosa to sing "La Llorona" (The Weeping Woman), and Concha Michel sang other favorites. After most of her friends had embraced her, the guests stood in a circle around the four-poster and sang:

> *Esta noche m'emborrachó*
> *Niña de mi corazón*
> *Mañana será otro día*
> *y verán que tengo razón.*
>
> (Tonight I will get drunk
> Child of my heart
> Tomorrow is another day
> And you will see that I am right.)

When Dr. Velasco y Polo told Diego that he thought Frida was getting tired and should be taken home, Diego was too caught up in the festivity to pay any attention. He brushed off the doctor with a mild curse: *"Anda, hijo, te voy a dar!"* (Beat it, kid, or I'll let you have it!)

Like the sugar skulls she loved, or the grinning Judas, Frida's opening was as macabre as it was gay. "All the cripples of Mexico came to give Frida a kiss," Andrés Henestrosa remembers, and he described the various Mexican painters who attended. "María Izquierdo arrived supported by friends and family because she was an invalid. She leaned over to kiss Frida's forehead. Goitia, sick and ghostly, arrived from his hut in Xochimilco with his peasant's clothes and his long beard. Also Rodríguez Lozano, who was crazy. Doctor Atl came. He was eighty years old. He had a white beard and crutches, because one of his legs had recently been amputated. But he was not sad. He leaned over Frida's bed and laughed boisterously at some witticism that made fun of death. He and Frida joked about his foot, and he told people not to look at him with pity, for his foot would grow again and be better than before. Death, he said, only exists if you fail to give it a little life. It was a procession of monsters, like Goya, or more like the pre-Columbian world with its blood, mutilation, and sacrifice."

"Frida was very fixed up, but tired and sick," Monroy recalls. "We were deeply moved to see all her work brought together and to see that she was loved by so many people." But her former pupils felt, as did many of Frida's friends, that the opening was exhibitionistic. "It was," Raquel Tibol observed, "a little spectacular, a little bit like a Surrealist act, with Frida like the Sphinx of the Night, presenting herself in the gallery in her bed. It was all theater."

"Everybody and his dog was there," Mariana Morillo Safa says. "Frida was so thrilled welcoming everybody. But she was a different Frida from the one I had known as a little girl. She was not as natural. It is as if she were thinking of something else. She acted happy, but she was trying very hard."

Certainly it is true that Frida's presence turned the opening into a display of personal sentiment and emotion, rather than an artistic celebration. But if Frida had to perform to conceal her pain, this was the kind of performance that she loved—colorful, surprising, intensely human, and a little morbid, very like her theatrical self-presentation in her art.

Frida was amazed at the success of her exhibition. So was her gallery. Lola Alvarez Bravo recalls that "we received calls from Paris, London, and from several places in the U.S.A. asking us for details about Frida's exhibition. . . . we were surprised that anyone outside Mexico should have heard of it." The gallery had to extend the show for a month because of popular demand, and the press loved it, extolling Frida's heroic presence at the opening as much as it admired her work.

The painter, poet, and prominent critic José Moreno Villa struck in *Novedades* the note that would resound over the years: "It is impossible," he wrote, "to separate the life and work of this singular person. Her paintings are her biography." *Time* magazine reported the news of Frida's show in an article called "Mexican Autobiography." Although her renown still had much to do with the fact that she was married to Diego Rivera, she was no longer "little Frida," but a celebrity in her own right. The *Time* reviewer told the story of Frida's accident, her marriage, her pride in her Communist convictions. The piece ends with this ominous assessment of her physical and moral state:

After seeing her show last week, Mexico could understand Frida Kahlo's hard reality. And it is getting even harder. Recently, her condition had been getting worse; friends who remember her as a plump, vigorous woman are shocked by her haggard appearance. She cannot stand for more than ten minutes at a time now, and there is a threat of gangrene in one foot. But each day, Frida Kahlo still struggles to her chair to paint—even if only for a short while. "I am not sick," she says. "I am broken. But I am happy to be alive as long as I can paint."

In his autobiography, Diego remembered Frida's exhibition with pride and pleasure: "For me, the most thrilling event of 1953 was Frida's one-man show in Mexico City during the month of April. Anyone who attended it could not but marvel at her great talent. Even I was impressed when I saw all her work together." But he also recalled that at her opening Frida hardly spoke: "I thought afterwards that she must have realized she was bidding good-bye to life."

She may have been tired and broken, but she was bidding goodbye to life in her own gallant style. In her diary Frida listed, as a kind of prose poem, some of the images—*The Little Deer, Flower of Life*—that hung on the walls of her exhibition. The last, separated deliberately from the others, is *Tree of Hope.*

La Vida callada . . .	The silent life . . .
dadora de mundos.	giver of worlds.
Venados heridos	Wounded deer
Ropas de Tehuana	Tehuana clothes
Rayos, penas, Soles	Lightning flashes, pains, Suns
ritmos escondidos	hidden rhythms
"La niña Mariana"	"The little girl Mariana"
frutos ya muy vivos.	Fruits that are very much alive.
la muerte se aleja—	death keeps its distance—

lineas, formas. nidos.
las manos construyen
los ojos abiertos
los Diegos sentidos
lágrimas enteras
todas son muy claras
Cósmicas verdades
que viven sin ruidos

lines, forms. nests.
hands build
open eyes
the Diegos full of feeling
whole tears
all are very clear
Cosmic truths
that live without sounds

Arbol de la Esperanza
mantente firme.

Tree of Hope
keep firm.

Chapter 24

Night Is Falling in My Life

"I HAD GONE to leave a ring for her," Adelina Zendejas remembers of the day in August 1953 when, after half a year of torturous uncertainty, Frida's doctors decided they would have to amputate her right leg. "She had always told me that she would like to have a peacock ring. I asked her to draw it. 'Look,' she told me, 'I have a few little stones here. Go out in the street and look for more.' I gathered a pile of little stones and took them to her.

"Dr. Farill arrived. He was in a great hurry and he said, 'Let's see the leg,' because by now the pain was unbearable. Diego was desperate, and the amount of drugs that she took was terrible.

"For the first time in many years, I saw her leg. It was so crippled, shrunk, degenerated, that I cannot understand how she was able to put her foot into her boot. Two toes were missing. Farill was examining it, touching it, and he became pensive. Frida said to him, 'What, Doctor, are you going to cut off? Another toe? Cut these two at once.' And he said to her, 'You know, Frida, I think that it is useless to just cut your toe, because of the gangrene. I think that the moment has come when it would be better to cut off your leg.'

412

"If you could have heard the scream that Frida let out! She said, 'No!' It came out of her guts. It was something pathetic. Her hair was loose, she was wearing a Tehuana costume, and she had bedclothes over her, but the foot stuck out from under the bedclothes. The leg was very thin, as if it were broken, as if it hung on her. And then she turned around and looked at me and said, 'What do you think? Tell me, *Timida*, what do you think?'

"And I kept looking at Diego. He was holding on to the end of the bed. I said, 'Well, Frida, you always used to call yourself *"Frida la coja, pata de palo"* [Frida the gimp, with the peg leg]. So you will be lame. Now you are lame with much suffering. Your leg does not allow you to walk, and now there are very good artificial legs, and you are a person who knows how to overcome this kind of thing very well. Probably you will be able to walk and move more normally than with this leg that no longer is much use to you and that also gives you so many pains and makes you an invalid. And the sickness won't spread. So you no longer have to be "Frida the gimp." Think about it. Why don't you let them operate on you?'

"Frida looked at Diego. He was on the verge of tears. He didn't want to look at me. Dr. Farill was looking at me as if to say, Thank you. Frida said, 'If you say so, I'll do it.' She turned, and said to Dr. Farill, 'Prepare me for the operation.' When Diego took me home, he said to me, 'She is going to die; this is going to kill her.'

"The day before the operation, I sent Frida a little clay deer, one of those that you plant with a chia seed. It had a little monkey on it. I sent a message that said, 'Here is your deer. I hope that you come out of the operation as gay as he is with his little monkey.' And she answered me, 'Adelina you always give me courage. Tomorrow I will go under the knife. Now I will be Frida the gimp, peg leg, from the city of the Coyotes.' "

Frida was putting on a brave face. "Do you know," she said gaily to friends, "they are going to cut off my paw?" She hated to be given pitying looks. But the entries in her diary during the six months preceding the operation, when, Frida recalled, "they were saying over and over again that they were going to amputate my leg, and I wanted to die," reveal both her anguish and the desperateness of her hope.

In one horrific drawing she depicted herself as a one-legged doll, toppling off what can only be seen as an ironic pedestal for a figure so lacking in the classical ideals of balance, unity, and harmony—a classical column. The doll's body is covered with splotches. A hand and a head are falling from it. Above this grim self-portrait are the even grimmer words "I am DISINTEGRATION."

But in July, a month before her amputation, while she was in Cuernavaca, where her nurse had taken her to see if the warmer climate could improve her health and spirits, Frida wrote:

Points of Support
On my whole body there is only *one;* and I want two. In order to have two they have to cut *one.* It is the *one* that I do not have that I have to have in order to be able to walk, the other will already be dead! For me, wings are more than enough. Let them cut it and off I'll fly!!

Two pages later, there is a drawing of a headless, winged nude with a dove perched where her head should be, and a cracked marble column in place of her spine. One leg is artificial, the other is her own. The legs are labeled "Support number 1" and "Support number 2." Frida's accompanying words are: "The dove made a mistake. He was mistaken . . . . instead of going north he went south. . . . He thought wheat was water. He made a mistake." In another drawing of the nude and winged Frida, her body is covered with a thicket of dots and cross-hatching. "Are you going? No," is written above the figure. Below is the reason: "BROKEN WINGS." In a different mood, Frida drew her feet on a pedestal. The right foot is severed at the ankle. From the place where it has been cut, thorny brambles grow. The legs are tinted yellow, and the background is a wash of ink the color of blood. There is a caption: "Feet what do I want them for if I have wings to fly. 1953."

In perhaps the most heart-wrenching drawing in the diary, Frida weeps beneath a dark moon, her recumbent body dissolving into the earth, turning into a network of roots. Above her are the words "color of poison," referring perhaps to gangrene. The sun is below the surface of the earth, and in the sky, next to a small disembodied foot, she has written: "everything backward sun and moon, feet and Frida." Opposite, there is a drawing of a bare, storm-tossed tree; the wind whips off its leaves. It is lacerated, bent but not broken, and its roots dig deep into the earth.

The theme of disintegration is reiterated in *The Circle,* a tiny, undated self-portrait. Done on a round piece of sheet metal, it shows Frida's naked torso, cracked at the chest and decomposing into the

Diary pages.

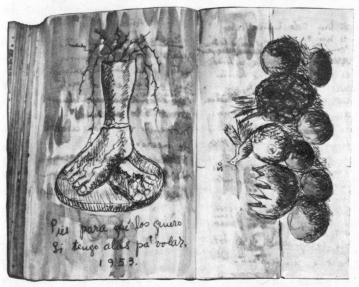

surrounding nocturnal landscape. Her lower legs metamorphose into a fungus. Her head has vanished into moss-green and earth-brown patterns behind which smoke rises. A streak of red slashes across her chest and crimson flames shoot from the place where her right shoulder has disappeared. So unlike *Roots'* sanguine vision of women's participation in life cycles, *The Circle*, like the drawing in the diary, is a fearful image of physical and psychological dissolution. To her old friend Andrés Henestrosa Frida said that she had replaced her motto "Tree of Hope, keep firm" with another: *"Esta anocheciendo en mi vida"* (Night is falling in my life).

When, in August, the doctors had finally made their decision and so had Frida, she wrote in her diary: "It is certain that they are going to amputate my right leg. I know few details, but the opinions are very serious. Dr. Luis Méndez and Dr. Juan Farill. I am very worried, but at the same time, I feel that it will be a liberation. I hope I will be able, when I am walking, to give all the strength that I have left to Diego, Everything for Diego."

On the eve of the operation, her friend Antonio Rodríguez, the art historian who had written so many laudatory articles about her art and her heroism, was by her bedside with a few other friends. Seeing how they suffered, Frida tried to cheer them up with stories and jokes. Rodríguez says, "We were almost in tears seeing this marvelous, beautiful and optimistic woman, and knowing they were going to amputate her leg. She, of course, noticed that we were suffering, and she gave us courage, saying, 'But what's the matter? Look at your faces, it's as if there were a tragedy! What tragedy? They are going to cut off my *pata*. So what?' " Later she dressed in an elegant Tehuana dress as if it were for a party, and she delivered herself to the surgeon's knife.

But Judith Ferreto was there after all the guests had gone, and Frida abandoned her façade of *alegría;* she had kept Frida company during the two days in the hospital prior to the operation, and she was at Frida's side when it was over. "The night before the operation when we were finally alone, Diego, Frida, and I, in her [hospital] room, the nurse came in to prepare her leg for surgery. It was just silent. . . . We didn't say a single word. And all the days after the operation it was silent. Even if she was furious—and I was anxious to see her furious, protesting—nothing. Just silence. Just the very few words that were completely necessary. She was not even interested in Diego's visits, and Diego was her life. The doctor came and he ordered me to force her to walk in the corridor, to go to Chapultepec Park with me, to paint, to paint, to paint. After the doctor left, she was completely upset. Then after a while, her psychiatric doctor came. He asked me what had happened. I said that she had been quiet, and that then the doctor came and ordered me to take her to the park to make her paint. The psychiatrist told me, 'Please, Judy. Don't force her to do anything. She doesn't want to live. We are forcing her to live.' "

The removal of her leg was a terrible offense to Frida's aesthetic sensibility: her sense of integrity and her self-esteem were linked with her vanity on the deepest level, and her vanity was shattered. She became so demoralized that she did not want to see people, even Diego. "Tell them I am sleeping," she would say. When she did see Diego, she ignored his presence, acting indifferent and detached. She was silent, listless, interested in nothing. "Following the loss of her leg," Rivera said in his autobiography, "Frida became deeply depressed. She no longer even wanted to hear me tell her of my love affairs, which she had enjoyed hearing about after our remarriage. She had lost her will to live."

When it came time to go home from the hospital, she at first refused to go. Ferreto recalled that "Diego had some person in his studio. Frida always respected his right to do whatever he wanted. She said, 'If I suffer because of that, it's my fault,' because he loved women and Frida just accepted it. But that person who was in his studio gave orders in Frida's house. You had to be very careful about giving orders in her house or in something related to her house. That woman did not have tact, and she made Frida suffer. That was why Frida refused to go to her house.

"One morning Frida had a crisis. The night before, Diego had been with her. It was during those bad days in the hospital. She had been very happy with Diego. But then the nurse on the floor came and said, 'Mr. Rivera, someone is waiting for you, because you have to go to the opening of an exhibition.' It was the person who was in his studio. I saw that Frida was not happy, because of that interruption, but anyway, Diego left her.

"The next morning I [got up and] went into the bathroom. She was sleeping. She had tried to kill herself that morning."

In a strange meditation on pain, loneliness, and suicide in her journal, Frida seems either to be welcoming the hand of death or expressing remorse over some recent suicide attempt. Death she calls an "enormous" and "very silent exit."

> Quietly, the pain
> Noisily the suffering
> the accumulated *poison*—
> Love was leaving me
> Now my world was a strange one
> of criminal silences
> of alert alien eyes
> mistaking the evils.
> Obscurity in the day
> I did not live the nights
> You are killing yourself!!
> with the morbid knife
> of those who are watching over you
> was it my fault?
> I admit my great guilt
> as great as the pain
> It was an enormous exit that I went through, my love.
> a very silent exit
> That carried me to death
> I had been so forgotten
> that that was my best luck
> You are killing yourself!
> YOU ARE KILLING YOURSELF
> There are those who *will no longer forget you*
> I accepted its strong hand
> *Here I am,* so that they should live.
>
> Frida

The poem's refrain, "You are killing yourself!" could be Frida talking to herself, or it could be words she heard from Diego, who despaired at all the narcotics she took to ease her suffering. When Frida says, "Here I am," at the end of the poem, she appears to be accepting either death's or life's hand.

About two months after the "person" in Rivera's studio moved out (she was Emma Hurtado, Rivera's dealer since 1946, and the woman who would become his fourth wife, in 1955), Frida went home to Coyoacán. Rivera did what he could to comfort her. Judith Ferreto recalled that he was a "wonderful collaborator" with her. Although they knew he hated being interrupted in his work, when no one else could calm Frida or stay her tears, Ferreto or Frida herself would call him, and Diego would go home and sit by Frida's side, entertaining her with stories of his adventures, reading poetry aloud, singing soft ballads, or simply holding her in his arms until medications made her sleep. As he told it in his autobiography:

> Often, during her convalescence, her nurse would phone to me that Frida was crying and saying she wanted to die. I would immediately stop painting and rush home to comfort her. When Frida was resting peacefully again, I would return to my painting and work overtime to make up for the lost hours. Some days I was so tired that I would fall asleep in my chair, high up on the scaffold.
>
> Eventually I set up a round-the-clock watch of nurses to tend to Frida's needs. The expense of this, coupled with other medical costs, exceeded what I was earning painting murals, so I supplemented my income by doing watercolors, sometimes tossing off two big watercolors a day.

Sometimes he did not rush back to his studio. Instead, he would sit in a kind of sleep watch until midnight, his great girth filling his chair and his face falling into folds of sadness and exhaustion, an old, wise, resigned, but not defeated bullfrog.

At first, Frida refused to wear her artificial leg. It was distasteful and painful to her, and when she tried to learn to walk on it she fell. Dr. Velasco y Polo recalls: "She sent to have a special boot made, because she didn't like the artificial leg. I told her, 'No one is going to notice it, because you always wear long skirts.' She answered me in foul language: 'You son of a . . . , don't meddle in what is not your business! You cut off my leg, but now I'm going to say what's to be done!' "

But after three months, she did learn to walk a short distance, and slowly her spirits rose, especially after she started painting again. To hide the leg, she had boots made of luxurious red leather with Chinese gold embroidered trim adorned with little bells. With these boots, Frida said, she would "dance her joy." And she twirled in front of friends to show off her new freedom of movement. The writer Carleta Tibón recalls that "Frida was very proud of her little red boots. Once I took Emilio Pucci's sister to see Frida, who was all dressed up as a Tehuana and probably drugged. Frida said, 'These marvelous legs! And how well they work for me!' and she danced the *jarabe tapatío* with her wooden leg."

One Sunday afternoon, Rosa Castro went to visit Frida, only to be presented with an odd spectacle. When she opened the door of the bedroom, there was Frida all dressed in white, except for her red boots; she was wearing white gloves with her many rings placed on top of her gloved fingers. Waving her hands in the air, she laughed, and said, "Don't you love them? They are the first gloves I have ever worn in my life!" She offered friends another, more somber spectacle as well. Just as in 1951 she had delighted in showing visitors her unhealing surgical wounds through the hole in her plaster cast, she now asked them to look at the stump of her leg. Mariana Morillo Safa recalls that "Frida used to joke about the amputation, but with the blackest humor. One day when I went to the house, she gave me a photograph of herself and she dedicated it: *'Su majestad es coja'* [this translates literally: "Her majesty is lame," but Frida was making a pun: *escoja* means "chooses"]. At that time she was having a fight with her old friend Dolores del Rio, and she joked, 'I will send her my leg on a silver tray as an act of vengeance.' "

In medical terms, the amputation was a simple procedure—the leg was removed at the knee—but despite the red boots and the laughter, Frida did not recover, not completely. Her diary entry for February 11, 1954, says: "They amputated my leg six months ago, they have given me centuries of torture and at moments I almost lost my 'reason.' I keep on wanting to kill myself. Diego is the one who holds me back because of my vanity in thinking that he would miss me. He has told me so and I believe him. But never in my life have I suffered more. I will wait a little while." On the next page is a flash of the old *alegría:*

I have achieved a lot.
I will be able to walk
I will be able to paint
I love Diego more
than I love myself.
My will is great
My will remains
Thanks to the magnificent love of Diego, to the honorable and intelligent work of Dr. Farill. To the purpose, so honest and loving, of Dr. Ramón Parres [Frida's psychiatrist] and to the darling persons of my whole life [Dr.] David Glusker and Dr. Eloesser.

Among the last drawings in her diary are two nude self-portraits in which she stands with her false leg. One is dedicated with love to her "child Diego." In the other, the leg is just a wooden pole, a *pata de palo*, and arrows that point to various places on her head and body suggest psychic and physical suffering.

Once Frida wrote in her diary that death was "nothing but a process in order to *exist*"; for her the process of dying—the slow decay caused by osteomyelitis and poor circulation—could not be stopped despite all the operations and other medical treatments she underwent. On April 27, 1954, her diary entry suggests that she has just recovered from a crisis, perhaps another suicide attempt, or simply a downturn in her health. She sounds as if she were in a drug-induced euphoria, but the urgency in her litany of thanks hints at an underlying despair, as if she knew her leave-taking from this world was imminent:

I came out healthy—I made the promise and I will keep it never to go backwards. Thanks to Diego, thanks to my Tere [Teresa Proenza], thanks to Gracielita and to the little girl, thanks to Judith, thanks to Isaua Mino, thanks to Lupita Zuñiga, thanks to Dr. Farill, to Dr. Polo, to Dr. Armando Navarro, to Dr. Vargas. thanks to me myself and to my enormous will to live among all the people who love me and for all those whom I love. Long live *alegría*, life, Diego, Tere, my Judith and all the nurses I have had in my life who have treated me so marvelously well. Thanks because I am a Communist and I have been all my life. Thanks to the Soviet people, to the Chinese, Czechoslovaks, and Polish people and to the people of Mexico, above all to the people of Coyoacán where my first cell was born, which was incubated in Oaxaca, in the womb of my mother, who had been born there, and married my father, Guillermo Kahlo—my mother Matilde Calderón, a brunette country girl from Oaxaca. Marvelous afternoon that we spent here at Coyoacán; the room of Frida, Diego, Tere and me. Señorita Capulina, Señor Xolotl, Señora Kosti. [The last three are names of Frida's dogs.]

She clung to notions of hope and gratitude as if she might otherwise sink into bitterness and despair. Perhaps, too, she felt that gratitude and *alegría* were, like *retablos* or prayers, rites of devotion that held some magic power: they, too, could connect her with those people she needed and loved.

Because of her loss of control, both physical and mental, terrible things happened to Frida. One accident occurred when she was confined to her bed, and needed something that lay beyond her reach. Hating not to be able to do things for herself, and not wanting to ask for help, she got up. As she told it in her diary: "Yesterday May 7 . . . when I fell on the stone floor tiles a needle entered one of my buttocks. They took me immediately to the hospital in an ambulance. I was suffering enormous pains and screaming all the way from the house to the English Hospital— They took an X-ray—various. They found the needle and they are going to take it out one of these days with a magnet. Thanks to my Diego love of all my life. Thanks to the doctors."

When she was neither drugged nor sleeping, she was often nervous to the point of hysteria. Her behavior was unpredictable. She became angry over little things, things that would not normally have bothered her. She flailed out at people, yelling abuse, even at Diego. Judith Ferreto remembers that "sometimes just a word, something like a thing done wrong, or something not clean, or even just an attitude, could make Frida explode because of her sensitivity. If they love you, they really love you, especially Frida. If she loved you, you could be sure that she loved you. She could never show a thing that she was not feeling, and she could not keep things inside, except for her pain, her suffering."

There were times when Frida's illness and wild behavior were more than Rivera could bear. Raquel Tibol tells of an occasion when Frida was extremely sick and lay upstairs in her bedroom, half unconscious from drugs. "Diego and I were downstairs in the living room. He had come home to eat, but he didn't want to eat. He began to cry like a child, and he said, 'If I were brave, I would kill her. I cannot stand to see her suffer so.' He cried like a child, cried and cried. It was a kind of pious love."

His misery at seeing Frida miserable drove him away from her. Often he stayed away for days at a time, and Frida became lonely, angry, desperate. "But the moment Diego appeared," Rosa Castro remembers, "she would change and say, 'My child, where have you been, my child?' in the most soft and loving voice. Then Diego would go and kiss her. There was a dish of fruit near the bed, and she would say, 'My darling child, do you want a little piece of fruit?' Diego would answer 'chi' instead of 'si,' as if he were a little boy."

Once when Adelina Zendejas and Carlos Pellicer were having lunch in the patio of the Coyoacán house, Frida threw a bottle of water at Diego. He ducked, and it just missed his head. The noise of glass crashing on the stone floor shocked her out of her rage. She began to cry. "Why did I do it?" she asked. "Tell me, why did I do it? If I continue like this, I would prefer to die!" Driving Adelina home after lunch,

Rivera said, 'I must have her put in a home. I must commit her. It is not possible to go on like this." Like everyone except Cristina, Diego withdrew from Frida. Judith Ferreto tried to explain to her that Diego had to run away from her because he loved her so much that he could not bear to witness her suffering. Sometimes this explanation was consoling, but usually Frida was bitter:

Every night he stays up. He does not come home early, even one night. Where does he go? I no longer even ask him anything. He may go to the theater with his architect friends, to lectures. Every day [he appears] at eleven or twelve o'clock; one or four in the afternoon. From where? Who knows! The next morning he gets up, he comes to say hello to me: "How are you, *linda* [pretty one]?" "Fine, and you?" "Better." "Are you coming home for lunch?" "I don't know, I'll send word." He generally eats in the studio. His lunch is sent with Oswaldo. I eat alone. At night I don't see him because he arrives so late. I take my pills, and I never see him, he is never with me, and he is a horror, and he doesn't like me to smoke, he doesn't like me to sleep, he makes such a scandal about everything that he wakes one up. He needs his liberty and he has it.

"Her relations with Diego in this final and tragic period were irregular," writer Loló de la Torriente remembers. "Some easy, sweet, and affectionate, others of tempestuousness and fury. Patiently, the maestro humored her, supported her in those rages, indulged her, but he ended by calling the doctor, who calmed her with palliatives. She would go to sleep and then everything in that large house was like a tomb. . . . During this period Frida spoke little. She lay or sat near the large window in her bedroom and watched the pigeons and branches and a fountain moving in the garden."

Frida's feelings toward Diego changed from hour to hour, from minute to minute. "No one knows how much I love Diego," she said. "But neither does anyone know how difficult it is to live with that *señor*. And he is so strange in his way of living that I have to guess whether he loves me; because I think that he does love me, even if it is 'in his way.' I always say this sentence when our marriage is discussed: that we have joined 'hunger with the desire to eat.'" Presumably she meant that she was hungry and Diego greedy: hunger takes what it can get; greed takes what it wants, here and there, for its own pleasure.

Her emotional excesses had much to do with her increased dependence on drugs. She had permission to acquire them from a government office, but her need now went beyond what she could purchase in this manner, and often she turned to Diego; he always knew how to find them. She sometimes became wild, and made desperate phone calls to friends to borrow money. At one point, Rivera tried to stop her drug addiction by substituting alcohol. Frida consumed two liters of cognac a day—without giving up the drugs.

She took huge doses and mixed them in the most unorthodox ways. Several times when Raquel Tibol was helping Cristina care for Frida, she watched her put three or more doses of Demerol into a large syringe and add various small vials of other narcotics. Frida would ask Tibol to inject her, and since her back was a mass of scabs from other injections as well as scars from operations, it was hard to find a place to insert the needle. Frida would cry, "Touch, touch, and where you find a soft place, inject!"

"Once I went to see her with Lupe Marín," Jesús Ríos y Valles remembers. "She was completely lost. She asked me to get her an injection. I asked, 'Where am I going to get it?' And I told her that Diego and her doctor had told me that she should not have any more injections. Frida was as if crazy. She said, 'Please! please!' I said, 'Anyway, where will I get it?' She said, 'Open that drawer.' In the drawer, behind a group of Diego's drawings, was a box with thousands of vials of Demerol."

Frida had painted almost nothing for a year when in the spring of 1954 she forced herself once more out of bed and into the studio. There, tied to her wheelchair with a sash to support her back, she worked at her easel for as long as she could stand the pain, then kept on painting in bed.

Painting was now a devotional act. She made paintings that communicate her political faith and several "alive still lifes"; all have a visionary quality and a kind of exuberance that has much to do with the euphoric effect of Demerol. One 1954 *Still Life* is divided into four quarters (earth and sky, day and night) and the sun's rays become a web of glowing red roots or veins that embrace both the fruits and the dove nesting in their midst. Where the roots end at the bottom of the painting, they spell the word "LUZ" (light) plus Frida's name. Although this painting is rough in facture, harsh in color, and unsubtle in concept, there is something gallant about the passion and hope that Frida projects upon oranges and melons. It is clear that as she was painting the embrace of life by light, she knew that the final night was near.

To find the scenario for her expression of political faith, Frida once again turned to *retablos*. In *Frida and Stalin*, she sits in front of a huge portrait of Stalin that is propped on her easel; like the painting of her doctor in *Self-Portrait with the Portrait of Doctor Farill*, the image of Stalin functions as the holy intercessor in an ex-voto. Likewise, in *Marxism Will Give Health to the Sick*, Frida, the protagonist dressed in an orthopedic corset, is saved by the miracle-making saint, Karl Marx (figure 80). His white-bearded head floats in the sky; a hand projecting from it strangles an American eagle, a caricature of Uncle Sam. Projecting from Marx's head on the other side, a white peace dove hovers protectively over Frida and over a globe that displays a huge red continent, no doubt Soviet Russia. The earth beneath her feet has been politicized too. Under the peace dove and Russia, rivers run blue. Beneath the night sky that surrounds the American eagle, rivers run red. Two enormous disembodied hands (one with the eye of wisdom in its palm) descend from the sky (from the vicinity of Marx) to support Frida. The Marxian hands and the red book, probably Marx's *Capital*, that she holds allow her to cast aside her crutches. Frida told Judith Ferreto that in this painting, "For the first time, I am not crying anymore."

Though flags may wave in these paintings, peace doves may fly, and Marxist heroes occupy the heavens, Frida's last works remained personal and self-identifying; they could never serve as political propaganda. Instead, like prayers, they affirmed faith. She knew this when she complained to her nurse in bitter frustration over her inability to make paintings with social value: "I cannot, I cannot, I cannot!" She knew she could not, indeed, even as she told Antonio Rodríguez: "I want my work to be a contribution to the struggle for peace and liberty"; and "if I do not transmit more ideas in my painting, it is because I have nothing to say, and I don't feel that I have the authority to give lessons; but it is never because I think that art should be something mute." Frida's paintings are hardly mute. They shriek their personal messages so passionately that there are no decibels left for propaganda.

Like *Showcase in Detroit*, the curious, ugly landscape called *The Brick Kilns* was inspired by something Frida happened to see on an outing. One spring day, Dr. Farill took her for a drive on the outskirts of the city. They passed a group of brick kilns, and something about the bleak, archaic beauty of these round ovens caught the attention of the crippled pair. Dr. Farill said he wanted to paint the kilns. Frida said she would do it. When her doctor suggested that she make a sketch on the spot, Frida replied that she did not need to, she would carry the sketch in her head. *The Brick Kilns* shows a group of kilns with a man in a sombrero sitting and stoking one of the ovens with a long stick. The style testifies to Frida's loss of control. Brushwork is messy; impasto is gritty; color is murky. The general unpleasantness of the scene is underscored by wretched, leafless trees and ominous clouds of smoke that billow from the brick ovens. Since it was Frida's expressed desire that she be cremated, the sight of the brick kilns on her outing with her surgeon probably turned her thoughts to her own end. Certainly the painting foreshadows death.

Raquel Tibol, who was with Frida at the time, recalls that when Frida finished it, she gave the work a solemn but reckless look and asked, "Haven't you seen the other? It's of my face inside a sunflower. It was a commission. I don't like the idea; it seems to me that I am drowning inside the flower." Tibol found the painting Frida mentioned, and brought it to her. It was, like *The Brick Kilns,* painted in a slapdash way with thick impasto. But unlike the other, it was full of movement, an expression of joy. Tibol remembers:

> Irritated by the vital energy that radiated from an object that she had created, an energy that she, in her own movements, no longer possessed, she took a knife made in Michoacán which had a straight and cutting edge, and overcoming the lassitude produced by her nocturnal injections, with tears in her eyes, and a convulsive grin on her tremulous lips, she began to scratch the painting slowly, too slowly. The noise of steel against very dry oil paint grew like a lament in the morning of this space of Coyoacán where she had been born. . . . She scratched, annihilating, destroying herself; it was her sacrifice and her expiation.

She may have been repelled by the radiant energy of the self-portrait as a sunflower, but as the darkness of her own twilight thickened, she wanted to be nearer to light. In June, she asked that her four-poster bed be moved from her small corner bedroom out into the adjacent passageway which led to her studio. She wished, she said, to be able to see more greenery; the tiny passageway had glass-paned metal doors that opened onto a flight of steps leading down to the garden. From this vantage point, she could see the pigeons that lived in the ceramic pots that Rivera had embedded in the pitted stone walls of the new wing of the house. When the summer rains came, she spent many hours watching the flutter of light on leaves, the branches moving in the wind, and the rain pelting onto the roof and pouring from the gutters.

Mariana Morillo Safa remembers: "In her last days she was lying down, unable to move. She was all eyes. I could not stand to see her again. Her character was totally changed. She fought with everyone. Since I stayed only a short while, she was nice to me, but it was as though she was thinking of something else, and just trying to be nice. She couldn't stand noise and didn't want too many people near her. She did not want to see children. Just her arms and hands moved, and she threw things at people. 'Stop bothering me! Peace!' she would cry as she beat people with her cane. She would yell, 'Bring me this! I'm talking to you!' Her cane was beside her bed, and if you didn't do things fast, she'd use it. She was very impatient because she couldn't do things by herself. All she could do was comb her hair and put on lipstick. Earlier, she had not worn makeup except lipstick. At the end of her life, she used makeup, and she could not control her colors. It was grotesque. She was a horrible imitation of the old Frida Kahlo."

Judith Ferreto: "During those days, she was going down rapidly. . . . I think that she foresaw that she was going down and down. . . . That morning she called me up. I always knew in her voice how she was; it's very easy to note in the voice when a person is completely desperate, and she was completely desperate that day. And she said, 'Oh, please, Judy, come! Can you come here, Judy, to help me? I cannot do anything. I am completely upset. Please come and help me.'

"I went and spent most of the day with her. She was painting in the studio . . . . she was always so beautiful, with very beautiful dresses. But that day was different. These pleats were separated from the dress in large part. Her hair was completely unarranged, her eyes out of their orbits. She was painting, and was all full of paint on her hands, knuckles, and everything. . . . I took her with all my love. I put her in bed and I said, 'Do you want me to fix you up?' She said, 'Yes.' I asked, 'Which dress do you want to wear?' 'Please bring me the one you prepared before you left, because all those things were done with love, and there is no love around here now. And you know that love is the only reason for living. So bring the one that was made with love.' I fixed her hair and everything, and she was resting . . . so sweet, so angry, so nasty."

The visit ended with a fight and a reconciliation. Some visitors had stayed too long, and Judith, seeing how they exhausted Frida, had asked them to leave. Frida was furious. Judith, she felt, was ordering her around in her own home. But they made up, and Frida tried to press her former nurse into accepting the gift of a ring and a Tehuana dress, both of which Judith refused. As she explained it: "I was exasperated that day, because I was convinced, as a nurse, that it was impossible to help Frida Kahlo. I had seen her in many crises in her life. In most of them I helped her, but then Frida had both legs, and I knew that without the leg it was impossible to help her anymore.

"During those days, sometimes some children came to the house to visit her . . . even the child of her sister, whom she loved very much. And after they left her she would say, 'Oh, Judy, I don't like children anymore. I don't want them. I can't tell them not to come, because it's not good, but I would prefer not to see children anymore.' After the amputation, she hated children. . . . The operation destroyed a personality. She loved life, she really loved life, but it was completely different after they amputated her leg.

"At the end of the day, Carlos Pellicer appeared. And I was so happy, because it was almost the time when I was supposed to leave her, and the day had been awful. I was so happy, because I knew how much they loved each other. At the last moment, Frida took a doll without a leg, and she said, 'That is me without my leg.' That was her last present, and also a little bunch of very beautiful flowers in a small glass. She said, 'Take it with you.' And I took a taxi, and on the way I dropped the flowers on the street. I was furious with life, and it was the last day that I saw her."

Toward the end of June, her health seemed to be improving. "What are you going to give me as a prize since I'm getting better?" she teased. Not waiting for the answer, she said, "I'd like a doll best." She was demanding with her friends, insisting, for example, when they talked to her on the telephone, that they promise to visit. "Soon" was not good enough; they had to assure her that they would come that very afternoon. She begged people to spend the night with her. She even invited Lupe Marín, with whom she had a weeping reconciliation. Lupe declined the invitation.

She was full of hopes and plans for the future. She said she wanted to adopt a child. She spoke of her longing to travel. An invitation to

Russia tantalized her, but she said that she did not want to go without Rivera, who had not been readmitted to the Communist party in spite of his several applications. She was excited about the prospect of traveling to Poland, where she planned to follow a medical treatment recommended to her by Dr. Farill. Diego, she said, thought it was a good idea; he had offered to accompany her. What Frida looked forward to most of all was her and Diego's silver wedding anniversary. On August 21 they would have been married twenty-five years. She told a friend, *"Traigan mucha raza* [Bring lots of people], because there will be a great Mexican fiesta!" Already she had acquired her anniversary present for Diego. It was a beautiful antique gold ring. She wanted the anniversary celebration to be a popular event, like a *posada.* All the people of Coyoacán would come.

It was one of those cold, dank rainy-season days when, on July 2, 1954, Frida disobeyed doctor's orders and left her bed in order to participate in a Communist demonstration. Although she was convalescing from bronchopneumonia, she wanted to express her feeling of solidarity with the crowd of more than ten thousand Mexicans who took to the streets, walking from Santo Domingo Plaza to the Zócalo to protest the ouster of Guatemala's left-leaning President Jacobo Arbenz and the CIA's imposition on that country of a reactionary regime headed by General Castillo Armas. This was her last public appearance, and Frida made herself into a heroic spectacle. As Diego pushed her wheelchair slowly through the bumpy streets, prominent figures in the world of Mexican culture followed in her wake.

As in so many of Rivera's murals, Frida was a living exemplar of moral fortitude, a rallying point for revolutionary zeal. Photographs taken during the demonstration show her holding a banner emblazoned with the peace dove in her left hand, her right hand clenched in a fighting fist. Her gaunt, weary face looks older than her years, a battlefield of suffering. Too sick to bother with coquetry, she had not arranged her hair in its usual crown of braids. Instead, she simply covered it with an old wrinkled kerchief. The only signs of her habitual flamboyance were the many rings that made her fist of protest sparkle like a scepter. Frida withstood the discomfort of sitting in her wheelchair for four hours, joining in the cry of the multitude: *"Gringos, asesinos, fuera!"* (Yankee assassins, get out!) When she finally went home, she had the satisfaction of knowing that her presence had meant much to her fellow demonstrators. She confided to a friend, "I only want three things in life: to live with Diego, to continue painting, and to belong to the Communist party."

She would not have any of these things for long. As a result of her participation in the protest her pneumonia hung on, and to make matters worse, a few days later she got out of bed at night and, again disobeying her doctor's orders, took a bath, thus making herself violently ill.

Frida knew she was dying. In one of the last pages of her diary, she drew skeletons in costumes like Posada's *Calaveras*. In bold letters, she wrote: "MUERTES EN RELAJO" (the dead having a fling). For her, death was a fact of life, part of an eternal cycle, something to be faced head on. "We look for calm or 'peace,' " she wrote in her diary, "because we anticipate death, since we die every moment." When Cachucha Manuel González Ramírez went to see her shortly before she died, she discussed the details of her demise openly. "It was not awkward to speak of her [death]," González Ramírez recalled, "because Frida was not afraid of it." What did worry her, though, was the thought of being lowered into the ground in a recumbent position. She had suffered so often, in so many hospitals, in this posture, Frida explained, that she did not want to go to her grave lying down. For this reason, she had asked to be cremated.

The night before Frida's birthday, she said to Teresa Proenza, "Let's start celebrating my birthday. I want, as a present, for you to stay here to accompany me so that you wake up here tomorrow." Teresa agreed, and early the next morning put on a record of "Las Mañanitas," Mexico's birthday song, so that Frida would awake to music. Frida spent the morning in bed, sleeping off the narcotics she had taken. When she awoke again, she received a few visitors. Later, dressed in her heavy white cotton Yalalag *huipil* with the lavender tassel, her face made up, she was carried downstairs to the dining room. There, surrounded by all her birthday flowers, she entertained her friends. People came and went. One hundred guests ate a luncheon of Mexican dishes—turkey *mole*, chilis, and *tamales* with *atole*. Frida was full of her old vivacity. At eight o'clock in the evening, she went upstairs and continued to hold court in her bedroom. A letter from the women of the Communist party gave her great pleasure. A sonnet sent by Carlos Pellicer delighted her too.

In the last pages of Frida's journal are strange winged female figures that are much more chaotically drawn than the winged self-portraits of a few months before. The final entry is a drawing of a black angel risen into the sky—surely the angel of death. Such figures point to a desire for transcendence that is a counterpart of the desire for earthy rootedness expressed in Frida's other drawings: even her idea of death was split between the Catholic and pagan traditions. The last words in her diary reveal most poignantly her will to look at the bleakest realities with *alegría*. "I hope the exit is joyful—and I hope never to come back— Frida."

These words and her last drawing suggest that Frida committed suicide, yet the cause of her death, on Tuesday, July 13, 1954, was reported as a "pulmonary embolism." Certainly Rivera's account of his wife's death does not preclude the possibility of suicide. But at the same time he maintains the image of Frida as indomitable in her battle for life. He said that the night before she died, Frida was critically ill with pneumonia.

I sat beside her bed until 2:30 in the morning. At four o'clock she complained of severe discomfort. When a doctor arrived at daybreak, he found that she had died a short time before of an embolism of the lungs.

When I went into her room to look at her, her face was tranquil and seemed more beautiful than ever. The night before she had given me a ring she had bought me as a gift for our twenty-fifth anniversary, still seventeen days away. I asked her why she was presenting it so early and she replied, "Because I feel I am going to leave you very soon."

But though she knew she would die, she must have put up a struggle for life. Otherwise why should death have been obliged to surprise her by stealing away her breath while she was asleep?

Many of Frida's friends do not believe that she would have taken her own life. To the very end, they say, she retained her hope and gallant will. Others suspect that she died from an overdose of drugs that may—or may not—have been accidental. It is true that her circulation was bad and that her recent bout with bronchopneumonia had left her frail.

After Frida died, her friend Bambi published a long report on her last hours in the *Excelsior*. It said that Frida had received no visitors the day before her death because she was in great pain. For a little while in the afternoon, Diego had been with her. They chatted and laughed together, and she told him that she had slept most of the morning, because Dr. Velasco y Polo had told her she should. She joked about a special feeding cup for invalids that her nurse, Señora Mayet (who was working for her again), had brought in order to feed her liquid foods. This, said Frida, was the "year of broth." It seemed to her that she had consumed nothing but soup.

That evening she gave Diego the ring which was to be his anniversary present, and told him that she wanted to say goodbye to him and to a few of her closest friends. At ten o'clock that night, Rivera called Dr. Velasco y Polo. "Frida is very sick, I would like you to come and see her." The doctor came and found Frida in critical condition from bronchopneumonia. When he left her bedside and went downstairs, Rivera was sitting and talking with a friend. The doctor said, "Diego, Frida is very sick." Diego replied, "Yes, I know." "But she is really sick, she has a high fever," the doctor insisted. "Yes," said Diego.

At 11:00 P.M., after being given fruit juice, Frida went to sleep, with Diego sitting by her side. Certain that she was fast asleep, he left to spend the rest of the night at his San Angel studio. At four o'clock, Frida awoke and complained that she was in pain. Her nurse calmed her and straightened her sheets. She stayed near Frida until she slept again. It was still dark at six in the morning when Señora Mayet heard someone knocking and, on her way to open the door, paused by Frida's bed to tuck in her covers. Frida's eyes were open and staring. She touched Frida's hands. They were cold. Señora Mayet called Rivera's chauffeur, Manuel, and told him what had happened. The old chauffeur who had worked for Guillermo Kahlo and had known Frida from birth, took the news to Diego. "Señor," he said, *"murió la niña Frida"* (Miss Frida has died).

Chapter 25

Viva la Vida

WHEN FRIDA DIED, Diego's usually ebullient, rotund face became haggard and gray. "He became an old man in a few hours, pale and ugly," one friend recalls. A reporter from *Excelsior* came to photograph him and to extract quotes, but Rivera refused to be interviewed. "I beg of you don't ask me anything," he said. He turned his face to the wall and remained silent.

The news of Frida's death traveled fast. Diego called Lupe Marín early in the morning, and she and Emma Hurtado, Rivera's soon-to-be fourth wife, drove together to his third wife's home. "Diego was completely alone," Lupe recalled. "I stayed near him, and took his hand. By 8:30 A.M. Frida's friends began to arrive, and I said goodbye and left."

Frida lay on her four-poster bed dressed in a black Tehuana skirt and in the white *huipil* from Yalalag. Her friends braided her hair with ribbons and flowers. They adorned her with earrings, necklaces of silver, coral, and jade, and placed her hands across her body; every finger wore a ring. A white pillow with starched bands of Mexican lace framed her face. Beside her head was a vase of roses. A single foot with bright red toenails protruded below the hem of her long skirt. Next to it were branches of red flowers. From the shelf by the bed, Chinese dolls and pre-Columbian idols stared over the scene.

Large numbers of people, many of them unable to restrain their tears, filed past Frida's bed that day. Olga Campos was among the early mourners: "It was terrible for me. Frida was still warm when I arrived at the house around ten or eleven in the morning. She got goose pimples when I kissed her, and I started screaming, 'She's alive! She's alive!' But she was dead."

Bernice Kolko arrived in the middle of the day: "Naturally, when I came there to that house, I was hysterical. I met her sister Cristina and she took me around and said, 'We lost our Frida.' And I went to her bed, and saw her there, and then we waited for some time. We couldn't see Diego, because Diego had locked himself in his room."

At 6:30 P.M., all her jewelry except for her rings, a Tehuantepec chain, and some cheap shiny beads was taken off Frida's body, and she was placed in a gray coffin and driven to the Palace of Fine Arts. "Diego went with his chauffeur all alone in his car," Bernice Kolko said. "He didn't want anybody to go with him."

There, in the spacious lobby of the grand neoclassical structure, Mexico's greatest cultural center, Frida Kahlo lay in state, Rivera in agitation at her side. He had asked Dr. Velasco y Polo for a death certificate, so that he could have Frida's body cremated, but the doctor had refused, for what seem to have been legalistic reasons. So Rivera obtained the certificate from his friend and ex-brother-in-law, Dr. Marín. But even with the certificate, he was still not convinced that his wife was dead.

Rosa Castro tells this story: "When she was lying in state in Bellas Artes, Diego was standing with Dr. Federico Marín, Lupe's brother. I went over and said, 'What's the matter, Diego?' He said, 'It's that we are not very sure that Frida is dead.' Dr. Marín said, 'Diego, I assure you that she is dead.' Diego said, 'No, but it horrifies me to think that she still has capillary action. The hairs on her skin still stand up. It horrifies me that we should bury her in this condition.' I said, 'But it's very simple. Let the doctor open her veins. If the blood doesn't flow, it's because she's dead.' So they cut Frida's skin, and there was no blood. They cut her jugular, and one or two drops came out. She was dead. Diego didn't want to believe that she was dead, because of his terrible desire not to separate himself from her. He loved her very much. When Frida died, he looked like a soul cut in two."

All that night and the following morning, Frida lay in the huge, high-ceilinged hall. Her coffin was set upon a black cloth spread on the floor, and surrounded by masses of red flowers.

Permission to honor Frida in this way had been given by Andrés Iduarte, her old schoolmate at the Preparatoria, who was then director of the National Institute of Fine Arts, on condition that Rivera promise to keep politics out of the ceremony. "No political banners, no slogans, no speeches, no politics," he had warned. Diego had nodded: "Yes, Andrés." But when the first honor guard, consisting of Iduarte and several other Department of Fine Arts officials, entered the vestibule where Frida's coffin was, Frida's disciple Arturo García Bustos emerged from a group clustered around Rivera and moved quickly toward the coffin. Suddenly the casket was covered with a shiny red flag emblazoned with a hammer and sickle set in the middle of a white star.

Iduarte and his aides retreated in consternation. From his office upstairs, he sent Rivera a message reminding him of his promise. A note brought word that Rivera was so stricken by grief that he could not be disturbed. Unfortunately for Iduarte, President Ruiz Cortínez was away from the capital at that time, so the director turned to the presidential secretary for advice. He must persuade Rivera to remove the Communist flag, he was told, but he must also avoid a scandal. Rivera, surrounded by his leftist friends, would have none of it. He threatened to take Frida's body out into the street and stand guard there if the flag was removed.

Iduarte was greatly relieved when former president Lázaro Cárdenas arrived to take his place in Frida's honor guard; if a man of such high rank was willing to tolerate the red flag, it might not be so improper after all. A telephone call to the presidential secretary confirmed his feelings. "If General Cárdenas is standing guard," he was told, "you should stand guard too."

Thus was a national idol transformed, at least temporarily, into a Communist heroine. One result of this "Russophile farce," as the press called it, was that Iduarte lost his directorship (he returned to his chair as professor of Latin American literature at Columbia University). For his part, Rivera was delighted to be readmitted to the Communist party two and a half months after Frida's funeral.

All through the night and the following morning, the honor guards stood at the four corners of Frida's coffin. They included Communist notables as well as intimate friends and family. Lola Alvarez Bravo was there, and Juan O'Gorman, Aurora Reyes, María Asúnsulo, and the muralist José Chávez Morado. Three of Frida's sisters stood watch too, and so did Rivera's daughters, Lupe and Ruth. Two representatives from the Russian embassy came for a few minutes. Diego, formally dressed in a dark suit, his face drawn with exhaustion and grief, stayed near Frida's coffin all evening and took part in several of the watches. He had pulled himself together sufficiently to shake hands with consolers and to cooperate with the press. He told one newspaper reporter that Frida had died of a lung embolism in the presence of an osteologist between three and four in the morning. He proudly said that his wife had painted about two hundred paintings in her lifetime, that Frida was the only Hispano-American painter to have conquered the Louvre, and that her last painting, done a month before, was a still life of watermelons, full of color and *alegría*.

The last honor guard consisted of Rivera, Iduarte, Siqueiros, Covarrubias, Henestrosa, and the prominent agronomist and leftist politician César Martino, plus the former president, Cárdenas, and his son Cuauhtémoc. By noon on July 14, more than six hundred people had honored Frida's coffin. At 12:10 P.M., Cristina Kahlo asked the assembled crowd to sing the national anthem and then the "Corrido de Cananea," a ballad that interweaves indignation at the injustices suffered by the Mexican people with an unhappy love story. With great solemnity, Cárdenas moved his arms to keep the beat. Rivera, Siqueiros, Iduarte, and others hoisted Frida's coffin onto their shoulders and carried it down the broad marble steps of the Palace of Fine Arts and out into the rain. A funeral procession of some five hundred mourners followed on foot as the hearse carrying Frida's coffin moved slowly down Avenida Juárez.

The crematorium at the Panteón Civil de Dolores (the civil cemetery) was small and extremely primitive. Crowded into the tiny hot room were friends and family, cultural representatives of various socialist countries, the secretaries of the Mexican Communist party and the Communist Youth Organization, as well as luminaries from the worlds of art and literature. Outside, hundreds of guests stood among the tombstones beneath the ceaseless rain. Frida's coffin was brought into the anteroom and opened. She lay with a diadem of red carnations around her head and a *rebozo* covering her shoulders. Someone placed an enormous bouquet of flowers at the head of the coffin. Then, standing next to Frida, and with Rivera by his side, Andrés Iduarte gave a grandiloquent funeral oration:

> Frida has died. Frida has died.
> The brilliant and self-willed creature who, in our day, lit up the classrooms of the National Preparatory School has died. . . . An extraordinary artist has died: alert spirit, generous heart, sensibility in living flesh, love of art even unto death, intimate of Mexico in vertigo and in grace. . . . Friend, sister of the people, great daughter of Mexico: you are still alive. . . . You live on. . . .

Carlos Pellicer read his sonnets to Frida. A verse from one of them says: "You will always be alive on the earth,/you will always be a mutiny full of auroras,/the heroic flower of successive dawns." Adelina Zendejas spoke about her memories of Frida at the Preparatoria and about Frida's life and work as an example of the "iron will to live." Juan Pablo Sainz, a member of the Central Committee of the Mexican Communist Party, spoke in the name of the party, seizing the occasion to discuss the problems of the contemporary world.

At a quarter past one, Rivera and various family members lifted Frida out of the coffin and laid her on an automatic cart that would carry her along iron tracks to the crematory oven. Rivera stood by her side with his hands clenched into fists, his face and body sunken in sorrow. He bent to kiss her forehead. Friends crowded near to say goodbye.

Rivera wanted to send Frida off with music. With arms held high and hands in fists, the gathering sang the *Internationale,* the national anthem, "The Young Guard," Lenin's funeral march, and other political songs. At one-fifty the door of the oven opened, and the cart carrying Frida's body began to move toward the fire. Now the mourners sang ballads of farewell: "Adios, Mi Chaparita," "Adios, Mariquita Linda," "La Embarcación," and "La Barca de Oro," which goes:

> I'm off now to the port where the golden ship lies
> Waiting to take me away.
> I'm leaving you now, this is goodbye.
> Farewell, my love, goodbye forever.
> You'll never see me again, nor hear my songs,
> But the seas will overflow with my tears
> Goodbye, my love . . . goodbye.

"Rivera stood with his hands in fists," Monroy recalls. "When the door to the oven opened to receive the cart with Frida in it, there was an infernal heat that forced us all to press up against the back wall of the room because we could not stand the heat. But Diego did not move."

It was at this point that something almost as grotesque as one of Goya's *Los Caprichos* took place. Adelina Zendejas remembers: "Everyone was hanging on to Frida's hands when the cart began to pull her body toward the oven's entrance. They threw themselves on top of her, and yanked at her fingers in order to take off her rings, because they wanted to have something that belonged to her."

People were crying. Cristina became hysterical and began to scream when she saw her sister's body slide toward the oven. She had to be carried outside. With good reason: at the moment when Frida entered the furnace, the intense heat made her sit up, and her blazing hair stood out from her face in an aureole. Siqueiros said that when the flames ignited her hair, her face appeared as if smiling in the center of a large sunflower.

The fires in the old-fashioned crematorium took four hours to do their job. During the wait, the crowd kept on singing. Diego wept and dug his nails into the palms of his hands again and again, making them bleed. Finally, the oven door opened, and the red-hot cart containing Frida's ashes slid out. A blast of suffocating heat sent people once again reeling back against the walls of the room, covering their faces for protection. Only Rivera and Cárdenas calmly stood their ground.

Frida's ashes retained the shape of her skeleton for a few minutes before being dispersed by currents of air. When Rivera saw this, he slowly lowered his clenched fist and reached into the right-hand pocket of his jacket to take out a small sketchbook. With his face completely absorbed in what he was doing, he drew Frida's silvery skeleton. Then he fondly gathered up her ashes in a red cloth, and put them in a cedar box. He asked that his ashes be mixed with Frida's when he died. (The request has never been fulfilled; it was deemed more fitting for the great muralist to lie in the resting place of Mexico's most famous citizens, the Rotonda de los Hombres Ilustres.)

In his autobiography, he wrote: "July 13, 1954, was the most tragic day of my life. I had lost my beloved Frida, forever. . . . Too late now, I realized that the most wonderful part of my life had been my love for Frida."

Not long after Frida died, Rivera's granddaughter was baptized in the Coyoacán house. For the occasion, Diego dressed up a Judas figure, perhaps a skeleton, in Frida's clothes, and a bag containing her ashes and her plaster corset was laid in a cradle. It was a gesture Frida would have applauded, a festive and *Mexicanista* approach to the ancient duality of birth as the cradle of death and death as the bearer of life.

When the Frida Kahlo Museum first opened, in July 1958, Frida's ashes were placed in a sack on her bed; over them was her plaster death mask, wrapped in one of her *rebozos*—a ghostly Frida sitting in bed. A garland of flowers formed an arc over the assemblage, the flowers echoed in the garland that decks the dead child in the antique painting above Frida's bed.

Later, the ashes were placed in a pre-Columbian jar in the shape of a rotund, headless female, and a bronze cast of the death mask was set on a pedestal above it. The urn seems pregnant with life, just like the clay idol in *Four Inhabitants of Mexico,* which Frida described as pregnant, "because, being dead, she has something alive inside."

Today, Frida's home is open, as it was in her lifetime, to visitors. Rivera gave the house, complete with its art collection, including the paintings by Rivera and others that Frida owned, and with all its folkloric furnishings, to the Mexican people in 1955, in order to perpetuate his wife's memory. "I made one other stipulation," said Rivera, "that a corner be set aside for me, alone, for whenever I felt the need to return to the atmosphere which recreated Frida's presence."

Some visitors to the museum are Frida's friends. Others never knew Frida, but they leave the house feeling that they did, for the relics displayed there—Frida's costumes, jewelry, toys, dolls, letters, books, art materials, her love notes to Diego, her marvelous collection of popular art—offer a vivid picture of her personality and of the ambience in which she lived and worked. They create the perfect setting for those of her paintings and drawings that hang in what was once her living room. Upstairs, in Frida's studio, her wheelchair is drawn up before her easel. One of her plaster corsets, decorated with plants and thumbtacks, sits on her four-poster bed with its mirror-lined canopy. The Chinese dolls that substituted for children still stare from the shelf. Beside her bed is a doll bed, now empty. A skeleton dangles from the canopy of another four-poster bed, and Frida's crutches lean against the footboard.

The museum does more than recreate an atmosphere; it serves to convince us of the specificity and realism of the fantastic imagery in Frida's paintings and of the intimate bond between her life and her art. Because she was an invalid, the house in Coyoacán became her world. Because she was an artist, the paintings hanging in that house were an expansion and a transformation of that world; they powerfully evoke and commemorate the remarkable life she lived within it.

Frida's last painting hangs on the living room wall (plate XXXV). In it, set against a brilliant blue sky that is divided into lighter and darker halves, are watermelons, the most loved of Mexican fruit, whole, halved, quartered, and otherwise carved into pieces. The paint is laid on with far more control than in other late still lifes; shapes are solidly defined and composed. It is as if Frida had gathered and focused what was left of her vitality in order to paint this final statement of *alegría*. Sliced and chopped, the pieces of fruit acknowledge the imminence of death, but their luscious red flesh celebrates the fullness of life. Eight days before she died, when her hours were darkened by calamity, Frida Kahlo dipped her brush in blood-red paint and inscribed her name plus the date and the place of execution, Coyoacán, Mexico, across the crimson pulp of the foremost slice. Then, in large capital letters, she wrote her final salute to life: VIVA LA VIDA.

ACKNOWLEDGMENTS

The good will and generous cooperation of many people contributed to the making of this book. In particular, I am deeply indebted to Dolores Olmedo, president of the Technical Committee of the Diego Rivera Trust, not only for her intelligent insights and continuous support, but also for giving me access to and permission to quote from Frida Kahlo's diary and personal archive. In addition, Mrs. Olmedo allowed me to reproduce her marvelous collection of Frida Kahlo's paintings. I owe an equal debt of gratitude to Alejandro Gómez Arias, who, in a series of conversations, threw light on Kahlo's early years. He also kindly trusted me with Frida's letters to him and read my manuscript with intelligence and care. Special thanks go also to Isolda Kahlo for showing me family photographs and for talking about her aunt Frida for many hours. Among others I wish to thank for letting me draw on Kahlo's correspondence and private papers are Joyce Campbell, Alberto Misrachi, Mariana Morillo Safa, Mimi Muray, Emmy Lou Packard, and Ella Wolfe. All of these were unstinting with their help in other ways as well.

Numerous people gave freely of their time and recollections in interviews with me in Mexico, the United States, and France. Lucienne Bloch, who knew Frida intimately during the 1930s, shared her diary written while she lived with Frida and Diego Rivera in Detroit, and her vivid anecdotes helped me to perceive Frida's wit, vitality, and passion. Jean van Heijenoort, Trotsky's secretary from 1932 to 1940, was invaluable in providing a perceptive and precise picture of Trotsky's friendship with the Riveras. Clare Boothe Luce, a brilliant raconteuse, told the story of Frida's friend Dorothy Hale's suicide with wit and an eye for the manners and mores of the 1930s. Isamu Noguchi's buoyant tales of Frida were both entertaining and insightful. In Mexico, the critic Raquel Tibol was unfailingly generous not only in sharing her memories of Frida, but also in lending intelligent advice and photographs. Frida's friend the art historian Antonio Rodríguez shared with me his penetrating and affectionate view of Frida both in his photographs of her and in his conversations and writings. Adelina Zendejas told me with great zest of her childhood friend Frida's schoolgirl pranks, and she lent me various of her own newspaper articles about Frida. Frida's students Arturo García Bustos, Arturo Estrada, Guillermo Monroy, and Fanny Rabel provided a fond and bright picture of Frida as a teacher and a woman, and her doctor Guillermo Velasco y Polo was both humorous and compassionate in his telling of Frida's illnesses and her relationship to Diego.

I am grateful as well to the following, whose memories were important in evoking a picture of Frida Kahlo: Margot Albert, Dolores Alvarez Bravo, Manuel Alvarez Bravo, Carmen Corcuera Baron, Beryl Becker, Roberto BeHar, Heinz Berggruen, Adolfo Bergrunder, Lucile Blanch, Suzanne Bloch, Paul Boatine, Elena Boder, Jacqueline Breton, Sophia Caire, Nicolas Calas, Mercédez Calderón, Olga Campos, Lya Cardoza, Rosa Castro, Olga Costa, Dolores del Rio, Stephen Pope Dimitroff, Baltasar Dromundo, Marjorie Eaton, Eugenia Farill, Dr. Samuel Fastlich, Judith Ferreto, Gisèle Freund, Fernando Gamboa, Enrique García, José Gómez Robleda, Ernst Halberstadt, Andrés Henestrosa, José de Jesús Alfaro, Margarita Kahlo, María Luisa Kahlo, Edgar Kaufmann, Jr., Katherine Kuh, Marucha Lavín, Parker Lesley, Julien Levy, Antonio Luna Arroyo, David Margolis, Lupe Marín, Elena Martínez, Concha Michel, Enrique Morales Pardavé, Guadalupe Morillo Safa, Annette Nancarrow, Dr. Armando Navarro, Margarita Nelkin, Juan O'Gorman, Mr. and Mrs. Pablo O'Higgins, Esperanza Ordóñez, Antonio Peláez, Michel Petitjean, Carmen Phillips, Alice Rahon, Aurora Reyes, Jesús Ríos y Valles, Lupe Rivera de Iturbe, Mala Rubinstein, Rosamund Bernier Russell, Peggy de Salle, Bernarda Bryson Shahn, Mary Sklar, Juan Soriano, Carleta Tibón, Elena Vásquez Gómez, Esteban Volkow, Hector Xavier.

For the privilege of reproducing works of art in their possession, I am grateful to the owners, private and public, of paintings, drawings, and photographs illustrated here. A special note of appreciation is due to Dolores del Rio, Dr. Samuel Fastlich, Eugenia Farill, Jacques Gelman, Isolda Kahlo, Edgar Kaufmann, Jr., Michel Petitjean, Mary Sklar, and Jorge Espinosa Ulloa for permitting me to see and have photographed their splendid collections of paintings by Frida Kahlo. My thanks go also to Noma Copley for her constant enthusiasm and encouragement; to Mary-Anne Martin of Sotheby Parke Bernet for her insights and expertise; to Max and Joyce Kozloff for bringing Frida Kahlo to my attention in the first place and for remaining interested in hearing about her over the years; to Frances McCullough for asking me to write this book; to Miriam Kaiser and the National Institute of Fine Arts in Mexico for sharing their knowledge of the whereabouts of Kahlo's works and other invaluable advice; to Professors Milton W. Brown, Linda Nochlin, Eugene Goossen, and Edward Sullivan for their judicious readings of the first draft of my manuscript, and to Karen and David Crommie for all their many kindnesses, which include lending me the taped interviews they made in 1968 for their award-winning film *The Life and Death of Frida Kahlo*.

My sincere thanks go also to the Graduate School and University Center of the City University of New york for all the help and encouragement I received, including a grant from the Art History Program Dissertation Fund. Various people have labored with good humor and tenacity over the typing of this book. They include Jean Zangus, Kriss Larsen, Leslie Palmer, and Liza Pulitzer (who extended many other courtesies as well). My thanks, too, to Toni Rachiele, the production editor, who spent many late hours making sure my manuscript would become a book. I want to give a special note of appreciation to my editor, Corona Machemer, for her commitment, enthusiasm, and constant understanding. Finally, and primarily, I am deeply grateful to my husband, Philip Herrera, and to our children, Margot and John, for their support and patience throughout the writing of *Frida*.

SELECTED BIBLIOGRAPHY

Books and Catalogues

Brenner, Anita. *Idols Behind Altars.* New York: Payson & Clarke, 1929.

Breton, André. *Surrealism and Painting.* Trans. Simon Watson Taylor. New York: Harper & Row, Publishers, 1972.

Charlot, Jean. *The Mexican Mural Renaissance: 1920–1925.* New Haven and London: Yale University Press, 1967.

del Conde, Teresa. *Vida de Frida Kahlo.* Mexico City: Secretaría de la Presidencia, Departamento Editorial, 1976.

Dromundo, Baltasar. *Mi Calle de San Idelfonso.* Mexico City: Editorial Guarania, 1956.

Flores Guerrero, Raúl. *Cinco Pintores Mexicanos.* Mexico City: Universidad Nacional Autónoma de México, 1957.

Gruening, Ernest. *Mexico and Its Heritage.* New York: Appleton-Century-Crofts, 1928.

Heijenoort, Jean van. *With Trotsky in Exile: From Prinkipo to Coyoacán.* Cambridge, Mass., and London: Harvard University Press, 1978.

Helm, MacKinley. *Modern Mexican Painters.* New York: Dover, 1968.

Henestrosa, Andrés. *Una Alacena de Alacenas.* Mexico City: Ediciones de Bellas Artes, 1970.

Museum of Contemporary Art. *Frida Kahlo.* Exhibition catalogue. Chicago: The Museum of Contemporary Art, 1978. Essay by Hayden Herrera.

Herrera, Hayden. *Frida Kahlo: Her Life, Her Art.* A dissertation submitted to the graduate faculty in art history in partial fulfillment of the requirements for the degree of Doctor of Philosophy, The City University of New York, 1981. To be made available by University Microfilms.

Instituto Nacional de Bellas Artes. *Diego Rivera: Exposición Nacional de Homenaje.* Exhibition catalogue. Mexico City: Instituto Nacional de Bellas Artes, 1977.

Instituto Nacional de Bellas Artes. *Frida Kahlo: Exposición Nacional de Homenaje.* Exhibition catalogue. Mexico City: Instituto Nacional de Bellas Artes, 1977. Essays by Alejandro Gómez Arias and Teresa del Conde.

Instituto Nacional de Bellas Artes. *Frida Kahlo Acompañada de Siete Pintoras.* Exhibition catalogue. Mexico City: Instituto Nacional de Bellas Artes, 1967.

Organizing Committee of the Games of the XIX Olympiad. *The Frida Kahlo Museum.* Catalogue with texts by Lola Olmedo de Olvera, Diego Rivera and Juan O'Gorman. Mexico City: Organizing Committee of the Games of the XIX Olympiad, 1968.

Paz, Octavio. *The Labyrinth of Solitude: Life and Thought in Mexico.* Translated by Lysander Kemp. New York: Grove, 1961.

Rivera, Diego, with March, Gladys. *My Art, My Life: An Autobiography.* New York: Citadel, 1960.

Rodríguez Prampolini, Ida. *El Surrealismo y el Arte Fantástico de México.* Mexico City: Instituto de Investigaciónes Estéticas, Universidad Nacional Autónoma de Mexico, 1969.

Schmeckebier, Laurence E. *Modern Mexican Art.* Minneapolis: University of Minnesota Press, 1939.

Technical Committee of the Diego Rivera Trust. *Museo Frida Kahlo.* Museum catalogue with texts by Carlos Pellicer and Diego Rivera. Mexico City, Technical Committee of the Diego Rivera Trust, 1958.

Tibol, Raquel. *Frida Kahlo.* Translated by Helga Prignitz. Frankfurt: Verlag Neue Kritik, 1980.

Tibol, Raquel. *Frida Kahlo: Crónica, Testimonios y Aproximaciones.* Mexico City: Ediciones de Cultura Popular, S.A., 1977.

Trotsky, Leon. *Writings of Leon Trotsky: 1936–1937 and 1938–1939.* 12 volumes covering 1929–1940. Ed. Naomi Allen and George Breitman. New York: Pathfinder, 1969–1975.

Westheim, Paul. *The Art of Ancient Mexico.* Trans. by Ursula Bernard. New York: Doubleday (Anchor), 1965.

Whitechapel Art Gallery. *Frida Kahlo and Tina Modotti.* Exhibition catalogue. London, 1982. Essay by Laura Mulvey and Peter Wollen.

Wolfe, Bertram D. *Diego Rivera: His Life and Times.* New York and London: Knopf, 1939.

Wolfe, Bertram D. *The Fabulous Life of Diego Rivera.* New York: Stein and Day, 1963.

Wolfe, Bertram D., and Rivera, Diego. *Portrait of Mexico.* Text by Bertram D. Wolfe. Illustrated with paintings by Diego Rivera. New York: Covici, Friede, 1937.

ARTICLES IN PERIODICALS, NEWSPAPERS AND PAMPHLETS

Bambi. "Frida Dice Lo Que Sabe." *Excelsior* (Mexico City), June 15, 1954, pp. 1,7.

Bambi. "Frida Kahlo Es una Mitád." *Excelsior* (Mexico City), June 13, 1954, p. 6.

Bambi. "Manuel, el Chófer de Diego Rivera, Encontró Muerta Ayer a Frida Kahlo, en su Gran Cama que Tiene Dosel de Espejo." *Excelsior* (Mexico City), July 14, 1954, pp. 1,5.

Bambi. "Un Remedio de Lupe Marín." *Excelsior* (Mexico City), June 16, 1954, p. 3.

"Bomb Beribboned." *Time,* Nov. 14, 1938, p. 29.

Cardona Peña, Alfredo. "Frida Kahlo." *Novedades* (Mexico City), Supplement, "México en la Cultura," July 17, 1955.

Cardoza y Aragón, Luis. "Frida Kahlo." *Novedades* (Mexico City), Supplement, "México en la Cultura," Jan. 23, 1955, p. 3.

Castro, Rosa. "Carta a Frida Kahlo." *Excelsior* (Mexico City), Supplement, "Diorama de la Cultura," July 31, 1955, p. 1.

Castro, Rosa. "Cartas de Amor: Un Libro de Frida Kahlo." *Siempre* (Mexico City), June 12, 1954, p. 70.

de la Torriente, Loló. "Recuerdos de Frida Kahlo." *El Nacional* (Mexico City), Supplement, "Revista Mexicana de Cultura," Apr. 8, 1979, pp. 1, 8–9.

de la Torriente, Loló. "Verdad y Mentira en la Vida de Frida Kahlo y Diego Rivera." Undated newspaper clipping in the Diego Rivera file in the library of the Museum of Modern Art, New York, pp. 8,21.

Dromundo, Baltasar. "Frida Kahlo, la Niña de la Mochila." *El Sol de México* (Section D), Apr. 22, 1974.

Flores Guerrero, Raúl. "Frida Kahlo: Su Ser y su Arte." *Novedades* (Mexico City), Supplement, "México en la Cultura," June 10, 1951.

Freund, Gisèle. "Imagen de Frida Kahlo." *Novedades* (Mexico City), Supplement, "México en la Cultura," June 10, 1951, p. 1.

Galerías de la Ciudad de Mexico in collaboration with the Frida Kahlo Museum. *Homenaje a Frida Kahlo*. Exhibition brochure. 1967.

Goméz Arias, Alejandro. "Un Testimonio Sobre Frida Kahlo." Essay included in *Frida Kahlo: Exposición Nacional de Homenaje*. Instituto Nacional de Bellas Artes, 1977.

González Ramírez, Manuel. "Frida Kahlo." Apr. 24, 1953. Unidentified newspaper clipping, Isolda Kahlo archive.

González Ramírez, Manuel. "Frida Kahlo o el Imperativo de Vivir." *Huytlate* 2 (1954): 7–25.

Henestrosa, Andrés. "Frida." *Novedades* (Mexico City), Supplement, "México en la Cultura," July 17, 1955, p. 5.

Herrera, Hayden. "Frida Kahlo." Essay in *Women Artists: 1550–1950*, by Ann Sutherland Harris and Linda Nochlin, Los Angeles County Museum of Art and Alfred A. Knopf, New York, 1976, pp. 335–37.

Herrera, Hayden. "Frida Kahlo: Her Life, Her Art." *Artforum* 14 (May 1976): 38–44.

Herrera, Hayden. "Frida Kahlo: 'Sacred Monsters'." *Ms.* 6 (February 1978): 29–31.

Herrera, Hayden. "Frida Kahlo's Art." *artscanda*, Issue No. 230–31 (October–November 1979): 25–28.

Herrera, Hayden. "Portrait of Frida Kahlo as a Tehuana." *Heresies*, winter, 1978, pp. 57–58.

Herrera, Hayden. "Portraits of a Marriage." *Connoisseur* 209 (March 1982): 124–128.

Kahlo, Frida. "The Birth of Moses." *Tin-Tan* 1 (summer–fall 1975): 2–6.

Kahlo, Frida. "Frida Habla de su Pintura." Undated newspaper clipping, Antonio Rodríguez's archive.

Kahlo, Frida. "Retrato de Diego." *Novedades* (Mexico City), Supplement, "México en la Cultura," July 17, 1955, p. 5.

Kozloff, Joyce. "Frida Kahlo." *Women's Studies* 6 (1978): 43–59.

"Mexican Autobiography," *Time*, Apr. 27, 1953, p. 90.

Monroy, Guillermo. "Homenaje de un Pintor a Frida Kahlo a los 22 Años de su Muerte." *Excelsior* (Mexico City), July 17, 1976, p. 8.

Monroy, Guillermo. "Hoy Hace 24 Años que Falleció Frida Kahlo." *Excelsior* (Mexico City), July 13, 1978, p. 2.

Monteforte Toledo, Mario. "Frida: Paisaje de Si Mísma." *Novedades* (Mexico City), Supplement, "México en la Cultura," June 10, 1951, p. 1–2.

Moreno Villa, José. "La Realidad y el Deseo en Frida Kahlo." *Novedades* (Mexico City), Supplement, "México en la Cultura," Apr. 26, 1953, p. 5.

O'Gorman, Juan. "Frida Kahlo." In *The Frida Kahlo Museum*. Catalogue published by the Organizing Committee of the Games of the XIX Olympiad, Mexico City, 1968, p. 12.

Oliver, Rosa María. "Frida la Unica y Verdadera Mitád de Diego." *Novedades* (Mexico City), Supplement, "México en la Cultura," August 1959, p. 7.

Orenstein, Gloria. "Frida Kahlo: Painting for Miracles." *Feminist Art Journal*, fall 1973, pp. 7–9.

Poniatowska, Elena. "El Museo Frida Kahlo." *Novedades* (Mexico City), Supplement, "México en la Cultura," July 7, 1958, p. 11.

Rivera, Diego. "Frida Kahlo: Biographical Sketch." Written for the National Institute of Fine Arts of Mexico in August 1954 for the exhibition of Mexican painting in Lima, Peru; excerpt reprinted in *The Frida Kahlo Museum* (catalogue published by the Organizing Committee of the Games of the XIX Olympiad in 1968), p. 8.

Rivera, Diego. "Frida Kahlo y el Arte Mexicano." *Bolitín del Seminario de Cultura Mexicana*, no. 2. Mexico City: Secretaría de Educación Pública (October 1943): 89–101.

Robles, Antonio. "La Personalidad de Frida Kahlo." Undated newspaper clipping, Isolda Kahlo archive.

Rodríguez, Antonio. "Frida Abjura del Surrealismo." Undated newspaper clipping, Antonio Rodríguez archive, n.p.

Rodríguez, Antonio. "Frida Kahlo." In "Pintores de Mexico" series. Undated newspaper clipping, Isolda Kahlo archive, p. 18.

Rodríguez, Antonio. "Frida Kahlo, Expresionista de su Yo Interno." *Mañana* (Mexico City). Undated newspaper clipping, Antonio Rodríguez archive, pp. 67–69.

Rodríguez, Antonio. "Frida Kahlo: Heroína del Dolor." *Novedades* (Mexico City), Supplement, "México en la Cultura," July 17, 1955, pp. 1,4.

Rodríguez, Antonio. "Frida Kahlo: El Homenaje Postumo de México a la Gran Artista." *Impacto* (Mexico City) 7 (1958): 49–51.

Rodríguez, Antonio. "Una Pintora Extraordinaria: La Vigorosa Obra de Frieda Kahlo, Surge de su Propia Tragedia, con Fuerza y Personalidad Excepcionales." Undated newspaper clipping, Antonio Rodríguez, archive, n.p.

Ross, Betty. "Como Pinta Frida Kahlo, Esposa de Diego, las Emociones Intimas de la Mujer." *Excelsior* (Mexico City), Oct. 21, 1942, p. 6.

Tibol, Raquel. "Frida Kahlo: En el Segundo Aniversario de su Muerte." *Novedades* (Mexico City), Supplement, "México en la Cultura," July 15, 1956, p. 4.

Tibol, Raquel. "Frida Kahlo, Maestra de Pintura." *Excelsior* (Mexico City), Supplement, "Diorama de la Cultura," Aug. 7, 1960.

Tibol, Raquel. "Fué Frida Kahlo una Pintora Surrealista?" *Siempre* (Mexico City), Supplement, "La Cultura en México," Aug. 5, 1970, pp. x–xi.

Westheim, Paul. "Frida Kahlo: Una Investigación Estética." *Novedades* (Mexico City), Supplement, "México en la Cultura," June 10, 1950, p. 3.

Wolfe, Bertram D. "Rise of Another Rivera." *Vogue*, Nov. 1, 1938, pp. 64, 131.

Zendejas, Adelina. "Frida Kahlo: En los Diez Años de su Muerte (1910–1954)." *El Día* (Mexico City), Supplement, "El Gallo Ilustrado," July 12, 1964, pp. 1–2, 64.

NOTES

PREFACE

x   "Where's the circus?": Julien Levy, *Memoir of an Art Gallery* (New York: Putnam, 1977), p. 16.

xi   "I don't want to share my toothbrush": Carmen Phillips, private interview, Pipersville, Pennsylvania, November 1979.

xi   "I hold the record for operations": Rafael Lozano, Mexico City dispatch to *Time*, Nov. 9, 1950.

xi   "I paint my own reality": Bertram D. Wolfe, "Rise of Another Rivera," p. 64.

xiii   "Frida embodied": Quoted in Ira Kamin, "Memories of Frida Kahlo," *San Francisco Examiner & Chronicle,* May 6, 1979, pp. 44–50.

xiii   "Neither Derain, nor I": Raquel Tibol, *Frida Kahlo: Crónica, Testimonios y Aproximaciones,* p. 96. All translations from the original Spanish, in letters, diaries, books, and articles, are by the author.

CHAPTER 1: THE BLUE HOUSE ON LONDRES STREET

4   as her birth certificate shows: Frida's birth was inscribed in the register of births in the town hall in Coyoacán.

5   the youth sustained brain injuries: This information comes from Frida Kahlo's medical records from birth to 1946, which were compiled by Dr. Henriette Begun, Frida's gynecologist, who emigrated to Mexico from Berlin in 1942. The medical record is published in Raquel Tibol, *Frida Kahlo,* a German translation of Tibol's *Crónica.* Tibol added this medical report in the German edition, published in 1980; see pp. 138–43. Henceforth, Begun, medical record.

5   he found a job: Alejandro Gómez Arias, private interviews, Mexico City, July 1977–January 1982. Gómez Arias says that Guillermo Kahlo emigrated to Mexico with the Diener brothers and that Kahlo helped them found La Perla.

5   "The night his wife died": Tibol, *Crónica,* p. 22.

6   "like a little bell from Oaxaca": Ibid., p. 20.

6   he "was very interesting": Ibid., p. 21.

6   her mother showed her a book: Ibid., p. 26.

7   her grandfather lent her father a camera: Ibid., p. 22.

7   "first official photographer": Felipe García Beraza, "La Obra Historica de Guillermo Kahlo," in *Homenaje a Guillermo Kahlo (1872–1941): Primer Fotógrafo Oficial*

del Patrimonio Cultural de México, exhibition catalogue published by El Instituto Mexicano Norteamericano de Relaciones Culturales, A.C. in August 1976, n.p. Some of the photographs later became the illustrations for the six monumental volumes of *Las Iglesias de México* (The Churches of Mexico), produced between 1924 and 1927 with the collaboration of the well-known painter Doctor Atl, the art historian Manuel Touissant, and the engineer José R. Benítez. The National Institute of Anthropology and History now possesses a collection of Kahlo's daguer-reotypes. It is said that Frida's sister Matilde had her father's glass plates after he died. A compulsively clean housekeeper like her mother, Matilde decided one day to wash them, and many of them were destroyed (Dolores Olmedo, private interview, Xochimilco, D.F., March 1977).

7 "Guillermo Kahlo specialist in landscapes": Ibid.
7 he said that he did not want: Maria Luisa Kahlo, private interview, Mexico City, November 1977.
7 "he had only two friends": Tibol, *Crónica,* p. 21.
8 she said she was about two: Frida Kahlo, interviewed by Parker Lesley, Coyoacán, D.F., Mexico, May 27, 1939. Henceforth, Lesley notes.
8 "I have my father's eyes": Tibol, *Crónica,* p. 23.
8 Her Mexican grandparents: Lesley notes.

CHAPTER 2: CHILDHOOD IN COYOACÁN

10 "I was nursed": Lesley notes.
10 she began to suffer: Tibol, *Frida Kahlo,* p. 138.
11 who had been placed in a convent: Not surprisingly, Margarita and María Luisa retain unpleasant memories of their stepmother, recalling a small-minded, vain, selfish woman (Margarita Kahlo and María Luisa Kahlo, private interview, Mexico City, November 1977). Another family member, Mercedes Calderón, recalls that she rarely saw Frida's parents when she visited on Londres Street: "They were always disappearing behind heavy wooden doors" (Mercedes Calderón, private interview, Mexico City, February 1980).
12 "it was with great difficulty": Tibol, *Crónica,* p. 22.
12 They mortgaged the house: Gómez Arias, private interviews.
12 "She did not know": Tibol, *Crónica,* pp. 20–21.
12 "My mother was hysterical about religion": Ibid., pp. 26–27.
13 "When I was three": Ibid., p. 24.
13 "In play I pushed her": Ibid., pp. 24–25.
13 calling him "Herr Kahlo": Gómez Arias, private interviews.
13 "When I was seven": Tibol, *Crónica,* p. 26.
14 Matilde used to come: Margarita and María Luisa Kahlo, private interview.
14 "Maty now comes": Frida Kahlo, letter to Alejandro Gómez Arias, July 22, 1927. Gómez Arias, personal archive.
14 "very nice, active, intelligent": Tibol, *Crónica,* pp. 21–21, 26.
14 "could not stop crying": Lucienne Bloch, private interview, San Francisco, November 1978.
14 stricken with polio: Frida Kahlo's medical history compiled by Dr. Begun says that Frida had a normal birth, and except for the usual childhood diseases—measles, chicken pox, and tonsilitis—was a healthy child until 1918, when she had an accident and hit her right foot against a tree stump. This caused a slight deformation of her foot, which turned outward. Several doctors diagnosed the problem as polio. Others said Frida had a "white tumor." The treatment consisted of sunbaths and calcium baths.
14 "It all began": Tibol, *Crónica,* p. 26.
15 "My toys": Ibid., p. 28.
15 "The leg remained": Ibid., p. 26.
15 "We were quite cruel": Aurora Reyes, private interview, Mexico City, November 1978.

16 "She was extremely well coordinated": Adelina Zendejas, "Frida Kahlo: En los Diez Años de su Muerte (1910–1954)," p. 1.

16 In a 1938 painting: The painting, entitled *They Ask for Planes and Only Get Straw Wings*, is lost, but it is recorded in a photograph in the personal archive of Michel Petitjean.

16 the painting recalls "the time": Wolfe, "Rise of Another Rivera," p. 131.

17 The village square is "empty": Lesley notes.

17 "which is the whole thing about Indians": Ibid.

17 "It is burnt up": Ibid.

17 "death: very gay": Ibid.

18 "because he is weak": Ibid.

18 *"Frida, lieber Frida"*: Gómez Arias, private interviews.

18 "Frida is the most intelligent": María Luisa Kahlo, private interview.

19 "philosophy makes men prudent": Ibid.

19 the link between his art and her own: Emmy Lou Packard, private interview, San Francisco, November 1978.

19 Guillermo Kahlo's . . . paintings: Three of Kahlo's watercolors are in the collection of Isolda Kahlo. One is a still life, another is a barnyard scene with two fuzzy calves that appear to be entranced by a mother hen who puffs up her chest proudly to protect her chicks, and the third is a copy of Caspar Metscher's *The Lace Maker*, in the Wallace Collection in London. The first and third are dated 1938. The barnyard scene is undated.

20 Frida is yet another instance: In her article "Why Have There Been No Great Women Artists?" (in Thomas B. Hess and Elizabeth C. Baker, *Art and Sexual Politics*, New York: Macmillan, 1973), Linda Nochlin observed that there are many examples in art history of women artists whose fathers were artists. Beyond that, women artists of the nineteenth and twentieth centuries often "had a close personal connection with a strong or dominant male artist" (p. 30). Frida obviously had the benefit of that as well.

20 a "kind of fearful mystery": Lesley notes.

20 "Many times when he went walking": Tibol, *Crónica*, p. 28.

20 used the word "tranquil": Ibid., p. 21.

21 effect of the staccato marks: The background conveys a feeling of anxiety in the same way that the flowered wallpaper in the background of Van Gogh's *La Berceuse* (1889), painted at one of the moments when Van Gogh became mentally ill and finished during his recovery, intimates distress. One senses in both Frida's portrait of her father and Van Gogh's *La Berceuse* that the image is a private icon, reflecting the painter's extreme need for the portrait subject. Writing about his intentions in this portrait, Van Gogh said that he wanted to create the kind of image that could comfort and ease the "mournful isolation" of fishermen. Like the Dutch master, Frida seems to have tried to create something that was at once commemorative and consoling.

CHAPTER 3: THE NATIONAL PREPARATORY SCHOOL

23 "will be our motto": Baltasar Dromundo, *Mi Calle de San Ildefonso*, p. 43.

24 "Idealists, persist": Ibid., p. 46.

24 to be founded on "our blood": Octavio Paz, *The Labyrinth of Solitude: Life and Thought in Mexico*, p. 152.

24 "Men are more malleable": Jean Charlot, *The Mexican Mural Renaissance: 1920–1925*, pp. 87, 93.

24 "The Spirit Shall Speak": Paz, *Labyrinth*, pp. 146–47.

24 "We do not speak of a time": Andrés Iduarte, "Imagen de Frida Kahlo," clipping from a Caracas newspaper (Aug. 12, 1954), Isolda Kahlo archive.

25 the school's cry: Dromundo, *Mi Calle*, p. 28.

25 "madhouse on wheels": Ibid., p. 78.

25 "Formidable Affray": Charlot, *Mexican Mural Renaissance*, pp. 115–16.

25 one father allowed his daughter: Elena Boder, private interview, Los Angeles, November 1978.

26 "a fragile adolesecent": Alejandro Gómez Arias, "Un Testimonio Sobre Frida Kahlo," n.p.

26 like a German high school student: Ibid. Gómez Arias says that before entering the Preparatoria Frida had studied briefly at the Colegio Alemán, the German School in Mexico City, but her parents found the tuition beyond their means and Frida found it too strict (Gómez Arias, private interviews). Frida is also said to have studied two years at the Normal School for Teachers, an institution founded in 1887 for the training of elementary school teachers (Teresa del Condé, *Vida de Frida Kahlo*, p. 13).

26 "Que niña tan fea!": Alicia Galant, quoted in Gabriela Rabago Palafox, "Frida Vive en Coyoacán," 1982 newspaper clipping in author's archive.

26 carried a schoolboy's knapsack: Gómez Arias, "Frida Kahlo," n.p.

26 Frida considered most girls to be *cursi:* Isolda Kahlo, private interview, Mexico City, October 1977.

27 Among the Contemporáneos: Zendejas, "Frida Kahlo," p. 1.

27 Frida's real *cuates:* For this account of the doings of Frida and the Cachuchas I have relied—unless otherwise noted—on the memories (both written and communicated in private interviews) of members of the group, especially Alejandro Gómez Arias, but including José Gómez Robleda, Manuel González Ramírez, and Jesús Ríos y Valles, and of such other contemporaries as Baltasar Dromundo, Adolfo Zamora, and Adelina Zendejas.

28 their escapades: Baltasar Dromundo, private interview, Mexico City, November 1978.

28 "it was the joking attitude": Manuel González Ramírez, "Frida Kahlo."

28 "we can't take it anymore": Zendejas, "Frida Kahlo," p. 2. It is hardly surprising that Antonio Caso did not want to investigate socialist thought in the Preparatoria classrooms. He did, however, make a critique of positivism, forming a philosophy of intuition and action, feeling and Christian charity. He was against imperialism and for constitutional government, but he felt that progress comes through outstanding individuals and that there was too much stress on the masses (J. Frederick Rippy, *Latin America: A Modern History*, Ann Arbor, University of Michigan Press, 1968).

28 "Gómez Arias . . . left the school building": José Gómez Robleda, private interview, Mexico City, April 1978.

29 Frida was expelled: Bertram D. Wolfe, *The Fabulous Life of Diego Rivera*, pp. 240–41.

29 "lend me your Spengler": Dromundo, private interview.

29 Zendejas . . . recalls: Zendejas, "Frida Kahlo," p. 2.

30 The two girls loved to loiter: Ibid.

30 Carmen Jaime: Ibid., and Dromundo, *Mi Calle*, pp. 153–60.

30 She could read a text once: Antonio Luna Arroyo, *Juan O'Gorman: Autobiografía, Antología, Juicios Críticos y Documentación exhaustiva sobre su Obra* (Mexico City: Cuadernos Populares de Pintura Mexicana Moderna, 1973), p. 103.

30 she would sit just outside a class: Adolfo Zamora, telephone interview, Mexico City, February 1980.

30 she handed Adelina Zendejas a note: Zendejas, "Frida Kahlo," p. 2.

31 "He is not a teacher": Arroyo, *Juan O'Gorman*, p. 103.

31 "We would set them on fire": Gómez Robleda, private interview.

31 She stole food: Wolfe, *Fabulous Life of Diego Rivera*, p. 241.

32 Frida liked to hide: Ibid., p. 242, and Diego Rivera, *My Art, My Life*, pp. 128–29.

32 "My ambition": Wolfe, *Fabulous Life of Diego Rivera*, p. 241.

32 When Adelina Zendejas protested: Adelina Zendejas, interviewed by Karen and David Crommie for their film *The Life and Death of Frida Kahlo*, 1968.

32 "Old Fatso": Antonio Rodríguez, "Frida Kahlo: El Homenaje Postumo de México a la Gran Artista," p. 49.

32 "One night": Rivera, *My Art, My Life,* pp. 128–29.

33 "Optimism, sacrifice, purity": Dromundo, *Mi Calle,* p. 262.

33 "a fresh, perhaps ingenuous and childlike manner": Gómez Arias, private interviews.

33 Alejandro wooed his "niña of the Preparatoria": Dromundo, private interview, and Zendejas, "Frida Kahlo," p. 1. The phrase "niña of the Preparatoria" comes from several of Frida's many letters to Gómez Arias written between 1922 and 1927. All of Frida's letters to Alejandro Gómez Arias are in Gómez Arias's personal archive.

34 the flow of the words is rarely measured: Frida wrote the way she talked. My translations of her words from the original Spanish follow her punctuation except where lack of punctuation makes the meaning unclear.

34 "One *tipo* ideal": Letter to Gómez Arias, Sept. 14, 1924.

34 Frida developed a personal emblem: González Ramírez, "Frida Kahlo."

35 "Tell me if you don't love me": Letter to Gómez Arias, c. Jan. 15, 1925.

36 It is said that on Christmas Eve: Dromundo, *Mi Calle,* p. 166.

36 "I am sad and bored": Letter to Gómez Arias, Aug. 4, 1924. The following quotation is from a letter dated July 25, 1925.

40 "sexually precocious": Gómez Arias, private interviews.

42 "I do not know what to do": Letter to Gómez Arias, 1924. Frida did not give the exact date, but instead wrote "Day of the gringos." My information about Frida's jobs comes from her letters to Gómez Arias as well as from his recollections.

43 "They pay 4 to 4.50": Letter to Gómez Arias, Jan. 8, 1925.

43 a woman employee: Gómez Arias, private interviews.

43 initiation into homosexual sex: Jean van Heijenoort, private interviews, Mexico City, New York City, and Cambridge, Massachusetts, Apr. 1978–May 1982.

43 "enormous talent": A statement Fernández wrote about his apprentice hangs today in the Frida Kahlo museum next to some of Frida's first drawings under Fernández's guidance. It says that Frida came to work with him because he was a close friend of her father's, and goes on: "In view of the enormous talent that she showed in drawing, I thought I would have her dedicate herself to etching and dry point engraving. I put into her hands a book with reproductions of the marvelous works by Anders Zorn and truly I was surprised by the skills of this marvelous artist. She copied directly, freehand with a pen without using any indications other than a few, very small pencil lines. She copied with an ease and accuracy that can be appreciated in these original drawings which I fortunately kept and which with pleasure I donate to Frida's Museum."

Enclosed in a frame with this statement are three pen-and-ink drawings by Frida juxtaposed with reproductions of the engravings by Zorn (1860–1920) that served as models. One can see Frida's skill, but her struggle to make a faithful copy is just as obvious: her line is looser and her hatching far more sketchy than in the original.

Chapter 4: Accident and Aftermath

48 "A little while": Tibol, *Crónica,* p. 31.

48 "The electric train": Gómez Arias, private interviews.

49 "It was a strange collision": Tibol, *Crónica,* p. 31.

49 Her spinal column: Begun, medical record.

49 "I lost my virginity": Tibol, *Crónica,* p. 32. Frida was probably speaking figuratively. According to Gómez Arias, she was no longer a virgin at the time of the accident (Gómez Arias, private interviews).

50 "They had to put her back together": Baltasar Dromundo, "Frida Kahlo: Vida Cercenada Mil Veces por la Muerte," *El Sol de México,* Apr. 23, 1974, p. D3.

50 "My mother was speechless": Tibol: *Crónica*, p. 32.
50 "They kept us in a kind of horrifying ward": Ibid.
50 "In this hospital": Gómez Arias, "Frida Kahlo," n.p.
51 "I am beginning to grow accustomed": Letter to Gómez Arias, Dec. 5, 1925. Letter to Gómez Arias.
53 "one of the sadder houses": Letter to Gómez Arias, Apr. 12, 1926.
58 "Although I have said I love you to many": Letter to Gómez Arias, Sept. 28, 1926.

CHAPTER 5: THE BROKEN COLUMN

62 thirty-two surgical operations: Olga Campos, telephone interview, Mexico City, February 1980.
62 "She lived dying": Andrés Henestrosa, "Frida."
62 the doctors at the Red Cross Hospital: Reyes, private interview.
62 "no one paid any attention": Tibol, *Crónica*, p. 32.
63 "The second plaster corset": Letter to Gómez Arias, May 31, 1927.
63 "Since I was young": Antonio Rodríguez, "Frida Kahlo, Expresionista de su Yo Interno," p. 67. This article is one of several given to me in the form of Xerox copies of clippings. Rodríguez does not recall the exact dates of his articles. Also, "Una Pintora Extraordinaria," n.p., and Antonio Rodríguez, private interview, Mexico City, August 1977.
63 She briefly entertained: Gómez Arias, private interviews.
63 She . . . never stopped drawing capricious interlaces: González Ramírez, "Frida Kahlo." Prophetically, González Ramírez saw that the webs of lines Frida drew looked like charts of the human circulatory system, a subject that would be, along with intertwining lines of all sorts, a constant preoccupation in her mature work. Similarly, the self-portrait as a triangle with a beard that she used as an emblem looks forward to her emphatic mustache in self-portraits from her adult years.
63 "I never thought of painting": Wolfe, "Rise of Another Rivera," p. 131. Frida told Parker Lesley that she had painted her first self-portrait in bed, using a special easel and looking at her reflection in a mirror suspended over her bed (Lesley notes), but the portrait is too large to have been painted in bed. Some people who knew her at the time say Frida began painting before the accident. In a 1953 interview, Frida told Raquel Tibol about an almost certainly fictitious exchange between herself and her mother: "As soon as I saw my mother I said to her: 'I have not died, and what's more, I have something to live for.' This something was painting. Since I had to remain lying down in a plaster corset from the clavicle to the pelvis, my mother managed to prepare for me a very funny apparatus from which hung a piece of wood which served as a support for my papers" (Tibol, *Crónica*, p. 33).
64 "My father had had": Rodríguez, "Frida Kahlo, Expresionista," p. 67.
64 Her first subjects: Adelina Zendejas remembers Frida lying in bed and producing little landscapes in watercolor or colored pencil on pieces of cardboard that Guillermo Kahlo brought her (Zendejas, private interview). No such landscapes exist, either from this time or from later in her career, but an undated 1926 letter to Gómez Arias testifies to the fact that she did sometimes paint in oil out of doors. "I do not think that I will go to the convent to paint," she wrote, "because I do not have any oil and haven't felt like buying it."
Frida's niece, Isolda Kahlo, owns a round tray painted with poppies that she says Frida made before her accident, as a gift for her grandmother. Although the flowers are skillfully depicted, they hardly seem original to Frida. They look as if they had been copied from some decorative art source such as a needlepoint pattern. Indeed, the tray was probably intended to be a handicraft object, not a work of art. In addition, there is a tattered and faded pencil *Self-Portrait* in the Frida Kahlo Museum on which is written "Frieda Kahlo 1927 In my house at

Coyoacán First Drawing in my Life." Given the fact that she started painting in 1926, it is unlikely that this inscription tells the truth. Perhaps she meant it was the first drawing of the new life that began when she met Diego, for both the pre-Columbian necklace and the work shirt she wears in it, and the background—in which she contrasts skyscrapers labeled "United States," "Large Houses," and "Without a style of their own" with mountains labeled "Coyoacán" and "Valley of Mexico"—surely indicate Rivera's influence.

The tray painted with poppies and other works discussed but not illustrated in *Frida* can be seen in the illustrations that accompany my dissertation, "Frida Kahlo: Her Life, Her Art."

64 "la Boticelinda Adriana" and "a cardboard cutout": from Frida's letters to Gómez Arias, June 24 and July 23, 1927.

65 spindly trees and scalloped clouds: The scalloped clouds might also derive from Botticelli, who painted similarly shaped clouds—for example, in his portrait entitled *Young Man with a Medal* in the Uffizi Gallery in Florence. Other possible sources for the first portraits, especially the first *Self-Portrait*, are Roberto Montenegro, whose Art Deco mural and decorative plaques in the Ibero American Library Frida knew well, and Doctor Atl, the Mexican painter best known for his intense self-portraits with the volcano Popocatépetl in the background; his influence on Frida's earliest paintings, remarked upon by Diego Rivera (Wolfe, *Fabulous Life of Diego Rivera*, p. 243), seems all the more likely, since he worked with her father in the mid-1920s on the books entitled *Las Iglesias de Mexico*.

Frida is said to have studied the Art Nouveau illustrations in a series of paperback books or reviews published by Editorial Aurora and collected by Guillermo Kahlo (Gómez Arias, private interviews). A few years after she completed her first *Self-Portrait*, she produced a highly stylized book illustration of her own—the frontispiece and the cover of Ernesto Hernández Bordes's volume of poems entitled *Caracol de Distancias*, privately printed in an edition of 250 in 1933 by Cachucha Miguel N. Lira. The illustration, which depicts two women, reveals Frida's familiarity with Art Deco design.

65 "How much I would like to explain": Letter to Gómez Arias, Apr. 31, 1927.

65 "pity is stronger than love": Edgar Kaufmann, Jr., private interview, New York City, May 1978.

66 "in order to cool off his close relationship": Tibol, *Crónica*, p. 35, note 4.

71 "It will be called 'Panorama' ": Miguel N. Lira's article was not published, but he did participate in the publication of a small pamphlet on Frida after her death, written by fellow Cachucha Manuel González Ramírez.

74 "I tease and laugh at death": Enrique Morales Pardavé, private interview, Mexico City, April 1978.

74 she had wanted to [paint the accident]: Lesley notes. Frida did have a *retablo* illustrating the scene. Some twenty years after the accident, when she came across an existing *retablo* showing a crash between a streetcar and a bus, a collision almost identical to her own, she, or one of her students, altered a few details so that the bus's sign says "Coyoacán," the streetcar says "Tlalpan," and the girl sprawled on the tracks has joined eyebrows like Frida's. They also added a dedicatory inscription: "The couple Guillermo and Matilde C. de Kahlo gives thanks to the Virgin of Sorrows for having saved their child Frida from the accident that occurred in 1925 on the corner of Cuahutemotzín and the Calzada de Tlalpan."

74 "I paint myself": Rodríguez, private interview, and "Una Pintora Extraordinaria," n.p.

74 "I look like many people": Mario Monteforte Toledo, "Frida: Paisaje de Sí Misma," p. 1.

74 "From that time": Antonio Rodríguez, "Frida Kahlo: Heroína del Dolor," p. 1.

75 "Frida is the only painter": Dolores Alvarez Bravo, interviewed by Karen and David Crommie.

75 "Why do you study so much?": Letter to Gómez Arias, Sept. 29, 1926. This letter was published in Zendejas, "Frida Kahlo," p. 64.

75 "no one in my house believes": Letter to Gómez Arias, Apr. 25, 1926.

76 "she always acted happy": Reyes, private interview.

76 "When we went to visit her": Adelina Zendejas, article by Zendejas dictated to the author in a private interview. The article was originally published in *Boletín del Grupo Preparatorio 1920–1924*, no. 44.

76 three months in the Red Cross Hospital: Tibol, *Crónica*, p. 32.

77 her hips wrapped in a cloth: According to Arturo García Bustos (private interview, Mexico City, March 1977), Frida's hips and thighs were originally left naked. Deciding that the depiction of her sex diverted attention from the painting as a whole, Frida painted a sheet wrapped around her hips.

CHAPTER 6: DIEGO: THE FROG PRINCE

79 "Samurai of my country": Dromundo, *Mi Calle*, p. 262.

79 "We will not be convinced": Alejandro Gómez Arias, "Aquella Generación; Esta Generación," essay published in *En Torno de una Generación: Glosa de 1929*, p. 75.

79 "Germancito el Campirano": Letter to Gómez Arias, June 24, 1927.

80 "Now as never before": Letter to Gómez Arias, June 14, 1928.

81 "I am not merely an 'artist' ": Wolfe, *Fabulous Life of Diego Rivera*, p. 342.

81 "It's like the tenderest young pig": Lucienne Bloch, private interview.

81 It is an odd work: In *Idols Behind Altars*, a delightful account of Mexican culture and history by Anita Brenner, there is a dialogue heard in 1923 at a gathering of intellectuals and university professors that took place in the home of Lombardo Toledano. Antonio Caso pronounced Rivera's mural to be "stupendous!" To his brother Alfonso Caso it showed "an excess of genius!" Lombardo Toledano said, "Mexico palpitates in his work." The verdict of Mrs. Caso and four female members of her family was that the mural whould be whitewashed. Alejandro Gómez Arias, who was also there, said Rivera had succeeded "by virtue of quantity, but certainly not by virtue of quality" (Wolfe, *Fabulous Life of Diego Rivera*, p. 139).

82 Mexican art "is great": MacKinley Helm, *Modern Mexican Painters*, p. 32.

83 "the art of the Mexican people": Ibid. The rise of folklorism in the 1920s was seen in other ways as well. On September 15, 1921, folk art was given a great boost by the first exhibition of popular art in Mexico, organized by the painter Doctor Atl (who three years later would collaborate with Frida's father on the six volumes of *Las Iglesias de Mexico*) in collaboration with painter Adolfo Best Maugard and Diego Rivera. (Doctor Atl was born in 1877 as Gerardo Murillo. He forsook his Spanish patronymic, taking as his pseudonym the Indian word for "water.") Doctor Atl's exhibition catalogue *Folk Arts of Mexico* remains to the this day the basic book on the subject; back then it served to make the richness of popular art available as a source to painters.

Not all Mexican artists supported the idea that for art to be Mexican it had to "return" to the naïve themes and primitive style of folk art. Orozco, recognizing the danger that such art could easily descend into trite picturesqueness or even exploitation of Indian themes and forms for self-promoting or tourist-enticing purposes, and as deft a debunker as Rivera was an eloquent enthusiast, scorned the cult of *retablos* and *pulquería* murals (the naïve murals that decorated bars selling the alcoholic beverage *pulque*) and sneered at the popularization of folklore: "Indeed we Mexicans are the first ones to blame for having concocted and nurtured the myth of the ridiculous *charro* and the absurd *china* as symbols of so-called Mexicanism. . . . At the sight of a *charro* or a *china*, at the opening notes of the horrible *jarabe* one is automatically reminded of the nauseating Mexican stage, and all this, amalgamated becomes our own" (Charlot, *Mexican Mural Renaissance*, p. 60).

83 "the principal imprint of the Indian": Aaron Copland, *Music and Imagination* (New York: New American Library, 1959), p. 98.

84 he fulminated against the "false artists": Diego Rivera, "Frida Kahlo y el Arte Mexicano," pp. 96–97.

85 He later claimed: Henry Beckett, "Rivera Denies Red 'Hate Hymns,'" *New York Evening Post*, Sept. 19, 1933.

85 "green eyes so transparent": Rivera, *My Art, My Life*, p. 126.

85 The cause of the separation: Alan Robinson, "Lupe Marín Recalls Life with Diego Rivera," *News* (Mexico City), Dec. 2, 1977, p. 12.

85 before an astonished group of guests: Wolfe, *Fabulous Life of Diego Rivera*, p. 186.

85 she smashed some of Diego's . . . idols: Robinson, "Lupe Marín," p. 12.

85 Diego had more love affairs: Wolfe, *Fabulous Life of Diego Rivera*, p. 245.

86 "Men are savages by nature": Undated newspaper clipping c. Dec. 27, 1931, private archive, New York City.

86 his reputation as a womanizer: There are many people who do not believe that Rivera actually became sexually engaged with the innumerable women who passed through his life. His obesity, his incredibly long hours of work, his concentration on art and politics, and, finally, his hypochondria and frequent bad health must have kept him from enjoying sex as often as the gossip columnists delighted in supposing he did. When painter Lucienne Bloch was living with the Riveras in Detroit, she recalls, "one morning Diego kissed me on the cheek and said to me, 'You know, in love, I'm not all what I'm made up to be'" (Lucienne Bloch, private interview).

José Gómez Robleda says that "Diego was full of sexual perversities and anomalies, and he was suspicious that he was deficient in normal sexual relations because of his fatness, etc." (Robleda, private interview).

86 "The meeting with Diego": Bambi, "Frida Kahlo Es una Mitád."

87 "He gave me an *abrazo*": Frida mentioned Orozco's response to her painting to a U.S. journalist, Robert Lubar. See also *Time*, "Mexican Autobiography," Apr. 27, 1953, p. 90. Frida had known Orozco at least since her days at the Preparatoria. His studio was near her home in Coyoacán, and it is said that he and she often traveled to and from Mexico City together, and that Orozco followed her and waited for her on corners so that they would be on the same bus. "He was a little fascinated by Frida, but he was also a little shy," says Rosa Castro, a writer and a friend of Frida's (Rosa Castro, private interview, Mexico City, November 1977).

87 "As soon as they gave me permission": Bambi, "Frida Kahlo Es una Mitád," and Rodríguez, "Frida Kahlo, Expressionista," p. 68.

87 Diego's version of the meeting: Rivera, *My Art, My Life*, pp. 169–72.

Chapter 7: The Elephant and the Dove

93 "When I went to the Secretary of Education": Radar, "Etcetera" column in a Mexico City newspaper. Undated clipping, Isolda Kahlo archive.

94 his fond recollection: Rivera, *My Art, My Life*, p. 175.

94 "He is irritated by only two things": Frida Kahlo, "Retrato de Diego." This essay was also published in *Hoy* (Mexico City), Jan. 22, 1949, and in the exhibition catalogue for Rivera's 1949 retrospective published in 1951, *Diego Rivera: 50 Años de su Labor Artística, Exposición de Homenaje Nacional,* Museo Nacional de Artes Plásticas. Parts of Kahlo's essay appeared in Rivera's *My Art, My Life*, pp. 301–3. More recently, the essay was reprinted in *Exposición Nacional de Homenaje a Diego Rivera,* Instituto Nacional de Bellas Artes, 1977, pp. 11–23.

94 "The trouble with Frida": Private interview with an old friend of Frida's who did not wish to be identified.

94 "her face was painted": Radar, "Etcetera."

94   "She no longer wore white blouses": Gómez Arias, private interviews.

95   "You have a dog face": Wolfe, *Fabulous Life of Diego Rivera*, p. 244. Unlike Lupe Marín, who was the model for Rivera's most vibrantly sensual nudes, Frida was never to be Rivera's ideal of feminine sensuality and charm. Only in a 1930 lithograph did he depict her nude. The picture has all the accouterments of eroticism: Frida sits on the edge of a bed. She is in the process of undressing. Her garter lies on the pillow. Stockings and high-heeled shoes and a necklace have not yet been removed. Her arms are raised above her head in a position that reveals her breasts to advantage. All this should be provocative, but it isn't. Frida's body is scrawny. She looks companionable, not sexy. A contemporaneous lithograph that was printed from the opposite side of the same stone shows Rivera's longtime friend Lola (Dolores) Olmedo. Where Frida looks self-possessed and of this world, Lola Olmedo is an idol to be possessed. Dolores Olmedo recalls that Rivera said she and Frida complemented each other (private interview). Presumably this was an excuse for him to love them both.

95   "I was terribly anxious": Tibol, *Crónica*, p. 49. The two following quotes are from the same source.

95   "Diego showed me": Rafael Lozano, Mexico City dispatch to *Time*, Nov. 10, 1950.

96   a figure from one of Diego's murals: Frida said that at the time when she took her first paintings to show to Rivera she was longing to paint murals. Although her physical frailty made the pursuit of a career as a muralist impossible, there exists an unfinished fresco panel, perhaps by Frida, showing a girl of about thirteen (possibly Frida) wearing a navy-blue tunic and a white blouse. The fresco panel is in the collection of Rivera's eldest daughter, who believes that Frida painted it at the time when she became reacquainted with Rivera in 1928 (Lupe Rivera de Iturbe, private telephone interview, Mexico City, July 1977). Very possibly Rivera helped Frida experiment with fresco technique, and this experimentation might have further encouraged Frida's turn toward a simplified realism in which a painting consists of a few relatively thinly painted color shapes. The fresco panel could also have been produced in 1934, when Frida mentioned in a letter that she was planning to paint a small fresco in a children's school near Tacuba in Mexico City.

96   Frida's [paintings of children] are always particularized: Only in *Portrait of Isolda Kahlo as a Baby*, 1929, did Frida paint a "cute" child—perhaps because Isolda was her goddaughter and niece and the painting was to be a gift to her sister Cristina.

98   "bright as an eagle": Wolfe, *Fabulous Life of Diego Rivera*, p. 244. The meaning of the juxtaposition of the clock set on the pedestal and the airplane in the sky in Frida's second *Self-Portrait* is uncertain. One possibility is that they refer to the modern technological world for which Rivera had such enthusiasm. Rivera said of a detail of his 1930 mural in the San Francisco Stock Exchange: "As a symbol of the future I showed a young Californian boy facing the sky with a model airplane in his hands" (*My Art, My Life*, p. 177). Or Frida could have intended the combination of airplane and clock to mean something as banal as "time flies"; she was perfectly capable of such visual puns.

98   "Marry him": Jesús Ríos y Valles, private interview, San Miguel de Allende, November 1978.

98   "By the time she became involved with Rivera": Dromundo, private interview.

99   Matilde Calderón de Kahlo . . . could not accept: Gómez Arias, private interviews.

99   "At seventeen": Bambi, "Frida Kahlo Es una Mitád." Frida's statement that she borrowed her wedding clothes from her maid is probably an embroidery on the truth. The dress she wears in her wedding photograph, though definitely Mexican, does not look like the "skirt and blouse" of a servant.

99   The couple were married in a civil ceremony: Rivera, *My Art, My Life*, p. 173.

99   *La Prensa* (Aug. 23, 1929): Newspaper clipping, Isolda Kahlo archive.

100   Betram Wolfe told the story: Wolfe, *Fabulous Life of Diego Rivera*, p. 249. The

story is also mentioned in Rivera's *My Art, My Life* (p. 173). Ella Wolfe remembers it well (private interview, Palo Alto, California, November 1978).

100 Frida's account of the post-wedding festivities: Bambi, "Frida Kahlo Es una Mitád."

100 As Andrés Henestrosa remembers the party: Henestrosa, private interview, Mexico City, March 1977. Henestrosa may be confusing the wedding celebration with the party at Modotti's where Frida met Diego.

CHAPTER 8: NEWLYWED: THE TEHUANA FRIDA

101 "as furniture we had": Bambi, "Frida Kahlo Es una Mitád." Since, when Frida and Diego got married, Siqueiros was in prison for taking part in a workers' demonstration that had been violently suppressed by the police in May 1929, Frida's account may indicate that she and Diego lived together before their marriage.

101 the charges against him: Wolfe, *Fabulous Life of Diego Rivera*, pp. 163–65.

102 "Diego arrived": Dromundo, private interview.

102 "I think his going out of the party": Modotti's letter is quoted in Mildred Constantine, *Tina Modotti: A Fragile Life* (New York: Paddington Press, Two Continents Publishing Group, 1975), pp. 162, 166.

102 "I did not have a home": Beckett, "Rivera Denies."

103 The teachers were . . . to be subject: Wolfe, *Fabulous Life of Diego Rivera*, p. 260.

103 she learned how to cater to his fancies: Bambi, "Frida Kahlo Es una Mitád." Lupe's solicitude for Frida did not last long; on November 2, 1929, she wrote from Veracruz, where she had gone to live with her new husband, the critic Jorge Cuesta: "Frida: It disgusts me to take pen in hand to write to you. But I want you to know that neither you nor your father nor your mother has a right to anything of Diego's. Only his children are the ones whom he has the obligation to maintain (and among them count Marcia [*sic*], to whom he has never sent a penny!) Guadalupe" (Wolfe, *Fabulous Life of Diego Rivera*, p. 249). Actually, Diego was extremely generous to Lupe and never stopped sending money to his illegitimate child, Marika, who lived in Paris.

Frida's portrait of Lupe Marín is now lost, but it is documented in a photograph. Though attractive and intelligent-looking, Lupe in Frida's conception does not seem to be at all the savage and sensuous beauty who appears in Rivera's portraits or in the famous photographs that Edward Weston took of her.

105 He loved . . . to tell the story: Zendejas, Crommie interview.

105 Luis Cardoza y Aragón . . . described his days in Cuernavaca: Luis Cardoza y Aragón, "Frida Kahlo."

106 "We could not have a child": Bambi, "Frida Kahlo Es una Mitád."

106 Frida had an abortion: Begun, medical record.

106 She mentioned the possibility: Letter to Dr. Leo Eloesser, May 26, 1932, Joyce Campbell, personal archive.

106 "I suffered two grave accidents": Gisèle Freund, "Imagen de Frida Kahlo."

108 "As is natural": Wolfe, *Fabulous Life of Diego Rivera*, pp. 395–96.

108 "the most important fact in my life": Rivera, *My Art, My Life*, p. 172.

108 "For lovely Fisita": "Fisita" was the name Frida's niece, Isolda Kahlo, called her aunt when Isolda was too young to pronounce "Frida" (Isolda Kahlo, private interview).

108 he returned . . . with a cartload of flowers: Mrs. Pablo O'Higgins, private interview, Mexico City, April 1978.

108 Mariana Morillo Safa . . . recalls: Mariana Morillo Safa, private interview, Mexico City, July 1977.

109 Carmen Jaime remembers: Orthón Lara Barba, "Sor Juana y Frida Kahlo: Paralelamente," *Boletín Bibliográfico*, Secretaría de Hacienda y Crédito Público (Mexico City), vol. XIII, no. 380 (Dec. 1, 1967), p. 8.

109 "In another period I dressed like a boy": Bambi, "Frida Dice Lo Que Sabe," June 15, 1954, p. 1.

110 "Does it work?": Lucile Blanch, telephone interview, Woodstock, New York, October 1978.

110 "coquettish masochism": Bambi, "Manuel, el Chófer de Diego Rivera, Encontró Muerta Ayer a Frida Kahlo, en su Gran Cama que Tiene Dosel de Espejo," p. 1.

111 "She is a person": Parker Lesley, transcription of notes taken during two conversations in Mexico City with Diego Rivera about Frida Kahlo and her work, in May 1939. Rivera's dealer Alberto Misrachi and New York art dealer Pierre Matisse were present and took part in the conversation.

111 "The classic Mexican dress": "Fashion Notes," *Time*, May 3, 1948, pp. 33–34. In the 1930s and 1940s, the virtues of the colonial, "homespun" past were sung, and native folk art was revered north of the border as well. From Greenwich Village to Santa Fe, sophisticated women (mainly artists or artists' wives) wore embroidered blouses, ruffled skirts, and huaraches. As is usual when folk costumes are adopted by sophisticated people, the peasant style did not catch on with men either in Mexico or in the United States. Diego Rivera, for example, chose to wear shabby, ill-fitting business suits. He would have felt ludicrous in the white *manta* shirt and pants that is virtually the uniform of the Mexican *campesino*. Only his Stetson hat and the pistol in his belt contradicted his citified appearance, linking him with the Mexican Revolution and activism. When working, he donned the denim overalls of the urban proletariat. "I searched my soul profoundly," said Rivera in 1929. "I found . . . I had sufficient strength to be a workman among other workmen" (Diego Rivera, in *Creative Art*, January 1929).

112 this magic power of clothes: The photographer Manuel Alvarez Bravo caught this mysterious vitality of empty clothing in his *Absent Portrait*, 1945, which shows an old-fashioned dress placed as if it were seated on a chair in an empty room. The dress charges the room with the owner's absence. Alvarez Bravo photographed Frida a number of times, and one of his portraits of her shows her on the roof of a Mexico City house, dressed in a Mexican costume and juxtaposed with empty clothes drying on a laundry line. When asked about the relationship of this image to those of Frida's paintings that depict empty clothes, he said that it was very possible that his knowledge of her work affected his decision to photograph her in this way (Manuel Alvarez Bravo, private interview, Mexico City, February 1978).

CHAPTER 9: GRINGOLANDIA

114 "whitewash those horrible frescoes": Wolfe, *Fabulous Life of Diego Rivera*, p. 203.

115 "the philosopher of the brush": Ibid., p. 301. Rivera resigned from the artists' syndicate in July 1924, because he did not want to ally himself with its protest over the wave of vandalism that had caused considerable damage to the Preparatory School murals. Later, in the Ministry of Education building, he painted a caricature of his old patron Vasconcelos as a dwarf straddling an elephant and dipping his pen in a spittoon.

115 As critic Max Kozloff put it: Kozloff, "The Rivera Frescoes of Modern Industry at the Detroit Institute of Arts: Proletarian Art Under Capitalist Patronage," *Artforum* 12 (November 1973): 60.

116 "one thing left for me": *New York Times*, May 17, 1933.

116 "There is so much beauty": Edward Weston, *The Daybooks of Edward Weston*, vol. I, "Mexico" (California: An Aperture Book, 1961), pp. 34–35. Rivera's positive attitude toward the United States is also revealed in an interview with him, possibly conducted by Bertram Wolfe or Frida Kahlo, in Bertram D. Wolfe archive, Hoover Institution, Stanford University.

116 "Frida dreamed": Rivera, *My Art, My Life*, p. 174. The self-portrait Frida gave Diego en route to San Francisco may be the pencil drawing in the Frida Kahlo

Museum that Frida falsely called her first drawing. It shows Frida in front of a background that is half U.S. skyscrapers and half Mexican mountains.

117 "Since they didn't have a phone": Blanch, private interview.

117 "Your game of football": Wolfe, *Fabulous Life of Diego Rivera,* p. 290.

117 Years later Frida told a friend: Loló de la Torriente, "Verdad y Mentira en la Vida de Frida Kahlo y Diego Rivera," p. 21.

118 "The city and bay are overwhelming": Frida Kahlo, letter to Isabel Campos (May 3, 1931), published in Tibol, *Frida Kahlo,* pp. 42–43.

118 "We were feted at parties": Rivera, *My Art, My Life,* p. 175.

118 The *Call-Bulletin* reported: Wolfe, *Fabulous Life of Diego Rivera,* p. 287.

119 "I don't particularly like the gringo people": Kahlo, letter to Isabel Campos, May 3, 1931.

119 "I am the adventurer": Weston, *Daybooks,* vol. 2, "California," p. xi.

119 "Why this tide of women?": Ibid., p. ix.

120 "I met Diego!": Ibid., pp. 198–99.

120 he diagnosed a congenital deformation of her spine: The diagnosis is an indication that not all Frida's subsequent problems with her spine were the result of her accident. Frida also apparently had symptoms of syphilis, for a Wassermann and Kahn test was administered. The results were "slightly positive," and she was treated for the disease. Subsequent tests in the 1930s and 1940s were (usually) negative (Begun, medical record).

120 At the age of forty-nine: This account of Dr. Eloesser's personality and life is from a private interview with Joyce Campbell, Tacambaro, Michoacán, Mexico, July 1977. Joyce Campbell was Dr. Eloesser's closest friend for many years.

121 "A few notes on the painting": Letter from Dr. Eloesser to Mr. William Zinn, the gifts and endowments officer of the University of California Hospital in San Francisco, in the hospital archive.

122 Lady Cristina Hastings: Lucienne Bloch, private interview.

122 Frida wrote of her exasperation: Letter to Dr. Leo Eloesser, Mar. 15, 1941. Frida Kahlo's letters to Dr. Eloesser from 1931 to 1946 are in Joyce Campbell's personal archive.

123 *Luther Burbank:* The element of fantasy in this painting, so different from the simpler, more straightforward portraits Frida did in San Francisco, may indicate that it was completed after Frida and Diego returned to Mexico (for a six-month period) in June 1931. Further evidence of this is a photograph (almost certainly taken in Mexico and now in the archives of Mexico's Institute of Fine Arts) of Luther Burbank, which shows the painting before it was finished.

123 *Frida and Diego Rivera:* The painting was exhibited at the sixth annual exhibition of the San Francisco Society of Women Artists at the California Palace of the Legion of Honor in 1932 and prominently reproduced in at least one local newspaper. It is now in the collection of the San Francisco Museum; the museum staff feel strongly that the title of the painting should accord with the spelling of the inscription and should therefore be *Frieda and Diego Rivera.*

124 "I spend most of my time painting": Kahlo, letter to Isabel Campos, 1931.

124 "His enormous stomach": Kahlo, *"Retrato de Diego."*

125 "Diego is beyond all limited . . . relations": Ibid.

125 At a dinner: Blanch, private interview.

126 "Rivera for Mexico City": Wolfe, *Fabulous Life of Diego Rivera,* p. 285.

126 Painter Kenneth Callahan's complaint: Ibid., p. 292. In later years the mural was covered, not because of Rivera's "fat rear" but because figurative art was out of fashion. Times have changed, and now it is once again proudly displayed.

128 Mexican Arts Association "to promote friendship": Wolfe, *Fabulous Life of Diego Rivera,* p. 297.

128 "Diego's very spinal column": Museum of Modern Art, *Diego Rivera,* Exhibition Catalogue (New York: Museum of Modern Art, 1931), p. 35.

128 Diego was on deck: The details of the Riveras' arrival in New York and Diego's

comments are from the *New York Herald Tribune*, Nov. 14, 1931. Bertram Wolfe's account of the arrival (*Fabulous Life of Diego Rivera*, p. 278) cites (erroneously) *"New York Times*, December 14, 1931."

129   She once asked him: Lucienne Bloch, private interview.
130   "I was sitting next to Diego": Ibid.
131   "We had lunch with Frieda": Diary of Lucienne Bloch. Lucienne Bloch read portions of the diary aloud to the author during their private interview.
132   "Had a delicious meal": Ibid., December 1931.
132   "As concerns what you asked me": Letter to Dr. Eloesser, May 26, 1932.

Chapter 10: Detroit: Henry Ford Hospital

133   To Diego Rivera, Detroit: Linda Downs, "The Rouge in 1932: The 'Detroit Industry' Frescoes by Diego Rivera," in the Detroit Institute of Arts, *The Rouge: The Image of Industry in the Art of Charles Sheeler and Diego Rivera* (Detroit Institute of Arts, 1978), pp. 47–48.
133   William Valentiner . . . met Rivera: Dr. Valentiner met Rivera through Helen Wills, and with his new friend had the terrifying experience of being driven by the athlete to one of her tennis matches: "I sat in the rumble seat next to Rivera. While we discussed balance and harmony in composition, we found ourselves pitched backwards to a horizontal position and looking directly at the sky, because Helen Wills took delight in driving us up the steepest of steep streets in San Francisco. Indeed Rivera's weight carried him so far backwards that I was afraid he might tumble out, and I with him" (Downs, "The Rouge," pp. 47–48).
133   "the great Saga of the machine and of steel": *Detroit News*, Jan. 19, 1933, p. 4.
133   They were met at the station: With the exception of the quotation "His name is Carmen," the description of the Riveras' arrival in Detroit is largely from *Detroit News*, April 22, 1932. Edgar P. Richardson, in a letter to the author (Jan. 30, 1978), remembered Diego's broken English.
135   the Wardell: Lucienne Bloch, private interview.
134   "I now placed the collective hero": Rivera, *My Art, My Life*, p. 183.
135   he called the . . . fountain *"horrorosa"*: *Detroit News*, Apr. 22, 1932.
135   "a wonderful symphony": Rivera, *My Art, My Life*, p. 187.
135   "Marx made theory": Ibid., p. 188.
135   she retaliated: This account of Frida's social life in Detroit is derived from private interviews or other communications with people who knew her there: Mrs. Barnett Malbin (private telephone interview, New York City, January 1978); Lenore de Martínez (Detroit, January 1978); Ernst Halberstadt (Onset, Massachusetts, September 1978); Edgar P. Richardson (letter to the author, Jan. 30, 1978); Peggy de Salle (Detroit, January 1978); Lucienne Bloch (private interview and diary).
135   "Mr. Ford, are you Jewish?": Lucienne Bloch, private interview.
136   In Mexico, Frida said, there was more sparkle: de Salle, private interview.
136   the matter of food: Lucienne Bloch, private interview.
136   When Frida chastised him: Ríos y Valles, private interview.
136   [Frida's] success at a folk dancing party: Rivera, *My Art, My Life*, pp. 188–89.
136   "When we went to Detroit": Bambi, "Frida Dice Lo Que Sabe," p. 7.
137   Actually, the car was a trade: Lucienne Bloch, diary, late October 1932, and private interview; Ernst Halberstadt, private interview.
140   When Lucienne Bloch came to Detroit: Lucienne Bloch, interviewed by Karen and David Crommie.
140   Lucienne worked . . . designing small figurines: Frida used to tell Lucienne that she should work in larger scale, that making such tiny sculptures was bad for her career. It was serving as Rivera's assistant that finally impelled Lucienne to abandon her plan to be a sculptor. Instead, she became a mural painter, and she has been painting frescoes ever since (Lucienne Bloch, private interview).
141   "She was just hoping to be pregnant": Lucienne Bloch, Crommie interview.

141 "I wish I were dead!": de Salle, private interview.
142 when Lucienne brought her a parody: Lucienne Bloch, private interview.
142 Frida wanted to draw her lost child: Lucienne Bloch Crommie interview.
144 Rivera noted the change: Rivera, *My Art, My Life*, p. 202.
144 "my idea of . . . the insides of a woman": Lesley notes.
144 The snail . . . refers to . . . the miscarriage: Ibid.
144 The meaning of the . . . machinery: Lucienne Bloch, private interview, and Wolfe, "Rise of Another Rivera," unedited draft in the Frida Kahlo archive, Frida Kahlo Museum, Mexico City.
144 "anything mechanical" always meant bad luck and pain: Lesley notes.
144 Frida herself told one friend: Helm, *Modern Mexican painters*, p. 169.
144 to another she said that she had "invented [it]": Lesley notes.
145 "Diego gave [the orchid] to me": Ibid.
145 she said she painted the ground . . . earth color: Ibid.
145 To help her combat depression: Lucienne Bloch, private interview.
145 Frida was "like the wildest animal": Lucienne Bloch, diary, July–August 1932.
146 "These proofs are not good and not bad": Muller's comments were written on the second proof of the lithograph, which was dated August 1932, and signed "Frieda Rivera" instead of "Frieda Kahlo," perhaps because Muller was Rivera's, not Frida's friend.
146 Frida returned to her easel: Lucienne Bloch, private interview, and Crommie interview.
146 Three more times . . . Frida was to try to have a child: Rivera, *My Art, My Life*, p. 201.
146 he "forbade her to conceive again": Ibid.
147 "Diego was very cruel." Ella Wolfe, private interview, Palo Alto, California, November 1978. Frida's inability to bear a child has most often been attributed to the accident. Certainly that played a role, but Frida's medical record says that in 1934, when Frida was pregnant for the third time, a Dr. Zollinger ordered an abortion after three months because of the "infantilism of Frida's ovaries." Both of Frida's older sisters also had "insufficient ovaries"; neither bore children (Adriana had three miscarriages), and both eventually had their ovaries removed because of cysts (Begun, medical report). Gómez Arias says that "once she told me that all her feminine organs kept certain infantile characteristics during her whole life. They were organs of a small girl in a grown woman" (Gómez Arias, private interview). Another possibility, a remote one, is that syphilis played some role. Ulcers on the feet are a symptom of secondary syphilis.
147 "bring me a doll": Bambi, "Manuel, el Chófer de Diego Rivera," p. 1.
148 "My painting carries within it": Tibol, *Crónica*, p. 50.
149 "Frida came in every day": José de Jesús Alfaro, private interview, Detroit, January 1978.
149 Stephen Dimitroff tried to charm his way: Stephen Pope Dimitroff, interviewed by Karen and David Crommie, and Lucienne Bloch, private interview.
149 She would stop suddenly and say: Lucienne Bloch, private interview.
149 At home, with Lucienne: Lucienne Bloch, private interview and diary.
150 "My paintings are well painted": Tibol, *Crónica*, p. 50.
151 "Frida's *retablos* do not look like *retablos*": Rivera, "Frida Kahlo y el Arte Mexicano," p. 101. *Retablos* have been made in Mexico from colonial times. Most often the saved person or his family commissions the work from a professional ex-voto painter, who considers himself an anonymous craftsman and does not sign the painting. The purchasers hang their *retablos* in chruches; sanctuaries dedicated to particularly effective saints are sometimes covered with these ex-voto paintings as well as with other votive offerings—crutches, photographs, trusses, and silver charms in the shape of the leg, heart, ear, or any part of the body that has been miraculously healed.
152 Lucienne Bloch remembers how the painting came to be: Lucienne Bloch, private interview and diary.

152   "In most nature religions" Bertram D. Wolfe and Diego Rivera, *Portrait of Mexico*, p. 49.
153   "To tell you the truth": Letter to Dr. Eloesser, July 29, 1932.
154   On September 3 she received a telegram: Lucienne Bloch, private interview and diary.
155   Frida wrote a letter to Diego: This letter was copied by Bertram Wolfe, and together with Diego's reply, it is in his papers in the archive at the Hoover Institution, Stanford University.
157   "Frida returned to Detroit": Rivera, *My Art, My Life*, pp. 193–94.
157   The first of the series suggested by Diego: Lucienne Bloch said Rivera suggested the series to Frida (private interview).
157   "how I imagined I was born": Lesley notes.
157   the Virgin of Sorrows . . . as "part of a memory image": Lesley notes.
158   "The mother's face": Rivera, "Frida Kahlo y el Arte Mexicano," p. 101.
158   "I wanted to make a series of pictures": Lesley notes
159   "Wife of the Master Mural Painter": Florence Davies, "Wife of the Master Mural Painter Gleefully Dabbles in Works of Art,": *Detroit News*, Feb. 2, 1933, p. 16.

CHAPTER 11: REVOLUTIONARIES IN THE TEMPLE OF FINANCE

161   "heartless hoax on his capitalistic employers": Wolfe, *Fabulous Life of Diego Rivera*, p. 312.
161   "I admire Rivera's spirit": Ibid., p. 314.
161   "the beginning of the realization": Rivera, *My Art, My Life*, p. 200.
162   teaching Mexican ballads: Lucienne Bloch, Crommie interview. Frida's favorite was about a train crash that took place in 1895 and killed large numbers of people. *Corridos*, like *retablos* or José Guadalupe Posada's engravings, often tell about real disasters. They are a form of musical journalism, with all the grisly details, plus date, place, and number of people killed and injured, set to verse. Besides accidents, *corridos* report on crimes, suicides, natural disasters, and weird occurrences such as ghostly apparitions, the arrest of forty-one male homosexuals, or the woman with one hundred husbands. Given their taste for the lurid, it comes as no surprise that both Diego and Frida loved to sing these songs.
162   "Frida did all the worst ones": Lucienne Bloch, private interview.
163   "She stuck it under the bedcovers": Suzanne Bloch, private interview, New York City, April 1977.
163   "Frida went through dime stores": Lucienne Bloch, private interview.
163   Once when she was passing a pharmacy: Mary Sklar, private interview, New York City, September 1977.
163   David Margolis . . . remembers: Margolis, private interview, New York City, June 1978.
163   preferred to go to Brooklyn: Beryl Becker, private interview, Cuernavaca, Mexico, August 1977.
163   "bored to tears": Lucienne Bloch, private interview.
164   "acted like the worst mischiefs": Lucienne Bloch, diary.
164   "Men at the Crossroads": Wolfe, *Fabulous Life of Diego Rivera*, p. 317.
164   "Rivera Paints Scenes": Ibid., p. 325.
164   "something could happen": Lucienne Bloch, diary.
165   "seriously offend a great many": Wolfe, *Fabulous Life of Diego Rivera*, p. 325.
165   "Workers Unite! Help protect": *Time*, May 22, 1933, p. 25.
165   "Save Rivera's Painting": Ibid.
166   "I Paint What I See": E. B. White, "I Paint What I See," *New Yorker*, May 20, 1933, p. 29. Also published in *Poems and Sketches of E. B. White* (New York: Harper & Row 1981), pp. 35–36.
166   Rockefeller Center mural was "reactionary": Rivera, *My Art, My Life*, p. 210.
167   Rockefeller came up to her: Lucienne Bloch, private interview.

167 "Señora Diego Rivera": Geraldine Sartain, "Rivera's Wife Rues Art Ban," *New York World Telegram,* June 10, 1933.

168 Rivera . . . announced: Wolfe, *Fabulous Life of Diego Rivera,* p. 334.

168 twenty-one movable panels: The panels are now in the dining hall of Unity House, the International Ladies' Garment Workers' Union Recreation Center in Forest Park, Pennsylvania.

168 "Diego Rivera, Mexican Artist": *New York Times,* May 16, 1933.

169 the Riveras' "house was always open": Louise Nevelson, *Dawns and Dusks,* taped conversations with Diana MacKown. (New York: Scribner's, 1976), p. 57.

169 "We will go to dinner": Marjorie Eaton, private interview, Palo Alto, California, November 1978.

169 "We used to carry on": Nevelson, *Dawns and Dusks,* p. 65.

170 He showed his gratitude: Eaton, private interview. According to Eaton, Nevelson was embarrassed about the gift and did not wear it that evening when she joined Frida and Diego for dinner. She was greatly relieved when Rivera turned to her in Frida's presence and asked, "Have you shown Frida your necklace?"

170 Rivera was . . . with Louise: Lucienne Bloch, private interview.

170 her right foot felt paralyzed: Begun, medical record.

170 "Frida did not go out": Lupe Marín, private interview, Mexico City, July 1977.

170 "Oh, I hate to be alone": Suzanne Bloch, private interview.

170 "he wanted to be independent": Lucienne Bloch, private interview.

172 a lot of "bunk": Lucienne Bloch, Crommie interview.

172 "New York is very pretty": Frida Kahlo, letter to Isabel Campos (Nov. 16, 1933), published in Tibol, *Frida Kahlo,* pp. 43, 46–47.

175 "the George Washington Bridge": *New York Times Magazine,* Apr. 2, 1933, p. 11.

175 a heated argument: Lucienne Bloch, private interview.

176 "We got together a group": Nevelson, *Dawns and Dusks,* p. 59.

Chapter 12: A Few Small Nips

179 "from a bohemian point of view": Ella Wolfe, private interview.

179 "[Diego's] architectural theories": Ric y Rac, "In-Mural," *Excelsior* (Mexico City), Aug. 14, 1949, sec. 2, p. 1.

180 *A Few Small Nips* is based on a newspaper account: The story behind this painting was told in Loló de la Torriente, "Verdad y Mentira en la Vida de Frida Kahlo y Diego Rivera," and in a private interview with a Spanish refugee painter, a friend of Frida's, who wishes to remain anonymous. The drawing for *A Few Small Nips* is lost, but it is documented in a photograph of several drawings by Frida that was displayed in Frida's retrospective at Mexico's Palace of Fine Arts in 1977. It shows the murdered woman naked on a bed with the murderer and a small boy standing over her and weeping. A dove holds a ribbon in its beak. On the ribbon are the words *"Mi chata ya no me quiere"* ("My cutie doesn't love me anymore"). In the upper right corner, the murderer's words are put into verse: "My cutie doesn't love me anymore, because she loves another bastard, but today she was snatched away for sure, now her hour has come." At the bottom of the page his words continue: "A few small 'nips.' It was not twenty stabs, mister."

180 "The verb [*chingar,* to screw]": Paz, *Labyrinth,* pp. 76–77, 86. Violence to women who reject, disobey, or betray a man is a familiar theme in Mexican life and culture. There are, for example, numerous ballads about men's violent retaliation against women; one that Frida kept among her papers tells the story of Rosita Alvarez, who was murdered by a man with whom she refused to dance (Frida Kahlo archive, Frida Kahlo Museum). In Mexico, crimes of passion like the one depicted in *A Few Small Nips* are often considered human foibles rather than heinous acts. Murders prompted by pride are deemed manly. "Murder," said Octavio Paz, "is still a relationship in Mexico, and in this sense it has the same liberating significance

as the fiesta or the confession. Hence its drama, its poetry and—why not say it?—its grandeur. Through murder we achieve a momentary transcendence" (*Labyrinth*, p. 61).

181 "because in Mexico killing is quite satisfactory": Lesley notes.
181 a doctor . . . ordered him to be "reinflated": Wolfe, *Fabulous Life of Diego Rivera*, p. 309.
181 He was "weak, thin, yellow": Frida Kahlo's letters to Ella Wolfe are in the Bertram Wolfe archive, Hoover Institution, Stanford University.
182 "My right foot": Letter to Dr. Eloesser, Oct. 24, 1934.
182 The foot was operated on: Begun, medical record. This was the first of several operations on Frida's right foot. In 1935 she had another, and the doctors discovered that she had problems with sesamoids (small bony or cartilaginous nodules that can develop in tendons). This time her foot took six months to heal. In 1936, with a third operation, the sesamoids were removed. Once again, healing was slow.
182 "she lives a little bit in . . . ether": Letter to Ella Wolfe, dated "Wednesday 13," 1938.
183 Frida had been told by her doctors: Tibol, private interview, Mexico City, August 1977.
183 "If I loved a woman": Rivera, *My Art, My Life*, pp. 287–88.
185 Frida actually consulted a lawyer: Gómez Arias, private interview.
185 he bought Frida a set of blue . . . "moderne" furniture: Eaton, private interview.
185 to furnish a flat for Cristina: Dr. Samuel Fastlich, private interview, Mexico City, November 1977.
185 her friends: Annette Nancarrow, private interview, New York City, November 1979.
185 "Look!" she cried: Gómez Arias, private interviews.
186 The trip: Sklar, private interview.
186 "As the flames of resentment died": Wolfe, *Fabulous Life of Diego Rivera*, p. 357.
186 "all these letters, liaisons": Ibid., pp. 357–58.
186 [Rivera] tells of an incident: Rivera, *My Art, My Life*, pp. 214–15.
187 Frida said they stood for good and evil: Ibid.
188 *Memory* . . . also may refer: In 1939, when Frida gave the painting to Michel Petitjean, she told him it was about how her 1925 accident had changed her (Petitjean, private interview, Paris, November 1981).
190 "lyrical bright Mexican colors": Kaufmann, private interview. Kaufmann also remembers that *Remembrance* "had a flat frame upholstered in velvet. The parallel sides were alternately upholstered in muted red and green which were less bright than the colors of the painting itself. It was all very lively."
190 She candidly told male friends: Julien Levy, private interview, Bridgewater, Connecticut, Apr. 1977, and Kaufmann, private interview.

Chapter 13: Trotsky

192 when Frida was angry at him: Sidney Simon, private interview, Wellfleet, Massachusetts, August 1978.
193 Diego provided the money: This account of the Riveras' financial affairs is derived from Wolfe, *Fabulous Life of Diego Rivera*, Ella Wolfe, private interview, and many interviews with Frida's friends.
193 when reprimanded, he would counter: Ella Wolfe, private interview.
193 "Frida used to scold me": Rivera, *My Art, My Life*, pp. 251–52.
193 "There were times": Ibid.
193 A typical message from Frida reads: Frida's letters to Alberto Misrachi and to his nephew (also Alberto Misrachi), dating from 1935 through 1946, are in the Alberto Misrachi, Central de Publicaciones, S.A., archive, Mexico City.

194 When all was well: This account of the Riveras' daily life is derived from van Heijenoort and Eaton, private interviews.

194 an excursion . . . "to some little village": Letter to Dr. Eloesser, July 12, 1936. In this same letter Frida mentioned the self-portrait: "I'm finishing my portrait for you painted by me, the one that you asked me for in your letter from Russia." On December 17 she wrote asking him if she should send the *pinturita* (little painting) to him.

195 "Always, from the age of four": Isolda Kahlo, private interview.

195 they wrote her loving letters: Isolda and Antonio Kahlo's letters to Frida from August and September 1940 are in the Frida Kahlo's archive.

196 "I came for lunch": Eaton, private interview.

196 The bold spider monkey: Ella Wolfe, private interview.

196 "some evenings": van Heijenoort, private interview.

197 Frida . . . began to carry a little flask: Frida's drinking habits were described by Jean van Heijenoort, Ella Wolfe, Julien Levy, and others in interviews with the author.

197 "You can tell Boit": Letter to Ella Wolfe, dated "Wednesday 13," 1938. Frida borrowed the witticism "I drank because I wanted to drown my sorrows, but now the damned things have learned to swim" from a close friend of hers, the poet José Frías (Wolfe, *Fabulous Life of Diego Rivera*, pp. 107–8).

198 Lucienne Bloch remembers: Lucienne Bloch, private interview.

198 "Frida had many girl friends": van Heijenoort, private interview.

198 Picasso . . . is reported to have said: Told to the author by Leo Steinberg, in fall 1973.

199 "the indigenous nude": Dolores del Rio, private interview, Mexico City, November 1977.

199 "[Diego] considered Frida's lesbian affairs a . . . safety valve": van Heijenoort, private interview.

200 "I loved her very much": Isamu Noguchi, private interview, Long Island City, New York, April 1977.

200 The two were planning: Eaton, private interview.

201 Others say the affair: Roberto BeHar, private interview, Mexico City, October 1977.

201 As Noguchi tells it: Noguchi, private interview. Frida was in the English Hospital for the operation on her foot.

201 As early as 1933 . . . Diego had declared his sympathies: Margolis, private interview.

202 Rivera decided to tell his side: Emanuel Eisenberg, "Battle of the Century," *New Masses*, Dec. 10, 1935, pp. 18–20. Siqueiros had launched a crusade of insults against Rivera in the early 1930s. On May 29, 1934, for example, he published a vituperative attack on his old friend in *The New Masses*, calling Rivera "counter-revolutionary," "painter of millionaires," and "esthete of imperialism." Rivera counter attacked, saying, in a December 1935 article entitled "Defense and Attack Against the Stalinists," that Siqueiros was a tool of the Stalinists. (Both Rivera's and Siqueiros's articles are reprinted in Raquel Tibol, *Documentación Sobre el Arte Mexicano*, Fondo de Cultura Económica, Mexico City, 1974, pp. 53–82.)

203 "the liveliest and strongest hope": Letter to Dr. Leo Eloesser, Jan. 30, 1937. Frida's political concern expressed itself in a strange painting, which is now lost, but was reproduced in the Mexico City newspaper *Novedades* on July 17, 1955. The reproduction shows a scene that corresponds with the title *Survivor* (the name of a painting listed in Frida's 1938 exhibition in New York) and with the title *The Air Crash*, given it by Bertram Wolfe in "Rise of Another Rivera," publication of which was timed to coincide with that exhibition. Beneath the newspaper illustration is the caption: "A testimony of sufferings of a world in war" (*Novedades*, Supplement, "México en la Cultura," July 17, 1955, p. 6). Very possibly the painting is an expression of Frida's reaction to the horrors she had heard about firsthand

from the Spanish militiamen. It shows a scene of carnage in which one lone survivor, a wounded man, looks at a burning, crashed airplane and at bloodied and mangled bodies—apparently civilians, since some are women—strewn on the ground.

204 [Trotsky] . . . came close to despair: Jean van Heijenoort, *With Trotsky in Exile: From Prinkipo to Coyoacán*, p. 89.

204 On November 21, Rivera: Octavio Fernández, "Cómo Se Obtuvo el Derecho de Asilo para Trotsky en México," *La Prensa* (Mexico City), Apr. 20, 1956, pp. 20–21, 39.

205 Trotsky told the police: Robert Payne, *The Life and Death of Trotsky* (New York: McGraw-Hill, 1977), p. 391.

205 a welcoming party: Leon Trotsky, *Writings of Leon Trotsky*, 1936–1937, p. 79.

205 "It was to him above all": Ibid., p. 80.

205 "After four months": Ibid., p. 79.

205 A special train: *Time*, Jan. 16, 1937, p. 16.

206 Trotsky embraced Rivera: Trotsky, *Writings (1936–1937)*, p. 80.

206 details of Trotsky's safety: Payne, *Trotsky*, pp. 391–92.

206 "We were on a new planet": Joel Carmichael, *Trotsky: An Appreciation of His Life* (New York: St. Martins, 1975), p. 432.

207 "Who are these people?": Gómez Arias, private interviews.

207 "At latest reports": *Time*, Jan. 16, 1937, p. 16.

207 "The experience of my life": Isaac Deutscher, *The Prophet Outcast, Trotsky: 1929–1940*, vol. 3 of a trilogy (London: Oxford University Press, 1963), p. 380.

208 During the months following the "trial": This account of the activities of the Riveras and the Trotskys comes from Jean van Heijenoort (private interview and *Trotsky in Exile*).

208 "If they were together": van Heijenoort, private interview.

209 In a *Partisan Review* article: The article is quoted in Wolfe, *Fabulous Life of Diego Rivera*, pp. 238–39.

209 He was also a man with a vigorous interest in sex: van Heijenoort, private interview.

210 "Frida did not hesitate to use the word love: van Heijenoort, private interview.

210 "I saw myself in a mirror": Jean van Heijenoort, "Correspondence of Leon and Natalia Trotsky, 1933–1938." This unpublished manuscript is van Heijenoort's English translation of the letters the Trotskys wrote to each other during the brief periods they were apart. The correspondence has been published in a French translation, also by van Heijenoort (Paris: Gallimard, 1980).

211 [Natalia] wrote her husband a letter: Ibid.

211 Trotsky's distinctly underplayed report: Ibid. The following day (July 12), Trotsky wrote that he had just received a letter Natalia had written on July 10, before she learned of Frida's trip. The July 10 letter is missing from the Trotsky archives, almost certainly because Natalia, feeling that it revealed too much about her pain over the affair, destroyed it after her husband's death.

211 "Now, let me tell you about the visit": Ibid.

212 "I remembered that yesterday": Ibid.

212 Ella Wolfe believes: Ella Wolfe, private interview.

212 "It was impossible to go on": van Heijenoort, private interview.

213 In a film showing Trotsky: The film was taken by Ivan C. F. Heisler, who was visiting Trotsky with his father, Francis Heisler. It is now in the Trotsky Collection, Hoover Institution, Stanford University. Natalia's approach to Frida was a rather odd combination of aloofness and affection. Sometimes when Diego and Frida came to the Coyoacán house, Natalia would not come out of her room. At other times, she would greet Frida with a kiss or give her flowers (van Heijenoort, private interview). Many photographs of outings in the environs of Mexico City show Natalia next to Frida, as if she were keeping an eye on someone she did not trust. A more subtle reason for Natalia's attentiveness to Frida might be that curious emotion that causes some people to love the person his or her loved one loves.

Loving the same man can create a kind of complicity between two women. Natalia's bond with Frida lasted even after Trotsky was killed and Natalia had not seen Frida for years. Natalia made a special point, for example, of taking a French Trotskyite visiting Mexico in the 1940s to see the frescoes in Coyoacán done by Frida's students under her supervision (van Heijenoort, private interview).

214 "I have for long admired": André Breton, "Frida Kahlo," in *Surrealism and Painting,* pp. 141–44.

CHAPTER 14: A PAINTER IN HER OWN RIGHT

215 a letter dated February 14, 1938: Frida's letter to Lucienne Bloch is in Mrs. Bloch's personal archive.

215 She wrote to Ella Wolfe in the spring: The letter is dated "Wednesday 13," 1938.

219 Mexico's ancient heritage is reborn in each new generation: Frida said she depicted herself with the body of an infant and her head as it looked at the time when she made the painting because she wanted to show the continuity of life (Lesley notes). In her perception of the continuity of Mexican culture, she would have agreed with Octavio Paz, who observed that the traditional Mexican attitude toward time is a passionate feeling of connection with the past. Mexico is a "land of super-imposed pasts. Mexico City was built on the ruins of Tenochtitlán, the Aztec city that was built in the likeness of Tula, the Toltec city that was built in the likeness of Teotihuacán, the first great city on the American continent. Every Mexican bears within him this continuity, which goes back two thousand years. It doesn't matter that this presence is almost always unconscious and assumes the naive forms of legend and even superstitution. It is not something known but something lived" (Paz, "Reflections: Mexico and the United States," *New Yorker,* Sept. 17, 1979, pp. 140–41).

220 the ducts and glands: Here, as on many other occasions, Frida used a medical illustration as a source for interior anatomy. Frida Kahlo's personal archive has a page from a catalogue selling "physiological supports scientifically designed" that illustrates the ducts and glands of a lactating breast. Another precedent for the idea of showing the ducts and glands inside the breast is the breast with its inner structure revealed as if by X-ray vision in Rivera's Palace of Fine Arts mural, the second version of his Rockefeller Center fresco.

220 "milk from the virgin": Lesley notes.

220 "I appear with the face": Ibid.

221 Dolores del Rio . . . says: Dolores del Rio, private interview. Frida painted the child with the death mask again in a very similar painting (now lost), which was reproduced in *Novedades* (Mexico City), supplement, "México en la Cultura," June 10, 1951, p. 2.

221 a family in Ixtapalapa: Bertram D. Wolfe's *Portrait of Mexico* illustrates several of Rivera's portraits of the children of the Rosas family (see, for example, *Portrait of Dimas,* 1935, plate 51), and Wolfe writes of the the family in Ixtapalapa on pp. 27–28. Alejandro Gómez Arias believes that Dimas was the son of one of the Riveras' household servants (Gómez Arias, private interviews). Dimas wears a cardboard crown: One can only hope that poor Dimas's festive apparel has nothing to do with the old Mexican custom that continued into the first quarter of the twentieth century and was described by Ernest Gruening in his *Mexico and Its Heritage,* published in 1928. Gruening speaks of the practice that was part of the wakes of poor families and consisted of suspending dead babies "for the edification of the neighbors, for twenty-four hours or more." And he quotes a report on Mexico by a French priest who lived in Mexico for twenty years in the mid-nineteenth century: "I have spoken of the custom of dressing up deceased children, of decorating them with silk wings, paper crowns, flowers and ribbons, of displaying them seated on a chair or stretched on a table, of burying them to the noise of petards, or of instruments playing polkas and quadriles. In Mexico

City, and in the interior, I have seen even more revolting things. *Pulque* merchants hired these corpses called *angelitos* (little angles) to attract trade: First there were prayers; then one drank; young girls made these occasions for rendezvous with their beaux. The corpse would serve several merchants and be buried only when putrefaction was well advanced." Gruening notes the resemblance of this custom to the Aztec practice of decorating the dead with various kinds of papers. The portrait of the dead Dimas dressed as an *angelito* retains something of the barbarism of such customs.

222   *se petateó* means: Wolfe, *Portrait of Mexico*, p. 22.

224   *Pitahayas* (now lost): *Pitahayas* was shown in the Golden Gate International Exposition and it was probably sold to someone in California in 1940. A letter to Frida (July 29, 1940) from Thomas Carr Howe, Jr., director of the California Palace of the Legion of Honor, says that a Mrs. Ryan (head of the sales department at the exposition) had an offer for $120 from an important collector. (The painting was priced at $150.) The result of this inquiry is not known.

224   "I never imagined": Breton, *Surrealism and Painting*, p. 143.

224   the tumultuous Mexican sky: Frida's intuition of nature's responsiveness to her emotions is also demonstrated in the way the knots of the wooden table on which the fruit is displayed in *Fruits of the Earth* are made to look like wounds. Old photographs of this painting show that it originally had a pale blue sky with fleecy white clouds. Some time after it was finished, Frida repainted the sky a dark gray with stormy clouds, leaving a strip of the original blue sky at the top, so that one section of the sky overlaps the other as if both were theatrical backdrops. Possibly she made this change in order to express her gloom after her separation from Diego in 1939. Like the tablecloth that metamorphoses into landscape and sky in *Tunas*, the double sky is a surrealistic device, the kind of thing Magritte might have done, and it underscores the fictional, mutable—indeed, the totally unreliable—nature of Frida's reality.

225   "She's working now": van Heijenoort, private interview.

225   "Diego always wants": Letter to Julien Levy, undated draft, Frida Kahlo archive.

225   she told Lucienne: Lucienne Bloch, private interview.

225   "For that price": Private interview with an old friend of Frida's who wished to remain anonymous.

225   "It must be because": Lucienne Bloch, private interview.

226   "I kept about twenty-eight paintings hidden": Bambi, "Frida Kahlo Es una Mitád," p. 6. A letter from Gladys Lloyd Robinson to Diego Rivera and Frida Kahlo (Sept. 7, 1938) in the Kahlo archive says: "Everybody raved about Frida's four paintings and yours. . . . They simply fell in love with 'Me and My Doll' and the portraits and were crazy about the way they were framed. . . . Everybody agreed that Frida is a great artist and are falling over themselves to see all the new additions to our collection."

226   "Surrealist place par excellence": This and the following quote are from Ida Rodríguez Prampolini, *El Surrealismo y el Arte Fantástico de México*, p. 54, and from an interview with Breton by Rafael Helidoro Valle that appeared in *Universidad* (Mexico, D.F.), 29 (June 1938): 5–8.

227   [Trotsky] became incensed: van Heijenoort, private interview.

227   "Conversations in Pátzcuaro": van Heijenoort, *Trotsky in Exile*, p. 127. The ideas explored in these "Conversations" led to the founding by Trotsky, Breton, and Rivera of an International Federation of Independent Revolutionary Artists (IFIRA) to resist totalitarian encroachments on art and literature and to counterbalance Stalinist organizations. They produced a manifesto entitled "Toward an Independent Revolutionary Art," stressing the need for artists to be free of political controls, provided that they not use this liberty to attack the revolution. Because it was directed to artists, it was signed not by Trotsky but by Breton and Rivera, even though Rivera had nothing to do with its writing.

227   "We acted like two pupils": Jacqueline Breton, private telephone interview, Paris, October 1980.

228   "My surprise and joy": Breton, *Surrealism and Painting,* p. 144.

228   "she led friends like Noguchi": Noguchi and Levy, private interviews.

229   "You ought to do a portrait of Mrs. Luce": Wolfe, *Fabulous Life of Diego Rivera,* pp. 358–59.

229   "I recommend her to you": Ibid., p. 360. The Lewisohns did befriend Frida and purchased a painting from her show. A letter to Frida from Mrs. Lewisohn (Frida Kahlo archive, Frida Kahlo Museum) says: "We love your painting which is much admired in my sitting room." Mr. and Mrs. Lewisohn's daughters have pleasant memories of Frida's visits to their parents' country house, but none of them recalls there being a Kahlo painting in their mother or father's collection. The sculptor Sidney Simon, once married to one of Lewisohn's daughters, does recall the painting, and says it was a still life. Stanton Loomis Catlin was kind enough to give me an old photograph of a 1937 still life of flowers in a vase that is decorated with the words "I Belong to My Owner." The photograph has "Mrs. Sam Lewisohn" written in pencil on the back. Presumably this painting was the one exhibited as *I Belong to My Owner* at Frida's Julien Levy show. Frida listed the Lewisohn purchase of one of her works from the Levy show in her application for a Guggenheim grant in 1940.

230   The press release: A copy of the press release is in the Frida Kahlo file in the Museum of Modern Art's library. Also in the library is the exhibition's catalogue, a brochure consisting of a single piece of folded yellow paper.

230   The catalogue listed these titles: The identity of some of these works can only be guessed at; others have been lost or are known by different titles. Frida saw nothing immutable about her paintings' titles, and according to Julien Levy, they were often made up on the spur of the moment during conversations with her various suitors (Levy, private interview). Obviously, *I with My Nurse* is *My Nurse and I. The Square Is Theirs* is *Four Inhabitants of Mexico. My Family* is *My Grandparents, My Parents and I. The Heart* is *Memory. My Dress Was There Hanging* is *My Dress Hangs There. Dressed Up for Paradise* is *The Deceased Dimas. Birth* is *My Birth. Burbank—American Fruit Maker* is *Luther Burbank.* Other identifications are less certain. *She Plays Alone* might be the version of *Girl with Masks* (now in Dolores del Rio's collection) that Levy exhibited, but it could as well be *Me and My Doll,* which, though not listed in the brochure as such, was one of the paintings Edward G. Robinson lent to the exhibition. *Passionately in Love* could be the *Portrait of Diego,* also lent by Robinson (Diego's portrait was reproduced in Wolfe's "Rise of Another Rivera"), but I suspect that this was Frida's ironical title for *A Few Small Nips,* which Wolfe, calling it "Just a Few Small Jabs," said was in the Levy exhibition. Robinson also lent the 1933 *Self-Portrait* with jade beads that Frida painted in Detroit. This might be the work listed as *Xochitl,* since Frida sometimes signed her name this way. (Xochitl was the name of a Toltec lady who popularized *pulque* in the ninth century B.C., and Frida also made Xochitl the name of one of her hairless Mexican dogs.) As for the painting called *Eye,* it could be the *Portrait of Diego,* whom we know she thought of as having a particularly acute eye. Or it could be a self-portrait, with the title a pun on the word "I."

231   "flutter of the week": *Time,* "Bomb Beribboned," Nov. 14, 1939, p. 29.

231   "more obstetrical than aesthetic": *New York Times,* Nov. 16, 1939, p. 10.

231   Another critic quibbled: Undated newspaper clipping, private archive, New York City.

232   one to . . . Chester Dale: Levy, private interview. Mrs. Elise V. H. Ferber, in the Art Information Service of the National Gallery of Art, Washington, D.C., wrote me on April 26, 1977, that no Frida Kahlo paintings came to the National Gallery with the Chester Dale bequest. Mrs. Chester Dale told me in a telephone

conversation (April 1977) that there were no Kahlos in her husband's collection. She added that she remembered Frida as a "slim little thing who sat on chaise longues a lot. She had humor, and was vivacious in a quiet way."

233   Frida said that art critic Walter Pach . . . purchased a painting: Frida Kahlo, list of patrons included in her application for a Guggenheim fellowship, 1940.

233   [Clare Boothe Luce] purchased the *Self-Portrait* dedicated to Trotsky: Mrs. Luce recalls that she was in Mexico in 1940 at the time of Trotsky's assassination. "What happened was this," she remembers: "I had commissioned a symphony in memory of my daughter who was killed from Carlos Chávez, who was at that moment minister of fine arts. I went to Mexico, and I saw a lot of Diego and Frida, who were close friends of Carlos Chávez. She showed me this self-portrait in her studio, which had been a birthday present to Trotsky. And the next day, or that night, Carlos told me that Trotsky had been murdered. Now Carlos said, "Frida cannot bear to look at it again," so I said, "Carlos, could you get it for me?" Carlos negotiated for me, and it left her studio, and I took it home. I kept the painting after I sold the rest of my collection, because it is very beautiful."

233   Frida received a commission: Sklar, private interview.
233   Conger Goodyear fell in love: Ibid.
233   "I did that: Levy, private interview.
233   "In a private collection": Letter to Gómez Arias, Nov. 1, 1938.
234   "arriving inside the bank": Levy, *Memoir.*
234   "I like this guy": Levy, private interview.
234   "fit completely the Surrealist ideal of woman" Nicolas Calas, private telephone interview, New York City, fall 1974.
234   "She didn't jump to it": Levy, private interview.
234   Her right foot: Begun, medical record.
235   Levy saw Frida as a kind of "mythical creature": Levy, private interview.
235   Edgar Kaufmann, Sr., . . . wanted to be Frida's patron: Levy, *Memoir,* p. 85.
235   She was "very cavalier with her men": Levy, private interview.
236   the Wednesday evening gatherings: Paul Gallico, "Memento Muray," essay in *The Revealing Eye: Personalities of the 20's in Photography,* by Nickolas Muray, with text by Paul Gallico, pp. 16–17.
236   letters Frida wrote: Frida Kahlo's letters to Nickolas Muray, 1930–1940, are in his daughter Mimi Muray's personal archive, Alta, Utah.
238   *Mi niñita chiquitita":* Wolfe, *Fabulous Life of Diego Rivera,* pp. 358–59.
240   "Do not stop giving thirst": In the diary there are seven lines crossed out after the word "blossoms." The poem's original ending was:

> Name of Diego—Name of love
> Do not stop giving thirst to
> the tree that loved you so much
> That treasured your seed
> That crystallized your life
> At six in the morning
> > Your Frida

CHAPTER 15: THIS PINCHISIMO PARIS

243   "You see, I had my belly full": Letter to Ella and Bertram Wolfe, Mar. 17, 1939.
243   "go back to the damn hotel": Letter to Nickolas Muray, Feb. 16, 1939.
244   "Marcel Duchamp has help me a lot": Letter to Nickolas Muray, Feb. 27, 1939.
244   Frida did . . . participate: Sources for this account of Frida's stay in Paris, in addition to her letters, are private interviews with Michel Petitjean, Jacqueline Breton, Alice Rahon (Mexico City, March 1977) and Carmen Corcuera Baron (interviewed by Elizabeth Gerhard at the request of the author, Paris, May 1978).
244   On one occasion Frida refused: Alice Rahon, private interview. Carmen Corcuera

Baron, who in 1939 was married to Frida's Paris dealer, Pierre Colle, says that Frida "always sat on the floor and she was constantly doing things with her hands," such as braiding the silk fringes of antique furniture (Gerhard interview).

245 The world of haute couture embraced her: *Time,* "Fashion Notes," May 3, 1948, pp. 33–4.

245 She went to the "thieves market": Letter to Nickolas Muray, Feb. 27, 1939.

245 "You have no idea": Letter to Nickolas Muray, Feb. 16, 1939.

246 "If you knew in what conditions": Letter to Ella and Bertram Wolfe, Mar. 17, 1939.

246 indeed, she had a brief affair: Petitjean, private interview.

246 "Diego has now fought": Letter to Bertram and Ella Wolfe, Mar. 17, 1939.

247 Personal and political conflicts: van Heijenoort, *Trotsky in Exile,* p. 136.

247 One incident points: Ibid., p. 132.

247 They disagreed about: This account is based on Payne, *Trotsky;* and van Heijenoort, *Trotsky in Exile* and private interview. Since Trotsky was closely associated with Rivera in the public eye, he felt it was necessary to disassociate himself from Rivera's political whims. Rivera characterized Lázaro Cárdenas as "an accomplice of the Stalinists" and he believed Mújica would continue the revolution in Mexico. When Mújica withdrew his candidacy, Rivera gave his support to the right-wing General Juan Andrew Almazán, who was closely tied to American business interests. This capricious act befuddled Rivera's leftist friends. But by this time (1940), the break between Rivera and Trotsky was complete.

247 "You know, I'm a bit of an anarchist": van Heijenoort, private interview.

247 "vainglorious gesture": Payne, *Trotsky,* p. 409.

247 Trotsky . . . took steps to limit his influence: van Heijenoort, private interview. van Heijenoort recalls that "the Mexican Trotskyite group was very small and it was divided into factions. All the members were very poor except Diego who had a lot of money. Thus he could impose his will on the others. If, for example, the group wanted to print a poster for something and Diego was in agreement with it, he would contribute money. If he decided that he did not like the project, he would hold back. This created chaos in the organization. Diego had the ambition to be actively involved in politics. He had a kind of guilt about just painting. Trotsky said several times: 'You are a painter, you have your work. Just help them, but do your own work' " (also, Trotsky, *Writings* [1938–1939], "Necessary Statement," Jan. 4, 1939.) The International Secretariat and the founding conference of the Fourth International resolved that Rivera should "not be a member of the reconstituted organization" but instead should work directly under the "control of the International Secretariat" (van Heijenoort, *Trotsky in Exile,* p. 133).

247 [Rivera] wrote Breton a letter: van Heijenoort, *Trotsky in Exile,* pp. 136–37.

247 Trotsky stated to the Mexican press: Deutscher, *Prophet Outcast,* pp. 444–45.

248 "We here are all very happy": Trotsky, *Writings* (1938–1939), p. 276–79.

249 Rivera refused: Diego Rivera, "Rivera Still Admires Trotsky: Regrets Their Views Clashed," *New York Times,* Apr. 15, 1939. According to Rivera, when Trotsky sent 200 pesos as rent payment, Rivera took this as an affront and would have rejected the money had he not been told that if he did, Trotsky would move his belongings out into the street. In the end, Rivera took the money and gave it to the Trotskyite magazine *Clave,* to which both he and Trotsky had contributed. In the *New York Times* article, Rivera said that his own letter to Breton had precipitated the incident with Trotsky, that he had left the Fourth International in order not to embarrass Trotsky. "The incident between Trotsky and myself is not a quarrel. It is a lamentable misunderstanding." Rivera called Trotsky "a great man . . . the man who, together with Lenin, gave victory to the proletariat of Russia," but he felt that Trotsky's circumstances and sorrows had made him "more and more difficult despite his huge reserve of goodness and generosity. I regret that fate should have decreed that I should collide against that difficult

side of his nature. But my dignity as a man precluded my doing anything to avoid it."

249 He left behind . . . a pen: van Heijenoort, *Trotsky in Exile*, p. 27.

249 [Frida] denied Rivera's demand: Wolfe, *Fabulous Life of Diego Rivera*, p. 396.

249 "absolutely impossible": Bambi, "Frida Kahlo Es una Mitád."

249 [Frida] recalled meeting . . . Ramón Mercader: Ibid.

250 the story "Mornard" told: Maria Craipeau, "Jai Connu l'Assassin de Trotsky," *France Observateur*, May 19, 1960, p. 12. Translated from the French by the author.

250 "if the show will be a successful one": This and the following quotation are from Frida's letter to Nickolas Muray, Feb. 27, 1939.

250 She canceled a London exhibition: In the Frida Kahlo archive, Frida Kahlo Museum, is a letter dated May 3, 1939, from Peggy Guggenheim: "I hope by now you are home safe and sound and that all your European troubles are over. It was a great disappointment to me that you did not come to London. Also I am very sad not to have the pleasure of showing your paintings here. I wear your beautiful earrings and they are greatly admired, and I like them better than any I have. The gallery closes here the end of June and next fall I hope the Modern Museum of Art will start in London in its stead. The Breton show gets more and more complicated. God knows how it will end." Some years later, Peggy Guggenheim did have a chance to exhibit a 1940 *Self-Portrait* by Frida.

250 Jacqueline Breton recalls . . . the opening: Jacqueline Breton, private interview.

251 a favorable review in *La Flèche*: L. P. Foucaud, "L'Exposition de Frida Kahlo," *La Flèche*, March 1939. Clipping in the Frida Kahlo archive. Translation from the French by the author.

251 Diego, naturally, had the most to say: Rivera, *My Art, My Life*, p. 224.

251 Picasso gave Frida a pair of earrings: Sklar, private interview. These must be the earrings that Frida wears in an extraordinary *Self-Portrait* drawing done in 1946.

251 He also taught her a Spanish song: Packard, private interview.

CHAPTER 16: WHAT THE WATER GAVE ME

254 "I never knew I was a Surrealist": Wolfe, "Rise of Another Rivera," p. 64.

254 Breton's definition of Surrealism: William S. Rubin, *Dada and Surrealist Art* (New York: Abrams, 1969), p. 121.

255 Miguel Covarrubias . . . categorized her as a Surrealist: Museum of Modern Art, *Twenty Centuries of Mexican Art* (New York, Museum of Modern Art, and Mexico City, Instituto de Antropología y Historia, 1940), p. 141.

255 "I adore surprise": Rodríguez, "Frida Kahlo, Expresionista," p. 68.

256 the inaugural fiesta "had the character": Rodríguez Prampolini, *El Surrealismo* pp. 55–56, quotes Mexican critic Ramón Gaya's "Divagaciones en Torno al Surrealismo."

256 Thoughtful reviewers noticed: Ibid.

256 "spiritual ingenuousness": Luis G. Basurto, Jr., "Crítica de Arte," an article in two parts published in *Excelsior* in January or February 1940. Undated newspaper clipping, Isolda Kahlo, personal archive.

256 [Frida] herself commented: Letter to Nickolas Muray dated January 1940.

256 she sent two paintings: Curiously, given their pride in their Mexican heritage, Frida and Diego were listed among the European participants rather than with the Mexicans (Catalogue of "International Exhibition of Surrealism," Galería de Arte Mexicano, 1940). It is said that this categorization had to do with the fact that both Riveras had had exhibitions outside Mexico and their reputations were international in scope. Another possible explanation is that at this particular moment they felt Mexican art should be less nationalistic and more open to foreign currents. In any case, neither was (then) averse to association with contemporary trends abroad.

256 dominance of the Mexican muralist movement: Rodríguez Prampolini, *El Surreal-ismo*, p. 44.

256 Mexico had its own magic and myths: Ibid., p. 95. Rodríguez Prampolini argues that Mexican artists reject abstraction or "pure art," and cling to the real, because of the "insecurity and ambivalence" in which they live; moreover, they want their art to transmit a message. The Mexican has a magic sense of life and an animistic perception of concrete reality. Thus, she says, there is no opposition between subject and object, between conscious and subconscious, between the symbol and the thing symbolized.

257 a painting she said had special importance: Levy and van Heijenoort, private interviews.

257 Like something in a horror movie: Perhaps Frida was influenced here by the insects and blood in Luis Buñuel and Salvador Dali's Surrealist film *Un Chien Andalou*, which was shown in Mexico City during Breton's visit in 1938, when she was working on *What the Water Gave Me*.

258 "*What the Water Yields Me* illustrated": Breton, *Surrealism and Painting*, p. 144.

259 paradigm of Surrealism described by . . . Lautréamont: Rubin, *Dada and Surrealist Art*, p. 36. Isidore Ducasse (the "Count of Lautréamont"), who died in 1870 at the age of twenty-four, was considered by the Surrealists to be their precursor.

259 "It's quite explicit": Levy, private interview.

260 Diego argued that Frida was a "realist": Rivera, "Frida Kahlo y el Arte Mexicano," p. 101.

261 "Surrealism . . . is the magical surprise": Frida Kahlo, diary.

261 "I use Surrealism as a means of poking fun": O'Gorman, "Frida Kahlo."

261 A piece that was surely hers: Gómez Arias, private interview.

262 "The trouble with *El Señor* Breton": Private interview with a friend of Frida's who wished to remain anonymous.

262 "Though André Breton": Wolfe, "Rise of Another Rivera," pp. 64, 131.

262 Parker Lesley wrote her: Letter from Parker Lesley, Frida Kahlo archive. The article was not published.

262 "painter deeply rooted in reality": Rodríguez, "Frida Kahlo: Heroína del Dolor," p. 4.

262 "Frida's work, instead of wanderings": Rodríguez, "Frida Kahlo, Expresionista," p. 68.

262 "the cock was crowing": Levy, private interview.

263 "Some critics have tried to classify me": Frida's letter is quoted in Antonio Rodríguez, "Frida Abjura del Surrealismo."

266 "They thought I was a Surrealist": *Time*, "Mexican Autobiography," Apr. 27, 1953.

CHAPTER 17: A NECKLACE OF THORNS

269 "Dear, Dear Frida": Nickolas Muray, letter to Frida Kahlo. This and the following letter, both undated, are in an envelope postmarked May 16, 1939, in the Frida Kahlo archive.

270 One friend recalls: Private interview with a Mexican friend of Frida Kahlo's who wishes not to be identified.

272 Others say Rivera was impotent: Gómez Robleda, private interview.

273 Frida once blamed Lupe Marín: Frida said this in a letter to a friend who wishes to remain anonymous.

273 "When Frida was good for nothing anymore": Marín, private interview. The painting is illustrated in Wolfe, *Diego Rivera*, fig. 69.

273 Another theory is: Private interview with an old friend of Frida's who did not wish to be identified.

273 Jean van Heijenoort thinks: van Heijenoort, *Trotsky in Exile*, p. 141.

273 a rumor that Rivera was planning to marry . . . Irene Bohus: *El Universal*, Oct. 19, 1939, newspaper clipping in Bertram D. Wolfe archive, Hoover Institution, Stanford University.

273 Rivera is widely believed to have been romantically involved with Paulette Goddard: Rivera himself intimated as much in *My Art, My Life,* p. 228.
273 New York's *Herald Tribune* noted: Rivera quoted in an Oct. 19, 1939, newspaper clipping in Bertram D. Wolfe archive.
273 "There is no change": *Time,* Oct. 30, 1939, p. 44.
273 "artistic difference": *New York Herald Tribune,* Oct. 20, 1939, newspaper clipping, in Bertram D. Wolfe archive.
273 "This is the tenth year of their marriage": Bertram D. Wolfe, *Diego Rivera, His Life and Times,* p. 394.
274 "Tell Bert that": Wolfe, *Fabulous Life of Diego Rivera,* p. 361.
274 "no trouble, no fuss": *El Universal* clipping, Oct. 19, 1939.
274 "We have been separated for five months": Ibid. See also *Art Digest* 14 (Nov. 1, 1939), p. 8.
274 Firestone wrote to Diego: Diego Rivera and Frida Kahlo, correspondence with Sigmund Firestone, 1940–41. The letters are now in the possession of Mr. and Mrs. Philip M. Liebschutz, Rochester, New York. (Mrs. Liebschutz is Sigmund Firestone's daughter.)

Firestone had to wait a long time for his pair of self-portraits, for Rivera was busy. In July he wrote a rather tart letter to Diego saying that he had received a catalogue of the art exhibition that appeared in the Palace of Fine Arts during the Golden Gate International Exhibition in San Francisco. To his complete surprise, the catalogue illustrated the *Self-Portrait* Frida had painted for but not delivered to him. The painting was listed as lent by himself. (Other works by Frida in the show were *Four Inhabitants of Mexico, Fruits of the Earth,* and *Pitahayas.*) It was wrong, Firestone pointed out, for Diego not to fulfill his end of the agreement, because Frida needed her share of the money, which he agreed to pay as soon as he was in receipt of both self-portraits. When Firestone received Frida's *Self-Portrait,* he wrote her that it was "lovely" but quibbled: "It is an excellent reproduction of yourself when in a pensive mood. Why didn't you smile a bit? The only criticism I have is that the canvas is too small. The figure looks crowded inside the frame. . . . I am enclosing a check for $150.00 and as soon as I receive Diego's portrait to match yours, as we decided in Mexico City, I will forward the balance to be divided as you wish."

A letter from Frida to Firestone (postmarked Nov. 1, 1940) thanked him for the payment and said: "Sigy, I would like to ask you a favor. I don't know if it is too much trouble for you. Could you send me the one hundred dollars balance of my painting here because I need them badly, and I promise you that as soon as I go to San Francisco I will make Diego send to you his self portrait. I am sure he will do it with great pleasure, it is only a question of time." Firestone complied. On December 9 Frida wrote: "I am very happy and proud because you like my portrait, it is not beautiful but I made it with a great pleasure for you." Finally, on January 31, 1941, Rivera wrote to Firestone that his self-portrait was finished and on its way. Firestone's next letter was duly appreciative: "It is excellent and perfect in every way. . . . Up to now I was in love with Frida's portrait. With your fine painting along side I must double my admiration because both are excellent, very much cherished and valued by Alberta and me."

275 "No one paid any attention": Lesley, private interview, New York City, June 1978.
275 She "loved the minuet": Kaufmann, private interview.
275 Spanish refugee Ricardo Arias Viñas: Gómez Arias, private interviews.

All that we know about this man comes from a letter Frida wrote to Edsel B. Ford on December 6, 1939, asking him to help her lover get a job with the Ford Motor Company in Mexico; there is a draft in the Frida Kahlo archive, Frida Kahlo Museum:

I am sure you must receive thousands of bothering letters. I feel really ashamed to send you one more, but I beg you to forgive me, because it is the first time I do so, and because I hope that what I will ask you, won't cause you too much trouble.

It is only to explain to you the special case of a very dear friend of mine, who was for many years a Ford's dealer in Gerona, Cataluña, and who for the circumstances of the recent war in Spain came to Mexico. His name is *Ricardo Arias Viñas*, he is now thirty-four years old. He worked for Ford Motor Co., for almost 10 years, he has a letter given by the European Central (Essex) which guarantees his actuation as a Ford worker, this letter is addressed to your plant in Buenos Aires. Also Mr. Ubach, the subdirector of your plant in Barcelona could give any kind of information about Mr. Arias. During the war, taking advantage of his charge as chief of transportation of Cataluña, he could get back to your factories several hundred units which were stolen at the beginning of the movement.

His problem is this, he couldn't go directly to Buenos Aires on account of economical difficulties, so he would like to stay here in Mexico and work in your plant. I am sure that Mr. Lajous your manager here, would give him a job knowing all about his experience and good acceptance as a Ford worker, but in order to avoid any difficulties I would appreciate very much if you were so kind just to send me a note which Mr. Arias could present to Mr. Lajous as a recommendation directly from you. That would facilitate enormously his entrance in the plant. He doesn't belong to any political party, so I imagine there is no difficulty for him to get this job and work honestly. I really would appreciate of you this big favor and hope there won't be much trouble for you in accepting my petition. Let me thank you in advance for anything you can so kindly do in this case.

276 she was drinking: Begun, medical record.

276 to Wolfgang Paalen, she wrote: Frida Kahlo, letter to Wolfgang Paalen, Dec. 6, 1939. A copy of this letter is in the Frida Kahlo archive, Frida Kahlo Museum.

276 "I don't see anybody": The letter is dated simply January 1940 and is postmarked January 11.

277 "I never was": Rivera, *My Art, My Life*, pp. 225–26.

277 "I had tea with Frida Kahlo": Helm, *Modern Mexican Painters*, pp. 167–68.

278 "I began painting it three months ago": *El Universal* clipping, Oct. 19, 1939.

279 "duality of her personality": Dolores Alvarez Bravo, private interview, Mexico City, September 1974.

280 *"la pintora mas pintor"*: Rivera, "Frida Kahlo y el Arte Mexicano," p. 101.

280 Levy said: Levy, private interview.

280 *The Wounded Table:* According to Frida's student Arturo García Bustos, this painting was part of a group of Mexican paintings given to a museum in Russia during the 1940s (García Bustos, private interview).

281 the Judas . . . on top of her bed's canopy: The skeleton with its head resting on two pillows appears in a photograph taken in 1940 by Emmy Lou Packard.

282 in Mexico, hummingbirds: Nancy Breslow, "Frida Kahlo: A Cry of Joy and Pain," *Americas* 32 (March 1980): 33–39. Breslow also quotes Fernando Gamboa, former director of Mexico City's Museum of Modern Art, as saying that the hummingbird was a pre-Columbian symbol of resurrection, as were the butterflies and thorns with which Frida has adorned herself in the 1940 *Self-Portrait.* That Frida identified with the hummingbird is certain, for friends compared her with one. Mrs. Eddie Albert, the wife of the movie actor, recalled her impression of Frida at a luncheon at the Covarrubias's house around 1943: "She had the quality of a hummingbird—a quick mind and swift but lovely movements. She was very beautiful and vulnerable" (Margot Albert, private interview, July 1978, Cuernavaca, Mexico).

283 the Aztecs . . . pricked their own skin: Anita Brenner, *Idols Behind Altars,* p. 138.

283 almost every Mexican church has frighteningly veristic Christ: In *The Mexican Mural Renaissance* (pp. 15–16), the muralist Jean Charlot made this observation about Mexican religious art: "A sublayer of Aztec ritual blood letting plus a layer of Spanish asceticism do not build up to squeamish prettiness. Coming late, the saint had to prove his mettle at least as impressively as had the pagan zealot. If

the latter threaded a knotted rope through his tongue in guise of a prayer, the newcomer had to go him one better to earn his welcome." Thus, said Charlot, Mexican religious art "overruled the rules of good taste in its desire to stir, to expostulate and to convert."

285 One story has it that Frida warned Diego: Private interview with Frida's Spanish lover, who wishes to remain anonymous.

285 she is dressed in a man's suit: Frida's donning men's clothes in this painting makes one think of the French painter Rosa Bonheur (1822–1899), who chose male attire to disguise her sex when she sketched from life at horse fairs and cattle markets, and of the American painter Romaine Brooks (1874–1970), whose self-portraits in men's clothes reveal a similar rejection of femininity as well as a strong note of lesbianism. According to Frida's friend Annette Nancarrow (private interview), Frida cut off her hair and wore men's clothes to assert her identity as an independent person dedicated to a career. "It was," says Mrs. Nancarrow, "a denial of her more passive role as wife and well-dressed woman." But while it is true that Frida wore blue jeans for working and made an issue about supporting herself through her painting, it seems unlikely that she had such consciously feminist motives for adopting men's clothes.

287 "I think you are quite right": Conger Goodyear, letter to Frida Kahlo, Frida Kahlo archive, Frida Kahlo Museum.

287 Anita Brenner wrote to offer help: Anita Brenner, letter to Frida Kahlo, Frida Kahlo archive, Frida Kahlo Museum.

288 "She is an excellent painter": Transcribed summary of Frida Kahlo's application, prepared by the foundation's staff, in the John Simon Guggenheim Memorial Foundation's 1940 Inter-American competition. The original application has not survived.

290 Clare Boothe Luce . . . says: Clare Boothe Luce, private interview, New York City, November 1978.

290 "She was a very beautiful girl": Noguchi, private interview.

290 "Dorothy Donovan Hale was": Luce, private interview. So Dorothy Hale's admirer took the painting away: Mrs. Luce went on to tell the denouement of the painting's saga: "My friend Frank Crowninshield, longtime editor of *Vanity Fair*, was also a well-known art collector. When the painting came back, with the legend removed, I took it to 'Crowny.' I asked him to hold the painting for a few years—until the Hale suicide was forgotten—and then to give it—without using my name—to the Museum of Modern Art, as an example of modern Mexican art.

"Twenty years later, I was living in Arizona when there suddenly arrived an object I had long since forgotten—the same crate that had once arrived from Mexico with the Kahlo painting of the suicide of Dorothy Hale. A letter from the nephew—and heir—of Frank Crowninshield accompanied it, saying that the painting had been found among other pictures belonging to the estate of the late Frank Crowninshield. His nephew remembered Crowninshield's telling him that the Kahlo picture was the property of Clare Luce, and so he was returning it to me.

"I then gave the picture to Mr. F. M. Hinkhouse, curator of the Phoenix Art Museum, with the express understanding that it would be listed as the gift of an *anonymous donor*. A few years later, Mr. Hinkhouse left the museum. Sometime in the early 1970s, his successor decided on a showing of the museum's Southwest and Mexican art. He telephoned (I suppose) Mexican friends of the Riveras for background on the Kahlo painting for the catalogue and they, it seems, informed him that from his description, this must be the picture that Clare Boothe Luce commissioned of the suicide of her friend Dorothy Hale! And that was the way the painting was described in the catalogue of the Museum's exhibition.

"Well, this whole episode led me to pen a phrase which has since been widely quoted:

'No good deed goes unpunished.' "

CHAPTER 18: REMARRIAGE

295   "They acted like firecracker makers": Bambi, "Frida Dice Lo Que Sabe," pp. 1, 7.

295   "[She] brought delicacies": This and the following quote are from Rivera, *My Art, My Life*, pp. 228, 237.

296   He planned to put Bohus in his mural: Packard, private interview.

296   [Rivera] became an impassioned advocate of inter-American solidarity: The Chilean poet Pablo Neruda tells of witnessing one of Rivera's and Siqueiros's fiery debates on the subject. Having run out of arguments, the sparring painters "drew huge pistols and fired almost as a man, not at each other, but at the wings of plaster-of-Paris angels on the theater's ceiling. When the heavy plaster wings started falling on the heads of the people in the audience, the theater emptied out and the discussion ended with a powerful smell of gunpowder in a deserted hall" (Pablo Neruda, *Memoirs*, trans. by Hardie St. Martin [New York: Farrar, Straus and Giroux, 1977], pp. 153–54).

296   He wanted to create: Timothy G. Turner, "What Happened to Diego Rivera?" *Los Angeles Times Sunday Magazine*, July 14, 1940, pp. 3, 8.

296   She represents "American girlhood": Rivera, *My Art, My Life*, p. 245.

296   "Frida Kahlo, [the] Mexican artist": Wolfe, *Diego Rivera*, p. 364.

297   "They killed old Trotsky": Bambi, "Frida Dice Lo Que Sabe," p. 7.

297   The police . . . interrogated her for twelve hours: Rivera, *My Art, My Life*, p. 239.

297   "They sacked Diego's house": Bambi, "Frida Dice Lo Que Sabe," p. 1.

297   Rivera proudly claimed: Tibol, private interview and other interviews.

297   he told . . . Pablo Neruda: Neruda, *Memoirs*, pp. 153–54.

298   "Raquelito, we must open a bottle": Tibol, private interview.

298   He ordered an armed guard: Packard, private interview.

298   "Diego loves you very much": Dr. Leo Eloesser, letter to Frida Kahlo, Frida Kahlo archive.

298   Dr. Eloesser rejected the grave diagnoses: According to Teresa del Conde, Dr. Eloesser diagnosed "poliomyelitis" (del Conde, *Vida de Frida Kahlo,* p. 29).

298   "I was very ill": Letter to Sigmund Firestone (undated; postmark Nov. 1, 1940).

300   "He took me to the hospital": Heinz Berggruen, private interview, New York City, November 1981.

301   warning her that Rivera would not reform: Rivera, *My Art, My Life*, p. 242.

301   "I'm going to marry her": Packard, private interview.

301   the separation . . . "was having a bad effect": Rivera, *My Art, My Life*, p. 242.

301   "He is basically a sad person": Anita Brenner, letter to Frida Kahlo, Sept. 25, 1940, Frida Kahlo archive.

302   She had seen old friends: Rivera, *My Art, My Life*, p. 241–42.

302   [she] managed to finish a few paintings: Frida Kahlo, letter to Emmy Lou Packard, Oct. 24, 1940, Packard personal archive. Frida said that she would return to San Francisco from New York as soon as she had finished one or two paintings.

302   "She would provide for herself": Rivera, *My Art, My Life*, p. 242. Two years after the remarriage, at a moment when Frida was showing *The Two Fridas* to a reporter, Rivera came into the room. He solemnly told the visitor that it had been painted during their divorce, and that was why Frida had painted her heart broken and bleeding. The visitor exclaimed, "How much she must have loved you! Did she, by any chance, give you the painting so that you would understand this?" "Oh, no!" Rivera replied. "It wasn't necessary. You see, I never stopped loving her; what's more, I divorced her because I thought that she would be happy if she recovered her freedom. But when I was convinced that it didn't do that, I returned to her and we got married again" (Betty Ross, "Como Pinta Frida Kahlo Esposa de Diego, las Emociones Intimas de la Mujer.").

303   The marriage was performed by: *Los Angeles Times*, Dec. 9, 1940, "Diego Rivera,

Mexican Mural Artist, Weds Former Wife," clipping in Karen and David Crommie file.

303 Rivera . . . went off to work at Treasure Island: Packard, private interview.

303 *"Emilucha linda":* Letter to Emmy Lou Packard (undated, 1941) Packard's personal archive.

303 the Treasure Island mural: The mural was eventually moved to the lobby of the Arts Auditorium of San Francisco Junior College.

305 according to Emmy Lou Packard: Except where otherwise noted, this account of the Riveras' daily life during the remarriage comes from the author's private interview with Emmy Lou Packard.

305 he was worried about his health: Emmy Lou Packard recalls the time when a blood vessel in one of Rivera's eyes broke, and he was sure that he would die at any moment. "He was very conscious of dying. He was sick a lot, and Frida took care of him," she says. Among Frida Kahlo's papers in her archive is a note from Diego to Frida, probably dated c. 1940, that says: "Niñita Fisita: my heart is hurting: I have in the Banco de Commercio $14,000 pesos. . . . Alberto Misrachi owes me $10,000, reclaim them for yourself the same as the pieces of land, the house and my idols and paintings. Diego Rivera. This has the value of a testament."

306 "The niña Fridita": Tibol, *Crónica,* p. 115.

306 "She loved them": Jacqueline Breton, private interview.

307 "Imagine, the little parrot, 'Bonito,' died": Frida Kahlo, letter to Emmy Lou Packard, Dec. 15, 1941, Packard's personal archive.

312 *Self-Portrait with Bonito:* This painting was purchased in 1941 by Mrs. Somerset Maugham (Syrie Maugham). Its present whereabouts are unknown.

312 "Frida and I started a strange kind of ranch": Rivera, *My Art, My Life,* pp. 249–52.

313 In a style he described as a composite: Ibid., p. 249.

313 Anahuacalli has been alternately called: Wolfe, *Diego Rivera,* p. 370.

313 She gave her husband title: Ibid.

313 "I have been worried about Diego": Frida Kahlo, letter to Marte R. Gómez, Frida Kahlo archive.

314 "The stupendous work": Kahlo, "Retrato de Diego."

CHAPTER 19: PORTRAITS, PATRONS, PUBLIC RECOGNITION

317 "Since the accident changed my path": Frida Kahlo, "Frida Habla de Su Pintura." Though published under Frida's name, the article was actually compiled from an interview with Frida conducted by Antonio Rodríguez.

317 "the most recent of Rivera's ex-wives": Frank Crowninshield, "New York Goes Mexican," *Vogue,* June 15, 1940, p. 82.

318 Guggenheim commented: Peggy Guggenheim, *Confessions of an Art Addict* (New York: Macmillan, 1960), pp. 166–67.

318 originally titled *Flame Flower: Flower of Life* was called *Flame Flower* when it was exhibited in the Salon de la Flor in the National Flower Show in 1944. Rivera was also wont to transform plants into male and female genitalia, to wit, the huge crocus-like flower in his 1929 Health Building mural, which, like Frida's *Flower of Life,* is a hybrid of male and female sexual organs.

319 Three concerns impelled her to make art: Frida's comments are contained in an article entitled "Frida Kahlo y la Melancolia de la Sangre" ("Frida Kahlo and the Melancholy of Blood") in the magazine *Rueca* (Mexico City, No. 10 [1944], p. 80. The author is identified only with the initials A.F. The clipping is in Isolda Kahlo's personal archive.

319 "The education minister asked me": Gómez Arias, private interview.

320 Frida was asked by . . . Miguel N. Lira: Miguel N. Lira, letter to Frida Kahlo, Jan. 7, 1943, Frida Kahlo archive.

320 her work for this organization: This information comes from various documents

and clippings concerning the Seminario de la Cultura Mexicana in the Frida Kahlo archive.

320 "The five Mexican women": Letter to Dr. Leo Eloesser, July 18, 1941.

321 "From what you tell me": Letter to Emmy Lou Packard, Packard's personal archive.

322 "I am going to battle for you": Emmy Lou Packard, undated letter to Frida Kahlo (undated), Frida Kahlo archive.

322 "I did not feel so sad": Letter to Dr. Eloesser, Mar. 15, 1941.

322 it was purchased . . . because Frida desperately needed money: Fernando Gamboa, private interview, Mexico City, November 1977.

322 *Doña Rosita Morillo* shows . . . an extremely refined miniaturistic realism: Frida's extreme realism at this time may have been inspired by the portraiture of Hermenegildo Bustos, the late-nineteenth-century painter from Guanajuato, whom she admired and whose work was shown along with her own in the January 1943 exhibition of one hundred years of Mexican portraiture. Bustos's portrait of his wife, *Joaquina Ríos Bustos,* must have especially delighted Frida, for its combination of detailed realism with primitivism, plus the undeviating frankness underlying its intense capturing of the sitter's emotional presence, are characteristics seen in her portrait of Doña Rosita.

324 *Portrait of Mariana Morillo Safa:* When Morillo Safa received this portrait of his daughter, he wrote to Frida, on Jan. 20, 1944: "I am sending you the thousand pesos for the one of Mariana, it turned out very well and it's very pretty. Listen, how much will you charge me for two more portraits? One of Lupe and another of Eduardo [Morillo Safa's other two children]? Let me know through them." Eduardo Morillo Safa, letter to Frida Kahlo, Frida Kahlo archive.

324 "turned into idiots": Kahlo, "Retrato de Diego."

324 "Diego got me a job": Bambi, "Frida Kahlo Es una Mitád."

324 Roberto BeHar remembers: Roberto BeHar, private interview.

325 "I loved her": Morillo Safa, private interview.

325 "From Coyoacán, so sad": Frida Kahlo, letter to Mariana Morillo Safa, Oct. 23, 1946, Morillos Safa's personal archive. The pet "name," *"Cachita, changa, maranga,"* is a nonsense rhyme.

326 The painting was the result of a chance conversation: José Domingo Lavin, interviewed by Karen and David Crommie.

326 "As this is the first time in my life": Frida Kahlo, "The Birth of Moses," p. 2. I have substituted my own translation for the one published alongside the Spanish original.

327 "Solar energy, the life source": Rivera, *My Art, My Life,* p. 131. In his explanation of the mural written shortly after he had finished it, Rivera called the central orb of light "The Light-One or Primal Energy," and noted that the hands at the end of the light rays have their index and ring fingers pointing toward the earth, while the other fingers are closed. This gesture, he said, signified "FATHER-MOTHER" (Wolfe, *Diego Rivera,* p. 136).

327 "the center of all religions": Kahlo, "Moses," p. 4.

327 Moses' birth stands for the birth of all heroes: Ibid. In her discussion of *Moses* (pp. 4–6), Frida listed the heroes, as well as the gods they invented because of their fear of death.

Like Moses [she said], there have been and there will be a great number of "higher-ups," transformers of religions and of human societies. It may be said that they are a species of *messengers* between people that they manage and the *gods* invented by them in order to manage them.

Of these "Gods" there are many, as you know. Naturally I could not fit them all in, and I placed those who have direct relation with the sun (whether you like it or not) on either side of the sun. To the right, those of the West and to the left, those of the East.

The winged bull Asirus, Amon, Zeus, Osiris, Horus, Jehova, Apollo, The Moon,

The Virgin Mary, Divine Providence, the Holy Trinity, Venus and . . . the devil.

To the left, Lightning, the Strike of Lightning and the Wake of Lightning, that is to say, Huarakan, Kukulkan and Gukumatz, Tlaloc, the magnificent Coatlicue, mother of all the gods, Quetzalcoatl, Tezcatlipoca, the Centeotl, the Chinese god (Dragon) and the Hindu, Brahma. I missed an African god, but I couldn't find him anywhere (but a little room can be made for him).

I cannot tell you something about each one of them, because my ignorance of their origin, importance, etc., *is too much for me.*

Having painted the gods that I could fit in, in their respective heavens, I wanted to divide the celestial world of the imagination and of poetry, from the terrestrial world of *fear of death,* and I painted the skeletons, human and animal, that you see here. . . .

On the same earth, but painting their heads larger, to distinguish them from the "mass," the heroes are pictured (very few of them, but well chosen), the transformers of religions, the inventors or creators of these, the conquerors, the rebels . . . in other words the real "big wigs."

To the right, and this figure I should have painted with much more importance than any other, Amenhotep IV can be seen, who was later called Akhenaten. . . .

Later, Moses, who according to Freud's analysis, gave his adopted people the *same religion as that of Akhenaten,* a little altered according to the interests and circumstances of his time. . . .

After Christ, follow Alexander the Great, Caesar, Mohammed, Luther, Napoleon and . . . "the lost infant" . . . Hitler.

To the left, marvelous Nefertiti, wife of Akhenaten, I imagine that besides having been extraordinarily beautiful, she must have been "a wild one" and a most intelligent collaborator to her husband. Buddha, Marx, Freud, Paracelsus, Epicure, Ghenghis Kahn, Gandhi, Lenin and Stalin (the order is in poor taste but I painted them according to my historical knowledge which is also bad).

Among those belonging to the "masses," I painted a sea of blood with which I signify "War," inevitable and fertile.

And finally, the powerful and "never well ponderated" mass of humanity, composed of all kinds of . . . rare types, the warriors, the pacifists, the scientists and the ignorant, the makers of monuments, the rebels, the flag-bearers, the medal carriers, the loudmouths, the sane and the insane, the gay and the sad, the healthy and the sick, the poets and the fools and all the rest of the race that you wish to exist in this powerful bunch.

Only the ones in the foreground are seen a little clearly, the rest *con el ruido . . . no se supo* [literally, they were drowned out by the noise; idiomatically, they were lost in the fog].

327   "On either side of the child": Kahlo, "Moses," p. 4.

328   "the trunk of age": Ibid., p. 6.

328   a conch symbolizes "love": Ibid.

329   Their aim was . . . to "prepare individuals": A copy of a 1943 booklet published by the Ministry of Education, announcing the school's purposes and program, is in the Frida Kahlo archive.

329   "in the beginning there were only about ten students": Guillermo Monroy, private interview, Cuernavaca, Mexico, March 1977.

329   "It is an old vice of women": Fanny Rabel, private interview, Mexico City, August 1977.

330   "brotherly, an extraordinary teacher": Monroy, private interview.

330   "I remember her entering the school": Guillermo Monroy, transcribed by María Idalia (Monroy's articles in *Excelsior* are usually signed by another writer), "Homenaje de un Pintor a Frida Kahlo a los 22 Años de su Muerte," p. 8.

331   "this should be a little stronger": Monroy, private interview.

331   "The only help she gave us": García Bustos, private interview.

331   "Frida's great teaching": Rabel, private interview.

332   "Muchachos," she would announce: Monroy, private interview.

332   "When we were leaving": Hector Xavier, private interview, Mexico City, November 1977.

333 "We got so used to Frida": Fanny Rabel, interviewed by Karen and David Crommie.

333 "The whole garden is ours": Monroy, private interview.

333 "I remember particularly": García Bustos, private interview.

333 Monroy was equally bewitched": Guillermo Monroy, "Hoy Hace 24 Años que Falleció Frida Kahlo."

334 "[She] constantly renewed the scenography": Rabel, Crommie interview.

334 "When she was ill": Ibid.

334 "root of our modern art": Arturo Estrada, private interview, Mexico City, March 1977. From Estrada, too, comes the list of Frida's favorite painters.

335 "great and many-sided painter": Ibid.

335 Fanny Rabel recalls: Rabel, private interview.

335 Posada-like broadside: A copy of the announcement is in the Frida Kahlo archive.

336 *corridos* written for the occasion: Copies of these *corridos* are in the Frida Kahlo archive.

337 Rivera was photographed . . . Frida . . . danced: *La Prensa* (Mexico City), June 20, 1943, p. 27. Clipping of an unsigned article about the inauguration of La Rosita in the Frida Kahlo archive.

338 "the greatest thing of that afternoon": Xavier, private interview.

338 All the dignitaries made speeches: *La Prensa* clipping, June 20, 1943, p. 27.

338 "Frida Kahlo, satisfied with her work": Ibid.

339 Another newspaper took a more skeptical view: Clipping (unidentified) in Frida Kahlo archive.

339 another mural project for the "Fridos": Arturo Estrada, "Recuerdo de Frida," text of lecture delivered on Aug. 11, 1967. Arturo Estrada's personal archive.

339 the laundresses contributed: Arturo García Bustos, interviewed by Karen and David Crommie.

339 "at the moment of definitive selection": Estrada, "Recuerdo de Frida."

340 "My particular project": García Bustos, private interview.

340 Each painter took responsibility: Estrada, "Recuerdo de Frida." This collective, anti-individualistic idea was, Estrada notes, very much in vogue at the time.

340 "dog without a master": Rabel, Crommie interview.

340 A photograph of the preparatory drawings: Photographs of these drawings are in a scrapbook on this mural project put together by Arturo García Bustos. It is in his personal archive.

340 A rather formal invitation: A copy of the invitation is in García Bustos's personal archive.

341 Fanny Rabel says: Rabel, private interview.

341 there was also music: García Bustos, Crommie interview.

341 As early as June 1943 . . . they had a show: There is an announcement for this show in the Frida Kahlo archive.

341 The "Fridos" contribution: Estrada, "Recuerdo de Frida." For a description of the painting, see Tibol, *Crónica*, pp. 135–37.

341 "She encouraged the development of a personalized style": Diego Rivera, "Frida Kahlo: Biographical Sketch."

341 "If Diego had said": Guillermo Velasco y Polo, private interview, Tepoztlán, Morelos, Mexico, October 1977.

342 Frida . . . was welcomed back into the Communist fold: Octavio Paz said that when Rivera rejected Trotsky and embraced Stalinism, his application for readmission to the Mexican Communist party was "an abject and uncalled for *mea culpa.*" Bertram Wolfe recalled that Frida "dragged her feet" when Rivera made his political switch. She could not, said Wolfe, bring herself to grovel or to admit to the wrongs of her past political behavior the way Rivera chose to do when he underwent the ritual of "self-criticism" that the Communist party required (Wolfe, *Diego Rivera*, p. 396). Octavio Paz would disagree. According to him, Frida did not abstain from humiliating statements in her written application for readmission

to the party: "Frida Kahlo's retraction, no doubt influenced by Rivera, was no less shameful" (Octavio Paz, "Social Realism in Mexico: The Murals of Rivera, Orozco and Siqueiros," *Artscanada* 36[December 1979–January 1980]: 63–64).

342 "She was a humanist": Rabel, private interview.

342 Painting . . . should play a role in society: This information on Frida's attitude toward the relationship between politics and art is from private interviews with García Bustos, Monroy, and Estrada.

342 "Her roots in the tradition of our people": Estrada, "Recuerdo de Frida."

343 "I'm going to be very sad": Monroy, private interview.

Chapter 20: The Little Deer

344 Dr. Alejandro Zimbíon . . . prescribed: Begun, medical record. All the details of Frida's medical history are from that report, unless otherwise noted.

345 Alejandro Gómez Arias recalls: Gómez Arias, private interview.

345 Frida described the succession of orthopedic corsets: Bambi, "Un Remedio de Lupe Marín."

346 She spent three months: Dromundo, private interview.

346 "We were horrified": Adelina Zendejas, private interview, Mexico City, October 1977.

346 "It was very exciting": Ella Paresce, interviewed by Karen and David Crommie. Actually, the plaster corset displayed on Frida's bed in her museum is not the same one that Ella Paresce helped to remove, for it shows no signs of having been cut in the front. Frida decorated it with decals, painted vegetal designs, and a broken classical column that runs down the middle. Until someone plucked them out, another "decoration" consisted of yellow thumbtacks stuck into the plaster's surface. They recall the nails driven into Frida's flesh in *The Broken Column*, and one can imagine her laughing as she pushed them in, but they look like points of pain.

347 Dr. Eloesser believed: Joyce Campbell, private interview.

348 "Now you can eat anything": Monteforte Toledo, "Frida: Paisaje de Sí Misma," p. 2.

348 the doctors made her eat puréed food: Jacqueline Breton, private interview.

348 Everything moves in time with what the belly contains: In her diary, Frida wrote a mysterious poem that ended with the same words:

> Numbers. economy,
> farce of the word,
> nerves are blue
> I don't know why—also red,
> but full of color
>
> From round numbers
> and red nerves
> stars are made
> and worlds are sounds.
>
> I would not want to nourish
> even the least hope,
> everything moves in time
> with what the belly contains.

348 the microscope and the solar system: Frida's vision of the world as a continuum and of herself as connected to a microcosm/macrocosm dialectic was, as we have seen, shared by her husband. Rivera's murals show the span of life from the cellular to the cosmic. To take one example, he described a portion of his Radio City mural in the following words: "In the center, the telescope brings to the vision and understanding of man the most distant celestial bodies. The microscope makes visible and comprehensible to man infinitesimal living organisms, connecting atoms and cells with the astral system" (Wolfe, *Diego Rivera*, p. 321).

351 The operation was performed in June: Dr. Philip Wilson's son, Dr. Philip D. Wilson, Jr., M.D., who works at the Hospital for Special Surgery, wrote to me (July 21, 1977) that he remembers his father speaking of Frida but could find no trace of either hospital records or office records bearing the name Kahlo or de Rivera.

351 "She was there with Cristina": Noguchi, private interview.

352 "My dear Engineer": Letter to Eduardo Morillo Safa, Oct. 11, 1946, Mariana Morillo Safa's personal archive.

354 Dr. Wilson fused the wrong vertebrae: Gómez Arias, Dr. Velasco y Polo, private interviews.

354 Cristina maintained that the operation . . . was so painful: Tibol, private interview.

355 Lupe Marín recalled: Marín, private interview.

355 She is said to have had osteomyelitis: del Conde, *Vida de Frida Kahlo*, p. 16.

356 "Tree of Hope, keep firm" was her ralling cry: Henestrosa, private interview. In his article "Frida," Henestrosa compared Frida to a tree when he said: "Frida Kahlo has died. And with her goes, silently, a lesson of firmness in the face of adversity; with her death comes the end of the spectacle of a woman who was like a tree, small and weak, but so deeply rooted in the earth of life that death struggled for years to pull her out."

357 "the agony of living with Diego": Ella Wolfe, private interview.

357 the arrows signify Frida's suffering due to male oppression: Frida's Spanish-refugee lover, private interview.

357 Once when a gardener brought her an old chair: Ibid.

357 "in the pre-Hispanic world": Rodríguez, private interview.

357 As Anita Brenner explained: Brenner, *Idols Behind Altars*, p. 155.

358 There is a popular song: García Bustos, private interview, March 1977. Sor Juana Inés de la Cruz: The connection between *The Little Deer* and this poem was pointed out by Laura Mulvey and Peter Wollen in their essay "Frida Kahlo and Tina Modotti" in Whitechapel Art Gallery, Exhibition Catalogue, *Frida Kahlo and Tina Modotti*, p. 25.

359 your Olinka: Olinka is the name of Isabel Villaseñor's daughter.

CHAPTER 21: PORTRAITS OF A MARRIAGE

360 "sacred monsters": Interview with Frida's Spanish-refugee friend who wishes to remain anonymous.

361 He would tell people: Rivera, "Frida Kahlo: Biographical Sketch." Frida's painting, purchased by the State of France in 1939, is now in the Musée National de Art Moderne, Centre Georges Pompidou, Paris.

361 "There is no artist in Mexico": Rosa María Oliver, "Frida la Unica y Verdadera Mitád de Diego." Undated newspaper clipping, Isolda Kahlo archive.

362 "We are all clods next to Frida": Private interview with an old friend of Frida's who wished to remain anonymous.

362 "In the panorama of Mexican painting": Rivera, "Frida Kahlo y el Arte Mexicano," p. 101. Frida's opinion of herself was humbler. To one friend who inquired about her art she said, "And how can you want me to have ambitions given the physical state in which I find myself? . . . They have performed eleven operations on me; and from each of them I come out with only one hope: to see Diego triumph again" (Antonio Robles, "La Personalidad de Frida Kahlo").

362 Diego was the "architect of life": Paul Boatine, private interview, Detroit, January 1978.

362 She listened to his stories: Ella Wolfe, private interview.

362 "His supposed mythomania"; Kahlo, "Retrato de Diego."

363 "Against the cowardly attacks": Ibid.

363 Once, in a restaurant: Wolfe, *Fabulous Life of Diego Rivera*, pp. 360–61.

364 *Diego and Frida 1929–1944:* There are, in fact, two versions of this painting. A visitor who saw the painting in 1944 described it as a "portable medallion" (Oliver, "Frida la Unica"). Frida did paint several oval miniatures, following a tradition

of miniature painting that flourished in Mexico in the nineteenth century; one of them, barely two inches high and painted about 1946, was a self-portrait that she gave to her Spanish-refugee lover. Although it is only five by three inches, the extant version of *Diego and Frida 1929–1944*, is not locket size. The other version (documented in a photograph that was probably taken during Frida's lifetime and is in the archive of Mexico's Department of Fine Arts) is signed, and because it is more minutely painted, less cramped in organization, and slightly more elaborate in detail, I believe it to be the original. The other, I think, is a slightly later copy, also by Frida.

364 she was, . . . the embryo that "engendered him": Frida Kahlo, diary.

364 shells were symbols of birth: Paul Westheim, "Frida Kahlo: Una Investigación Estética."

364 "the two sexes": Kahlo, "Moses," p. 6.

364 the notion of showing duality: Frida was not the only twentieth-century artist to borrow the idea of the duality contained in a single figure from pre-Cortesian culture. Her friend Roberto Montenegro picked up on the idea in his *Así es la Vida* (Thus Is Life), 1937, where an elegant woman holding a mirror is divided vertically into half skeleton and half flesh-and-blood woman.

365 intertwined branches look like Christ's crown of thorns: The allusion to Christ's martyrdom is obvious enough; Frida did, after all, transform Christ's crown of thorns into a necklace in two 1940 self-portraits. On the other hand, Frida may have also intended the necklace-tree to be a symbol of the strong and vital bond between herself and Rivera—for Frida, trees were usually auspicious symbols denoting the perseverance of life against terrible odds.

365 "To the celebrated painter": The note is in the Frida Kahlo archive.

365 "Being the wife of Diego": Lozano, dispatch to *Time*, Nov. 9, 1950.

365 "I will not speak of Diego as 'my husband' ": Kahlo, "Retrato de Diego."

366 "when I was alone with her": Ella Wolfe, private interview.

368 "The marvelous Nefertiti": Kahlo, "Moses," p. 5.

368 "I've never seen anyone": Interview with a lover of Frida's who wishes to remain anonymous.

370 "she consoled herself": Tibol, private interview.

370 her "Zapata" mustache: One wonders which of Frida's courtiers (or was it Frida herself) wrote the rhyme scribbled on a scrap of paper that Frida always kept and that is now in the Frida Kahlo archive, Frida Kahlo Museum: "When I see you with a mustache, and like a little bald kid, I feel that I would like to turn into a homosexual." The complete Spanish is: "Me gusta tu nombre, Frida,/ pero tú me gustas más/ en lo 'free' por decidida/ y en el final porque das./ Cuando te veo con tu bozo/ y como chico pelón/ siento que sería mi gozo/ el volverme maricón."

370 "Of his chest it must be said": Kahlo, "Retrato de Diego."

370 The press posed the question: "Un Retrato de Escandalo," undated newspaper clipping, Isolda Kahlo archive.

371 Three leading papers published the "news": *Time* dispatch from Mexico, Aug. 14, 1949.

371 "I adore Frida": Ibid.

371 Frida took an apartment: Reyes and Rabel, private interviews.

371 Rivera kept her informed: Rosa Castro, private interview.

371 [Frida] even wrote María Félix: Ríos y Valles, private interview.

371 Rivera also had an affair [with Pita Amor]: Ric y Rac, "In-Mural."

371 Adelina Zendejas tells of the time: Zendejas, private interview.

372 "miserable and hurt": Rivera, *My Art, My Life,* pp. 264–65.

372 *Diego and I* was just a sketch: Samuel A. Williams, private telephone interview, November 1981.

375 "Women . . . amongst them I": Kahlo, "Retrato de Diego."

375 He holds a maguey plant: Frida compared Rivera's resilient strength to that of a

cactus: "Like the cacti of his land, he grows strong and astonishing, equally well in sand as in rock. . . . Even if they yank him from the earth, his roots live. . . . He rises up with surprising strength and, like no other plant, he flowers and gives fruit" (Kahlo, "Retrato de Diego," p. 5). Rivera used a plant similar to the one in *The Love Embrace*, and likewise, sprouting upward, as a sexual symbol in his mural *The Fecund Earth*: "My symbol for Nature was a colossal, dreaming woman. Securely clasped in her hands was an equally symbolic phallic plant" (My Art, My Life, p. 139). The nude Lupe Marín was Rivera's model for fertility here. Frida, on the other hand, chose her naked husband as her model for a similar subject. The orange hue of the cactus in Rivera's hand also recalls Frida's *Flower of Life*, 1944.

375 "His form: with his Asiatic-type head": Ibid.

375 "Oh, that boy": Rabel, Crommie interview.

376 Antonio Rodríguez remembers": Rodríguez, private interview.

376 "The images and ideas flow": Kahlo, "Retrato de Diego."

377 *ojo avisor:* Isolda Kahlo, private interview. Frida herself wrote "ojo avisor" on a large disembodied eye that she drew in the 1940s (Collection Rafael Coronel, Mexico City). And in her discussion of her *Moses*, she said she gave Moses an "ojo avisor" because he was "more alert and sharper than other people" (Kahlo, "Moses," p. 4).

378 Frida once drew her notion of love: In 1950, Frida and Diego each made a series of drawings expressing their responses to various human emotions. This was partly a game and partly a psychological experiment (Olga Campos, private interview).

378 "If I had died without knowing her": Lara Barba, "Sor Juana y Frida Kahlo: Paralelamente," p. 8.

Chapter 22: Naturaleza Viva

383 "the calvary that would lead to the end": González Ramírez, "Frida Kahlo o el Imperativo de Vivir," p. 22.

383 Dr. Eloesser . . . scribbled some notes: The notes are among Dr. Eloesser's letters from Frida in Joyce Campbell's personal archive.

384 "Forgive me the trouble": Frida Kahlo, letter to Dr. Fastlich, Dr. Fastlich's personal archive.

385 "Today I answer your letter": Matilde Kahlo, letter to Dr. Leo Eloesser, Joyce Campbell's personal archive.

388 Diego could be extraordinarily tender: Reyes, private interview.

388 According to Dr. Velasco y Polo: Velasco y Polo, private interview.

388 "she never complained": Ibid.

388 "With my new bone": Velasco y Polo, private interview, and Lozano, dispatch to *Time*, Nov. 9, 1950.

388 She also liked to let friends peek: Campos, private interview.

389 Campos . . . had plans to write: Ibid.

389 "when I leave the hospital": Lozano, dispatch to *Time*, Nov. 9, 1950.

389 Dr. Velasco y Polo recalls her fear of solitude: Velasco y Polo, private interview.

390 "We healthy people": Elena Vásquez Gómez, private interview, Mexico City, August 1977.

390 "She did not concentrate on herself": Rabel, private interview.

390 "He has great talent": Lozano, dispatch to *Time*, Nov. 9, 1950.

390 When she had seen the whole series: Antonio Luna Arroyo, private interview, Mexico City, March 1977.

390 "Cristina brought a big basket": Campos, private interview.

390 "I never lost my spirit": Bambi, "Un Remedio de Lupe Marín."

391 [Dr. Farill] had founded a hospital: Dr. Armando Navarro, private interview, Mexico City, March 1977.

391 Frida called him *"chulito"*: Eugenia Farill de Pastor, private interview, Mexico City, July 1977.
391 she was especially attached to him: Velasco y Polo, private interview.
392 She could propel herself in her wheelchair: Elena Martínez, private interview, Mexico City, October 1978.
393 Her day began with tea: Ibid.
393 *"Chaparrita,* what are you up to?": Ibid.
393 "María Félix was very intimate": Ibid.
393 Dr. Velasco y Polo would pick her up: Velasco y Polo, private interview.
394 "in one moment you would see a multitude": Judith Ferreto, interviewed by Karen and David Crommie.
394 "We'd dance and sing": Bernice Kolko, interviewed by Karen and David Crommie.
394 "I love him for many things": Ferreto, Crommie interview.
394 He would undress her very tenderly: Tibol, private interview.
394 "I very much love": Tibol, *Crónica,* p. 32.
394 "I'm going to be a little old woman": Rabel, private interview.
395 "Because she was immobile": Rabel, private interview.
395 "If one refused to accept a present": Ríos y Valles, private interview.
396 "One day . . . Diego said to me": Bambi, "Frida Es una Mitád."
396 "I was a member of the Party before I met Diego": Rosa Castro, "Cartas de Amor: Un Libro de Frida Kahlo."
396 "Many things in this life now bore me": Robles, "La Personalidad de Frida Kahlo."
399 "The style of her last paintings": Velasco y Polo, private interview.
399 she now got her hands and clothes covered with pigment: Ferreto, Crommie interview.
399 "I must paint tomorrow": Ibid.
399 Her house, Frida said, was theirs: The words on Frida's wall begin: "House of . . ."
399 Several among her old friends were put off: Lupe Marín, private interview.
400 One friend was so shocked: Private interview with a friend of Frida's who wishes to remain anonymous.
400 Raquel Tibol recalls Frida's fury: Tibol, private interview.
400 she tried to hang herself: Ferreto, Crommie interview.
400 Tibol also tells of the suicide of a brain-damaged girl: Tibol, private interview. It has also been said that the girl was not a suicide but was actually killed by Frida, who, in a fit of rage, struck her with her crutch (private interview with a friend of Frida's and Diego's who wishes to remain anonymous).
  Judith Ferreto told Karen and David Crommie a story that may very well be a third version of the same death. According to Ferreto, a girl died in Frida's house from contagious encephalitis. "Frida was in a state of crisis and was almost impossible to calm down. We had to leave the house in quarantine and move to my apartment for about a month."
400 Alejandro Gómez Arias remembers [Ferreto]: Gómez Arias, private interview.
400 "You are like a fascist": Ferreto, Crommie interview.
401 "I think I have cultivated your feelings": Ibid.
401 "I started working with her": Ibid.
402 "They lived together": Ibid.
402 he had cancer of the penis: Rivera, *My Art, My Life,* p. 234.
402 "he needs someone to take care of him": Castro, private interview.
402 "I love Diego more than ever": Bambi, "Un Remedio de Lupe Marín," p. 3.
403 Frida herself chose the grouping: Julio García Scherer, "Satira Fina, Nunca En-mohina," undated newspaper clipping, Isolda Kahlo archive.
403 "for pure pleasure": Ibid.
403 there was even talk of changing the *pulquería*'s name: Monroy, private interview.
404 dazzling but grotesque afternoon: Rosa Castro, "Galería del Mundo"—"Recordando a Frida Kahlo," *El Día* (Mexico City), July 19, 1966.

CHAPTER 23: HOMAGE TO FRIDA KAHLO

405 "They had just performed a bone transplant": Dolores Alvarez Bravo, Crommie interview.

405 folkloric invitations: Arturo García Bustos has an invitation in his personal archive.

406 The gallery also printed a brochure: A copy is in the Frida Kahlo archive. The show was called "Primicias para un Homenaje a Frida Kahlo" (Preliminaries for an Homage to Frida Kahlo), because a larger retrospective was being planned by the National Institute of Fine Arts. As things turned out, it was never held. Rodríguez (private interview) said that it was canceled because of the scandal that ensued when Frida's funeral was turned into a political act. The exhibition was to have taken place in the summer of 1954—the time when Frida died.

406 When the night of the opening approached: This account is based on the Crommie interview with Dolores Alvarez Bravo, and Dolores Alvarez Bravo, private interview.

407 "There was a traffic jam outside": Dolores Alvarez Bravo, Crommie interview.

407 "The photographers and reporters were so surprised": Ibid.

407 "We asked people to keep walking": Ibid.

408 Carlos Pellicer acted as traffic policeman: Morillo Safa, private interview.

408 "Stay with me": Monroy, private interview.

408 Carlos Pellicer had tears in his eyes; Morillo Safa, private interview.

408 She asked the writer Andrés Henestrosa to sing La Llorona: Henestrosa, private interview.

408 "Anda, hijo": Velasco y Polo, private interview.

408 "All the cripples of Mexico": Henestrosa, private interview, and Andrés Henestrosa, Una Alacena de Alacenas, pp. 87–89.

409 "Frida was very fixed up": Monroy, private interview.

409 "It was . . . a little spectacular": Tibol, private interview.

409 "Everybody and his dog was there": Morillo Safa, private interview.

409 "we received calls": Dolores Alvarez Bravo, Crommie interview.

410 "It is impossible . . . to separate the life and work": J. Moreno Villa, "La Realidad y el Deseo en Frida Kahlo."

410 Time magazine reported the news: Time, "Mexican Autobiography."

410 "For me, the most thrilling event": Rivera, My Art, My Life, pp. 283–84.

410 some of the images . . . that hung on the walls: According to the press (Excelsior, unsigned review, Apr. 12, 1953), there were some thirty-six paintings, all from private collections and none for sale. The exhibition brochure listed only thirty-one items, one entry being a group of drawings and another, Frida's diary. Also included in the exhibition were Frida's 1927 Self-Portrait drawn in pencil, many of Morillo Safa's Kahlos, and two works belonging to Marte R. Gómez. Several works listed in the brochure are not attributed to specific owners, and some cannot be identified (for example, Mujer de Sarape, lent by the late Frederick Davis; Self-Portrait, lent by Sra. Emilia Moreschi; and Frida in Flames, lent by Teresa Proenza. La Tierra Misma (The Earth Itself) is listed as lent by Dolores del Rio. Perhaps it is Two Nudes in a Forest, identified by another title.

CHAPTER 24: NIGHT IS FALLING IN MY LIFE

412 "I had gone to leave a ring": Zendejas, private interview.

413 "Do you know": Elena Poniatowska, "El Museo Frida Kahlo."

413 "they were saying over and over again": Bambi, "Un Remedio de Lupe Marín."

416 The circle . . . is a fearful image: Such an image is also seen in a strange, unfinished painting of a body in a rocky landscape that hangs today in Frida's bedroom in her museum. Though it is unsigned and is not listed in the museum's catalogue, I believe it is a work from Frida's last years. Except for the rough painting technique, the landscape is almost identical to the landscape in Roots. A small hill

and a ravine are similarly situated in both paintings. The proportion of earth to sky is the same. The painting seems, like *Roots*, to depict a sleeping figure, but there the resemblance ends. Instead of a neatly executed self-portrait, we see an amorphous body that appears to merge with, or decompose into, the earth. In one corner of the painting there is a cactus—that hardy symbol of the persistence of life. Next to it, a face or a cast-off mask stares plaintively at the sky.

416 she said that she had replaced her motto: Henestrosa, private interview.

416 Frida tried to cheer them up: Rodríguez, "Frida Kahlo: El Homenaje," p. 50, and private interview.

416 "The night before the operation": Ferreto, Crommie interview.

417 "Tell them I am sleeping": Ibid.

417 "Following the loss of her leg": Rivera, *My Art, My Life*, p. 284.

417 "Diego had some person in his studio": Ferreto, Crommie interview.

418 [Diego] was a "wonderful collaborator": Ferreto, Crommie interview.

419 "often during her convalescence": Rivera, *My Art, My Life*, p. 284.

419 "She sent to have a special boot made": Velasco y Polo, private interview. It was Dr. Velasco y Polo, not Dr. Farill, who amputated Frida's leg. Because he was lame, Dr. Farill did not perform amputations.

419 Frida said she would "dance her joy": Flores Guerrero, *Cinco Pintores Mexicanos*, p. 16.

419 she twirled in front of friends: Castro, "Carta a Frida Kahlo."

419 "Frida was very proud": Tibón, private interview, Cuernavaca Morelos, Mexico, July 1977.

419 Rosa Castro went to visit: Castro, "Carta a Frida Kahlo."

420 "Frida used to joke": Morillo Safa, private interview.

421 not wanting to ask for help: Martínez, private interview.

421 "Yesterday, May 7": The text reads 1953, but I believe Frida wrote the wrong year, since the entry follows one dated April 1954.

422 "sometimes just a word": Ferreto, Crommie interview.

422 Raquel Tibol tells of an occasion: Tibol, private interview.

422 "But the moment Diego appeared": Castro, private interview.

422 "Why did I do it?": Zendejas, private interview.

423 Judith Ferreto tried to explain: Ferreto, Crommie interview.

423 "Every night he stays up": Bambi, "Frida Dice Lo Que Sabe," p. 7.

423 "Her relations with Diego": Loló de la Torriente, "Recuerdos de Frida Kahlo," p. 9.

423 "No one knew how much I love Diego": Robles, "La Personalidad de Frida Kahlo."

423 she had permission: Tibol, private interview.

424 "Once I went to see her": Ríos y Valles, private interview.

425 probably Marx's *Capital:* This was a book she treasured. In a list of things she wanted to accomplish, which is displayed in the Frida Kahlo Museum, Frida noted that she wanted *Capital* sent out to be rebound.

425 "For the first time": Ferreto, Crommie interview. Frida did, in fact, cast aside her crutches at the time she produced *Marxism Will Give Health to the Sick*, but after walking a few steps, she fell, aggravating her already critical condition (García Bustos, private interview).

425 "I cannot": Ibid.

425 "I want my work to be a contribution": Rodríguez, "Frida Abjura del Surrealismo."

426 One spring day, Dr. Farill: Eugenia Farill, private interview.

426 "Haven't you seen the other?": Tibol, "Frida Kahlo: En el Segundo Aniversario de su Muerte." As Tibol described the painting, it was a self-portrait showing Frida wearing tweed pants and a *rebozo* and standing guard next to a crematorium. Tibol also recalled that Frida painted it on a small piece of wood. Although this description does not entirely coincide with the extant painting entitled *The Brick Kilns*, it seems likely that the painting Tibol watched Frida paint in 1954 is the same one. The painting of Frida's face inside a sunflower may be the one (recorded

in a photograph) that shows the nude Frida holding in one hand a sunflower that hides her genitals, and, in the other, paintbrushes and a mask that bears her features. Her own face has lost its features and been transformed into four petals that radiate light out onto other flowers, which fill the background. Dolores Olmedo said (private interview) that this painting depicts her body and Frida's face (as a mask) and that the portrait relates to Rivera's idea that there was a duality between Dolores Olmedo and Frida—they were opposites that complemented each other.

427 "In her last days": Morillo Safa, private interview.
427 "During those days": Ferreto, Crommie interview.
427 "I went and spent most of the day": Ibid. Because of her own poor health, Ferreto was not working for Frida at this time.
428 "What are you going to give me as a prize": Bambi, "Manuel, el Chófer," p. 5.
428 She even invited Lupe Marín: Radar, "Etcetera," July 15, 1954.
429 She said she wanted to adopt a child: Zendejas, private interview.
429 An invitation to Russia: Bambi, "Manuel, el Chófer," p. 1.
429 She was excited about . . . traveling to Poland: Ibid.
429 "Traigan mucha raza": Ibid.
429 "Gringos asesinos": Tibol, Crónica, illustration caption, n.p.
430 "I only want three things": J.O., "Frida Kahlo, Una Vida de Martiro," July 22, 1954, newspaper clipping, Isolda Kahlo archive.
430 she got out of bed: Rivera, My Art, My Life, pp. 284–85.
430 "It was not awkward to speak": González Ramírez, "Frida Kahlo o el Imperativo de Vivir," p. 25.
430 "Let's start celebrating": Bambi, "Manuel, el Chófer," p.1.
431 "pulmonary embolism": El Nacional, July 14, 1954.
431 "I sat beside her bed": Rivera, My Art, My Life, pp. 284–85.
431 Bambi published a long report: Bambi, "Manuel, el Chófer," pp. 1, 5.
432 Rivera called Dr. Velasco y Polo: Velasco y Polo, private interview.
432 At 11:00 P.M.: Bambi, "Manuel, el Chófer," p. 5.
432 "Señor," he said: Ibid., p. 1. Dr. Velasco y Polo recalled (private interview) that when he returned to the house after Frida was dead, "Frida was lying in her bed. They told me that Frida had been found dead in the bathtub. Apparently what happened was that her leg was troubling her, and she got up and went into the bathroom. Then she fell and died."

CHAPTER 25: VIVA LA VIDA

433 "He became an old man": Ella Paresce, letter to Bertram D. Wolfe (July 23, 1954), Hoover Institution, Stanford University.
433 "I beg of you": Wolfe, Fabulous Life of Diego Rivera, p. 400.
433 "Diego was completely alone": Marín, private interview.
434 "It was terrible for me": Campos, private interview.
434 "Naturally, when I came there": Kolko, Crommie interview.
434 "Diego went with his chauffeur": Ibid.
434 He had asked . . . for a death certificate: Velasco y Polo, private interview.
434 "When she was lying in state": Castro, private interview.
435 "No political banners": Wolfe, Fabulous Life of Diego Rivera, p. 400. This account of Frida's funeral comes largely from Wolfe's Fabulous Life of Diego Rivera, from Press accounts in the Isolda Kahlo archive, and from interviews with Arturo García Bustos and Dr. Velasco y Polo.
435 He threatened to take Frida's body: Foto-Gión, 48, undated clipping from a magazine, Isolda Kahlo archive.
435 "If General Cárdenas": Wolfe, The Fabulous Life of Diego Rivera, p. 401.
435 "Russophile farce": Undated newspaper clipping, Isolda Kahlo archive.
436 He told one newspaper reporter: Rodolfo Contreras A., "Frida Kahlo, la Artista

del Pincel, Dejó de Existir Ayer," *Novedades* (Mexico City), July 14, 1954, p. 19.

436 "Frida has died": Iduarte, "Imagen de Frida Kahlo."

436 "You will always be alive": The Pellicer poem has never been published in English. I have translated the last three lines from the original Spanish; the first line reads, *"Si en tu vientre acampo la prodigiosa."*

436 "iron will to live": "El Cadáver de la Artista Frida Kahlo, Incinerado en Dolores," *Novedades* (Mexico City), July 15, 1954, p. 26.

436 At quarter past one: Ibid.

437 Rivera wanted to send Frida off with music: Monroy, private interview, and Guillermo Monroy, "Vayan a la Cámara del Horno a Despedir a Frida Kahlo," *Excelsior* (Mexico City), July 13, 1975, pp. 1, 5, 8.

438 "Rivera stood with his hands in fists": Monroy, private interview.

438 "Everyone was hanging on to Frida's hands": Zendejas, private interview.

438 Cristina became hysterical: Paresce, letter to Bertram Wolfe.

438 when the flames ignited her hair: Tibol, "Frida Kahlo: Segundo Aniversario."

438 A blast of suffocating heat: Monroy, "Vayan a la Cámara del Horno." See also *Novedades*, "El Cadáver de la Artista," p. 17.

438 With his face completely absorbed: Estrada, private interview.

438 He asked that his ashes be mixed with Frida's: Some time after Frida's death, Antonio Peláez asked Rivera to write a few words to accompany Peláez's portrait of Frida to be published in his *21 Mujeres de Mexico* (21 Mexican Women, Editorial Fournier, S.A., 1956, p. 21). One paragraph from Rivera's contribution said: "Whoever had the matchless luck to be close to Frida, inside her love, can—at the hour when she changed her presence through the fire—fall deeper and deeper into the endless abyss that left worlds, understanding them better each instant, in the hopes of gaining complete happiness by having his own ashes mixed well, molecule against molecule with hers."

438 "July 13, 1954, was the most tragic day of my life": Rivera, *My Art, My Life*, pp. 285–86.

439 a bag containing her ashes: Juan Soriano, interviewed by Elizabeth Gerhard at the author's request, Paris, June 1978. Another story has it that Rivera ate some of Frida's ashes.

439 pregnant "because being dead": Lesley notes.

439 paintings by Rivera and others: Frida's art collection included works by Paul Klee, Yves Tanguy, Marcel Duchamp, José María, Velasco, and José Clemente Orozco.

439 "I made one other stipulation": Rivera, *My Art, My Life*, pp. 285–86.

440 Eight days before she died: Rodríguez, "Frida Kahlo: El Homenaje," p. 50.

ILLUSTRATIONS

Color plates following page 210

493

XVI   *Self-Portrait*, 1940. Oil on canvas, 24½″ x 18¾″. Iconography Collection, Humanities Research Center, The University of Texas at Austin.

Color plates following page 290

Black-and-white illustrations following page 146

28. *Self-Portrait on the Borderline Between Mexico and the United States,* 1932. Oil on sheet metal, 12½ x 13¾". Collection Mr. and Mrs. Manuel Reyero, New York. Photo courtesy Christie's, New York.
29. Painting *Self-Portrait on the Borderline.*
30. *Self-Portrait,* 1933. Collection Mr. and Mrs. Jacques Gelman, Mexico City. Oil on sheet metal, 13½ x 11½". Photo Raúl Salinas.
31. Rivera's Rockefeller Center mural as repainted in the Palace of Fine Arts, Mexico City, 1934. Photo Raúl Salinas.
32. With Diego and an unidentified friend at the New Workers' School, New York City, 1933.
33. With Nelson Rockefeller and Rosa Covarrubias in 1939.
34. *My Dress Hangs There,* 1933. Oil and collage on masonite, 18 x 19¾". Estate of Dr. Leo Eloesser, Courtesy Hoover Gallery, San Francisco.
35. Rivera's portraits of Frida, Cristina, and Cristina's children, in his mural at the National Palace, 1935.
36. With Ella Wolfe in New York 1935.
37. *Self-Portrait,* 1935. Oil on sheet metal. Private collection, California.
38. Isamu Noguchi. Photograph by Edward Weston, 1935.
39. *Memory,* 1937. Oil on sheet metal, 15¾ x 11". Collection Michel Petitjean, Paris.
40. *Remembrance of an Open Wound,* 1938. Oil, destroyed by fire. Photo courtesy Raquel Tibol.
41. With her niece and nephew, Isolda and Antonio Kahlo.
42. With Diego in front of the organ cactus fence at San Angel.
43. The Riveras' linked houses in San Angel.

Black-and-white illustrations *following page 354*

Figure

44. The Trotskys arriving at Tampico, 1937.
45. Frida and Trotsky, 1937.
46. With, from left, Trotsky (seated), Diego, Natalia Trotsky, Reba Hansen, André Breton, and Jean van Heijenoort, on an outing near Mexico City, June 1938.
47. A gathering in Lupe Marín's apartment in 1938. From left, Luis Cardoza y Aragón, Frida, Jacqueline and André Breton, Lupe, Diego, and Lya Cardoza.
48. *Me and My Doll,* 1937. Oil on sheet metal, 15¾ x 12¼". Collection Mr. and Mrs. Jacques Gelman, Mexico City. Photo Raúl Salinas.
49. *Escuincle Dog with Me,* c. 1938. Oil. Whereabouts unknown. Photo courtesy Unidad de Documentación Dirección de Artes Plásticas. INBA.
50. *What the Water Gave Me,* 1938. Oil on canvas, 38 x 30". Collection Tomás Fernández Márquez, Mexico City. Photo Raúl Salinas.
51. At the New York exhibition, 1938. Photo by Elinor Mayer.
52. With Nickolas Muray. Photograph by Nickolas Muray, c. 1938.
53. *Two Nudes in a Forest,* 1939. Oil on sheet metal, 9 x 12". Collection Dolores del Rio, Mexico City. Photo Raúl Salinas.
54. *Suicide of Dorothy Hale,* 1939. Oil on masonite, 23¼ x 19". Phoenix Art Museum, Phoenix, Arizona.
55. *The Wounded Table,* 1940. Oil on canvas. Whereabouts unknown. Photo courtesy Excelsior Archive.
56. *Self-Portrait,* 1940. Oil on masonite, 23½ x 15¾". Estate of Dr. Leo Eloesser, courtesy Hoover Gallery. Photo courtesy Sotheby Parke Bernet.
57. *Self-Portrait with Braid,* 1941. Oil on masonite, 20 x 15¼". Collection Mr. and Mrs. Jacques Gelman, Mexico City. Photo Raúl Salinas.

58. Ceramic clocks, one with the date of the divorce (Frida wrote on it "The hours were broken"), the other with the date of the remarriage. Photo Hayden Herrera.
59. Frida and Diego with Caimito de Guayabal. Photo courtesy Excelsior Archive.
60. During World War II. Photograph by Nickolas Muray.
61. In the dining room of the blue house in Coyoacán. Photograph by Emmy Lou Packard.
62. *Diego and Frida 1929–1944*, 1944. Oil on cardboard. Whereabouts unknown. Photo courtesy Unidad de Documentación Dirección de Artes Plásticas, INBA.
63. *Self-Portrait*, drawing, 1946. Pencil on paper, 15¼ x 12¾″. Collection Marte Gómez Leal, Mexico City. Photo José Verde.
64. *Flower of Life*, 1944. Oil on masonite, 11½ x 9″. Collection Dolores Olmedo, Mexico City. Photo Raúl Salinas.
65. *Still Life*, 1942. Oil on sheet metal, 24¾″ diameter. The Frida Kahlo Museum, Mexico City. Photo Raúl Salinas.
66. *Fruits of the Earth*, 1938. Oil on masonite, 16¼ x 23½″. Collection Banco Nacional de Mexico, Mexico. Photo Larry Bercow.
67. *Portrait of Mariana Morillo Safa*, 1944. Oil on canvas, 10½ x 15″. Collection Ruth Davidoff, Mexico City. Photo courtesy Unidad de Documentación Dirección de Artes Plásticas, INBA.
68. *Doña Rosita Morillo*, 1944. Oil on masonite, 30½ x 28½″. Collection Dolores Olmedo, Mexico City. Photo Raúl Salinas.
69. *Moses*, 1945. Oil on masonite, 37 x 20″. Collection Jorge Espinosa Ulloa, Mexico City. Photo Raúl Salinas.
70. With Granizo ("the little deer") when he was a fawn, c. 1939. Photograph by Nickolas Muray.
71. With Diego at a political rally, c. 1946.
72. With three of her students, c. 1948. From left, Fanny Rabel, Arturo Estrada, and Arturo García Bustos.
73. Frida, c. 1947.
74. Detail from Rivera's 1947–1948 Hotel del Prado mural, in which he depicted himself as a boy; Frida's hand rests protectively on his shoulder.
75. Diego with María Félix, 1949.
76. Frida's year in the hospital, 1950–1951. Above left, holding a sugar skull with her name on it; above, right, painting one of the succession of plaster corsets she endured; left, with Diego. Photo Juan Guzmán.
77. Painting *Naturaleza Viva*, at home, 1952. Photo Antonio Rodríguez.
78. With her servants, c. 1952.
79. Being carried into the gallery at the opening of the Homage to Frida Kahlo in 1953. Looking on are (left to right) Concha Michel, Antonio Peláez, Dr. Roberto Garza, Carmen Farell, and (lower right), Doctor Atl. Photo courtesy Excelsior Archive.
80. *Marxism Will Give Health to the Sick*, 1954. Oil on masonite, 30 x 24″. The Frida Kahlo Museum, Mexico City. Photo Raúl Salinas.
81. Frida's studio as she left it, the unfinished portrait of Stalin on the easel. Photo Raúl Salinas.
82. Protesting the ouster of Guatemalan president Jacobo Arbenz Guzmán by the CIA in July 1954. Juan O'Gorman is beside Frida, Diego behind her.
83. On her deathbed.
84. Diego flanked by Lázaro Cárdenas (left) and Andrés Iduarte following the hearse to the crematorium. Photo courtesy Excelsior Archive.
85. Frida's bed, Frida Kahlo Museum. Photo Raúl Salinas.

Other black-and-white illustrations

Part Titles

INDEX

504   Index

ALSO AVAILABLE BY HAYDEN HERRERA

ARSHILE GORKY: HIS LIFE AND WORK

The result of over three decades of scholarship: the definitive biography of the man André Breton called 'the most important painter in American history'

Born in Turkey around 1900, Vosdanik Adoian escaped the massacres of Armenians in 1915 only to watch his mother die of starvation and his family scatter in their flight from the Turks. Arriving in America in 1920, Adoian invented the pseudonym Arshile Gorky – and obliterated his past. Claiming to be a distant cousin of the novelist Maxim Gorky, he found work as an art teacher and undertook a program of rigorous study, schooling himself in the modern painters he most admired, especially Cézanne and Picasso. His masterpieces influenced the great generation of American painters in the late forties, even as Gorky faced a series of personal catastrophes: a studio fire, cancer, and a car accident that temporarily paralyzed his painting arm.

A sympathetic, sensitive account of artistic and personal triumph as well as tragedy, Hayden Herrera's biography is the first to interpret Gorky's work in depth.

'Hayden Herrera has written the definitive biography of Arshile Gorky – lucid, persuasive, meticulous, intimate and refreshingly clear-eyed'
NEW YORK TIMES

'Extraordinary'
LONDON REVIEW OF BOOKS